T0203015

Lecture Notes in Computer Science **11818**

More information about this series at http://www.springer.com/series/7412

Zhenan Sun · Ran He · Jianjiang Feng ·
Shiguang Shan · Zhenhua Guo (Eds.)

Biometric Recognition

14th Chinese Conference, CCBR 2019
Zhuzhou, China, October 12–13, 2019
Proceedings

Editors
Zhenan Sun
Chinese Academy of Sciences
Beijing, China

Ran He
Chinese Academy of Sciences
Beijing, China

Jianjiang Feng
Tsinghua University
Beijing, China

Shiguang Shan
Chinese Academy of Sciences
Beijing, China

Zhenhua Guo
Tsinghua University
Shenzhen, China

ISSN 0302-9743 ISSN 1611-3349 (electronic)
Lecture Notes in Computer Science
ISBN 978-3-030-31455-2 ISBN 978-3-030-31456-9 (eBook)
https://doi.org/10.1007/978-3-030-31456-9

LNCS Sublibrary: SL6 – Image Processing, Computer Vision, Pattern Recognition, and Graphics

This Springer imprint is published by the registered company Springer Nature Switzerland AG
The registered company address is: Gewerbestrasse 11, 6330 Cham, Switzerland

Preface

Reliable recognition of person identity has a number of applications in modern society. Biometric technology, which performs automatic person recognition based on biological or behavioral traits, provides substantial advantages over traditional password- or token-based solutions. In recent years, biometric recognition systems have been extensively deployed worldwide in law enforcement, government, and consumer applications. In China, thanks to the huge population using the Internet and smart phones as well as to the great investment of the government in security and privacy protection, the biometric market is rapidly growing and biometric research has attracted the attention of numerous scholars and practitioners. These researchers have been addressing various scientific problems in biometrics, developing diverse biometric techniques, and making significant contributions to the biometrics field. The Chinese Conference on Biometric Recognition (CCBR), an annual conference held in China, provides an excellent platform for biometric researchers to share their progress and thoughts in the development and applications of biometric theory, technology, and systems.

CCBR 2019 was held in Zhuzhou during October 12–13, 2019, and was the 14th in the series, which has been successfully held in Beijing, Hangzhou, Xi'an, Guangzhou, Jinan, Shenyang, Tianjin, Chengdu, Shenzhen, and Urumqi since 2000. CCBR 2019 received 74 submissions, each of which was reviewed by at least two experts from the Program Committee. Based on the rigorous review process, 56 papers were selected for presentation. These papers comprise this volume of the CCBR 2019 conference proceedings, which covers a wide range of topics: face recognition and analysis; hand-based biometrics; eye-based biometrics; gesture, gait, and action; emerging biometrics; feature extraction and classification theory; and behavioral biometrics.

We would like to thank all the authors, reviewers, invited speakers, volunteers, and Organizing Committee members, without whom CCBR 2019 would not have been successful. We also wish to acknowledge the support of the Chinese Association for Artificial Intelligence, Institute of Automation of Chinese Academy of Sciences, Springer, and Hunan University of Technology for sponsoring this conference.

October 2019

Yimin Tan
Jie Zhou
Yunhong Wang
Zhenan Sun
Ran He
Jianjiang Feng
Shiguang Shan
Zhenhua Guo

Organization

Advisory Committee

Anil K. Jain	Michigan State University, USA
Tieniu Tan	Institute of Automation, Chinese Academy of Sciences, China
David Zhang	The Hong Kong Polytechnic University, China
Jingyu Yang	Nanjing University of Science and Technology, China
Xilin Chen	Institute of Computing Technology, Chinese Academy of Sciences, China
Jianhuang Lai	Sun Yat-sen University, China

General Chairs

Yimin Tan	Hunan University of Technology, China
Jie Zhou	Tsinghua University, China
Yunhong Wang	Beihang University, China
Zhenan Sun	Institute of Automation, Chinese Academy of Sciences, China

Program Committee Chairs

Ran He	Institute of Automation, Chinese Academy of Sciences, China
Jianjiang Feng	Tsinghua University, China
Shiguang Shan	Institute of Computing Technology, Chinese Academy of Sciences, China
Zhenhua Guo	Graduate School at Shenzhen, Tsinghua University, China

Program Committee Members

Caikou Chen	School of Information Engineering, Yangzhou University, China
Cunjian Chen	Canon Information Technology (Beijing), China
Fanglin Chen	National University of Defense Technology, China
Weihong Deng	Beijing University of Posts and Telecommunications, China
Yuchun Fang	Shanghai University, China
Lunke Fei	Guangdong University of Technology, China
Keren Fu	Shanghai Jiaotong University, China
Quanxue Gao	Xidian University, China

Shenghua Gao	Shanghai Tech University, China
Yongxin Ge	Chongqing University, China
Xun Gong	Southwest Jiaotong University, China
Zhe Guo	Northwestern Polytechnical University
Hu Han	Institute of Computing Technology, Chinese Academy of Sciences, China
Zhenyu He	Harbin Institute of Technology Shenzhen Graduate School, China
Qingyang Hong	Xiamen University, China
Dewen Hu	National University of Defense Technology, China
Di Huang	Beihang University, China
Wei Jia	Hefei University of Technology, China
Xiaoyuan Jing	School of Computer Science, Wuhan University, China
Wenxiong Kang	South China University of Technology, China
Kurban Ubul	Xinjiang University, China
Zhihui Lai	Shenzhen University, China
Huibin Li	Xian Jiaotong University, China
Qi Li	Institute of Automation, Chinese Academy of Sciences, China
Weijun Li	Institute of Semiconductors, Chinese Academy of Sciences, China
Wenxin Li	School of Information Science and Technology, Peking University, China
Zhifeng Li	Institute of Advanced Technology, Chinese Academy of Sciences, China
Dong Liang	Nanjing University of Aeronautics and Astronautics, China
Shengcai Liao	Abu Dhabi Artificial Intelligence Innovation Institute, UAE
Eryun Liu	Zhejiang University, China
Feng Liu	School of Computer and Software, Shenzhen University, Institute of Computer Vision, China
Heng Liu	Anhui University of Technology, China
Manhua Liu	Shanghai Jiao Tong University, China
Yiguang Liu	Sichuan University, China
Zhi Liu	Shandong University, China
Guangming Lu	Harbin Institute of Technology Shenzhen Graduate School, China
Jiwen Lu	Tsinghua University, China
Xiao Luan	Key Laboratory of Computational Intelligence Chongqing, Chongqing University of Posts and Telecommunications, China
Bo Peng	Institute of Automation, Chinese Academy of Sciences, China
Haifeng Sang	Shenyang University of Technology, China
Chao Shen	Xi'an Jiaotong University, China

Fumin Shen	University of Electronic Science and Technology of China, China
Linlin Shen	Shenzhen University, China
Kejun Wang	Harbin Engineering University, China
Wei Wang	Institute of Automation, Chinese Academy of Sciences, China
Yiding Wang	North China University of Technology, China
Yi Wang	Hong Kong Baptist University, SAR China
Yunlong Wang	Institute of Automation, Chinese Academy of Sciences, China
Xiangqian Wu	Harbin Institute of Technology, China
Lifang Wu	Beijing University of Technology, China
Xiaohua Xie	Sun Yat-sen University, China
Yuli Xue	Beihang University, China
Haibin Yan	Beijing University of Posts and Telecommunications, China
Gongping Yang	Shandong University, China
Jinfeng Yang	Shenzhen Polytechnic, China
Jucheng Yang	Tianjin University of Science and Technology, China
Wankou Yang	Southeast University, China
Yingchun Yang	Zhejiang University, China
Shiqi Yu	Shenzhen University, China
Weiqi Yuan	Shenyang University of Technology, China
Baochang Zhang	Beihang University, China
Lei Zhang	The Hong Kong Polytechnic University, SAR China
Lin Zhang	Tongji University, China
Man Zhang	Institute of Automation, Chinese Academy of Sciences, China
Yongliang Zhang	Zhejiang University of Technology, China
Zhaoxiang Zhang	Institute of Automation, Chinese Academy of Sciences, China
Cairong Zhao	Tongji University, China
Qijun Zhao	Sichuan University, China
Weishi Zheng	Sun Yat-sen University, China
Xiuzhuang Zhou	Capital Normal University, China
Wangmeng Zuo	Harbin Institute of Technology, China
En Zhu	National University of Defense Technology, China
Kunbo Zhang	Institute of Automation, Chinese Academy of Sciences, China

Publicity Chairs

Jing Dong	Institute of Automation, Chinese Academy of Sciences, China
Wei Jia	Hefei University of Technology, China

Doctoral Consortium Chairs

Shiqi Yu	Shenzhen University, China
Zhaoxiang Zhang	Institute of Automation, Chinese Academy of Sciences, China

Publication Chairs

Angelo Marcelli	University of Salerno, Italy
Qi Li	Institute of Automation, Chinese Academy of Sciences, China
Jinfeng Yang	Shenzhen Polytechnic, China

Organizing Committee Chair

Wenqiu Zhu	Hunan University of Technology, China

Organizing Committee Members

Yunlong Wang	Institute of Automation, Chinese Academy of Sciences, China
Zhigao Zeng	Hunan University of Technology, China

Contents

Eye-Based Biometrics

Hand-Based Biometrics

Local Discriminative Direction Extraction for Palmprint Recognition

Zhanchun Qiu[1], Lunke Fei[1(✉)], Shaohua Teng[1], Wei Zhang[1], Dongning Liu[1], Yan Hou[1], and Wei Jia[2]

[1] School of Computer Science and Technology, Guangdong University of Technology, Guangzhou, China
flksxm@126.com

[2] School of Computer and Information, Hefei University of Technology, Hefei, China

Abstract. Direction features server as one of the most important features of palmprint and there have been a number of direction-based palmprint recognition methods. However, most existing direction-based methods extract the dominant direction features, which are possibly not the most discriminative features due to the influence of the neighboring directions. In this paper, we present a straightforward example to show that the direction with a large neighboring direction response difference (NDRD) is more stable so as to be more robust and discriminative. Inspired by that, we propose a new feature descriptor by extracting multiple direction features with the competitive NDRDs for palmprint recognition. Extensive experiments conducted on three widely used palmprint databases, including the PolyU, IITD and CASIA databases, demonstrate the effectiveness of the proposed method.

Keywords: Biometric · Palmprint recognition · Direction feature · Neighboring direction response difference

1 Introduction

Biometrics refers to automatic recognizing a subject by using ones physiological or behavioral traits. To date, a variety of biometric traits such as face, fingerprint, iris and gaits have been studied and applied to the authentication of individuals [1–3]. As one of new and promising biometrics, palmprint recognition has recently attracted widely research attention due to its rich discriminative features and high user acceptability [4,5]. Over the past decades, various palmprint recognition technologies have been developed, such as low-resolution [6], high-resolution [7] and three-dimension (3D) palmprint recognition [8,9], which focus on different levels of palmprint features. In this paper, we focus on 2D low-resolution palmprint recognition due to its potential for civilian applications and low acquisition cost [10].

In recent years, a number of feature extraction methods have been proposed for palmprint recognition, and they can be mainly grouped into three categories:

Z. Sun et al. (Eds.): CCBR 2019, LNCS 11818, pp. 3–11, 2019.
https://doi.org/10.1007/978-3-030-31456-9_1

holistic features, local features and hybrid methods. Representative holistic feature methods include principal component analysis (PCA), linear discriminant analysis (LDA) [11] and sparse representation (SR) [12]. While these holistic methods have achieved encouraging performance, their performance is still far from satisfactory due to the neglect of much special and intrinsic features of the palmprint. To this end, many efforts have concentrated on the local palmprint feature extraction [6,10,13]. For example, Huang et al. [14] proposed a palmprint recognition method by extracting the principal lines. Zhang et al. [15] proposed a palmcode method by encoding a spectral direction of palmprint. Wong et al. [16] proposed a competitive code method by encoding the most dominant direction features of a palmprint based on the winner-take-all principle. Similarly, Jia et al. [17] proposed a dominant direction method by using modified finite radon transform (MFRAT). Moreover, Jia et al. [18] extracted the histogram of oriented line (HOL) as feature representation for palmprint recognition. Fei et al. [19] proposed an ALDC method by exploring double-layer dominant direction features of palmprint. To extract more direction features, Sun et al. [20] proposed an ordinal code method by encoding the filtering responses on three orthogonal directions. Guo et al. [21] proposed a binary orientation co-occurrence vector (BOCV) method to extract the binary codes on six orientations, and Zhang et al. [22] extended the BOCV method by incorporating the fragile bit with the original direction feature maps. More local feature methods can be found in a survey of palmprint feature extraction [23]. In addition, Zhang et al. [24] proposed a hybrid method by sparse representing the block-wise statistical features of the competitive code.

It can be seen that the direction information have served as one of the most important features for palmprint recognition. However, most existing methods are hand-crafted, which usually encode the dominant direction features of palmprint without considering ones stability. In this paper, we first analyze the stability of a direction. Then, we propose a new palmprint descriptor by encoding multiple directions with high stability as well as strong discriminability. Experimental results on three baseline palmprint databases show that the proposed method outperforms the state-of-the-art palmprint representation methods.

The rest of the paper is organized as follows: Sect. 2 briefly reviews the related work. Section 3 details the proposed method. Section 4 presents the experimental results and Sect. 5 offers the conclusion.

2 Related Work

A palmprint image usually contains a number of lines such as principal lines and wrinkles so as to carries informative direction features. To this end, there have been many methods that extracted the direction features for palmprint recognition. Representative direction-based methods include the competitive code [16] and RLOC [17] methods, which extracted the dominant direction features of a palmprint image. Specifically, they first define a bank of direction-based templates, such as Gabor filters and MFRAT, to convolve a palmprint image.

Then, they extracted the direction of the template that produces the maximum filtering response as the dominant direction of the palmprint image, as follows.

$$c = f(\operatorname{argmax} \operatorname{res}(T, I)), \tag{1}$$

where res represents the convolution responses between the direction-based templates (i.e. T) and a palmprint sample (i.e. I). f is a mapping function that encodes the directions with the maximum response into the feature codes.

Different from the competitive code, the BOCV method proposes to preserve multiple direction feature of a palmprint. Specifically, the BOCV method uses Gabor filters with six different orientations to convolve with a palmprint image. The direction responses on six orientations are encoded into binary codes. Thus, six-bit code planes can be formed for a palmprint. Moreover, the E-BOCV method filters out the fragile bits with small direction responses from the BOCV code maps.

3 Local Discriminative Direction Code

3.1 Direction Discriminability Analysis

It is seen that the typical palmprint recognition methods usually extract the most dominant direction feature based on the winner-take-all rule. However, they dont answer the question whether the most dominant direction is the most discriminative direction feature. In the following, we give a detailed example to analyze the stability as well as the discriminability of the direction features.

Figure 1(a) shows the procedure of twelve Gabor templates convolving a palmprint image on twelve different directions, and Fig. 1(b) depicts the distribution of the convolved responses. The conventional methods such as the competitive code will extracted the third direction (red circle) due to its maximum convolved responses. It is seen that the second direction (blue circle) can produce a convolved response that is very close to the maximum one. In other word, the direction with the maximum responses could be easily influenced by the external factors such as small rotation and noise because the two neighboring directions can produce almost the largest responses. By contract, some other directions such as the first and the forth directions (green circles) are hard to be replaced because they have large response distance to their neighboring directions. Therefore, the direction that has a larger neighboring direction response difference (NDRD) is more stable so as to be more discriminative. Inspired by this, we extract and encode the directions with large NDRDs as the palmprint features.

3.2 LDDC Extraction

Suppose $\mathrm{T}(\theta_j)$ represents the direction-based templates with the directions of $\theta_j (j = 1, 2, ..., N_\theta)$, and I is a palmrint image, the convolution of the templates with the palmprint image can be represented as follows:

$$r_j(x, y) = T(\theta_j) * I(x, y), \tag{2}$$

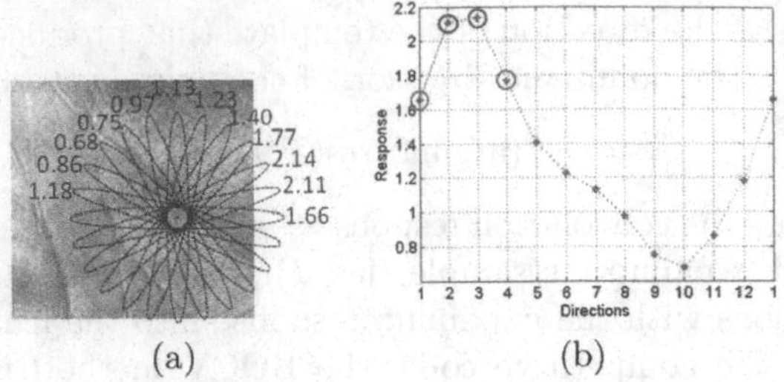

(a) (b)

Fig. 1. An example of the convolution between the Gabor templates and a palmprint image. (a) The convolution results of the twelve Gabor filters with a palmprint image. (b) The distribution of the convolution results, where the x-axis is the direction index and the y-axis is the corresponding convolution response. (Color figure online)

where "*" represents the convolution operation and r_j is the convolution response of the template and the palmprint image on the $j-th$ direction. Then, we define the $NDRD$ of a direction as follows:

$$NDRD_j(x,y) = |r_j(x,y) - r_{\varphi(j)}(x,y)| + |r_j(x,y) - r_{\phi(j)}(x,y)|, \tag{3}$$

where $\varphi(j)$ equals N_θ if $j = 1$, and $(j-1)$ otherwise. $\phi(j)$ equals 1 if $j = N_\theta$, and $(j+1)$ otherwise. So $\varphi(j)$ and $\phi(j)$ represent the clockwise and anti-clockwise neighboring directions. So the $NDRD$ of a direction is the sum of the response differences between the direction and its two neighboring directions. In this paper, we define the templates $T(\theta_j)$ based on the real parts of the Gabor filters with twelve different directions [25], i.e. $\theta_j = (j-1)\pi/N_\theta$ and $N_\theta = 12$. Finally, to make a good trade-off between the feature size and discriminative ability, we extract the two directions with the largest two $NDRDs$ as the local discriminative direction features and encode them into a code, named as local discriminative direction code (LDDC):

$$LDDC(x,y) = d_1 \times N_\theta + d_2, \tag{4}$$

where

$$d_1 = \arg\max_j r_j\{j = 1, 2, ..., N_\theta\}, \tag{5}$$

and

$$d_2 = \arg\max_j r_j\{j = 1, 2, ..., d_1 - 1, d_1 + 1, ..., N_\theta\}. \tag{6}$$

In order to achieve invariant of palmprint image and overcome the small misalignment, we form the LDDC histogram-based vector as the palmprint descriptor. Specifically, given a palmprint image, we first calculate the LDDC feature map. Then, we divide the LDDC map into non-overlapping blocks and compute the LDDC histogram for each block. Finally, we concatenate the histograms of each block forming the feature vector as the palmprint descriptor. In this paper, the block size is empirically set to 16×16 pixels.

3.3 LLDC-Based Palmprint Matching

In palmprint matching, we use the simple and efficient Chi-distance metric to calculate the similarity of two palmprint descriptors. Suppose P and Q are the two compared palmprint descriptors, the distance of them can be computed as follows:

$$d(P, Q) = \sum_{i=1}^{S} \frac{(p_i - q_i)^2}{p_i + q_i}, \tag{7}$$

where p_i and q_i represent $i-th$ bin of the P and Q, respectively. S is the feature size of the palmprint descriptors.

4 Experiments

In this section, we conduct both palmprint identification and verification on three widely used palmprint databases, including the PolyU, IITD and CASIA databases, to evaluate the effectiveness of the proposed method. The experimental platform includes a PC with Intel(R) i7-7700CPU@3.60HZ, 16G RAM and Matlab R2014a.

4.1 Palmprint Databases

PolyU Palmprint Database [26]**:** The PolyU database includes 7752 palmprint images collected from 386 volunteers, both the left and right palm of which provided about 20 palmprint images in two different sessions. All the palmprint images had been cropped into region of interests (ROI) with the sizes of 150×150 pixels.

IITD Palmprint Database [27]**:** The IITD database consists of 2601 images collected from 460 palms of 230 individuals. Each palm provided 5 to 7 samples with various rotations and translations. The ROIs of all samples with the sizes of 150×150 pixels have also been included in the database.

CASIA Palmprint Database [28]**:** The CASIA database contains 5502 palmprint images collected from 312 subjects, each palm of which provided 8 to 10 samples. In this experiment, we employ the palmcode method to crop the ROIs of all the CASIA images with the size of 128×128 pixels.

Figure 2 shows some typical examples selected from the PolyU, IITD and CASIA databases.

4.2 Palmprint Identification

Palmprint identification is to determine the class label of a query palmprint image by comparing it with the labeled samples in the training set. In this experiment, for a database, we first randomly select $n (n = 1, 2, 3)$ palmprint image(s) per each palm to form the training set and use the rest as the query samples.

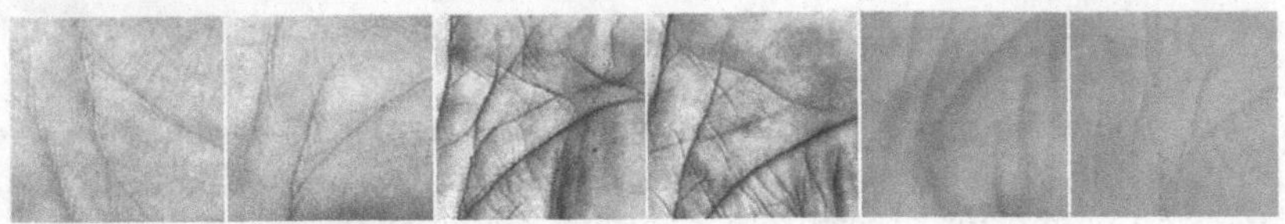

Fig. 2. The typical palmprint images. The first two images are selected from the PolyU database. The middle two and last two images are from the IITD and CASIA databases, respectively.

Then, we run the proposed method 10 times to calculate the average rank-one identification accuracy. Moreover, we also implement the state-of-the-art methods and compare them with the proposed method, including the competitive code [16], HOL [18], E-BOCV [22], Comp_CR [24] and ALDC [19] metehods. Table 1 tabulates the identification results of the proposed method and the five compared methods on the three databases. It is seen that the proposed method can achieve a higher accuracy than the state-of-the-art methods with a significant improvement. This is because the proposed LDDC method encodes the multiple and stable direction features so that more discriminative features can be extracted.

Table 1. The identification accuracy (average accuracy ± standard error) of different methods on the PolyU, IITD and CASIA databases.

Database	n	Competitive	HOL	E-BOCV	Comp_CR	ALDC	LDDC
PolyU	1	95.32 ± 0.38	98.71 ± 0.77	92.20 ± 0.60	96.77 ± 0.84	99.35 ± 0.08	**99.47 ± 0.10**
	2	97.48 ± 0.40	99.61 ± 0.16	95.29 ± 1.85	99.15 ± 0.61	99.63 ± 0.20	**99.80 ± 0.14**
	3	98.08 ± 0.85	99.77 ± 0.15	95.38 ± 0.42	99.33 ± 0.43	**99.85 ± 0.12**	**99.85 ± 0.08**
IITD	1	45.92 ± 2.60	84.88 ± 0.90	60.73 ± 1.04	78.14 ± 1.32	85.07 ± 0.10	**88.69 ± 0.41**
	2	65.16 ± 1.55	93.19 ± 0.20	74.31 ± 2.28	91.43 ± 0.98	93.54 ± 1.02	**95.31 ± 0.44**
	3	72.25 ± 2.40	95.12 ± 0.47	84.10 ± 1.24	93.69 ± 1.21	96.15 ± 0.91	**97.04 ± 0.55**
CASIA	1	55.21 ± 0.61	83.03 ± 0.47	60.50 ± 6.18	79.90 ± 1.92	86.16 ± 1.03	**88.63 ± 2.61**
	2	66.49 ± 6.69	88.37 ± 2.44	75.55 ± 4.83	85.54 ± 1.56	92.03 ± 0.97	**93.93 ± 2.10**
	3	79.45 ± 1.44	92.45 ± 2.88	82.83 ± 1.35	88.05 ± 1.90	93.65 ± 2.18	**96.36 ± 0.56**

4.3 Palmprint Verification

Different from identification, palmprint verification is a one-to-one comparison to determine whether a query palmprint image is captured from the same palm as another palmprint image. The comparison is named as a genuine match if the two compared palmprint images are from the same palm, or an impostor match otherwise. In our verification experiment, we compare each pair of the palmprint images in a database to calculate the false acceptance rate (FAR) and genuine acceptance rate (GAR). Then, we draw the ROC curves, i.e., FAR versus GAR, of different methods to compare the proposed method with the conventional representative methods, as shown in Fig. 3. It can be observed that the proposed method consistently achieve a higher GAR again the same FRR than the other methods on all databases, demonstrating the promising effectiveness of the LDDC method.

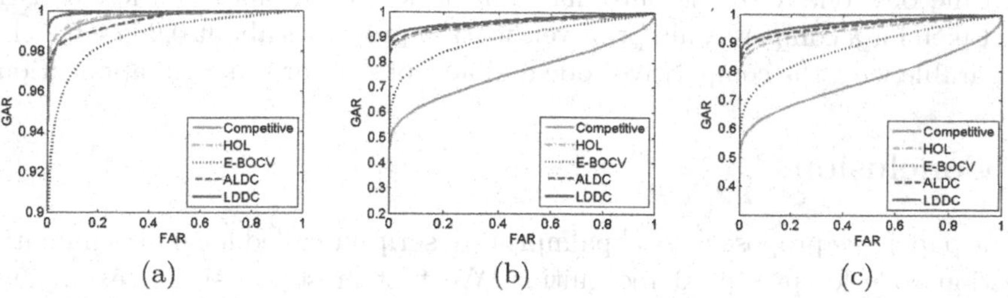

Fig. 3. The ROC curves of different methods on the (a) PolyU, (b) IITD and (c) CASIA databases.

4.4 Difference Between LDDC and the Competitive Code

LDDC is extracted based on the competitive NDRD and the conventional competitive code is extracted based on the competitive filtering response. To better show the difference of the LDDC and the competitive code, we extract the direction with the maximum NDRD (e.g. d_{NDRD}) and the maximum filtering response (e.g. d_{comp}) for each pixel of a palmprint image, respectively. Then, we calculate the distance of them: $dis = |d_{NDRD} - d_{comp}|$. Figure 4 shows the distributions of the dis on the three databases. It can be seen the LDDC extracts completely different direction code from the conventional winner-take-all scheme.

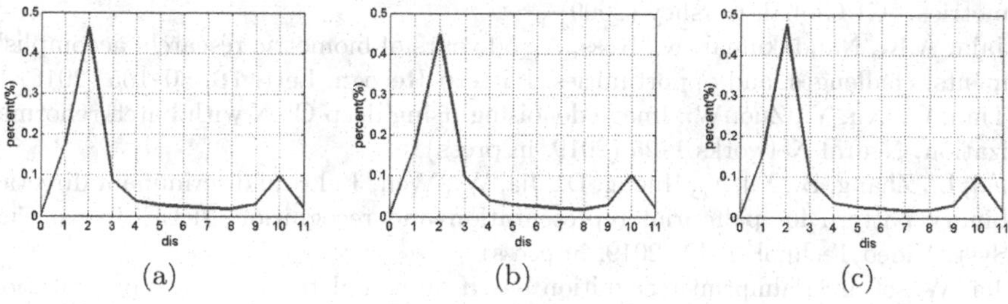

Fig. 4. The distribution of difference between the direction with the maximum NDRD and the maximum filtering response on the (a) PolyU, (b) IITD and (c) CASIA databases.

4.5 Computational Complexity Analysis

The proposed LDDC method first performs some convolution operation and then simply encodes double directions, where the first step is the most time-consuming for the feature extraction. Actually, both steps can be efficiently performed by the existing function. For example, the computational time of extracting the LDDC for a palmprint image is about 0.032 s. In addition, the proposed method has a fast matching speed due to its simple and efficient distance measurement. The time of a one-to-one feature matching is less than 0.001 s. Therefore, the time taken for a complete palmprint verification process is about 0.065 s, which is comparable with the competitive code and acceptable for practical applications.

5 Conclusion

In this paper, we propose a novel palmprint descriptor called local discriminative direction code for palmprint recognition. We first present a simple example to show that the direction with a large NDRD is more stable so as to be more robust to the influence such as rotation and noise. Then, we extract and encode the multiple direction features with the competitive NDRDs. Finally, we cluster and pool the local discriminative direction code into histogram-based feature as the final palmprint descriptor. Extensive experimental results show that the LDDC is completely different from the conventional competitive code and moreover our proposed method outperforms the state-of-the-art.

Acknowledgment. This work was supported inpart by the National Natural Science Foundation of China under Grants 61702110 and 61972102 and inpart by the Guangzhou Science and Technology Program under Grants 201802010042 and 201804010278.

References

1. Zhang, D.: Advanced Pattern Recognition Technologies with Applications to Biometrics. IGI Global, Hershey (2009)
2. Jain, A.K., Nandakumar, K., Ross, A.: 50 years of biometric research: accomplishments, challenges, and opportunities. Pattern Recogn. Lett. **79**, 80–105 (2016)
3. Tian, C., Xu, Y., Zuo, W.: Image denoising using deep CNN with batch renormalization. Neural Networks 1–25 (2019, in press)
4. Fei, L., Zhang, B., Xu, Y., Huang, D., Jia, W., Wen, J.: Local discriminant direction binary pattern for palmprint representation and recognition. IEEE Trans. Circ. Syst. Video Technol. 1–13 (2019, in press)
5. Jia, W., et al.: Palmprint recognition based on complete direction representation. IEEE Trans. Image Process. **26**, 4483–4498 (2017)
6. Zhang, D., Zuo, W., Yue, F.: A comparative study of palmprint recognition algorithms. ACM Comput. Surv. **44**, 1–37 (2012)
7. Jain, A.K., Feng, J.: Latent palmprint matching. IEEE Trans. Pattern Anal. Mach. Intell. **30**, 1032–1047 (2009)
8. Fei, L., Lu, G., Jia, W., Wen, J., Zhang, D.: Complete binary representation for 3-D palmprint recognition. IEEE Trans. Instrum. Meas. **17**, 2761–2771 (2018)
9. Fei, L., Zhang, B., Xu, Y., Jia, W., Wen, J., Wu, J.: Precision direction and compact surface type representation for 3D palmprint identification. Pattern Recogn. **87**, 237–247 (2019)

10. Kong, A., Zhang, D., Kamel, M.: A survey of palmprint recognition. Pattern Recogn. **42**, 1408–1418 (2009)
11. Ribaric, S., Fratric, I.: A biometric identification system based on eigenpalm and eigenfinger features. IEEE Trans. Pattern Anal. Mach. Intell. **27**, 1698–1709 (2005)
12. Imad, R., Somaya, A., Arif, M., Ahmed, B., Sambit, B.: Palmprint identification using an ensemble of sparse representations. IEEE Access. **6**, 3241–3248 (2018)
13. Fei, L., et al.: Learning discriminant direction binary palmprint descriptor. IEEE Trans. Image Process. **28**, 3808–3820 (2019)
14. Huang, D.S., Jia, W., Zhang, D.: Palmprint verification based on principal lines. Pattern Recogn. **41**, 1316–1328 (2008)
15. Zhang, D., Kong, W.-K., You, J., Wong, L.M.: Online palmprint identification. IEEE Trans. Pattern Anal. Mach. Intell. **25**, 1041–1050 (2003)
16. Kong, A.W.K., Zhang, D.: Competitive coding scheme for palmprint verification. In: Proceeding of International Conference on Pattern Recognition, pp. 520–523 (2004)
17. Jia, W., Huang, D., Zhang, D.: Palmprint verification based on robust line orientation code. Pattern Recogn. **41**, 1504–1513 (2008)
18. Jia, W., Hu, R.X., Lei, Y.K.: Histogram of oriented lines for palmprint recognition. IEEE Trans. Syst. Man Cybern. Syst. **44**, 385–395 (2014)
19. Fei, L., Zhang, B., Zhang, W., Teng, S.: Local apparent and latent direction extraction for palmprint recognition. Inf. Sci. **473**, 59–72 (2019)
20. Sun, Z., Tan, T., Wang, Y., Li, S.: Ordinal palmprint representation for personal identification. Comput. Vis. Pattern Recogn. **1**, 279–284 (2005)
21. Guo, Z., Zhang, D., Zhang, L., Zuo, W.: Palmprint verification using binary orientation co-occurrence vector. Pattern Recogn. Lett. **30**, 1219–1227 (2009)
22. Zhang, L., Li, H., Niu, J.: Fragile bits in palmprint recognition. IEEE Sig. Process. Lett. **19**, 663–666 (2012)
23. Fei, L., Lu, G., Jia, W., Teng, S., Zhang, D.: Feature extraction methods for palmprint recognition: a survey and evaluation. IEEE Trans. Syst. Man Cybern. Syst. **49**, 346–363 (2019)
24. Zhang, L., Li, L., Yang, A., Shen, Y., Yang, M.: Towards contactless palmprint recognition: a novel device, a new benchmark, and a collaborative representation based identification approach. Pattern Recogn. **69**, 199–212 (2017)
25. Fei, L., Wen, J., Zhang, Z., Yan, K., Zhong, Z.: Local multiple directional pattern of Palmprint images. In: Proceeding of International Conference on Pattern Recognition (ICPR), pp. 3013–3018 (2016)
26. PolyU palmprint image database. http://www.comp.polyu.edu.hk/~biometrics/
27. IITD palmprint image database. http://www4.comp.polyu.edu.hk/~csajaykr/IITD/Database_Palm.html
28. CASIA palmprint image database. http://biometrics.idealtest.org/

Fingerprint Presentation Attack Detection via Analyzing Fingerprint Pairs

Meng Zhang, Jianjiang Feng[(✉)], and Jie Zhou

Department of Automation, Tsinghua University, Beijing, China
jfeng@tsinghua.edu.cn

Abstract. With the ever growing deployments of fingerprint recognition systems, presentation attack detection has become the new bottleneck. In order to make full use of the difference in materials between the fake fingerprint and the real fingerprint, we proposed to utilize two images of a finger for classification. A pair of fingerprints are first aligned using a deformable registration algorithm and then are fed into MobileNet-v2 networks to perform the classification. Experimental results on the public dataset LivDet 2011 show that the performance of the proposed approach is promising and prove the effectiveness of fusing two fingerprints rather than using the fingerprints separately.

Keywords: Fingerprint presentation attack · Distortion · Thin-plate spline model · Mobilenet-v2

1 Introduction

Fingerprint recognition has been more often deployed in mobile and desktop solutions due to the convenience, uniqueness and stability such as unlocking a smartphone, mobile payments and international border control. On the other hand, fingerprint capture systems are very vulnerable while they are under the risk of attacks [1]. A determined person can effectively steal someone's fingerprint via the latent print on the keyboard or the cellphone screen, which is called uncooperative spoofing. These fake fingers can be realized by a number of fabrication materials such as PlayDoh, Gelatin, Wood Glue and Silicone, utilizing 2D or 3D printing techniques. More and more new, challenging fake fingers are generalized due to the unknown materials.

The fingerprint presentation attacks have called the attention of the researchers as a consequence. Different fingerprint presentation attack detection approaches were proposed and evaluated. The fingerprint presentation attack detection methods are usually classified to two groups: the methods based on hardware and the ones based on software. Hardware-based techniques always embed special sensors to the fingerprint capture systems to detect particular properties such as odor, vein, heartbeat or fingerprint sweat [2–4]. The software-based techniques use the standard capture system and detect the fake fingers

Z. Sun et al. (Eds.): CCBR 2019, LNCS 11818, pp. 12–19, 2019.
https://doi.org/10.1007/978-3-030-31456-9_2

through extracting the features combined with a classifier such as a trained Convolutional Neural Network (CNN) in recent years [6–10].

While many fingerprint scanners are capable of capturing a series of fingerprint images, most of the liveness detection methods only make use of one frame. For the purpose of fully extracting the features of real and fake fingers, we propose to utilize two frames of images that the finger is supposed to lift and then press. The information extracted from two captures is divided into two parts, one of which is the intensity changes of corresponding points while the other part is the distortion of the structures. Both types of information are related to characteristics of the material and thus useful for spoof detection. This work mainly takes advantage of the intensity changes. The proposed approach, utilizing two fingerprint captures, (i) obtains a series of paired minutiae as landmarks, (ii) calculates a thin-plate-spline model and aligns the two captures, (iii) trains a MobileNet-v2 network to distinguish a fake finger from a live one. The output of the MobileNet-v2 is a confidence score in the range [0,1]. Fingers whose scores are higher than the threshold are judged as live fingers, and the threshold is set to be 0.5.

The rest of this paper is organized as follows: Sect. 2 introduces the related fingerprint presentation attack detection works, Sect. 3 describes the details of the proposed approach and Sect. 4 reports the experiments evaluated in the LivDet datasets. Finally, we draw our conclusion in Sect. 5.

2 Related Work

2.1 Fingerprint Presentation Attack Detection

A great number of works have been done in the field of fingerprint presentation attack detection almost since the early attacks appeared. Some hardware-based approaches gained special features such as blood flow [2], odor [3] and electrical properties [4]. Engelsma et al. designed an open source fingerprint reader named RaspiReader to gain both direct images and FTIR images to reinforce the classifier [5]. The software-based approaches extracted texture features through handcrafted ways or filter banks [6,7]. With the further employment of Convolutional Neural Networks in extracting features from images, recent works trained neural networks for classification [8–10]. Chugh et al. [11] utilized local patches centered and aligned using fingerprint minutiae to train CNN and provided a start-of-the-art accuracy. Engelsma et al. [12] proposed a one-class classifier through training multiple generative adversarial networks (GANs) on live fingerprint images. However, most of above approaches took advantage of one of the images acquired but left the information between two images.

2.2 Liveness Detectoin Method Based on Distortion

Even though the novel fabrication materials are highly elastic, it seems difficult to make the fake fingers deform just like the real fingers because the distortion model depends on the underlying derma and shape of the finger bone in addition to the surface material. Zhang et al. [13] calculated the TPS model of distortion to compute the bending energy vector. The similarity of the bending energy vector to fuzzy feature set was calculated to distinguish the fake fingers from the live ones. Antonelli et al. [14] required users to move their fingers on the readers to produce skin distortion and computed the optical flow as the distortion model, which is encoded as DistortionCodes to determine the authenticity of the finger. Bao et al. [15] proposed a face attack detection method based on optical flow field as well. These methods employed clustering or SVM to classify and only gained the spatial information. Our approach trained the CNN and used the intensity changes between two images to get a more promising classifier.

3 Proposed Method

The flowchart of the proposed method is shown in Fig. 1. Phase based fingerprint registraion algorithm is used to calculate the thin-plate spline (TPS) model [16]. For each point (x, y), the TPS model describes the corresponding point (x', y') in the other image as $(f_x(x, y), f_y(x, y))$. Obtained the displacement of each point, we deform the point back and keep the intensity constant. As for a point (x, y) in the deformed fingerprint, the intensity is $\phi_2(x', y')$ before and is changed to $\phi_2'(x, y) = \phi_2(f_x(x, y), f_y(x, y))$ after the deformation, so the intensity of the aligned fingerprint pair is $\phi_1(x, y)$ and $\phi_2'(x, y)$. The intensity of points whose source points are out of range is set to 255 as padding. The registered fingerprint pair is showed in the Fig. 2 and then the fingerprint pairs are fed to train MobileNet-v2 networks.

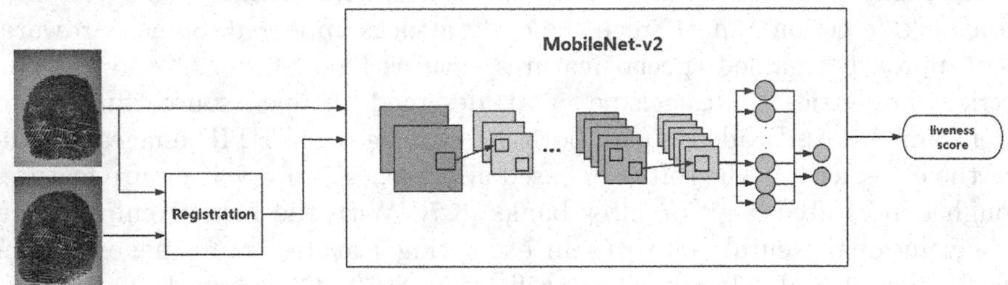

Fig. 1. The process of proposed method. We obtain the liveness scores utilizing the registered fingerprint pairs. The schematic diagram of MobileNet-v2 is just part of the full architecture.

Since the successful deployments of different CNN architectures in recent years, a great number of works have used the CNN to extract features from images such as AlexNet, VGG, GoogleNet, ResNets and MobileNet. We utilize the MobileNet-v2 [17] architecture in our study. The basic building block of MobileNet-v2 architecture is a bottleneck depth-separable convolution

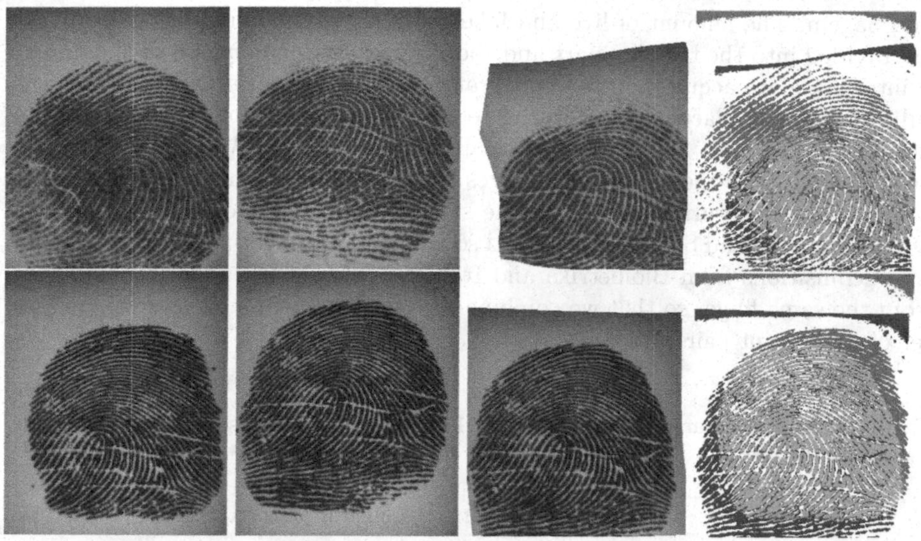

Fig. 2. Example of the aligned fingerprint pairs for live fingers (above) and spoof fingers (below). The first two columns is the origin fingerprints, the third column is the second fingerprint aligned to the first one. The last column presents the overlapping part of the aligned pair after binarization.

with residuals. The depth-separable convolutions decrease the model size to 8.67 M while the model size of VGG is over 100 M. The training time is reduced as the block with residuals maintains a better performance.

We concatenate the aligned fingerprint pairs as the two-channel input to train the MobileNet-v2 networks. A 1000-unit softmax layer which is the last layer of the original version is replaced by a 2-unit softmax layer for the fake or live detection. The first element of the softmax layer's output is recognized as the liveness score. The threshold of classifying the fake and the live fingers is set to 0.5, even though the performance will be slightly better when we select a specific threshold.

4 Experiments and Results

The experiments are performed on a computer with a Intel Xeon CPU E5-2620 and a NVIDIA GeForce GTX1080Ti with 12G memory. The training and evaluating of MobileNet-v2 are based on the PyTorch 1.0.

4.1 Dataset

In order to evaluate the performance of the proposed approach, we utilized LivDet 2011 datasets [18]. This dataset contains 16,000 fingerprint images acquired using four different sensors as Biometrika, Italdata, Digital Persona and Sagem. The amount of live and fake fingerprints are equal and the images are divided into the training part and the testing part equally. All of the fingerprint images are acquired in the cooperative subject scenario, which means the subject willingly places the fingerprint to get a fingerprint mold. The fabrication materials vary from 2D to 3D such as Ecoflex, Gelatine, Wood Glue and Silgum. We only use the fingerprint images from Biometrika and Italdata because we need the fingerprint pairs from the same fingers and the acquisitions from Digital Persona and Sagem are shuffled so we can hardly get paired fingerprints. The acquisitions from Biometrika and Italdata in the same folder are acquired from the same finger so that we combine the first image and each of others as a set of fingerprint pairs (Table 1).

Table 1. The summary of the LivDet 2011 dataset and the resolution of all of the sensors is 500 dpi.

Sensor	Biometrika	Italdata	Digital persona	Sagem
Image Size	312 × 372	640 × 480	355 × 391	352 × 384
#Live Images Train/Test	1000/1000	1000/1000	1000/1000	1000/1000
#Fake Images Train/Test	1000/1000	1000/1000	1000/1000	1000/1000
Fabrication Materials	Ecoflex, Gelatine, Latex, Silgum, Wood Glue		Gelatine, Latex, PlayDoh, Silicone, Wood Glue	

4.2 Training Parameters

We utilize the Adam optimizer to train our networks and the hyper parameters are set as following: the initial learning rate $lr = 0.0001$, $betas = (0.9, 0.99)$. The batch size is 10 and we apply the data augmentation techniques such as random cropping, random rotation, vertical flipping and horizontal flipping while training to avoid overfitting and the batch size is set to 10. We train the MobileNet-v2 with 1500 epochs and select the best evaluation model.

4.3 Results

The performance of proposed approach is evaluated by the metrics of average classification error (ACE):

$$ACE = \frac{FRR + FAR}{2} \tag{1}$$

where FAR (False Acceptance Rate) represents the percentage of the instances of classifying the fake fingers to be live and FRR (False Rejection Rate) represents the percentage of rejecting the live fingers falsely. To prove the effectiveness of fusing fingerprint pairs while some other studies get a good performance utilizing only one image, we conduct the experiment with an comparative experiment. For the first comparative experiment, we feed the original fingerprint pairs to train the MobileNet-v2 networks and evaluate it with fingerprint pairs. In the second comparative experiment, we train a best single fingerprint image MobileNet-v2 model, and then evaluate the model with fingerprint pairs. Two fingerprint images are fed into the best single model separately, which generates two liveness scores and we judge the classification to be right as long as one of the liveness scores distinguishes the finger correctly.

Table 2. Experimental results.

Dataset	LivDet 2011		
Sensor	Original fingerprint pairs	Single fingerprint	Proposed approach
Biometrika	7.505	7.836	1.447
Italdata	8.734	9.118	4.792

Our experimental results in Table 2 show that the proposed method fusing the aligned fingerprint pairs performs quite well on the dataset LivDet 2011. Compared to the original fingerprint pairs, our approach deforming the fingerprint eliminates the spatial interference. The alignment makes it easier to learn the difference of intensity changes between two images for MobileNet-v2 networks.

As showed in the Table 2, even the single fingerprint approach adopts two chances to detect the fingerprints, the proposed approach reaches a higher level accuracy. In the experiment of utilizing fingerprint image separately, we notice that the classification results of two images are almost the same which means that the model treat them similarly regardless of the information of finger distortion.

Note that the performance in Table 2 cannot be compared with performances of other PAD methods since the evaluation protocol is different. We utilize two images of the finger while most of other methods utilize one image, and they employ some complicated algorithms while our approach feeds the images into the CNNs directly. It is possible to apply our approach to other PAD methods to boost their performances.

5 Conclusion

In this paper, we propose a novel method to detect the fingerprint presentation attack. A set of aligned fingerprint pairs are fed into MobileNet-v2 networks while other study make use of images separately. The distortion of fingerprint pairs implies the difference in materials between the fake fingerprint and the real fingerprint. Our experimental results show that the intensity changes of corresponding points can conduce to fingerprint presentation attack detection and the method of fusing two aligned fingerprints get a promising performance on the LivDet 2011. In future work, we will apply the distortion of structure which may be same across different sensors to generalize the model and a more suitable dataset will be the key point.

Acknowledgments. This work is supported by the National Natural Science Foundation of China under Grants 61622207, 61527808, and Shenzhen fundamental research fund (subject arrangement) (Grant No. JCYJ20170412170438636).

References

1. Marcel, S., Nixon, M.S., Fierrez, J., Evans, N. (eds.): Handbook of Biometric Anti-Spoofing. ACVPR. Springer, Cham (2019). https://doi.org/10.1007/978-3-319-92627-8
2. Lapsley, P., Less, J., Pare, D., Hoffman, N.: Anti-fraud biometric sensor that accurately detects blood flow (1998)
3. Baldisserra, D., Franco, A., Maio, D., Maltoni, D.: Fake fingerprint detection by odor analysis. In: Zhang, D., Jain, A.K. (eds.) ICB 2006. LNCS, vol. 3832, pp. 265–272. Springer, Heidelberg (2005). https://doi.org/10.1007/11608288_36
4. Martinsen, O.G., Clausen, S., Nysather, J.B., Grimmes, S.: Utilizing characteristic electrical properties of the epidermal skin layers to detect fake fingers in biometric fingerprint systems-a pilot study. IEEE Trans. Biomed. Eng. **54**, 891–894 (2007)
5. Engelsma, J.J., Kai, C., Jain, A.K.: RaspiReader: open source fingerprint reader. IEEE Trans. Pattern Anal. Mach. Intell. **PP**(99), 1–1 (2017)
6. Jain, A.K., Prabhakar, S., Hong, L., Pankanti, S.: Filterbank-based fingerprint matching. IEEE Trans. Image Process. **9**(5), 846–859 (2000)
7. Jain, A., Ross, A., Prabhakar, S.: Fingerprint matching using minutiae and texture features. In: 2001 Proceedings of the 2001 International Conference on Image Processing, vol. 3, pp 282–285. IEEE (2001)
8. Nogueira, R.F., de Alencar Lotufo, R., Machado, R.: Fingerprint liveness detection using convolutional neural networks. IEEE Trans. Inf. Forensics Secur. **11**(6), 1206–1213C (2016)
9. Gottschlich, C.: Convolution comparison pattern: an efficient local image descriptor for fingerprint liveness detection. PLoS ONE **11**(2), e0148,552 (2016)
10. Kim, S., Park, B., Song, B.S., Yang, S.: Deep belief network based statistical feature learning for fingerprint liveness detection. Pattern Recognit. Lett. **77**, 58–65 (2016)
11. Chugh, T., Cao, K., Jain, A.K.: Fingerprint spoof buster: use of minutiae-centered patches. IEEE Trans. Inf. Forensics Secur. **13**(9), 2190–2202 (2018)
12. Engelsma, J.J., Arora, S.S., Jain, A.K., Paulter, N.: Universal 3D wearable fingerprint targets: advancing fingerprint reader evaluations. IEEE Trans. Inf. Forensics Secur. (2018). doi:https://doi.org/10.1109/TIFS.2018.2797000
13. Zhang, Y., Tian, J., Chen, X., Yang, X., Shi, P.: Fake finger detection based on thin-plate spline distortion model. In: Lee, S.-W., Li, S.Z. (eds.) ICB 2007. LNCS, vol. 4642, pp. 742–749. Springer, Heidelberg (2007). https://doi.org/10.1007/978-3-540-74549-5_78
14. Antonelli, A., Cappelli, R., Maio, D., Maltoni, D.: A new approach to fake finger detection based on skin distortion. In: Zhang, D., Jain, A.K. (eds.) ICB 2006. LNCS, vol. 3832, pp. 221–228. Springer, Heidelberg (2005). https://doi.org/10.1007/11608288_30

15. Bao, W., Li, H., Li, N., et al.: A liveness detection method for face recognition based on optical flow field. In: IEEE International Conference on Image Analysis and Signal Processing (2009)
16. Cui, Z., Feng, J., Li, S., Lu, J., Zhou, J.: 2-D phase demodulation for deformable fingerprint registration. IEEE Trans. Inf. Forensics Secur. **13**(12), 3153–3165 (2018)
17. Sandler, M., Howard, A., Zhu, M., et al.: MobileNetV2: Inverted Residuals and Linear Bottlenecks (2018)
18. Yambay, D., Ghiani, L., Denti, P., Marcialis, G.L., Roli, F., Schuckers, S.: LivDet 2011–Fingerprint liveness detection competition 2011. In: Proceedings 5th IAPR ICB, pp. 208–215 (2012)

Finger Vein Recognition Based on Double-Orientation Coding Histogram

Yuting Lu[1], Mo Tu[1], Hao Wang[1], Junhong Zhao[1](✉), and Wenxiong Kang[1,2]

[1] School of Automation Science and Engineering, South China University of Technology, Guangzhou 510641, China
auwxkang@scut.edu.cn

[2] School of Automation, Guangdong University of Petrochemical Technology, Maoming 525000, China

Abstract. More and more handcraft finger vein recognition algorithms have been proposed successively in recent years, and the orientation coding-based finger vein recognition has great research significance. In the paper, we offer a double orientation coding (DOC) method for finger vein recognition to represent the direction of vein texture using two orientation values. To strengthen the discrimination ability and robustness of the direction description, we further convert the DOC into the double orientation coding histogram (DOCH). Subsequently, since the proposed DOCH method cannot represent vein information adequately, we fuse DOCH with LBP scores. Finally, we propose a weighted score fusion strategy to improve recognition performance, which integrates the DOCH score and the LBP score with the chi-square distance and SVM respectively. Experimental results on two public databases (i.e., the MMCBNU_6000 and the FV-USM databases) demonstrate the effectiveness of our method for finger vein recognition, which has achieved 0.55% and 0.16% EERs.

Keywords: Finger vein recognition · Double orientation coding histogram · LBP · Score fusion

1 Introduction

In recent years, the increasing security demand of the public for identity recognition or verification has drawn substantial attention to biometrics [1]. Among the biometrics, finger vein recognition is regarded as a promising biometric technology because of its advantages, including difficult to counterfeit, living body recognition and the ability to be implemented in a compact device. And many practical finger vein recognition algorithms have been proposed successively. Generally, finger vein recognition consists of four steps: image acquisition, image preprocessing, feature extraction and matching, of which, feature extraction is the most crucial step. Additionally, most existing finger vein feature extraction methods can be divided into three groups, i.e. local texture structure-based, minutiae-based and orientation coding-based.

As for methods that extract local texture structure-based and minutiae-based features, there have been plenty of adequate studies, such as local directional code (LDC) [2] and

Z. Sun et al. (Eds.): CCBR 2019, LNCS 11818, pp. 20–27, 2019.
https://doi.org/10.1007/978-3-030-31456-9_3

discriminative binary codes (DBC) [3], singular value decomposition (SVD) [4] and so on. Although the abovementioned methods can achieve high accuracy, most of these methods have lower robustness against rotation than orientation coding-based methods. However, most existing orientation coding-based methods are mainly used for palmprint recognition [5–8], only exists a small number of orientation coding-based methods for finger vein feature extraction, like [9]. Moreover, the most challenging problem about orientation coding is that it is challenging to represent the orientation of finger vein patterns accurately and sufficiently due to the poor imaging quality and irregular shape of finger vein patterns.

Hence, to overcome the abovementioned problems, we propose an efficient orientation coding-based algorithm DOCH for finger vein recognition. This study can fully extract direction information from vein texture for finger vein recognition. And then, to represent the vein information adequately and boost the recognition performance, we fuse DOCH with LBP [10] in the score-level. Experimental results demonstrate the effectiveness of our method for finger vein recognition against finger rotation.

2 The Proposed Method

The framework of the proposed finger vein recognition method consists of three parts: image preprocessing, feature extraction, matching, and score-level fusion, as shown in Fig. 1. First, we obtain the ROI from the original image. Then, taking into account the vein texture deformation caused by finger rotation or translation, we use gradient alignment to get the most similar parts between the two matching images, which reduces the intra-class distance to some extent. Subsequently, we extract the orientation and structure features of the vein texture using DOCH and LBP methods, respectively. And then, the Chi-square distance and SVM classification are used to obtain the DOCH score and LBP score. Finally, we use a weighted score level fusion strategy to fuse the two scores.

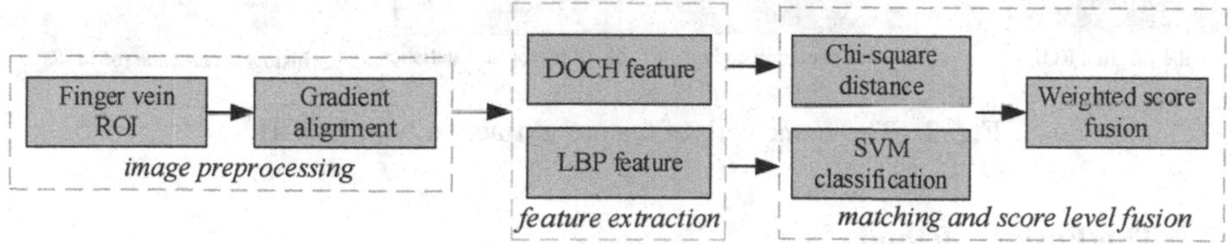

Fig. 1. The framework of the proposed method

2.1 Double-Orientation Coding Histogram Algorithm

As is known to us all, most existing orientation coding-based methods for finger vein recognition use the winner-take-all rule, which take the orientation corresponding to the maximum filter response value as the main direction of vein points. However, since the vein texture is curved in most cases and the orientation values used to describe the vein direction are discrete, it is not accurate to use only one orientation to describe the vein texture direction. Therefore, it is sufficient and reliable to obtain the orientation information of the vein texture with two different directions between 0° and 360°. Furthermore, double orientation has better robustness against slight rotation than a single orientation. Hence, it is more reasonable to describe the vein texture with the top-two largest filter response values rather than that only corresponds to the largest filter response value. Therefore, a method called double-orientation coding histogram (DOCH) is proposed to describe the finger vein features better.

As shown in Fig. 2, we first obtain the double-orientation coding of the entire ROI and then divide the coding map into 16 blocks according to trial and error, where the size of each block is 16×32. Subsequently, to further strengthen the robustness of the features, we use histogram statistics to represent the double-orientation coding of all blocks. Finally, we concatenate the histograms of all blocks together to form DOCH features (dimensions: 66×16). To show the pipeline clearly, we take one of the blocks as an example, as shown in the dashed box in the upper part of Fig. 2. Since each pixel has two different orientation values, we use twelve half-Gabor filters [8] to obtain the double-orientation values of all pixels in the image. There are twelve different orientation values and 66 types of double-orientation coding, that is, each set of double-orientation values can be converted to a number between 1 and 66. In the upper panel of Fig. 2, the first part (a) shows the double-orientation values of the pixels in the block, and then, we convert the double-orientation values to one number between 1 and 66, which is shown in part (b); finally, the coding values of the block are generated into a 66-dimensional histogram, which is shown in part (c).

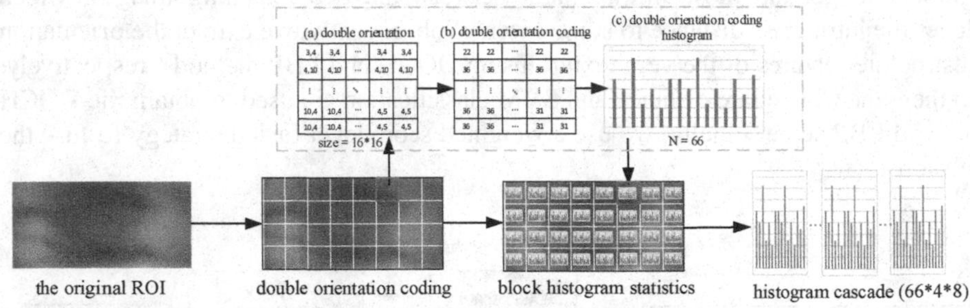

Fig. 2. The framework of feature extraction with DOCH

2.2 The Fusion Method

Although we can achieve a competitive result by extracting the DOCH feature for finger vein recognition, the proposed DOCH feature only contains the orientation information of the finger vein texture and lacks the structure information of finger vein texture, such as grayscale information and intensity changes, which can be supplemented by LBP feature. Therefore, to further increase the recognition accuracy, we fuse the DOCH with the LBP because of some degrees of compatibility and complementarity between these two features. That is, DOCH is dedicated to extracting the direction information, while LBP mainly extracts the structural information of the texture.

It is commonly known that most multimodal biometric fusion methods are mainly divided into feature-level fusion and score-level fusion. It is inappropriate to use a feature-level fusion strategy in our experiment since the relationship between DOCH and LBP feature spaces is unknown, and the concatenation of the two feature vectors can lead to huge dimensions. Moreover, score-level fusion is simpler and more convenient, and it is more effective to highlight the effectiveness of the fusion result using a simple score-level fusion than a feature-level fusion. The flowchart of fusion recognition is shown in Fig. 3.

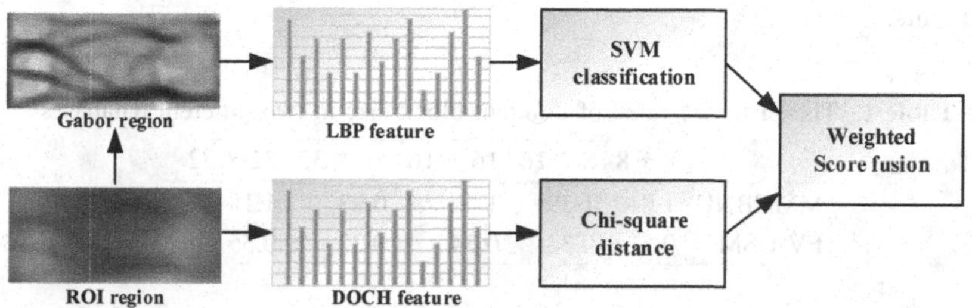

Fig. 3. The diagram of fusion recognition

In the score-level fusion, we first classify the LBP features using SVM, and then calculate the distance from all class feature vectors to the classification hyperplane as the LBP score according to the classification result. At the same time, the DOCH score is obtained by using the chi-square distance. Complementary weights are set for the two scores respectively. After traversing the weights with a certain step length, the weight with the minimum equal error rate was taken as the final weight.

3 Experimental Results and Discussion

In this paper, two public databases (i.e., MMCBNU_6000 [11], FV-USM [12]) and are used to evaluate the performances of the proposed DOCH method and the fusion method.

The MMCBNU database [11] consists of 6000 images which were captured from 83 males and 17 females, a total of 100 subjects, who come from 20 countries. The images of each subject were captured from the index finger, middle finger and ring finger of both hands; each finger was captured ten times. We utilize the provided ROI images of the database to conduct our experiment.

The FV-USM database [12] contains 5904 finger vein images in total, which is captured from 83 males and 40 females, a total of 123 subjects. The images of each subject were captured from the index finger and middle finger of both hands. Each finger was captured six times in each session and each subject was captured from two sessions between two weeks. Therefore, the database contains. Then, we utilized the provided ROI images in our experiments.

3.1 Performance of Different Block Size

To reduce the matching error caused by the alignment error, we introduce the histogram statistics into the DOC to generate the DOCH. In this conversion process, we first divide the DOC into non-overlapping blocks, and then the histogram statistics are performed on all blocks to generate DOCH. Here, the purpose of blocking is to preserve the local structure information of the original DOC. As shown in Table 1, the first row showed the different block sizes, while the first column refers to the different databases. It can be seen from Table 1 that the block size of 16 * 32 corresponds to the lower EER value. Therefore, the block size is set as 16 * 32 in the rest of the experiments.

Table 1. The EER (%) value of different block size in two different databases

	8 * 8	8 * 16	16 * 16	16 * 32	32 * 32
MMCBNU	1.81	1.39	1.42	0.93	1.15
FV-USM	0.51	0.33	0.34	0.22	0.35

3.2 Comparison of Single- and Double-Orientation Coding

To verify the accuracy and anti-rotation robustness of double-orientation coding and the effectiveness of our histogram statistics, we evaluate its performance by comparing the typical single-orientation coding method, Competitive Code [9], with our proposed double-orientation coding methods, DOC and DOCH on two open databases: MMCBNU_6000 and FV-USM. As shown in Table 2, it can be seen that our proposed DOCH method has the lowest EER value among the three methods in two databases. Moreover, the DOC method performs better than competitive coding in all two databases, which indicates that double-orientation coding is more effective for finger vein recognition than single-orientation coding. Furthermore, it can be seen from the comparison results of DOC and DOCH that the histogram statistics extracts the more discriminative finger vein information, which can significantly improve the recognition accuracy.

Table 2. The performance of single- and double-orientation coding on two different databases (EER%)

Methods	MMCBNU	FV-USM
Competitive Code	2.70	1.09
DOC	2.09	0.88
DOCH	0.93	0.22

3.3 The Effectiveness of the Proposed Fusion Method

As mentioned above, the DOCH method only extracts the orientation feature of finger veins, which not fully represent adequate vein texture information. Therefore, we proposed a weighted score-level fusion method that fuses the DOCH score with the

LBP score, which integrates the DOCH feature with chi-square distance and the LBP feature with SVM. We conduct comparison experiments on two public databases (i.e., MMCBNU_6000, FV-USM). For the SVM classification used on LBP feature, we adopt the same experimental protocol as that in the literature [12], i.e., data from the first session of the FV-USM database are used to train the SVM parameters, and data from the second session are used to evaluate the performance of our proposed fusion method. The trained parameters are also directly applied to MMCBNU. The performance of our proposed fusion method on four databases is shown in Table 3. It can be seen that the fusion method can improve the recognition performance to a certain extent compared with only using DOCH.

Table 3. The performance of our proposed fusing method on two different databases (EER%)

Methods	MMCBNU	FV-USM
DOCH	0.93	0.22
DOCH+LBP	0.55	0.16

3.4 Comparison with State-of-the-Art Algorithms

In this paper, we conduct our experiments on two public databases (i.e., MMCBNU_6000 and FV-USM) and. Tables 4 and 5 provide comparisons between the existing methods and our proposed method on two public databases. Comparison results shows that our proposed method has a better performance than most existing methods on two public finger vein databases. This is because our proposed fusion method combines the orientation information with the structure information of the texture to extract sufficient vein information,. Although the EER value of the two-channel convolutional network learning proposed in the literature [13] is lower than that of our proposed method in Table 4, it needs a more massive time consumption for pre-training the network and larger memory for storing the network. Therefore, to improve recognition performance and efficiency, we fuse the texture-based feature LBP with the orientation coding-based feature DOCH, which is proven effective in Tables 4 and 5.

Table 4. Comparison with the state-of-the-art in MMCBNU_6000

Reference	Methodology	EER%
Xie et al. [14]	Guided filter-based single scale retinex	1.5
Meng et al. [2]	Local directional code	1.03
Lu et al. [15]	Histogram of salient edge orientation map	0.9
Fang et al. [13]	Two-channel convolutional network learning	0.2
The proposed method	DOCH+LBP	**0.55**

Table 5. Comparison with the state-of-the-art in FV-USM

Reference	Methodology	EER%
Wang et al. [16]	Gabor wavelet features	4.75
Asaari et al. [12]	Band limited phase correlation	2.34
Qiu et al. [17]	Dual-sliding window and pseudo-elliptical transformer	2.32
Qin et al. [18]	Deep representation-based feature extraction	1.69
The proposed method	DOCH+LBP	**0.16**

4 Conclusion

Most existing finger vein recognition methods mainly focus on texture-based features or minutiae-based features, while orientation coding-based finger vein recognition algorithms are relatively few. However, orientation coding-based features are more robust against rotation than most texture-based and minutiae-based features. In the paper, we utilize double-orientation coding (DOC) to represent finger vein patterns; then, to further strengthen the discrimination ability of the direction description, a global histogram statistic is introduced to form the double-orientation coding histogram (DOCH). Furthermore, to represent the vein information adequately, we fuse LBP with our proposed DOCH because of the strong complementary and compatibility between the two features, that is, the chi-square distance is used to compute the DOCH score, and the SVM classification is used to obtain the LBP score. Furthermore, we conduct a series of rigorous contrast experiments on two public databases. The results show that the proposed methods have lower EERs than most existing methods when using the same database, which demonstrates the efficiency of our proposed methods. In the future, we will focus on developing more robust and effective orientation coding-based methods to obtain more finger vein information, thus improving recognition performance.

References

1. Jain, A.K., Ross, A., Prabhakar, S.: An introduction to biometric recognition. IEEE Trans. Circ. Syst. Video Technol. **14**(1), 4–20 (2004)
2. Meng, X., Yang, G., Yin, Y., Xiao, R.: Finger vein recognition based on local directional code. Sensors **12**(11), 14937–14952 (2012)
3. Xi, X., Yang, L., Yin, Y.: Learning discriminative binary codes for finger vein recognition. Pattern Recogn. **66**, 26–33 (2017)
4. Liu, F., Yang, G., Yin, Y., Wang, S.: Singular value decomposition based minutiae matching method for finger vein recognition. Neurocomputing **145**, 75–89 (2014)
5. Wei, J., Zhang, B., Lu, J., Zhu, Y., Yang, Z., Zuo, W., et al.: Palmprint recognition based on complete direction representation. IEEE Trans. Image Process. **26**(9), 4483–4498 (2017)
6. Fei, L., Wen, J., Zhang, Z., Yan, K., Zhong, Z.: Local multiple directional pattern of palmprint image. In: International Conference on Pattern Recognition (2017)
7. Fei, L., Xu, Y., Tang, W., Zhang, D.: Double-orientation code and nonlinear matching scheme for palmprint recognition. Pattern Recogn. **49**, 89–101 (2016)

8. Fei, L., Xu, Y., Zhang, D.: Half-orientation extraction of palmprint features. Elsevier Science Inc., New York (2016)
9. Yang, W., Huang, X., Zhou, F., Liao, Q.: Comparative competitive coding for personal identification by using finger vein and finger dorsal texture fusion. Inf. Sci. **268**, 20–32 (2014)
10. Lee, E.C., Jung, H., Kim, D.: New finger biometric method using near infrared imaging. Sensors **11**(3), 2319–2333 (2011)
11. Lu, Y., Xie, S.J., Yoon, S., Wang, Z., Dong, S.P.: An available database for the research of finger vein recognition. In: International Congress on Image and Signal Processing, pp. 410–415 (2014)
12. Asaari, M.S.M., Suandi, S.A., Rosdi, B.A.: Fusion of band limited phase only correlation and width centroid contour distance for finger based biometrics. Expert Syst. Appl. **41**(7), 3367–3382 (2014)
13. Fang, Y., Wu, Q., Kang, W.: A novel finger vein verification system based on two-stream convolutional network learning. Neurocomputing **290**(17), 100–107 (2018)
14. Xie, J.S., Lu, Y., Yoon, S., et al.: Intensity variation normalization for finger vein recognition using guided filter based singe scale retinex. Sensors **15**(7), 17089–17105 (2015)
15. Lu, Y., Yoon, S., Xie, S.J., Yang, J., Wang, Z., Park, D.S.: Efficient descriptor of histogram of salient edge orientation map for finger vein recognition. Appl. Opt. **53**(20), 4585–4593 (2014)
16. Wang, R., Wang, G., Chen, Z., Zeng, Z., Wang, Y.: A palm vein identification system based on Gabor wavelet features. Neural Comput. Appl. **24**(1), 161–168 (2014)
17. Qiu, S., Liu, Y., Zhou, Y., Huang, J., Nie, Y.: Finger-vein recognition based on dual-sliding window localization and pseudo-elliptical transformer. Expert Syst. Appl. **64**, 618–632 (2016)
18. Qin, H., El-Yacoubi, M.A.: Deep representation-based feature extraction and recovering for finger-vein verification. IEEE Press **12**(8), 1816–1829 (2017)

Fingerprint Classification Based on Lightweight Neural Networks

Junying Gan(✉), Ling Qi, Zhenfeng Bai(✉), and Li Xiang(✉)

Intelligent Manufacturing Department,
Wuyi University, 529020 Jiangmen, China
junyinggan@163.com, baizhenfeng1212@163.com,
xianglizaa@163.com

Abstract. Fast and accurate fingerprint classification is very important in large-scale fingerprint identification system. At present, fingerprint classification model has many problems such as complicated operation, lots of parameters, massive data. In this paper, we present a lightweight neural network for automatic extraction features and classification of fingerprint images. Fingerprint Region of Interest (ROI) images is regarded as the input of the network and fused with the shallow feature map to obtain accurate trend information of the shallow middle line. Transfer learning and fingerprint directional field map are combined to pre-train the lightweight network, then the parameters of the network are optimized and experimentally verified. Experimental results show that the fingerprint ROI is integrated into the deep features, which can improve the fingerprint classification effect. The transfer of the lightweight network model can reduce the network requirements for the target domain data and improve the classification performance of small sample fingerprint images.

Keywords: Fingerprint classification · Fingerprint feature fusion · Lightweight neural network · Transfer learning

1 Introduction

Deep learning has made great strides in recent years, especially in the Convolutional Neural Networks (CNNs). Training a deep network requires a lot of sample data. For the study of small sample problems, trainsfer learning methods have received extensive attention in recent years.

In 2010, Pan et al. [1] summarized the history, classification and challenges of transfer learning. In 2015, Hu et al. [2] presented a transfer learning algorithm for single-sample face recognition. In 2016, Geng et al. [3] designed a network framework based on transfer learning for Person Re-identification (ReID), which is used to solve the challenge of deep learning by ReID. In 2017, Yang Qiang et al. [4] presented transitive transfer by face and airplane, was realized in two completely different domains, which has brought broader application prospects in the domains of transfer learning, machine learning and even artificial intelligence. In 2018, Xu et al. [5] used transfer learning for face beauty prediction, removed the last fully connected layer of the trained VGG-16, and used it as a depth feature extractor.

Z. Sun et al. (Eds.): CCBR 2019, LNCS 11818, pp. 28–36, 2019.
https://doi.org/10.1007/978-3-030-31456-9_4

Fingerprint authentication is manually checked at the beginning. If the number of fingerprints is large, searching work will be monotonous, boring and error-prone. In the early research, the main way to extract feature point is based on geometric. The development of computers and the emergence of new algorithms have driven the rapid development of fingerprint authentication. Currently, there are four categories studied, such as endpoints, forks, triangles, and centers. We present a lightweight neural network for extracting features and classification of fingerprint images automatically. And we build feature fusion model and transfer classification model to improve the performance of fingerprint classification.

2 Algorithm Structure

2.1 Network Framework

CNNs are very effective in images classification and recognition. However, there is a contradiction between model performance and network parameter quantity in the process of images classification and recognition. This is one of the reasons why a good performance neural network is difficult to apply on the mobile terminal. The SqueezeNet [6] network model obtains the same accuracy as CNNs on the ImageNet datasets, but only requires 1/50 of the parameters.

We presented a Finger-SqueezeNet network, which is mainly composed of fire modules. The detailed structure includes: (1) The overall structure consists of two convolutional layers, five fire modules, four pooling layers and a softmax classifier for classification. (2) The first layer is a simple convolutional layer with a size of 7×7. (3) The fire module consists of compressed convolutional layer with the resolution of 1×1 and an extension layer of two hybrid filters with the resolution of 1×1 and 3×3, respectively. (4) H, W, and C are the height, width, and number of channels of the input images, respectively. S1 is the number of filters in the Squzze layer, e1 and e2 are the number of filters of 1×1 and 3×3, respectively. When the number of filters increases gradually with the number of layers, they were both satisfied with e1 = e2 = 4S1, the size entered by the fire module is represented as H * W * C. After fusion, the output feature map size is represented as H * C * (e1 + e2), as shown in Fig. 1.

2.2 Feature Fusion Model

The overall block diagram of fingerprint feature fusion classification is shown in Fig. 2. Firstly, we should refine and enhance fingerprint image, then put them into the top three layers of Finger-SqueezeNet for feature extracting. Secondly, the ROI images are obtained and convolved. It is ensured that the image size is the same as the size of the feature map extracted in the top three layers of the Finger-SqueezeNet network. Finally, the fingerprint feature map and the obtained fingerprint ROI images are merged in the network. On the other words, the merged fingerprint feature map is continued to be trained in the fourth layer of Finger-SqueezeNet to obtain the classification result.

Fingerprint classification method presented is mainly based on the pattern type. ROI of fingerprint is the local information of the ridge trend, which has a positive

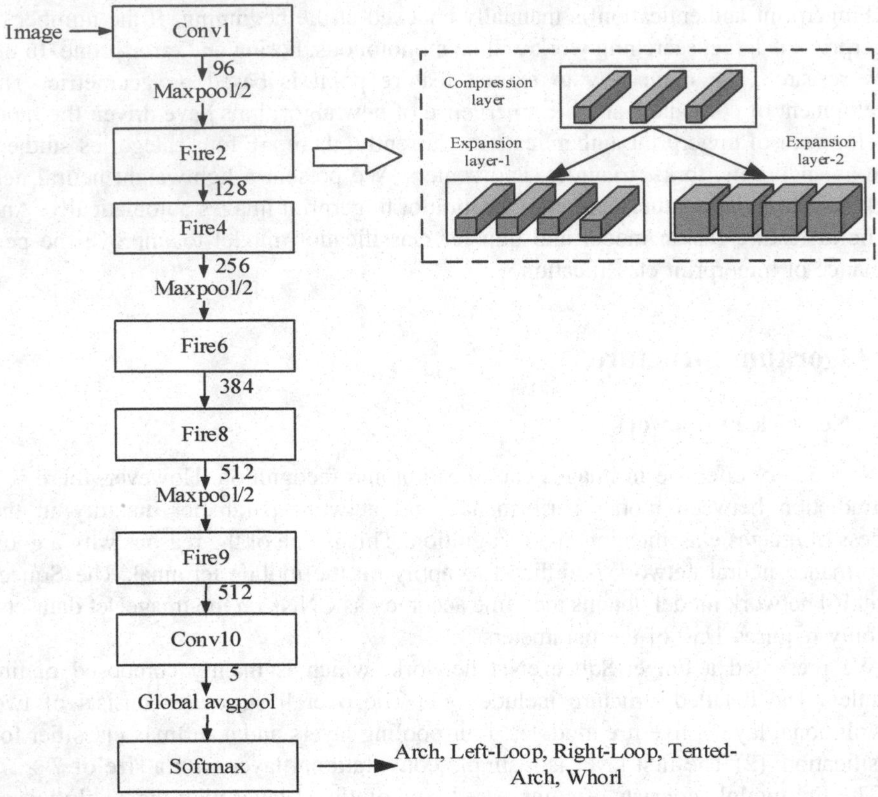

Fig. 1. Finger-squeezeNet network

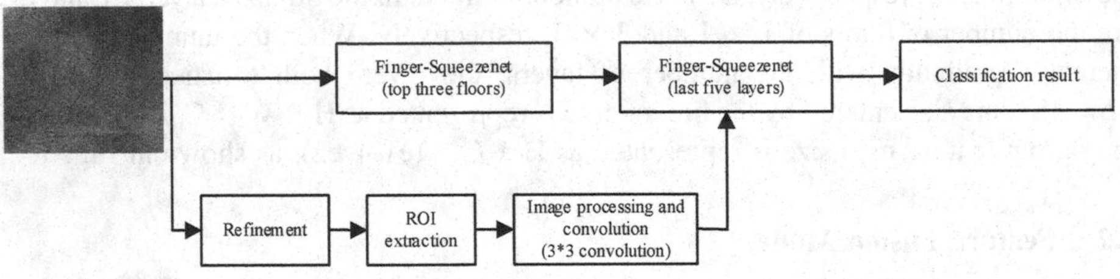

Fig. 2. Algorithm block diagram

enhancement effect on the division of the pattern. In order to emphasize the main features such as the pattern and direction, we first obtain the refined images of fingerprint and then extract the ROI images. ROI extraction includes edge detection, region segmentation, and threshold processing. After fingerprint images is refined, its pattern and direction are enhanced. The ROI images of fingerprint can be segmented more clearly by using reasonable threshold. Threshold processing is to calculate the gradient of fingerprint images, and then we can set a threshold by the gradient to extract the ROI. However, the threshold segmentation method has different effects on fingerprint segmentation with different quality. In order to avoid this phenomenon, we select the improved gradient method to extract the ROI, which was presented by Usman Akram et al. [7]. The gradient is no longer approximation, but is obtained by step-by-step summation. Firstly, the means of the gradient components M_x and M_y are expressed by

$$M_x = \frac{1}{\omega^2} \sum_{i=-\omega/2}^{\omega/2} \sum_{j=-\omega/2}^{\omega/2} \partial_x(i,j) \tag{1}$$

$$M_y = \frac{1}{\omega^2} \sum_{i=-\omega/2}^{\omega/2} \sum_{j=-\omega/2}^{\omega/2} \partial_y(i,j) \tag{2}$$

Secondly, calculate the gradient deviation D_x and D_y, expressed by

$$D_x = \sqrt{\frac{1}{\omega^2} \sum_{i=-\omega/2}^{\omega/2} \sum_{j=-\omega/2}^{\omega/2} (\partial_x(i,j) - M_x(I))^2} \tag{3}$$

$$D_y = \sqrt{\frac{1}{\omega^2} \sum_{i=-\omega/2}^{\omega/2} \sum_{j=-\omega/2}^{\omega/2} (\partial_y(i,j) - M_y(I))^2} \tag{4}$$

Finally, the final gradient deviation D is expressed by

$$D = D_x + D_y \tag{5}$$

When it is larger than the set threshold, it is the ROI; otherwise, it is the background that needs to be removed. According to the ROI process, the refined images and the ROI images are obtained as shown in Fig. 3.

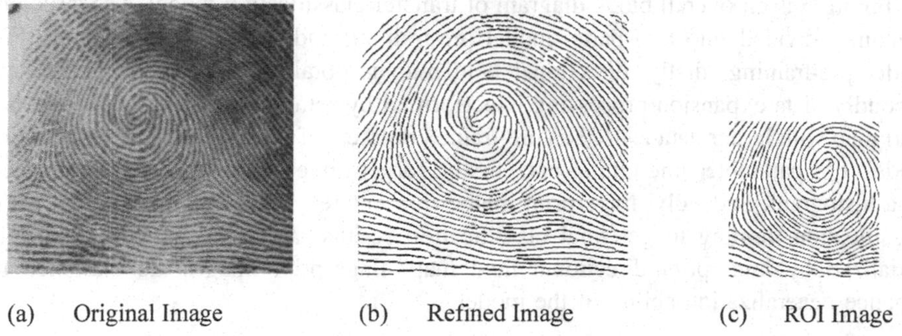

Fig. 3. (a) Original image, (b) refinement image, (c) ROI image

2.3 Transfer Classification Model

Transfer learning can use the similarity between data, tasks and models, and can transform the models learned in the past to the target tasks, making the model more personalized and more concise. Fine-tuning is the simplest transfer method [8], it not only can reduce time consumption and resource loss for the greater part, but also can make the model have stronger robustness and generalization ability.

Fingerprint can complete the transfer learning at the feature level because the map of fingerprint directional images belongs to two different feature spaces. Transfer learning not only makes full use of feature information, but also effectively enhances the generalization ability and robustness of the network. As shown in Fig. 4. We use the directional field map as the source domain and the fingerprint images as the target domain. The model-based transfer method refers to finding the shared parameters from the source domain and target domain. The premise of transfer method is that model parameters of source domain and target domain can be shared. The ellipse calibration in Fig. 4 is the parameter information that can be shared by two domains. When we determine the fingerprint feature information, the model parameters of the source domain can be retained, and we only use the target domain data to fine-tune model.

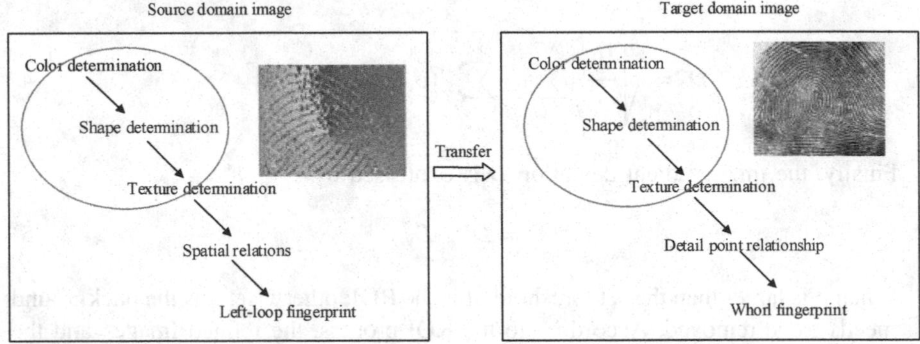

Fig. 4. Schematic diagram of transfer learning algorithm

Figure 5 is an overall block diagram of transfer classification model. The structure is mainly divided into two parts: model pre-training and parameter fine-tuning. For model pre-training, firstly, directional field map is obtained for fingerprint images. Secondly, data expansion processing is performed by rotation. Finally, the directional field map with larger data is used as pre-trained datasets of Finger-SqueezeNet network model. For parameter fine-tuning part, firstly, target fingerprint datasets are enhanced by a histogram. Secondly, fingerprint images are entered into pre-trained network for classification training to get final classification results. After the network model is initialized by fingerprint directional field map, fingerprint images are classified to enhance generalization ability of the model.

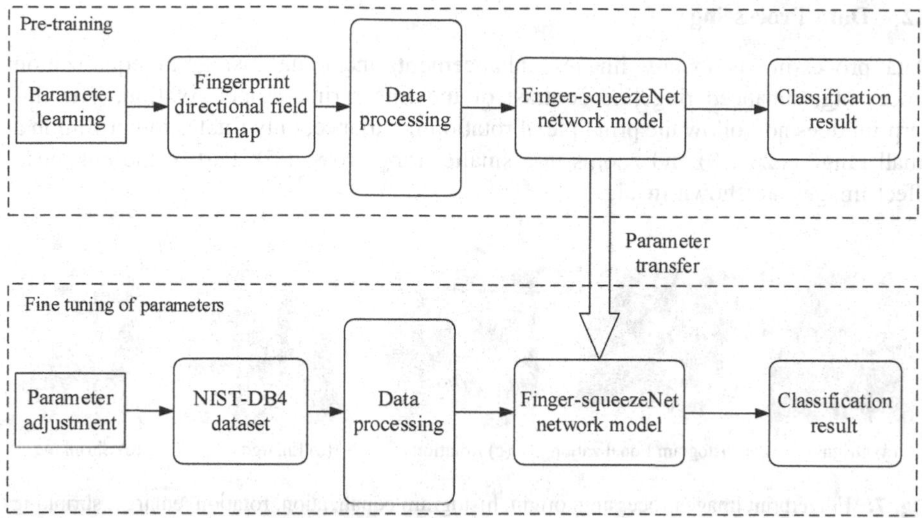

Fig. 5. Overall block diagram of model

3 Experimental Analysis

3.1 Experimental Object

Computer CPU in the experiment is InterCore i3-7350k, GPU is GeForce GTX1080 with 16G memory, operating system is Windows10, deep learning framework is Tensorflow, acceleration library is CUDA Toolkit 8.0.

In this paper, we use NIST-DB4 dataset, which contains 2000 pairs fingerprints with the resolution of 512 × 512. There are five categories: Arch, Left-loop, Right-loop, Tented-Arch, and Whorl. This dataset is widely used in many fingerprint identification studies, because the images quality is acceptable, and the reliability is high. Some experimental samples are shown in Fig. 6.

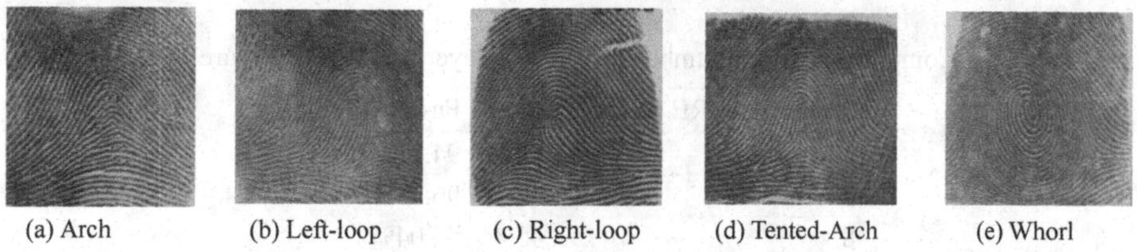

Fig. 6. Five types of fingerprints: arch, left-loop, right-loop, tented-arch, whorl

In NIST-DB4 dataset, each fingerprint has an independent pattern label, and the quality is within the acceptable limits. However, NIST-DB4 dataset has a 17.5% fuzzy label, the same type of fingerprint is assigned to two labels. Usually, the fuzzy label is Arch and Tented-Arch.

3.2 Data Processing

Data processing is mainly images enhancement, including histogram equalization processing, enhanced ridgeline contrast of the fingerprint, proper rotation. The fingerprint does not follow the principle of rotation invariance, only rotates fingerprint in a small range (−20, 20) and zooms in a smaller range (0.8, 1.5). Part of the enhanced effect images are shown in Fig. 7.

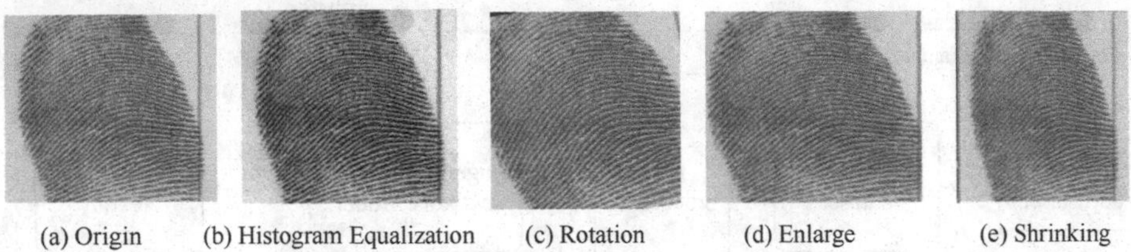

(a) Origin (b) Histogram Equalization (c) Rotation (d) Enlarge (e) Shrinking

Fig. 7. Fingerprint image processing: origin, histogram equalization, rotation, enlarge, shrinking

3.3 Experimental Results

3.3.1 Feature Fusion Experiment

We start from the trainable fire layer and discusses the optimal network layer suitable for fingerprint classification. We have fused ROI images of fingerprint to compensate for shallow features in deep network. Table 1 shows the results of five-category experiments. The verification standard is average accuracy of fingerprint classification. Trainable network is the fire module of the network structure. The number of fire modules in the 3, 5 and SqueezeNet is selected, obtained from Table 1. It is not the deeper the network is, the better the classification effect is. For fingerprint classification, best network layer for training is 5 Finger-fire layers, classification results obtained is the best, up to 96.81%. From the analysis of ROI feature and its fusion classification effect is better than unfused feature map. It is inferred that the fusion processing of fingerprint ROI images can compensate for shallow feature loss in the network, improving classification accuracy.

Table 1. Comparison of the number of network layer and fusion feature accuracy

Trainable FIRE layer	Unfused	Fusion ROI
3	91.14%	94.35%
5	95.52%	96.81%
8	95.45%	96.04%

Table 2 is images-enhanced NIST-DB4 dataset, fingerprint five-category test results after multi-features fusing. The average accuracy of five fingerprint types is 94.57%. The best classification effect is Whorl fingerprint, which can achieve an accuracy of 97.86%.

Table 2. Multi-features fusion with five types of fingerprint classification results

Types	Arch	Left-loop	Right-loop	Tented-Arch	Whorl
Arch	443	7	3	20	2
Left-loop	11	448	0	4	5
Right-loop	5	3	444	7	8
Tented-Arch	31	7	4	426	0
Whorl	2	4	3	1	458
Accuracy: 94.57%					

3.3.2 Transfer Classification Experiment

Table 3 shows training accuracy of NIST-DB4 dataset dividing two categories F and S into transfer learning model, in which F and S is the training accuracy of entire NIST-DB4 dataset. When training on dataset, a part of fingerprint is randomly extracted from the dataset for verifying, data enhancement processing is needed, enhanced images will be more abundant, and the network generalization ability is improved.

Table 3. Comparison of different datasets

Datasets category	Accuracy
F	97.37%
S	96.52%
F and S	98.45%

Table 4 is classification results of classification model based on transfer learning. The average accuracy of five fingerprint types is 95.73%. Best classification effect is Whorl fingerprint, up to 98.72%. The classifications of Arch and Tented-Arch are more difficult to complete in testing. What causes the problem is dataset, in which there exist two classification labels for some images.

Table 4. Five types of fingerprint classification results of transfer learning model

Types	Arch	Left-loop	Right-loop	Tented-Arch	Whorl
Arch	443	5	2	17	1
Left-Loop	7	452	1	5	3
Right-Loop	4	2	450	5	7
Tented-Arch	27	5	3	433	0
Whorl	0	4	2	0	462
Accuracy: 95.73%					

4 Conclusion and Future Work

Experiments show that when the Finger-SqueezeNet network contains 5 Finger-fire modules and 2 convolution modules, fingerprint classification model has highest accuracy and least parameter. According to the results of two algorithms, fingerprint classification model obtained by transfer learning has a deeper impact on classification generalization ability of neural networks due to multi-features fusion fingerprint classification algorithm.

With the popularity of mobile wearable devices, the implementation of algorithms on the mobile terminal has opened up a new direction for fingerprint classification research.

Acknowledgement. This Work is Supported by National Natural Science Foundation of China (No. 61771347), Basic Research and Applied Basic Research Key Project in General Colleges and Universities of Guangdong Province (No. 2018KZDXM073).

References

1. Pan, S.J., Yang, Q.: A survey on transfer learning. IEEE Trans. Knowl. Data Eng. **22**(10), 1345–1359 (2010)
2. Hu, J., Lu, J., Zhou, X., et al.: Discriminative transfer learning for single-sample face recognition, pp. 272–277. In: International Conference on Biometrics (ICB). IEEE (2015)
3. Geng, M., Wang, Y., Xiang, T., et al.: Deep transfer learning for person re-identification. arXiv preprint arXiv:1611.05244 (2016)
4. Tan, B., Zhang, Y., Pan, S.J., et al.: Distant domain transfer learning. In: Thirty-First AAAI Conference on Artificial Intelligence (2017)
5. Xu, L., Xiang, J., Yuan, X.: Transferring rich deep features for facial beauty prediction [EB/OL], 20 March 2018. https://arxiv.org/pdf/1803.07253.pdf
6. Iandola, F.N., et al.: SqueezeNet: AlexNet-level accuracy with 50x fewer parameters and <0. 5 MB model siz. arXiv preprint arXiv:1602.07360 (2016)
7. Akram, M.U., Nasir, S., Tariq, A., et al.: Improved fingerprint image segmentation using new modified gradient based technique. In: Canadian Conference on Electrical and Computer Engineering, CCECE. IEEE (2008). 001967-001972
8. Wang, J.: Transfer Learning Tutorial. Technical report 2018. 4. http://jd92.wang

3D Fingerprint Gender Classification Using Deep Learning

Haozhe Liu[1,2,3], Wentian Zhang[1,2,3,4], Feng Liu[1,2,3](✉), and Yong Qi[4]

[1] The National Engineering Laboratory for Big Data System Computing Technology, Shenzhen University, Shenzhen 518060, China
liuhaozhest@gmail.com, zhangwentianml@gmail.com, feng.liu@szu.edu.cn

[2] The Guangdong Key Laboratory of Intelligent Information Processing, Shenzhen University, Shenzhen 518060, China

[3] College of Computer Science and Software Engineering, Shenzhen University, Shenzhen 518060, China

[4] College of Electrical and Information Engineering, Shaanxi University of Science and Technology, Shaanxi 710021, China
qiyong@sust.edu.cn
http://cv.szu.edu.cn

Abstract. Optical Coherence Tomography (OCT) is a high resolution imaging technology, which provides a 3D representation of the fingertip skin. This paper for the first time investigates gender classification using those 3D fingerprints. Different with current fingerprint gender classification methods, the raw multiple longitudinal(X-Z) fingertip images of one finger can be applied instead of studying features extracted from fingerprints, and the model can be trained effectively when the training data set is relatively small. Experimental results show that the best accuracy of 80.7% is achieved by classifying left fore finger on a small database with 59 persons. Meanwhile, with the same data size and method, the accuracy of classification based on 3D fingerprints is much higher than that based on 2D fingerprints: the highest accuracy is increased by 46.8%, and the average accuracy is increased by 26.5%.

Keywords: 3D Fingerprint · Gender Classification · OCT

1 Introduction

Fingerprint, as the main biological feature of finger, has several ideal characteristics such as universality, salience, permanence, collectibility, acceptability

---

The work is partially supported by the Natural Science Foundation of China (61672357, 61573248, 61802267, 61732011 and U1713214), the Science and Technology Funding of Guangdong Province (2017A030313367 and 2018A050501014), Shenzhen Fundamental Research fund (JCYJ20180305125822769), the Education Department of Shaanxi Province (15JK1086), and Shaanxi University of Science and Technology Dr. Foundation (BJ14-07).

Z. Sun et al. (Eds.): CCBR 2019, LNCS 11818, pp. 37–45, 2019.
https://doi.org/10.1007/978-3-030-31456-9_5

and anti-circumvention, and it is widely used in personal identification system [1]. Fingerprint-based gender classification, as one of the important identification of human, is of great significance for forensic anthropology, tracking and identification of unknown populations, census of population data, etc. [2,3].

Currently, fingerprint-based gender classification can be roughly divided into two categories. One refers to identify human gender by classifying artificial annotation features extracted from fingerprint images, such as ridge count, ridge density, ridge thickness to valley thickness ratio, white lines count [4–6]. These studies show that ridge density has the strongest distinguishability among those gender artificial annotation features to classify genders. In general, the fingerprint of man demonstrates the lower density of the ridge line, and the higher is mostly female [7,8]. The public best accuracy is about 97.25% based on a dataset with 3000 fingerprints using multilayer perceptron neural network [6]. The other one is classifying gender by extracting features automaticly from fingerprints. The feature extraction methods include discrete wavelet transform (DWT), Canny algorithm, singular value decomposition (SVD) and so on [2,9–11], while K nearest neighbor (KNN) [2,9], backpropagation (BP) [10], artificial neural network (ANN) [11] are usually taken as classifiers. Based on self-built and undisclosed 2D fingerprint databases, of which the minimum number is 550 [9] and the maximum is 22000 [12], the best accuray can reach to 98.42% [9].

It can be seen that both types of methods mentioned above have a limitation: Features, no matter whether they are manually labelled or automatically extracted, must be accurate enough for the subsequent classification task. This will make the classification result relies heavily on image quality. Moreover, current fingerprint-based gender classification builds on 2D fingerprint images with ridge and valley patterns. The limited information provided by 2D fingerprints impedes the development of gender classification. Recently, optical coherence tomography (OCT) proposed a new way to imaging fingerprints [13]. A 3D representation with depth information of fingerprints can be provided using OCT. This paper for the first time directs a gender classification method based on such 3D fingerprints. The motivations and contributions of this paper are summarized as follows:

1. The depth information, which is not available on 2D fingerprint images, is considered for gender classification.
2. Since multiple longitudinal(X-Z) fingertip images of one finger are provided, the deep learning method can be adopted and the model can be trained effectively when the training data set is relatively small. In this paper, a best accuracy of 80.7% is achived by classifying 59 left fore fingers using the proposed discriminate model. The size of database is only one-tenth of the smallest one ever.
3. By using the proposed learning method, it is no need to extract features from original fingerprint image, which solved the problem existed in current gender classification methods.

4. In the case of the same data size, the proposed 3D fingerprint gender classification can improve an average accuracy of 26.5% when compared with the method based on 2D fingerprints.

2 Acquisition Device and Data Description

Since the 3D fingerprints used in this paper is quite different with traditional 2D fingerprints, we then introduce our acquisition device and data in detail. The prototype of the acquisition device is shown in Fig. 1(a). It equips with a super luminescent diode (SLD) and two identical telecentric lenses. A source light centred at 840 nm is emitted by the SLD. Two identical telecentric lenses are used as a focusing lens and a scanning lens. High-resolution tomography imaging of the internal microstructure of the biological tissue is performed by measuring the interference signal of the sample backscattered light. Spectral information along the depth direction of fingertip skin, denoted by A-line as labelled in Fig. 1(b), is then obtained using a rate of 18 kHz, which reach to a depth of about 1.8 mm into the skin corresponding to 500 pixels. The number of A-line in this paper is 1500, so as to finally get a longitudinal(X-Z) fingertip images with spatial size of $500 * 1500$ pixels, as shown in Fig. 1(b). For 3D scanning, a slow scanning galvanometer is employed to obtain 400 B-scans. Thus, the 3D fingerprint image captured by our device consists of four hundreds longitudinal(X-Z) fingertip images with spatial size of $500 * 1500 * 400$ pixels to quantify a real fingerprint area of 15 mm $*$ 15 mm $*$ 1.8 mm, as the example given in Fig. 1(b). Figure 1(c) shows the X-Y tomographic images of the 3D fingerprint, which is the same as traditional 2D fingerprint image but imaging at different depth.

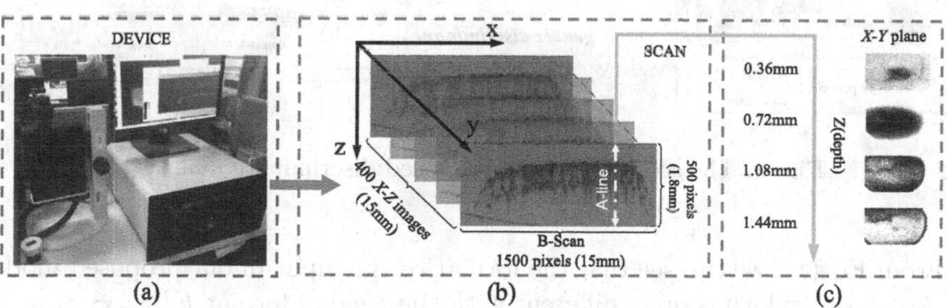

Fig. 1. An example of a 3D Fingerprint image captured by our device: X-Y corresponds to our observation of traditional 2D fingerprint and Z is the additional depth direction of the 3D fingerprint. (a). The 3D fingerprint acquistion device using OCT in the paper. (b). The captured 400 longitudinal(X-Z) fingertip images of one finger along Y direction, (c). The X-Y tomographic images of the 3D fingerprint.

3 Gender Classification Based on Deep Learning

3.1 The Proposed Discriminate Model

As we known, deep Convolutional Neural Networks play an important role on image classification since they can handle complex image classification tasks and can achieve high accuracy without any preprocessing [14–16]. Among those Deep CNNs, ResNet outstands due to its superior performance to solve the vanishing/exploding gradients problem in model training [16,17]. Thus, in this paper, we proposed a discriminate model based on ResNet-17 to solve gender classification problem using 3D fingerprints imaging by OCT. Figure 2 shows the framework of our proposed gender discriminate model. It can be seen that the input of the model is the longitudinal(X-Z) fingertip images and the output is gender category. Then, the model is formulated as

$$F_i(FI_{\sum x,y,\sum z}) = label \tag{1}$$

F_i represents the discriminate model. FI is defined as a matrix of a finger and $FI_{\sum x,y,\sum z}$ refers to the representation of 3D fingerprints in the form of x-z plane. The *label* is the output of the ModelF_i.

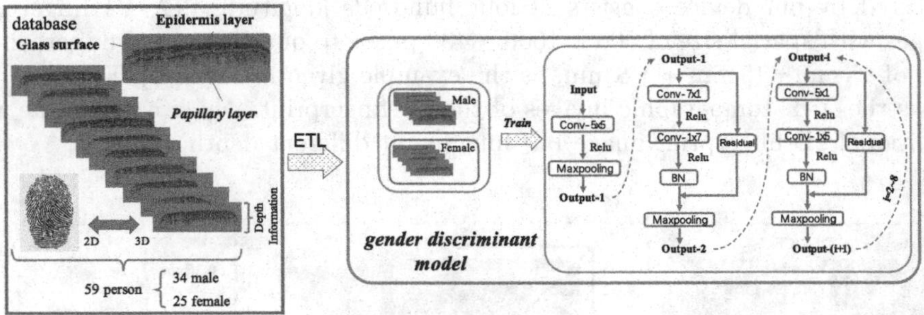

Fig. 2. The structure of the proposed discriminate model.

From Eq. (1), we can see that the format of the input in our proposed model is $FI_{\sum x,y,\sum z}$, which is quite different with the general format $FI_{\sum x,\sum y,z=C}$ in traditional models. This is because the data size of each finger is $500 * 1500 * 400$ pixels. The growth of data volume caused by the increase of data dimension makes our model more efficient and stronger, and also effectively reduces the risk of over-fitting problem in model training. Furthermore, with the increase of Dot Per Inch (*dpi*) in x, y and z directions of image, the training data of 3D image will be much higher than that of 2D images, as expressed by Eq. (2).

$$\lim_{dpi_{xyz} \to +\infty} \frac{FI_{2D}}{FI_{3D}} = 0 \tag{2}$$

This means that 3D images have more features and information than 2D with the support of a certain dpi. However, the training-time of the model will be prolonged thereupon.

To solve this problem, we fine tuned the structure: the traditional convolution structure of $A * A$ is replaced by $A * 1$ and $1 * A$ as shown in Fig. 2. By doing so, the storage space occupied by the network structure learning from inception algorithm [18] was reduced and the model can be trained effectively.

3.2 Model Training and Parameter Setting

Algorithm 1 gives the training process of this paper. We trained eight times so as to adapt to the characteristics of different fingers. The ratio of test set to training for each group is 0.25.

```
Algorithm: Model Training
    for each i in finger[1, 8] do
        initialize a model Fi;
        for each num in epochcount do
            for each data in traindata do
                data := Shuffle(data);
                Fi := Train(Fi,data);
            end for
        end for
        Return Fi;
    end for
```

The training implementation details are stated as follows. First, initializing the weights in each layer from a zero-mean Gaussian distribution with standard deviation 0.02. Training adopted Adam as optimization method with 0.99 β_1 and 0.999 β_2. The mini-batch is set to 10, base learning-rate is set to 0.001 and the max-iteration is set to 32 million. Tensorflow framework was used to implement the network training and testing. Workstation's CPU is 2.8 GHz RAM 32 GB and GPU is NVIDIA TITAN Xp. All methods were implemented using python.

4 Results and Analysis

4.1 Database and Protocols

The experimental data is collected from of 25 Asian females and 34 Asian males aged from 18 to 35 years old. Each volunteer provides 8 fingerprints, including thumb, fore finger, middle finger and ring finger from both hands. For each finger, we have 400 longitudinal(X-Z) fingertip images collected by our device using OCT and one 2D image collected by a commercial optical 2D fingerprint sensor (i.e. URU4000B). Thus, two databases are established. One is 3D fingerprint database of 200 female fingers and 272 male fingers, which corresponds to 80000 female longitudinal(X-Z) images and 108800 male longitudinal(X-Z) images respectively. The other one is 2D fingerprint database of 200 female fingers and 272 male fingers.

Nine sets of data classified by finger type, expressed with L-thumb, L-forefinger, L-middle, L-ringfinger, R-thumb, R-forefinger, R-middle, R-ringfinger, and AllFingers are used for experiments. The ratio of test set to training is 1:4. Recognition accuracy and Loss value are used to evalute the performance of classification. The *Loss* can show the gap between predicted gender labels and real labels. The lower the Loss value is, the more similar the predicted result to be with the real label.

In order to fairly compare the proposed 3D fingerprint gender classification method with 2D fingerprint-based gender classification, the KNN, BP and ANN methods used in current 2D fingerprint-based gender classification are replaced by deep learning methods. Meanwhile, different networks, such as VGG, AlexNet, ResNet, with same or similar networks were adopted to perform 2D fingerprint-based classification [14–16].

4.2 Gender Classification Performance

To show the performance of the proposed method, we calculated the recognition accuracy and loss value for nine experiments we organized, as shown in Table 1. From Table 1, we can see that different accuracy are achieved by different fingers. The best accuracy of 80.7% and Loss value of 0.496 is obtained based on left fore finger, which shows the feasibility of the proposed method. The worst accuracy of 54.4% is obtained when considering all fingers(the training and testing set are made up of all kinds of fingers), which indicates that it is better to propose to use the same finger for a gender classification system.

Table 1. Results: nine sets of 3D fingerprint dataset using the proposed method.

Finger-Kinds	Acc	Loss	Epoch-Num
L-thumb	78.5%	0.967	66
L-forefinger	80.7%	0.496	28
L-middle	70.0%	0.830	129
L-ringfinger	56.4%	3.112	54
R-thumb	54.7%	0.686	11
R-forefinger	71.1%	2.048	123
R-middle	73.4%	0.620	121
R-ringfinger	65.8%	5.143	10
All-Fingers	54.4%	0.684	200

In order to verify the usefulness of the additional depth information of 3D fingerprints to gender classification, we tested 2D fingerprint-based gender classification using different networks on the collected 2D fingerprint database. The experimental results are given in Table 2. In order to compare the advantage and disadvantage of 3D and 2D fingerprint images in gender classification, we define I_{rate},

$$I_{rate} = \frac{Acc_{3D} - \max\limits_{F} Acc_{2D}}{\max\limits_{F} Acc_{2D}} \quad (3)$$

On the one hand, it can be seen that all of the results based on 2D fingerprints are worse than those based on 3D fingerprints. The accuracy of the recognition fluctuates around 50%, which means that deep learning algorithm is ineffective in such small data case. The above results indicate a problem that the deep learning models can not capture the classification features in the data. On the other hand, the highest accuracy of 3D fingerprint-based gender classification is increased by 46.8% (I_{rate}), and the average accuracy is increased by 26.5% (I_{rate}). Those results have proved the usefulness of the additional depth information of 3D fingerprints to gender classification. By comparing with the accuracy of 2D fingerprint-based gender classification using different networks, we further demonstrated the effectiveness of the proposed 3D fingerprint-based gender classification.

Table 2. Results based on different networks implemented on 2D fingerprint datasets.

Finger-Kinds	AlexNet	VGG	ResNet	I_{rate}
L-thumb	54.4%	54.5%	54.0%	44.0%
L-forefinger	60.0%	50.0%	50.0%	34.5%
L-middle	50.0%	50.0%	50.0%	40.0%
L-ringfinger	55.6%	55.8%	55.6%	1.10%
R-thumb	50.0%	50.0%	50.0%	9.40%
R-forefinger	45.5%	54.5%	54.5%	30.5%
R-middle	44.4%	44.4%	50.0%	46.8%
R-ringfinger	50.0%	50.0%	44.4%	31.6%
AllFingers	52.2%	53.6%	51.4%	0.20%

5 Conclusion

The different representation of fingerprints imaged by OCT opens up a new research domain for fingerprint recognition. This paper for the first time investigated gender classification using X-Z depth fingerprints. By making full use of the multiple longitudinal(X-Z) fingertip images of one finger, the discriminate model was trained effectively utilizing deep learning method and was then applied in gender classification. In the experiments, the proposed 3D fingerprint-based gender classification method can classify gender effectively on a database of 25 female fingers and 34 male fingers without separation between feature extraction and classification, but the 2D method with the same data size is not ideal. There are two reasons for this result: The first is that, with a small number of data, learning algorithms are difficult to achieve good results and the second is that we believe there are a lot of undiscovered features in the 3D fingerprints imaged by OCT, which are worth to study and discover.

References

1. Jain, A.K., Dass, S.C., Nandakumar, K.: Can soft biometric traits assist user recognition? In: Biometric Technology for Human Identification. International Society for Optics and Photonics, vol. 5404, pp. 561–573 (2004)
2. Gnanasivam, P., Muttan, S.: Fingerprint gender classification using wavelet transform and singular value decomposition. arXiv preprint arXiv:1205.6745 (2012)
3. Gupta, S., Prabhakar Rao, A.: Fingerprint based gender classification using discrete wavelet transform & artificial neural network. Int. J. Comput. Sci. Mob. Comput. **3**(4), 1289–1296 (2014)
4. Hossain, S., Habib, A.: Improving fingerprint based gender identification technique using systematic pixel counting. In: International Conference on Electrical Engineering & Information Communication Technology (2015)
5. Abdullah, S.F., Rahman, A.F.N.A., Abas, Z.A., Saad, W.H.M.: Fingerprint gender classification using univariate decision tree (j48). Network (MLPNN) **96**(95.27), 95–95 (2016)
6. Abdullah, S.F., Rahman, A.F.N.A., Abas, Z.A., Saad, W.H.M.: Multilayer perceptron neural network in classifying gender using fingerprint global level features. Indian J. Sci. Technol. **9**9 (2016)
7. Li, X., Zhao, X., Fu, Y., Liu, Y.: Bimodal gender recognition from face and fingerprint. In: 2010 IEEE Conference on Computer Vision and Pattern Recognition (CVPR), pp. 2590–2597. IEEE (2010)
8. Ceyhan, E.B., Sağiroğlu, Ş.: Gender inference within Turkish population by using only fingerprint feature vectors. In: 2014 IEEE Symposium on Computational Intelligence in Biometrics and Identity Management (CIBIM), pp. 146–150. IEEE (2014)
9. Shinde, S.R., Thepade, S.D.: Gender classification with KNN by extraction of HAAR wavelet features from canny shape fingerprints. In: 2015 International Conference on Information Processing (ICIP), pp. 702–707. IEEE (2015)
10. Sheetlani, J., Pardeshi, R.: Fingerprint based automatic human gender identification. Threshold **170**(7), 1–4 (2017)
11. Kanojia, M., Gandhi, N., Armstrong, L.J., Suthar, C.: Fingerprint based gender identification using digital image processing and artificial neural network. In: Abraham, A., Muhuri, P.K., Muda, A.K., Gandhi, N. (eds.) ISDA 2017. AISC, vol. 736, pp. 1018–1027. Springer, Cham (2018). https://doi.org/10.1007/978-3-319-76348-4_98
12. Mishra, A., Khare, N.: A review on gender classification using association rule mining and classification based on fingerprints. In: 2015 Fifth International Conference on Communication Systems and Network Technologies (CSNT), pp. 930–934. IEEE (2015)
13. Auksorius, E., Boccara, A.C.: Fast subsurface fingerprint imaging with full-field optical coherence tomography system equipped with a silicon camera. J. Biomed. Opt. **22**(9), 1 (2017)

14. LeCun, Y., Bottou, L., Bengio, Y., Haffner, P.: Gradient-based learning applied to document recognition. Proc. IEEE **86**(11), 2278–2324 (1998)
15. Krizhevsky, A., Sutskever, I., Hinton, G.E.: Imagenet classification with deep convolutional neural networks. In: International Conference on Neural Information Processing Systems, pp. 1097–1105 (2012)
16. He, K., Zhang, X., Ren, S., Sun, J.: Deep residual learning for image recognition, pp. 770–778 (2015)
17. Tian, C., Xu, Y., Fei, L., Yan, K.: Deep learning for image denoising: a survey. arXiv preprint arXiv:1810.05052 (2018)
18. Yu, X., et al.: Contrast enhanced subsurface fingerprint detection using high-speed optical coherence tomography. IEEE Photon. Technol. Lett. **PP**(99), 1 (2017)

A Novel Method for Finger Vein Recognition

Junying Zeng, Yao Chen, Chuanbo Qin(✉), Fan Wang, Junying Gan, Yikui Zhai, and Boyuan Zhu

Faculty of Intelligent Manufacturing, Wuyi University, Jiangmen 529020, Guangdong, China
zengjunying@126.com, sunnyshenyao@163.com, tenround@163.com, victorwf1219@163.com, junyinggan@163.com, yikuizhai@163.com, zhuboyuan586@163.com

Abstract. Benefiting from CNN's strong feature expression ability, the finger vein recognition systems using the convolutional neural network (CNN) currently have shown a good performance. However, these systems usually adopt such large networks or complex step-by-step processes that they cannot be applied to the hardware platform with limited computing power and small memory. To address this limitation, this research proposes a finger vein recognition network based on difference image and 3C image for cascade fine-tuning. First, a difference image from the image pair for authentic matching or imposter matching is obtained by difference operation and a 2C image is acquired by regarding this image pair as a two-channel image; furthermore, a 3C image is gained with the channel connection of the difference image and 2C image. Then, the SqueezeNet (this network has been pre-trained on ImageNet) that receives the 3C image as input is fine-tuned and the best fine-tune manner is determined. Finally, a cascade fine-tune framework is designed to integrate the difference images and 3C image. In this paper, the size of SqueezeNet which is cascade fine-tuned on the basis of the pre-training weights is 5.63 MB, and the corresponding equal error rate(EER) acquired on the dataset MMCBNU_6000 and SDUMLA-HMT is 1.889% and 4.906% respectively. The experimental results fully prove that the proposed method achieves not only high recognition accuracy but also the simplification of network.

Keywords: Finger vein recognition · Convolutional neural network · Difference image · SqueezeNet

1 Introduction

At present, vein recognition, as a kind of biometric authentication technology with high anti-counterfeiting, has attracted much attention. Compared with traditional biometrics such as fingerprints, faces, and irises, vein recognition has two significant advantages:

This work is supported by NNSF (No. 61771347), Characteristic Innovation Project of Guangdong Province (No. 2017KTSCX181), Young innovative talents project of Guangdong Province (2017KQNCX206), Jiangmen science and technology project ([2017] No. 268), Youth Foundation of Wuyi University (No. 2015zk11).

Z. Sun et al. (Eds.): CCBR 2019, LNCS 11818, pp. 46–54, 2019.
https://doi.org/10.1007/978-3-030-31456-9_6

internal features and liveness detection [1]. Finger vein recognition has been applied to ATM machines, access control systems, vending machines, and various login products in some countries or regions [2]. At the same time, it is difficult to capture high-quality finger vein images during the acquisition of finger vein images, which is still a great challenge for the subsequent recognition process. Due to unique advantages, broad application scenarios and existing challenges, finger vein recognition has attracted more and more researchers' attention.

Traditional finger vein recognition systems mostly use hand-craft features, which are generally sensitive to image quality and finger attitude changes; besides, the pre-processing process is too complicated and the final performance is still limited of the system. To overcome the shortcomings of this method, a few researchers have proposed the CNN-based finger vein recognition, which can automatically learn and extract features with stronger distinguishing ability from the original region of interest (ROI) image. There is no need to filter and enhance the ROI image and the pre-process of image is greatly simplified with CNN. Nevertheless, existing CNN-based finger vein recognition methods mostly adopt such large networks [3] or complex step-by-step processes [4] that they cannot be applied to the hardware platform with limited computing power and small memory.

Considering the weakness of existing CNN-based finger vein recognition methods, this paper introduces a finger vein verification system using cascade fine-tuning CNN, which achieves not only high recognition accuracy but also the simplification of network.

2 Related Works

In recent years, a few researchers have used CNN for finger vein recognition [4–11]. At present, CNN-based finger vein recognition can be roughly classified into the following categories: (1) Finger vein recognition is regarded as a multiclass classification problem [6–8]. In [6], they proposed a reduced complexity CNN with four convolutional layers for finger vein recognition. In [7], using CNN of the same structure as the one used in [6], they retrain the fully connected layer regardless of the pre-training weights. However, these types of methods use finger-vein images of the same class both for training and testing, and for this reason, they only work for 1:N recognition scene on some fixed small databases because they cannot recognize the finger-vein images of classes that have not been trained. (2) CNN is trained to extract the vein structure of a single image and template matching is applied to the obtained binary vein pattern image for verification [9]. This method can identify classes that have not been trained, but the vein pattern extraction and matching process are carried out step by step and the traditional algorithm is still used in the matching with this method. (3) A pair of homologous or heterogeneous images is treated as a single sample whose label is one or zero [4, 5, 10]. In [4], difference image of the image pair is taken as the input of CNN to fine-tune VGGNet-16 [12]. In [5], they design a two-channel network and a two-stream network with a two-channel image as the CNN's input, but in this paper, some images of the same finger both are used for training and others are used for testing in the experiment and there is no definite conclusion when finger images that have not been trained are tested. In addition to the above, the literature [11] proposes a template image generation model of finger vein based on deep learning and random mapping according to the practical application. Of course, some of the CNN techniques in the above have also achieved good results in the fields of face recognition and image matching [13–15].

Therefore, how to train a finger vein recognition model with high precision and small model size is the focus of this paper, when there are only limited finger vein images. The main contributions of this paper are as follows:

1. This paper is the first to use 3C image as the input of CNN for finger vein verification, which not only make it possible to fine-tune the ImageNet pre-training model but also make full use of finger vein images. In addition, this paper compares the performances of the same network with difference image, 2C image and 3C image as the input, and makes a conclusion that the network performs best with 3C image as the input.
2. Considering that the finger vein recognition algorithm is often embedded in a small portable device, people maybe tend to the network with small size compared with that method using VGGNet-16. For this reason, this paper fine-tunes the light-weight SqueezeNet [16] with 3C image as the input and analyses the performance of SqueezeNet when we fine-tune it in different ways.
3. In order to make full use of the difference and self-information of the image pair to recognize and simultaneously fine-tune the light-weight SqueezeNet, this paper designs a cascade fine-tune framework to train difference images and 3C images hierarchically, further improving the performance of network.

The remainder of the paper is organized as follows: Sect. 3 introduces the proposed method, including how to obtain the 3C image, make use of SqueezeNet, design the cascade fine-tune framework for finger vein recognition. Section 4 describes our experiments as well as analysis on the experimental results. Finally we present conclusions in Sect. 5.

3 Proposed Method

3.1 Acquirement of the 3C Image

There are two methods of a CNN structure's identifying finger vein images of the untrained classes. (1) Using the trained CNN network to extract features from the original single finger vein image, Fig. 1(a) shows this flowchart. (2) Considering a pair of images to be verified as one sample. They use the difference image that is obtained with the difference operation between the input and enrolled image as the input to the CNN in [4], which is shown in Fig. 1(b). They use the 2C image that is obtained with the channel connection between the input and enrolled image as the input to the CNN in [5], which is shown in Fig. 1(c). If we try to fine-tune the ImageNet pre-training model with the difference image as the input, we have to copy the channel of the difference image. It is impossible to fine-tune the ImageNet pre-training model with the 2C image as the input because 2C image is a two-channel image. In addition, copying channel of difference images is only the simple repetition of difference information and does not fully utilize the information about the image pair themselves. In order to fine-tune the ImageNet pre-training model and avoid copying the channel of the difference image, this paper combines the difference image with the 2C image in channel to acquire the 3C image, which is uses as the input of CNN. This flowchart is shown Fig. 1(d).

3.2 SqueezeNet-Based Finger Vein Recognition

In Fig. 2, the input of the network is a 3C image, and the output of the network is the category, that is, authentic matching or imposter matching. The SqueezeNet employed

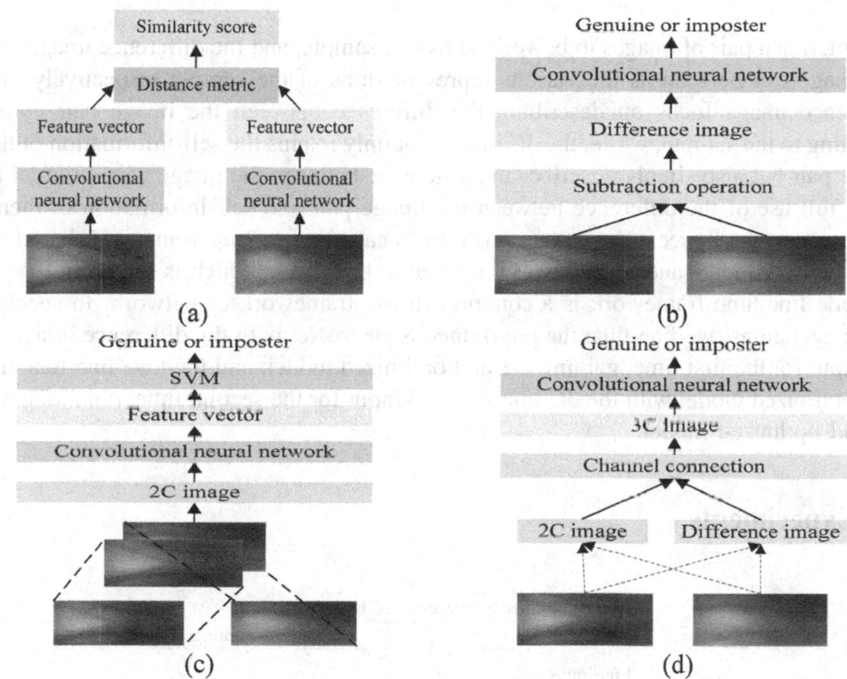

Fig. 1. The CNN structure with the finger vein image as the input

in this paper starts with the convolution layer (conv1), then uses 8 Fire Modules (fire2-fire9), and finally ends with the convolution layer (conv10). The number of filters in each Fire Module is gradually increased, and the layers conv1, fire3, and fire5 are all followed by the max-pooling with the step size of two. Like face recognition, finger vein recognition also consists of the 1:1 verification and the 1:N recognition. When the accuracy of 1:1 verification is high enough, the verification method will be applied to the 1:N recognition. Our method is aimed at solving the 1:1 verification problem that when there is a pair of images, the trained network can output the probability of this image pair's being authentic matching or imposter matching. (The probability of this image pair's being authentic matching is regarded as the similarity between them in this paper.)

3.3 Cascaded Fine-Tune Framework Based on Difference Image and 3C Image

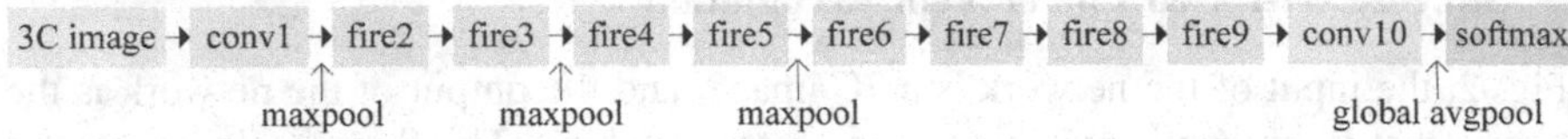

Fig. 2. Finger vein recognition network based on SqueezeNet

Considering a pair of images to be verified as one sample, and the difference image and 3C image can be seen as the various representations of the sample respectively: the difference image focus on describing the difference between the image pair corresponding to the sample; while, the 3C image not only retains the self-information of the image pair but also simply describes the difference between the image pair. In order to make full use of the difference between the image pair and self-information of them, and fine-tune the SqueezeNet at the same time, a cascade fine-tune framework based on the difference image and 3C image is proposed in this paper, which is shown in Fig. 3. Cascade fine-tune framework is a common fusion framework of network. In specific implementations, we fine-tune the pre-trained SqueezeNet with the difference image as the input for the first time, gaining the first optimized model, and then we fine-tune the first optimized model with the 3C image as the input for the second time, obtaining the second optimized model.

4 Experiments

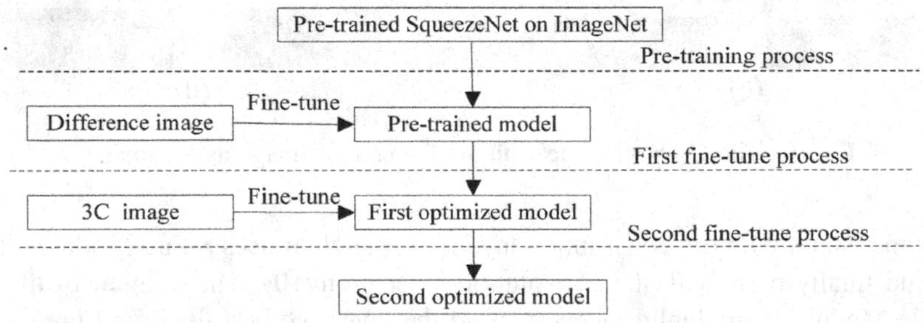

Fig. 3. Cascaded fine-tune framework for finger vein recognition

4.1 Experimental Environment and Data

The MMCBNU_6000 dataset has a total of 6000 images consisting of 100 people with 2 hands and 3 fingers, and 10 images per each finger. This dataset provides the original finger vein images whose resolution is 640 × 480 and corresponding ROI regional images whose resolution is 128 × 60. In order to compare with other algorithms conveniently and fairly, we directly employ the ROI images of this dataset.

The SDUMLA-HMT dataset has a total of 3816 images consisting of 106 people with 2 hands and 3 fingers, and 6 images per each finger. All finger vein images in the dataset are gray-scale images with the resolution of 320 × 240. Moreover, using the existing ROI extraction algorithm [18], we obtain the corresponding ROI images which are normalized to the size of 128 × 60.

4.2 The Performance of Fine-Tuning Different Pre-Trained Models

The experimental results are shown in Table 1. C-1 is the method in reference [4] and the input of this method is replaced by the 3C image in this paper, namely, the C-2 method It can be seen that the EER of C-2 method is lower than that of C-1 method on both datasets, which also shows that when fine-tuning the same network, inputting 3C image is better than inputting difference image. Then, this paper takes 3C image as input to fine-tune the SqueezeNet. In the process of transfer learning, there is no fixed choice that which layer weight of the pre-training model is used. In order to make the best transfer learning on two datasets, this paper further carries out experiments: the pre-training weights of SqueezeNet's pre-fire9, pre-fire8, pre-fire7 and pre-fire6 are taken as the initial weights respectively, and the weights of the other layers are randomly initialized. Then, the 3C images are used as input to fine-tune the SqueezeNet on the two datasets, respectively. The experimental results are shown in Table 2. On MMCBNU_6000, the EER of D-3 method is the lowest, while that of D-4 method is the lowest on SDUMLA-HMT. Thus, fine-tuning the same network is different on different datasets. Based on the previous experiments, the cascade fine-tune framework is tried in the experiment. The experimental results are shown in Table 3. This result is compared with those above. As shown in Fig. 4, the EER of this method is lower than that of the above on both datasets. So cascade fine-tuning the SqueezeNet based on difference images and 3C images will have the best performance.

Table 1. EER of fine-tuning VGGNet-16 with different inputs

Method name	Input image	Layer for recognition	EER(%)	
			MMCBNU	SDUMLA
C-1(VGGNet-16)	Difference image	Output layer	2.333	5.825
C-2(VGGNet-16)	3C image	Output layer	1.845	5.535

Table 2. EER of fine-tuning SqueezeNet with different ways (Here fine-tune means that pre-trained weights of some layers are as initial weights)

Method name	Input image	Fine-tune	Layer for recognition	EER(%)	
				MMCBNU	SDUMLA
D-1(SqueezeNet)	3C image	Conv1-fire9	Output layer	2.304	5.406
D-2(SqueezeNet)		Conv1-fire8	Output layer	2.185	5.136
D-3(SqueezeNet)		Conv1-fire7	Output layer	1.967	5.281
D-4(SqueezeNet)		Conv1-fire6	Output layer	2.162	5.115

Table 3. EER based on cascaded fine-tune framework

Method name	Implementation process	Layer for recognition	EER(%)	
			MMCBNU	SDUMLA
E(cascaded fine-tune SqueezeNet)	See Part 3.3	Output layer	1.889	4.906

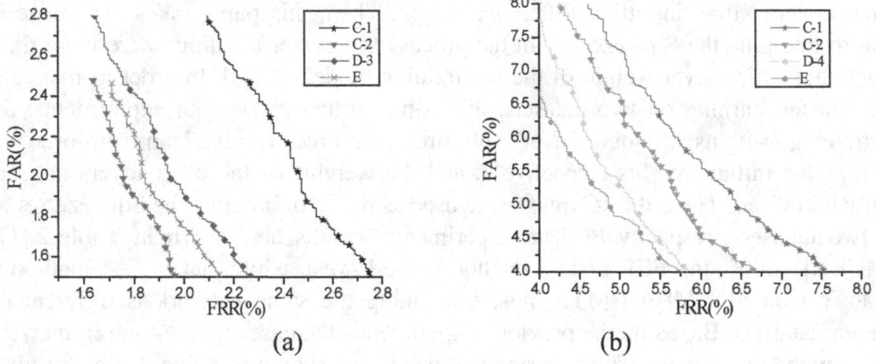

Fig. 4. EER of fine-tuning various pre-training models

4.3 Comparisons with Other Methods

Comparing the best E method with other existing algorithms, the results of comparing our E method with other finger vein recognition methods based on CNN are shown in Table 4. In Table 4, we can see that the proposed method has the best performance on MMCBNU_6000 and a little worse performance on SDUMLA-HMT than other methods. As mentioned above, image quality and ROI extraction process will affect subsequent recognition. In addition, the size of the model proposed in this paper is only 5.63 MB, which is much smaller than that of other methods. Considering the comprehensive performance and practical value, the proposed method is superior to other algorithms.

Table 4. Compare our method with other CNN methods in comprehensive performance

	EER(MMCBNU)	EER(SDUMLA)	Model Size
Hong et al. [3]	2.33	5.83	>500 MB
Kang et al. [4]	2.1	3.84	–
(proposed method)	1.89	4.91	5.63 MB

5 Conclusion

In this paper, 3C image is first proposed as CNN's input and we fine-tune the pre-trained SqueezeNet. Furthermore, a cascade fine-tune framework of network based on difference image and 3C image is proposed to improve the recognition accuracy of finger vein recognition. Firstly, the finger vein feature expression ability of three pre-training models is validated on two datasets. Secondly, the performance of the same network under different inputs is compared and the experimental results show that the 3C image has a good effect when it is used as the input of network. Finally, fine-tune is implemented in different ways based on SqueezeNet, and the performance of the model is further improved by using cascade fine-tune framework. Compared with other traditional methods, this method is obviously superior to the traditional feature extraction method. Compared with other CNN methods, this method has good comprehensive performance and high recognition accuracy. How to further improve the recognition accuracy on low-quality image datasets is still a challenging problem on the premise of smaller model. The next step is to consider further improving the recognition accuracy by data enhancement and more refined ROI extraction.

References

1. Yang, G., Xiao, R., Yin, Y., et al.: Finger vein recognition based on personalized weight maps. Sensors **13**(9), 12093–12112 (2013)
2. Yang, G., Xi, X., Yin, Y.: Finger vein recognition based on a personalized best bit map. Sensors **12**(12), 1738–1757 (2012)
3. Hong, H.G., Lee, M.B., Park, K.R.: Convolutional neural network-based finger-vein recognition using NIR image sensors. Sensors **17**(6), 1297 (2017)
4. Fang, Y., Wu, Q., Kang, W.: A novel finger vein verification system based on two-stream convolutional network learning. Neurocomputing **290**, 100–107 (2018)
5. Yang, L., Yang, G., Xi, X., et al.: Tri-branch vein structure assisted finger vein recognition. IEEE Access **5**, 21020–21028 (2017)
6. Radzi, S.A., Hani, M.K., Bakhteri, R.: Finger-vein biometric identification using convolutional neural network. Turk. J. Electr. Eng. Comput. Sci. **24**(3), 1863–1878 (2016)
7. Itqan, K.S., Syafeeza, A.R., Gong, F.G., et al.: User identification system based on finger-vein patterns using Convolutional Neural Network. ARPN J. Eng. Appl. Sci. **11**(5), 3316–3319 (2016)
8. Das, R., Piciucco, E., Maiorana, E., et al.: Convolutional neural network for finger-vein-based biometric identification. IEEE Trans. Inf. Forensics Secur. **14**(2), 360–373 (2019)

9. Qin, H., El-Yacoubi, M.A.: Deep representation-based feature extraction and recovering for finger-vein verification. IEEE Trans. Inf. Forensics Secur. **12**(8), 1816–1829 (2017)
10. Kim, W., Song, J., Park, K.: Multimodal biometric recognition based on convolutional neural network by the fusion of finger-vein and finger shape using near-infrared (NIR) camera sensor. Sensors **18**(7), 2296 (2018)
11. Liu, Y., Ling, J., Liu, Z., et al.: Finger vein secure biometric template generation based on deep learning. Soft. Comput. **22**(7), 2257–2265 (2018)
12. Simonyan, K., Zisserman, A.: Very deep convolutional networks for large-scale image recognition. arXiv preprint arXiv:1409.1556 (2014)
13. Zagoruyko, S., Komodakis, N.: Learning to compare image patches via convolutional neural networks. In: Proceedings of the IEEE Conference on Computer Vision and Pattern Recognition, pp. 4353–4361 (2015)
14. Han, X., Leung, T., Jia, Y., et al.: Matchnet: unifying feature and metric learning for patch-based matching. In: Proceedings of the IEEE Conference on Computer Vision and Pattern Recognition, pp. 3279–3286 (2015)
15. Taigman, Y., Yang, M., Ranzato, M.A., et al.: Deepface: closing the gap to human-level performance in face verification. In: Proceedings of the IEEE Conference on Computer Vision and Pattern Recognition, pp. 1701–1708 (2014)
16. Iandola, F.N., Han, S., Moskewicz, M.W., et al.: Squeezenet: alexnet-level accuracy with 50x fewer parameters and <0.5 mb model size. arXiv preprint arXiv:1602.07360 (2016)
17. Lu, Y., Xie, S.J., Yoon, S., et al.: An available database for the research of finger vein recognition. In: 2013 6th International Congress on Image and Signal Processing (CISP), vol. 1, pp. 410–415. IEEE (2013)
18. Kumar, A., Zhou, Y.: Human identification using finger images. IEEE Trans. Image Process. **21**(4), 2228–2244 (2012)

Rolled Fingerprint Mosaicking Algorithm Based on Block Scale

Yongliang Zhang[1(✉)], Minghua Gao[1], Xiaosi Zhan[2], Yifan Wu[1], and Shengyi Pan[1]

[1] College of Computer Science and Technology, Zhejiang University of Technology, Hangzhou 310023, China
titanzhang@zjut.edu.cn

[2] School of Science and Technology, Zhejiang International Studies University, Hangzhou 310023, China

Abstract. In the mosaicking process of rolled fingerprint, there will be a certain positional offset between adjacent two frames of fingerprint images due to the large elastic deformation of the fingertip portion, which results in a significant mosaicking gap in the rolled fingerprint. Aiming at the problem, a block scale based rolled fingerprint mosaicking algorithm is proposed in this paper. Firstly, the fingerprint image is divided into many small blocks, and the center areas are extracted by the binary search. Then the corresponding lines of the segmented images are mosaicked and all lines are optimized according to the sequence of frames captured in the fingerprint rolling process. Finally, all line sequences are combined to a complete rolled fingerprint. The experimental results show that the proposed algorithm can effectively eliminate the mosaicking gap and the positional deviation of misalignment and reprint, and improve the accuracy of fingerprint recognition.

Keywords: Rolled fingerprint · Image mosaic · Block scale · Binary search

1 Introduction

With the development of computer technology, biometric technology has become the preferred method of identity authentication, and fingerprint authentication is the most common method [1]. The fingerprint collectors on the market usually capture small areas of fingerprint with plane pressing. It is difficult for collectors to capture the same fingerprint area every time, increasing the rejection rate of fingerprint authentication. By rolling the same finger to capture a sequence of fingerprint images and mosaicking them to obtain a complete rolled fingerprint, the drawback above can be overcome. Compared with flat fingerprint, the effective area of the rolled fingerprint is increased and more fingerprint feature information is provided in the fingerprint rolling process, which makes identity authentication more accurate [2].

The traditional method uses ink pressing to collect the rolled fingerprint. The ink-stained finger rolls on the paper, and then the ink stays on the paper, resulting in a rolled fingerprint. With the invention of the fingerprint collector, we can easily collect the fingerprint sequence when the finger is rolling on fingerprint collector. The fingerprint

Z. Sun et al. (Eds.): CCBR 2019, LNCS 11818, pp. 55–62, 2019.
https://doi.org/10.1007/978-3-030-31456-9_7

sequence can obtain a complete rolled fingerprint through the fingerprint mosaicking algorithm. At present, there are many rolled fingerprint mosaicking algorithms [3–7]. In [3], a covering-based mosaicking algorithm was proposed Where the images were synthesized by calculating the confidence of each pixel, and five synthetic schemes were given. Literature [4] proposed a waveform matching algorithm to extract the waveform information of the reference region and compared the waveform similarity of two adjacent frames to estimate displacement. Literature [5, 6] located the mosaicking line and processed the area near the mosaicking line to obtain better results. In [7], a real-time mosaicking algorithm based on key columns was proposed for the mosaicking of rolled fingerprints, using the selection of key columns to obtain the column sequences. At the same time, the column sequences were divided into upper and lower sequences by calculating the position of the centroid point to eliminate the influence of the deformation of the finger during the fingerprint rolling process. These algorithms obtain rolled fingerprints by combining pixels or columns. However, it can be found through experiments that it is easy to produce reprinting and misalignment because of the elastic distortion when the finger is placed and rolled on the sensor. The accuracy of subsequent fingerprint recognition is difficult to improve.

Therefore, a rolled fingerprint mosaicking algorithm based on block scale is proposed in this paper. There are two advantages: the fingerprints in each small block are coherent, and the influence due to the elastic deformation of the fingertips is eliminated because of the independence of the blocks.

2 Algorithm

In the process of real-time rolling fingerprint mosaicking, the sensor generates a blank image, and then mosaic the fingerprint images captured later into the blank image by frame number until a complete rolled fingerprint image is formed.

2.1 Finger Detection

The collection of images is a continuous process. The fingerprint mosaicking starts when the fingerprint image is first captured and ends when a blank image is captured.

The image is detected by the method of literature [7]. The background frame is collected when the finger is not placed on the collector, and then every frame captured is compared with the background frame. The number of pixels $N(I_i)$ whose gray scale difference is greater than a given threshold T_1 is counted as follow:

$$N(I_i) = |\{(x,y)||I_i(x,y) - I_0(x,y)| > T_1, 1 \le x \le W, 1 \le y \le H\}| \quad (1)$$

I_i and I_0 represent the ith frame and the background frame respectively. $I_i(x,y)$ denotes the gray of the pixel *(x, y)* in the ith frame and $W \times H$ is the size of each frame, where H is the height of the frame and W is the width. $|\{\bullet\}|$ is the number of the elements in the set. I_i is considered a fingerprint image when $N(I_i)$ is more than the given threshold T_2. Here, the value of T_1 and T_2 are 50 and 15000 respectively.

2.2 Image Segmentation

The fingerprint can be divided into two regions: the fingertip and the finger belly [5]. The finger belly region has almost no deformation during the rolling process. However, the fingertip region is prone to deformation, resulting in misalignment and reprinting. In order to eliminate the mosaicking gap caused by the deformation of the fingertip region, we proposed a fingerprint mosaic algorithm based on block scale.

The images are divided into many small blocks of size $w \times h$, where h is the height of the block, which determines the number of line sequences after the whole image is segmented; w is the width, which determines the number of blocks contained in each line sequence. The size of the block is selected as 10×80 according to the experimental results in this paper. Provided that the image of the ith frame is segmented, the segmented image is $I_i^{'}$ and the size of $I_i^{'}$ is $W^{'} \times H^{'}$.

The gray value of each block in $I_i^{'}$ is the sum of the gray values of all points in the corresponding position in I_i:

$$I_i^{'}(x,y) = \sum_{(a,b)\in L(x,y)} I_i(a,b) \tag{2}$$

$$L(x,y) = \{(a,b)|(x-1) \times h + 1 \leq a \leq x \times h, (y-1) \times w + 1 \leq b \leq y \times w\} \tag{3}$$

2.3 Center Area Calibration

For the fingerprint image which has been segmented, each column of the image is composed of a plurality of small blocks. Assuming that the finger only rolls in the left and right direction, the column with the largest fingerprint area will be retained in the rolled fingerprint during the mosaicking process. We define the column as the center area of the fingerprint image, and it has the smallest grayscale. In this paper, the binary search is used to locate the center areas of fingerprints.

Firstly, the fingerprint image is divided into two parts, and the value of each part is the sum of the pixel values in the respective part. The part with smaller value is selected to be segmented. Repeat this process until the center area of the fingerprint image is found. It is necessary to calculate the pixel value of the target area repeatedly in the segmentation process, so the integral map is used to reduce the amount of calculation. In the image integration map, the value of each point is the sum of all pixel values in the upper left corner of the point in the original image:

$$SAT(x,y) = \sum_{x_i \leq x, y_i \leq y} I(x_i, y_i) \tag{4}$$

Where $I(x_i, y_i)$ represents the pixel value of the image at position (x_i, y_i).

First of all, the whole image is defined as the area to be divided, defined four parameters: l, r, m and d. They are defined as follows:

(1) l is the leftmost column of the area to be divided, and the initial value is 1;
(2) r is the rightmost column of the area to be divided, and the initial value is $W^{'}$;

(3) m is the middle column of the area to be divided, $m = \lfloor (l+r)/2 \rfloor$, and "$\lfloor \ \rfloor$" is a rounding down symbol;
(4) d is the width of the area to be divided, $d = |r - l + 1|$, and "$| \ |$" is an absolute value symbol.

The gray of the left half area is defined as G_l, and the gray of the right half area is G_r. They are calculated by formula (6) and (7), considering the situation that the image cannot be equally divided:

$$G_l = SAT\left(H', m\right) - SAT\left(H', l\right) \tag{5}$$

$$G_r = \begin{cases} SAT(H', r) - SAT(H', m), d\%2 = 1 \\ SAT(H', r) - SAT(H', m+1), d\%2 = 0 \end{cases} \tag{6}$$

If $G_l \geq G_r$, the right half area is selected as the area to be divided, otherwise the left half area is selected. After determining the area to be divided, the values of the four parameters l, r, m, and d are re-determined, then recalculate G_l and G_r and continue to divide until the value of d is 1. At the same time, the area to be divided has only one column. Assume it is the j column of ith frame and this column is the center area, record as $C(i) = j$.

2.4 Image Mosaicking

Provided that the finger is rolling from left to right and the current frame is I_k. Each block of the image is marked by the frame number of source image. The segmented image can be regarded as a combination of line sequences $J = \{J_1, J_2, \cdots, J_{H'}\}$, and $J_i(j)$ represents the frame number of the jth block of the ith line. The mosaicking process can be regarded as the update of the frame number of the block, and we choose the block frame number with smaller grayscale:

$$J_i(j) = \mathop{\arg\min}_{m=1,2,\ldots,k} \left\{ I'_m(i,j) \right\} \tag{7}$$

Where $I'_m(i,j)$ denotes the grayscale sum of the block at position (i,j) in the mth frame, and $\arg\min_m f(m)$ denotes the value of m which takes $f(m)$ as the minimum value.

The center area of the segmented image I'_k is the $C(k)$ column, and each block in $C(k)$ column is defined as the reference block. Such as, the reference block position of the ith row is $(i, C(k))$. Define the blocks on the left of the reference block as spliced region and other blocks as the unspliced region in each line. We want to reduce the modification of the spliced area and make the fingerprint image of the unspliced area more complete, so different strategies are adopted for the two areas.

For the spliced area, if the frame number is satisfied the update condition, the frame number need to be updated and continue to judge the blocks on the left. The splicing is stopped when the update condition is not satisfied. All blocks in unspliced area should be judged. At last, the sources of all blocks that make up the rolled fingerprint are known.

2.5 Sequence Optimization Based on Rolling Direction

The rolled direction of the ith frame is determined by the value of $R(i)$ which is obtained by comparing the positions of the central blocks of two adjacent frames:

$$R(i) = \begin{cases} 0, C(k) < C(k-1) \\ 1, C(k) > C(k-1) \\ R(i-1), C(k) = C(k-1) \end{cases} \tag{8}$$

Where i is the frame number, $R(i) = 0$ means the finger rolls from right to left, $R(i) = 1$ means the finger scrolls from left to right, and $R(i) = R(i-1)$ means the direction does not change.

The line sequences are optimized according to the different conditions of the finger scrolling, so that the rolled fingerprint is more complete. The main conditions are as follows:

(1) Normal rolling ($R(k) = R(k-1)$). Optimization rule: traverse each line sequence separately in the rolling direction. Taking J_i as an example, if the rolled direction is from left to right, there should be $J_i(j) \geq J_i(j-1)$ in the ideal case. If a frame number is smaller than the former, we update the frame number to the same of former.

(2) A rollback occurs ($R(k) \neq R(k-1)$). In order to avoid unintentional rollback, the optimization is stopped when the rolling direction is changed. This can protect the spliced area. But if the rolled direction of the next frame remains unchanged, it is judged as a rollback operation, and optimization can overwrite the current mosaicking result and re-splicing.

3 Experimental Results

To evaluate the proposed construction algorithm, a HighLand PU-JY301U roll fingerprint sensor (each frame with 640 × 640 pixels and 500 dpi) is used [8]. The sensor continuously collects images when a finger is rolling on the sensor. A typical rolled fingerprint sequence is shown in Fig. 1.

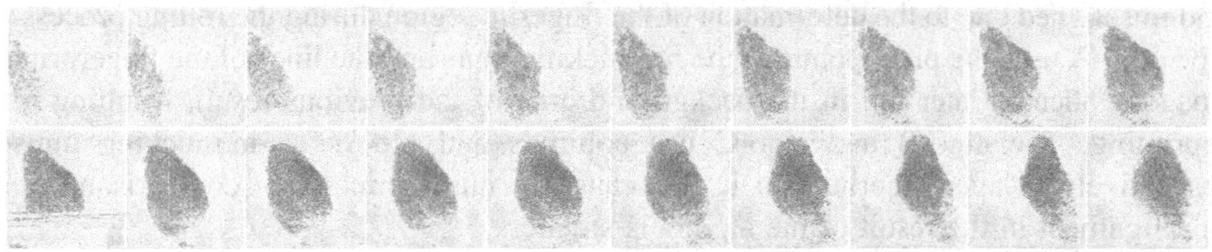

Fig. 1. Image sequence of rolled fingerprint

In this paper, the image needs to be block-processed firstly because the scale of the block directly affects the mosaicking effect. The width of the small block is the number of columns occupied by the mosaicking unit. It is most suitable for one to two ridge widths. In this paper, the width of the small block is 10, and the height of the small block determines the number of line sequences, which means how many lines the image is divided into. It is the most important factor to eliminate the impact of fingertip deformation on the whole. Therefore, we focus on different values of block height when comparing experimental results. Figure 2 shows the results of the algorithm for four different height values on blocks.

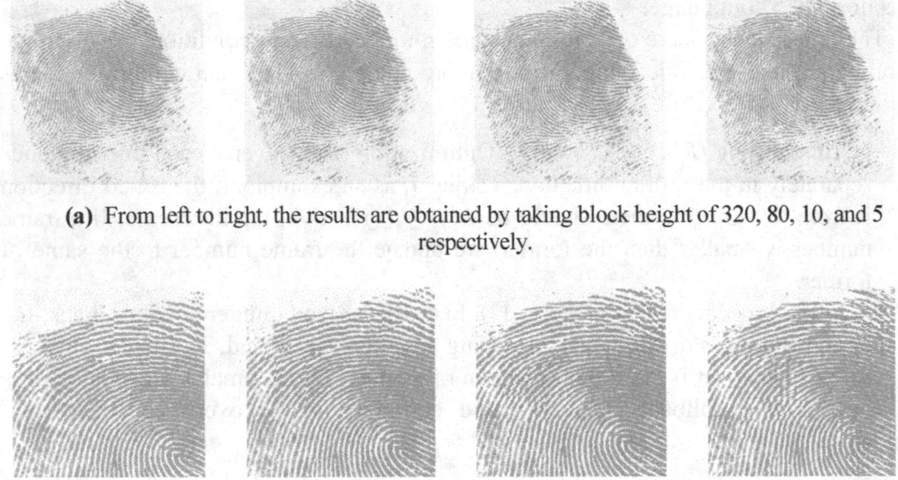

(a) From left to right, the results are obtained by taking block height of 320, 80, 10, and 5 respectively.

(b) Magnified view of the fingertip area in (a).

Fig. 2. Results of the algorithm for four different block height values.

For the same set of images collected, the algorithms in literature [3] (called algo-A), literature [7] (called algo-B) and this paper (called algo-C) are used for mosaicking. For algo-A, the minimum compositing method is applied. The results obtained by three algorithms for the fingerprint sequences in Fig. 1 are shown in Fig. 3.

It can be seen from Fig. 3 that the upper portions of the fingerprints are reprinted and misaligned due to the deformation of the fingertip region during the rolling process. The algo-A uses the pixel points as the mosaicking units and the lines of the fingerprint images collected later fall in the background area of the previous result, resulting in reprinting. The algo-B and algo-C use columns and blocks as mosaicking units respectively to avoid reprint, but it also causes a misalignment. In comparison, the misalignment in the result of the algo-C is smaller.

In this paper, the equal error rate (EER) is used as the evaluation metric [9], which is the error rate when the error acceptance rate (FAR) and the error rejection rate (FRR) are the same. The rolled fingerprints are used as the template library, and the corresponding fingerprint sequences are used as the sample library. Under the same set

(a) The fingerprint images from left to right are the results of the algo-A, algo-B, algo-C on the same fingerprint image sequences (in Fig.1) respectively.

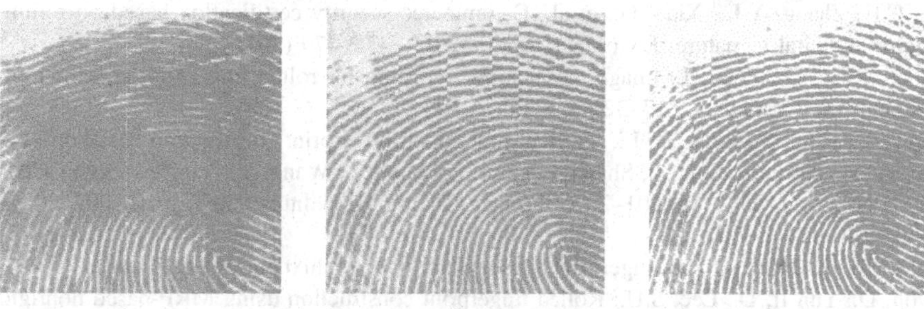

(b) Magnified view of the fingertip area in (a).

Fig. 3. The rolled fingerprints obtained by the algo-A, algo-B and algo-C.

of fingerprint identification algorithms and thresholds, the EER indicators obtained by the three algorithms are shown in the Table 1. It can be seen that the EER of algo-C is less than half of the other two algorithms. The algorithm in this paper has better recognition performance.

Table 1. The EER of three algorithms

algo-A	algo-B	algo-C
4.04%	3.11%	1.24%

4 Conclusions

Based on block scale, a rolled fingerprint mosaicking algorithm is proposed in this paper. The images are divided into blocks to reduce the negative impact of fingertips during scrolling. Compared with the previous two algorithms, the experimental results show that the rolled fingerprint image obtained by the algorithm in this paper has fewer mosaicking gaps and better performance in recognition.

Acknowledgement. This work was supported by the Public Welfare Technology Research Program of Zhejiang Province under Grant LGF18F030008.

References

1. Wang, J.S., Zhang, W.M.: The category of biometric chip and its application in identity. Henan Sci. Technol. **15**, 34–35 (2017)
2. Kumar, A.: Introduction to trends in fingerprint identification. In: Kumar, A. (ed.) Contactless 3D Fingerprint Identification. ACVPR, pp. 1–15. Springer, Cham (2018). https://doi.org/10.1007/978-3-319-67681-4_1
3. Ratha, N.K., Connell, J.H., Bolle, R.M.: Image Mosiacing for rolled fingerprint construction. In: Proceedings of the International Conference Pattern Recognition, pp. 1651–1653 (1998)
4. Wang, P., Zhang, Y.G.: A wave matching based algorithm for fingerprint image series mosaicking. J. Comput. Aided Des. Comput. Graphics **21**(10), 1467–1471 (2009)
5. Liu, C.F., Zhang, Y.L., Xiao, G., et al.: E-commerce security certification based on rolling fingerprint digital signature. J. Comput. Appl. **32**(02), 475–479 (2012)
6. He, D., Rong, G., Zhou, J.: Image mosaicking algorithm for rolled fingerprint construction. Tsinghua Sci. Technol. **3**, 317–321 (2002)
7. Zhang, Y., Fang, S., Bian, Y., Li, Y.: Real-time rolled fingerprint construction based on key-column extraction. In: Sun, Z., Shan, S., Yang, G., Zhou, J., Wang, Y., Yin, Y. (eds.) CCBR 2013. LNCS, vol. 8232, pp. 201–207. Springer, Cham (2013). https://doi.org/10.1007/978-3-319-02961-0_25
8. HighLand. PU-JY301U roll fingerprint sensor. http://www.bjhlxt.com
9. Kwon, D., Yun Il, D., Lee, S.U.: Rolled fingerprint construction using MRF-based nonrigid image registration. IEEE Trans. Image Process. **19**(12), 3255–3270 (2010)

Study and Realization of Partial Fingerprint Mosaicking Technology for Mobile Devices

Yumeng Wang[1], Xiangwen Kong[1], Rongsheng Wang[1], Changlong Jin[1(✉)], and Hakil Kim[2]

[1] Department of Computer Science, Shandong University at Weihai, Weihai, Shandong Province, China
kt2meng@163.com, kxwkaoyan@163.com, wangrsl412@mails.jlu.edu.cn, cljin@sdu.edu.cn

[2] School of Information and Communication Engineering, INHA University, Incheon, Korea
hikim@inha.ac.kr

Abstract. To obtain a large fingerprint template from several partial fingerprints, we propose a novel partial fingerprint mosaicking scheme, which includes a coarse-to-fine alignment stage and a fusion stage, to build a synthetic template from multiple partial fingerprints. In the alignment stage, firstly, a central patch is determined after pair-wised patch matching, then the rest patches are coarsely aligned based on the central patch, thirdly, the locations of patches are optimized globally. In the feature fusion stage, not only minutiae, but also ridge sampling points are fused to increase the information in the synthetic template. The proposed algorithm is tested on two datasets of FVC2002 and the experimental results show that it can achieve a great fingerprint mosaicking performance.

Keywords: Mosaicking · Partial fingerprint · Global optimization · Feature fusion · Template construction

1 Introduction

Among the various applications of fingerprint recognition, the most concerned is its application on mobile devices. In order to embed in devices and reduce cost, the sensor is usually made very small, which lead to limited sensing area with insufficient fingerprint information. Therefore, overlapping areas between multiple fingerprints are relatively small, which results in a high False Non-Match Rate (FNMR) and False Match Rate(FMR).

In order to solve this problem, the fingerprint mosaicking scheme has been extensively studied, that is, a system that acquires multiple partial fingerprints(which are called patches in this paper) from one finger as input and then generates an integrated template as an output. The synthesized template contains relatively complete fingerprint feature information and requires less storage space than storing multiple partial fingerprint templates. It also helps shorten the matching time because the query fingerprint only needs to match one template.

Z. Sun et al. (Eds.): CCBR 2019, LNCS 11818, pp. 63–72, 2019.
https://doi.org/10.1007/978-3-030-31456-9_8

Generally, the fingerprint mosaicking algorithm mainly includes two stages, an alignment stage and a fusion stage. The methods used in alignment stage can be divided into two categories: based on minutiae and based on non-minutiae feature. The methods used in fusion stage can be roughly divided into four categories: image level, feature level, score level, and decision level fusion.

Jain *et al.* [1] used the Iterative Closest Point(ICP) method to align two fingerprint images and then performed fusion at image level. Due to the plastic distortion, Dongjae Lee *et al.* [2] and Kyoungtaek Choi *et al.* [3] both used non-rigid transforms in their algorithms. Ratha *et al.* [4] and Zhou *et al.* [5] proposed a mosaicking technique for another situation which is to mosaic a series of fingerprint images acquired by an optical scanner into a complete fingerprint image. For very small sensors, Choi *et al.* [6] stitched multiple fingerprint images acquired by sliding a finger on the sensor's surface. Yamazaki *et al.* [7] used SIFT algorithm in the alignment stage and fused at image level. Mathur *et al.* [8] proposed an enrollment protocol on mobile devices using the Accelerated KAZE method.

In this paper, a novel fingerprint mosaicking scheme is proposed. After coarsely estimating the initial transformation by a patch matching algorithm, all pair-wised information of patches are used for global alignment optimization. In the feature fusion phase, a novel feature fusion method is proposed for both minutiae and ridge sampling points(briefly named as ridge points in the rest of this paper), while the existing feature fusion methods are all focused on the minutiae.

The rest of this paper is organized as follows, the proposed method is described in detail in Sect. 2, the experimental results are reported in Sect. 3, and finally, Sect. 4 concludes the proposed algorithm.

2 Proposed Method

2.1 Overall Flow and Preprocessing Procedure

The algorithm proposed in this paper includes three stages. In the preprocessing stage, the ridges are sampled and the minutiae and their ridge points' structures are stored. In the alignment phase, a coarse-to-fine alignment method is used. Firstly, estimate the initial transformation of patches by a matching algorithm, and then use a global optimization method to calculate the accurate transformation. In the fusion stage, the minutiae and the ridge points are merged into a synthetic feature template, respectively. The flowchart of the proposed algorithm is shown in Fig. 1.

In the preprocessing procedure, the ridges are sampled and the corresponding structures of minutiae and their ridge points are established. This paper uses a new ridge points sampling method which inspired from the reference [9]. Firstly, for a minutia m_i, search the ridges connected to it. Ending minutia has one connected ridge, while bifurcation minutia has three connected ridges. Draw a line segment centered at m_i, perpendicular to the direction of m_i, and the two nearest ridges intersecting the line segment are each divided into two sub-ridges. Each ridge is labeled and sampled at a constant interval, as shown in Fig. 2. Take m_i as the center, make a circle with radius r, store the ridge sample points located in the circle in a list R_i, the ridge points are

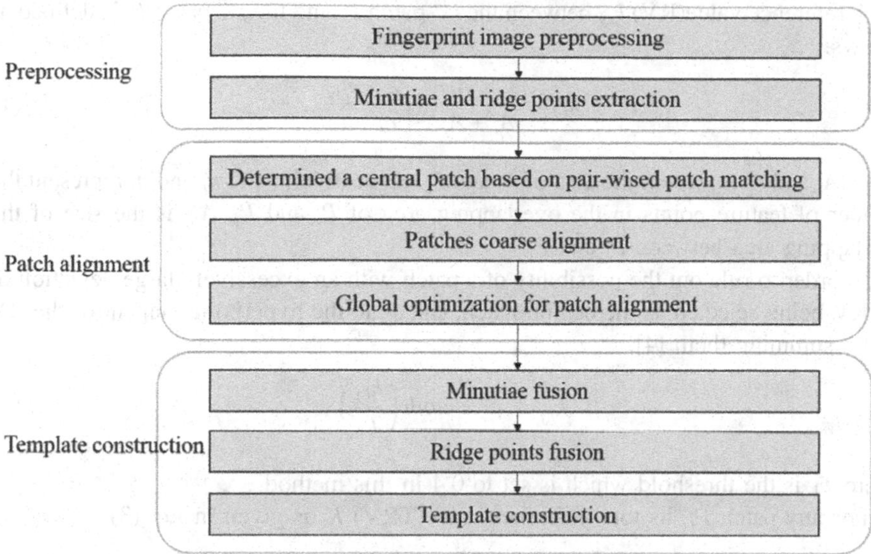

Fig. 1. Flowchart of the proposed method.

represented as $(x_r, y_r, \theta_r, mp_r, r_r)$, which denote the x-coordinates, y-coordinates and angles of the ridge points, the labels of minutiae to which they belong, and the labels of sub-ridges to which they belong, respectively.

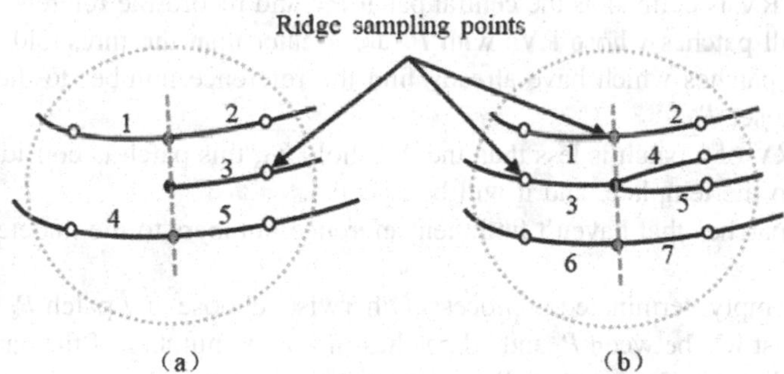

Fig. 2. The sampling method of ridge points.

2.2 Patch Alignment

The initial alignment is performed using the Modified Feature Point Cylinder Code (MFPCC)-based partial fingerprint matching algorithm which is developed by our lab. Then this paper proposes a global optimization method for accurate alignment.

Firstly, some factors should be considered when selecting the central patch as a baseline: which two patches have overlap and the size of the overlapping area, and the number of matched feature points(include minutiae and ridge points) in these overlapping areas.

A reference value(RV) $k_{i,j}$ between the ith patch P_i and the jth patch P_j is defined as follows:

$$k_{i,j} = \frac{2 \times A_{i,j}}{A_i + A_j} + \frac{2 \times n_{i,j}}{n_i + n_j} \tag{1}$$

where A_i and A_j represent the area of P_i and P_j, respectively, and n_i and n_j represent the number of feature points in the overlapping area of P_i and P_j. $A_{i,j}$ is the size of the overlapping area between P_i and P_j.

In order to rule out the possibility of a patch with an excessively large deviation of the RV being selected as the central patch, calculate the hyperbolic tangent of the RV before summing them [4].

$$k_{i,j}^{'} = \gamma_2 \times tanh\left(\frac{k_{i,j}}{T_1}\right) \tag{2}$$

where T_1 is the threshold which is set to 0.4 in this method.

For any patch P_i, its total reference value(TRV) K_i is given in Eq. (3).

$$K_i = \sum\nolimits_{j=1}^{N} k_{i,j}^{'}, j \neq i. \tag{3}$$

where N is the number of patches.

The central patch P_c and the reference number of the non-central patches are determined as follows.

(1) match all patches in pairs and calculate the RVs between them, the patch with the largest TRV is defined as the central patch P_c, and record the reference number f as c of all patches whose RVs with P_c are greater than the threshold T_2.
(2) Add the patches which have already find the reference number to the candidate reference set T_P.
(3) If the TRV of a patch is less than the threshold T_3, this patch is considered not to belong to the template, and it will be rejected.
(4) Add all patches that haven't find their reference numbers to the undetermined set D_P.
(5) if D_P is empty, terminate the process. Otherwise, choose any patch P_i in D_P, find the biggest RV between P_i and all patches in T_P, the number of the patch in T_P is set as P_i's reference number. Repeat this step.

Next, the parameters of transforming all patches to the coordinate system of the central patch need to be calculated.

T_{ij} is the transformation matrix of the P_i transformed into the coordinate system where its reference patch P_j is located. All patches can be iteratively transformed into the coordinate system of P_c. Therefore, for any patch P_i, it can be calculated by the following equation to find the joint transformation matrix T_{ic} of P_c.

$$T_{ic} = T_{zc} \cdot \ldots \cdot T_{jk} \cdot T_{ij} \tag{4}$$

The relationship between all patches are shown in Fig. 3. Use the RVs as the weights of the relationship. Only non-zero weighted relationship is drawn.

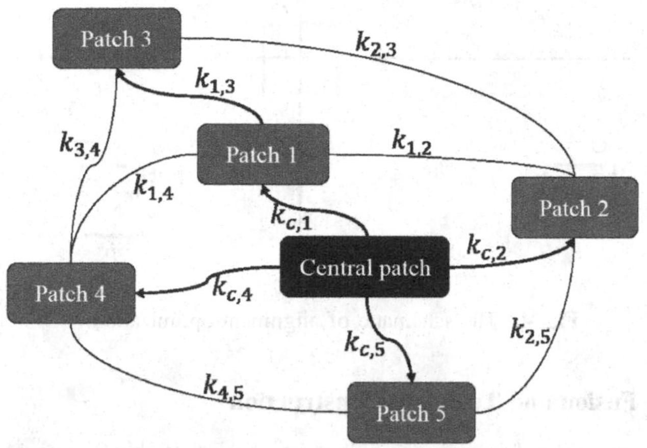

Fig. 3. The relationships of all patches. Thick arrow lines represent reference relationships, and thin lines represent correlation relationships. The correlation relationships refer to the meaning that the two patches are not reference patch for each other, and their RVs are non-zero.

For any non-central patch P_i, its initial feature points set is F_i, F_{ic} is the F_i transformed to the coordinate system of central patch. The alignment error is defined in the following way:

$$E_{rel}(T_{ic}) = \sum\nolimits_{i=1}^{N} \sum\nolimits_{j \in R_i} \lambda_{ij} d_{ij}. \tag{5}$$

$$d_{ij} = d^2\left(F_{im}^{j'}, F_{jm}^{i'}\right). \tag{6}$$

Where R_i represents the non-zero weighted relationship of $P_i.F_{im}^{j'}, F_{jm}^{i'}$ are the F_{im}^{j} and F_{jm}^{i} transformed into the central coordinate system, respectively.

$$d_{ij} = \sum\nolimits_{(t,k) \in M_{ij}} \left\| dx\left(m_t^i, m_k^j\right)^2 \right\| + \left\| d\varnothing\left(m_t^i, m_k^j\right)^2 \right\|. \tag{7}$$

where $\left(m_t^i, m_k^j\right)$. is a pair of matching points of P_i and P_j, and $dx\left(m_t^i, m_k^j\right)$ is the Euclidean distance between these two points. $d\varnothing\left(m_t^i, m_k^j\right)$ is the difference in angle between these two points.

The alignment error is optimized using the LM algorithm [10].

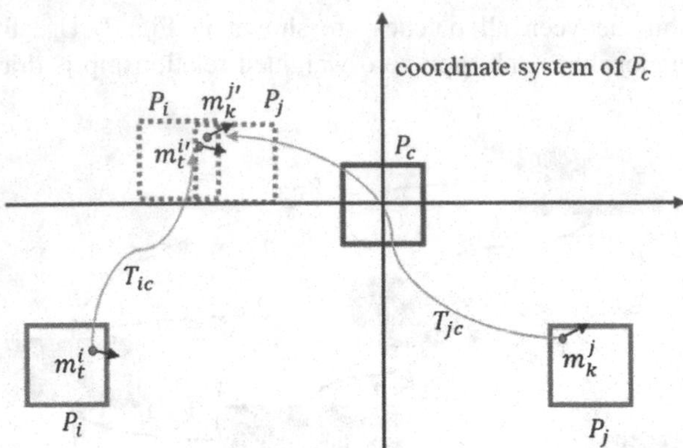

Fig. 4. The schematic of alignment optimization.

2.3 Feature Fusion and Template Construction

Fingerprint fusion technology is a very important part of the fingerprint mosaicking technology. Choosing a reasonable fusion algorithm can greatly improve the reliability of the mosaicking results.

Start with the central patch, the RVs betwe the unfused patches and the already fused patches are sorted, the patches are fused in descending order of RVs.

For any two minutiae, if their distance and angle difference are respectively less than the corresponding thresholds T_4 and T_5, they can be merged. When the fusion is performed, calculate the median value of their positions and angles. It should be noted that if the types of these two minutiae are inconsistent, the merged minutia is stored as a bifurcation. Conversely, minutiae that cannot be merged are added directly to the template.

The corresponding ridge points are merged after the minutiae are merged. It should be noted that when the merged minutiae are different types, their corresponding ridge points have two possible fusion strategies, as shown in Fig. 5.

(1) A bifurcation type minutia's 5th ridge were disconnected with its 3rd and 4th ridge in a certain fingerprint image, causing the change of minutia type from bifurcation to ridge ending, as shown in Fig. 4(a) and (b). In this situation, the corresponding ridge pairs is shown in Fig. 4 (c). The left column is the number of ridges of the bifurcation minutia, and the right column is the number of ridges of the ridge ending minutia.

(2) A bifurcation type minutia's 4th ridge were disconnected with its 3rd and 5th ridge in a certain fingerprint image, causing the change of minutia type from bifurcation to ridge ending, as shown in Fig. 4(d) and (e). In this situation, the corresponding ridge pairs is shown in Fig. 4(f). The left column is the number of ridges of the bifurcation minutia, and the right column is the number of ridges of the ridge ending minutia.

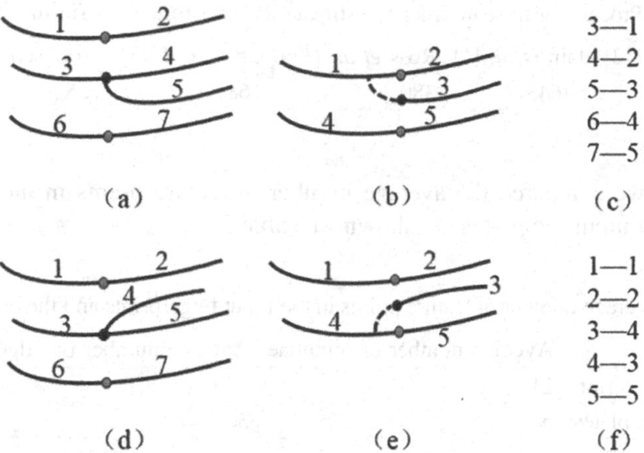

Fig. 5. The schematic of ridge points fusion strategy. (a) and (d) are the structures of bifurcation minutiae. (b) and (e) are the structures of ridge ending minutiae which are occasionally become ridge ending minutiae. (c) and (f) are the labels of pair-wised ridges in (a), (b) and (d), (e).

3 Experimental Results and Analysis

The partial fingerprint registration process on the mobile device requires the user to input multiple fingerprint images, and in the process of inputting, a prompt will be given to guide the user to input in accordance with the prescribed manner, so as to ensure the full coverage of the entire finger by the patches. Due to the fact that there is no publicly available datasets that satisfy requirements of partial fingerprint registration, this paper uses the FVC2002db1 and FVC2002db3 datasets to construct a simulation dataset, which simulates the fingerprint registration process by cutting the full fingerprints of the datasets into patches.

The method of constructing the simulation dataset is in the following way: For the eight fingerprints of one finger in the datasets, three of them are selected as template materials, and the remaining five are used as test materials. In the template material set, two patches are cut out from each fingerprint image as template patches. When cutting, it is necessary to ensure that these template patches of one finger can cover most areas of the entire finger. In the test material library, two patches are randomly cut out from each fingerprint image, and the foreground rate of the cutting patches is required to exceed 90% when cutting. The size of the cutting patches is 192 × 192.

Firstly, we compared several algorithms in terms of processing time performance. Table 1 shows the comparison of the processing time in order to estimate the transformation given in paper [3]. The last column of this table is the time of the algorithm in this paper. Besides, the average time of fusing two 128 × 128 patches in Yamazaki's method [7] is 300 ms, while the average time of fusing two 192 × 192 patches in our method is 6.6 ms, which is far faster than Yamazaki's, despite the size of patches in our algorithm is a little larger than Yamazaki's. In summary, the time performance of our algorithm is both very good in the alignment stage and the fusion stage.

Table 1. Processing time in order to estimate the transformation (in milliseconds).

Lee *et al.* [2]	Jain *et al.* [1]	Ross *et al.* [11]	Choi *et al.* [3]	Proposed method
2685	84643	380	1681	165

Secondly, we compared the average number of feature points in the input fingerprints and the output templates, as shown in Table 2.

Table 2. The average number of feature points in the input fingerprints and the output templates.

	Average number of minutiae	Average number of ridge points
Input fingerprints	21	106
Output templates	56	361

Finally, we compared the recognition performances, as shown in Figs. 6 and 7. Figure 6 shows the recognition performance when the test patches are matched to the templates, the EER(Equal Error Rate) is 3.19% and 1.9% of 2002db1 and 2002db3, respectively. In Choi's [3] experimental results, the EER can be inferred from their figures. When patches of similar size to those used in our experiment are matched to their templates, the EER is about 14%, which is much higher than the proposed algorithm. Figure 7 shows the ROC curves of the proposed method when the complete fingerprint images in test material library are matched to the template, the EER is 1.2% and 2.63% of 2002db1 and 2002db3, respectively. Compared to the several methods mentioned above, the proposed algorithm can achieve an improved recognition performance.

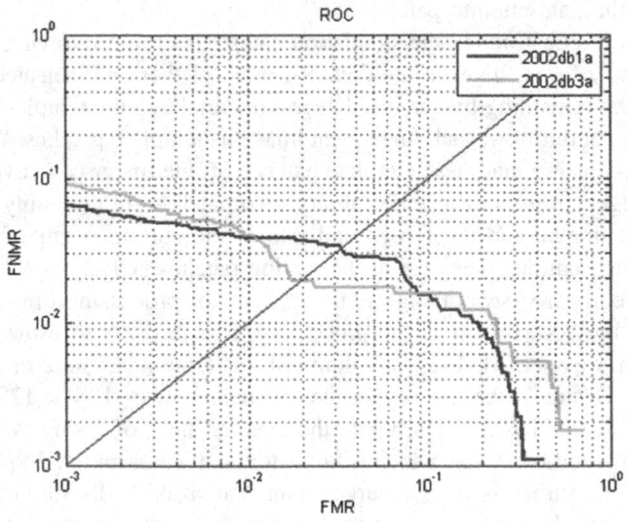

Fig. 6. Roc curves of the proposed method.

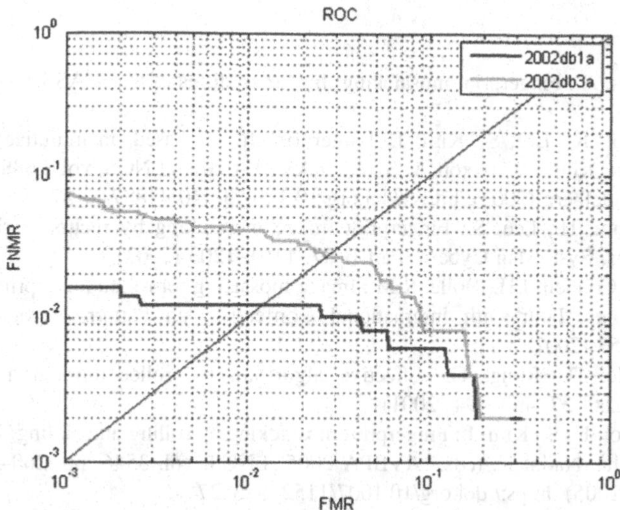

Fig. 7. Recognition performances based on the complete fingerprints in test material library.

4 Conclusions

Based on a large number of researches and literature readings, this paper proposes a novel fingerprint mosaicking scheme. The algorithm mainly studies on two aspects: partial fingerprint alignment and partial fingerprint fusion. Through a great of experimental tests, it is verified that this algorithm can ensure the correctness and timeliness of partial fingerprint mosaicking.

Although the partial fingerprint mosaicking algorithm proposed in this paper has achieved relatively satisfactory results, there is still room for improvement which is also the direction of future researches:

(1) Further improvement in the fingerprint pre-processing process: The current pre-processing process works best on FVC2002 datasets, but it is slightly less effective on other datasets and still needs further improvement to adapt it to any dataset.
(2) Add more features in fusion stage: at present, the proposed algorithm only integrates minutiae and ridge points. If necessary, more features can be added for fusion.
(3) When the patches is very small, the recognition performance of the mosaicking template still has much room for improvement.

Acknowledgments. This work is supported by the Natural Science Foundation of Shandong Province, China (No. ZR2014FM004).

References

1. Jain, A., Ross, A.: Fingerprint mosaicking. In: Proceedings of the ICASSP, vol. 4, pp. 406–4067 (2002)
2. Lee, D., Choi, K., Lee, S., Kim, J.: Fingerprint fusion based on minutiae and ridge for enrollment. In: Kittler, J., Nixon, M.S. (eds.) AVBPA 2003. LNCS, vol. 2688, pp. 478–485. Springer, Heidelberg (2003). https://doi.org/10.1007/3-540-44887-X_57
3. Choi, K., Choi, H., Lee, S.: Fingerprint image mosaicking by recursive ridge mapping. J. IEEE Trans. Syst. Man Cybern. Part B **37**, 1191–1203 (2007)
4. Ratha, N.K., Connell, J.H., Bolle, R.M.: Image mosaicing for rolled fingerprint construction. In: Proceedings. Fourteenth International Conference on Pattern Recognition, vol. 2, pp. 1651–1653 (2002)
5. Zhou, J., He, D., Rong, G.: Effective algorithm for rolled fingerprint construction. J. Electron. Lett. **37**, 492–494 (2001)
6. Choi, K., Choi, H.-S., Kim, J.: Fingerprint mosaicking by rolling and sliding. In: Kanade, T., Jain, A., Ratha, Nalini K. (eds.) AVBPA 2005. LNCS, vol. 3546, pp. 260–269. Springer, Heidelberg (2005). https://doi.org/10.1007/11527923_27
7. Yamazaki, M., Li, D., Isshiki, T., Kunieda, H.: SIFT-based algorithm for fingerprint authentication on smartphone. In: Information and Communication Technology for Embedded Systems, pp. 1–5 (2015)
8. Mathur, S., Vjay, A., Shah, J., Das, S., Malla, A.: Methodology for partial fingerprint enrollment and authentication on mobile devices. In: International Conference on Biometrics, pp. 1–8 (2016)
9. Feng, J., Ouyang, Z., Cai, A.: Fingerprint matching using ridges. Pattern Recogn. **39**, 2131–2140 (2006)
10. Madsen, K., Nielsen, H.B., Tingleff, O.: Methods for Nonlinear Least Squares Problems. J. Soc. Indu. Appl. Math. 2012, 1409–1415 (2004)
11. Ross, A., Dass, S.C., Jain, A.K.: Fingerprint warping using ridge curve correspondences. IEEE Trans. Pattern Anal. Mach. Intell. **28**, 19–30 (2006)

Gesture, Gait and Action

Multiscale Temporal Network for Video-Based Gait Recognition

Xinhui Wu[1,2](✉), Shiqi Yu[1,2](✉), and Yongzhen Huang[3,4](✉)

[1] College of Computer Science and Software Engineering, Shenzhen University, Shenzhen, China
wuxinhui2017@email.szu.edu.cn, shiqi.yu@szu.edu.cn

[2] Shenzhen Institute of Artificial Intelligence and Robotics for Society, Shenzhen, China

[3] National Laboratry of Pattern Recognition, Institute of Automation, Chinese Academy of Sciences, Beijing, China

[4] Watrix Technology Co., Ltd., Beijing, China
yongzhen.huang@nlpr.ia.ac.cn

Abstract. Gait is a kind of advanced feature for human identification at a distance. It also contains rich temporal information. In the paper an innovative gait recognition model, Multiscale Temporal Network (MSTN), is designed to extract discriminative feature at multiple scales in the temporal domain. MSTN can build a temporal pyramid from four different temporal resolutions. That means the human body motion can be described from coarse to fine by the four pathways in the network. The method is verified on a popular databset, CASIA-B. The experimental results show that the proposed MSTN can observably improve the recognition rate and MSTN is a straightforward and effective solution. It also shows that there is great potential in gait feature extraction from the temporal domain.

Keywords: Gait recognition · Multiscale feature · Temporal feature

1 Introduction

Gait is a kind of popular biometric for human identification at a distance. It should be the only biometric that can be collected at a far distance. Because of its unique advantages and great potential in video surveillance, a lot of researchers worked on it in the past 20 years. Especially in these several years, gait recognition has been improved greatly with the development of deep learning. Among the methods for gait recognition, Gait Energy Image (GEI) [9] should be the most popular feature because of its effectiveness and robustness. But the temporal information is lost during the computation of GEI. It is reasonable to use both spatial information and temporal information in gait recognition since gait is a kind of behavioral features and contains some unique moving patterns of the subjects in the temporal domain.

Z. Sun et al. (Eds.): CCBR 2019, LNCS 11818, pp. 75–83, 2019.
https://doi.org/10.1007/978-3-030-31456-9_9

Compared with the traditional learning methods, deep learning based method can obviously improve the performance of gait recognition. Deep learning based methods can handle the input data in a very high dimensional space. To input a sequence of silhouettes into a CNN model can achieve higher recognition rates than to input a GEI because of the dynamic information in the sequence. Experimental results in [20] also proved that.

We were inspired by SlowFast network in [4]. In SlowFast there are two pathways for different temporal resolutions. The higher resolution pathway can extract feature for fast-motion, and the lower resolution pathway is for slow-motion. The discriminative feature in gait recognition includes the body shape, the obvious motion patterns and some minor motion patters. To better extract these kinds of features, we expand SlowFast network to four pathways and propose a Multiscale Temporal Network (MSTN). That means the features can be extracted in four different temporal resolutions. Surely it should have better feature extraction capability.

The remaining part of the paper is organized as follows. We firstly introduce some related methods for gait recognition in recent years, and also show how gait recognition was improved in deep learning era. Then the proposed method is introduced in Sect. 3 and the network designing details are also included. The next section is for the experimental design and results. The last section, Sect. 5, conclues the paper.

2 Related Work

Generally, there are two categories for gait recognition, model-based methods and appearance-based methods. Model-based methods [1,13] normally build one 2D or 3D model for a human body and joints. It is a challenging task especially when the resolution and image quality are not high. Compared with model-based methods, appearance-based ones are normally easy to implement since they extract features directly from 2D human silhouettes. Such as in [12], Makihara *et al.* extract frequency-domain features first, construct view transformation model. In [11], Kusakunniran *et al.* consider correlations between gaits across views. Among these methods, the gait energy image (GEI) [9] may be the most popular feature because of its small amount of calculation and data. Wu *et al.* [16] achieved really good classification results using GEI. However, GEI is an average of all images in a sequence, a lot of temporal information will be lost.

In order to make the use of temporal information effectively in the sequences, researchers have proposed many methods to process temporal information. One of the possible solutions is 3D convolution. C3D [3] proposed by Du *et al.* employs 3D convolution to extract temporal information. On the other hand, LSTM can intrinsically handle temporal information in the input data. In [6], a Recurrent Neural Network (RNN) is employed to extract feature from silhouette sequences. There are more related works [8,10,14,16] which use CNN to extract features in the temporal domain. Multiple frames of silhouettes construct a multiple channel data blob, that is sent to a CNN network to train a classifier.

In addition, some researchers have also proposed two-stream architectures. A two-stream network usually consists a temporal network and a spatial network. The spatial network is a common CNN network and the temporal network choose a method of processing temporal information as mentioned above, or divide a long gait sequence into several segments. Such as in [5], Feichtenhofer *et al.* studied many ways of fusing ConvNet towers both spatially and temporally, and proposed a network for combining the appearance and motion information. In [15], Wang *et al.* proposed TSN network, which extract short snippets from a long video sequence by sparse sampling, and then capture the long-range temporal structure. SlowFast Network [4] is also a two-stream architecture. It included a slow pathway to capture spatial information at low frame rate, and a fast pathway to capture motion at fine temporal resolution.

3 Proposed Method

3.1 The Network Architecture

The network designed for temporal feature extraction in the paper is named as Multiscale Temporal Network (MSTN). The framework of MSTN is shown in Fig. 1. There are 4 different pathway in it for 4 different temporal scales. Different frame rates are selected for each scale, and the frame rates decrease step by step. So the 4 pathways can help extract temporal feature in different scales. The structures of the CNN in the 4 pathways are similar. The only difference is that the number of kernels in each convolutional layer.

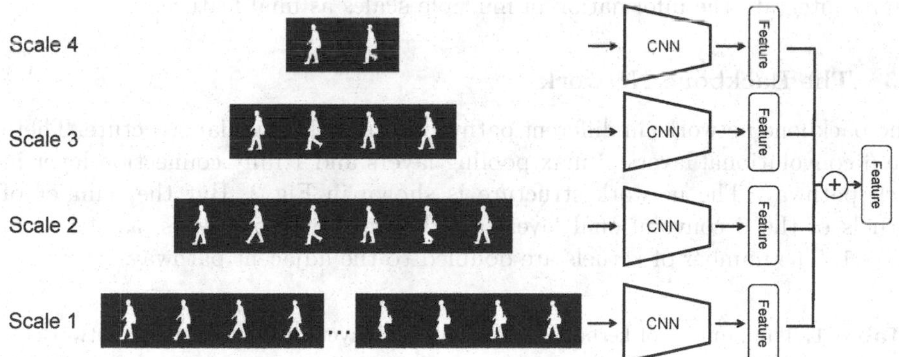

Fig. 1. The framework of the proposed method. There are 4 pathways designed for temporal feature extraction in different scales, and the number of convolutional kernels are different. CNN module stands for our backbone network as shown in Fig. 2. At last the features at different scales are concatenated to one feature vector for gait recognition.

3.2 Multiscale Temporal Network

As SlowFast network in [4], the multiple temporal network can extract temporal feature in different scales. There are more scales in the proposed network than SlowFast network. That means the temporal feature can be better extracted in more temporal resolutions, and it surely can benefit gait recognition.

The first pathway is a fine-grained one, and it can extract feature from some motion patterns which only last in a very short time period. In the first pathway, all silhouettes in a gait cycle are all inputted into the backbone CNN network. The size of the input data is $T_1 \times 1 \times H \times W$, where T_1 is the number of successive frames from one sequence, H is the height of the silhouettes in pixels, and W are the width. The silhouettes are inputted into the backbone network one by one or in a batch. Then the feature vector is obtained by averaging the output of the network from different silhouettes. In the second pathway, the number of frames decreases from T_1 to αT_1. That means $T_2 = \alpha T_1$. The network can focus on the motion pattern which last $1/\alpha$ times of the patterns in the first pathway. The frame rates in the remaining pathways are in the same manner.

$$T_i = \alpha T_{i-1}, i \in \{2, 3, 4\} \tag{1}$$

MSTN proposed in the paper can extract features in 4 different resolutions which are 1, α, α^2 and α^3 times of the original resolution. This idea is similar to the classical image pyramid, which are usually used for target detection tasks in image processing. The image pyramid scales the image at different scales in a spacial space, and then input them to the network. Finally, the features of different size images are fused as final prediction feature. The proposed MSTN scale the temporal information at different scales, build a temporal pyramid, and finally integrate the information of multiple scales as final feature.

3.3 The Backbone Network

The backbone networks in different pathways are with a similar structure. There are 6 convolutional layers, 3 max pooling layers and 1 fully connection layer in each pathway. The network structure is shown in Fig. 2. But the number of kernels of the 6 convolutional layers are different in 4 pathways, as shown in Table 1. The number of kernels are doubled to the adjacent pathway.

Table 1. The number of kernels of convolutional layers in the backbone networks.

Pathway	C_1	C_2	C_3	C_4	C_5	C_6
1	32	32	64	64	128	128
2	64	64	128	128	256	256
3	128	128	256	256	512	512
4	256	256	512	512	1024	1024

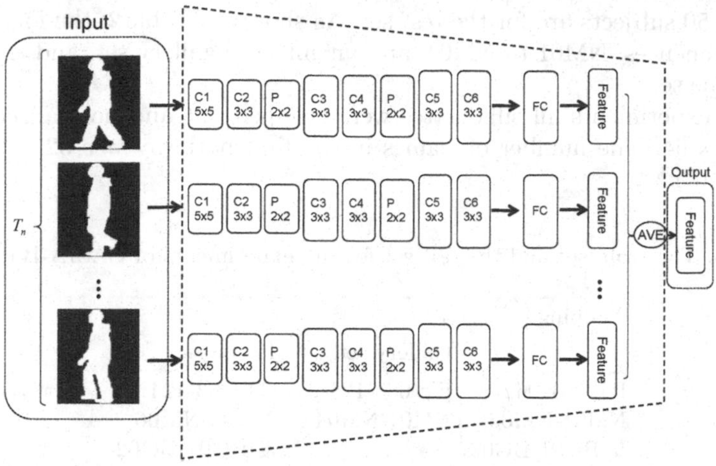

Fig. 2. The backbone CNN network. The final feature vector is obtained by averaging the feature vectors of frames.

4 Experimental Design and Results

4.1 The Gait Dataset

To evaluate our proposed method, we selected the popular gait dataset CASIA-B [19]. This dataset contains these variations, namely view, clothing, and carrying and it is a challenging dataset. Some sample images in this datasets are shown in Fig. 3. CASIA-B is a large multi-view gait database, which was collected indoorsis in January 2005. There are 13640 gait videos, 124 subjects, 10 sequences (NM01-06, BG01-02, CL01-02) for each person, and the gait data was captured from 11 views (000, 018, ..., 180). Three variations, namely view angle, clothing and carrying condition changes, are separately considered.

Fig. 3. Sample images in CASIA Dataset B

4.2 Experimental Design

The samples in CASIA-B are divided into two sets, the training set and the test set. The samples from the first 74 subjects are put into the training set, and the remaining 50 subjects are for the test set. As shown in Table 2, the four normal walking sequences, NM01 to NM04, are put into the gallery set, and the others in the probe set.

In the experiments all silhouettes were cropped out and normalized to the size of 64×64. The number of frames in the first pathway was 32. α in Eq. 1 was set to 0.5.

Table 2. The train set and the test set for the experiments of CASIA-B dataset

Training	Test	
	Gallery set	Probe set
ID: 001-062 NM01-NM06 & BG01-BG02 & CL01-CL02	ID: 063-124 NM01-NM04	ID: 063-124 NM05-NM06 & BG01-BG02 & CL01-CL02

4.3 Effectiveness of the Multiple Temporal Scales

In [2,20], it is shown that inputting silhouettes nor GEI can achieve better performance. Here we want to prove that inputting silhouettes at different frame rates can improve the performance more. To evaluate the effectiveness of combining the multiple temporal scales, we designed four sets of experiments. They are (1) One-scale, only the first scale is involved; (2) Two-scales, there are two scales, Scale 1 and 2; (3) Three-scales, there are three scales, from Scale 1 to 3; (4) Four-scales(The proposed MSTN), there are four scales as illustrated in Fig. 1.

The correct classification rates (CCR) include all views of 62 subjects in test set. The CCR of these four methods are listed in Table 3. It can be easily found that the CCR will increase when more scales are added. The proposed MSTN which contains four scales reaches the best recognition rate. From the last row in Table 3 it can also be found that MSTN achieves greater improvements when there are carrying condition and clothing variations. The CCR is improved 4.6% under carrying changing and clothing changing. There is more redundant information in the input data when more scales are involved. So it can make the recognition method be more robust to variations. It also should be the reason why the proposed MSTN is more robust when there are some variations.

4.4 Comparisons with State-of-the-Arts

To evaluate the performance of the proposed method, we also compared the proposed MSTN with some state-of-the-art ones. They are ViDP [8], C3A [17], AE [18], MGAN [7], CNN [16]. Because of the limitation of space, only 5 views from 11 views are listed in Table 4. There are several methods in [16], and CNN-LB is the best one among them. So we chose CNN-LB among the methods

Table 3. Correct classification rates on CASIA-B dataset of the four methods, One-scale, Two-scales, Three-scales and Four-scales (MSTN)

Method	CCR(%)		
	NM	BG	CL
One-scale	84.5	70.9	53.0
Two-scales	85.7	73.0	56.0
Three-scales	86.3	73.9	55.2
Four-scales (MSTN)	**86.7**	**75.5**	**57.6**
Improvement of MSTN to One-scale	2.2	4.6	4.6

in [16]. The method GaitSet in [2] achieved a really high classification rate. But the feature fusion strategy in it is different from that in the proposed method. So we did not compare the proposed MSTN with GaitSet. From the results in Table 4 it can be found that MSTN achieves very good performance. Especially there are some variations, MSTN achieves the best recognition rates. It shows that MSTN is more robust to variations.

Table 4. Comparisons with some state-of-the-arts on CASIA-B dataset

Gallery NM01-04		0°–180°					Mean
Probe	Method	0°	54°	90°	126°	180°	
NM05-06	ViDP [8]	–	59.1	50.2	57.5	–	–
	C3A [17]	–	64.5	58.1	65.7	–	–
	AE [18]	49.3	63.6	58.1	66.5	44.0	59.3
	MGAN [7]	54.9	74.8	65.7	75.6	53.8	68.1
	CNN-LB [16]	**79.1**	**92.8**	**87.0**	**92.1**	**75.4**	**88.4**
	MSTN (Proposed)	76.7	90.7	80.1	91.4	75.0	86.7
BG01-02	AE [18]	29.8	40.5	37.5	42.7	28.5	37.2
	MGAN [7]	48.5	58.0	49.8	61.3	43.1	54.7
	CNN-LB [16]	64.2	76.9	63.1	76.9	61.3	72.4
	MSTN (Proposed)	**68.4**	**81.6**	**66.3**	**76.9**	**61.5**	**75.5**
CL01-02	AE [18]	18.7	25.1	26.3	30.0	19.0	24.2
	MGAN [7]	23.1	33.3	32.7	37.6	21.0	31.5
	CNN-LB [16]	37.7	61.0	54.6	59.1	39.4	54.0
	MSTN (Proposed)	**47.8**	**61.0**	**57.9**	**59.2**	**39.7**	**57.6**

5 Conclusions and Future Work

In the proposed MSTN there are four pathways to extract temporal feature for gait recognition at different temporal resolutions. The experimental results show that MSTN can improve the correct classification rate obviously. It can also improve the robustness to different kinds of variations greatly because it is effective to extract robust feature from redundant data.

It is essential and important to extract temporal feature efficiently in gait recognition. The proposed MSTN show the effectiveness of feature extraction at different temporal resolutions. We will train the model using larger datasets. We also believe that there are some other models needed to design which can extract temporal feature more efficiently than MSTN.

References

1. Ariyanto, G., Nixon, M.S.: Model-based 3D gait biometrics. In: International Joint Conference on Biometrics, pp. 1–7 (2011)
2. Chao, H., He, Y., Zhang, J., Feng, J.: Regarding gait as a set for cross-view gait recognition. In: AAAI, GaitSet (2019)
3. Du, T., Bourdev, L., Fergus, R., Torresani, L., Paluri, M.: Learning spatiotemporal features with 3D convolutional networks. In: IEEE International Conference on Computer Vision, pp. 4489–4497 (2015)
4. Feichtenhofer, C., Fan, H., Malik, J., He, K.: Slowfast networks for video recognition. arXiv:1812.03982 (2018)
5. Feichtenhofer, C., Pinz, A., Zisserman, A.: Convolutional two-stream network fusion for video action recognition. In: Computer Vision & Pattern Recognition (2016)
6. Feng, Y., Li, Y., Luo, J.: Learning effective gait features using LSTM. In: International Conference on Pattern Recognition, pp. 325–330 (2017)
7. He, Y., Zhang, J., Shan, H., Wang, L.: Multi-task gans for view-specific feature learning in gait recognition. IEEE Trans. Inf. Forensics Secur. **14**(1), 102–113 (2018)
8. Hu, M., Wang, Y., Zhang, Z., Little, J.J., Huang, D.: View-invariant discriminative projection for multi-view gait-based human identification. IEEE Trans. Inf. Forensics Secur. **8**(12), 2034–2045 (2013)
9. Han, J., Bir, B.: Individual recognition using gait energy image. IEEE Trans. Pattern Anal. Mach. Intell. **28**(2), 316 (2006)
10. Kusakunniran, W., Wu, Q., Zhang, J., Li, H.: Support vector regression for multi-view gait recognition based on local motion feature selection. In: Computer Vision & Pattern Recognition (2010)
11. Kusakunniran, W., Qiang, W., Zhang, J., Li, H., Wang, L.: Recognizing gaits across views through correlated motion co-clustering. IEEE Trans. Image Process. **23**(2), 696–709 (2014)
12. Makihara, Y., Sagawa, R., Mukaigawa, Y., Echigo, T., Yagi, Y.: Gait recognition using a view transformation model in the frequency domain. In: Leonardis, A., Bischof, H., Pinz, A. (eds.) ECCV 2006. LNCS, vol. 3953, pp. 151–163. Springer, Heidelberg (2006). https://doi.org/10.1007/11744078_12

13. Urtasun, R., Fua, P.: 3D tracking for gait characterization and recognition. In: IEEE International Conference on Automatic Face and Gesture Recognition, pp. 17–22 (2004)
14. Wang, C., Zhang, J., Pu, J., Yuan, X., Wang, L.: Chrono-gait image: a novel temporal template for gait recognition. In: Daniilidis, K., Maragos, P., Paragios, N. (eds.) ECCV 2010. LNCS, vol. 6311, pp. 257–270. Springer, Heidelberg (2010). https://doi.org/10.1007/978-3-642-15549-9_19
15. Wang, L., Xiong, Y., Zhe, W., Yu, Q., Van Gool, L.: Temporal segment networks for action recognition in videos. IEEE Trans. Pattern Anal. Mach. Intell. **PP**(99) (2017)
16. Wu, Z., Huang, Y., Wang, L., Wang, X., Tan, T.: A comprehensive study on cross-view gait based human identification with deep CNNs. IEEE Trans. Pattern Anal. Mach. Intell. **39**(2), 209–226 (2017)
17. Xing, X., Wang, K., Yan, T., Lv, Z.: Complete canonical correlation analysis with application to multi-view gait recognition. Pattern Recognit. **50**(C), 107–117 (2016)
18. Yu, S., Chen, H., Wang, Q., Shen, L., Huang, Y.: Invariant feature extraction for gait recognition using only one uniform model. Neurocomputing **239**(C), 81–93 (2017)
19. Yu, S., Tan, D., Tan, T.: A framework for evaluating the effect of view angle, clothing and carrying condition on gait recognition. In: International Conference on Pattern Recognition, pp. 441–444 (2006)
20. Zhang, Y., Huang, Y., Wang, L., Shiqi,Y.: A comprehensive study on gait biometrics using a joint CNN-based method. Pattern Recognit. **93**(9), 228–236 (2019)

Global and Local Spatial-Attention Network for Isolated Gesture Recognition

Qi Yuan[1], Jun Wan[2(✉)], Chi Lin[3], Yunan Li[4], Qiguang Miao[4], Stan Z. Li[2], Lihua Wang[1], and Yunxiang Lu[1]

[1] School of Software, Beihang University, Beijing, China
{qiyuan,wanglihua}@buaa.edu.cn, yxlu_2000@163.com

[2] National Laboratory of Pattern Recognition, Institute of Automation, Chinese Academy of Sciences, Beijing, China
{jun.wan,szli}@nlpr.ia.ac.cn

[3] University of Southern California, Los Angeles, CA, USA
linchi@usc.edu

[4] School of Computer Science and Technology, Xidian University & Xi'an Key Laboratory of Big Data and Intelligent Vision, Xi'an, China
yn_li@stu.xidian.edu.cn, qgmiao@mail.xidian.edu.cn

Abstract. In this paper, we focus on isolated gesture recognition from RGB-D videos. Our main idea is to design an algorithm that can extract global and local information from multi-modality inputs. To this end, we propose a novel attention-based method with 3D convolutional neural network (CNN) to recognize isolated gesture recognition. It includes two parts. The first one is a global and local spatial-attention network (GLSANet), which takes into account the global information that focuses on the context of the frame and the local information that focuses on the hand/arm actions of the person, to extract efficient features from multi-modality inputs simultaneously. The second part is an adaptive model fusion strategy to fuse the predicted probabilities from multi-modality inputs. Experiments demonstrate that the proposed method has achieved state-of-the-art performance on the IsoGD dataset.

Keywords: Gesture recognition · Fusion strategy · RGB-D video

1 Introduction

Video based dynamic gesture recognition plays an important role in human-computer interaction (HCI) [1]. Isolated gesture recognition and continuous gesture recognition are two major tasks [2]. The former focuses on gesture classification merely while the latter also pays attention to temporal segmentation that needs to separate each gesture from a video containing continuous gestures.

In this paper, we focus on isolated gesture recognition. In the task of isolated gesture recognition, most of the deep learning based methods [3–7] are adapted from general action recognition. However, the general action recognition task

Z. Sun et al. (Eds.): CCBR 2019, LNCS 11818, pp. 84–93, 2019.
https://doi.org/10.1007/978-3-030-31456-9_10

that based on widely used action recognition datasets, such as HMDB51 [8], UCF101 [9], and Kinetics [10] focuses more on the general human activity in the videos. But gesture recognition is a fine-grained action recognition task that focuses more on detailed hand gestures and arm movements, it is hard to extract distinguishable features to classify different gestures from the entire frame in spatial with general action recognition derived methods.

Therefore, we propose a global and local spatial-attention network, dubbed as GLSANet, which considered the global information that focuses on the global context and local information that focuses on the hand actions from multi-modality inputs simultaneously, to classify the isolated gestures on publicly used large-scale gesture recognition dataset IsoGD [2]. Besides, we propose an adaptive fusion strategy to fuse the probabilities of multi-modality inputs. The results show that we achieve state-of-the-art performance. The main contributions of this work can be summarized as follows:

- We propose an attention based network that not only embedded the global information into 3D CNNs along with the original RGB-D videos, but also focused on the local hand/arm regions based on the skeleton points.
- We develop a class-constrained fusion strategy to fuse the predicted probabilities of all the global/local attention models from multi-modality inputs.
- We achieve state-of-the-art performance on the IsoGD dataset.

2 Related Work

Most of deep learning based gesture recognition methods are adapted from action recognition tasks. Generally, action recognition models can be roughly divided into two categories. One is 2D CNN based methods that extract spatial features from several video frames followed by a temporal reasoning scheme to extract temporal features from these spatial features, and the other one is 3D CNN based methods that treat the spatial dimension the same as the spatial dimension and extract spatio-temporal features uniformly with 3D convolutional kernels.

2D CNN Based Methods. Wang *et al.* [11] proposed three representations of depth sequences, referred to respectively as Dynamic Depth Images (DDI), Dynamic Depth Normal Images (DDNI) and Dynamic Depth Motion Normal Images (DDMNI) that are constructed from a sequence of depth maps using bidirectional rank pooling [12] to capture the spatio-temporal information. 2S-RNN [13] used an LSTM layer to fuse the color and depth features extracted by a 2D CNN separately. Kopuklu *et al.* [14] proposed a data level fusion strategy to fuse optical flow information into static images as better representatives of spatio-temporal states of action.

3D CNN Based Methods. C3D [15] was first proposed to extract spatio-temporal features with a single model in action recognition, C3D treat the spatial dimension the same as the spatial dimension by using 3D convolution kernel in the network. Li *et al.* [7] used C3D to extract features from multi-modality inputs. Miao *et al.* [3] proposed a multi-modality gesture recognition method based on the ResC3D network which leverages the advantages of both residual network [16] and C3D model. Zhu *et al.* [17] presented a pyramidal 3D convolutional network framework for gesture recognition, in which the author used a pyramid input scheme to extract multi-scale contextual information and a pyramid fusion scheme to fuse the features from pyramid input.

3 The Proposed Method

In this section, we describe the proposed GLSANet algorithm to handle the isolated gesture recognition problem. The overall structure of our framework is illustrated in Fig. 1.

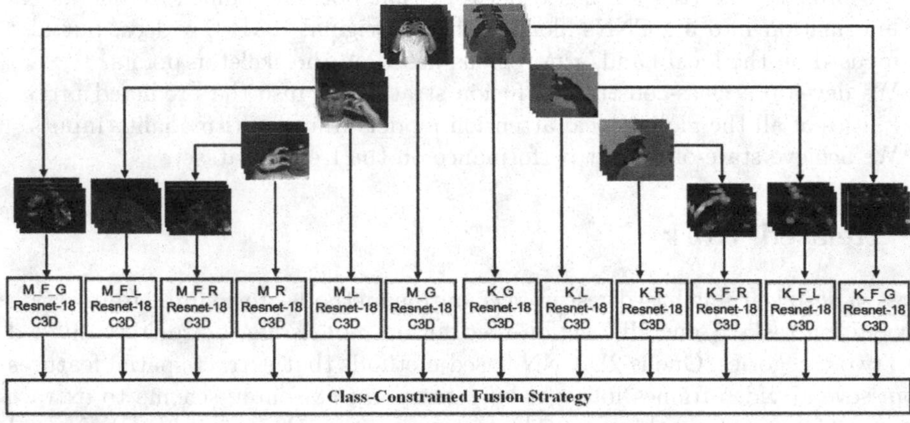

Fig. 1. The overview of our GLSANet network, which includes 12 sub-branches. A weight fusion layer is designed to merge the predictions of all branches to get the final results (M: RGB, K: depth, L: the left hand region, R: the right hand region, F: optical flow, G: global information (the whole image)).

3.1 Global and Local Spatial Attention Network

Intuitively, the motions of body parts (*e.g.*, arms and hands) are important to gesture recognition. Thus, as shown in Fig. 1, we design the GLSANet to focus on the local context with attention mechanism, especially for the left and right hands, together with the global context provided by the entire video for better extracting the essential features of the gesture.

Considering the outstanding performance of C3D and ResNet models in the recognition task [18], we use them to extract features for both original global or local videos. The C3D model with a 3D convolutional and pooling structure can describe a video concurrently from both spatial and temporal domains, while the

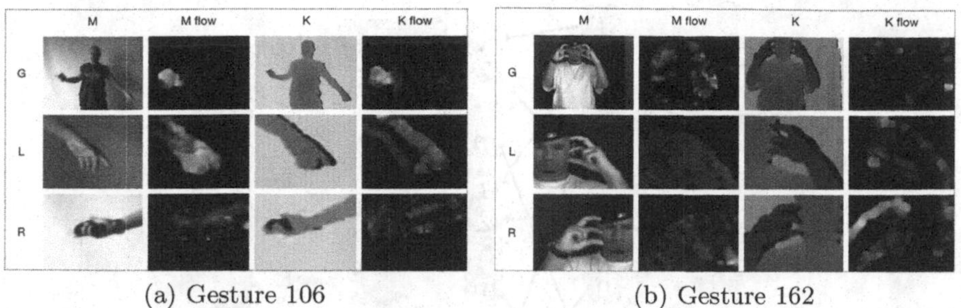

(a) Gesture 106 (b) Gesture 162

Fig. 2. Two samples of the training data in the IsoGD dataset. M, M flow, K, K flow are correspond to RGB, RGB flow, depth and depth flow data respectively; G, L, R are correspond to a frame of global, left and right hand attention respectively

ResNet has a better convergence performance with the deep network. Integrating them can help to achieve a good result for video based gesture recognition.

We can obtain the gesture and body keypoints via CPM [19] algorithm. Therefore, for each sub-model of GLSANet, we can get the regions of hands via the coordinates of hands/body. The cropping region size is determined related to the shoulder's width ϕ_w, which is set to $2 \times \phi_w \times c$, c is a parameter used to control the size. Thus, the cropping area $\mathcal{A}$ is:

$$\mathcal{A} = \Big\{(x - \phi_w \cdot c, y - \phi_w \cdot c), (x + \phi_w \cdot c, y + \phi_w \cdot c)\Big\} \tag{1}$$

where the first point is the top left coordinate and the second one is the bottom right coordinate. We adjust the parameter c to ensure that it not only includes the hand but is also smaller than 112×112 (we set $c = 0.6$ in our experiments).

The cropped left and right hand regions are shown in the second and third rows of Fig. 2. Besides, we also extract the optical flow for both RGB and depth videos after cropping operation on all of the videos.

Global Spatial Information. Although dynamic gesture recognition is most relevant to the arm or hands, the global information from other parts of the performer's body and environments (*i.e.*, face, background) also provides useful information to increase the robustness of our method. Thus, the raw RGB and depth videos are fed into the C3D network, respectively to capture the global context. Similarly, the optical flow from raw RGB and depth video encode the dynamic gesture in sequences, which refers to temporal information of the video. So optical flow information is also encoded by the C3D network.

Local Spatial Information. To extract more precise information of the gesture, we attempt to focus on the hands, and crop the videos with centroids on the hands, which is helpful to draw local attentions to the hands and extract details of complex gestures. Similar to the global one, the optical flow of the cropped right/left hand is also calculated and fed to the C3D network.

In this way, we can obtain the predictions of 12 C3D models. Then we use an adaptive loss weight layer to fuse the results to get the final prediction.

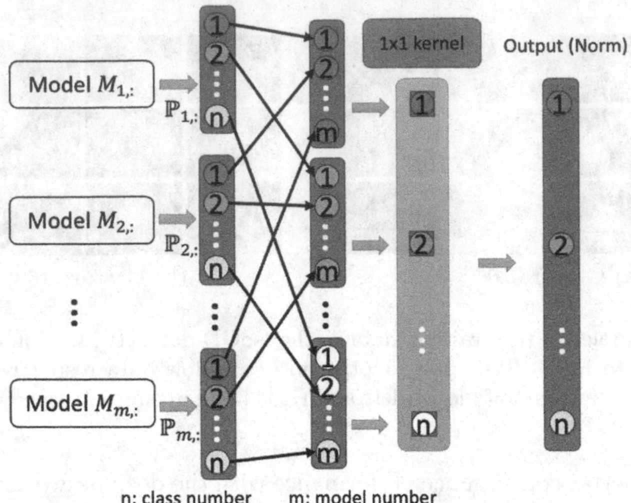

Fig. 3. The class-constrained weight fusion strategy. The 1st column: the classification model; the 2nd column: the output probability vectors of the input models; the 3rd column: class-constrained vector for each class; the 4th column: the 1×1 kernel for convolutional operation; the 5th column: the final predicted result.

3.2 Class-Constrained Fusion Strategy

Inspired by our previous fusion method [20], we also applied a similar fusion strategy for the final prediction. However, compared with [20], the class-constrained fusion strategy has two traits. First, because of the lack of right or left hand in some gestures (*i.e.*, Fig. 3), it would lead to the unavailable local model for the prediction voting. Therefore, we develop a more general scheme for adaptive fusion of all models even if some models are missing. Second, we employ a series of mathematical expressions to derive the fusion processing.

We suppose there are m classification models used for final result fusion, and the $P_{i,j}$ is the predicted probability value of the i-th model $\mathcal{M}_i$ for the j-th class, and n is the class number. The final fusion value for the j-th class can be calculated as:

$$y_j = \sum_{i=1}^{m} (\omega_{i,j} \times \mathbb{P}_{i,j}) = \mathbb{P}_{:,j} \bigotimes \mathbb{K} \; for \; j = 1, \cdots, n$$
$$\mathbb{P}_{i,j} = \begin{cases} P_{i,j}, \; j = 1, \cdots, n & P_{i,j} \text{ exist} \\ 0 & P_{i,j} \text{ not exist} \end{cases} \tag{2}$$

where y_j is the final result for the j-th class and $\omega_{:,j}$ is the weight vector for the j-th class. It can be achieved by using a convolution with a 1×1 kernel $\mathbb{K}$ ($\bigotimes$ is the convolution operation). $\mathbb{P}_{i,j} \in R^{m \times n}$ is a piecewise function which means if the j-th model is missing, then we can directly set $\mathbb{P}_{i,j}$ to zero. We can see that no matter what value for the weight w, it doesn't influence the final weight fusion voting as shown in Eq. (2). Because y_j is only calculated by its corresponding j-th probabilities of m models in Eq. (2), we call it as the class-constrained fusion strategy. Finally, we normalize $y_j, j = 1, \cdots, n$ via normalized exponential function in the range [0, 1] and then get the final fusion result. The structure are show in Fig. 3

4 Experiments

In this section, we illustrate our experiments on IsoGD dataset. First, the experimental setup is presented, including the running environments and settings. Then, the performances and comparisons on the IsoGD dataset is given. At last, an ablation study analyzes and discusses the effect of each strategy including our spatial attention mechanism and weight scheme.

4.1 Experiment Setup

Our experiments are conducted on three NVIDIA Titan Xp GPUs with PyTorch [21]. For the GLSANet algorithm, we utilize the stochastic gradient descent (SGD) optimization strategy and train the model for up to 20 epochs with the batch size 32, and the initial learning rate and the momentum are set as 0.001 and 0.9, respectively. For the fusion network, we utilize the SGD algorithm to optimize the model with the initial learning rate 0.01, momentum 0.9, and 100 epochs (batch size is 128).

4.2 Experiments on the IsoGD Dataset

Table 1 shows all the results of different combinations of either data modalities or global/local attention models. In the header, M, K and F represent the modalities of RGB, $depth$ and $flow$, while L and R represent attention model on either the left or right hand, respectively. We divide our experiments into four groups according to different attention strategies, namely only global models (marked as g), global and right-hand-attention models (marked as gr), global and left-hand-attention models (marked as gl), and finally the global and both right/left-hand-attention models (marked as glr). Each group (*i.e.*, g) has nine models that have used varied data modalities.

Effectiveness of Local Attention Models. As shown in Table 1, the global and left hand attention model gl_9 achieves an improvement at 2.52% from 70.56% (g_9) to 73.08% (gl_9), while the global and right hand attention model gr_9 has improved 1.14% from 70.56% (g_9) to 71.70%(gr_9). It also shows that the global and left hand attention model gl_9 works better than the right hand attention model gr_9 because most gestures from the IsoGD dataset are with the left hand Moreover, we also can see an improvement of about 0.92% from 73.08% (gl_9) to 74.00% (glr_9). The same similar can be found in the other pairs of the result

Table 1. Accuracies of different fusion combinations on the IsoGD dataset. Column header (varied data modality): M: RGB image, K: depth image, L: local attention image from the left hand, R: local attention image from the right hand, F: optical flow image; Row header (model ID using different training data): g: the model using global data, gr: the model using both the global and right hand data; gl: the model using both the global and left hand data; glr: the model using the globe, left hand and right hand data.

ID	Data													
	M_G	M_L	M_R	K_G	K_L	K_R	M_F_G	M_F_L	M_F_R	K_F_G	K_F_L	K_F_R	Valid	Test
g_1	√												56.52%	59.56%
g_2				√									56.21%	64.55%
g_3							√						56.95%	60.90%
g_4										√			56.31%	64.76%
g_5	√						√						57.59%	61.62%
g_6				√						√			57.35%	65.59%
g_7	√			√									64.75%	68.94%
g_8							√			√			65.30%	69.81%
g_9	√			√			√			√			66.08%	70.56%
gr_1	√		√										56.79%	60.15%
gr_2				√		√							56.90%	65.22%
gr_3							√		√				57.22%	61.22%
gr_4										√		√	57.11%	65.08%
gr_5	√		√				√		√				58.18%	62.43%
gr_6				√		√				√		√	58.21%	66.34%
gr_7	√		√	√		√							65.53%	69.99%
gr_8							√		√	√		√	66.17%	70.47%
gr_9	√		√	√		√	√		√	√		√	67.39%	71.70%
gl_1	√	√											57.26%	60.93%
gl_2				√	√								57.92%	65.87%
gl_3							√	√					57.88%	61.41%
gl_4										√	√		57.56%	65.68%
gl_5	√	√					√	√					59.04%	62.86%
gl_6				√	√					√	√		58.80%	67.80%
gl_7	√	√		√	√								66.72%	70.44%
gl_8							√	√		√	√		66.39%	70.99%
gl_9	√	√		√	√		√	√		√	√		68.45%	73.08%
glr_1	√	√	√										57.50%	61.17%
glr_2				√	√	√							58.58%	66.46%
glr_3							√	√	√				58.02%	61.98%
glr_4										√	√	√	58.00%	66.11%
glr_5	√	√	√				√	√	√				59.42%	63.85%
glr_6				√	√	√				√	√	√	60.15%	68.20%
glr_7	√	√	√	√	√	√							67.58%	71.50%
glr_8							√	√	√	√	√	√	66.98%	71.39%
glr_9	√	√	√	√	√	√	√	√	√	√	√	√	**69.76%**	**74.00%**

such as g_7, gr_7, gl_7, glr_7. This proves that both of our left- and right-hand local attention can improve the accuracy of the whole framework.

Effectiveness of Model Fusion. We use the last group models (from glr_1 to glr_9) to illustrate the effectiveness of different data modalities in Table 1. The model glr_1 is trained via global RGB images and glr_2 using global depth images. The performance of the depth model (glr_2, 66.46%) is better than the RGB model (glr_1, 61.17%) about 5%. Similarly, the depth optical flow model (glr_4) is also better than the RGB flow model glr_3 by about 4%. When the RGB and optical flow of the RGB data have used (*i.e.*, glr_5), the performance can also be improved compared with only RGB data used (i.e., glr_1). When all the multiple data modalities are used, namely the RGB-depth-flow model can significantly improved a high accuracy of 74.00%.

Comparison with State-of-the-Arts. Table 2 gives the comparisons with the previous methods, in which our proposed method performs better than all published methods on both the validation set and the testing set. The best accuracy published before on the validation set is 64.40% from Miao *et al.* [3], and the best accuracy on the testing set is 68.42% from Lin *et al.* [20]. Our result of the GLSANet achieves 69.76% on the validation set and 74.00% on the testing set, which improves the accuracy at 5.36% and 5.58%, respectively.

Table 2. Comparison of different methods on the IsoGD dataset.

Method	Backbone	Fusion strategy	Modality of data	Evaluation	
				Valid	Test
Li *et al.* [5] '16	C3D	SVM	RGB-D	49.20%	56.90%
Wang *et al.* [11] '16	VGG-16	Score fusion	depth (DDI+ DDNI+DDMNI)	39.23%	55.57%
Zhu *et al.* [17] '16	pyramidal C3D	Score fusion	RGB-D	45.02%	50.93%
Zhu *et al.* [22] '17	C3D, convLSTM	Score fusion	RGB-D	51.02%	/
Li *et al.* [7] '17	C3D	SVM	RGB-D flow	54.50%	60.93%
Miao *et al.* [3] '17	ResC3D	SVM	RGB-D flow	64.40%	67.71%
Wang *et al.* [23] '17	convLSTM, Resnet-50, C3D	Score fusion	RGB-D saliency	60.81%	65.59%
Zhang *et al.* [24] '17	convLSTM, C3D	Score fusion	RGB-D flow	58.00%	60.47%
Duan *et al.* [4] '17	2S CNN, C3D	Score fusion	RGB-D saliency	49.17%	67.26%
Lin *et al.* [20] '18	Skeleton LSTM, C3D	Adaptive weight fusion	RGB-D Skeleton	64.34%	68.42%
GLSANet (Ours)	C3D	Adaptive weight fusion	RGB-D flow, skeleton	**69.76%**	**74.00%**

4.3 Weight Fusion Analysis

Besides the weight fusion strategy, we also show the maximum and average fusion strategies. The maximum fusion is to select the maximum probability as the predicted result, while the average fusion is to calculate the average value of all the models as the final fusion result. The comparisons among three fusion strategies on the IsoGD dataset are shown in Table 3. We can see that the weight fusion strategy get the best performance on both the validation and testing sets, which is much better than the max and average fusion strategies.

Table 3. Comparisons among different fusion methodologies on the IsoGD dataset.

Fusion method	Validation set	Testing set
Max fusion	61.67%	65.51%
Average fusion	62.02%	65.97%
Weight fusion	**69.76%**	**74.00%**

5 Conclusion

In the paper, we propose a novel gesture recognition architecture GLSANet and an improved adaptive fusion strategy. On the one hand, resnet based C3D network plays an important role in extracting global and local spatial attention features. On the other hand, the proposed adaptive fusion strategy fuses results of each category from different morality input efficiently. The state-of-the-art performance demonstrates the effectiveness of our method. Although the proposed method shows remarkable results, several venues still need further exploration.

Acknowledgments. This work has been partially supported by the Chinese National Natural Science Foundation Projects #61876179, #61872367, and by Science and Technology Development Fund of Macau (Grant No. 0025/2018/A1). We acknowledge the support of NVIDIA Corporation with the donation of the GPU used for this research.

References

1. Rautaray, S.S., Agrawal, A.: Vision based hand gesture recognition for human computer interaction: a survey. Artif. Intell. Rev. **43**(1), 1–54 (2015)
2. Wan, J., Zhao, Y., Zhou, S., Guyon, I., Escalera, S., Li, S.Z.: ChaLearn looking at people RGB-D isolated and continuous datasets for gesture recognition. In: CVPRW, pp. 56–64 (2016)
3. Miao, Q., et al.: Multimodal gesture recognition based on the ResC3D network. In: ICCVW, pp. 3047–3055 (2017)
4. Duan, J., Wan, J., Zhou, S., Guo, X., Li, S.: A unified framework for multi-modal isolated gesture recognition. TOMM **9**(4) (2017)

5. Li, Y., et al.: Large-scale gesture recognition with a fusion of RGB-D data based on the C3D model. In: ICPR, pp. 25–30. IEEE (2016)
6. Li, Y., et al.: Large-scale gesture recognition with a fusion of RGB-D data based on optical flow and the C3D model PRL (2017)
7. Li, Y., et al.: Large-scale gesture recognition with a fusion of RGB-D data based on saliency theory and C3D model. TCSVT **28**, 2956–2964 (2017)
8. Kuehne, H., Jhuang, H., Garrote, E., Poggio, T., Serre, T.: HMDB: a large video database for human motion recognition. In: ICCV, pp. 2556–2563. IEEE (2011)
9. Soomro, K., Zamir, A.R., Shah, M.: Ucf101: a dataset of 101 human actions classes from videos in the wild arXiv preprint arXiv:1212.0402 (2012)
10. Kay, W., et al.: The kinetics human action video dataset arXiv preprint arXiv:1705.06950 (2017)
11. Wang, P., Li, W., Liu, S., Gao, Z., Tang, C., Ogunbona, P.: Large-scale isolated gesture recognition using convolutional neural networks. In: ICPR, pp. 7–12. IEEE (2016)
12. Fernando, B., Gavves, E., Oramas, J., Ghodrati, A., Tuytelaars, T.: Rank pooling for action recognition. TPAMI **39**(4), 773–787 (2017)
13. Chai, X., Liu, Z., Yin, F., Liu, Z., Chen, X.: Two streams recurrent neural networks for large-scale continuous gesture recognition. In: ICPR, pp. 31–36. IEEE (2016)
14. Kopuklu, O., Kose, N., Rigoll, G.: Motion fused frames: data level fusion strategy for hand gesture recognition. In: CVPR, pp. 2103–2111 (2018)
15. Tran, D., Bourdev, L., Fergus, R., Torresani, L., Paluri, M.: Learning spatiotemporal features with 3D convolutional networks. In: ICCV, pp. 4489–4497 (2015)
16. He, K., Zhang, X., Ren, S., Sun, J.: Deep residual learning for image recognition. In: CVPR, pp. 770–778 (2016)
17. Zhu, G., Zhang, L., Mei, L., Shao, J., Song, J., Shen, P.: Large-scale isolated gesture recognition using pyramidal 3D convolutional networks. In: ICPR, pp. 19–24. IEEE (2016)
18. Tran, D., Ray, J., Shou, Z., Chang, S.F., Paluri, M.: ConvNet architecture search for spatiotemporal feature learning arXiv preprint arXiv:1708.05038 (2017)
19. Wei, S.E., Ramakrishna, V., Kanade, T., Sheikh, Y.: Convolutional pose machines. In: CVPR (2016)
20. Lin, C., Wan, J., Liang, Y., Li, S.Z.: Large-scale isolated gesture recognition using masked Res-C3D network and skeleton LSTM. In: FG (2018)
21. Paszke, A., et al.: Automatic differentiation in pytorch (2017)
22. Zhu, G., Zhang, L., Shen, P., Song, J.: Multimodal gesture recognition using 3D convolution and convolutional LSTM. IEEE Access **5**, 4517–4524 (2017)
23. Wang, H., Wang, P., Song, Z., Li, W.: Large-scale multimodal gesture recognition using heterogeneous networks. In: ICCVW, pp. 3129–3137 (2017)
24. Zhang, L., Zhu, G., Shen, P., Song, J., Shah, S.A., Bennamoun, M.: Learning spatiotemporal features using 3DCNN and convolutional LSTM for gesture recognition. In: ICCV, pp. 3120–3128 (2017)

Authentication System Design Based on Dynamic Hand Gesture

Chang Liu[1], Wenxiong Kang[1,2(✉)], Linpu Fang[1], and Ningxin Liang[1]

[1] School of Automation Science and Engineering, South China University of Technology, Guangzhou 510641, China
auwxkang@scut.edu.cn

[2] School of Automation, Guangdong University of Petrochemical Technology, Maoming 510641, China

Abstract. Due to biometric immutability, an authentication system that depends on irrevocable biometric data (faces and fingerprints) is vulnerable to vicious attacks. Gestures, as short actions that contain static and dynamic behavioral information, are gradually replacing traditional biometrics. Compared to body gestures, hand gestures are more flexible and do not require the user's entire body to appear in front of the camera. However, most existing feature extraction algorithms rely on the key point of a hand in motion or the image analysis of a static hand gesture, thereby making the authentication less real-time and less effective in the real-word. To alleviate these problems, we propose a user authentication system based on dynamic hand gestures jointly models the silhouette and skeletal properties of moving hands for user authentication. Our system obtains an average 0.105% false acceptance rate (FAR) and an average 3.40% false rejection rate (FRR) on the public Dynamic Hand Gesture 14/28 dataset.

Keywords: Biometrics · Dynamic hand gestures · User authentication system

1 Introduction

In the information age, how to accurately identify a person to protect information security has become a key social problem. Traditional authentication methods, such as alphanumeric passwords, are easy to forge and lose. At present, the most convenient and safe authentication method is biometric identification technology. Biometric identification refers to the identification of individuals based on their unique biological characteristics. In general, biological characteristics can be divided into physiological features (e.g., irises, fingerprints, etc.) and behavioral features (e.g., gait, voice, handwriting, etc.).

However, there are obvious weaknesses in user authentication systems based on physiological features such as fingerprints and irises. Once registered, these modalities are difficult to change, and these modal data are often exposed in public, which can be easily stolen or copied. An authentication system based on such biological characteristics has irreparable defects. Dynamic gestures, as biological features with rich information, not only contain individual physiological characteristics but also contain

Z. Sun et al. (Eds.): CCBR 2019, LNCS 11818, pp. 94–103, 2019.
https://doi.org/10.1007/978-3-030-31456-9_11

unique behavioral characteristics. If the biometric input is attacked or destroyed, the user can change the dynamic gesture to maintain the security of the system at any time. This paper focuses on a hand gesture-based user authentication system given the flexibility and ubiquity of dynamic hand gestures.

We capture the silhouette and skeletal information simultaneously to extract the features for the prediction. As shown in Fig. 1, the system is separated into three parts. The first part is denoted as the silhouette module, which is applied on a sequence of images of dynamic hand gestures to extract the contour features of a moving hand. The second part is denoted as the skeletal module. This part mainly focuses on the motions of the hand joints in a dynamic hand gesture. Compared with silhouette features, skeletal features are more focused on recording the dynamic characteristics of hand gestures. The third part is named the fusion module. To combine the information from both the hand silhouette and hand skeleton, we fuse the scores of the aforementioned two modules as the final results using a fusion module.

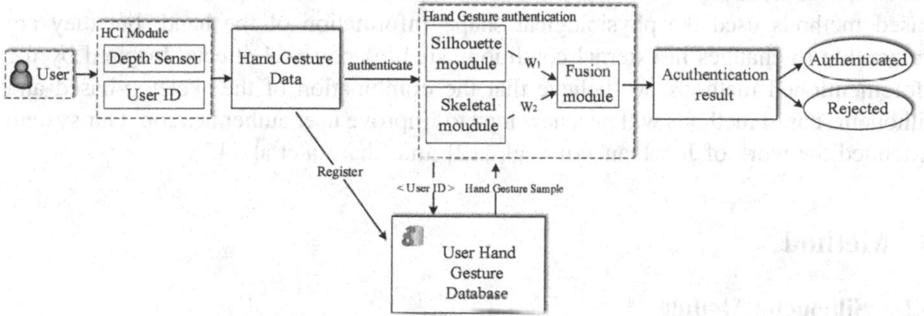

Fig. 1. The overview of the authentication system based on dynamic hand gestures

The main contributions of our work are threefold: (1) we propose a unified framework that combines silhouette features and skeletal features for hand gesture-based user authentication, (2) we present a fusion module to adaptively integrate different predictions for the final authentication, and (3) our method obtains state-of-the-art results on the Dynamic Hand Gesture 14/28 dataset.

The rest of the paper is organized as follows. In Sect. 2, we review some works on dynamic hand gesture-based authentication. In Sect. 3, we introduce our proposed system. In Sect. 4, we present the experimental results and the comparison with previous studies. Finally, the paper is concluded in Sect. 5.

2 Related Work

Although there exists a vast amount of literature on gesture recognition and estimation [1–6], there has been little work on dynamic hand gesture authentication. In [8], Simon Fong et al. proposed a novel hand biometric authentication method based on measurements of the user's stationary hand gestures for sign language. In [11],

Igor Kviatkovsky et al. presented a generative model describing the action instance creation process and derived a probabilistic identity inference scheme, which implicitly includes the action type inference as one of its components. Islam Aumi et al. used in-air hand gesture inputs to authenticate users, and their system tracks individual finger tips and the center of the user's hand in 3D space for biometric authentication [10]. In recent years, some methods were proposed that use the skeleton for user authentication. Some works apply the dynamic time-warping (DTW) based framework to the Kinect's skeletal information for user access control [9, 13]. Many of these skeleton-based methods only use the coordinate information in space for authentication. As a result, some unique physiological shape information of the hand is lost. It is still challenging to distinguish different users who are performing the same dynamic hand gesture. Some silhouette-based methods have been proposed to authenticate users. In [7], the empirical feature covariance matrix framework that has previously been used for tracking and action recognition is applied to extract silhouette features for gesture verification. Jonathan Wu et al. also presented an approach to user authentication from such gestures by leveraging the temporal hierarchy of the depth aware silhouette covariance [12]. These silhouette-based methods used the physiological shape information of the hand, but they are vulnerable to changes in external conditions such as personal effects. Inspired by the aforementioned methods, we believe that the combination of the skeleton-based and silhouette-based methods will be a new idea to improve user authentication. Our system extended the work of Jonathan Wu et al. [12] and Sharma et al. [13].

3 Method

3.1 Silhouette Module

The depth sensor's growing popularity has led to a wide assortment of depth-based applications. In this module, we mainly explain how to obtain the silhouette features of dynamic hand gestures for user authentication, which is mainly divided into three parts: hand gesture extraction, silhouette feature extraction, and authentication. For each set of dynamic hand gesture sequences, the hand gesture of each frame can be extracted according to the depth information of the sequence, and the specific methods are as follows.

1. Perform the morphological opening on each depth image of the dynamic hand gesture sequence.
2. Each pixel is traversed to obtain the minimum depth value, which is the minimum depth of the hand gesture contour. The initial hand gesture contour in the image is extracted from the minimum depth and depth range of the palm.
3. Calculate the connected domain of the extracted hand gesture contour and remove the non-gesture region.

After extracting the hand mask of each frame, the hand gestures of multi-frame images constitute a complete dynamic hand gesture channel, as shown in Fig. 2. To extract the unique features from dynamic hand gesture channels, we rely on a heuristic similar to [14].

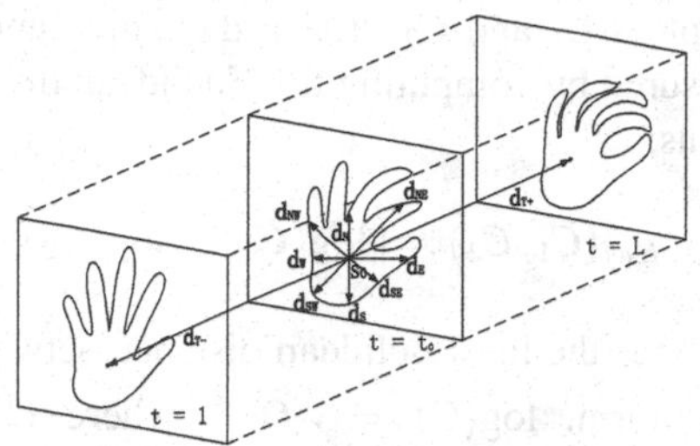

Fig. 2. Example of hand gesture extraction

For each pixel in the dynamic hand gesture channel, we define its feature vector as follows:

$$f^n = [x, y, z, t, \delta_E, \delta_W, \delta_N, \delta_S, \delta_{NE}, \delta_{SW}, \delta_{SE}, \delta_{NW}, \delta_{T+}, \delta_{T-}]' \tag{1}$$

Where n = 1, $\cdots$, N is the pixel in the dynamic hand gesture channel. x, y and t represent the spatial coordinates of pixel n in frame t, and z represents the depth value of the pixel. δ_{DIR} is the distance between the pixel n and the most distant edge pixel on the direction DIR. In particular, δ_{T+} and δ_{T-} are the distances in the temporal domain (forward and backward in time), which describe the dynamic features of hand gestures.

By traversing all the pixel points in the dynamic hand gesture channel, we can get the final feature matrix of 14 × N, $F = [f^1, f^2, \cdots, f^N]$

In authentication system, the obtained features should be independent of the distance between the gesture and camera. Therefore, we normalize the feature matrices as follows:

$$F_{norm}[\text{i}, \text{j}] = \frac{F[i,j] - \min_k F[i,k]}{\max_k F[i,k] - \min_k F[i,k]} \tag{2}$$

We calculate the empirical covariance matrix C of the dynamic hand gesture features F_{norm}, which can preserve the effective features and greatly reduce the dimensions of features.

$$\text{C} := \frac{1}{N} \sum_{1}^{N} \left(f^n_{norm} - \mu\right) \left(f^n_{norm} - \mu\right)^T \tag{3}$$

where μ is the mean value of f^n_{norm}. C is a symmetric matrix, and the upper triangular part size is $(D^2 + \text{D})/2$, which can be used as a unique descriptor for a dynamic hand gesture.

For the unique descriptors C_1 and C_2 of two dynamic hand gestures, the distance between them can be measured by computing the Euclidean distance between their log-transformed representations:

$$\mathrm{d}_{Log-Eucl}(C_1, C_2) := \|\log(C_1) - \log(C_2)\|_2 \tag{4}$$

Where $\mathrm{d}_{Log-Eucl}(C_1, C_2)$ is the log-Euclidean distance between C_1 and C_2, and $\|\cdot\|_2$ is the matrix Frobenius norm. $\log(\mathrm{C}) := V\widetilde{D}V'$, where $\mathrm{C} = \mathrm{VDV}'$ is the eigen decomposition of C. $\widetilde{D}$ is the variant of D by replacing the diagonal element with the logarithm of the diagonal element of D.

To enhance the time constraint between image sequences and avoid misjudging similar dynamic hand gestures with different sequences (such as open the door and close the door), the dynamic hand gesture channel with a frame length of L is split into 16 frames with 8 frames of overlap between two consecutive clips. These clips use the feature extraction algorithm that we previously mentioned to obtain the features.

When a new user accesses the system, all covariance feature descriptors of the dynamic hand gesture samples of the new user are respectively extracted and compared with the features of the verified samples in the dynamic hand gesture database. If the Log-Euclidean distance θ_s' is smaller than θ_s (θ_s is the class distance of the same hand gesture multiple samples, which has been calculated in the user dynamic hand gesture registration), the gesture will pass the authentication; otherwise, it will be rejected.

3.2 Skeleton Module

Compared to the silhouette features, the advantage of skeletal features is that they are relatively insensitive to changes in external conditions such as clothing and personal effects. Hand skeletal information can be extracted from some depth sensors such as Kinect and Intel RealSense cameras. The Intel RealSense Software Development Kit (SDK) [15] provides real-time 22-joint skeletal tracking by using depth information. These skeleton models track the following center-hand joints: Tip, Articulation a, Articulation b, Base, Palm and Wrist joints. These joints are shown in Fig. 3(a).

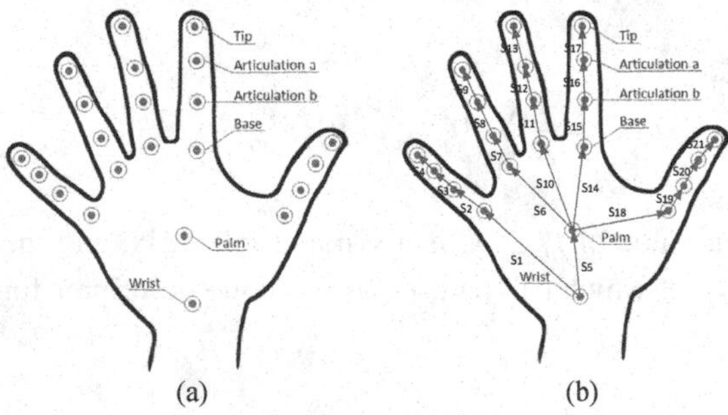

Fig. 3. (a) Hand skeleton points obtained using an Intel RealSense camera; (b) Feature vector constructed from hand skeleton

For each dynamic hand gesture sample, the dynamic hand gesture skeleton information in frame t can be expressed as follows:

$$f^t := \left[s_1^t, s_2^t, \cdots, s_{22}^t\right]' \quad t = 1, 2, \cdots, T \tag{5}$$

where T represents the total number of frames, $s_i^t = \left(x_i^t, y_i^t, z_i^t\right) \in R^3$ represents the spatial coordinates of the i_{th} skeleton point in frame t, and f^t represents the hand skeleton at frame t.

For dynamic hand gesture samples that are T frames long, we use $F = [f^1, f^2, \cdots, f^T]$ to represent the skeletal sequence of a dynamic hand gesture sample.

The skeletal sequence that is extracted from the depth sensor only represents the position of the independent skeletal points at each time, which does not consider the shape of the hand and the connection between the knuckles. Therefore, different from [9], in order to describe the shape of the hand, we construct the feature vector of the gesture according to the structure of the hand, as shown in Fig. 3(b).

The skeletal features of all frames are calculated to form the feature matrix $G = [g^1, g^2, \cdots, g^T]$ (63 * T), where $g^t = \left[S_1^t, S_2^t, \cdots, S_{21}^t\right]'$.

Considering that the frame numbers T of different dynamic hand gestures are not equal, we use the DTW algorithm for hand skeleton-based user authentication, which could find a nonlinear warping path between two time-varying sequences.

The DTW algorithm has been clearly described and thoroughly investigated in several publications [16]. For simplicity, we only introduce how to adopt it to our dynamic hand gesture authentication system without elaborating on its principle.

Let $G_{g_1} = \left[g_{g_1}^1, g_{g_1}^2 \cdots, g_{g_1}^{T_1}\right]$ and $G_{g_2} = \left[g_{g_2}^1, g_{g_2}^2 \cdots, g_{g_2}^{T_2}\right]$ be the skeletal feature matrix of gesture g_1 and gesture g_2, respectively; and g_1 and g_2. are T_1 and T_2 frame-length gesture sequences, respectively. To align the feature matrices G_{g_1} and G_{g_2}, we construct the distance matrix Cos of $T_1 \times T_2$:

$$\mathrm{Cost}(i,j) = \mathrm{Cost}\left(g_{g_1}^i, g_{g_2}^j\right) = \sum_{n=1}^{21} \left\| S_{n,g_1}^i - S_{n,g_2}^j \right\|_2 \tag{6}$$

The alignment path P for hand gesture g_1 and hand gesture g_2 is defined as follows:

$$\mathrm{P} = \left\{(i_a, j_b)_p\right\} \tag{7}$$

where $p = 1, 2, \cdots P; i_1 = j_1 = 1; \max(i_a) = T_1; \max(j_b) = T_2; \forall a, i_{a+1} - i_a \in (0,1); \forall b, j_{b+1} - j_b \in (0,1)$; and $max(T_1, T_2) \leq P \leq T_1 + T_2$

The distance between hand gesture g_1 and hand gesture g_2 is defined as follows:

$$\mathrm{Pathcost}\left(P, G_{g_1}, G_{g_2}\right) = \sum_{(i_a, j_b) \in P} Cost\left(g_{g_1}^{i_a}, g_{g_2}^{j_b}\right) \tag{8}$$

The minimum distance between the two hand gestures is the optimal matching distance determined by DTW:

$$d_{DTW}(G_{g_1}, G_{g_2}) = min(\text{Pathcost}(P, G_{g_1}, G_{g_2})) \tag{9}$$

3.3 Fusion Module

The aforementioned silhouette module and skeletal module authenticate dynamic hand gestures by capturing silhouette and skeletal features. We represent the authentication results from these two module as R_{sil} and R_{ske}, respectively. Then, we use a fusion method to adaptively integrate the different results for the final prediction.

As shown in Eq. 10, the fusion module fuses two predictors, and gives the final result as follows:

$$R_{out} = w_1 \odot R_{sil} + w_2 \odot R_{ske} \tag{10}$$

where $w_1 + w_2 = 1$. The final result R_{out} is the weighted sum of two sub results, w_1 and w_2 are confidence of the two predictions.

In the system initialization stage, for the two cases of denied and passed, we calculate the R_{sil} and R_{ske} of each user in original database, and the real value R_{truth} of whose access result, then we use the binary linear regression model to obtain the values of w_1 and w_2.

We summarize our proposed system in Algorithm 1.

Algorithm 1: Summary for The Authentication System Based on Dynamic Hand Gesture

---

Input: The query user's dynamic hand gesture sample user ID
Output: The query user's authentication results
/* Registration stage */
Step1: The features of the dynamic hand gesture samples and corresponding user Id are saved in the system database, calculate the distance θ between classes of the features of the same set of samples;
Step2: Use the binary linear regression model to obtain w_1 and w_2;
/* Authentication stage */
Step3: Forward the dynamic hand gesture information and user ID into system, then extract the silhouette features and skeleton features. Calculate the distance between the query user and its ID corresponding feature, and get the sub result R_{sil} and R_{ske};
Step4: Calculate the final result via Equation 6.

---

4 Experiment and Discussion

4.1 Experiment Setting

We evaluate our method using the Dynamic Hand Gesture 14/28 dataset [14], which contains 14 dynamic hand gestures, and each of which includes 5 samples that are collected from 20 users. All participants are right-handed. Each sample contains the depth image sequence of a dynamic hand gesture and the sequence of 22 skeletal points of the hand.

Two kinds of errors are considered in this case: false acceptance rate (FAR) and false rejection rate (FRR). As mentioned above, we suppose $A_i = \{S_1, S_2, \cdots, S_m\}$ is the set of m dynamic hand gesture samples of user i, and U_i is the set of hand gesture samples that do not belong to user i. We define FRR and FAR as follows:

$$\mathrm{FRR} = \frac{\sum_{Q \in A_i} 1(D(Q, A_i \backslash \{Q\}) \geq \theta)}{|A_i|} \tag{11}$$

$$\mathrm{FAR} = \frac{\sum_{Q \in U_i} 1(D(Q, A_i) < \theta)}{|U_i|} \tag{12}$$

where $D(\cdot,\cdot)$ is the distance between a single query sample Q and the authorized set A_i. The FRR is found by comparing the samples in A_i among themselves (each sample in A_i is treated as a query sample Q). I.e., Q is compared to the set $A_i \backslash \{Q\}$ with itself removed. In addition, the FAR is found by comparing the samples in U_i to the samples in A_i (each sample in U_i is treated as a query sample Q).

4.2 Experiment Result

The Dynamic Hand Gesture 14/28 dataset is divided into 2 meaningful sets of short dynamic hand gestures where the coarse one can be better described using the movement of the hand through space and the fine one can be better described using the palm translation and subtle finger movements. We want to use the dynamic hand gestures that contain more information of the user. Therefore, in the experiment in this section, we use five groups of dynamic hand gestures that are defined in the database as "Fine" (as shown in Table 1): Grab, Expand, Pinch, Rotation, CW and Rotation CCW. The experimental results are shown in Tables 1 and 2.

Table 1. False acceptance rates (FARs) for various methods and dynamic hand gestures using the Dynamic Hand Gesture 14/28 dataset.

	Grab	Expand	Pinch	Rotation CW	Rotation CCW	Average
[Sil]	11.24%	1.16%	0.76%	0.86%	1.28%	3.06%
[Ske]	14.62%	20.15%	14.2%	15.25%	9.63%	14.77%
Our Sil	4.91%	0.0526%	0	0.579%	0	1.1082%
Our Ske	13.74%	17.95%	15.84%	10.89%	8.842%	13.452%
Our Fus	0.5263%	0	0	0	0	0.105%

From the experimental results, we can see that the performance of our method is considerable compared with the baseline. Integrating the silhouette module with the skeleton module can improve the performance of dynamic hand gesture authentication. The false acceptance rate (FAR) is close to zero, which means that the system can

Table 2. False rejection rates (FRRs) for various methods and dynamic hand gestures using Dynamic Hand Gesture 14/28 dataset.

	Grab	Expand	Pinch	Rotation CW	Rotation CCW	Average
[Sil]	16%	12%	12%	6%	13%	11.8%
[Ske]	22%	22%	22%	20%	22%	21.6%
Our Sil	14%	11%	10%	3%	13%	10.2%
Our Ske	22%	21%	25%	20%	22%	22%
Our Fus	6%	5%	1%	2%	3%	3.4%

determine almost all illegal users, and in such a case, the probability of legal users being misjudged is also significantly reduced. It shows that this system is effective.

5 Conclusions

In this paper, we propose a system for dynamic hand gesture-based authentication that combines the dynamic hand gesture features of silhouettes and skeletons. The registration and authentication of users is simple, robust and easy to implement. Moreover, the authentication algorithm we used does not require large amounts of running time, thus our system is easily deployable on desktop systems. The experiment provided encouraging results. Even in the case in which the attacker knows the user's dynamic hand gestures, the system has a FAR of 0.105%, which demonstrates that our system is feasible.

Acknowledgments. This work was supported in part by the National Natural Science Foundation of China under Grants 61573151, in part by Science and Technology Planning Project of Guangdong Province under Grant 2018B030323026, and in part by the Fundamental Research Funds for the Central Universities under Grant 2018PY24.

References

1. Narayana, P., Beveridge, J.R., Draper, B.A., et al.: Gesture recognition: focus on the hands. In: IEEE/CVF Conference on Computer Vision and Pattern Recognition, pp. 5235–5244 (2018)
2. Zhang, P., Lan, C., Xing, J., et al.: View adaptive recurrent neural networks for high performance human action recognition from skeleton data. In: IEEE International Conference on Computer Vision, pp. 2136–2145, August 2017
3. Chen, X., Guo, H., Wang, G., Zhang, L.: Motion feature augmented recurrent neural network for skeleton-based dynamic hand gesture recognition. In: IEEE International Conference on Image Processing, pp. 2881–2885, August 2017
4. Wu, Y., Ji, W., Li, X.: Context-aware deep spatio-temporal network for hand pose estimation from depth images. IEEE Trans. Cybern. arXiv:1810.02994v1 [cs.CV], 6 October 2018
5. Yuan, S., Stenger, B., Kim, T.-K.: RGB-based 3D hand pose estimation via privileged learning with depth images. arXiv:1811.07376v1 [cs.CV], 18 November 2018

6. Hu, T., Wang, W., Lu, T.: Hand pose estimation with attention-and-sequence network. In: Pacific Rim Conference on Multimedia PCM 2018. Advances in Multimedia Information Processing, pp. 556–566 (2018)
7. Lai, K., Konrad, J., Ishwar, P.: Towards gesture-based user authentication. In: 2012 IEEE Ninth International Conference on Advanced Video and Signal-Based Surveillance (2012)
8. Fong, S., Zhuang, Y., Fister, I., Fister Jr., I.: A biometric authentication model using hand gesture images. Biomed. Eng. Online **12**, 111 (2013)
9. Wu, J., Konrad, J., Ishwar, P.: Dynamic time warping for gesture-based user identification and authentication with kinect. In: 2013 IEEE International Conference on Acoustics, Speech and Signal Processing, pp. 2371–2375 (2013)
10. Aumi, Md.T.I., Kratz, S.: AirAuth: evaluating in-air hand gestures for authentication. In: MobileHCI 2014, Toronto, ON, CA, 23–26 September 2014
11. Kviatkovsky, I., Shimshoni, I., Rivlin, E.: Person Identification from action styles. In: 2015 IEEE Conference on Computer Vision and Pattern Recognition Workshops (2015)
12. Wu, J., Christianson, J., Konrad, J., Ishwar, P.: Leveraging shape and depth in user authentication from in-air hand gestures. In: 2015 IEEE International Conference on Image Processing, pp. 3195–3199 (2015)
13. Sharma, A., Sundaram, S.: An enhanced contextual DTW based system for online signature verification using vector quantization. Pattern Recognit. Lett. **84**, 22–28 (2016)
14. Guo, K., Ishwar, P., Konrad, J.: Action recognition from video using feature covariance matrices. IEEE Trans. Image Process. **22**(6), 2479–2494 (2013)
15. Wang, W., Zhang, J., Wu, W.: An automatic approach for retinal vessel segmentation by multi-scale morphology and seed point tracking. J. Med. Imaging Health Inform. **8**, 262–274 (13) (2018)
16. Lee, M., Lee, S., Choi, M.-J., et al.: Hybrid FTW: hybrid computation of dynamic time warping distances. IEEE Access **6**, 2085–2096 (2017)

Feature Extraction and Classification Theory

Structure Feature Learning: Constructing Functional Connectivity Network for Alzheimer's Disease Identification and Analysis

Qinghua Zhao[1(✉)], Zakir Ali[2], Jianfeng Lu[2], and Hichem Metmer[3]

[1] College of Information Engineering, Nanjing University of Finance and Economics, Nanjing, Jiangsu, China
qhzhao@nufe.edu.cn

[2] School of Computer Science and Engineering, Nanjing University of Science and Technology, Nanjing, China

[3] National Laboratory of Pattern Recognition, Institute of Automation, University of Chinese Academy of Sciences, Beijing, China

Abstract. Functional connectivity network, which as a simplified representation of functional interactions, it has been widely used for diseases diagnosis and classification, especially for Alzheimer's disease (AD). Although, many methods for functional connectivity network construction have been developed, these methods rarely adopt anatomical prior knowledge while constructing functional brain networks. However, in the neuroscience field, it is widely believed that brain anatomy structure determining brain function. Thus, integrating anatomical structure information into functional brain network representation is significant for disease diagnosis. Furthermore, ignoring the prior knowledge may lose some useful neuroscience information that is important to interpret the data, and lose information could be important for disease diagnosis. In this paper, we propose a novel framework for constructing the functional connectivity network for AD classification and functional connectivity analysis. The experimental results demonstrate the proposed method not only improves the classification performance, but also found alteration functional connectivity.

Keywords: Alzheimer's disease · Functional connectivity · Group sparsity learning · Functional connectivity networks

1 Introduction

Alzheimer's disease (AD) is a progressive neurodegenerative disorder, the early characteristic is loss of short-term memory function following by a progressive decline in other cognitive domains including language, attention, orientation, visuospatial skills, executive function, emotional and behavioral disturbances. With the aging population living longer than ever before, AD is now a major public health concern and the number of affected patients is estimated to triple and reaches 13.4 million, in the United States by the year 2050 [1]. The early stage of AD is called Mild cognitive

Z. Sun et al. (Eds.): CCBR 2019, LNCS 11818, pp. 107–115, 2019.
https://doi.org/10.1007/978-3-030-31456-9_12

impairment (MCI), which is an intermediate state of brain cognitive decline between normal aging and dementia, with the progress of the disease, more than half individuals with MCI to dementia within 5 years. Therefore, accurate diagnosis of MCI and AD is important for early treatment and delay of the progression of AD.

Recent evidence shows constructing functional connectivity network from neuroimaging data hold great promising for classification of MCI and AD. The theoretical assumption of brain connectivity network is can be represented as a graph, which comprise nodes and edges, in the neuroscience community, the brain regions or regions of interests (ROIs) from predefined atlas as nodes are natural selection, and the functional connectivity between pair-wise of brain regions usual as edges. Functional connectivity have been applied to individual with a variety of neuropsychiatric disorder for diagnosis and classification [2, 3].

Previous studies on functional connectivity modeling for AD and MCI classification include correlation, partial-correlation, graphical models and sparse representation-based methods. In these methods, correlation-based method is one of the most frequent application methods, any two brain regions of the time courses correlation, allows one to infer whether the regions are functionally connected. Although, correlation-based methods used widely, this method can only capture pairwise information and cannot fully reflect the interactions among multiple brain regions [4]. Recent studies show sparse representation method has been successfully applied to construct sparse brain network model for disease classification. For example, Huang et al. [5] proposed sparse inverse covariance estimation method for functional connectivity analysis. Lee et al. [6] employed the sparse linear regression model with L1 norm penalty for estimating sparse brain connectivity. Wee et al. [7] proposed a novel approach to infer functional connectivity networks from R-fMRI data for classification via group-based sparsity $\ell_{2,1}$ norm penalization.

Inspired by these works, in this work we propose a novel anatomical guided group sparse representation (AG2SR) method to construction functional network for Alzheimer's disease identification. Specifically, the group information of fMRI signals are defined by the anatomical structure information according to AAL template, the 116 brain regions naturally represent as 116 groups, each brain region as an independent group. The group information will be used to guide the coefficient learning. The group sparsity variable selection problem is achieved by introducing the regularized Euclidean projection. Afterward, we achieved functional connectivity network, then extract edges as features for classification and estimating functional connectivity.

2 Materials and Methods

2.1 Data Acquisition and Pre-processing

Data used in this work are taken from the Alzheimer's disease Neuroimaging Initiative (ADNI2) database (http://adni.loni.usc.edu). ADNI2 resting state MRI data include 209 cognitively normal elderly subjects (CN), 208 subjects with early stage mild cognitive impairment (EMCI), 183 subjects in a more advanced stage of MCI (LMCI), and 121 subjects with AD dementia. In this work, we employed AD subjects and CN subjects as test samples.

In this study, all imaging were performed on a 3.0 T Philips MRI scanner. The R-fMRI images acquisition parameters as follow: Field Strength = 3.0 T; Flip Angle = 80.0°; Matrix X = 64.0 pixels; Matrix Y = 64.0 pixels; Pixel Spacing X = 3.3125 mm; Pixel Spacing Y = 3.3125 mm; Pulse Sequence = GR; Slices = 6720.0; Slice Thickness = 3 mm; TE = 30 ms; TR = 3000.0 ms. Data preprocessing was carried out with FSL [8]. The detail processing as follow: head motion correction by using MCFLIRT, non-brain removal by using BET, Spatial smoothing by using a Gaussian kernel of FWHM 5 mm; Registration of each subject's FMRI data to MNI152 standard space was achieved by using FLIRT affine registration, and then via de-trended and band-pass filtered (0.01–0.08 Hz) to remove the extremely low and high-frequency artifacts. The registered to MNI152 space FMRI data were divided into 116 regions, then extracted the mean time series by averaging the fMRI time series all voxels in the regions.

2.2 Partial Correlation Linear Regression Represent Functional Connectivity

Suppose that $\{y_1, \ldots, y_p\}$ is the n-dimensional data vector measured at the p selected ROIs on the fMRI images of n subjects. The observed data vector y_i is the random variable, y_i at the i th ROI fMRI time series. The collection of measurements y_i(the *fMRI time series*) are assumed to be normally distributed with mean 0 and covariance $\sum$, where $\sum$ is a p by p positive definite matrix and $\sum^{-1}$ as concentration matrix. Denote the partial correlation between y_i and y_j by $\rho_{ij}(1 \leq i \leq p)$ and denote the concentration matrix $\sum^{-1} = (\sigma_{ij})_{p \times p}$. So that partial correlation coefficient ρ_{ij} is given as follows:

$$\rho_{ij} = -\frac{\sigma_{ij}}{\sqrt{\sigma_{ii}\sigma_{jj}}} \tag{1}$$

The estimation of partial correlations to a regression problem as following:

$$y_i = \sum_{j \neq i} \beta_{ij} y_j + \varepsilon_i \tag{2}$$

where β_{ij} is the measure of relationship between y_i and y_j given all other data vectors. When $\mathrm{var}(\varepsilon_i) = \frac{1}{\sigma_{ii}}$ and $\mathrm{cov}(\varepsilon_i, \varepsilon_j) = \frac{\sigma_{ij}}{\sigma_{ii}\sigma_{jj}}$ the partial correlation as follows [6, 11]:

$$\rho_{ij} = \beta_{ij}\sqrt{\frac{\sigma_{ii}}{\sigma_{jj}}} \tag{3}$$

Now, we write the linear regression model in (2) to explicitly show the relationship between partial correlations and linear regression, we denote $\mathrm{A} = [y_1, \ldots, y_p] \in R^{n \times p}$

and $\beta = [\mathrm{W_{ij}}] \in R^{p\times p}$, then (2) can be rewritten as $\mathrm{A} = AW$, here vectorize the both sides as $vec(\mathrm{A}) = vec(\mathrm{AW})$, then can be written in a matrix form as follows:

$$y = \mathrm{AW} + \varepsilon = \sum_{j=1}^{p} \mathrm{A_j W_j} + \varepsilon \tag{4}$$

where $y = vec(\mathrm{A})$, $\mathrm{A} = (y_1, \ldots, y_p)^T$ and $\mathrm{W} = [\mathrm{W_{ij}}] \in R^{p\times p}$.

2.3 Estimating Sparse Functional Connectivity via L1-Norm Penalty Model

The Eq. (4) is a linear representation model, the solution of linear model (4) is usually obtained by the least squares minimization

$$\min_{\mathrm{W}\in R^p} \sum_{i=1}^{n} (y_i - \sum_{j=1}^{p} \mathrm{A}_j W_j)^2 \Leftrightarrow \min_{w\in R^p} \|y - \mathrm{AW}\|_2^2 \tag{5}$$

Where $\|\cdot\|_2$ is L2-norm. To obtain a unique solution, we need to add the sparseness constraint. The sparsest solution is obtained by the $\mathrm{L_0}$ norm penalty, which measures the number of nonzero elements as follows:

$$\hat{\mathrm{W}}_{\mathrm{L0}} = \arg\min_{W} \|y - \mathrm{AW}\|_2^2 \ \text{s.t.} \|\mathrm{W}\|_0 \le k \tag{6}$$

Since this optimization problem is generally NP-hard, in practice, one often consider the following $\mathrm{L_1}$ norm regularization problem, which is the standard convex relaxation of $\mathrm{L_0}$:

$$\hat{\mathrm{W}}_{\mathrm{L1}} = \arg\min_{\mathrm{W}} \|y - \mathrm{AW}\|_2^2 + \lambda \|\mathrm{W}\|_1 \tag{7}$$

where λ is an appropriately chosen regularization parameter. The solving this problem is often as LASSO problem to estimate sparse correlation. The problem of functional connectivity between two ROIs are transformed into solving the $\mathrm{L_1}$ sparse problem.

2.4 $\mathrm{L_1}/\mathrm{L}_q$ Anatomical Guided Group Sparsity Functional Connectivity

In conventional approaches, brain regions or ROI usual as nodes, between ROIs functional connectivity as edges, the pair-wise functional connectivity was transferred to solve coefficient matrix of linear regression problem, Eq. (7) can rewrite as follows:

$$\min_{\beta\in R^n} f(x) = \ell(x) + \lambda\Omega(x) \tag{8}$$

where $\ell(x)$ is the loss function, and $\Omega(x)$ is the regularization term, which could regularize feature selection while achieving sparse regularization, and $\lambda > 0$ is the regularization parameter. The group sparsity problem is achieved by introducing the regularization function $\lambda > 0$ as follows:

$$\Omega(x) = \lambda \sum_{j=1}^{r} \lambda_j \|x_{G_j}\|_2 \quad (9)$$

In Eq. (9), $\Omega(x)$ defines the regularization on the weight. In the group lasso, the L2-norm is adopted as the regularization term, where $G_1, G_2, \ldots G_m$ are m disjoint groups such that $\cup_{j=1}^{m} G_j = \{1, 2, \ldots n\}$ and $G_i \cap G_j = \emptyset$ when $i \neq j$, α_{G_j} denotes the variables of α indexed by the j th G_j, λ_j is a positive weight, and $\|\cdot\|_2$ represents the ℓ_2 norm.

In this paper, we solve Eq. (9) via the ℓ_1/ℓ_q regularized Euclidean Projection algorithm [9]. Therefore, Eq. (9) can be rewritten as Eq. (10)

$$\pi_{1q}(V, \lambda) = \arg\min_{X \in R^n} \frac{1}{2} \|X - V\|_2^2 + \lambda \sum_{i=1}^{n} \|x_i\|_q \quad (10)$$

Here $\pi_{1q}(\cdot)$ as the ℓ_1/ℓ_q regularized Euclidean projection problem, the groups in (10) are independent. Thus the optimization in (10) decouples into a set of s independent ℓ_q-regularized Euclidean projection problems:

$$\pi_q(v) = \arg\min_{X \in R^n} \{\frac{1}{2} \|x - v\|_2^2 + \lambda \|x\|_q\} \quad (11)$$

Here, the group information of fMRI signals are defined by the anatomical structure according to AAL template [12], each brain regions voxels could be categorized and labeled as 116 AAL groups. The group sparsity of variable selection problem is achieved by introducing the ℓ_1/ℓ_q regularized Euclidean projection as following:

$$X^* = \arg\min_{w} \frac{1}{2} \|AW - Y\|_2^2 + \lambda_j \sum_{j=1}^{m} \|W_{G_j}\|_q \quad (12)$$

where are $G_1, G_2, \ldots G_m$ disjoint groups such that $\cup_{j=1}^{m} G_j - \{1, 2, \ldots p\}$ and $G_i \cap G_j = \emptyset$ when $i \neq j$, W_{G_j} denotes the variables of W indexed by the j th G_j, λ_j is a positive weight, $\|\cdot\|_2$ represents the ℓ_2 norm. Thus, Eq. (12) can be also viewed as the structured sparse penalized least squares problem. Functional connectivity measurement can as solve this structured problem is summarized as in Eq. (12).

3 Experimental Results

3.1 Classification Performance

In this study, we adopt 10-fold cross-validation to evaluate the classification performance of the proposed method. The linear SVM classifier is implemented using LIBSVM toolbox [10] with a different parameter value. The weights in our proposed method are determined based on the training subjects through a grid search with the range from 0 to 1 at a step size of 0.5. We evaluated the classification performance of a method by measuring the classification accuracy, sensitivity, specificity, and area under receiver operating characteristic (ROC) curve (AUC).

Table 1 lists the results of classifications on ADNI dataset. From Table 1, we can see that our proposed method outperforms the other methods in the mainly performance measures for AD classifications. Specifically, our method achieves the classification accuracy of 96.48% and a balanced accuracy of 98.68%, while the best accuracy of other method is only 89.39% and the best balanced accuracy is 90.78%. In addition, our proposed method achieves high AUC values of 0.9881, which indicate our proposed method has better identification power than the other methods for AD classifications.

Table 1. Classification performances comparison of different methods on ADNI dataset

Method	Acc (%)	Sen (%)	Spe (%)	BAC	AUC	F-Score
PC	80.30	89.29	72.50	81.48	93.23	79.36
SR [13]	62.12	71.42	55.00	63.34	70.11	61.53
LRR [14]	89.39	89.11	82.05	90.78	98.31	88.89
SICE [15]	86.36	87.30	76.92	88.15	91.54	86.15
SGL [16]	77.27	85.71	70.00	78.38	91.73	76.19
AG2SR	**96.48**	**94.70**	**97.43**	**98.68**	**98.81**	**98.24**

3.2 Functional Connectivity Analysis Based on Our Proposed Method

To compare the differences of functional connectivity our proposed method and State-of-art methods, six different functional connectivity matrices are shown in Fig. 1. The Fig. 1(a), and (d) can capture pairwise ROI interaction of 116 regions obviously, but, there are a great quantity of non-zero elements. Figure 1(b), (e) and (c) methods are relatively sparsity and has fewer non-zero elements. Figure 1(c) and (d) shows plenty of irrelevant functional connectivity that leads to difficulty to distinguish the important functional connectivity. Our proposed method Fig. 1(f) not only capture pairwise of functional connectivity, but also keep mainly connectivity and remove irrelevant connectivity.

In addition, to evaluate functional connectivity difference between NC and AD, two categories of functional connectivity matrices are shown as follow. Figure 2(a) is a NC subject and Fig. 2(b) is an AD, Fig. 2(a) and (b) with at same scale and parameters.

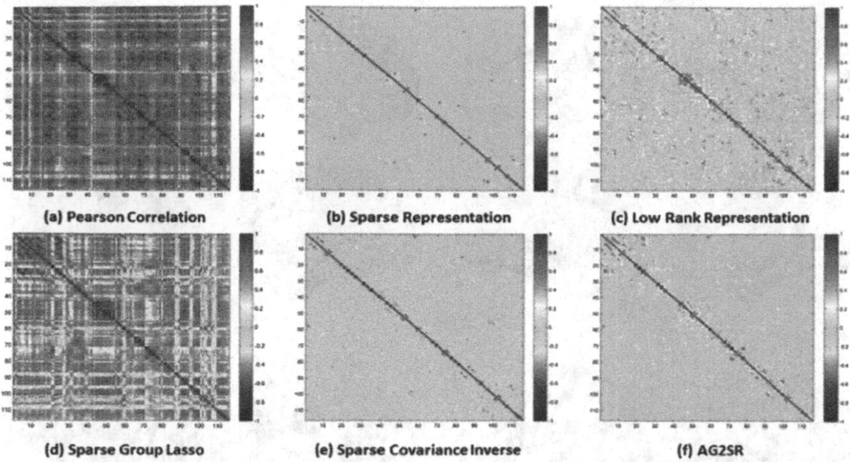

Fig. 1. Six differences of functional connectivity matrices.

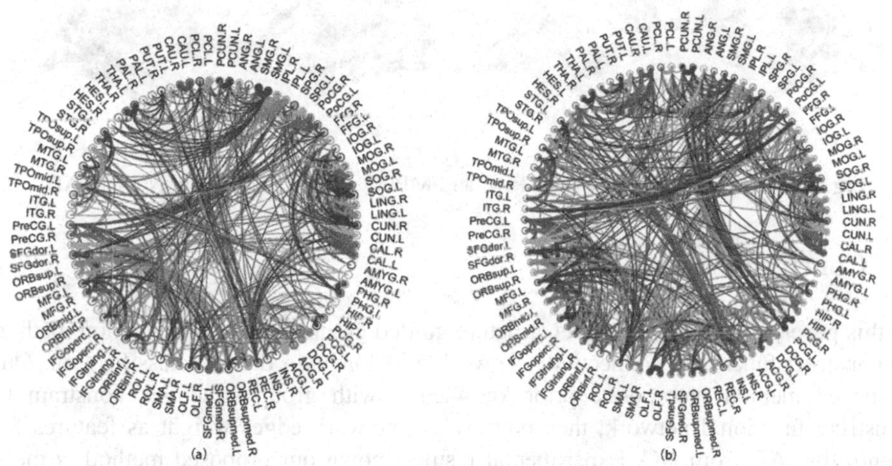

Fig. 2. Functional connectivity of NC (a) and AD (b) based on our proposed method.

3.3 Analysis of Intrinsic Connectivity Network

Figure 3 shows functional connectivity of PCC and MPFC regions of default mode network (DMN) in normal subject and AD. Figure 3(a) is the MPFC regions of Normal control, Fig. 3(b) is the MPFC region of AD. Compared with Fig. 3(a), the functional connectivity (Fig. 3(b)) of MPFC region shows significantly increased. Figure 3(c) is the PCC regions of Normal Control, Fig. 3(d) is the PCC region of AD. Comparison the PCC region (Fig. 3(d)) between AD patient and Normal control (Fig. 3(c)), the result show functional connectivity in PCC region has significant increased.

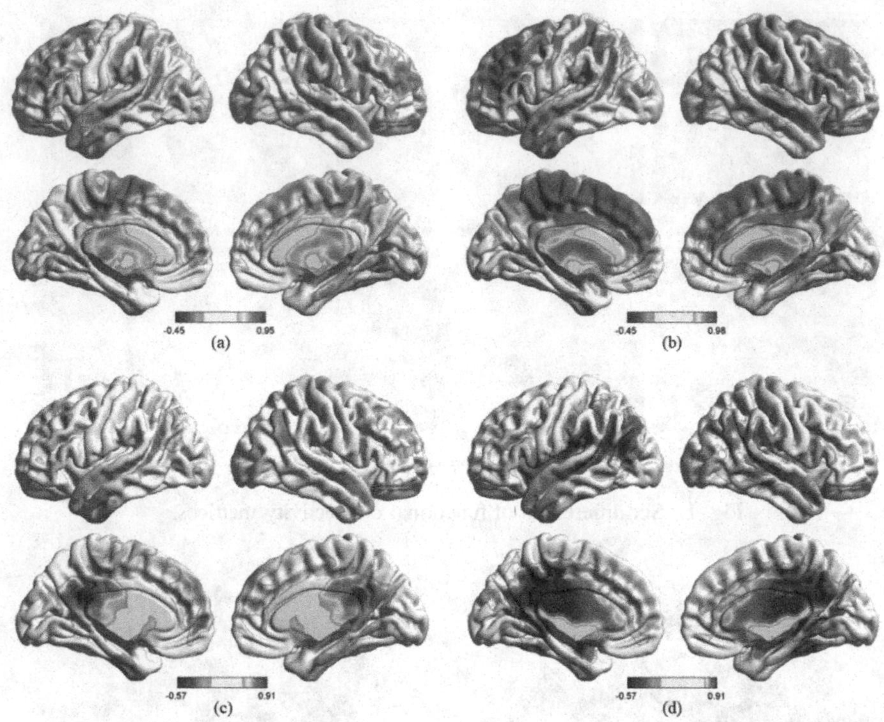

Fig. 3. Functional connectivity of PCC and MPFC regions of DMN in NC and AD.

4 Conclusion

In this paper, we proposed a novel structure guided group sparse representation method to construct functional connectivity network and for brain disease classification. Our proposed method incorporate prior knowledge with group structures constrain to construct functional network, then employ the network edges weight as features for identifying AD from NC. Experimental results shown our proposed method is more effective and accurately. In the future, we plan to apply and test this AG2SR method in larger sample datasets and to further improve the classification performance.

Acknowledgments. This work is partly supported by the 111 Project (No. B13022). J Lu was supported by the 111 Project (No. B13022) and the Natural Science Foundation of Jiangsu Province of China under Grant (No. 20131351).

References

1. Mueller, S.G., et al.: Ways toward an early diagnosis in Alzheimer's disease: the Alzheimer's Disease Neuroimaging Initiative (ADNI). Alzheimer's Dement. **1**, 55–66 (2005)

2. Pievani, M., et al.: Functional networks connectivity in patients with Alzheimer's disease and mild cognitive impairment. J. Neurol. **258**, S170 (2011)
3. Wang, J., He, Y., et al.: Disrupted functional brain connectome in individuals at risk for Alzheimer's disease. Biol. Psychiatry **73**, 472–481 (2013)
4. Wee, C.-Y., Yap, P.T., Shen, D., et al.: Group-constrained sparse fMRI connectivity modeling for mild cognitive impairment identification. Brain Struct. Funct. **219**, 641 (2014)
5. Huang, S., Li, J., Ye, J., et al.: Learning brain connectivity of Alzheimer's disease from neuroimaging data. In: Advances in Neural Information Processing Systems, pp. 808–816 (2009)
6. Lee, H., Lee, D.S., Chung, M.K., et al.: Sparse brain network recovery under compressed sensing. IEEE Trans. Med. Imaging **30**, 1154–1165 (2011)
7. Smith, S.M., et al.: Functional connectomics from resting-state fMRI. Trends Cogn. Sci. **17**, 666–682 (2013)
8. Jenkinson, M., Smith, S.M., et al.: Fsl. Neuroimage **62**, 782–790 (2012)
9. Liu, J., Ye, J.: Efficient L1/Lq norm regularization. arXiv preprint arXiv:1009.4766 (2010)
10. Chang, C.-C., Lin, C.-J.: LIBSVM: a library for support vector machines. ACM Trans. Intell. Syst. Technol. (TIST) **2**, 27 (2011)
11. Peng, J., Wang, P., Zhou, N., Zhu, J.: Partial correlation estimation by joint sparse regression models. J. Am. Stat. Assoc. **104**, 735–746 (2009)
12. Tzourio-Mazoyer, N., Landeau, B., et al.: Automated anatomical labeling of activations in SPM using a macroscopic anatomical parcellation of the MNI MRI single-subject brain. Neuroimage **15**, 273–289 (2002)
13. Wright, J., Yang, A.Y., Ganesh, A., Sastry, S.S., Ma, Y.: Robust face recognition via sparse representation. IEEE Trans. Pattern Anal. Mach. Intell. **31**(2), 210–227 (2008)
14. Liu, G., Lin, Z., Yan, S., Sun, J., Yu, Y., Ma, Y.: Robust recovery of subspace structures by low-rank representation. IEEE Trans. Pattern Anal. Mach. Intell. **35**(1), 171–184 (2012)
15. Huang, S., Li, J., Sun, L., Ye, J., et al.: Learning brain connectivity of Alzheimer's disease by sparse inverse covariance estimation. Neuroimage **50**, 935–949 (2010)
16. Qiao, L., Shen, D., et al.: Estimating functional brain networks by incorporating a modularity prior. NeuroImage **141**, 399–407 (2016)

Weakly Supervised Learning of Image Emotion Analysis Based on Cross-spatial Pooling

Guoqin Peng(✉) and Dan Xu(✉)

School of Information Science and Engineering,
Yunnan University, Kunming 650504, China
{pengguoqin, danxu}@ynu.edu.cn

Abstract. Convolutional neural networks (CNNs) simulate the structure and function of the nervous system based on biological characteristics. CNNs have been used to understand the emotions that images convey. Most existing studies of emotion analysis have focused only on image emotion classification, and few studies have paid attention to relevant regions evoking emotions. In this paper, we solve the issues of image emotion classification and emotional region localization based on weakly supervised deep learning in a unified framework. We train a fully convolutional network, followed by our proposed cross-spatial pooling strategy, to generate an emotional activation map (EAM), which represents the relevant region that could evoke emotion in an image and is only labelled with an image-level annotation. Extensive experiments demonstrate that our proposed method has the best performance in the accuracy of classification and emotional region localization.

Keywords: Convolutional neural networks · Weakly supervised · Visual sentiment analysis · Emotion classification · Emotional region localization

1 Introduction

A CNN is a network formed by extensive connected artificial neurons to simulate the structure and function of the human nervous system. Artificial neurons have the same structure as the basic neurons in biology. CNNs based on the simulation of biological neuron characteristics have been used in many fields of artificial intelligence, including image emotion analysis. Automatically understanding the emotion implied in images can be useful in many fields, such as education, entertainment and public opinion monitoring. CNNs have become state-of-the-art methods for computer visualization tasks and have also been applied in image sentiment analysis [1–5].

Visual sentiment analysis is more challenging than conventional recognition tasks due to a higher level of subjectivity in the human recognition process; in addition, human emotional responses to images are evoked by local regions. Classification performance is usually improved with accurate annotations (e.g., bounding boxes) in conventional classification tasks. However, there are still problems in emotion classification with bounding boxes. First, these rectangular proposal boxes tend to find only

Z. Sun et al. (Eds.): CCBR 2019, LNCS 11818, pp. 116–125, 2019.
https://doi.org/10.1007/978-3-030-31456-9_13

the foreground objects in an image. However, the regions evoking emotion are related not only to the foreground regions but also to the context regions that convey emotion. In addition, pixels in the bounding boxes make the same contribution to evoking emotions, but the contribution of each pixel varies across different regions. Second, manual labelling is expensive.

To address these problems, we perform the weakly supervised learning of image emotion classification and emotional region localization in a unified CNN framework using only image-level label information. Here, emotional region localization means annotating regions that evoke emotion in an image. In this paper, we use an emotion activation map (EAM) to indicate the result of emotional region localization. The EAM provides a fine-grained, pixel-level image emotional annotation. Figure 1 illustrates in detail the overall framework of our proposed method, which is based on RestNet-101 [7].

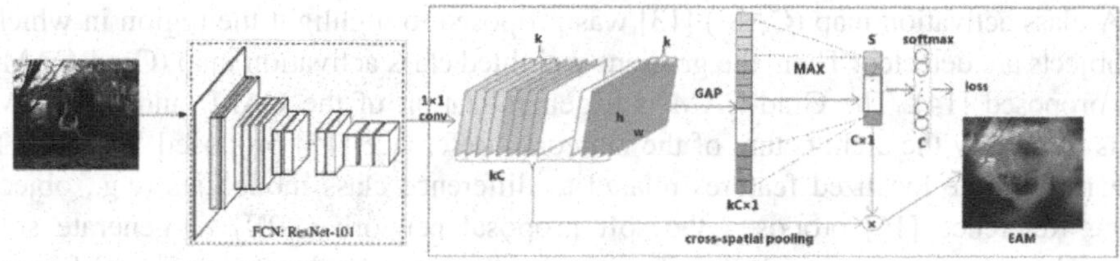

Fig. 1. Overview of the proposed network

The main contributions of this paper are summarized as follows.

First, we design a new CNN that learns discriminative features in an end-to-end manner. Obviously, this approach greatly improves the classification accuracy.

Second, our model integrates visual emotional classification and localization in a unified weakly supervised CNN framework, generating the EAM that represents the emotional region evoking human emotion. The EAM can show the contribution of each pixel. Finally, a fine-grained, pixel-level annotation can be obtained with our method using only image-level annotation information.

2 Related Works

2.1 Visual Sentiment Analysis

Recently, many deep models [6] have considered more cues for image sentiment analysis. References [7, 8] proposed visual sentiment ontologies consisting of adjective noun pairs (ANP) as a mid-level visual representation. Moreover, some high-level features are considered in image sentiment analysis. The emotional gap is bridged between the image content and the emotional response of the viewer by using high-level concepts (HLCs) (e.g., scenes and places) [9]. Context information is considered to analyse the emotions of characters in images [10]. Reference [5] proposed EmotionROI datasets, which label the regions that evoke emotion with bounding boxes. A fully convolutional network with Euclidean loss (FCNEL) was trained to predict an emotion stimuli map (ESM). Reference [5] is the first research study on sentiment analysis with full supervision. These models mentioned above try to develop more cues that are related to evoking emotions to improve classification performance. Moreover, gaining these relevant cues requires a greater cost.

2.2 Emotional Region Localization

The conventional weakly supervised localization of CNNs is defined as detecting the objects (e.g., cats or dogs) in an image with only image-level label information. Given the recent success of deep learning in large-scale object recognition, several weakly supervised CNNs have been proposed for the object detection task using a multiple instance learning (MIL) algorithm [11, 12]. However, since sentiment is subjective, and assuming that an instance only appears in a single category, MIL is suboptimal for sentiment detection.

A class activation map (CAM) [13] was proposed to highlight the region in which the objects are detected. Then, the gradient-weighted class activation map (Grad-CAM) was proposed [14]. The Grad-CAM is a generalization of the CAM, and the CAM needs to modify the architecture of the network. Reference [15] proposed WILDCAT to learn multiple localized features related to difference class modalities (e.g., object parts). Reference [16] proposed the soft proposal network (SPN) to generate soft proposals and aggregate image-specific patterns by coupling the proposal and feature maps. These methods mentioned above are designed to detect the relative regions of a specific class and tend to distinguish the foreground objects from the surroundings for the conventional recognition task. However, emotional region localization is more challenging because the emotional semantics of the image are related not only to the foreground but also to the overall semantics of the image.

Recently, [17] proposed WSCNet with two branches. The second branch is used for classification and takes advantage of the emotion region that is produced by the first branch. Reference [18] designed a CNN network to predict emotional saliency by using eye movement data. These studies are the most relevant works on emotional region localization. Our method, based on a simple architecture, can obtain a better result with only image-level annotation.

3 Our Method

3.1 Cross-spatial Pooling Strategy

Let $\{(x_i, y_i)\}_{i=1}^{N}$ be a collection of emotional training examples, where x_i is an emotional image, N is the sample size, and $y_i \in \{1, \cdots, C\}$ is the corresponding sentiment label. For each instance, let $F \in \mathbb{R}^{w \times h \times n}$ be the feature maps of conv5 in ResNet-101, where n is the number of channels and w and h are the width and height, respectively, (the spatial size) of the feature maps. First, we add a 1×1 convolutional layer to capture multiple channel information for each emotional category that has a high response to certain discriminative regions. Supposing k convolutional filters are applied to each sentiment category, for C emotion categories, resulting feature maps F' will have dimensions of $w \times h \times kC$. The confidence coefficient, denoted as S^c, is computed from F' as follows:

$$S^c = \max_{j \in \{1,\cdots,k\}}(G_{ave}(f_j^c)), c \in \{1,\cdots,C\} \tag{1}$$

where f_j^c represents the j-th feature map for the c-th category label from F' and $G_{ave}(\bullet)$ denotes the GAP. Here, GAP is employed to identify the global information in the same emotional class. The Softmax function is used for this classification problem, and p_c, the probability of the emotion category c, is defined as:

$$p_c = \frac{e^{S^c}}{\sum_{l=1}^{C} e^{S^l}} \tag{2}$$

The training loss is defined as:

$$loss = -\frac{1}{N}\sum_{i=1}^{N}\sum_{c=1}^{C} 1(y_i == c)\log S^c \tag{3}$$

if $y_i == c$ is true; in other words, if the i-th sample is labeled by c, then $1(y_i == c)$ is 1; otherwise, $1(y_i == c)$ is 0. The parameters are updated during the training process with stochastic gradient descent (SGD). Finally, an optimal model, which has the highest classification accuracy, is obtained. Thus, our proposed cross-spatial pooling method can extract more discriminative features for each emotion class, and the emotion classification performance is improved.

3.2 The Emotion Activation Map

First, we generate the classwise activation maps for each emotional class (i.e., emotion feature map) through an averaging operation. There are C emotion feature maps. The C emotion feature maps are combined with the corresponding weights to capture the comprehensive localization information instead of using the emotion feature map with the largest response from a specific class. Thus, the EAM is generated using S^c as the weight of the response map of class c:

$$M = \sum_{c=1}^{C} S^c\left(\frac{1}{k}\sum_{j=1}^{k} f_j^c\right) \tag{4}$$

Intuitively, we expect that each unit is activated by some visual patterns within its receptive field. The EAM is a weighted linear sum of the presence of these visual patterns at different spatial locations, as shown in Fig. 2. The resulting EAM is represented by a heat map. Our cross-spatial spooling method can prevent the fully connected layer from ignoring the spatial information of the objects in the image. Every feature map extracted from CNNs can express some of the features of the entire network. The information associated with an object or the contextual information in different feature maps can be effectively utilized through the cross-spatial pooling strategy. With this approach, more discriminative information can be extracted, and we can better localize the relative regions that evoke emotion.

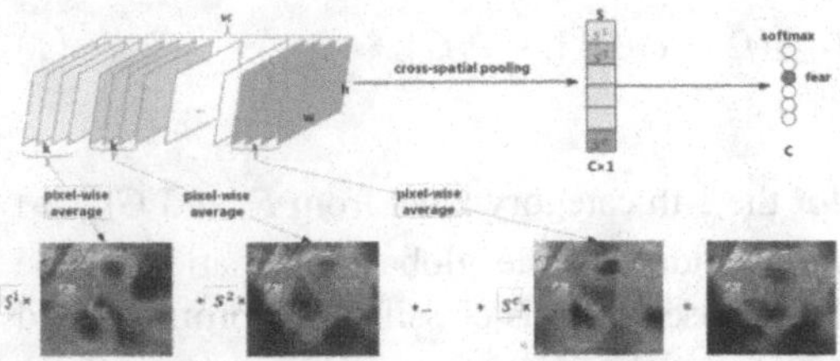

Fig. 2. Generation of the emotion activation map (EAM). The redder the colour is, the greater the contribution to emotion classification. (Color figure online)

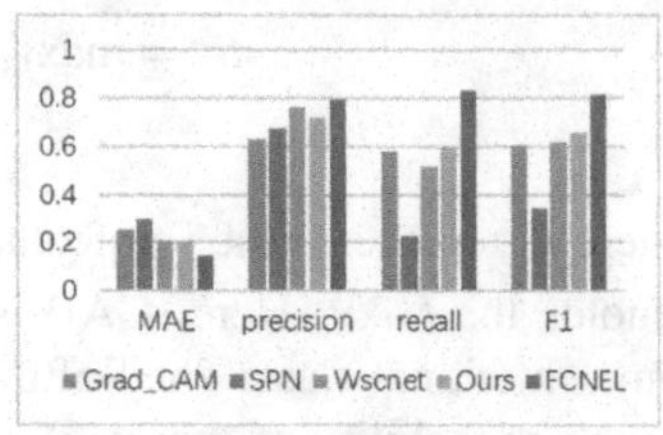

Fig. 3. Comparison of the emotional region localization performance.

4 Experiments and Analysis

4.1 Datasets and Experimental Setting

The proposed method is evaluated based on two available datasets: Twitter I and EmotionROI. The Twitter I dataset consists of 1269 images, which are labeled with positive and negative emotions. In the EmotionROI dataset, there are 1980 images labeled with the six basic emotions of Ekman by 15 AMT workers. The workers were asked to draw a rectangle (bounding box) to enclose the region that most influences the evoked emotion in the image. The influence of each pixel on evoked emotions is the ratio of bounding boxes covering the pixel to all bounding boxes. The EmotionROI and Twitter I datasets were split into training and testing sets at ratios of 7:3 and 8:2, respectively.

We initialize our model with a pretrained model of visual recognition base on the ImageNet dataset. In addition, we apply random horizontal flips and crop a random 448 × 448 patch as a form of data augmentation to reduce overfitting. Our framework is implemented using PyTorch [19]. All our experiments are performed on an NVIDIA 1080 TI GPU with 16 GB on-board memory.

Table 1. Comparison of the classification accuracy (%)

Methods	Twitter I	EmotionROI
AlexNet	66.11	34.85
VGG16	68.35	37.71
ResNet101	72.55	40.40
Fine-tuned AlexNet	72.83	41.58
Fine-tuned VGG16	76.47	47.31
Fine-tuned ResNet101	79.27	52.69
WILDCAT [15]	80.67	55.39
SPN [16]	81.79	52.86
WSCNet [17]	84.25	58.25
Our method	84.87	60.44

Fig. 4. Every emotion feature map and the generated EAM. The predicted probability of each category is marked.

4.2 Experimental Analysis and Comparison

Classification Accuracy. As illustrated in Table 1, the classification accuracy of our method is obviously better than that of the fine-tuned method and is also better than that of the weakly supervised WILDCAT and SPN methods. Our method improves upon their classification performance by at least 3% and 5% for these two datasets. Our proposed method also improved upon the classification accuracy of WSCNet by 2% for EmotionROI.

Emotional Region Localization. We employ the same evaluation metrics as [5] (i.e., the mean absolute error (MAE), precision, recall, and F_1 score). All the detected regions or maps and ground truth are first normalized to 0 to 1. The MAE corresponds to the mean absolute pixelwise error between the predicted proposal and ground truth. Before computing precision and recall, we adaptively binarize each predicted map using Otsu thresholding [20]. Thus, precision and recall represent the percentages of detected emotionally involved pixels out of all the pixels identified in the predicted region and the ground truth. The F_1 score, defined as $F_1 = 2pr/(p+r)$, measures the harmonic mean of the precision and recall.

Figure 3 compares several evaluation metrics. FENCEL is a fully supervised method that trains the network with emotional region annotation. This approach has the best performance based on all the evaluation metrics. Our method is suboptimal compared to FENCEL. Additionally, WSCNet has higher precision than our method, our method has a larger value of recall, and the harmonic evaluation metric F_1 of our method is larger than that of WSCNet, which suggests that more ground-truth emotional regions have been localized by the proposed method. More results are shown in Fig. 5.

4.3 Hyperparameter Analysis

There is a hyperparameter k in (1), which is defined as the number of response feature maps for each emotion category. As seen in Table 2, with an increasing number of feature maps, our method can achieve better performance compared with the standard classification strategy in the CNN (i.e., k = 1), which captures multiple views for each emotion category. However, overamplifying the feature maps results is suboptimal performance, mainly due to overfitting. For the two datasets, our method achieves the best performance with k = 4. Therefore, we set k = 4 in all experiments.

Table 2. The classification accuracy for different numbers of response feature maps (k)

Datasets	k = 1	k = 2	k = 4	k = 8	k = 16
EmotionROI	56.73	55.89	60.44	56.06	56.73
Twitter I	84.03	83.19	84.87	82.35	81.51

4.4 Visualization

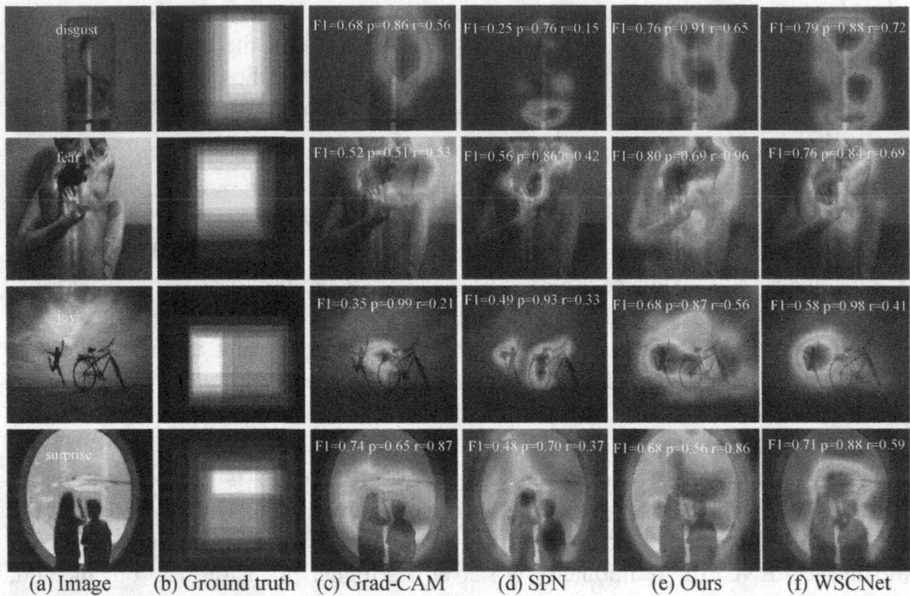

(a) Image (b) Ground truth (c) Grad-CAM (d) SPN (e) Ours (f) WSCNet

Fig. 5. The results of emotional region localization. Some evaluation metrics are marked on the images. Precision and recall are abbreviated as p and r, respectively.

Figure 5 illustrates the results of emotional region localization for the EmotionROI testing sets. Compared with Grad-CAM and SPN, our proposed method and WSCnet can better detect the relevant regions that evoke emotion (not only the foreground objects). The detected regions contain scenes, objects or action semantic regions related to the evoked emotion. A comparison of Fig. 5(e) and (f) shows that our method can detect more ground truth emotional regions than other methods and maintain a high recall. As shown in Fig. 6, WSCnet leads to a 0.94 precision but only a 0.15 recall. In contrast, our method achieves a precision of 0.82 and a recall of 0.85. Obviously, our proposed method localizes large regions that evoke emotion in Fig. 6(d). Generally, precision and recall are contradictory, so F_1 is used as a comprehensive evaluation metric. A larger F_1 is gained with our proposed method than with the other methods.

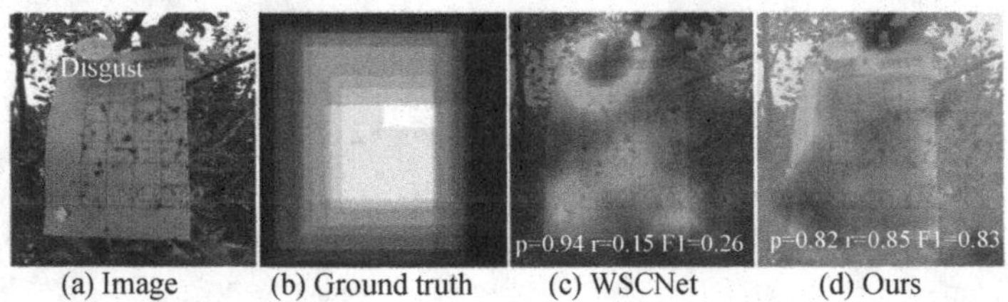

(a) Image (b) Ground truth (c) WSCNet (d) Ours

Fig. 6. Examples of emotion region localization

The CNNs of deep learning are regarded as black boxes. Why can the CNNs predict such results, and which features make the CNNs generate such results? The EAM proposed in this paper can partly answer these questions. The EAM highlights the regions that contribute to emotion classification by a heat map, and these regions directly influence the results of the classification. The closer to the EAM the emotion feature heat map is, the greater the contribution to emotion classification. As shown in Fig. 7, the emotion feature maps in (c) are the closest to the EAM in (d), and the emotion category corresponding to the feature map has a high predicted value.

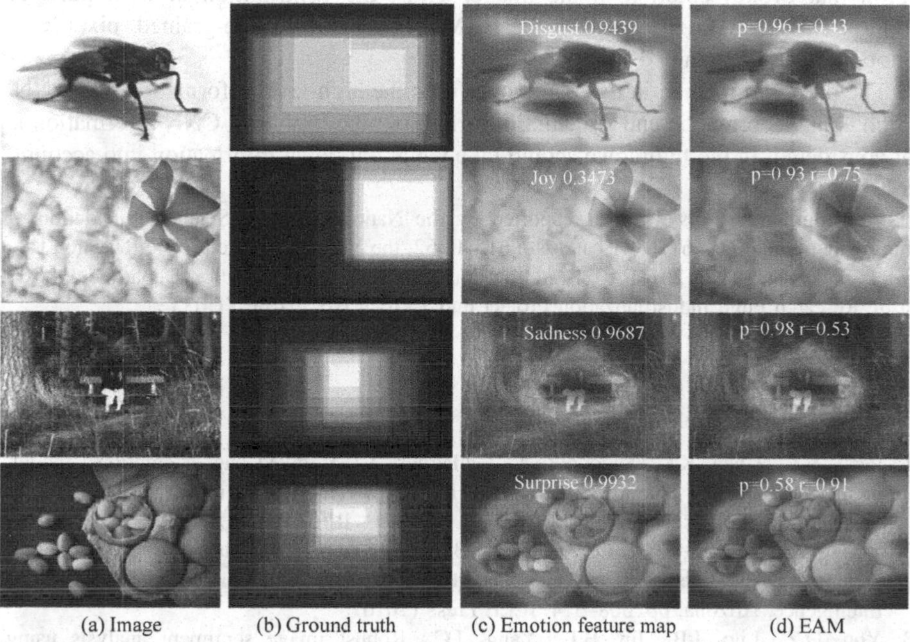

Fig. 7. The emotion feature maps of the highest predicted value of the category and the generated EAM

Figure 4 illustrates an image with the EAM and emotion feature map of each emotion category. Although surprise has the highest predicted value, the emotion feature map of joy is the closest to the EAM. More information from the emotion feature map of joy is used for classification. The main emotion of this image should be joy, the same as for its ground-truth label. However, the predicted category is surprise. Part of the reason is the fuzziness of emotion labels. Joy and surprise may share some common features, so it is hard to distinguish them from each other. Our EAM can correct the predicted result. Thus, our EAM, which is the weighted sum of the emotional feature maps of each category of emotion, is more intelligible than other methods, and it can more robustly localize the regions that evoke emotion and detect discriminative information for emotion analysis.

5 Conclusions

This paper proposes a weakly supervised emotion classification and localization method with a cross-spatial pooling strategy. We solve image emotion classification and region localization problems in a unified convolutional neural network framework. Extensive experiments on the EmotionROI and Twitter I datasets demonstrate that the proposed method performs favourably against the state-of-the-art methods of visual emotional analysis. The relevant regions that influence an evoked emotion are localized with the EmotionROI dataset. The EAM of the image is generated to represent the region that evokes emotion in the image. Thus, the contribution of each pixel to emotion classification is labeled in the EAM. As a result, a fine-grained, pixel-level annotation can be obtained.

The proposed method in this paper only uses the high-level information of a CNN, which contains semantic and structural information; the low-level CNN information is not considered. In the future, we should take CNN low-level information into account.

Acknowledgments. This work is supported by the National Natural Science Foundation of China under Grant Nos. 61163019 and No. 61540062, the Yunnan Applied Basic Research Key Project under Grant No. 2014FA021, and the Yunnan Provincial Education Department's Scientific Research Fund Industrialization Project under Grant No. 2016CYH03.

References

1. Peng, K.C., Chen, K.C., Sadovnik, A., Gallagher, A.: A mixed bag of emotions: model, predict, and transfer emotion distributions. In: The 2015 IEEE Conference on Computer Vision and Pattern Recognition, Boston, pp. 860–868. IEEE Press (2015)
2. You, Q.Z., Luo, J.B., Jin, H.L., Yang, J.C.: Building a large scale dataset for image emotion recognition: the fine print and the benchmark. In: The 30th Conference on Artificial Intelligence, Arizona, pp. 308–314. IEEE Press (2016)
3. You, Q.Z., Luo, J.B., Jin, H.L., Yang, J.C.: Robust image sentiment analysis using progressively trained and domain transferred deep networks. In: The 29th Conference on Artificial Intelligence, Austin, pp. 381–388. IEEE Press (2015)
4. Victor, C., Brendan, J., Giró-i-Nieto, X.: From pixels to sentiment: fine-tuning CNNs for visual sentiment prediction. Image Vis. Comput. **65**, 15–22 (2017)
5. Peng, K.C., Sadovnik, A., Gallagher, A., Chen, T.: Where do emotions come from? Predicting the emotion stimuli map. In: The 2016 IEEE International Conference on Image Processing, Phoenix, pp. 614–618. IEEE Press (2016)
6. Yang, J.F., She, D.Y., Lai, Y.k., Yang, M.H.: Retrieving and classifying affective images via deep metric learning. In: the 30th innovative Applications of Artificial Intelligence, New Orleans, pp. 491–498. IEEE Press (2018)
7. Borth, D., Ji, R.R., Chen, T., et al.: Large-scale visual sentiment ontology and detectors using adjective noun pairs. In: The 2013 ACM Multimedia Conference, Barcelona, pp. 223–232. ACM Press (2013)
8. Chen, T., Borth, D., Darrell, T, et al.: DeepSentibank: visual sentiment concept classification with deep convolutional neural networks. arXiv preprint arXiv:1410.8586 (2014)

9. Ali, A.R., Shahid, U., Ali, M., et al.: High-level concepts for affective understanding of images. In: The 2017 IEEE Winter Conference on Applications of Computer Vision, Santa Rosa, pp. 678–687. IEEE Press (2017)
10. Kosti, R., Alvarez, J.M., Recasens A., et al.: Emotion recognition in context. In: The 2017 IEEE Conference on Computer Vision and Pattern Recognition, Honolulu, pp. 1960–1968. IEEE Press (2017)
11. Bilen, H., Vedaldi, A.: Weakly supervised deep detection networks. In: The 2016 IEEE Conference on Computer Vision and Pattern Recognition, Las Vegas, pp. 2846–2854. IEEE Press (2016)
12. Cinbis, R.G., Verbeek, J., Schmid, C.: Weakly supervised object localization with multi-fold multiple instance learning. IEEE Trans. Pattern Anal. Mach. Intell. **39**(1), 189–203 (2016)
13. Zhou, B.L, Aditya, K., Agata, L., Aude, O., Antonio, T.: Learning deep features for discriminative localization. In: The 2016 IEEE Conference on Computer Vision and Pattern Recognition, Las Vegas, pp. 2921–2929. IEEE Press (2016)
14. Selvaraju, R.R, Cogswell, M., Das, A., et al.: Grad-CAM: visual explanations from deep networks via gradient-based localization. In: The 2017 IEEE International Conference on Computer Vision, Venice, pp. 618–626. IEEE Press (2017)
15. Durand, T., Mordan, T., Thome, N., et al.: WILDCAT: weakly supervised learning of deep convnets for image classification, pointwise localization and segmentation. In: The 2017 IEEE Conference on Computer Vision and Pattern Recognition, Honolulu, pp. 5957–5966. IEEE Press (2017)
16. Zhu, Y., Zhou, Y., Ye Q., et al.: Soft proposal networks for weakly supervised object localization. In: The 2017 IEEE International Conference on Computer Vision, Italy, pp. 1859–1868. IEEE Press (2017)
17. Yang, J.F., She. D.Y., Lai, Y.K., Rosin, P.L.: Weakly supervised coupled networks for visual sentiment analysis. In: The 2018 IEEE Conference on Computer Vision and Pattern Recognition, Salt Lake City, pp. 7584–7592. IEEE Press (2018)
18. Fan, S.J., Shen, Z.Q., Jiang, M., Koening L., et al.: Emotional attention: a study of image sentiment and visual attention. In: The 2018 IEEE Conference on Computer Vision and Pattern Recognition, Salt Lake City, pp. 7521–7531. IEEE Press (2018)
19. Paszke, A., Gross, S., Chintala, S., et al.: Pytorch. https://pytorch.org/ (2017)
20. Otsu, N.: A threshold selection method from gray-level histograms. IEEE Trans. Syst. Man Cybern. **9**(1), 62–66 (1979)

Embarrassingly Easy Zero-Shot Image Recognition

Wenli Song, Lei Zhang(✉), and Jingru Fu

School of Microelectronics and Communication Engineering, Chongqing University, Chongqing, China
{swl,leizhang,jrfu}@cqu.edu.cn

Abstract. Zero-shot Learning (ZSL) aims to transfer knowledge from seen image categories to unseen ones by leveraging semantic information. It is generally assumed that the seen and unseen classes share a common semantic space. A number of methods propose to design a common space to accomplish the projection between image and class embeddings by learning a compatibility function, which make up sample pairs to train the object function. However, considering the drawbacks of previous compatibility function, we design a new compatibility function in this paper. Different from previous compatibility pattern, our proposed compatibility function is more discriminative by employing label vectors, which can measure the similarity between the projected image features and all seen class prototypes. Extensive experiments on four benchmark datasets show the effectiveness of our proposed approach.

Keywords: Zero-shot learning · Knowledge transfer · Semantic embedding

1 Introduction

At present a general strategy for ZSL is that both seen and unseen classes share a common semantic space. In this way, some knowledge learned during the training stage is able to transfer to the testing stage. Semantic space can be semantic attribute space [7,8] or semantic word vector space [4]. In semantic space, the labels of seen and unseen classes can be represented as vectors called class prototypes [5].

Considering the projection from visual to semantic space may cause loss of available features, a large number of previous methods propose to employ a parameter to connect the image and semantic embedding [1,8,17]. The parameter is the visual-semantic mapping matrix to be learned which most existing approaches of ZSL construct the common space in this way. The differences of them mainly focus on how to represent the image and semantic vectors and how to design different regularization terms. However, the formulation of the bilinear compatibility is always fixed. Though it is a general framework that can be applied to any learning problem with more than one modality, ZSL solves

Z. Sun et al. (Eds.): CCBR 2019, LNCS 11818, pp. 126–133, 2019.
https://doi.org/10.1007/978-3-030-31456-9_14

the problem which the visual and semantic space are completely independent to each other. Therefore, it is doubtful whether the common space with this compatibility function of applying a parameter is discriminative enough to complete classification. In addition, almost all of the object functions are designed by employing a ranking formulation. Due to arranging a corresponding and a non-corresponding semantic vector for each visual vector, the choose of sample pairs may cause discriminative information loss on the other different classes. Besides, how to choose and how much to choose positive and negative pairs are key to the bilinear compatibility function. When the number of sample pairs is not appropriate, it is easy to cause overfitting to seen classes while invalid to unseen classes.

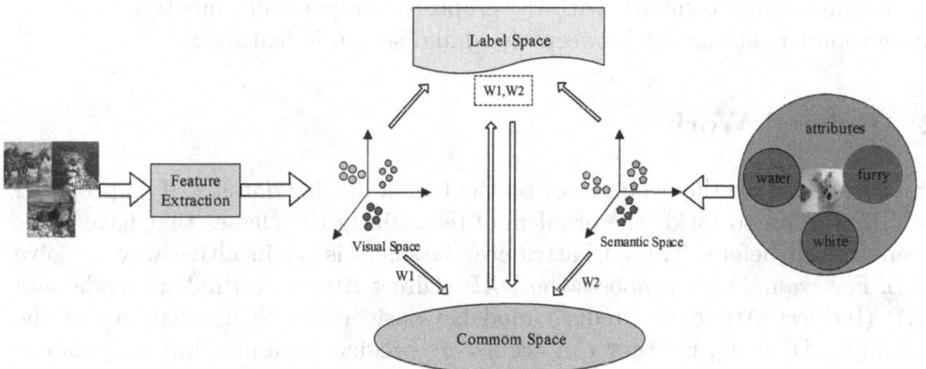

Fig. 1. The framework of our proposed method. In the flowchart, we can see that we first construct the visual and semantic space by feature extraction and attribute annotations. Then we build up a common space to align visual and semantic space by applying two parameters W_1 and W_2 separately. To make the common space discriminative, we combine the common space with the label space which design a compatibility function by also applying W_1 and W_2. Different from previous compatibility function, we don't design positive and negative pairs and avoid the overfitting of the training stage. Our method aims to utilize labels of all seen samples to construct robust relationship between visual and corresponding semantic feature.

Under these circumstances, it is natural for us to consider whether only using a parameter to accomplish the procedure of compatibility is reasonable. In addition, designing a objection function which can reduce the discriminative information loss during the process of compatibility and generalize well to test examples is encouraging. To address above mentioned pitfalls, as is illustrated in Fig. 1, we propose to construct a common embedding space and explore structure for both visual and semantic representations simultaneously. Specifically, the proposed method utilizes two parameters to denote the projection for visual feature and semantic feature separately. They align the structure of visual and semantic space in the common space, at the same time a linear transformation is utilized to attributes, which can combine different attributes and make attributes of different object classes more discriminative. To make the common space discriminative enough to complete classification, we propose a compatibility function by using the same two parameters in the common space. Different from the previous compatibility methods, we expect our compatibility function can represent each sample's true label which we add label space to our model as seen class classifiers. Our compatibility function no longer takes a sample of positive and negative pairs, instead we make a similarity contrast between each seen sample to all seen class prototypes which ensures that the compatibility between projected visual feature and corresponding class prototype is higher than that of all other class prototypes and thus can preserve the discriminative information for different classes. In this way, each seen sample can get close to corresponding class prototype and get far away any other class prototypes. We confirm that the common space combines with the proposed compatibility function can learn more robust relationships between visual and semantic features.

2 Related Work

In order to reduce the dependency on the lots of labeled datas, ZSL is proposed by [10]. It aims to tackle the problem of recognizing the classes that have never been trained before. Training attribute classifiers is an intuitive way to solve ZSL. For example, [9] proposes the DAP (Direct Attribute Predict) model and IAP (Indirect Attribute Predict) model. Considering the unreliability of the attribute classifiers, i.e. they can accurately predict attributes but they maybe poorly classify, lots of methods then solve ZSL based on label embedding. [4] and [8] both employ a ranking formulation for zero-shot learning using visual and semantic representations and recognize an image by the score of ranking formulation. Then [1] relates the image and semantic features linearly in a joint embedding space with several compatibility functions.

3 Proposed Method

3.1 Mathematical Notations

Suppose there are c_s seen classes with n_s labeled samples $\Phi_s = \{X_s, A_s, Z_s\}$ and c_u unseen classes with n_u unlabeled samples $\Phi_u = \{X_u, A_u, Z_u\}$. $X_s \in \mathbb{R}^{N_s \times d}$ and $X_u \in \mathbb{R}^{N_u \times d}$ are seen and unseen images visual feature vectors. N_s is the number of seen samples and N_u is the number of unseen samples, d is the dimension of visual features. $A_s \in \mathbb{R}^{N_s \times m}$ and $A_u \in \mathbb{R}^{N_u \times m}$ are seen and unseen samples corresponding semantic features, m is the dimension of semantic features. Z_s and Z_u are the prototype semantic representations of the seen and unseen classes. In zero-shot recognition settings, the seen and unseen classes are disjoint: $Z_s \cap Z_u = \oslash$. A_s and A_u are composed of prototype semantic representations of the seen and unseen classes respectively. The task of ZSL is to estimate A_u and then get labels of unseen samples.

3.2 Model Formulation

The key to solve ZSL task is to build up relationship between visual space and semantic space. Considering there exists lots of typical problems when using ridge regression to accomplish the projection from the visual space to semantic space, we explore a common space using two parameters to contact the visual space with semantic space. One matrix completes the dimension transformation from the visual space to common space. [6] points out that due to there are correlations among the attributes, it is necessary to build up relationship between attributes and attributes. Similarly, we use a linear transformation matrix to deal with the semantic vectors. In this way, the other matrix accomplishes the projection from the semantic space to common space and gets more discriminative semantic features. Then the objective function can be

$$\min_{W_1,W_2} \left\| W_1 X_s^T - W_2 A_s^T \right\|_F^2 \tag{1}$$

where $\|.\|_F$ denotes the Frobenius norm, W_1 and W_2 denote the learned projection matrix for visual feature X_s and semantic feature A_s respectively. Thus the visual space and semantic space can be projected to common space.

Considering the discriminative information loss on the other different classes by using previous compatibility function of applying a parameter, we want to design a compatibility function to preserve the discriminative information for different classes and make the common space more discriminative. Thus we design our compatibility function by utilizing the seen samples' labels. Specifically, the relationship between projected visual and semantic features is learned with labels by applying the same two parameters of the projection process, as is shown in Fig. 1:

$$\min_{W_1,W_2} \left\| X_s W_1^T W_2 Z_s^T - Y \right\|_F^2 \tag{2}$$

where $Y = [y_1, y_2, \cdots, y_{N_s}] \in \mathbb{R}^{N_s \times c_s}$ and y_i is a one-hot vector which represents the true label of x_i. Z_s is the prototype semantic representations of the seen classes. Thus, the common space can connect with the label space which makes the common space more discriminative. In addition, the proposed compatibility function preserve the discriminative information for different classes.

Then we consider combining the two proposed terms to accomplish more effective classification by using two parameters. The final object function can be

$$\begin{aligned} \min_{W_1,W_2} & \left\| W_1 X_s^T - W_2 A_s^T \right\|_F^2 + \beta \left\| X_s W_1^T W_2 Z_s^T - Y \right\|_F^2 \\ & + \lambda_1 \|W_1\|_F^2 + \lambda_2 \|W_2\|_F^2 \end{aligned} \tag{3}$$

λ_1 and λ_2 are the coefficient of the regularizers, β is a weighting coefficient to control the importance of the first and second terms.

In summary, we learn a discriminative common space which can accomplish the projection of visual and semantic features respectively and force $W_1 x_i^T$ to be as close as $W_2 a_j^T$ in the common space if a_j is x_i corresponding semantic indication, i.e. $i = j$. Besides, considering the case that a_j is not x_i corresponding semantic indication, i.e. $i \neq j$, we make a similarity contrast between each seen sample to all seen class prototypes which ensures that the compatibility between projected visual feature and corresponding class prototype is higher than that of all other class prototypes. Thus we can preserve the discriminative information for different classes and get a good recognition effect.

3.3 Optimization

It is obvious that Eq. (3) is not convex for W_1 and W_2 simultaneously, but it is convex for each of them separately. To optimise the objective in Eq. (3), we use an alternating optimization method. Specifically, we alternate between the following subproblems:

Fix W_2 and Update W_1. To optimise Eq. (3), we can calculate derivative of W_1 and set it zero, then can get the Sylvester equation:

$$\begin{aligned}&(\beta W_2 Z_s^T Z_s W_2^T) W_1 + W_1(\lambda_1 (X_s^T X_s)^{-1} + I)\\&= (W_2 A_s^T X_s + \beta W_2 Z_s^T Y^T X_s)(X_s^T X_s)^{-1}\end{aligned} \tag{4}$$

where I is the identity matrix, $A_1 = \beta W_2 Z_s^T Z_s W_2^T$, $B_1 = \lambda_1 (X_s^T X_s)^{-1} + I$, $C_1 = (W_2 A_s^T X_s + \beta W_2 Z_s^T Y^T X_s)(X_s^T X_s)^{-1}$. The Sylvester equation can be solved easily in MATLAB:

$$W_1 = sylvester(A_1, B_1, C_1) \tag{5}$$

Fix W_1 and Update W_2. This problem can be solved in the same way as the solution to W_1, then can get the Sylvester equation:

$$\begin{aligned}&(\beta W_1 X_s^T X_s W_1^T) W_2 + W_2 (A_s^T A_s + \lambda_2 I)(Z_s^T Z_s)^{-1}\\&= (W_1 X_s^T A_s + \beta W_1 X_s^T Y Z_s)(Z_s^T Z_s)^{-1}\end{aligned} \tag{6}$$

where $A_2 = (\beta W_1 X_s^T X_s W_1^T)$, $B_2 = (A_s^T A_s + \lambda_2 I)(Z_s^T Z_s)^{-1}$, I is the identity matrix, $C_2 = (W_1 X_s^T A_s + \beta W_1 X_s^T Y A_s)(Z_s^T Z_s)^{-1}$. The Sylvester equation can be solved easily in MATLAB:

$$W_2 = sylvester(A_2, B_2, C_2) \tag{7}$$

In our experiments, the optimization process always converges after seven iterations, usually less than 25.

3.4 ZSL Classification

Due to we have two fields of restriction on the common space, we can perform ZSL in two methods.

Classification Applying the Compatibility Function. We can employ the learned W_1 and W_2 to build up relationships between the test sample x^u and unseen classes A_u. Specifically, considering the dimension of visual space is higher than semantic space, we classify in the visual space:

$$f(x_i^u) = \arg\min_j d(x_i^u, a_j^u W_2^T W_1) \tag{8}$$

Classification Applying the Projected Function. We can utilize the learned W_1 to accomplish the projection of original image data. For the unseen class prototypes, we project their attribute representations to the common space by the transformation matrix W_2.

$$f(x_i^u) = \arg\min_j d(x_i^u W_1^T, a_j^u W_2^T) \tag{9}$$

where x_i^u is the visual represent of the i-th unseen sample, W_1 and W_2 are the compatibility parameters, a_j^u is prototype attribute vector of the j-th unseen class, d is a cosine distance function, and $f()$ returns the predicted label of the unseen sample.

4 Experiments

4.1 Datasets and Settings

Datasets. We perform experiments on four benchmark ZSL datasets, i.e. Animals with Attributes (AwA) [9], Caltech-UCSD Birds-200-2011 (CUB-200) [16], aPascal & aYahoo (aP&Y) [3], and SUN Attribute (SUN) [12]. The summary of these datasets is given in Table 1.

Table 1. Statistics of different datasets: AWA, CUB, aP&Y, SUN in terms of instance numbers, dimension of semantic vector, seen and unseen classes numbers

Database	Instance	Attributes	Seen/Unseen
AwA	30475	85	40/10
CUB-200	11788	312	150/50
aP&Y	15339	64	20/12
SUN	14340	102	707/10

Parameter Settings. In our experiments, we use GoogleNet features [15] which is the 1024D activation of the final pooling layer as in [1]. We use attribute annotations as the semantic space for the datasets.

4.2 Evaluations of the Proposed Framework

We compare our method with previous methods in Table 2. Our proposed model improves the state-of-the-art performance on the datasets. For AWA dataset, our model achieves 85.16% and 85.03% separately by using proposed two recognition methods. Both of them obtain comparative results and achieve the best performance. For CUB dataset, our result is lower than SAE [7] (61.4%) and SCoRe [11] (58.4%). Compared with the previous models that applying traditional compatibility function, such as ALE [8] and SJE [1], our proposed method observes a significant improvement, which demonstrates the effectiveness of the common space. For aP&Y dataset, our result ranks the second. The split of aP&Y dataset is 20/12. The reason may lie in a smaller number of seen classes, which causes less discriminative on label space. For SUN dataset, our model achieves 92.0%, which is higher than almost all previous methods. The encouraging result further confirms that it is effective to employ label vectors in the common space.

Table 2. Zero-shot recognition results on AWA, CUB, aP&Y, SUN (%). CF means that we use compatibility function to classify and PF means that we use projected function to classify. '*' denotes the visual features are extracted by the imagenet-vgg-verydeep-19 [14] pre-trained model.

Method	AWA	CUB	aP&Y	SUN
DAP* [9]	57.2	44.5	38.2	72.0
IAP [9]	57.2	36.7		40.8
SynC [2]	72.9	54.5		62.8
SJE [1]	66.7	50.1		
LatEM [17]	71.9	45.5		
ALE [8]	49.7	35.8	30.9	38.2
ESZSL* [13]	75.3		24.2	82.1
DeViSE [4]	56.7	33.5		
SCoRe [11]	78.3	58.4		
SAE [7]	84.7	**61.4**	**55.4**	91.0
CF(Ours)	**85.16**	54.71	50.80	**92.00**
PF(Ours)	85.03	56.06	47.50	90.00

5 Conclusion

In this paper, we use attributes as semantic vector to construct semantic space and evaluate our method on four datasets. We employ two parameters to separately embed the visual and semantic features into a common embedding space and the common space is combined with the label space. In this way, the learned compatibility parameters will be discriminative with category information. It is reasonable to think that the common space combined with label space is the key to effective ZSL. The explicit and closed solution makes the method efficient to optimize. Our method obtains competitive results on the four benchmark datasets.

References

1. Akata, Z., Reed, S., Walter, D., Lee, H., Schiele, B.: Evaluation of output embeddings for fine-grained image classification. In: Computer Vision & Pattern Recognition (2015)
2. Changpinyo, S., Chao, W.L., Gong, B., Sha, F.: Synthesized classifiers for zero-shot learning. In: Computer Vision & Pattern Recognition (2016)
3. Farhadi, A., Endres, I., Hoiem, D., Forsyth, D.: Describing objects by their attributes. In: IEEE Conference on Computer Vision & Pattern Recognition (2009)
4. Frome, A., et al.: Devise: a deep visual-semantic embedding model. In: International Conference on Neural Information Processing Systems (2013)
5. Fu, Y., Hospedales, T.M., Xiang, T., Fu, Z., Gong, S.: Transductive multi-view embedding for zero-shot recognition and annotation. In: Fleet, D., Pajdla, T., Schiele, B., Tuytelaars, T. (eds.) ECCV 2014. LNCS, vol. 8690, pp. 584–599. Springer, Cham (2014). https://doi.org/10.1007/978-3-319-10605-2_38
6. Jiang, H., Wang, R., Shan, S., Yi, Y., Chen, X.: Learning discriminative latent attributes for zero-shot classification. In: IEEE International Conference on Computer Vision (2017)
7. Kodirov, E., Xiang, T., Gong, S.: Semantic autoencoder for zero-shot learning (2017)
8. Lampert, C.H., Hannes, N., Stefan, H.: Attribute-based classification for zero-shot visual object categorization. IEEE Trans. Pattern Anal. Mach. Intell. **36**(3), 453–465 (2014)
9. Lampert, C.H., Nickisch, H., Harmeling, S.: Learning to detect unseen object classes by between-class attribute transfer (2009)
10. Larochelle, H., Erhan, D., Bengio, Y.: Zero-data learning of new tasks. In: AAAI Conference on Artificial Intelligence (2014)
11. Morgado, P., Vasconcelos, N.: Semantically consistent regularization for zero-shot recognition (2017)
12. Genevieve Patterson, X., Hang, C.S., Hays, J.: The sun attribute database: beyond categories for deeper scene understanding. Int. J. Comput. Vis. **108**(1–2), 59–81 (2014)
13. Romera-Paredes, B., Torr, P.H.S.: An embarrassingly simple approach to zero-shot learning. In: International Conference on International Conference on Machine Learning (2015)
14. Simonyan, K., Zisserman, A.: Very deep convolutional networks for large-scale image recognition. Comput. Sci. (2014)
15. Szegedy, C., et al.: Going deeper with convolutions (2014)
16. Wah, C., Branson, S., Welinder, P., Perona, P., Belongie, S.: The caltech-ucsd birds200-2011 dataset. In: Advances in Water Resources - ADV WATER RESOUR, July 2011
17. Xian, Y., Akata, Z., Sharma, G., Nguyen, Q., Hein, M., Schiele, B.: Latent embeddings for zero-shot classification. In: 2016 IEEE Conference on Computer Vision and Pattern Recognition (CVPR), pp. 69–77, June 2016

On the Generalization of GAN Image Forensics

Xinsheng Xuan, Bo Peng, Wei Wang, and Jing Dong(✉)

Center for Research on Intelligent Perception and Computing, National Laboratory of Pattern Recognition, Institute of Automation, Chinese Academy of Sciences, Beijing, China
xinsheng.xuan@cripac.ia.ac.cn, {bo.peng,wwang,jdong}@nlpr.ia.ac.cn

Abstract. Recently GAN generated face images are more and more realistic with high-quality, even hard for human eyes to detect. On the other hand, the forensics community keeps on developing methods to detect these generated fake images and try to ensure the credibility of visual contents. Although researchers have developed some methods to detect generated images, few of them explore the important problem of generalization ability of forensics model. As new types of GANs are emerging fast, the generalization ability of forensics models to detect new types of GAN images is absolutely an essential research topic, which is also very challenging. In this paper, we explore this problem and propose to use preprocessed images to train a forensic CNN model. By applying similar image level preprocessing to both real and fake images, unstable low level noise cues are destroyed, and the forensics model is forced to learn more intrinsic features to classify the generated and real face images. Our experimental results also prove the effectiveness of the proposed method.

Keywords: Image forensics · GAN · Fake image detection

1 Introduction

Generative Adversarial Networks (GANs) [2] are generative models that learn the distribution of the data without any supervision. Currently, GANs are the most popular and effective generative models for image generation and the generated images could reach very high quality, even human eyes could not tell them apart from real images. Some examples are shown in Fig. 1. Owing to the advancement image synthesis of GAN, it also brings a serious forensics problem if we could not distinguish fake image from real ones. For example, DeepFake is a GAN-based technology that can replace a person's face with another person's or animal's face [3]. Criminals can use the generated images to make fake news,

This work is funded by the National Natural Science Foundation of China (Grant No. 61502496, No. 61303262 and No. U1536120) and Beijing Natural Science Foundation (Grant No. 4164102).

Z. Sun et al. (Eds.): CCBR 2019, LNCS 11818, pp. 134–141, 2019.
https://doi.org/10.1007/978-3-030-31456-9_15

and the rumors brought by fake news can have a serious negative impact on our community. In addition, if the generated face can be used to deceive the face recognition system, it will challenge the system security and may cause the collapse of the entire recognition system.

Fig. 1. Generated face image examples with PG-GAN [1].

Although there have been some methods proposed in the literature for detecting AI generated images, existing methods are almost exclusively for the detection of one type of generated images, but the detection performance of other unseen types of generated images is not addressed. As new types of GAN models are emerging quickly, the generalization ability of forensics method to other unseen types of generated fake images is becoming more important for the forensic analysis.

The improvement of generalization performance has always been an arduous task. To improve the generalization ability of image forensics model, some primary studies are done in this paper. We adopt a novel method of image preprocessing, e.g. Gaussian Blur and Gaussian Noise, in the training phase to enhance the generalization ability of our forensics Convolutional Neural Network (CNN) model. Our method is quite different from traditional forensics method, the purpose of the general forensic method is to enhance high frequency pixel noise and to focus on the clues in low level pixel statistics. Whereas our work is to destroy or depress these unstable low level high frequency noise cues. The motivation behind using image preprocessing is to improve pixel level statistical similarity between real images and fake images, so that the forensic classifier is forced to learn more intrinsic and meaningful features, rather than the style of the generation model. Hence the classifier will have better generalization ability for the aim of forensic. The experimental results we conduct in this paper also validate the idea of the proposed method.

2 Related Work

There are some related work proposed to detect AI generated fake images or videos using deep networks. To detect DeepFake video, different detection methods have been proposed [4–8]. In addition, some works focus on the detection of GAN generated images [9–12]. In [9], the authors present a study on the detection of images translation from GANs. But some of them show dramatic impairments on Twitter-like compressed images. Tariq et al. [10] use ensemble classifiers to detect fake face images created by GANs. A method based on color statistical features is proposed in [11], and several detection schemes are designed according to the practicability. Nhu et al. [12] proposed another model based on convolutional neural network to detect gernerated face images, which is based on transfer learning from a deep face recognition network. These image forensics methods can perform well on test dataset that is homologous to the training dataset.

However, most of the above work do not pay attention to the generalization ability of their forensics models. They only train and test their methods on the same type of generated image, but the generalization ability to other fake images generated by new GANs models are unknown. An exception is the ForensicTransfer work proposed by Cozzolino et al. [13]. The authors use a new autoencoder-based architecture which enforces activations in different parts of a latent vector for the real and fake classes. They devise a learning based forensic detector which adapts well to new domains, and they handle scenarios where only a handful of target domain fake examples are available during training. However, in a real application, we may not have an example images from an unknown generation model. Thus, in this work we propose to improve the generalization ability without using any target domain fake images.

3 Proposed Method

The improvement of model generalization ability has always been an important and difficult issue, and we propose a method based on image preprocessing to solve this problem. A key difference of our proposed method from other GAN forensics work is that we use an image preprocessing step in the training stage to destroy low level unstable artifact of GAN images and force the forensics discriminator to focus on more intrinsic forensic clues. In this way, our method is a quite different exploration to existing image forensics or image steganalysis networks [14–16], where the network is designed to enhance high frequency pixel noise and to focus on the clues in low level pixel statistics. Whereas we intentionally destroy or depress these low level high frequency clues by introducing a preprocessing step using smoothing filtering or noise. By doing this we can improve the low level similarity between real images and fake images, so that

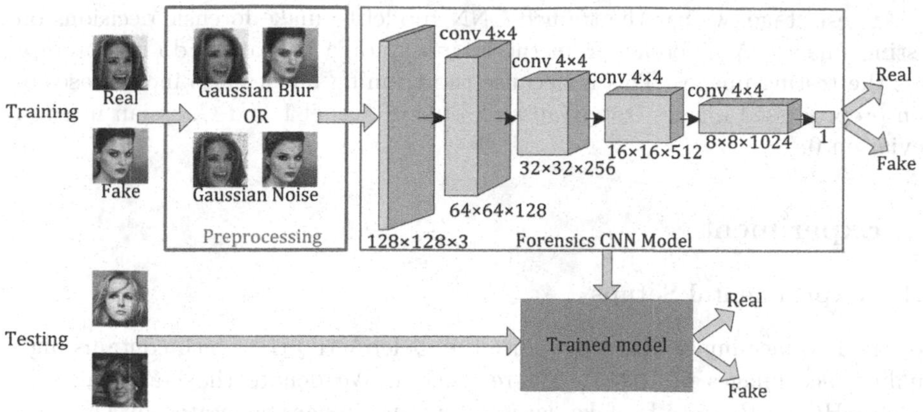

Fig. 2. The overall framework of the proposed method.

the forensic classifier is forced to learn more intrinsic features that have better generalization ability.

From a machine learning perspective, training and testing are two different phases. In the training stage, the training workflow is as shown in Fig. 2. We add an image preprocessing operation in front of the entire network architecture, where image preprocessing operation can be smoothing filtering or adding noise. In the testing stage, we used the network architecture shown in Fig. 2. At this stage, we abandon the preprocessing operation, and directly use original images as input.

In this work, Gaussian blur and Gaussian noise are used as our image preprocessing methods. Adding Gaussian blur and Gaussian noise can both change low level pixel statistics, which serve well for our purpose of depressing low level unstable clues. In order to increase the diversity of training samples, we apply random extent of these preprocessings. The kernel size of Gaussian blur is randomly chosen from 1, 3, 5 and 7 for each training batch. Similarly, the standard deviation of Gaussian noise is randomly set between 0 and 5 for each batch. Note that Gaussian blur of kernel 1 and Gaussian noise of 0 deviation result in no change to the original images.

As our main focus is to verify the effectiveness of proposed preprocessing operation on improving generalization ability, we do not design a complex CNN network architecture. The network architecture of our approach uses a simple DCGAN [17] network's discriminator network. The whole CNN network architecture is shown in Fig. 2. The input of the network are real and fake images, with image size of 128×128. The network is a binary classifier, with four convolutional layers, and all convolutions have stride 2 and padding 1, and all convolution kernel size is 4×4. For the four convolutional layers, we use the Batch Normalization except the first layer, and use Leaky Rectified Linear Unit activation functions that introduce non-linearities. The loss function and optimization algorithm are Binary Cross Entropy Loss and Adaptive Moment Estimation respectively.

At test stage, we use the trained CNN model to make forensic decisions on testing images. A difference from the training stage is that we do not preprocess the testing images. This is because the training images also inclue cases of non-preprocessed images from Gaussian blur of kernel 1 and Gaussian noise of deviation 0.

4 Experiments

4.1 Experimental Setups

For the real face image dataset, we use the CelebA-HQ [1], which contains high quality face images of 1024×1024 resolution. We denote the real images in CelebA-HQ as R_{cel}. As for fake datasets, we use images generated by DCGAN [17], WGAN-GP [18] and PGGAN [1], and they are respectively denoted as F_{dc}, F_{wg} and F_{pg}. For DCGAN and WGAN-GP, we first train the generative models using CelebA [19] dataset, and then use these trained GAN models to generate fake face images. The PGGAN model is a high quality image generation model based on progressive growing. Due to the long training time of the PGGAN model, we directly download fake image dataset provided by authors [1]. The size of images generated by DCGAN and WGAN-GP models is 128×128, and this is the input image size that our CNN model requires. However, the size of both real images and PG-GAN generated images is of high resolution 1024×1024, so we resize them to 128×128.

In our experiments, we train our CNN forensics model on only F_{pg} and R_{cel} datasets, and the rest two generated datasets F_{dc} and F_{wg} are just used for testing the generalization ability of trained model. Here images in F_{dc} and F_{wg} are treated as unseen generated images from new GANs that are different from the training data. The F_{pg} and R_{cel} datasets each has 20K images, where the first 10K images are used for model training and the last 10K for testing. The F_{dc} and F_{wg} datasets each contains 10K images for testing generalization ability.

The model trained on R_{cel} and F_{pg} without any image preprocessing is denoted as M. For the other two models, the training dataset is processed by Gaussian blur or Gaussian noise, which respectively are denoted as M_{GB} and M_{GN}. Then, we use testing images in R_{cel}, F_{pg}, F_{dc} and F_{wg} to test M, M_{GB} and M_{GN} separately. The performance is measured by overall accuracy (ACC), true positive rate (TPR) and true negative rate (TNR), where positive means real images and negative means fake images.

4.2 Improvement of Model Generalization

The experimental results are shown in Table 1. The experiment is divided into three parts by different test datasets. The test datasets of the first row to the third row are F_{pg} and R_{cel}, the test datasets of the fourth row to the sixth row are F_{wg} and R_{cel}, and the test datasets of the seventh row to the ninth row are F_{dc} and R_{cel}. Compare the M model without image preprocessing operation

Table 1. Detection results of models in different preprocessing operations.

No.	Detector model	Testing set	ACC(%)	TPR(%)	TNR(%)
1	M	$F_{pg} + R_{cel}$	95.45	95.12	95.77
2	M_{GB}	$F_{pg} + R_{cel}$	94.28	93.08	95.47
3	M_{GN}	$F_{pg} + R_{cel}$	95.02	94.65	95.38
4	M	$F_{wg} + R_{cel}$	64.62	95.12	34.12
5	M_{GB}	$F_{wg} + R_{cel}$	68.07	93.08	**43.06**
6	M_{GN}	$F_{wg} + R_{cel}$	68.28	94.65	**41.91**
7	M	$F_{dc} + R_{cel}$	60.55	95.12	25.98
8	M_{GB}	$F_{dc} + R_{cel}$	64.05	93.08	**35.02**
9	M_{GN}	$F_{dc} + R_{cel}$	66.38	94.65	**38.11**

on row 1 and the M_{GB} and M_{GN} models with image preprocessing operations on row 2 and row 3, ACC, TPR and TNR are almost constant after adding preprocessing. And this means that the proposed method does not damage the model and is relatively stable. From the first three row, it can also be seen that testing on the data which is from the same domain as training data can achieve very high classification performance.

From the data of row 1 we can observe that the detection ACC, TPR and TNR are all higher than 95% on testing dataset of the same type as training dataset, but the ACC and TNR on rows 4 and 7 are both significantly lower than those in row 1. This result means that the generalization ability of the model on unseen types of fake images is bad.

Compare row 4 and rows 5, 6 in Table 1, with the test dataset is F_{wg} and R_{cel}, we can see that our trained model can improve the TNR by around 10% and the overall ACC is also improved. And this can show that the method of preprocessing operation is effective for improving generalization ability on unseen generated images. Similarly, comparing row 7 and rows 8, 9, TNR also has an improvement of about 10%. Although the performance increment is not all that large due to the inherent difficulty of this problem, it is sufficient to show that our methods can improve generalization ability on unseen types of fake image datasets.

Different from other forensic methods, our method uses an image preprocessing to suppress unstable noise cues. From the experimental results, it can be seen that the proposed image preprocessing method can actually lead to a certain improvement of generalization, although the increment is not quite large. After our analysis, we believe that the reason for the difficulty in forensics generalization may be as shown in Fig. 3. There are many types of generator models, and likely to be more in the future, and the distribution of images generated by each model may vary greatly. As shown in Fig. 3, Fake1, Fake2 and Fake3 belong to differently distributed fake images. Although they are all fake images, the distribution difference between them is quite large. Therefore, to train a forensics

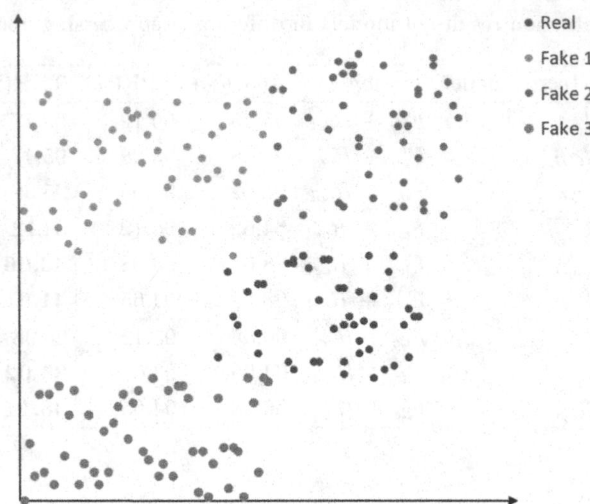

Fig. 3. Possible distribution of real and fake images simplified on a two-dimensional feature space.

model which can generalize to future unknown generated fake images is a very challenging task. We hope researchers can carry on in this line of research in the future to develop more and more effective solutions.

5 Conclusion

In this paper, we have investigated the issue of generalization ability of detection model for generated images. Perhaps because of the difficulty of generalization capabilities improvement, we found that most of the existing detection models did not pay attention to the improvement of generalization capabilities. Based on the observations, we propose to improve the generalization ability of a CNN forensics model by adding an image preprocessing step before training to force the discriminator to learn more intrinsic and generalizable features. To evaluate the performance of the proposed method, extensive experiments have been conducted. The experimental results show that our approach is effective in improving generalization, although the performance increment is not all that large due to the inherent difficulty of this problem. Observed from the experiments, the distribution of fake images generated by different models may be quite different. In short, the improvement of generalization is quite difficult, and we take a very different strategy compared to existing, but only achieved some preliminary results. We hope to inspire more work in this direction. In the future, we will continue to optimize the generalization of the detection model in other ways.

References

1. Karras, T., Aila, T., Laine, S., Lehtinen, J.: Progressive growing of GANs for improved quality, stability, and variation. arXiv preprint arXiv:1710.10196 (2017)
2. Goodfellow, I., et al.: Generative adversarial nets. In: Advances in Neural Information Processing Systems, pp. 2672–2680 (2014)
3. Deepfake. https://github.com/deepfakes/faceswap
4. Güera, D., Delp, E.J.: Deepfake video detection using recurrent neural networks. In: IEEE International Conference on Advanced Video and Signal-Based Surveillance (2018, to appear)
5. Li, Y., Lyu, S.: Exposing deepfake videos by detecting face warping artifacts. arXiv preprint arXiv:1811.00656 (2018)
6. Li, Y., Chang, M.C., Farid, H., Lyu, S.: In Ictu Oculi: exposing AI generated fake face videos by detecting eye blinking. arXiv preprint arXiv:1806.02877 (2018)
7. Yang, X., Li, Y., Lyu, S.: Exposing deep fakes using inconsistent head poses. arXiv preprint arXiv:1811.00661 (2018)
8. Afchar, D., Nozick, V., Yamagishi, J., Echizen, I.: MesoNet: a compact facial video forgery detection network. arXiv preprint arXiv:1809.00888 (2018)
9. Marra, F., Gragnaniello, D., Cozzolino, D., Verdoliva, L.: Detection of GAN-generated fake images over social networks. In: 2018 IEEE Conference on Multimedia Information Processing and Retrieval (MIPR), pp. 384–389. IEEE (2018)
10. Tariq, S., Lee, S., Kim, H., Shin, Y., Woo, S.S.: Detecting both machine and human created fake face images in the wild. In: Proceedings of the 2nd International Workshop on Multimedia Privacy and Security, pp. 81–87. ACM (2018)
11. Li, H., Li, B., Tan, S., Huang, J.: Detection of deep network generated images using disparities in color components. arXiv preprint arXiv:1808.07276 (2018)
12. Do Nhu, T., Na, I., Kim, S.: Forensics face detection from GANs using convolutional neural network, October 2018
13. Cozzolino, D., Thies, J., Rössler, A., Riess, C., Nießner, M., Verdoliva, L.: Forensictransfer: weakly-supervised domain adaptation for forgery detection. arXiv preprint arXiv:1812.02510 (2018)
14. Qian, Y., Dong, J., Wang, W., Tan, T.: Deep learning for steganalysis via convolutional neural networks. In: Media Watermarking, Security, and Forensics 2015, vol. 9409, p. 94090J. International Society for Optics and Photonics (2015)
15. Bayar, B., Stamm, M.C.: A deep learning approach to universal image manipulation detection using a new convolutional layer. In: Proceedings of the 4th ACM Workshop on Information Hiding and Multimedia Security, pp. 5–10. ACM (2016)
16. Yang, P., Ni, R., Zhao, Y.: Recapture image forensics based on Laplacian convolutional neural networks. In: Shi, Y.Q., Kim, H.J., Perez-Gonzalez, F., Liu, F. (eds.) IWDW 2016. LNCS, vol. 10082, pp. 119–128. Springer, Cham (2017). https://doi.org/10.1007/978-3-319-53465-7_9
17. Radford, A., Metz, L., Chintala, S.: Unsupervised representation learning with deep convolutional generative adversarial networks. arXiv preprint arXiv:1511.06434 (2015)
18. Gulrajani, I., Ahmed, F., Arjovsky, M., Dumoulin, V., Courville, A.C.: Improved training of wasserstein GANs. In: Advances in Neural Information Processing Systems, pp. 5767–5777 (2017)
19. Liu, Z., Luo, P., Wang, X., Tang, X.: Deep learning face attributes in the wild. In: Proceedings of the IEEE International Conference on Computer Vision, pp. 3730–3738 (2015)

Face

Deep Residual Equivariant Mapping for Multi-angle Face Recognition

Wei Liu[1], Lintai Wu[1], Yong Xu[1(✉)], and Dan Wang[2]

[1] Bio-Computing Research Center, Harbin Institute of Technology, Shenzhen, China
laterfall@hit.edu.cn
[2] IFLYTEK Co., Ltd., Hefei, China

Abstract. Face recognition has caught a lot of attention and plenty of valuable methods have been proposed during the past decades. However, because it is hard to learn geometrically invariant representations, existing face recognition methods still perform relatively poorly in conducting multi-angle face recognition. In this paper, we hypothesize that there is an inherent mapping between the frontal and non-frontal faces, and the non-frontal face representations can be converted into the frontal face representations by an equivariant mapping. To carry out the mapping, we propose a Multi-Angle Deep Residual Equivariant Mapping (MADREM) block which adaptively maps the non-frontal face representation to the frontal face representation. It can be considered the MADREM block carry out face alignment and face normalization in the feature space. The residual equivariant mapping block can enhance the discriminative power of the face representations. Finally, we achieve an accuracy of 99.78% on the LFW dataset and 94.25% on CFP-FP dataset based on proposed multiscale-convolution and residual equivariant mapping block.

Keywords: Face recognition · Feature equivariance · Residual equivariant mapping · Multiscale convolution

1 Introduction

Convolutional Neural Networks (CNNs) are widely used in computer vision tasks, such as object detection [1, 2], image classification [3] and image denoising [4]. As an important task in computer vision community, face recognition always catches a lot of attentions [5–7]. In recent years, the combination of large datasets and CNNs has greatly improved the performance of face recognition. As we know, CNN was first introduced into face recognition by DeepFace [8]. With the development of deep learning, various network structures [11] and loss functions [12–14] have been proposed for face recognition and the performance of face recognition has achieved a breakthrough. For example, the Facenet [9] illustrated the effectiveness of the triple loss for face recognition. The triple loss minimizes the distance between an anchor embedding and a positive embedding, while maximizes the distance between an anchor embedding and a negative embedding. Besides, various margin softmax loss functions are proposed based on standard softmax loss, such as SphereFace [12], CosFace [13] and ArcFace [14]. These margin softmax loss functions optimize the decision boundary in angular space or cosine space to obtain more discriminative deep features.

Z. Sun et al. (Eds.): CCBR 2019, LNCS 11818, pp. 145–154, 2019.
https://doi.org/10.1007/978-3-030-31456-9_16

Although previous methods have achieved good results for near-frontal face recognition, the facial pose variation is still a challenge for face recognition in real unconstrained environments. Some commonly used approaches to address this problem are to normalize face images to frontal pose before recognition [15–17]. For instance, Yim et al. [17] proposed a multi-task deep neural network, which aims to rotate a face from an arbitrary pose to a target pose. The aforementioned methods often costs many computing resources and the synthesized faces often contain artificial trace due to the non-rigid deformation of face. Other approaches attempt to train specific models for specific poses [18] or for specific parts [19]. These approaches would consume more storage and time due to the use of multiple models.

Different from the above methods, Cao et al. [20] proposed a novel method based on feature equivariance [21] for profile face recognition. Cao et al. hypothesize that the profile face domain possesses an underlying connection with the frontal face domain in the deep feature space. Based on the hypothesis, they proposed a novel module called Deep Residual EquivAriant Mapping (DREAM) block, which adaptively transforms a profile face representation to a frontal face representation to simplify face recognition. Figure 1 graphically illustrates the idea of the proposal.

In the DREAM block only the yaw of the face is considered, so it only transforms the profile representation to frontal representation. However, the pose of a face in the unconstrained environment tends to be complicated, which contains not only the variation of yaw but also pitch and roll.

To explore multi-angle face recognition in unconstrained environment, we proposed a Multi-Angle Deep Residual Equivariant Mapping (MADREM) block for multi-angle face recognition. Our major contributions are summarized as follows: First, we propose a MADREM block based on deep residual equivariant mapping, which considers not only yaw but also roll and pitch when adaptively mapping the non-frontal face representation to the fontal face representation. Second, we propose a multiscale convolution network as Stem CNN to extract discriminative face features. Third, we conduct extensive experiments to verify the effectiveness of the proposed method for multi-angle face recognition.

2 Previous Works and Preliminaries

Because our proposed method is based on the DREAM block [20] which utilizes the idea of feature equivariance [21], in this section we introduce the feature equivariance and the idea of the DREAM block.

We consider a CNN as a function ϕ that maps an image $x \in \chi$ to a vector $\phi(\mathrm{x}) \in R^d$. The representation ϕ is said equivariant with a transformation g of the input image if the transformation can be converted into the representation output [21]. That is, equivariance with the transformation is obtained when there exists a $\mathrm{M_g}: \mathrm{R^d} \rightarrow \mathrm{R^d}$ such that

$$\forall x \in \chi : \phi(gx) \approx M_g \phi(x) \tag{1}$$

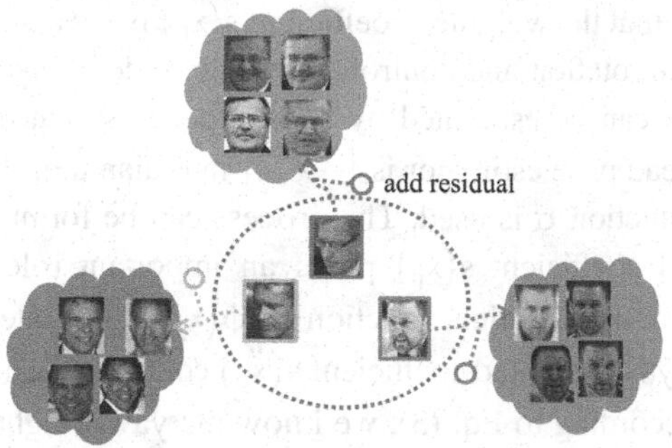

Fig. 1. The effect of pose variation and adding residuals. The distances between features of profile faces of different persons may be smaller than the distances between profile and frontal faces of the same persons. The samples which are from different category in the circle will be classified into the same category mistakenly. Adding residuals to the profile features will map the profile faces to frontal faces which are easier to recognition in the feature space.

For clarity, we describe the meaning of Eq. (1) in non-frontal face recognition task. x is a non-frontal face image, and g is a transformation which transforms a non-frontal face to a frontal face. Thus, we can use g to transform the non-frontal face to the frontal face which is denoted as gx, and then we use feature extractor ϕ to extract the feature of gx to get the result denoted by $\phi(gx)$. However, generating frontal face is a challengeable task. But we can accomplish this in feature space as the right part of Eq. (1) shows, which seems to be a simpler task. $\phi(x)$ denotes the feature extracted from non-frontal face image x. M_g is a transformation which transforms the features of non-frontal faces to the features of frontal faces. Applying the transformation M_g to the $\phi(x)$ we can obtain the feature of frontal face $M_g\phi(x)$. If there exists a M_g makes $M_g\phi(x)$ is approximately equal to $\phi(gx)$, we consider the transformation g has equivariance with respect to ϕ. Therefore, the most significant step of our task is to find M_g which meets this condition.

Motivated by Eq. (1), the DREAM block is aimed to transform the representation $\phi(x_p)$ of the profile face image x_p into the representation $\phi(x_f)$ of the frontal face image x_f via mapping function M_g. For cooperation with stem CNN, the mapped feature $M_g\phi(x_p)$ is formulated as a sum of the original profile feature with residuals given by a residual function $R(\phi(x_p))$ weighted by a yaw coefficient $s(x_p)$. We formulate this idea as follows [20]:

$$\begin{gathered} \phi(gx_p) = M_g\phi(x_p) \\ = \phi(x_p) + s(x_p)R(\phi(x_p)) \\ \approx \phi(x_f) \end{gathered} \tag{2}$$

$$s(x_p) = \sigma\left(\frac{4}{\pi}|yaw| - 1\right) \tag{3}$$

It is worth noticing that the weighted coefficient $s(x_p)$ plays a role of soft gate, which reflects the level of face rotation and controls the magnitude of residuals to be added to $\phi(x_p)$. The yaw angle can be estimated by a head pose estimator. The range of yaw angle obtained from head pose estimator is $\left[-\frac{\pi}{2}, \frac{\pi}{2}\right]$ in radian unit. In order to transform it to [0, 1] a sigmod function σ is used. The process can be formulated as Eq. (3).

The yaw weighted coefficient $s(x_p)$ plays an important role for arbitrary angle profile face recognition. The residual function $R(\phi(x_p))$ generates residuals between $\phi(x_f)$ and $\phi(x_p)$. The yaw weighted coefficient $s(x_p)$ controls the amount of residuals to be added to $\phi(x_p)$. According to Eq. (3), we know the yaw weighted coefficient $s(x_p)$ will be one for an complete profile face image, but for an almost frontal face image $s(x_p)$ will be about zero. For a complete profile face image, its representation has the greater discrepancy from the frontal representation. Therefore, in order to transform the complete profile presentation to the frontal representation, more residuals should be added.

3 The Proposed Approach

In this section, we first introduce the overall framework of the proposed multi-angle face recognition method. Then, we describe the details of our Multi-Angle Deep Residual Equivariant Mapping (MADREM) block which is useful for recognition of faces with unrestricted poses.

3.1 The Overall Framework

As shown in Fig. 2 the overall framework contains a Stem CNN, a Head Pose Estimator and the MADREM block. The Stem CNN is used to extract the original feature from the input face image x. The head pose estimator can estimate the yaw, pitch and roll of face from face landmarks [22] or deep feature [23] of face image. The MADREM block takes the original feature and angles as input to learn the residuals. Finally, the residuals are adaptively added to the original feature to obtain the more discriminative final feature.

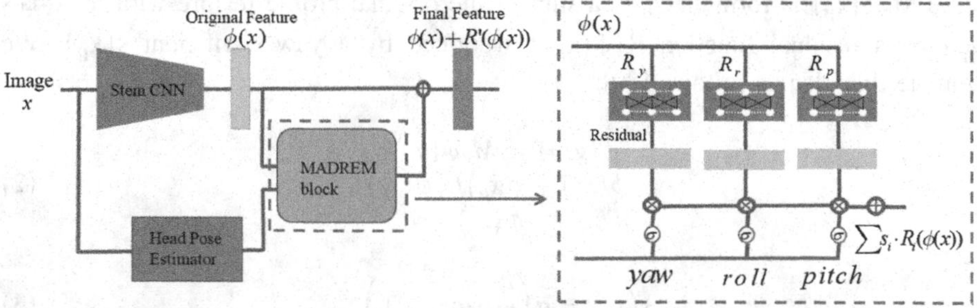

Fig. 2. Illustration of the overall framework and detail of MADREM block. The overall framework contains a Stem CNN, a Head Pose Estimator and The MADREM block. The final feature is the sum of the original feature and the residuals obtained from the MADREM block.

3.2 Multi-angle Deep Residual Equivariant Mapping

The DREAM block in [20] is proposed for profile-frontal face recognition, but it is not effective for face recognition with other pose variations. The facial pose in the unconstrained environment is various, which is caused by the variations of not only the yaw but also pitch and roll. We attempt to learn residuals for roll and pitch variations in this paper as Cao et al. did for yaw variation in [20]. We propose a Multi-Angle Deep Residual Equivariant Mapping (MADREM) approach. The MADREM block considers not only the yaw but also roll and pitch when learning residuals for face representation in unconstrained environment. The combination of different yaw, roll and pitch is directly associated with pose variation, so the block can map the face representation of an arbitrary pose face to the representation of the frontal face.

We propose the MADREM block to takes all the three dimensions pitch, roll and yaw into account for multi-angle face recognition. The details of the structures of the block are shown in Fig. 2. We design a separate residual branch for the yaw, roll and pitch variation respectively in the block. The advantage of the structure is that the MADREM block can learn residuals separately for each angle variation. The final representation can determine which angle variation the residuals come from. We aim to obtain a new representation of a face image x_m with arbitrary pose via a mapping function M_g, which satisfies $M_g\phi(x_m) \approx \phi(x_f)$. As shown in Eq. (4), we formulate the new representation as the sum of the original representation and the residuals given by the residual function $R_y(\phi(x_m))$, $R_r(\phi(x_m))$ and $R_p(\phi(x_m))$ respectively.

$$\begin{aligned} \phi(gx_m) &= M_g\phi(x_m) \\ &= \phi(x_m) + y_sR_y(\phi(x_m)) + r_sR_r(\phi(x_m)) + p_sR_p(\phi(x_m)) \\ &\approx \phi(x_f) \end{aligned} \tag{4}$$

$$y, r, p = e(x_m) \tag{5}$$

The $R_y(\phi(x_m))$, $R_r(\phi(x_m))$ and $R_p(\phi(x_m))$ are the residual functions of the yaw, roll and pitch respectively. Each residual function is represented by a two-layer neural network branch. The e is a head pose estimator which estimates the yaw denoted as y, roll denoted as r and pitch denoted as p of the face. The y, r and p are nonlinearly mapped to y_s, r_s and p_s within the range of [0, 1] respectively, according to Eq. (3) as the same manner of $s(x_p)$ in Sect. 2. The weighted coefficients y_s, r_s and p_s play the roles of soft gate, which control the amount of the residuals being added to the final representation. To be specific, the block generates more residuals for complete non-frontal face, but fewer residuals for an almost frontal face. Finally, by performing the transformation in Eq. (4), the representation $\phi(x_m)$ of non-frontal face will be adaptively mapped to the frontal face representation $\phi(x_f)$.

4 Experiments

The experimental settings are given in Sect. 4.1. In Sect. 4.2 we explore the powerful Stem CNN architecture. Experiments are conducted on the LFW [24] and the CFP [25] dataset in Sect. 4.3 to verify the effectiveness of the MADREM block.

4.1 Data and Processing

We train models on cleaned MS-Celeb-1M dataset [26] which are cleaned by trillionpairs consortium. The cleaned MS-Celeb-1M contains 86,876 identities and 3,923,399 aligned images.

We employ Labeled Face in the Wild (LFW) dataset [24] and Celebrities in Frontal-Profile (CFP) [25] as our test data. LFW dataset contains 13,233 web-collected images of 5749 different identities, with large variations in pose, expression and illumination. We report the accuracy on given 6000 face pairs. CFP [25] consists of 500 celebrities each with ten frontal and four profile images. The evaluation follows the standard 10-fold protocol for frontal-frontal (FF) and frontal-profile (FP) face verification, each having 10 folders with 350 same-person pairs and 350 different-person pairs generated from 50 individuals. We just report the performance on the challenging task Frontal-Profile (CFP-FP) face verification.

We detect the faces in the images and their landmarks with MTCNN [27]. For our proposal, based on the detected landmarks, we estimate the head pose (yaw, roll, pitch) by using the method in [22]. Then we map the roll, yaw and pitch to the nonlinear angle through Eq. (3). For face alignment in original image space, we perform face alignment with similarity transformation.

Similarity of two feature vectors is measured by Cosine Distance [28]. The last face verification task is conducted by the nearest neighbor. We use the loss function proposed by ArcFace [33], and other loss functions are also appropriate.

4.2 Stem CNN

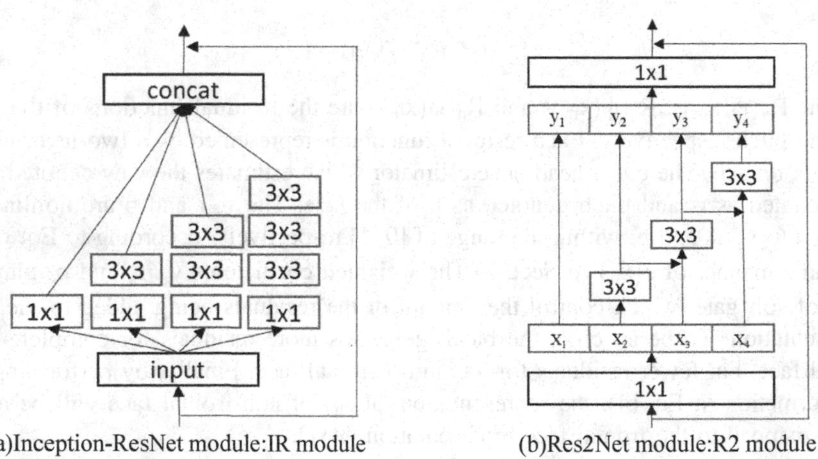

Fig. 3. The structures of Inception-ResNet module and Res2Net module.

Table 1. The architecture of IRes2Net.

Layer name	conv1	conv2_x	conv3_x	conv4_x	conv5_x
Module	3 × 3, 64, stride 1	IR module	IR module	R2 module	R2 module

Table 2. Verification accuracy (%) under different Stem CNN.

Stem CNN	LFW	CFP-FP
Restnet-50	99.68	92.00
Inception-ResNet-V2	99.57	91.83
Res2Net-50	99.71	92.26
IRes2Net-50	99.73	92.52

Our solution consists of two main components: Stem CNN and MDREM block. Multiscale features are important for face recognition and other computer vision tasks. First, we will explore a more powerful Stem CNN, which utilizes multiscale convolution and skip connection idea. The Inception-ResNet [35] and Res2Net [36] are two kinds network to extract multiscale features. These two modules are shown in Fig. 3. The Inception-ResNet module extracts the multiscale features independently and then stack them together. In the Res2Net module the multiscale features are fused progressively, and then multiscale features are stacked. In order to extract discriminative features, we use these two modules to construct the Stem CNN. In the network we use Inception-ResNet module and Res2Net module in early stage and late stage respectively to construct our Stem CNN, and the architecture of the network is shown in Table 1.

In the Table 2 we give the comparison of accuracy under different Stem CNNs. The proposed network IRes2Net has the best performance. In the early stage, the Inception-ResNet module can preserve the independence of multiscale features, and in the later stage Res2Net module can increase the receptive field rapidly under the condition of constant computation quantity.

4.3 Ablation and Evaluation

We employ IRest-Net-50 as our stem CNN and report the accuracy on the LFW dataset and the CFP-FP dataset to verify the effectiveness of the MADREM block. We give the accuracies of different models in Table 3.

The model proposal-0 in Table 3 does not use MADREM block. The proposal-1 just uses the yaw residual branch as [20]. The model proposal-2 uses the proposed MADREM block, which takes into account the yaw, roll, and patch information simultaneously.

From the results in Table 3, we have the following observations: The model proposal-1 with yaw residuals branch has better performance than proposal-0, which proves the effectiveness of the residual mapping strategy. The model proposal-2 with MADREM block has better performance than proposal-0 and proposal-1, which shows that it is an effective strategy to consider three angles at the same time in equivariant mapping block. The residual mapping structure will transform the representations of outliers (non-frontal faces) to the representations closed to the class center. Compared with LFW dataset, CFP-FP dataset has more obvious pose variation. Thus, our method has more effect improvement on CFP-FP dataset.

Table 3. Verification accuracy (%) of different methods on LFW and CFP-FP dataset.

Methods	LFW	CFP-FP
Proposal-0	99.73	92.52
Proposal-1	99.76	93.93
Proposal-2	99.78	94.25

We compare our method with other methods on CFP-FP dataset for frontal to profile face recognition. Chen et al. [37] combines the Fisher vector representation and the DCNN features for unconstrained face verification. Peng et al. [38] propose to generate non-frontal views and disentangle identity and pose. DR-GAN [17] and UV-GAN [39] which try to generate frontal faces from non-frontal faces. The comparison between our proposal and other methods is also shown in Table 4. Benefiting from residual mapping structure, our proposal has better performance than these methods.

Table 4. Varification accuracy (%) comparision on CFP-FP dataset.

Methods	CFP-FP
Chen et al. [37]	91.97
DR-GAN [17]	93.41
Peng et al. [38]	93.76
DREAM [20]	93.92
UV-GAN [39]	94.05
Proposal-2	94.25

5 Conclusion

In this paper, we propose a MADREM block for multi-angle face recognition. By attaching the MADREM block to the Stem CNN, we can adaptively map the non-frontal face representation to the fontal face representation and enhance the discriminative power of pose-variation face representations. In addition, we propose a Stem CNN which extract multiscale features for face recognition. Extensive experiments on the LFW and CFP-FP benchmarks have convincingly proved the effectiveness of the proposed MADREM block and the multiscale Stem CNN.

Acknowledgement. This work was funded by Economic, Trade and information Commission of Shenzhen Municipality (20170504160426188) and National Natural Science Foundation of China (U1836205).

References

1. Girshick, R.: Fast R-CNN. Computer science. arXiv preprint arXiv:1504.08083 (2015)
2. Liu, W., et al.: SSD: single shot multibox detector. In: Leibe, B., Matas, J., Sebe, N., Welling, M. (eds.) ECCV 2016. LNCS, vol. 9905, pp. 21–37. Springer, Cham (2016). https://doi.org/10.1007/978-3-319-46448-0_2
3. He, K., Zhang, X., Ren, S.: Delving deep into rectifiers: surpassing human-level performance on ImageNet classification. arXiv preprint arXiv:1502.01852 (2015)
4. Tian, C., Xu, Y., Fei, L.: Deep learning for image denoising: a survey. arXiv preprint arXiv: 1810.05052v1 (2018)
5. Xu, Y., Zhang, D., Yang, J.: A two-phase test sample sparse representation method for use with face recognition. IEEE Trans. Circuits Syst. Video Technol. **21**(9), 1255–1262 (2011)
6. Xu, Y., Zhu, X., Li, Z.: Using the original and 'symmetrical face' training samples to perform representation based two-step face recognition. Pattern Recognit. **46**(4), 1151–1158 (2013)
7. Guo, K., Wu, S., Xu, Y.: Face recognition using both visible light image and near-infrared image and a deep network. CAAI Trans. Intell. Technol. **2**(1), 39–47 (2017)
8. Taigman, Y., Yang, M., Ranzato, M.: DeepFace: closing the gap to human-level performance in face verification. In: 2014 IEEE Conference on Computer Vision and Pattern Recognition, Columbus, OH, pp. 1701–1708. IEEE (2014)
9. Schroff, F., Kalenichenko, D., Philbin, J.: FaceNet: a unified embedding for face recognition and clustering. arXiv preprint arXiv:1503.03832 (2015)
10. Sun, Y., Wang, X., Tang, X.: Deeply learned face representations are sparse, selective, and robust. In: 2015 IEEE Conference on Computer Vision and Pattern Recognition, Boston, pp. 2892–2900. IEEE (2015)
11. Wu, X., He, R., Sun, Z.: A light CNN for deep face representation with noisy labels. IEEE Trans. Inf. Forensics Secur. (2015)
12. Liu, W.: SphereFace: deep hypersphere embedding for face recognition. In: 2017 IEEE Conference on Computer Vision and Pattern Recognition, Honolulu, HI, pp. 6738–6746 (2017)
13. Wang, H., Wang, Y., Zhou, Z.: CosFace: large margin cosine loss for deep face recognition. arXiv preprint arXiv:1801.09414 (2018)
14. Deng, J., Guo, J., Zafeiriou, S.: ArcFace: additive angular margin loss for deep face Recognition.arXiv preprint arXiv:1801.07698 (2018)
15. Yim, J., Jung, H., Yoo, B.I.: Rotating your face using multi-task deep neural network. In: 2015 IEEE Conference on Computer Vision and Pattern Recognition, Boston, pp. 676–684. IEEE (2015)
16. Jourabloo, A., Liu, X.: Large-pose face alignment via CNN-based dense 3D model fitting. In: 2016 IEEE Conference on Computer Vision and Pattern Recognition, Las Vegas, NV, pp. 4188–4196. IEEE (2016)
17. Tran, L., Yin, X., Liu, X.: Disentangled representation learning GAN for pose-invariant face recognition. In: 2017 IEEE Conference on Computer Vision and Pattern Recognition, pp. 1283–1292. Springer, Honolulu (2017)
18. Masi, I., Rawls, S., Medioni, G.: Pose-aware face recognition in the wild. In: 2016 IEEE Conference on Computer Vision and Pattern Recognition, Las Vegas, pp. 4838–4846. IEEE (2016)
19. Liao, S., Jain, A.K., Li, S.Z.: Partial face recognition: alignment-free approach. IEEE Trans. Pattern Anal. Mach. Intell. **35**, 1193–1205 (2013)

20. Cao, K., Rong, Y., Li, C.: Pose-robust face recognition via deep residual equivariant Mapping. arXiv preprint arXiv:1803.00839 (2018)
21. Lenc, K., Vedaldi, A.: Understanding image representations by measuring their equivariance and equivalence. In: 2015 IEEE Conference on Computer Vision and Pattern Recognition, Boston, pp. 991–999 (2015)
22. Zhang, X., Sugano, Y., Fritz, M.: Appearance-based gaze estimation in the wild. In: 2015 IEEE Conference on Computer Vision and Pattern Recognition, Boston, MA, pp. 4511–4520 (2015)
23. Ruiz, N., Chong, E., Rehg, J.M.: Fine-grained head pose estimation without keypoints. arXiv preprint arXiv:1710.00925 (2017)
24. Huang, G.B., Mattar, M., Berg, T.: Labeled faces in the wild: a database for studying face recognition in unconstrained environments. In: Workshop on Faces in 'Real-Life' Images: Detection, Alignment, and Recognition, Marseille (2008)
25. Sengupta, S., Chen, J., Castillo, C.: Frontal to profile face verification in the wild. In: 2016 IEEE Winter Conference on Applications of Computer Vision, Lake Placid, pp. 1–9 (2016)
26. Guo, Y., Zhang, L., Hu, Y., He, X., Gao, J.: MS-Celeb-1M: a dataset and benchmark for large-scale face recognition. In: Leibe, B., Matas, J., Sebe, N., Welling, M. (eds.) ECCV 2016. LNCS, vol. 9907, pp. 87–102. Springer, Cham (2016). https://doi.org/10.1007/978-3-319-46487-9_6
27. Zhang, K., Zhang, Z., Li, Z.: Joint face detection and alignment using multitask cascaded convolutional networks. IEEE Signal Process. Lett. **23**(10), 1499–1503 (2016)
28. Nguyen, H.V., Bai, L.: Cosine similarity metric learning for face verification. In: Kimmel, R., Klette, R., Sugimoto, A. (eds.) ACCV 2010. LNCS, vol. 6493, pp. 709–720. Springer, Heidelberg (2011). https://doi.org/10.1007/978-3-642-19309-5_55
29. Parkhi, O.M., Vedaldi, A., Zisserman, A.: Deep face recognition. bmvc **1**(3), 6 (2015)
30. Liu, J., Deng, Y., Bai, T.: Targeting ultimate accuracy: face recognition via deep embedding. arXiv preprint arXiv:1506.07310 (2015)
31. Chen, J., Patel,V. M., Chellappa, R.: Unconstrained face verification using deep CNN features. arXiv preprint arXiv:1508.01722 (2015)
32. Sankaranarayanan, S., Alavi, A., Castillo, C.: Triplet probabilistic embedding for face verification and clustering. arXiv preprint arXiv:1604.05417 (2016)
33. Sun, Y., Wang, X., Tang, X.: Deep learning face representation by joint identification-verification. arXiv preprint arXiv:1406.4773 (2014)
34. Wen, Y., Zhang, K., Li, Z., Qiao, Yu.: A discriminative feature learning approach for deep face recognition. In: Leibe, B., Matas, J., Sebe, N., Welling, M. (eds.) ECCV 2016. LNCS, vol. 9911, pp. 499–515. Springer, Cham (2016). https://doi.org/10.1007/978-3-319-46478-7_31
35. Szegedy, C., Ioffe, S., Vanhoucke, V.: Inception-v4, Inception-ResNet and the impact of residual connections on learning. arXiv preprint arXiv:1602.07261 (2016)
36. Gao, S.-H., Cheng, M.-M., Zhao, K., et al.: Res2Net: a new multi-scale backbone architecture. arXiv preprint arXiv:1904.01169 (2019)
37. Chen, J.C., Zheng, J., Patel, V.M., et al.: Fisher vector encoded deep convolutional features for unconstrained face verification. In: IEEE International Conference on Image Processing (2016)
38. Peng, X., Yu, X., Sohn, K., et al.: Reconstruction-based disentanglement for pose-invariant face recognition. arXiv preprint arXiv:1702.03041 (2017)
39. Deng, J., Cheng, S., Xue, N., et al: UV-GAN: adversarial facial UV map completion for pose-invariant face recognition. arXiv preprint arXiv:1712.04695 (2017)

The Impact of Data Correlation on Identification of Computer-Generated Face Images

Taifeng Tan[1,2], Xin Wang[1], Yuchun Fang[1(✉)], and Wei Zhang[1]

[1] School of Computer Engineering and Science, Shanghai University, Shanghai, China
ycfang@shu.edu.cn

[2] The College of Information Engineering of Xiangtan University, Xiangtan, China

Abstract. The traditional image discriminating methods can accurately identify forged pictures generated by splicing, tampering, etc. But most methods cannot identify the forged pictures generated by the GAN models. In this paper, we specially explore to identify forged face created with the GAN models. Our target is to analyze the effect of data correlation on identification of computer created face images. In this work, we mainly test on false face datasets generated by StyleGAN and DCGAN. Both datasets are divided into two experimental control groups. We use the convolutional neural network models such as ResNet-18, VGG, and GoogLeNet to perform classification experiments on the control experimental groups. The results show that the models used in this paper can accurately distinguish the real faces and the forged faces generated with GAN. The validation analysis shows that the data correlation has a low influence on identification of forged faces with specific models.

Keywords: Neural networks · Face identification · Data correlation · Generative Adversarial Networks

1 Introduction

Interests in the use of biological signals have been rapidly growing in the past decades. Personal privacy is particularly important on the social networking platform. Biometrics-based recognition has become a hotspot. Fingerprints [1], irises, retinas, faces [2] and even odors [3] are all used to identify individual traits, which are known as biometrics. Among them, face plays an essential role in many different applications, such as access control and other means of authentication.

Derived from the branch of artificial neural networks in machine learning, the deep learning algorithms achieve the purpose of machine intelligence that is initially guaranteed by simulating the human brain. Particularly, there have been many face researches on Generative Adversarial Networks (GAN), including style migration, image restoration, etc. These research directions are inseparable from the excellent extraction effect of deep learning on facial features. With the development of deep learning, the methods based on the neural networks become more and more effective.

Z. Sun et al. (Eds.): CCBR 2019, LNCS 11818, pp. 155–162, 2019.
https://doi.org/10.1007/978-3-030-31456-9_17

Dang-Nguyen et al. [4] proposed a model for facial expression analysis, which distinguished computer-generated faces and natural faces by using neural networks. Peng et al. [5] found that the pulse signal generated by the human body in the activity could produce effects in the detection field. They identified the real content in the video containing face through checking the frequency waveform of the extracted pulse signal and the computer graphics [5]. Bayar and Stamm [6] found that most of the Convolutional Neural Networks (CNN) currently in use learned to capture features of image content rather than forged detection features as dominant features. They developed a new CNN architecture to suppress the content of images, and the model could adaptively learn the operation detection function from training data [6]. Cai et al. [7] chose a probabilistic cooperative representation classifier (ProCRC), which was innovative in the identification algorithm. Rao and Ni [8] used the convolutional neural network to learn the hierarchical representation of the input RGB color images automatically. The proposed CNN architecture was specially designed for detecting image stitching and copy-move [8]. Zhou et al. [9] proposed a two-stream network for facial tamper detection. The first stream GoogLeNet detected tampering artifacts in the facial identification stream, and the second stream of patch-based triple network captured local noise residuals and vectors of camera features [9]. Raghavendra et al. [10] used the transferable features of pre-trained deep convolutional neural networks to detect digital images and scanned faces. Rahmouni et al. [11] presented a new CNN model to distinguish between computer-generated images and real photographic images. Tariq et al. [12] proposed using the classifiers based on neural networks to detect false faces created by machines and created by humans.

Previous researches on identifying forged faces have shown the feasibility of the technologies in several aspects. Leykin and Cutzu [13] found that the forged images had more pronounced color-only edges by analyzing the image intensity and the color of the edges of the images. Huang and Long [14] discriminated the images by recognizing the demosaicing correlation of real images and forged images. Wang et al. [15] divided the tested image into non-overlapping blocks. They extracted features to each block with both discrete cosine transform (DCT) and discrete wavelet transform (DWT). The statistics of the image block is used to compare the copy areas [15]. Wang and Xuan [16] adopted a local blur estimation at each edge pixel of the image to expose the defocus blur inconsistency and thereby reveal the traces of tampering.

The previous researches concentrate on the accuracy of identification, time complexity, redundancy reduction, and reliability of algorithms. With the development of GAN models, more and more forged faces can be created easily based on any source datasets. However, it is interesting to explore how the correlation between source datasets and the forged datasets will affect the identification algorithms. In this paper, we perform tests for data correlation on controlled datasets. Based on transfer learning, the CNN models such as Residual Neural Network (ResNet), VGG, and Google Inception Net (GoogLeNet) are used to perform forged face identification on the experimental groups. The identification models are affected more by the content of the forged faces than by the data-independent face identification. Moreover, the data correlation has no noticeable impact on identifying forged faces.

2 Method

2.1 Framework of Forged Face Identification

To analyze the influence of data correlation to forged image identification, we design a framework shown in Fig. 1. As any general classification system, the framework consists of the training and testing stages. In the flow chart, both training and testing processes consist of data preprocessing. The training of neural network models aims at optimizing the parameters for feature annotation. In the testing stage, the final decision is the output of the best model based on the process of model selection. The correlation analysis is realized through model adjustment and transfer learning across databases.

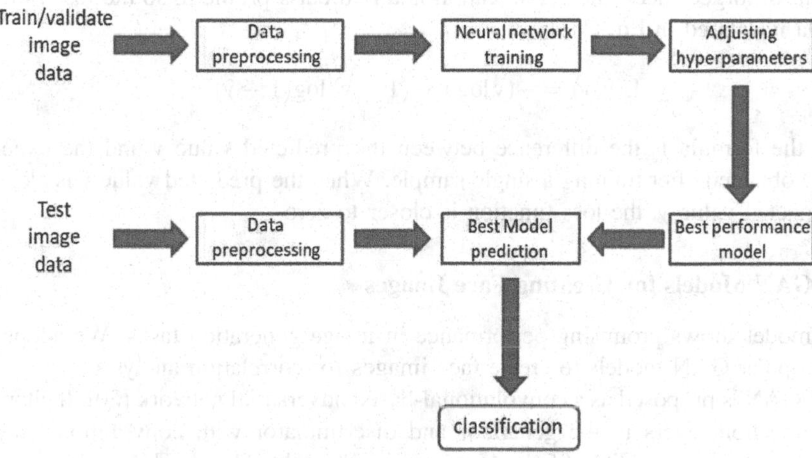

Fig. 1. The framework of forged face identification.

2.2 The Architecture of Neural Network Models

We adopt three types of basic neural network models in our work, namely ResNet-18, VGG-16 and GoogLeNet (Inception V3).

ResNet-18, an 18-layer residual network [17], is one of the ResNet series networks. With the residual blocks, the ResNet-18 can learn the residual portion of the previous layers instead of learning only from the original output. Shortcuts are added to ensure the robustness of information transmission.

Simonyan et al. [18] proposed VGGNet focusing on building convolutional layers. VGG-16 is one of the versions that use a continuous convolutional layer. The convolution layers of VGG-16 need to retain fewer parameters than those in other models. The adjusting of parameters of VGG-16 mainly concentrates on the three fully connected layers. Hence, the training process is fast.

GoogLeNet has several variations and contains filters of different sizes [19]. The multi-scale filters are spliced and fused. The network automatically chooses whether to use convolution or pooling. We adopt the third version of GoogLeNet, which splits a large two-dimensional convolution into two smaller one-dimensional convolutions. Hence, the parameters are significantly reduced and the operation is faster.

2.3 The Training of Models

We classify the extracted features with the basic networks and compare their identification effect with the simple cross-entropy classifier.

The initial value of the hyperparameter learning rate α is 0.001, which gradually decreases with the increase of the number of iterations epoch. The learning rate is one-tenth of every seven iterations. The number of epoch is set to 25. At the same time, the normalized mean and standard deviation parameters are sampled from the Imagenet.

The loss function of the three basic networks is the cross-entropy. For identification problem of forged faces, the classification is a two-class problem, so the loss function formula is defined in Eq. (1).

$$\mathrm{L}(\hat{y}, y) = -(y \log \hat{y} + (1 - y) \log(1 - \hat{y})). \tag{1}$$

where the formula is the difference between the predicted value $\hat{y}$ and the expected value y obtained after training a single sample. When the predicted value $\hat{y}$ is closer to the expected value y, the loss function is closer to zero.

2.4 GAN Models for Creating Face Images

GAN model shows promising performance in image generation tasks. We adopt two most popular GAN models to create face images for correlation analysis.

DCGAN is proposed as a convolutional-based adversarial network [20]. It alters the full-connection layers in the generator and discriminator with convolutional layers, which improves the quality of forged images significantly. The training tricks for stable adversarial training of DCGAN are practical to avoid the model collapse in GANs training.

The forged images always present some visual drawbacks that can be distinguished by human observers. StyleGAN is proposed as a style-based generator based on progressive network architecture [21]. The generator of StyleGAN adds style information to the generator progressively so that most of the image style information can be inserted into feature maps in a different scale. Besides, the style-generator utilizes the mapping networks and the adaptive instance normalization to detangle attribute features and enhance feature representation.

3 Experiment

We conduct control experiments on a total of three data sets to test the impact of data correlation on face identification.

3.1 Dataset Sources and Data Preprocessing

CelebA is from the Chinese University of Hong Kong[1], including open source images. The pictures are all clear face or side face images above the neck. This article does not consider the properties of the CelebA data set. Only the image itself is used as the real face set to experiment. In our laboratory, some false faces generated by DCGAN can be obtained as an experimental group using the CelebA real faces as the raw images. By extracting the features of different face images, Google has obtained a lot of generated faces and open source display these face images on the website[2]. In this paper, we use the false face images as a control experiment object, and obtain a total of 2,000 face images from the site. These images are all different, and they have been manually screened, eliminating the fact that the background portion is too mismatched to make it extremely easy to identify.

The data set of this article has two control groups. The group A includes the CelebA and the false faces generated by Google using StyleGAN. Also, group B consists of the CelebA real face data set and false faces created by DCGAN that the raw images of false faces are CelebA.

Each group contains 2000 real faces and 2000 false faces, a total of 4,000. Since the number of experimental data is small, we use the classic ratio which train set/validate set/test set is 6: 2: 2. For example, 1200 real faces and 1200 fake faces for each group are used for training.

The size of the image data is not uniform. Different image sizes cannot be used uniformly for image processing operations. Meanwhile, the face area is cropped to ensure that the face features are preserved as much as possible. The center crop is performed on CelebA images and Google images, as shown in Fig. 2.

Fig. 2. CelebA real faces and StyleGAN false faces cropping.

3.2 Results and Analysis

To explore the impact of data correlation on face identification, we use three different neural networks for testing and use training time and final identification average accuracy as the evaluation criterion. We use Figs. 3 and 4 to show the validating loss during training.

For loss, when the same experimental group used different models for training, the overall loss function values of the three models are not large. Only the verification loss

[1] http://mmlab.ie.cuhk.edu.hk/projects/CelebA.html.

[2] https://thispersondoesnotexist.com/.

value of GoogLeNet is larger and more unstable than the other models. It can be seen that the cross-entropy loss function can be applied to any experimental group, which proves the applicability of neural network identification in this experiment. When the same model was used for training in different experimental groups, the ResNet-18 model and the VGG-16 model of group A and group B are both stable, and the losses were low. The group B of the GoogLeNet model is better than group A. It is concluded that the GoogLeNet model has a reduced verification loss as the data correlation increases.

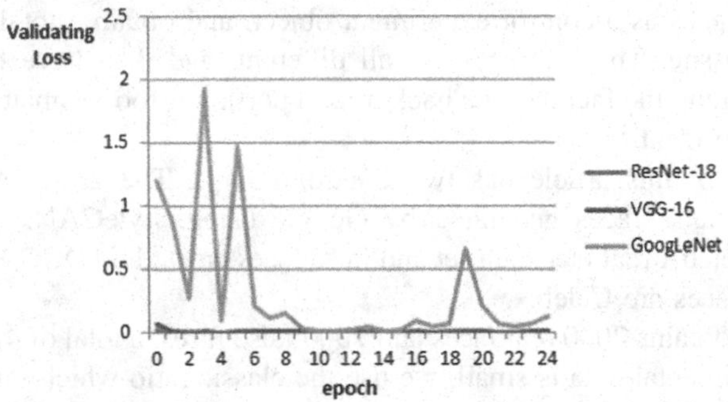

Fig. 3. Loss function line chart of group A.

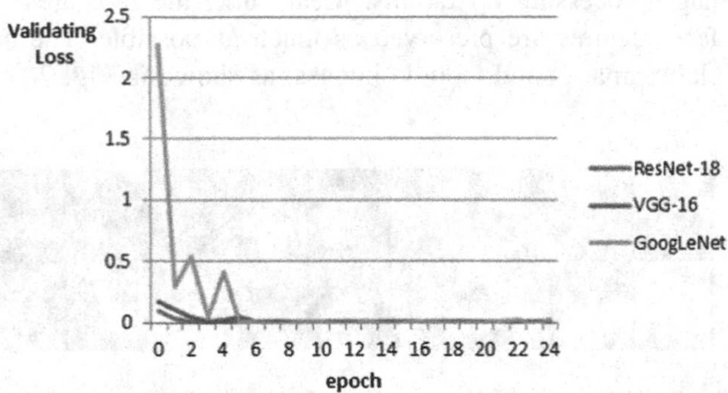

Fig. 4. Loss function line chart of group B.

We summarize the results in Table 1, including training time and average accuracy. From the results, we can obtain the following observations. Firstly, the training time of the same experimental group is different when using different networks. The training time of ResNet-18 is the shortest, and the VGG-16 and GoogLeNet training time are not much different. The reason for the shortest training time of ResNet is because the residual network structure dramatically reduces the training time under the same amount of data. When the same network is used for training in different experimental groups, the training time difference is within 2 min. It is concluded that the difference in data correlation has little effect on the training time of the experiment. Considering the average testing accuracy of identification, the same experimental group used different networks for training. The best identification accuracy network for the two groups is ResNet-18, but the overall gap is not large, both reaching more than 96%. Therefore, the famous neural network methods can be used for identifying forged faces. The results and conclusions for face identification are authentic. Three models are applied to our two experimental groups, and the results are all the better in the B experimental group than in the A experimental group. However, it can be seen that the overall difference is not large. Hence, under the training of these three models, data correlation has little effect on face image identification.

Table 1. Different data correlation results of test sets.

Test set	Method	Training time (min)	Average testing accuracy
Group A	ResNet-18	16.53	98% ± 1%
	VGG-16	54.35	98% ± 1%
	GoogLeNet	49.15	97% ± 1%
Group B	ResNet-18	16.85	98% ± 1%
	VGG-16	52.45	98% ± 1%
	GoogLeNet	51.40	98% ± 1%

Although we experiment with two data sets with different correlation, it could not guarantee whether the original resolution of the image will affect the identification accuracy. If the resolution is too high or too low, it may cause identification problems.

4 Conclusion

In this paper, the face images generated by generative adversarial networks and real faces are classified. And the identification results are analyzed. The influence of the data correlation on the face identification is discussed. In addition to the widely used CelebA face dataset, we get reliable two false faces with different data correlation through our laboratory generation and the website. These images are divided into two experimental groups and apply to three neural networks widely used for face identification currently. The results show that the experimental model used in this paper can accurately distinguish the real face and the face generated based on GAN. Moreover, the data correlation has a lower influence on image identification when using specific models. In addition to the training model used in this article, there may be more different results shown in different models. Extension of this research is necessary in the future.

References

1. Cao, K., Yang, X., Chen, X., et al.: A novel ant colony optimization algorithm for large-distorted fingerprint matching. Pattern Recogn. **45**(1), 151–161 (2012)
2. Shin, A., Lee, S.W., Bulthoff, H., et al.: A morphable 3D-model of Korean faces. In: IEEE International Conference on Systems. IEEE (2012)

3. O'Dwyer, T.W., Nevitt, G.A.: Individual odor recognition in procellariiform chicks: potential role for the major histocompatibility complex. Ann. N. Y. Acad. Sci. **1170**(1), 442–446 (2010)
4. Dang-Nguyen, D.T., Boato, G., Natale, F.D.G.B.: Identify computer generated characters by analysing facial expressions variation. In: WIFS. IEEE (2012)
5. Peng, B., Wang, W., Dong, J., et al.: Detection of computer generated faces in videos based on pulse signal. In: IEEE China Summit & International Conference on Signal and Information Processing. IEEE (2015)
6. Bayar, B., Stamm, M.C.: A deep learning approach to universal image manipulation detection using a new convolutional layer. In: The 4th ACM Workshop. ACM (2016)
7. Cai, S., Zhang, L., Zuo, W., et al.: A probabilistic collaborative representation based approach for pattern classification. In: 2016 IEEE Conference on Computer Vision and Pattern Recognition (CVPR). IEEE Computer Society (2016)
8. Rao, Y., Ni, J.: A deep learning approach to detection of splicing and copy-move forgeries in images. In: 2016 IEEE International Workshop on Information Forensics and Security (WIFS). IEEE (2016)
9. Zhou, P., Han, X., Morariu, V.I., et al.: Two-stream neural networks for tampered face detection (2018)
10. Raghavendra, R., Raja, K.B., Venkatesh, S., et al.: Transferable deep-CNN features for detecting digital and print-scanned morphed face images. In: CVPRW. IEEE Computer Society (2017)
11. Rahmouni, N., Nozick, V., Yamagishi, J., et al.: Distinguishing computer graphics from natural images using convolution neural networks. In: Information Forensics and Security. IEEE (2018)
12. Tariq, S., Lee, S., Kim, H., et al.: Detecting both machine and human created fake face images in the wild. In: Proceedings of the 2nd International Workshop on Multimedia Privacy and Security - MPS 2018, Toronto, Canada, 15–19 October 2018, pp. 81–87 (2018)
13. Alex Leykin, F.C.: Differences of edge properties in photographs and paintings. In: International Conference on Image Processing. IEEE (2003)
14. Huang, Y.: Demosaicing recognition with applications in digital photo authentication based on a quadratic pixel correlation model. In: IEEE Conference on Computer Vision and Pattern Recognition. IEEE (2008)
15. Wang, X., Zhang, X., Li, Z., et al.: A DWT-DCT based passive forensics method for copy-move attacks. In: Third International Conference on Multimedia Information Networking and Security. IEEE (2011)
16. Wang, X., Xuan, B., Peng, S.L.: Digital image forgery detection based on the consistency of defocus blur. In: International Conference on Intelligent Information Hiding and Multimedia Signal Processing. IEEE Computer Society (2008)
17. He, K., Zhang, X., Ren, S., et al.: deep residual learning for image recognition (2015)
18. Simonyan, K., Zisserman, A.: Very deep convolutional networks for large-scale image recognition. Computer Science (2014)
19. Szegedy, C., Liu, W., Jia, Y., et al.: Going deeper with convolutions. In: 2015 IEEE Conference on Computer Vision and Pattern Recognition (CVPR). IEEE (2015)
20. Yu, Y., Gong, Z., Zhong, P., Shan, J.: Unsupervised representation learning with deep convolutional neural network for remote sensing images. In: Zhao, Y., Kong, X., Taubman, D. (eds.) ICIG 2017. LNCS, vol. 10667, pp. 97–108. Springer, Cham (2017). https://doi.org/10.1007/978-3-319-71589-6_9
21. Karras, T., Laine, S., Aila, T.: A style-based generator architecture for generative adversarial networks. In: Proceedings of the IEEE Conference on Computer Vision and Pattern Recognition, pp. 4401–4410 (2019)

Face Image Deblurring Based on Iterative Spiral Optimazation

Yukun Ma[1(✉)], Yaowen Xu[2], Lifang Wu[2], Tao Xu[1], Xin Zhao[3], and Lei Cai[1]

[1] School of Artificial Intelligence, Henan Institute of Science and Technology, Xinxiang 453003, Henan, China
yukuner@126.com, xutao@hist.edu.cn, cailei2014@126.com
[2] Faculty of Information Technology, Beijing University of Technology, Beijing 100124, China
xuyao_wen@126.com, lfwu@bjut.edu.cn
[3] School of Information and Engineering, Henan Institute of Science and Technology, Xinxiang 453003, Henan, China
314965740@qq.com

Abstract. The motion blurred image is caused by the relative motion between the target and the capturing device during the exposure time. It's difficult to analyze the face information of the motion blurred face image, therefore motion deblurring is needed. However, the existing algorithms cannot deal with the diversity of motion blur kernels well. Based on that, this paper proposes an iterative spiral optimization algorithm for blind motion blurring. The algorithm makes the blurred image spirally approximate the sharp image by calling the deblurring generator multiple times. It is proved that the algorithm can effectively restore the motion blurred image with diverse blurred kernels in the approximate natural state, and improve the visual effect of the image.

Keywords: Iterative spiral optimization · Generative Adversarial Network · Motion blur · Image blind restoration

1 Introduction

In recent years, face recognition technology [1] has been widely used in various fields. However, in the stage of image acquisition, due to the machine shake [2] or positional movement with the target, the captured images are usually motion blurred [3], which are more common in surveillance video. Deblurring can improve the accuracy of image information extraction to the benefit of subsequent analysis.

Due to the diversity of blurred kernels, the existing deblurring models cannot deal with all kinds of blurred images accurately. To make the restored image closer to the sharp image when the diverse blurred kernel is unknown, an iterative spiral optimization-based algorithm is proposed in this paper. Proposed method builds a GAN-based deblurring model, and the output of the deblurring model is input into the model iteratively, then compared with the first output, the restored image can approximate the sharp image spirally spirally (Fig. 1).

Z. Sun et al. (Eds.): CCBR 2019, LNCS 11818, pp. 163–170, 2019.
https://doi.org/10.1007/978-3-030-31456-9_18

Main contributions of this paper are as follows:

(1) On the GAN framework, an iterative spiral optimization-based method is proposed. It can effectively restore the motion blurred face image;
(2) Applying the proposed method on the motion blurred image generated with both the averaging and natural random kernels, the experimental results show that the proposed method perform well in two kinds of motion blurred images.

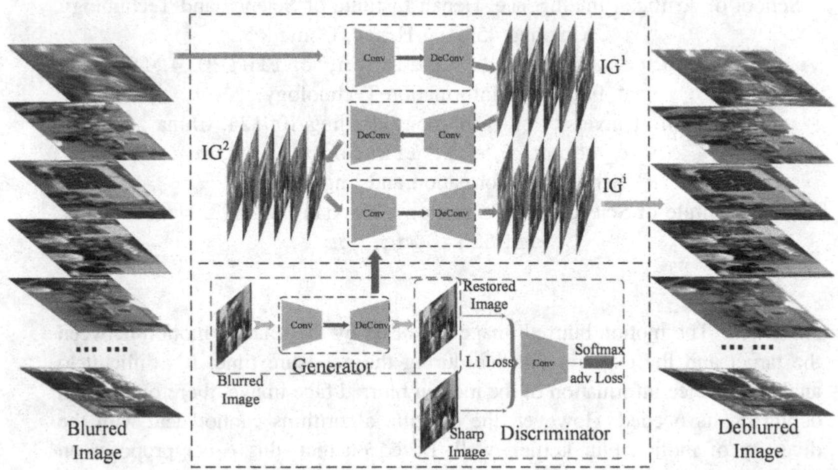

Fig. 1. The algorithm schematic diagram. In order to restore the input blurred images, the GAN-based algorithm is designed. The generator is used to approach the sharp images spirally and iteratively.

2 Related Work

The restoration method of motion blurred image can be divided into non-blind restoration and blind restoration algorithm according to the different grasping conditions of blurred kernel [4]. The non-blind restoration algorithm refers to the restoration when blurred kernel is known. This kind algorithm can get a satisfied effect, but the blurred kernel is unknown in most cases. So, the blind restoration algorithm [5] is needed. It mainly estimates the blurred kernel by transforming the blurred image into spatial matrix, and the space transformation matrix are used as the parameters of the blurred kernel to restore the image.

In recent years, deep learning was widely used because of its capability of feature extraction. In recent years, there were several works that applying deep learning on image blind motion deblurring. Ren et al. [6] used the combination of Convolutional Neural Networks (CNN) and Fourier domain for image blind restoration, which was the first deblurring work based on deep learning. Nah et al. studied a spatially variable cyclic neural network that performs blind restoration by combining CNN with the Recurrent Neural Network (RNN) [7]. Zhang et al. combined a code-decoding residual network block with convolutional neural networks to propose a scaled-loop network that greatly simplified the network training process [8]. The birth of Generative Adversarial Networks (GAN) [9] brought a new technical solution for deblurring, because image deblurring is a special case of image-to-image.

Based on the above analysis, we can see that the blind deblurring methods combined with deep learning can be divided into two categories. One is the blind image restoration algorithm based on the blurred kernel estimation [10], which extract blurred kernel information automatically with the deep learning method. Secondly, the end-to-end blind image restoration algorithm completely ignores the blurred kernel [11–13], and uses conditional GAN in most cases.

Because of the diversity of blurred kernels, the single deep learning model cannot deal with all kinds of blurred images accurately, but can only make the restored image closer to the sharp image. So, the problem is how to get the restored image closer and closer to the sharp image in the absence of dealing with the diverse blurred kernel well.

3 The Proposed Algorithm

3.1 Iterative Spiral Optimization

Iterative Spiral Optimization deblurring means that the output of the model is input into the model iteratively, then compared with the first output, the restored image will be much closer to the sharp image. The starting position of spiral optimization represents the blurred image, and the target position of the spiral is the sharp image. The optimization is shown in Fig. 2

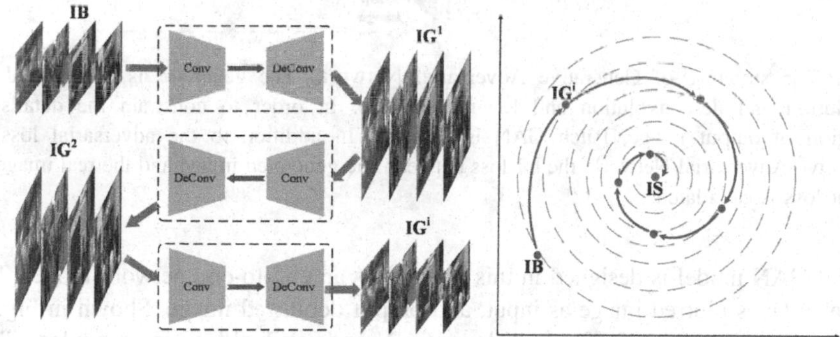

Fig. 2. Iterative spiral optimization. Initially, the blurred image is input into the network, and the output image is input into the generator network again. The process is cycled until the restored image approaches the sharp image.

The trained network is used as the basic model of spiral optimization, and its parameters are fixed. The blurred image IB is input into the network at the first execution to generate the restoration image IG^1, and the IG^1 is called again as the input of the network. After i cycles, the restored image IG^i will approximate the sharp image IS infinitely. In this process, the generated image IG^i is always centered on the sharp image *IS*, and the distance to *IS* is getting closer and closer, so the optimization process from *IB* to *IS* is spiral.

3.2 Model Structure

We use the deblurring algorithm based on GAN in this paper. GAN can learn the probability distribution of pixels in sharp image and generate data samples similar to sharp image. If the discriminator can't classify the generated image accurately, the training is completed, and then the generator can simulate the distribution of sharp image. Then the generator is saved as the deblurring model. The schematic diagram is shown in Fig. 3.

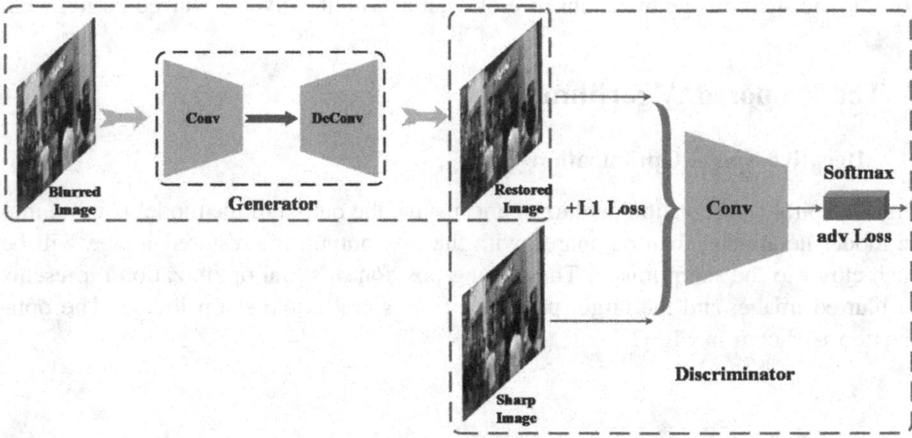

Fig. 3. The structure of Generative Adversarial Network. The generator is constructed by convolution and de-convolution and Res-net module. In order to constrain the details in subregion of output image, Patch GAN is adopted. In addition to the adversarial loss of Generative Adversarial Network, the L1 loss between the generated image and the real image as content loss is calculated.

The GAN model is designed in this method as an end-to-end network model. The generator takes blurred image as input, and output deblurred image. Shown in Fig. 4, the generator is composed of a multi-layer CNN and residual learning modules. CNN can extract features of an image, which generally consists of an input layer, convolutional layers, pooling layers, activation layers, and an output layer. After learning through multiple residual learning modules, the features are extracted, and the deconvolutional layers are used to output restored image. When the GAN reaches the Nash equilibrium, it can be considered that the generator has learned the probability distribution of the sharp image.

The discriminator model is to judge whether the generator can generate a restored image with similar content in the sharp image. In order to generate images with better local detail information, Patch GAN structure is used as the discriminator [14–16]. The structure of the discriminator is shown in Table 1.

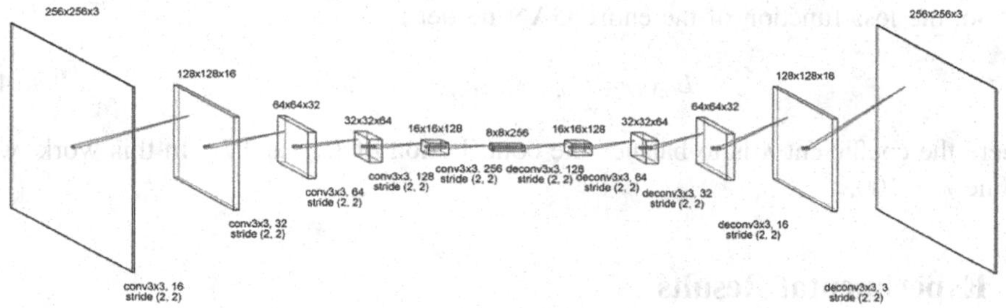

Fig. 4. The detailed structure of the generator

Table 1. The structure of the discriminator.

Output Size	Layers
256 × 256 × 3	Input images
128 × 128 × 64	4 × 4 CONV, stride = 2, padding = 2, Leaky ReLU
64 × 64 × 128	4 × 4 CONV, stride = 2, padding = 2, Leaky ReLU
32 × 32 × 256	4 × 4 CONV, stride = 2, padding = 2, Leaky ReLU
32 × 32 × 512	4 × 4 CONV, stride = 1, padding = 2, Leaky ReLU
32 × 32 × 1	4 × 4 CONV, stride = 1, padding = 2, Leaky ReLU

3.3 Loss Function

The basic structure of the model is composed of a generator and a Patch GAN discriminator, so the loss function contains the adversarial loss and the perceived loss.

The adversarial loss function in GAN is:

$$L_{adv} = p_{IS}(-\log(D(IS))) + p_{IB}(-\log(1 - D(G(IB)))) \quad (1)$$

Where *IS* represents a sharp image, *p* represents probability. If the input of discriminator is sharp image, $p_{IS} = 1$, $p_{IB} = 0$, else when the input of discriminator is a restored image, $p_{IS} = 0$, $p_{IB} = 1$. *G* is the generator, *G(IB)* is the restored image while input blurred image *IB*, *D* represents the prediction probability of discriminator. Because the discriminator network is a Patch GAN model in this paper, the adversarial loss function is actually:

$$L_{adv-PatchGAN} = \sum\nolimits_{n=1}^{N} L_{adv}(n) \quad (2)$$

Here, suppose the Patch GAN has *N* patches totally, and $L_{adv}(n)$ means the adversarial loss of *n*-th patch, which is calculated as formula (1).

At the same time, in order to make the generator fit the probability distribution of *IS*, the content loss between IG^1 and *IS* is introduced as follow:

$$L_c = \left\| IG^1(x, y) - IS(x, y) \right\| \quad (3)$$

So, the loss function of the entire GAN model is:

$$L_{GAN} = L_{adv-PatchGAN} + \lambda \cdot L_c \tag{4}$$

where the coefficient λ is to balance the contribution of L_{adv} and L_c. In this work, we define $\lambda = 100$.

4 Experimental Results

4.1 Database and Pre-processing

We use the GoPro database [7] in our experiments, which is a video frame in high-speed video captured by a GoPro camera. The training set uses the GoPro_Large database, which consists of 3,214 sharp-blurred image pairs (2103 pairs of training data and 1111 pairs of test data). The GoPro_Small database (containing 1000 pairs of sharp-blurred image pairs) was used as test set. At the same time, the Labeled Faces in the Wild (LFW) database [1] was used to test the generalization ability of the proposed method in face deblurring.

Because LFW database has not sharp-blurred image pairs, we generate the blurred kernel by a Markov random process, and the blurred image can be obtained by the convolution of sharp image and random blurred kernel [11].

In the network model training process, the blurred images in the database were randomly clipped into 256 × 256 pixels size as the GAN model input sample, which are also as the initial input sample of the iterative optimization of the generator.

4.2 Experimental Setup

The implementation of this algorithm is based on the PyTorch deep learning framework in the Ubuntu Server 18.04 operating system. The training and verification of algorithm in the experiment are performed on two Intel Xeon E5-2640 CPU and one NVIDA Tesla K40c GPU. The initial learning rate was set to 1×10^{-4}. After 180 epochs, the learning rate was linearly attenuated, and the attenuation coefficient was 0.9 for each 30 epochs. The total number of epochs was 300. In the experiment, the choice of optimizer was the adaptive moment estimation optimization strategy, namely Adam optimization algorithm [17].

4.3 Result

Figure 5 shows the experimental comparison of iterative spiral optimization algorithm. The line *IB* means blurred images, line IG^1 means the first output of the deblurring model with blurred image input, line IG^{10} means the output of the spiral optimization after calling the model 10 times, and line *IS* means the sharp images. Figure 5(a) shows the experimental results in the GoPro database, and Fig. 5(b) shows the test results in the LFW database. It can be found that the visual effect of IG^{10} has been significantly improved compared with IG^1, and the sharp image is gradually approached after iterative invocation.

(a) GoPro Database (b) LFW Database

Fig. 5. The experimental comparison of iterative spiral optimization algorithm.

5 Conclusion

In this paper, an iterative spiral optimization image deblurring algorithm based on GAN was proposed. In the restoration process of blurred image, the trained network was used multiple times, so that the restored image approximates the sharp image spirally. The proposed algorithm uses the end-to-end method, and doesn't need to estimate the blurred kernel, so it directly inputs the blurred image to model and outputs restored image. This method improves the blind recovery effect of the image to some extent for different blurred kernels. The only fly in the ointment is that some low-frequency noise is introduced into the restored image while enhancing the edge information. The next research will focus on how to remove low-frequency noise from the restored image to improve the efficiency and robustness of the algorithm.

Acknowledgments. This research was financially supported by the Science and Technology Foundation of Henan Province of China (182102210302), Research Foundation for Talented Scholars of Henan Institute of Science and Technology, National Natural Science Foundation of China (61703143), Science and Technology Project of Henan Province (192102310260), Scientific and Technological Innovation Talents in Xinxiang (CXRC17004), young backbone teacher training project of Henan University (2017GGJS123), and Science and Technology Major Special Project of Xinxiang City (ZD18006).

References

1. Huang, G.B., Ramesh, M., Berg, T., Learned-Miller, E.: Labeled faces in the wild: a database for studying face recognition in unconstrained environments. Technical report 07-49, University of Massachusetts, Amherst, October, 2007
2. Ji, Y., Liu, G., Chen, T., et al.: Classical restoration algorithm for motion blurred images. J. Southwest Univ. (Nat. Sci. Ed.) **40**(8), 168–177 (2018). (in Chinese)
3. Wang, S.: An image blind motion deblurring method. Dalian University of Technology (2018). (in Chinese)

4. Liu, G., Bodi, W., Jian, H., et al.: Research progress and prospect of motion blurred image restoration technology. Laser Mag. **4**, 1–8 (2019)
5. Jun, Z., Sen, H.: Comparison of two improved methods for detecting motion blur angle. Opt. Instrum. **41**, 218–226 (2019). (in Chinese)
6. Ren, J., Fang, X., Chen, S., et al.: Image deblurring based on fast convolution neural network. J. Comput. Aided Des. Graph. **8**, 1444–1456 (2017). (in Chinese)
7. Nah, S., Kim, T.H., Lee, K.M.: Deep multi-scale convolutional neural network for dynamic scene deblurring. In: Computer Vision and Pattern Recognition, vol. 1, no. 2, pp. 3883–3891 (2017)
8. Zhang, J., Pan, J., Ren, J., et al.: Dynamic scene deblurring using spatially variant recurrent neural networks. In: IEEE Conference on Computer Vision and Pattern Recognition, pp. 2521–2529 (2018)
9. Tao, X., Gao, H., Wang, Y., et al.: Scale-recurrent network for deep image deblurring. In: IEEE Conference on Computer Vision and Pattern Recognition, pp. 1–9 (2018)
10. Goodfellow, I.J., Pouget-Abadie, J., Mirza, M., et al.: Generative adversarial nets. In: International Conference on Neural Information Processing Systems, pp. 1–9 (2014)
11. Kupyn, O., Budzan, V., Mykhailych, M., et al.: DeblurGAN: blind motion deblurring using conditional adversarial networks. In: IEEE Conference on Computer Vision and Pattern Recognition, pp. 1–10 (2017)
12. Isola, P., Zhu, J.Y., Zhou, T., et al.: Image-to-image translation with conditional adversarial networks. In: IEEE Conference on Computer Vision and Pattern Recognition, pp. 5967–5976 (2017)
13. Radford, A., Metz, L., Chintala, S.: Unsupervised representation learning with deep convolutional generative adversarial networks. In: International Conference on Learning Representation (2016)
14. Zhu, J.-Y., Krähenbühl, P., Shechtman, E., Efros, A.A.: Generative visual manipulation on the natural image manifold. In: Leibe, B., Matas, J., Sebe, N., Welling, M. (eds.) ECCV 2016. LNCS, vol. 9909, pp. 597–613. Springer, Cham (2016). https://doi.org/10.1007/978-3-319-46454-1_36
15. Zhu, J.-Y., Park, T., Isola, P., Efros, A.: Unpaired image-to-image translation using cycle-consistent adversarial networks. In: International Conference on Computer Vision, pp. 2223–2232 (2017)
16. Xiao, H., Feng, J., Lin, G., Liu, Y., Zhang, M.: MoNet: deep motion exploitation for video object segmentation. In: IEEE Conference on Computer Vision and Pattern Recognition, pp. 1140–1148 (2018)
17. Kingma, D.P., Ba, J.: Adam: a method for stochastic optimization. In: International Conference on Learning Representation, pp. 1–15 (2016)

AdaptiveNet: Toward an Efficient Face Alignment Algorithm

Xiehe Huang and Weihong Deng(✉)

School of Information and Communication Engineering,
Beijing University of Posts and Telecommunication, Beijing, China
{xiehe.huang,whdeng}@bupt.edu.cn

Abstract. Face alignment, a challenging task in computer vision, has witnessed its tremendous improvement on the 300W benchmark. However, state-of-the-art algorithms are suffering from computational expense and therefore cannot apply in real-time. In this paper, we propose a time-efficient face alignment algorithm while maintain a sufficient algorithmic accuracy. Specifically, we adopt *MobileNet-V2* as our backbone architecture to deal with easy samples, accompanied by a *ResNet* branch to handle hard examples. This combination leads to a low-latency and yet agreeable-performance design as our extensive experiment shows.

Keywords: Face alignment · Time-efficient · MobileNet · ResNet

1 Introduction

Face alignment, a.k.a. facial landmark detection, serves as an essential role in many face analysis applications, including face verification and recognition [1], face morphing [2], expression recognition [3], and 3D face reconstruction [4]. More and more fancy face alignment algorithms have been emerging to handle the task and achieved considerable performance on various datasets.

MobileNetV2 [5], thanks to its tiny model size and low computational cost, is best adapted to practical applications such as face alignment and object detection. It proposes a novel layer module, *i.e.* the inverted residual with linear bottleneck, that can reduce the memory footprint needed for inference. Moreover, it can be further optimized by quantization.

Referred to as an **easy branch** in our work, a MobileNetV2 architecture is applied to predict the landmarks of easy face image samples, whereas a ResNet [6] branch is meant to predict those of hard samples when it is beyond the easy branch's capability. We also add an easy sample indicator (or a confidence score) to suggest whether the prediction of the easy branch is convincingly accurate. If the prediction is shown to be acceptable, we go with the easy branch. Otherwise, we choose that of the **hard branch** as the final result.

Face alignment undergoes the same problem data imbalance as with many other tasks, where a dataset often shows an unbalancing distribution among

Z. Sun et al. (Eds.): CCBR 2019, LNCS 11818, pp. 171–179, 2019.
https://doi.org/10.1007/978-3-030-31456-9_19

classes or attributes. Besides, a takeaway L2 loss tends to minimize loss over a whole set of landmarks and therefore become sensitive to outliers. So we must go for a carefully designed loss function if we want every point to be exactly in their supposed position. To address all these issues, we design a novel loss function, termed as **combinational wing loss**. It makes network branches to work in tandem and to train in an end-to-end fashion.

2 Related Work

Traditional methods such as ASM [7], AAM [8], CLM [9] and their variations seek to obtain a descriptor that can represent local features so as to locate facial landmarks using heuristic rules. Inspired by previous work of coarse-to-fine regression models [10], cascaded regression models (CRM) [11–13] have been popular during the first few years when deep learning began to prevail in computer vision. Replacing classic machine learning algorithms with convolutional neural network (CNN) and refining keypoint coordinates step by step (or even facial-part-wise), CRMs prove themselves to outperform traditional methods and one of them, MTCNN [14], is still welcomed by many developers. However, they are still far from a robust and accurate landmark localization model when we are confronted with unconstrained face images in the wild impacted by a slew of factors, *e.g.* pose, occlusion, expression, illumination, make-up, blurring, *etc.*

Recently, interest of the field has been largely focusing on two mainstream approaches, *i.e.* coordinate regression and heatmap regression, though with various model designs.

Coordinate regression models attempt to construct a mapping between input face image domain and coordinate domain, a naive and explicit fashion in terms of end-to-end learning. TCDCN [15] thinks learning face attributes can facilitate keypoint localization because these attributes, such as wearing glasses, smiling, and head pose, indicate landmark distribution. Assisted by head pose estimation, Pose-RCPR [16] and PFLD [17] perform face alignment task respectively in separate and combinational way. MDM [18], though in a cascaded form, proposes for the first time to train in an end-to-end way and combat descent direction cancellation and handcrafted features. LAB [19] incorporates facial boundary information as prior knowledge for landmark regressor via attention mechanism.

Heatmap regression models, functioning on the basis of a fully convolution network (FCN), try to maintain structure information throughout the whole network and therefore dwarf coordinate regression models in their state-of-the-art performance. MHM [20] implements face detection and face alignment consecutively and leverages stacked hourglass model to predict landmark heatmaps. Wing [21] and AWing [22] both modify L1 loss to derive so-called wing loss and prove their superiority in CNN-based facial landmark localization.

3 Approach

Intuitively, we want our backbone network, *i.e.* MobileNet, to handle easy samples most of the time, since they dominate a dataset and are most likely to

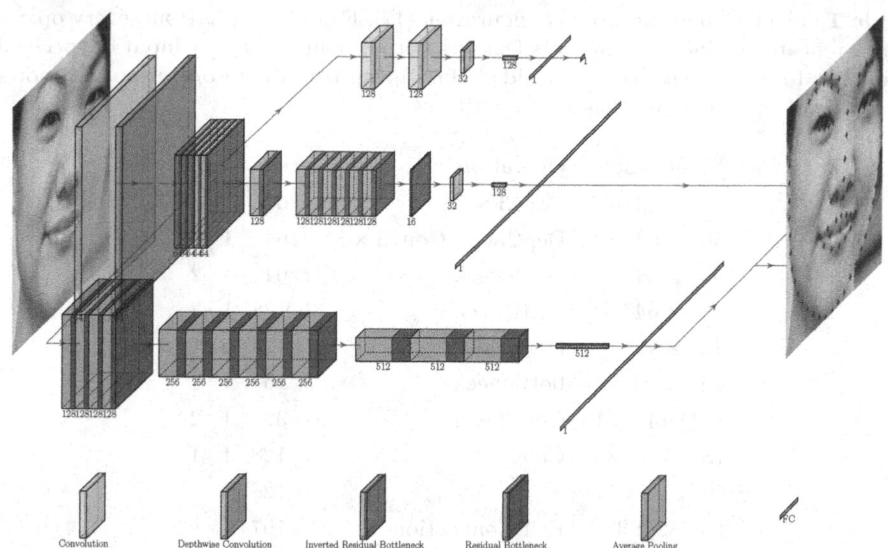

Fig. 1. From left to right, *common sharing layers* extract some low-level features. The *outermost branch*, mainly composed of residual blocks, is what we call a hard branch. The *middle branch* is our backbone easy branch, featured by its bottleneck design. The *innermost branch* is used for head pose estimation and abandoned during inference time. This figure is drawn using PlotNeuralNet [23].

happen in practice. The output of backbone network will be replaced by that of hard branch when hard examples come in. Hence we term our model as **AdaptiveNet**.

But how do we distinguish a face image sample as an easy or hard example? That is, how do we label images when training the model? Since the dataset WFLW [19] we are using in our experiments contains labels of facial attributes, such as head pose, occlusion, and make-up, we have three best candidates for indicating the difficulty of a sample, respectively **learning-based indicator**, **all-attribute indicator**, and **head pose indicator**. After trial and error (which we will formulate in more details in the following experiment section), we propose head pose to measure confidence of easy branch output.

In the following subsections, we will dive deep into our approach in details. First comes the network architecture, as illustrated in Fig. 1 and next is our design of loss function in order to train the network end-to-end.

3.1 Two Runtime Branches

The architectures of two runtime branches are shown in Tables 1 and 2. Similar to most CNN-based models, we first employ a number of convolutional feature extractors to derive some common sharing features and then feed them into different branches. For the backbone branch, we add a full connection unit to predict the confidence score of its output of coordinates.

Table 1. The backbone network configuration [17]. From top to bottom, every operation is repeated n times and outputs features with c channels. Every input of specified shape has to expand channels at t folds before being fed into an operation. s denotes the stride of the first operation of n repetitions.

Input shape	Operation	t	c	n	s
$112^2 \times 3$	Conv3 × 3	–	64	1	2
$56^2 \times 64$	Depthwise Conv3 × 3	–	64	1	1
$56^2 \times 64$	bottleneck	2	64	5	2
$28^2 \times 64$	bottleneck	2	128	1	2
$14^2 \times 128$	bottleneck	4	128	6	1
$14^2 \times 128$	bottleneck	2	16	1	1
(S1) $14^2 \times 16$	Conv3 × 3	–	32	1	2
(S2) $7^2 \times 32$	Conv7 × 7	–	128	1	1
(S3) $1^2 \times 128$	–	–	128	1	–
S1, S2, S3	Full Connection	–	197	1	–

3.2 Head Pose Estimation

Considering almost no facial landmark dataset comes with head pose ground-truth labels, we have to generate the data on ourselves. Concretely, we work with HopeNet [24] pretrained model to obtain the yaw, roll, and pitch angles for every face in WFLW dataset. Since all we need is a coarse estimation of head pose which helps the network learn some information of head pose, an agreeable range of error does not actually affect our model's performance too much. For head pose branch design, we follow PFLD's [17] design, as shown in Table 3.

Table 2. The hard branch configuration. Here we only use conv3_x and beyond blocks specified in a ResNet-34 [6].

Input shape	Operation	s
$56^2 \times 64$	$\begin{bmatrix} 3 \times 3, 128 \\ 3 \times 3, 128 \end{bmatrix} \times 3$	1
$28^2 \times 128$	$\begin{bmatrix} 3 \times 3, 256 \\ 3 \times 3, 256 \end{bmatrix} \times 6$	2
$14^2 \times 256$	$\begin{bmatrix} 3 \times 3, 512 \\ 3 \times 3, 512 \end{bmatrix} \times 3$	2
$7^2 \times 512$	Average pool	–
$1^2 \times 512$	Full Connection	–

3.3 Combinational Wing Loss

Wing loss [21] is basically a variant of smooth L1 loss except that the smooth quadratic curve is replaced by a logarithmic curve. It is piecewise-defined as Eq. (1), where $\Omega = \omega - \omega ln(1 + \omega/\epsilon)$ is a constant and ω and ϵ are hyper-parameters that affect the none-L1 range and the gradient between it.

Table 3. The head pose branch configuration. From top to bottom, input of specified shape is fed to an operation of a stride s and it has output of c channels.

Input shape	Operation	c	s
$28^2 \times 64$	Conv3 × 3	128	2
$14^2 \times 128$	Conv3 × 3	128	1
$14^2 \times 128$	Conv3 × 3	32	2
$7^2 \times 32$	Conv7 × 7	128	1
$1^2 \times 128$	Full Connection	32	–
$1^2 \times 32$	Full Connection	3	–

$$wing(x) = \begin{cases} \omega ln\left(1 + |x|/\epsilon\right), & |x| < \omega \\ |x| - \Omega, & |x| \geq \omega \end{cases} \tag{1}$$

Wing loss is best suited for landmark localization tasks, compared to L1, L2, Smooth L1 loss functions. We hereby use it in our loss function design. Besides, we intend to address data imbalance and include head pose estimation as part of landmark prediction task. So we have:

$$L_{landmark} = \frac{1}{N}\sum_{n=1}^{N}\sum_{c=1}^{C}\sigma_n^{(c)}\sum_{p=1}^{P}\left(1 - cos\theta_n^{(p)}\right)\sum_{k=1}^{K}CombWing\left(x_n^{(k)}, y_n^{(k)}\right) \tag{2}$$

where N, C, P, K respectively denote batch size, number of classes (attributes), number of head pose angles, and number of coordinates. In our case, $C = 5$ for 5 attributes: expression, illumination, make=up, occlusion, and blurring; $P = 3$ for 3 angles, yaw, pitch, and roll; $K = 196$ for 98 landmarks that are considered. $\sigma_n^{(c)}$ is the reciprocal of fraction of class c in a batch; $\theta_n^{(p)}$ is the p-th angle of the n-the sample; $x_n^{(k)}$ and $y_n^{(k)}$ separately stand for the output of easy branch and that of hard branch; and $CombWing(\cdot)$ is combinational loss defined as:

$$CombWing(x_n, y_n) = \begin{cases} \beta \cdot wing(x_n - z_n) + wing(y_n - z_n), & s = 1 \\ wing(x_n - z_n) + \beta \cdot wing(y_n - z_n), & s = 0 \end{cases} \tag{3}$$

where $\beta > 1$ is a hyper-parameter, s is predicted confidence score, and z_n is ground-truth landmark coordinates. For a sample labeled as easy ($s = 1$), we hope the model to penalize the easy branch for its error more than the hard branch. We do not remove hard branch's prediction when $s = 1$ because the classifier is not 100% correct in practice, which means a hard example might fall into the easy branch (or vice versa).

For sample classification in our model, we simply adopt the cross entropy loss. Finally we obtain the holistic loss function as:

$$Loss = L_{landmark} + \alpha \cdot L_{classification} \quad (4)$$

where α is a hyper-parameter for balancing two tasks.

4 Experiments

Dataset. We perform both training and testing of our model on the challenging dataset WFLW [19] which consists of 10,000 faces (7,500 for training and 2,500 for testing) with 98 fully manual annotated landmarks and is probably the largest open dataset for face alignment yet.

Evaluation Metric. We conduct evaluation of our algorithm using popular metric in face alignment community, i.e. Normalized Mean Error (NME) and Failure Rate (FR). Noteworthy, we normalize landmark distance error over outer-eye-corner distance, following [25] and [18].

Indicators. We mentioned 3 different types of hard sample indicator in previous passage. *Learning-based indicator* works by assigning an example as easy when its NME is less than 0.1, the same way as what a sample is defined a failure in FR calculation. It is intuitively reasonable but cannot make it as the more adapted easy branch becomes to the dataset, the more extreme imbalance will ensue between positive and negative sample, and therefore, the less training samples will be fed into hard branch. Our experiments demonstrate that the model trained this way tends to predict every sample in test set as easy. On the other hand, *all-attribute indicator* suffers from the same problem, though in an opposite way. It basically attempts to recognize samples with any one of the aforementioned attribute in WFLW, as these samples do not present better performance than the rest. Most examples, however, more or less fall into an attributes, meaning most samples will escape from easy branch to hard branch. That results in longer inference time, which is not what we want. Finally, we go for the *head pose indicator* and as shown in our experiment, it works fine.

Implementation Details. All images are cropped and resized to 112×112 and enhanced with data augmentation when training, including random scaling ($-15 \sim 15\%$), random crop ($-15 \sim 15$ pixels), and random horizontal flip. We implement our algorithm and test it using Pytorch [26] with its built-in Adam optimizer parameterized as base learning rate 1×10^{-4}, weight decay 1×10^{-6}, and others on default. Empirically, we set hyper-parameters in our loss function to be: $\alpha = 1.5$, $\beta = 10$, $\omega = 10$, $\epsilon = 2$.

As shown in Tables 4 and 5, our proposed AdaptiveNet outperforms all of the state-of-the-art algorithms except LAB, which we come close at, considering evaluation metrics but leave far behind, with respect to time-efficiency and model size. Noticeably, C denotes being tested on i7-6700K CPU, C* i5-7360U CPU, G NVIDIA GTX 1080Ti GPU, G* TITAN X GPU, and G** Tesla P40 GPU.

Table 4. Evaluation of AdaptiveNet and other state-of-the-arts on WFLW testset and its subsets.

Metric	Method	Testset	Pose subset	Expression subset	Illumination subset	Make-up subset	Occlusion subset	Blur subset
NME (%)	ESR [27]	11.13	25.88	11.47	10.49	11.05	13.75	12.20
	SDM [28]	10.29	24.10	11.45	9.32	9.38	13.03	11.28
	CFSS [29]	9.07	21.36	10.09	8.30	8.74	11.76	9.96
	LAB [19]	5.27	10.24	5.51	5.23	5.15	6.79	6.12
	Ours	6.11	10.51	6.25	5.94	6.33	7.48	6.67
FR (%)	ESR [27]	35.24	90.18	42.04	30.80	38.84	47.28	41.40
	SDM [28]	29.40	84.36	33.44	26.22	27.67	41.85	35.32
	CFSS [29]	20.56	66.26	23.25	17.34	21.84	32.88	23.67
	LAB [19]	7.56	28.83	6.37	6.73	7.77	13.72	10.74
	Ours	9.72	36.81	8.28	7.88	12.62	17.26	11.25

Table 5. Model size and speed comparison

Model	SDM [28]	SAN [30]	LAB [19]	AdaptiveNet
Size (Mb)	10.1	270.5 + 528	50.7	8.4 + 81
Speed (ms)	16(C)	343(G)	2,600(C)/60(G*)	171.59(C*)/9.95(G**)

Acknowledgments. This work was partially supported by the National Natural Science Foundation of China under Grant Nos. 61573068 and 61871052.

References

1. Wang, M., Deng, W.: Deep face recognition: a survey. CoRR abs/1804.06655 (2018)
2. Hassner, T., Harel, S., Paz, E., Enbar, R.: Effective face frontalization in unconstrained images. In: Proceedings of the IEEE Conference on Computer Vision and Pattern Recognition, pp. 4295–4304 (2015)
3. Li, S., Deng, W.: Deep facial expression recognition: a survey. CoRR abs/1804.08348 (2018)
4. Dou, P., Shah, S.K., Kakadiaris, I.A.: End-to-end 3D face reconstruction with deep neural networks. In: Proceedings of the IEEE Conference on Computer Vision and Pattern Recognition, pp. 5908–5917 (2017)
5. Sandler, M., Howard, A., Zhu, M., Zhmoginov, A., Chen, L.C.: MobileNetV2: inverted residuals and linear bottlenecks. In: Proceedings of the IEEE Conference on Computer Vision and Pattern Recognition, pp. 4510–4520 (2018)
6. He, K., Zhang, X., Ren, S., Sun, J.: Deep residual learning for image recognition. In: Proceedings of the IEEE Conference on Computer Vision and Pattern Recognition, pp. 770–778 (2016)

7. Cootes, T.F., Taylor, C.J., Cooper, D.H., Graham, J.: Active shape models-their training and application. Comput. Vis. Image Underst. **61**(1), 38–59 (1995)
8. Cootes, T.F., Edwards, G.J., Taylor, C.J.: Active appearance models. IEEE Trans. Pattern Anal. Mach. Intell. **6**, 681–685 (2001)
9. Cristinacce, D., Cootes, T.F.: Feature detection and tracking with constrained local models. In: BMVC, vol. 1, p. 3. Citeseer (2006)
10. Dollár, P., Welinder, P., Perona, P.: Cascaded pose regression. In: 2010 IEEE Computer Society Conference on Computer Vision and Pattern Recognition, pp. 1078–1085. IEEE (2010)
11. Sun, Y., Wang, X., Tang, X.: Deep convolutional network cascade for facial point detection. In: Proceedings of the IEEE Conference on Computer Vision and Pattern Recognition, pp. 3476–3483 (2013)
12. Zhou, E., Fan, H., Cao, Z., Jiang, Y., Yin, Q.: Extensive facial landmark localization with coarse-to-fine convolutional network cascade. In: Proceedings of the IEEE International Conference on Computer Vision Workshops, pp. 386–391 (2013)
13. Kowalski, M., Naruniec, J., Trzcinski, T.: Deep alignment network: a convolutional neural network for robust face alignment. In: Proceedings of the IEEE Conference on Computer Vision and Pattern Recognition Workshops, pp. 88–97 (2017)
14. Zhang, K., Zhang, Z., Li, Z., Qiao, Y.: Joint face detection and alignment using multitask cascaded convolutional networks. IEEE Signal Process. Lett. **23**(10), 1499–1503 (2016)
15. Zhang, Z., Luo, P., Loy, C.C., Tang, X.: Facial landmark detection by deep multi-task learning. In: Fleet, D., Pajdla, T., Schiele, B., Tuytelaars, T. (eds.) ECCV 2014. LNCS, vol. 8694, pp. 94–108. Springer, Cham (2014). https://doi.org/10.1007/978-3-319-10599-4_7
16. Yang, H., Mou, W., Zhang, Y., Patras, I., Gunes, H., Robinson, P.: Face alignment assisted by head pose estimation. arXiv preprint arXiv:1507.03148 (2015)
17. Guo, X., et al.: PFLD: a practical facial landmark detector. arXiv preprint arXiv:1902.10859 (2019)
18. Trigeorgis, G., Snape, P., Nicolaou, M.A., Antonakos, E., Zafeiriou, S.: Mnemonic descent method: a recurrent process applied for end-to-end face alignment. In: Proceedings of the IEEE Conference on Computer Vision and Pattern Recognition, pp. 4177–4187 (2016)
19. Wu, W., Qian, C., Yang, S., Wang, Q., Cai, Y., Zhou, Q.: Look at boundary: a boundary-aware face alignment algorithm. In: Proceedings of the IEEE Conference on Computer Vision and Pattern Recognition, pp. 2129–2138 (2018)
20. Deng, J., Trigeorgis, G., Zhou, Y., Zafeiriou, S.: Joint multi-view face alignment in the wild. IEEE Trans. Image Process. **28**(7), 3636–3648 (2019)
21. Feng, Z.H., Kittler, J., Awais, M., Huber, P., Wu, X.J.: Wing loss for robust facial landmark localisation with convolutional neural networks. In: Proceedings of the IEEE Conference on Computer Vision and Pattern Recognition, pp. 2235–2245 (2018)
22. Wang, X., Bo, L., Fuxin, L.: Adaptive wing loss for robust face alignment via heatmap regression. arXiv preprint arXiv:1904.07399 (2019)
23. Iqbal, H.: HarIsiqbal88/PlotNeuralNet v1.0.0, December 2018
24. Ruiz, N., Chong, E., Rehg, J.M.: Fine-grained head pose estimation without keypoints. In: The IEEE Conference on Computer Vision and Pattern Recognition (CVPR) Workshops, June 2018
25. Sagonas, C., Tzimiropoulos, G., Zafeiriou, S., Pantic, M.: 300 faces in-the-wild challenge: the first facial landmark localization challenge. In: Proceedings of the IEEE International Conference on Computer Vision Workshops, pp. 397–403 (2013)

26. Paszke, A., et al.: Automatic differentiation in PyTorch. In: NIPS-W (2017)
27. Cao, X., Wei, Y., Wen, F., Sun, J.: Face alignment by explicit shape regression. Int. J. Comput. Vis. **107**(2), 177–190 (2014)
28. Xiong, X., De la Torre, F.: Supervised descent method and its applications to face alignment. In: Proceedings of the IEEE Conference on Computer Vision and Pattern Recognition, pp. 532–539 (2013)
29. Zhu, S., Li, C., Change Loy, C., Tang, X.: Face alignment by coarse-to-fine shape searching. In: Proceedings of the IEEE Conference on Computer Vision and Pattern Recognition, pp. 4998–5006 (2015)
30. Dong, X., Yan, Y., Ouyang, W., Yang, Y.: Style aggregated network for facial landmark detection. In: Proceedings of the IEEE Conference on Computer Vision and Pattern Recognition, pp. 379–388 (2018)

Cross-Dimension Transfer Learning for Video-Based Facial Expression Recognition

Kailun Zhong, Yi Li(✉), Li Fang, and Ping Chen

College of Information and Communication Engineering,
Beijing University of Posts and Telecommunications, Beijing, China
{karenz,liyi,fangli,rab1106}@bupt.edu.cn

Abstract. Dynamic Facial Expression Recognition (FER) in videos is currently a topic of broad concern. Considering the fact that 3-dimensional convolutional networks (3D ConvNets) have recently demonstrated poor performance in this task, we propose a simple, yet effective approach to solve this problem within limited emotion data, which we call cross-dimension transfer learning (CTL). By transferring parameters learned from 2D ConvNets into 3D, network can be initialized reasonably, making it possible to avoid training 3D ConvNets from scratch. We introduce several transfer strategies and experiment results show that, CTL methods can bring considerable improvement to 3D ConvNets and compared with training from scratch, recognition accuracy on AFEW (Acted Facial Emotion in the Wild) has improved by 12.79%. We further extend our method to CK+ (The Extended CohnKanade) dataset and the classification performance shows the generalized ability of our approach.

Keywords: Transfer learning · Emotion · 3D convolution

1 Introduction

Video-based FER is an emerging research area. Recent works have concentrated on applying ConvNets to classify emotions. However, dynamic FER has not yet seen the excellent performance that achieved in other areas dominated by ConvNets. Current advanced results almost benefit from spatial performance, temporal relationships between consecutive frames are sometimes ignored.

Part of reason for such neglect is current databases are too small, making it difficult to model spatiotemporal features simultaneously. Compared to image classification, video-based FER has additional challenge of variations in motion, so more training samples are needed. As can be seen from Fig. 1, some frames can be distinguished by its individual appearance. For others, though, emotion may be ambiguous because video is annotated as a whole expression, while frames may have different labels, so the motion information is absolutely necessary.

Z. Sun et al. (Eds.): CCBR 2019, LNCS 11818, pp. 180–189, 2019.
https://doi.org/10.1007/978-3-030-31456-9_20

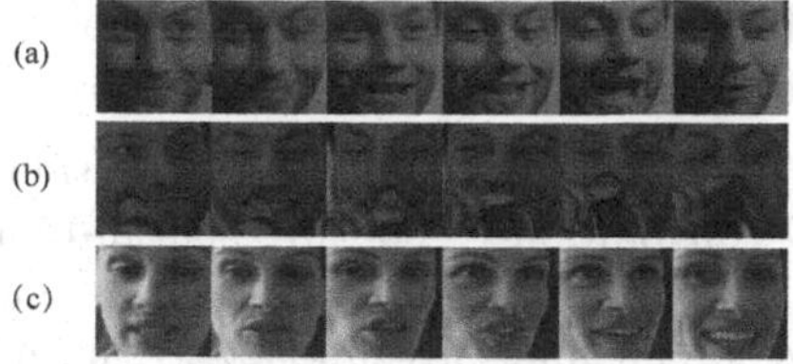

Fig. 1. Several frames from AFEW. Video (a), (b) and (c) are all annotated as happy.

Optical flow is a crucial method to capture position changes [1]. For FER, however, existing optical-flow algorithms are difficult to accurately capture tiny changes on facial organs. For action recognition, 3D convolution is widely used to capture motion implicitly. For FER, previous studies show the 3D performance is unsatisfactory for its increasing parameters and limited emotion data. Additionally, it seems to preclude the benefits of pre-training because currently, it is difficult to find a public large-scale dataset for video emotion. For dynamic FER, 3D ConvNets suffer from a significant amount of over-fitting.

In this paper we introduce a strategy to solve the overfitting problem of 3D ConvNets in video-based FER. This can be done by starting with a 2D architecture and padding all filters with an additional temporal dimension. Similarities of 2D features are well persevered and training time is greatly saved. Our contributions are two-fold: (i) we make an attempt on Cross-dimension Transfer Learning (CTL) for video-based FER and proved its effectiveness in a new domain. (ii) transfer strategies are optimized and we find that for spatiotemporal tasks with small datasets, the more complete spatial information is retained, the easier to learn seamless spatiotemporal features. We name such integrity of features as Spatial Retention Rate (SR-Rate). Without using any additional training data, CTL shows considerable results on AFEW [2] and CK+ [3] datasets.

2 Related Work

Designing deeper network becomes the mainstream of classification tasks. For video-based FER, though, the amount of training data is rather small compared to the number of parameters in standard deep models currently. In the case of no over-fitting, a more effective classifier will be the clue to research.

Video-Based FER. Some researchers treat dynamic FER as static FER. HoloNet [4] uses Concatenated Rectified Linear Unit to improve non-saturated nonlinearity. [5] introduces Supervised Scoring Ensemble (SSE) learning strategy in diverse layers. [6] focuses on the high intra-class variation and proposes novel loss functions. Other works aim to capture spatiotemporal relationships among frames and distinguish it from static image classification. [7] extracts spatial information and optical flow from peak emotional and neutral faces. [8] first classifies emotions based on 3D structures and trains the model from scratch. [9] makes modifications on the initialization and they fine-tune network weights with action pre-trained models. [10] also uses 3D convolution and [11] optimizes Recurrent Neural Network (RNN) to learn spatiotemporal contacts.

3D Convolution. 3D ConvNets are first applied to action recognition. [12] first propose to perform 3D convolution to capture spatial-temporal features. However, the problems of more parameters and lack of pre-learnt models make the application of 3D ConvNets far inferior than two-stream models [13]. Therefore, [14] introduces Two-Stream Inflated 3D ConvNets (I3D) based on 2D ConvNets and successfully employs ImageNet architecture and their parameters. [15,16] combine 2D and 3D convolution to reduce calculation.

For video-based FER, small datasets make it difficult for us to design complex networks. Meanwhile, the lack of large video emoticon datasets drives researchers using action pre-trained models. However, in [9], cross-domain pre-learnt model has seen degradation in performance. The role of action model is negligible due to the broader difference between actions and emotions both in spatial and temporal dimensions. For tasks with small datasets, divergence between target domain and source domain can not be ignored. Therefore, the selection source of pre-learnt parameters can be of importance, together with its processing procedure.

3 Cross-Dimension Transfer Learning

3.1 Where to Get Pre-learnt Models?

3D convolution is mostly used for action recognition recently. But transferring parameters from action to emotion directly seems ineffective due to their wide discrepancies. Action recognition focus on the movements of limbs while emotion recognition prefers to pay more attention on minor changes in facial organs.

For video-based FER, organ motions are not obvious sometimes, so spatial features are still important. Temporal information can be seen as a complement to enhance the expression of video sequences. Obtaining 2D parameters from large-scale face or expression datasets is the easiest solution. However, the change on convolution kernel dimension will inevitably bring about some randomness, so on the other side, we can also treat 2D models learnt on the target data as the migration source. Comparative experiment can be seen in Sect. 4.3.

3.2 Cross-Dimension Transfer Learning Strategies

Suppose that we have pre-learnt 2D convolutional kernel $W_{c_{in},c_{out},w,h}$ and bias kernel $B_{c_{out}}$, one goal is to create 3D kernel $K_{c_{in},c_{out},t,w,h}$ with additional time dimension T. At initialization, the output of 3D convolution layer remains to be approximately as the output of originally 2D convolution layer. For simplicity, we keep the sum of K be equal to W, i.e. $\sum_{i=1}^{T} K_{c_{in},c_{out},i,w,h} = W_{c_{in},c_{out},w,h}$. The initialization problem becomes the weights distribution of W on T dimensions.

Weight a_i can be positive or negative and be any size, as long as guaranteeing sum requirement. But exaggerating weight in one dimension will make the rest play a negligible role. Additionally, the bias kernel shares the same shape in 2D and 3D structure. We simply define 3D bias kernel $B'_{c_{out}} = B_{c_{out}}$ at initialization.

Average Transfer. This can be done by repeating W for T times along the time dimension and dividing them by T. $K_{c_{in},c_{out},i,w,h}$ is exactly the same with each other and very similar spatial representations are expect to be extracted from consecutive faces. More formally, it can be expressed as:

$$K_{c_{in},c_{out},i,w,h} = \frac{W_{c_{in},c_{out}w,h}}{T}. \tag{1}$$

Weight Transfer. There should be some variations in different time dimensions, so the range of parameters can vary greater during training. $K_{c_{in},c_{out},i,w,h}$ is initialized with a proportion of W. a_i can be arbitrary, but within a certain range. We take two situations into account. (i) All a_i are positive. Different frames contribute differently. (ii) a_i can be positive or negative. Some frames are counterproductive. $K_{c_{in},c_{out},i,w,h}$ can be defined as:

$$K_{c_{in},c_{out},i,w,h} = a_i \cdot W_{c_{in},c_{out},w,h}. \tag{2}$$

Zero Transfer. As the most special case, one time dimension is initialized as W while the others are set to zero matrix. Only one image feature can be preserved among T because other signals are multiplied with zero matrix. More formally, $K_{c_{in},c_{out},i,w,h}$ is defined as Eq. (3). O represents zero matrix.

$$K_{c_{in},c_{out},i,w,h} = \begin{cases} W_{c_{in},c_{out},w,h}, & \textit{any one time dimension}, \\ O, & \textit{other time dimensions}. \end{cases} \tag{3}$$

4 Experiments

4.1 Dataset

We evaluate CTL on AFEW and CK+. In AFEW, since the correct label for the test set has not been published, we adopt the training and validation splits for evaluation. CK+ includes six basic and one non-basic facial expressions. We divide these videos into 10 folds according to its subjects by ID in ascending order for cross-validation experiments on six basic expressions.

4.2 Training Details

VGG-M model has been modified in our experiments. To make full use of parameters on fully-connected (fc) layers, temporal size of feature need to reduce to 1 before the first fc layer. We follow [17] and temporal kernel size is set to 3. Temporal stride for the first pooling layer is set to 1 with the intention of not to merge the temporal signal too early, for other pooling layers it set to 2. All convolution layers are applied with spatial and temporal padding.

In AFEW, we select 16 frames per video and padding the last frame if the original length is less than 16. For CK+, we select fewer images for its shorter sequence length and plenty of neutral faces, so the input length is set to 4.

4.3 Results with Different CTL Strategies

Two sets of controlled experiments are evaluated whether obtaining 3D parameters directly from large emotion datasets, RAF-DB [18]. Exact results are shown in Table 1. Direct means obtaining 3D parameters from RAF-DB 2D models while Non-Direct means from 2D models trained on target datasets fine-tuned with RAD-DB. When adopting weight transfer, two typical weights are selected. We choose training from scratch as our baseline. Compared to baseline, we gain 12.75% performance boost in AFEW and 5.38% performance boost in CK+.

Table 1. Performance with cross-dimension transfer strategies.

Method: weight	Rate1	Direct	Non-Direct	Rate2	Direct	Non-Direct
Dataset	AFEW			CK+		
From scratch	39.69			93.99		
Average: $(1/3, 1/3, 1/3)$	65.84	46.74	47.52	39.51	95.21	95.76
Weight: $(1/4, 1/2, 1/4)$	74.71	46.21	48.04	52.73	95.15	96.24
Weight: $(-1/3, 5/3, -1/3)$	17.21	42.30	40.99	29.78	93.48	95.01
Zero: $(1, 0, 0)$	0	38.38	40.47	0	93.43	95.23
Zero: $(0, 1, 0)$	100	**49.35**	**52.48**	100	**98.46**	**99.37**
Zero: $(0, 0, 1)$	0	40.21	42.30	0	93.99	94.94

Transfer Source. Compared to using RAF-DB 2D models directly, obtaining parameters from the target dataset itself will almost improve the performance in every transfer strategies. When migrating parameters across dimensions, obtaining spatial parameters from target domain itself seems more helpful.

Spatial Retention Rate. Different strategies differ significantly in performance. Even with the same strategy, e.g. zero-transfer, assigning W on different time position also varies greatly. We think it is related to the preservation degree of spatial information at initialization, which we call it Spatial Retention Rate. To simplify the interpretation, we only select four frames as input and no longer consider the spatial difference in frames. Every frame is marked as fea and zero matrix is used to represent padding. We choose positive weights and very simple network structure, 3 convolution layers and 3 max pooling layers, to explain our SR-Rate. Suppose the weight vector is (a_1, a_2, a_3), the input is defined as $[fea, fea, fea, fea]$ and output feature of each layer is defined in following equations.

Firstly, influenced by padding, edge weights are multiply with zero matrix, so the feature output by $conv_1$ is:

$$\begin{aligned}[a_2 \cdot fea + a_3 \cdot fea, (a_1 + a_2 + a_3) \cdot fea, (a_1 + a_2 + a_3) \cdot fea, a_1 \cdot fea + a_2 \cdot fea] \\ = [(a_2 + a_3) \cdot fea, fea, fea, (a_1 + a_2) \cdot fea)]. \end{aligned} \quad (4)$$

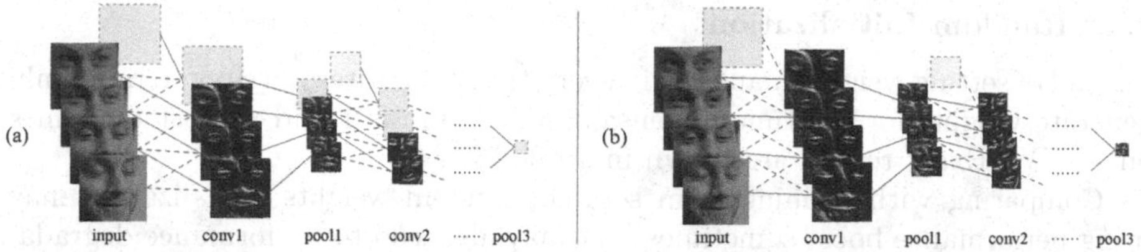

Fig. 2. (a), (b) shows the process when time weights is $(1, 0, 0)$, $(0, 1, 0)$. Light-colored block represents zero matrix. In (a), after each *conv* layer, it loses a spatial feature. At initialization, (a) outputs zero matrix and (b) outputs fusion of input signals.

Then the max pooling with temporal stride 1 is implemented and no reduce on time dimension, the output of $pool_1$ is the same with Eq. (4). Following Eq. (4), we continue the convolution operation and the output of $conv_2$ is:

$$[(a_2^2+a_2\cdot a_3+a_3),(a_1\cdot a_2+a_1\cdot a_3+a_2+a_3),(a_1+a_2+a_1\cdot a_3+a_2\cdot a_3),(a_1+a_1\cdot a_2+a_2^2)]\cdot fea. \quad (5)$$

Subsequently, max pooling with stride 2 is conducted on temporal dimension. We assume all weights are positive here, so the feature difference between $index_1$ and $index_0$, between $index_3$ and $index_2$ can be respectively expressed as:

$$(a_1\cdot a_2+a_1\cdot a_3+a_2+a_3-a_2^2-a_2\cdot a_3-a_3)\cdot fea = [a_2\cdot(a_1+1-a_2-a_3)+a_1\cdot a_3]\cdot fea > 0. \quad (6)$$

$$(a_1+a_1\cdot a_2+a_2^2-a_1-a_2-a_1\cdot a_3-a_2\cdot a_3)\cdot fea = [a_2\cdot(a_1+a_2-1-a_3)-a_1\cdot a_3]\cdot fea < 0. \quad (7)$$

Thus, the feature of $index_1$ and $index_2$ are retained and output of $pool_2$ is:

$$[(a_1 \cdot a_2 + a_1 \cdot a_3 + a_2 + a_3) \cdot fea, (a_1 + a_2 + a_1 \cdot a_3 + a_2 \cdot a_3) \cdot fea]. \quad (8)$$

Calculation process in $conv_3$ is analogous and we use x and y to represent the two values in Eq. (8), respectively. So the output of $conv_3$ is defined in Eq. (9) and the maximum of them is the output of $pool_3$.

$$[(a_2 \cdot x + a_3 \cdot y) \cdot fea, (a_1 \cdot x + a_2 \cdot y) \cdot fea]. \quad (9)$$

Above equations is a simple explanation. When network becomes more complicated and input sequence gets longer, calculation process is similar. When the weight appears negative, there will be a little different because the output of *pool*3 may be larger than original feature. So we take the reciprocal as SR-Rate, which also represents the relationship between the output of last pooling layer and original feature. In Table 1, Rate represents SR-Rate. When weights become $(1, 0, 0)$, x is zero but y not, but y multiply with weight 0 so the output of $pool_3$ is zero matrix. When weights become $(0, 0, 1)$, y is zero but x not, but x multiply with weight 0 at $conv_3$. Calculation process is shown in Fig. 2. The results on AFEW and CK+ both show the performance of 3D convolution is closely related to SR-Rate.

4.4 Random Initialization

Instead of setting weights manually in every transfer strategy, we try to randomly generate weights for the time dimension. Their sum is 1 and we test ten times on AFEW. Exact results are shown in Table 2.

Comparing with training from scratch, random weights initialization may bring performance boost sometimes, but may also lead to performance degradation. It is related to the value of weight, e.g. weights of group 8 and group 10 are similar with $(0, 1, 0)$, so their results are better. To be more precise, it's related to SR-Rate we describe in Sect. 4.3. For the video-based emotion, keeping spatial features as complete as possible will simplify the learning of temporal association between consecutive frames.

Table 2. Random initialization results.

Weight	Direct	Non-Direct
$(+0.72, -0.80, +1.08)$	27.94	31.85
$(-0.13, +0.21, +0.92)$	41.51	47.00
$(-0.50, +1.23, +0.27)$	40.47	44.65
$(+0.47, +0.71, -0.18)$	41.25	49.09
$(-0.93, +0.85, +1.08)$	27.68	26.11
$(-0.36, +0.43, +0.93)$	44.29	50.13
$(-0.11, +0.95, +0.16)$	45.12	49.87
$(+0.13, +0.92, -0.05)$	47.38	49.09
$(-0.36, +0.43, +0.93)$	37.34	38.12
$(-0.16, +0.82, +0.34)$	46.33	51.17

Table 3. AFEW perfromance.

Method	ACC
From scratch [8]	39.69
UCF101 init [9]	32.10
Window weights [19]	42.10
VGG-BRNN [20]	44.46
ResNet-LSTM [21]	46.40
HoloNet-B [4]	44.57
HoloNet-SSE [5]	46.48
Ours: Direct	**49.35**
Ours: Non-Direct	**52.48**

4.5 Comparison with State-of-the-Arts

For AFEW, we take other state-of-the-art models into consideration. Exact results are shown in Table 3. The first three models are based on 3D ConvNets and the middle two all use recurrent neural networks and the last two treat video-based FER as static FER. Compared to these models, we achieve excellent classification performance. For CK+, our method takes frames with neutral expression into account and methods which only evaluate the peak frame are not considered in this part. Exact results are shown in Table 4.

4.6 Model Fusion on AFEW

To further demonstrate the effectiveness of our approach on AFEW, we fuse different features such as Histogram of Oriented Gradients hand-crafted descriptor, audio extractor and LSTM module. Classification results of the three branches are 47.52%, 35.51% and 39.16% respectively. Fusion results are shown in Table 5. With fewer models, we achieve performance of state-of-the-art.

Table 4. CK+ performance

Method	ACC
Cascaded network [22]	96.70
Network ensemble [7]	97.28
Zero-bias CNN [23]	98.30
FaceNet2ExpNet [24]	98.60
Fine-tune [25]	98.90
Ours: Direct	98.46
Ours: Non-Direct	**99.37**

Table 5. Model fusion on AFEW

Method	ACC
3D ConvNets [8]	51.96
HoloNet [4]	51.96
VGG, LSTM [9]	55.30
SSE-Net [5]	59.01
Multimodal [10]	59.42
LEMD-Net [26]	56.13
Ours:	**59.53**

5 Conclusion

In this paper, we mainly focus on the over-fitting problem in 3D ConvNets in dynamic FER scenario. We propose CML learning to initialize 3D kernels from 2D parameters learned on the dataset itself and show the migration capacity between 2D and 3D models. Meanwhile, we put forward SR-Rate, which establishes relationships between spatial-temporal classification performance and spatial features. The training time has been significantly shortened and compared with training from scratch, we achieve remarkable classification performance. The problem of over-fitting is well retarded and on two standard benchmark datasets, AFEW and CK+, our approach demonstrates promising results.

References

1. Simonyan, K., Zisserman, A.: Two-stream convolutional networks for action recognition in videos, pp. 568–576 (2014)
2. Dhall, A., Goecke, R., Ghosh, S., Joshi, J., Hoey, J., Gedeon, T.: From individual to group-level emotion recognition: EmotiW 5.0. In: The ACM International Conference, pp. 524–528 (2017)
3. Lucey, P., Cohn, J.F., Kanade, T., Saragih, J., Ambadar, Z., Matthews, I.: The extended Cohn-Kanade dataset (CK+): a complete dataset for action unit and emotion-specified expression. In: Computer Vision and Pattern Recognition Workshops, pp. 94–101 (2010)
4. Yao, A., Cai, D., Hu, P., Wang, S., Sha, L., Chen, Y.: HoloNet: towards robust emotion recognition in the wild. In: ACM International Conference on Multimodal Interaction, pp. 472–478 (2016)
5. Hu, P., Cai, D., Wang, S., Yao, A., Chen, Y.: Learning supervised scoring ensemble for emotion recognition in the wild. In: The ACM International Conference, pp. 553–560 (2017)
6. Cai, J., Meng, Z., Khan, A.S., Li, Z., Tong, Y.: Island loss for learning discriminative features in facial expression recognition (2017)

7. Sun, N., Li, Q., Huang, R., Liu, J., Han, G.: Deep spatial-temporal feature fusion for facial expression recognition in static images. Pattern Recogn. Lett. **119**, 49–61 (2017)
8. Fan, Y., Lu, X., Li, D., Liu, Y.: Video-based emotion recognition using CNN-RNN and C3D hybrid networks. In: ACM International Conference on Multimodal Interaction, pp. 445–450 (2016)
9. Fan, L., Ke, Y.: Spatiotemporal networks for video emotion recognition (2017)
10. Lu, C., et al.: Multiple spatio-temporal feature learning for video-based emotion recognition in the wild. In: Proceedings of the 20th ACM International Conference on Multimodal Interaction, pp. 646–652 (2018)
11. Wang, H., Zhou, G., Hu, M., Wang, X.: Video emotion recognition using local enhanced motion history image and CNN-RNN networks. In: Zhou, J., et al. (eds.) CCBR 2018. LNCS, vol. 10996, pp. 109–119. Springer, Cham (2018). https://doi.org/10.1007/978-3-319-97909-0_12
12. Shuiwang, J., Ming, Y., Kai, Y.: 3D convolutional neural networks for human action recognition. IEEE Trans. Pattern Anal. Mach. Intell. **35**, 221–231 (2013)
13. Feichtenhofer, C., Pinz, A., Zisserman, A.: Convolutional two-stream network fusion for video action recognition. In: Computer Vision and Pattern Recognition, pp. 1933–1941 (2016)
14. Carreira, J., Zisserman, A.: Quo vadis, action recognition? A new model and the kinetics dataset, pp. 4724–4733 (2017)
15. Xie, S., Sun, C., Huang, J., Tu, Z., Murphy, K.: Rethinking spatiotemporal feature learning: speed-accuracy trade-offs in video classification. In: Proceedings of the European Conference on Computer Vision (ECCV), pp. 305–321 (2018)
16. Zhou, Y., Sun, X., Zha, Z.J., Zeng, W.: MiCT: mixed 3D/2D convolutional tube for human action recognition. In: The IEEE Conference on Computer Vision and Pattern Recognition (CVPR), June 2018
17. Du, T., Bourdev, L., Fergus, R., Torresani, L., Paluri, M.: Learning spatiotemporal features with 3D convolutional networks. In: IEEE International Conference on Computer Vision, pp. 4489–4497 (2015)
18. Li, S., Deng, W., Du, J.P.: Reliable crowdsourcing and deep locality-preserving learning for expression recognition in the wild. In: IEEE Conference on Computer Vision and Pattern Recognition, pp. 2584–2593 (2017)
19. Vielzeuf, V., Pateux, S., Jurie, F.: Temporal multimodal fusion for video emotion classification in the wild. In: The ACM International Conference, pp. 569–576 (2017)
20. Yan, J., et al.: Multi-clue fusion for emotion recognition in the wild. In: ACM International Conference on Multimodal Interaction, pp. 458–463 (2016)
21. Ouyang, X., et al.: Audio-visual emotion recognition using deep transfer learning and multiple temporal models. In: The ACM International Conference, pp. 577–582 (2017)
22. Liu, P., Han, S., Meng, Z., Tong, Y.: Facial expression recognition via a boosted deep belief network. In: IEEE Conference on Computer Vision and Pattern Recognition, pp. 1805–1812 (2014)
23. Khorrami, P., Paine, T.L., Huang, T.S.: Do deep neural networks learn facial action units when doing expression recognition? pp. 19–27 (2015)

24. Ding, H., Zhou, S.K., Chellappa, R., Ding, H., Zhou, S.K., Chellappa, R.: FaceNet2ExpNet: regularizing a deep face recognition net for expression recognition, pp. 118–126 (2016)
25. Zhang, Z., Luo, P., Chen, C.L., Tang, X.: From facial expression recognition to interpersonal relation prediction. Int. J. Comput. Vis. **126**, 550–569 (2018)
26. Liu, C., Tang, T., Lv, K., Wang, M.: Multi-feature based emotion recognition for video clips. In: Proceedings of the 20th ACM International Conference on Multimodal Interaction, pp. 630–634 (2018)

Exploring Shape Deformation in 2D Images for Facial Expression Recognition

Jie Li, Zhengxi Liu, and Qijun Zhao(✉)

College of Computer Science, Sichuan University, Chengdu, China
qjzhao@scu.edu.cn

Abstract. Facial expression recognition (FER) using 2D images has been rapidly developed in the past decade. However, existing 2D-based FER methods seldom consider the impact of identity factors, and do not utilize shape features which have been proven to be effective complement to texture features. Built upon latest 3D face reconstruction methods, this paper proposes to generate expression-induced shape deformation map (ESDM) from the 3D face reconstructed from the input 2D face image, and then extract shape feature from ESDM by using a deep network. The shape feature is then combined with the texture feature on the input 2D face image, resulting in a fused feature, based on which the expression of the input 2D face image is recognized by using a softmax classifier. Evaluation experiments on BU-3DFE, MMI and CK+ databases show that our proposed shape feature effectively improves the 2D-based FER accuracy, and our method using the fused feature achieves state-of-the-art accuracy.

Keywords: Facial expression recognition · Expression-induced shape deformation map · 3D face reconstruction

1 Introduction

Facial expression is one of the most powerful ways for humans to express their emotions. Thanks to its potential wide applications, facial expression recognition (FER) has attracted increasing attention from researchers and practitioners [3, 4]. Many methods have been proposed in the past decades for facial expression recognition based either on static images [11, 25, 26] or on videos [21–23], either on 2D data [7, 8, 11] or on 3D data [17–20]. Among these different source data, 3D data usually have higher recognition accuracy because 3D data can provide shape features in addition to texture features. However, acquiring 3D face data is much more expensive than acquiring 2D face images. In this paper, we focus on recognizing facial expressions based on single static face images, and aim to utilize the shape features recovered from 2D images to facilitate facial expression recognition.

Conventional 2D-image-based facial expression recognition methods extract either hand-crafted features [7, 8, 10] or deeply-learned features [11, 21–24]. These methods seldom consider the impact of identity factors; as a consequence, the extracted features would be more sensitive to identity differences than to expression differences. Being aware of this problem, some researchers proposed to decompose faces into identity, expression and other components by using tensor representation [2]. They showed that

Z. Sun et al. (Eds.): CCBR 2019, LNCS 11818, pp. 190–197, 2019.
https://doi.org/10.1007/978-3-030-31456-9_21

facial expression itself can be represented by a neutral component plus an expressive one. According to this, a number of facial expression recognition methods [7, 8] have been proposed by exploring the differences between expressive face images and neutral face images. Despite the impressive performance achieved by these methods, they mostly require the availability of neutral face images of specific subjects or an average neutral face image. Besides, these methods usually consider only 2D features, and thus could be affected by variations in illumination and head pose.

Recent studies using 3D faces, on the other hand, show that shape features can effectively improve facial expression recognition accuracy [17–20]. Motivated by the success of 3D shape features, and thanks to the advancement in 3D face reconstruction [5, 6, 13], we propose in this paper a novel method for recognizing expressions on 2D face images by exploring expression-induced shape deformation that can be extracted from 2D images via 3D face reconstruction. Such shape deformation is in essence independent from the facial identity, and can serve as effective complement to texture features.

2 Related Work

Existing methods for extracting identity-independent expression features can be roughly divided into two categories according to whether reference neutral or expressive face images are needed or not. Bazzo et al. [7] assume that an averaged neutral face image is available and utilize Gabor Wavelets to analyze the difference image between the query image and the averaged neutral face image. Zafeiriou et al. [8] study sparse image representations through generating difference images obtained by the query image subtracted from the corresponding reference face image. Lee et al. [10] construct intra-class variation images that are similar to the query face image in identity or illumination other than expression. Then, they subtract the intra-class variation images from the query face image and use the obtained difference images for recognizing expression of the query face image. Instead of computing difference images between query images and the available reference images, Yang et al. [11] employ Generative Adversarial Networks to generate corresponding neutral face images from expressive face images and utilize the deposition that remains in generative model to recognize expression. All these methods consider only 2D texture features. Chang et al. [12] propose an end-to-end network for directly regressing identity coefficients and expression coefficients from the input face image based on an expressive 3D morphable model (3DMM), and recognize its expression based on the obtained expression coefficients. While this method utilizes 3D-derived identity-independent features, it relies on a statistical parametric 3D face model that has to be built in advance based on a sufficient number of annotated 3D face samples. In this paper, in contrast, we directly generate shape deformation maps from 2D face images and train a deep network to extract identity-independent shape features from the deformation maps for FER. Our method requires neither reference face images nor statistical 3D face models.

3 Proposed Method

3.1 Overview

Given a 2D face image, our proposed method extracts both shape and texture features. The shape feature is obtained by first generating expression-induced shape deformation map (ESDM) and then applying a deep network to ESDM. The texture feature is obtained by first aligning the input face image and then applying another deep network to it. The shape and texture features are concatenated into a fused feature, which is used as the input to a softmax classifier to produce the facial expression recognition result. Figure 1 shows the overall flowchart of the proposed method. In the following subsections, we first introduce how ESDM is defined and extracted, and then give the detail of the shape and texture features.

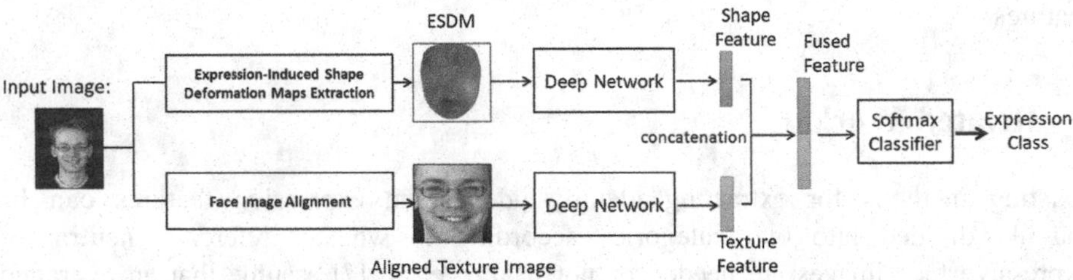

Fig. 1. The flowchart of our proposed facial expression recognition method

3.2 Expression-Induced Shape Deformation Maps

According to [9], 3D face shape can be reconstructed from a 2D face image under the assumption that 3D face shape consists of identity and expression components

$$S = \bar{S} + \Delta S_{Id} + \Delta S_{Exp}. \tag{1}$$

The identity component ΔS_{Id} describes the deviation of the 3D face shape of a subject with neutral expression from the mean 3D face shape $\bar{S}$. The expression component ΔS_{Exp} represents the shape deformation to the 3D face of the subject due to the expression on the face, which is defined by the vertex-wise difference between the expressive 3D face shape and its corresponding neutral 3D face shape. In this paper, we employ the method in [13] to recover the expression component of the input 2D face image.

Once the expression component ΔS_{Exp} is obtained, we can generate the expression-induced shape deformation map (ESDM). Suppose the 3D face shape is composed by n vertices, then its expression component ΔS_{Exp} can be denoted by

$$\Delta S_{Exp} = \begin{pmatrix} \Delta x_1 & \Delta x_2 & \cdots & \Delta x_n \\ \Delta y_1 & \Delta y_2 & \cdots & \Delta y_n \\ \Delta z_1 & \Delta z_2 & \cdots & \Delta z_n \end{pmatrix} \in \mathbb{R}^{3\times n}. \tag{2}$$

Each column in ΔS_{Exp} specifies the motion of a vertex with respect to its location under neutral expression. ESDM is a three-channel 2D image which is of the same spatial size as the input 2D face image. We project the *mean 3D face shape* $\bar{S}$ onto ESDM to determine the foreground pixels on ESDM, and set the value of each foreground pixel as the value of the corresponding vertex in ΔS_{Exp}. Algorithm 1 summarizes the procedure of generating ESDM from the expression component reconstructed from a 2D face image.

Algorithm 1 Generate ESDM

Require: $\Delta S_{Exp} \in \mathbb{R}^{3\times n}$, $\bar{S} \in \mathbb{R}^{3\times n}$ and *scale*: the transformation scale from ΔS_{Exp} to color space (0-255).

OutPut: ESDM

for $i\_channel = 1:3$

    //k: transformation ratio from ΔS_{Exp} to color space.

    $k_{pos} = (255 - 128)/(scale_{max} - 0)$

    $k_{neg} = (128 - 0)/(0 - scale_{min})$

    for $i = 1 : n$

    if $\Delta S_{Exp_{i\_channel,i}} \geq 0$

        $gray_i = 128 + k_{pos} * \Delta S_{Exp_{i\_channel,i}}$

    end

    if $\Delta S_{Exp_{i\_channel,i}} < 0$

        $gray_i = k_{neg} * (\Delta S_{Exp_{i\_channel,i}} - scale_{min})$

    end

    $gray$ = floor($gray$)

    $img_{:,:,i\_channel}$ = ZBuffer($\bar{S}$, $gray$) //project to a 2D image

end

return img

Converting ΔS_{Exp} to 2D ESDM has the following advantages: (i) The development of CNN is relatively mature. It's much easier to extract features than in 3D shape space. (ii) The form of ΔS_{Exp} has lost the spatial location information of the vertexes. ESDM retains both spatial location information and motion information. (iii) Since the position of the ESDM is determined by the same mean 3D face, the map itself has high alignment.

3.3 Shape and Texture Features

The aforementioned ESDM encodes the facial motion caused by expression variation. It enables the extraction of shape feature that is complementary to texture feature in characterizing facial expressions. Therefore, we use a deep network with ESDM as input to learn shape feature. As for texture feature, we use another deep network with aligned face image as input. Alignment of the face image is done by first detecting five facial landmarks (i.e., two eye centers, nose tip, and two mouth corners), then translating, rotating and scaling the face image such that the landmarks in each image can best conform others, and finally cropping the facial region as a 220 * 220 image.

4 Experiments

4.1 Data Augmentation Strategy

In this paper, we use DLib [1] to detect the facial landmarks, and ResNet-50 and ResNet-18 as the deep networks for extracting texture and shape features, respectively. During training of the proposed method, we first train the two deep networks separately, both with a softmax loss. After they converge, we further train the softmax classifier while keeping the feature extraction deep networks fixed.

4.2 Experimental Results on 3D Data

We first validate the effectiveness of our proposed ESDM in recognizing facial expressions by using real 3D face data. Since we have 3D data, we can compute the ground truth shape deformation maps directly by subtracting neutral 3D face shapes from expressive 3D face shapes, and then use the trained shape feature extraction deep network to extract shape features from the ESDM. In this experiment, we use the BU-3DFE database, and compare our method with some state-of-the-art 3D and 2D+3D facial expression recognition methods.

BU-3DFE Database: The BU-3DFE database [14] contains 100 subjects (56 females and 44 males). Each subject has 25 3D faces (6 expression $\times$ 4 intensities + a neutral face) and corresponding texture images. In our experimental design, 2,500 (2400 expressive face and 100 neutral face) 3D data and 2,400 texture images are used to recognize the six basic expressions in a subject-independent 10-fold cross-validation manner. Table 1 compares the recognition accuracy of different methods, and Fig. 2(a) shows the confusion matrix of our proposed method. As can be seen, our proposed shape features improve the facial expression recognition accuracy by 3 to 4%, which proves the effectiveness of ESDM in facial expression recognition.

Table 1. Comparisons of different methods on the BU-3DFE database

Method	Average accuracy	Intensity	Data	An	Di	Fe	Ha	Sa	Su
DMCMs [17]	76.6	3, 4	3D	72.0	74.9	62.3	86.4	72.0	92.1
SIM+NOM [18]	80.9	3, 4	3D	80.4	80.3	73.2	90.1	68.5	93.1
DF-CNN [19]	81.3	1–4	2D+3D	–	–	–	–	–	–
BBN+SFAM [20]	82.3	3, 4	2D+3D	71.7	85.0	71.4	89.9	81.7	93.8
Ours (Texture only)	80.8	1–4	2D	79.3	73.5	72.0	90.3	76.8	92.8
Ours (Shape only)	81.5	1–4	3D	79.5	79.8	63.8	**93.5**	79.3	93.5
Ours (Texture +Shape)	**85.3**	1–4	2D+3D	**85.5**	**81.8**	**72.0**	93.3	**84.0**	**95.3**

4.3 Experimental Results on 2D Data

We then evaluate the performance of our proposed method on 2D face images. MMI and CK+ databases are used in this experiment, and a number of state-of-the-art 2D facial expression recognition methods are considered as counterparts.

Table 2. Comparisons of different methods on the MMI database

Method	Average accuracy	An	Di	Fe	Ha	Sa	Su
Island loss [25]	69.6	66.7	78.1	57.1	92.9	59.4	63.4
(N+M)-tuplet clusters loss [26]	73.5	81.8	71.9	41.4	92.9	73.4	79.6
DeRL [11]	73.2	70.-	73.-	53.-	96.-	68.-	76.-
Ours (Texture only)	64.3	63.6	65.6	**59.5**	81.8	52.1	63.4
Ours (Shape only)	73.3	**71.7**	67.7	47.6	88.1	77.1	81.8
Ours (Texture+Shape)	**74.5**	64.7	**68.8**	53.6	**96.8**	**77.1**	**86.2**

MMI Database: The MMI database [15] includes 208 video sequences with frontal view faces for 31 subjects. Sequences in MMI are onset-apex-offset labeled. We select three frames in the middle of each image sequence (i.e., peak frames) for expression recognition. We also adopt person-independent 10-fold cross validation strategy on this database. As shown in Table 2, on average, our method achieves 10 percent higher accuracy when using both texture and shape features compared with using only texture feature. Moreover, our method overwhelms the state-of-the-art counterpart methods in terms of the average recognition accuracy.

CK+ Database: The CK+ database [16] collects 593 expression video sequences from 123 subjects. Among them, 327 sequences corresponding to seven categories of expression (anger, contempt, disgust, fear, happiness, sadness and surprise) are used in our experiment. We choose the last three frames of each video sequence and adopted person-independent 10-fold cross validation strategy. As we can see from the result in Table 3, although our method on average performs worse using only shape feature than using only texture feature, by combing the two features the average accuracy is successfully improved to 93.3%, which is comparable to the state-of-the-art.

Table 3. Comparisons of different methods on the CK+ database

Method	Average accuracy	An	Co	Di	Fe	Ha	Sa	Su
DTGN [21]	92.4	–	–	–	–	–	–	–
Cov3D [22]	92.3	94.4	100.0	95.5	90.0	96.2	70.0	100.0
3DCNN [23]	78.0	77.8	61.1	96.6	60.0	95.7	57.1	97.6
3DCNN-DAP [23]	87.9	91.1	66.7	96.6	80.0	98.6	85.7	96.4
VSLem [24]	**95.0**	97.8	88.2	96.6	92.0	97.1	87.9	97.4
Ours (Texture only)	91.3	**88.1**	83.3	93.8	86.7	**100.0**	88.1	**98.8**
Ours (Shape only)	85.4	81.5	90.4	92.1	90.7	97.1	69.1	97.2
Ours (Texture+Shape)	**93.3**	83.0	**92.6**	**97.7**	**96.0**	98.1	**88.1**	97.6

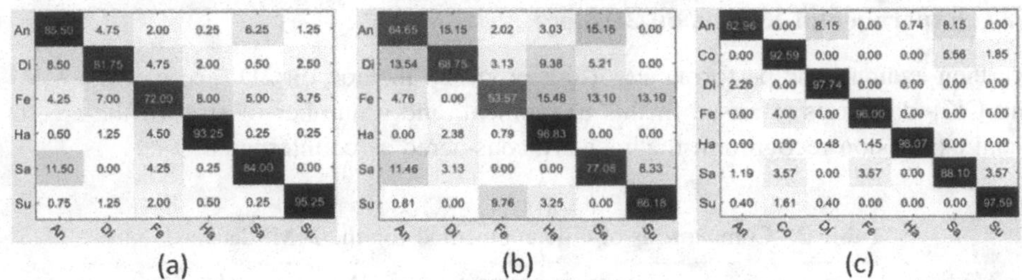

Fig. 2. Confusion matrix of our method on BU3DFE, MMI and CK+ (from left to right)

5 Conclusion

In this paper, we utilize 3D face reconstruction method to extend the information in the image to 3D space and extract the expression component caused by the expression. And we propose ESDM to convert expression component to 2D image called ESDM for FER task. The shape feature and texture feature which extract from ESDM and texture image respectively are concatenated into a fused feature for classification. The experimental results on three databases prove that the proposed method can improve the FER performance. The reconstruction module and expression recognition module used in our current work are independent. In future works, an end-to-end network will be applied and the expression label will be used to supervise the face reconstruction module to capture 3D expression component more precisely.

Acknowledgments. This work is supported by the National Natural Science Foundation of China (61773270, 61703077), and the Miaozi Key Project in Science and Technology Innovation Program of Sichuan Province, China (No. 2017RZ0016).

References

1. Kazemi, V., Sullivan, J.: One millisecond face alignment with an ensemble of regression trees. In: CVPR, pp. 1867–1874 (2014)
2. Wang, H.: Facial expression decomposition. In: ICCV, pp. 958–965 (2003)
3. Khan, R.A., Meyer, A., Konik, H., Bouakaz, S.: Pain detection through shape and appearance features. In: ICME, pp. 1–6 (2013)
4. Saradadevi, M., Bajaj, P.: Driver fatigue detection using mouth and yawning analysis. Int. J. Comput. Sci. Netw. Secur. **8**(6), 183–188 (2008)
5. Nirkin, Y., Masi, I., Tuan, A.T., Hassner, T., Medioni, G.: On face segmentation, face swapping, and face perception. In: FG 2018, pp. 98–105 (2018)
6. Chang, F.J., Tran, A.T., Hassner, T., Masi, I., Nevatia, R., Medioni, G.: ExpNet: landmark-free, deep, 3D facial expressions. In: FG, pp. 122–129 (2018)
7. Bazzo, J.J., Lamar, M.V.: Recognizing facial actions using gabor wavelets with neutral face average difference. In: FG, pp. 505–510 (2004)
8. Zafeiriou, S., Petrou, M.: Sparse representations for facial expressions recognition via l_1 optimization. In: CVPRW, pp. 32–39 (2010)

9. Liu, F., Zhao, Q., Zeng, D.: Joint face alignment and 3D face reconstruction with application to face recognition. IEEE Trans. Pattern Anal. Mach. Intell. (2018, to appear)
10. Lee, S.H., Plataniotis, K.N.K., Ro, Y.M.: Intra-class variation reduction using training expression images for sparse representation based facial expression recognition. IEEE Trans. Affect. Comput. **5**(3), 340–351 (2014)
11. Yang, H., Ciftci, U., Yin, L.: Facial expression recognition by de-expression residue learning. In: CVPR, pp. 2168–2177 (2018)
12. Chang, F.J., Tran, A.T., Hassner, T., Masi, I., Nevatia, R., Medioni, G.: ExpNet: landmark-free, deep, 3D facial expressions. In: FG, May 2018, pp. 122–129 (2018)
13. Liu, F., Zeng, D., Li, J., Zhao, Q.J.: On 3D face reconstruction via cascaded regression in shape space. Front. Inf. Technol. Electron. Eng. **18**(12), 1978–1990 (2017)
14. Yin, L., Wei, X., Sun, Y., Wang, J., Rosato, M.J.: A 3D facial expression database for facial behavior research. In: FG, pp. 211–216 (2006)
15. Valstar, M., Pantic, M.: Induced disgust, happiness and surprise: an addition to the MMI facial expression database. In: Proceedings of 3rd International Workshop on EMOTION (Satellite of LREC): Corpora for Research on Emotion and Affect, p. 65 (2010)
16. Lucey, P., Cohn, J.F., Kanade, T., Saragih, J., Ambadar, Z., Matthews, I.: The extended Cohn-Kanade dataset (CK+): a complete dataset for action unit and emotion-specified expression. In: CVPRW, pp. 94–101 (2010)
17. Lemaire, P., Ardabilian, M., Chen, L., Daoudi, M.: Fully automatic 3D facial expression recognition using differential mean curvature maps and histograms of oriented gradients. In: FG, pp. 1–7 (2013)
18. Yang, X., Huang, D., Wang, Y., Chen, L.: Automatic 3D facial expression recognition using geometric scattering representation. In: FG, pp. 1–6 (2015)
19. Li, H., Sun, J., Xu, Z., Chen, L.: Multimodal 2D+3D facial expression recognition with deep fusion convolutional neural network. IEEE Trans. Multimedia **19**(12), 2816–2831 (2017)
20. Zhao, X., Huang, D., Dellandrea, E., Chen, L.: Automatic 3D facial expression recognition based on a Bayesian belief net and a statistical facial feature model. In: PR, pp. 3724–3727 (2010)
21. Jung, H., Lee, S., Yim, J., Park, S., Kim, J.: Joint fine-tuning in deep neural networks for facial expression recognition. In: ICCV, pp. 2983–2991 (2013)
22. Liu, M., Li, S., Shan, S., Wang, R., Chen, X.: Deeply learning deformable facial action parts model for dynamic expression analysis. In: CV, pp. 143–157 (2014)
23. Sanin, A., Sanderson, C., Harandi, M.T., Lovell, B.C.: Spatio-temporal covariance descriptors for action and gesture recognition. In: WACV, January 2013, pp. 103–110 (2013)
24. Walecki, R., Rudovic, O., Pavlovic, V., Pantic, M.: Variable-state latent conditional random fields for facial expression recognition and action unit detection. In: FG, pp. 1–8 (2015)
25. Cai, J., Meng, Z., Khan, A. S., Li, Z., O'Reilly, J., Tong, Y.: Island loss for learning discriminative features in facial expression recognition. In: FG 2018, pp. 302–309 (2018)
26. Liu, X., Vijaya Kumar, B.V.K., You, J., Jia, P.: Adaptive deep metric learning for identity-aware facial expression recognition. In: CVPRW, pp. 20–29 (2017)

Facial Attractiveness Prediction by Deep Adaptive Label Distribution Learning

Luyan Chen and Weihong Deng(✉)

School of Information and Communication Engineering,
Beijing University of Posts and Telecommunications, Beijing, China
{chenluyan,whdeng}@bupt.edu.cn

Abstract. One of the biggest challenges in the problem of facial attractiveness prediction is the lack of reliable labeled training data. It is very hard to apply a well defined concept to describe the attractiveness of a face. In fact, facial attractiveness prediction is a label ambiguity problem. In order to solve the problem, we propose a novel deep architecture called Deep Adaptive Label Distribution Learning (DALDL). Different from previous works, we use discrete label distribution of possible ratings rather than single label to supervise the learning process of facial attractiveness prediction, and update the label distribution automatically during training process. Our approach provides a better description for facial attractiveness, and experiments have shown that DALDL achieves better or comparable results than the state-of-the-art methods.

Keywords: Facial attractiveness prediction · Deep learning · Label distribution learning

1 Introduction

Facial attractiveness is an ever-lasting issue. Since ancient times, studies of face attractiveness have attracted interest of psychologists and philosophers. Some researchers hold the view that the attractiveness of face has objective criteria, independent of gender, age, ethnicity, etc [1,2]. Some studies even found that as early as in infancy, human beings tend to choose more attractive face [3] (when the baby see the beautiful face, eyes will stay for longer). This means that facial attractiveness can be quantitatively studied.

In early studies, face attractiveness prediction was basically a combination of hand-crafted features and shallow predictors. The hand-craft features include geometric features [4], texture features [5,6], and the combination of the both kind features. However, These traditional methods are inconvenient and lack universality. Recently, a lot of deep learning based methods have been proposed [7,8], and shown great performance.

Despite the breakthroughs in previous works, facial attractiveness prediction still face many challenges. Different from other facial analysis tasks such as face

Z. Sun et al. (Eds.): CCBR 2019, LNCS 11818, pp. 198–206, 2019.
https://doi.org/10.1007/978-3-030-31456-9_22

recognition [9] and facial expression recognition [10], it is hard to apply a well-defined concept to describe the attractiveness of faces. In previous studies, facial attractiveness was generally described with a single score, that is, the average score given by the raters. However, the perception towards facial attractiveness is complicated. For example, as shown in Fig. 1, although the average score of the two faces are the same, the label distribution given by the raters are different, which means that people's perception towards the attractiveness of these two faces is not exactly the same.

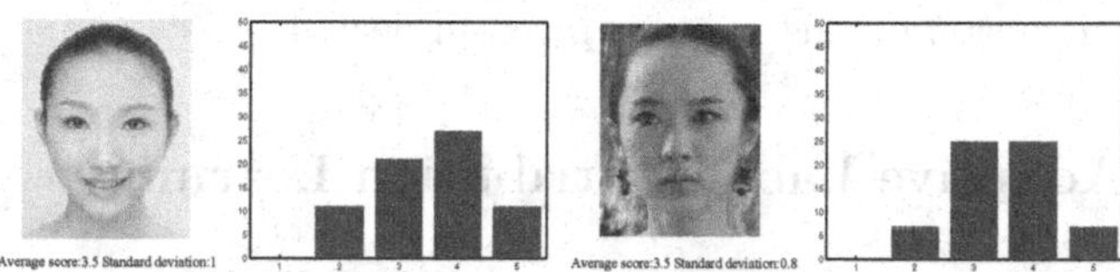

Fig. 1. Two images from SCUT-FBP [11] with the same average score. The histogram shows the number of raters giving the corresponding scores.

In other words, facial attractiveness prediction is a learning progress with label ambiguity, there is interaction between different labels. To tackle this problem, methods based on label ambiguity were proposed. Ren et al. [12] represent the human sense towards facial attractiveness by a label distribution, and proposed a learning method called Structural-Label-Distribution-Learning (SLDL) based on structural Support Vector Machine. Liu et al. [13] combine label distribution learning with deep learning. The label distribution used in these methods are calculated by the ratings from the database or generated on the basis of strong assumption. In general, it is assumed that the label distribution satisfies the Gaussian distribution, but there are some problems when the distributions of different faces are generated with the same parameters. For example, a face with high attractiveness should have a smaller deviation variance compare to "ordinary" face. Inspired by this, we propose Deep adaptively Label distribution learning (DALDL), to update the key parameters of the generated label distribution during the training process to obtain a more reliable label distribution.

We conduct our methods in SCUT-FBP [11], SCUT-FBP500 [14] and CelebA [15]. The sample distribution in the dataset is not balanced enough, lacking samples with high scores and low scores. To solve this problem, we propose a weighted Euclidean loss. The main contribution of our work can be summarized as following:

(1) We abstract facial attractiveness prediction into a label ambiguity problem, using a label distribution rather than a single label to describe the attractiveness of each face image.

(2) We propose a novel method called Deep Adaptive Label Distribution Learning (DALDL), which automatically updates the label distribution during training process to find better description for face attractiveness and show greater performance compare to previous works.
(3) Based on our label distribution learning algorithm, we improved the traditional Euclidean loss to balance the sample distribution of data, and experiments showed that the improved loss performs better.

The rest of this paper is organized as follows. Section 2 introduces the DALDL method we propose. Section 3 reports the experimental details and results. Finally, the conclusion of this paper is given in Sect. 4.

2 Deep Adaptive Label Distribution Learning

The overview of our framework is illustrated in Fig. 2. Each face is first annotated with a label distribution initialized with the same variance, and then automatically updated by end-to-end learning. The baseline network used in our method is VGGFace [16], and can be replaced by any other deep networks. We also compare the performance of other deep networks, details will be introduced behind.

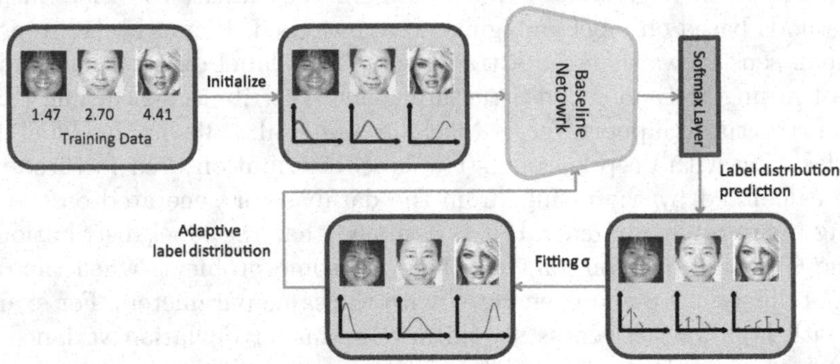

Fig. 2. The framework of DALDL. The label distribution of training data is first initialized with the same predefined standard deviation, then updated during training process.

2.1 Label Distribution Presentation

In previous studies, average score of all the raters is the most popular ground-truth label. Different from previous studies, we use the label distribution rather than a single label to describe the attractiveness of human face. The human sense towards facial attractiveness is complicated, using a single value can not fully describe the beauty of a face. Label distribution learning can utilize the label ambiguity, reflecting the interaction between adjacent labels.

Given an image $\boldsymbol{x}_n$, instead of using a single value y as its label, we try to quantify the range of possible y values. For the problem of facial attractiveness prediction, we assume there are 5 levels, i.e., "poor", "ordinary", "fair", "good", "excellent", corresponding to the numerical 1, 2, 3, 4, 5. The l-th label is denoted by y_l, in a label distribution, each label will be assigned a specific real number $d_{\boldsymbol{x}_n}^{y_l}$ to describe the description degree of y_l to the sample $\boldsymbol{x}_n$. It is obviously that $d_{\boldsymbol{x}_n}^{y_l} \in [0,1]$, and $\sum_l d_{\boldsymbol{x}_n}^{y_l} = 1$, since all the labels in the set can always fully describe the instance. Then the label distribution of image $\boldsymbol{x}_n$ can be denoted by $\boldsymbol{d}_n = \{d_{\boldsymbol{x}_n}^{y_1}, d_{\boldsymbol{x}_n}^{y_2}, d_{\boldsymbol{x}_n}^{y_3}, d_{\boldsymbol{x}_n}^{y_4}, d_{\boldsymbol{x}_n}^{y_5}\}$. It should be noted that, the meaning of $d_{\boldsymbol{x}_n}^{y_l}$ is not the probability that y_l correctly labels the instance x_n, but the proportion of y_l in a full description of the instance $\boldsymbol{x}_n$, which is different from previous studies since there is only one correct label for each instance.

A challenge lies in the research of facial attractiveness prediction is the lack of standard benchmark dataset. A very crucial reason is that collecting reliable annotated information is a huge amount of work. In previous work, researchers generally collected a small face aesthetics dataset, and then let a group of raters annotate each face in the dataset, then calculate the average of all rater's score as a label. For a dataset that can provide a large number of different annotations, similar to the method in [12], we can directly compute the label distribution by:

$$d_{\boldsymbol{x}_n}^{y_l} = \frac{\sum_{i=1}^{m^{(n)}} I(r_i^{(n)} = y_l)}{m^{(n)}} \tag{1}$$

where $m^{(n)}$ denotes the total number of raters giving ratings to $\boldsymbol{x}_n$, $r_i^{(n)}$ indicates the label of $\boldsymbol{x}_n$ given by the i-th rater. $I(*)$ returns 1 if $r^{(n)}$ equals to y_l, returns 0 else.

But for larger datasets, such as [7], collecting a lot of annotated data is very difficult. Obviously, the reliable ground-truth based label distribution representation is not available in most existing datasets, which means that we must construct a virtual label distribution under proper assumption. The constructed label distribution should satisfy the following two conditions: (1) The average score calculated from the original annotations should correspond to the highest point of the label distribution to ensure that the real label occupies the dominant position in the label distribution. (2) The label distribution of other labels should decreases with the distance away from the average score.

Among many possible distributions, the label distribution satisfying the discretized Gaussian distribution centered at the average score might suit face attractiveness representation. We first calculate the weighted average of the already existing scores and then calculate the label distribution by the following formulation:

$$d_{x_n}^{y_l} = \frac{1}{Z\sqrt{2\pi}\sigma_n} exp\left(-\frac{(y_l - \mu_n)^2}{2{\sigma_n}^2}\right) \tag{2}$$

Where μ_n represents the average score of x_n, σ_n is the standard deviation of the Gaussian distribution, and Z is a normalization factor that makes sure $\sum_l d_{\boldsymbol{x}_n}^{y_l} = 1$. The standard deviation controls the shape of label distribution. We found that the standard deviations of different faces are not exactly the same. For example, the scores of very attractive faces are more concentrated, the standard deviation is relatively small. In our method, σ is first initialized to the same value 0.5 and then updated during the training process.

2.2 Deep Adaptive Label Distribution Learning

As shown above, we use $\boldsymbol{d_n} = \{d_{\boldsymbol{x}_n}^{y_1}, d_{\boldsymbol{x}_n}^{y_2}, d_{\boldsymbol{x}_n}^{y_3}, d_{\boldsymbol{x}_n}^{y_4}, d_{\boldsymbol{x}_n}^{y_5}\}$ generated by Eq. (2) to represent the label distribution of sample x_n. Then the problem of Deep Label Distribution Learning can be described as follows:

Let $X = R^{h \times w \times d}$ denotes the input space, where h, w and d are the height, width and number of channels of the input image, respectively. $Y = \{y_1, y_2, y_3, y_4, y_5\}$ denotes the set of labels. $\boldsymbol{d_n} = \{d_{\boldsymbol{x}_n}^{y_1}, d_{\boldsymbol{x}_n}^{y_2}, d_{\boldsymbol{x}_n}^{y_3}, d_{\boldsymbol{x}_n}^{y_4}, d_{\boldsymbol{x}_n}^{y_5}\}$ is the label distribution of sample x_n, where $d_{\boldsymbol{x}_n}^{y_l} \in [0, 1]$ and $\sum_l d_{\boldsymbol{x}_n}^{y_l} = 1$. Given a training set with N instances $D = \{(\boldsymbol{x}_1, \boldsymbol{d}_1), (\boldsymbol{x}_2, \boldsymbol{d}_2), \ldots, (\boldsymbol{x}_N, \boldsymbol{d}_N)\}$, the goal of Deep Adaptive Label Distribution Learning is to learn a conditional probability mass function $\hat{\boldsymbol{d}} = p(\boldsymbol{d}|X; \boldsymbol{\theta})$ from D, where $\boldsymbol{\theta}$ is the parameters in the framework. There are two targets to be optimized, one is $\boldsymbol{\theta}$ and the other is σ in Eq. (2).

The training data is first initialized with the same predefined standard deviation, we set as 0.5 in our experiments. After initialization, each training image $\boldsymbol{x}_n$ is associated with a label distribution $\boldsymbol{d}_n$. Next, during each round of training, the first step is to find a θ that can generate label distribution $\hat{\boldsymbol{d}}$ most similar to $\boldsymbol{d}_n$. During the training process, we can assume that $a = \phi(\boldsymbol{x}|\boldsymbol{\theta})$ is the activation of the last fully connected layer in the deep network we used, then a softmax function is used to turn the activation into a probability distribution as:

$$\hat{d}_{\boldsymbol{x}_n}^{y_j} = \frac{exp(a_j)}{\sum_l exp(a_l)} \tag{3}$$

We use weighted Euclidean distance to measure the similarity of distributions. The loss function can be calculated by:

$$L(\boldsymbol{d}, \hat{\boldsymbol{d}}) = \sqrt{\sum_l \lambda_l * \left(d_{\boldsymbol{x}_n}^{y_l} - \hat{d}_{\boldsymbol{x}_n}^{y_l}\right)^2} \tag{4}$$

Where λ_l is the weight of the label y_l, depending on the number of samples in the dataset, the principle is that the smaller the number of samples, the bigger the weight. Then the best $\boldsymbol{\theta}$ can be determined by minimize the loss function:

$$\boldsymbol{\theta}^* = \arg\min_{\boldsymbol{\theta}} L(\boldsymbol{d}, \hat{\boldsymbol{d}}) \tag{5}$$

This process can be called Deep Label Distribution Learning (LDL). After the DLDL step, the σ in Eq. 2 can be updated by:

$$\boldsymbol{\sigma}_n = \arg\min_{\boldsymbol{\sigma}_n} \left(\alpha_1 * L(\boldsymbol{d}, \hat{\boldsymbol{d}}) + \alpha_2 * \left(\sum_l d_{\boldsymbol{x}_n}^{y_l} y_l - \mu_n\right)\right) \tag{6}$$

Where α_1 and α_2 represent the weights of the two optimization targets, which are set to 0.7 and 0.3 in our experiment. In order to prevent the error of σ_n from being too large when the network is not trained enough, the difference between the weighted average of the new label distribution and the original label is also one of the optimization goals. After σ_n is determined, the label distribution of all training samples can be updated. Then the training set with the new label distribution is send to the DLDL step to begin the next iteration. The whole process repeat until the loss is no longer reduced. Once the training is complete, the predict label distribution $\hat{\boldsymbol{d}}$ of any new input instance X can be generated by a forward run of the network. We can also predict a single score by weighted average of the label distribution:

$$y_{single} = \sum_{l} d_{x_n}^{y_l} y_l \tag{7}$$

This indicates that DALDL is suitable for both classification and regression tasks.

3 Experiments

3.1 Settings

Database. We conduct experiments on three public facial attractiveness prediction datasets. The first one is SCUT-FBP [11], which contains 500 frontal faces with around 70 attractivenes scores between [1, 5]. The second one is SCUT-FBP500 [14], a updated version of SCUT-FBP, which contains 5500 frontal faces of different races, ages and genders. For both SCUT-FBP and SCUT-FBP5500, 5-fold cross validation is used in our experiments. The third dataset is CelebA [15], a large-scale face attributes dataset with more than 200k images. Face attractiveness is one of the 40 binary attributes in CelebA dataset. We test the classification performance of our method on this dataset. Following the standard settings, 80% images are randomly selected as the training set, and the rest 20% as testing set.

Details of Training. Our experiments are implemented with Pytorch. In all the experiments, we use SGD optimizer to train the network for 100 epoches. We fix the batch size as 16, the weight decay as $1e-5$, the momentum as 0.96. The learning rate is first initialized as 0.001, and then gradually decreased by 0.1 per 20 epoches.

Evaluation Criteria. We use three widely used criteria to evaluate the performance of face attractiveness prediction on SCUT-FBP and SCUT-FBP5500, including Pearson Correlation (PC), Root Mean Squared Error (RMSE) and Mean Absolute Error (RMSE). In general, greater PC values while lower RMSE and MAE values indicate better performance. For CelebA, we use accuracy as the criteria.

Table 1. Results of ablation study.

Method	SCUT-FBP			SCUT-FBP5500		
	PC	MAE	RMSE	PC	MAE	RMSE
VGG+single score	0.866	0.297	0.490	0.881	0.246	0.476
VGG+DLDL	0.892	0.271	0.336	0.906	0.224	0.297
VGG+DALDL	0.901	0.248	0.328	0.910	0.219	0.286
VGG+DALDL+WeightedLoss	**0.903**	**0.227**	**0.312**	**0.915**	**0.210**	**0.278**

Table 2. Performance comparison on SCUT-FBP5500.

Method	PC	MAE	RMSE
LBP+GR [14]	0.674	0.391	0.509
Gabor+SVR [14]	0.807	0.401	0.518
AlexNet [14]	0.863	0.265	0.348
ResNet18 [14]	0.890	0.242	0.317
ResNeXt50 [14]	0.900	0.229	0.302
Ours+VGG	0.915	0.210	0.278
Ours+ResNeXt50	**0.920**	**0.200**	**0.269**

3.2 Results and Analysis

We performed abundant and reasonable experiments to prove that our method is effective. For both SCUT-FBP and SCUT-FBP5500, we conduct ablation study based on VGGFace [16], including the following three variants of our model: (1) single label: train the deep network with single label (average score); (2) DLDL: train the deep network with label distribution which is generated with the same standard deviation; (3) DALDL: train the model with automatically updated label distribution; (4) DALDL+weighted Euclidean loss: train the model with automatically updated label distribution and weighted Euclidean loss. Ablation study results are shown in Table 1. The experimental results show that the model trained using label distribution outperforms the model training with single label by a large margin. Notably, on all evaluation criterias, our proposed adaptive label distribution performs better than the label distribution initialized with the same parameters.

We also compared our method with several classic methods in [14]: (1) LBP+GR: Local binary pattern features+Gausian regression; (2) Gabor+SVR: Gabor features+Support Vector Regression; (3) three deep networks including Alexnet, ResNet-18 and ResNext50. Table 2 shows the comparison results on SCUT-FBP5500. Our methods outperforms all the classic methods. In addition, we replace the baseline network in DALDL with ResNeXt50, and the results show that the deeper architecture performs better.

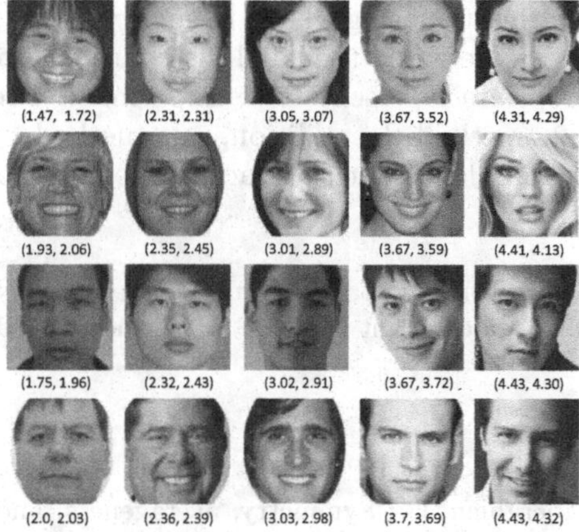

Fig. 3. Prediction results of our method, the numbers below each image corresponding $(groundtruth, prediction)$.

Table 3. Performance comparison on CelebA.

Method	Accuracy (%)
PANDA [17]	81.0
MOON [15]	81.7
Ding [18]	82.9
Ours	**83.9**

There are no face attractiveness prediction methods have been test on the dataset. We compare our methods with several advanced attributes classification methods as shown in Table 3. During training process, we convert the original binary label, which relative to "attractive" and "unattractive", to 5 and 1 following the settings in SCUT-FBP and SCUT-FBP5500. When predicting, we classify the images satisfied $y_{single} > 3$ as "attractive", where y_{single} is the weighted average label distribution calculated by Eq. 7. As shown in Table 3, DALDL outperforms the existing methods.

Figure 3 show some results predicted by DALDL+ResNext50, all the images are selected from SCUT-FBP5500. It can be seen that the scores predicted by our model are highly correlated with the ground-truth labels. Besides, the performance of the model did not fluctuate with changes in other facial attributes, such as gender, race or even facial expression.

4 Conclusions

This paper propose a new method called Deep Adaptive Label Distribution Learning (DALDL). The main purpose of our method is to solve the label ambiguity in face attractiveness prediction. Different from the previous studies, we use label distribution rather than single label to supervise the process of training. During the training of the network, the label distribution is adaptively updated to find the most appropriate representation. Experimental results demonstrate the effectiveness of our method. In addition, our method can be extended to other label ambiguity problems, such as face age estimation, face expression estimation, and so on.

Acknowledgments. This work was partially supported by the National Natural Science Foundation of China under Grant Nos. 61871052 and 61573068.

References

1. Baudouin, J.Y., Tiberghien, G.: Symmetry, averageness, and feature size in the facial attractiveness of women. Acta Psychologica **117**(3), 313–332 (2004)
2. Komori, M., Kawamura, S., Ishihara, S.: Effect of averageness and sexual dimorphism on the judgment of facial attractiveness. Vis. Res. **49**(8), 862–869 (2009)
3. Rubenstein, A.J., Kalakanis, L., Langlois, J.H.: Infant preferences for attractive faces: a cognitive explanation. Dev. Psychol. **35**(3), 848 (1999)
4. Eisenthal, Y., Dror, G.: Learning facial attractiveness (2007)
5. Whitehill, J., Movellan, J.R.: Personalized facial attractiveness prediction. In: IEEE International Conference on Automatic Face and Gesture Recognition, pp. 1–7 (2008)
6. Gray, D., Yu, K., Xu, W., Gong, Y.: Predicting facial beauty without landmarks. In: European Conference on Computer Vision, pp. 434–447 (2010)
7. Wang, S., Shao, M., Fu, Y.: Attractive or not?: beauty prediction with attractiveness-aware encoders and robust late fusion, pp. 805–808 (2014)
8. Gan, J., Li, L., Zhai, Y., Liu, Y.: Deep self-taught learning for facial beauty prediction. Neurocomputing **144**(1), 295–303 (2014)
9. Wang, M., Deng, W.: Deep face recognition: a survey. CoRR abs/1804.06655 (2018)
10. Li, S., Deng, W.: Deep facial expression recognition: a survey. CoRR abs/1804.08348 (2018)
11. Xie, D., Liang, L., Jin, L., Xu, J., Li, M.: SCUT-FBP: a benchmark dataset for facial beauty perception **9**(6), e98879 (2015)
12. Ren, Y., Geng, X.: Sense beauty by label distribution learning. In: Twenty-Sixth International Joint Conference on Artificial Intelligence, pp. 2648–2654 (2017)
13. Fan, Y.Y., et al.: Label distribution-based facial attractiveness computation by deep residual learning. IEEE Trans. Multimedia **20**(8), 2196–2208 (2016)
14. Liang, L., Lin, L., Jin, L., Xie, D., Li, M.: SCUT-FBP5500: a diverse benchmark dataset for multi-paradigm facial beauty prediction (2018)
15. Liu, Z., Luo, P., Wang, X., Tang, X.: Deep learning face attributes in the wild (2014)
16. Simonyan, K., Zisserman, A.: Very deep convolutional networks for large-scale image recognition. Computer Science (2014)
17. Zhang, N., Paluri, M., Ranzato, M., Darrell, T., Bourdev, L.: PANDA: pose aligned networks for deep attribute modeling (2014)
18. Hui, D., et al.: A deep cascade network for unaligned face attribute classification (2017)

LWFD: A Simple Light-Weight Network for Face Detection

Huan Liang, Jiani Hu, and Weihong Deng(✉)

Beijing University of Posts and Telecommunications, Beijing, China
sherryliang39@163.com, {jnhu,whdeng}@bupt.edu.cn

Abstract. In the latest field of object detection, whatever it is one-stage approach or two-stage approach, both of them are using the CNNs with complex calculations to guide the detection performance better. But this also greatly limits our use of the platform (only available on the GPU), so we propose a simple light-weight network for face detection based on the well performance light-weight network backbone which can run on CPU or ARM. In our approach, we have a light-weight network that combine a simple but effective detection framework, a hyperparameter to control the number of channels. It makes our model allowed to have smaller model, faster speed and better accuracy. LWFD can perform CNN inference on mobile devices, and 1.0x run at 90 ms on 2.4 GHz CPU with f-score of 89% on FDDB dataset.

Keywords: Light-weight network · Face detection · Compression

1 Introduction

With the popularity of deep convolutional neural networks, more and more people use convolutional neural networks to solve related visual problems. In recent years, research on CNNs models has emerged in an endless stream, resulting in excellent network structures such as VGG [1], GoogLeNet [2], ResNet [3], Xception [4] and so on, even surpassing humans in multiple visual tasks. However, these successful models are always based on huge computational complexity. This limits the ability of such models, so that they only to be used for high-performance server devices, and not for many mobile devices.

Therefore, many researchers have emerged to focus on researching more light-weight network structures, such as SqueezeNet [5], MobileNet [6,7], ShuffleNet [8,9]. Detection tasks are more complicated than classification tasks, so the requirements for equipment performance are higher, which greatly limits our available scenarios. Therefore, a light-weight and also good performance detection model which can be used on the mobile devices has become a hot topic in the industry and researchers.

Face detection is one of the most studied problems in all object detection sub-directions. Face detection is a fundamental problem in a large number of face-related applications in computer vision tasks, such as face recognition [10],

Z. Sun et al. (Eds.): CCBR 2019, LNCS 11818, pp. 207–215, 2019.
https://doi.org/10.1007/978-3-030-31456-9_23

facial expression recognition [11] and so on. So we always choose the methods of object detection to solve the problems of face detection.

The approach we proposed is to provide some solutions of this problem and apply on face detection task. The major contributions of this work are summarized as follows:

(1) Our approach use light-weight network backbone combining a simple but effective detection framework. Actually, in order to get better performance, many light-weight network use Light-Head R-CNN [12] or Faster R-CNN [13] detection framework (such as ShuffleNet) so that some special parts such as ROI-pooling cannot apply on CPU or ARM. So we construct a framework that is easy to implement on mobile devices, combined with the advantages of the current single-stage detection method [14–16], and use some skills that can improve the accuracy without affecting the speed of the model, making this light-weight model get better Performance.
(2) Generating anchor by data clustering [16] so that anchor can fit our object better and training a pretrain model for face detection, to make it get better performance. Light-weight model is hard to train due to the small amount of parameters and we know from ImageNet [17] that a better pre-training model can make the model training converge faster.
(3) Introducing the hyperparameter control channel number [7]. It likes the concept of channel clipping, but much easier. We control the number of channels by hyperparameter, so that this model can better meet our needs. It depends on whether we choose speed or accuracy.

2 Related Work

Face detection has also been widely studied and applied in the past two decades. Early research are deformable part models (DPM) based methods and cascaded AdaBoost classifier based on Haar-like features for face detection. The recent advances in face detection are mainly focused on deep learning-based methods, because of the success of convolutional neural networks. CNNs is quickly used for face detection. [18,19] introduces cascaded CNNs to learn face detectors with a coarse-to-fine strategy. [20] introduces the intersection-over-union (IoU) loss function, to directly minimize the IoUs of the predictions and the ground-truths. More recently, face detector always use latest detection algorithm as base, such as two-stage detection (Faster R-CNN [13], Mask R-CNN [21], Light-Head R-CNN [12]), one-stage detection (YOLO series [15,16], SSD [14]). And make some modifications, which can achieve good results.

If we choose to use the suitable CNNs combined detection algorithm to achieve the face detection task, we need to consider the choice of backbone which greatly affects speed and accuracy of the model. Since we need a light-weight model, we prefer a light-weight network like [6–9]. What's more, considering what type of detection framework we should use, one-stage or two-stage. Since we would like to implement on mobile devices, it should be more like an end-to-end detection framework [14–16]. further more, we should think how the loss function should be designed. The loss function is very important in CNNs, because it decides what kind of information the whole network has learned. And what else can we do besides these key points to make this network work better and fit our expectations better.

3 Our Approach

Under the premise that our two-stage detection and one-stage detection have achieved well performances, we should pay more attention to improve the other aspects of detection. When we face the real-word scene problems, we can not have high-computation devices (such as GPU) all the time. Motivated by the great success of the state-of-the-art light-weight framework ShuffleNet series [6,9] and MobileNet series [6,7], We design a simple detection algorithm based light-weight network to construct a face detection module that can be run on CPU or ARM.

3.1 Network Architecture

The backbone of a model mainly play the role of feature extraction, so the choice of backbone is related to the performance of the entire model. In Table 1, we can see the classification results, speeds, and flops of several popular light-weight backbone model [4,6–9]. After comparing, we chose the shufflenetV2 [9] which has a good balance between accuracy and complexity as the backbone of our light-weight detection model.

Table 1. Comparison of several popular light-weight network architectures over classification error, arm speed and complexity. All architectures is 1.0x.

Network	Top-1 err. (%)	ARM speed/FPS	Complexity/MFlops
Xception	34.1	19.5	145
mobilenetv1	29.4	6.5	569
mobilenetv2	28.3	8.9	300
shufflenetv1 (g = 3)	32.6	21.8	140
shufflenetv2	30.6	24.4	146

The detection framework we use is based on single-stage detection method that like SSD [14] and YOLO [15,16]. We introduce the concept of anchor according to SSD [14], YOLO [16] and Faster R-CNN [13]. After deep convolution feature extraction, each pixel point of the last feature map is mapped to the original image to generate several boundingbox which related with location of object. The number and the aspect ratio of each anchor can be set. We do not use the SSD multi-scale feature map extraction anchor because the multi-scale feature extraction speed is slow, and the scene we are facing is some simple face scenes (FDDB dataset). So only a single layer feature map is used to generate anchors. We further use convolution to extract features for obtaining finer location and classification of each location based on generated anchor, and send these predictions to our Multi-task Loss for back-propagation learning. The main difference between our detection model and the general one-stage detection model is that we focus on its light-weight so that model can performance on CPU or ARM. What's more, we can adjust the number of anchors and the aspect ratio according to the face scale [16], and compress or increase the number of channels by our own needs through some hyperparameter [7]. Besides we can use some tricks such as a better pre-training model for face detection and multi-scale training for better performance (Fig. 1).

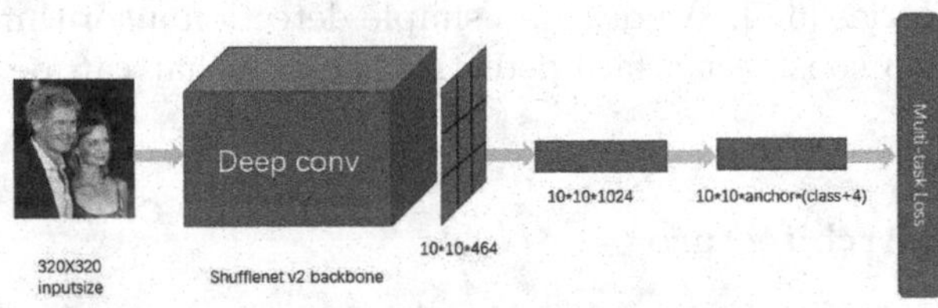

Fig. 1. An overview of our Network Architecture. We first extract features through conv with a pre-trained ConvNet which trained by CelebA.

3.2 Multi-task Loss Function

Loss function is important in our model training. The formulation of the loss function is directly related to what our network learn. In the detection, we have two tasks, one is to find the location of the object, and the other is to confirm which category the object belongs to. So this loss function is the combination of the box-classification loss and the box-regression loss. In addition, we add a loss function that corrects the anchor in the early stage of training [16], making the anchor more suitable for our goal. The entire loss function is formulated as follow:

$$L(p_i, t_i, anchor_i) = \sum_{j=0}^{n} L_{cls}(p^*, p_i) + \lambda * L_{loc}(t^*, t_i) + \alpha *_{(i<12800)} L_{anchor}(t^*, anchor_i) \quad (1)$$

L_{cls} is softmax loss over background/foreground classes, L_{loc} is SmoothL1 [13], L_{anchor} is MSE. p_i is the predicted probability of the proposal region being a face. The ground-truth label p^* is 1 if the proposal is positive, and is 0 if the proposal is negative. t_i is a vector representing the 4 parameterized coordinates of the predicted bounding box and t^* is that of the ground-truth. λ, α is used to balance weights between three loss.

3.3 Anchor

The biggest difference between detection and classification is that you need a location for the detection object, which is our boundingbox. The early region proposal in R-CNN which based on Selective Search, but its speed is too slow and the effect is not very good. An anchor was proposed at [13], Subsequently, anchor was also introduced in the one-stage detection [14,16]. And we decide use clustering to generate anchor to obtain a more accurate object aspect ratio and size which can improve the object detection performance [15,16].

3.4 Channel Compression

Two hyperparameters were introduced in [7]: the width hyperparameter α and resolution hyperparameter ρ. The main function of these two hyperparameters is to control the number of channels in the downsampling process and the inputsize of image. In our approach, we introduce the width factor α, which can be used to increase or compress the number of channels to let our model suits our needs better. Increasing the number of channels can increase parameters of the whole model, making the information it learns richer and the effect will be relatively better, but it is easy to cause a problem that the saddle point of the model will increase, the training is difficult, and the performance of the model may be affected. Decreasing the number of channels can make the whole model less parameter and faster, but it will loss some accuracy. We can constantly adjust this parameter to get the most suitable model for us.

3.5 Multi-scale Training

This multi-scale training method was proposed in [16]. During training, the input size of the network was fine-tuned per 10 iterations, and we randomly selected one of the resize scales we provide for training. Considering the range of the face size and the image size we used, we set the resize size from 288 to 416, which allows the network to adapt to different scale inputs. To some extent, accuracy can also be slightly improved [16].

4 Experiments

4.1 Dataset

WIDER FACE. In our approach, we focus on a light-weight network face detection task, It means that there are less parameters in our CNNs so that it's hard to directly train on complete WIDER FACE dataset. Therefore, we decided to according annotations filter some difficult samples (too small or dense faces) to train on our detection model. We call this small dataset WIDERFACE-refine which including 8879 images for training set and 872 images for val set.

FDDB. FDDB has a total of 2845 images and 5171 marked faces. It is the most commonly used database for the face detection task. The scenes in this data set can basically meet the needs of daily face detection, which our light-weight network for face detection focus on. So we decide to use FDDB dataset as our test set that reflects the performance of our model.

CelebA. CelebA each picture has a lot of marked features, such as face bbox labels, 5 face key points labels and 40 face attribute labels. It is widely used in face-related computer vision training tasks, and can be used for face attribute identification training, face detection training, and facial landmark detection training. Due to the difficult training characteristics of our light-weight network, we need a better pre-train model to learn some low-level features, so we choose CelebA as the dataset for our pre-training model training.

It's necessary for raw data to be pre-processed for experimentation, which is an effective step to simplify complexity and improve the effectiveness of the method. Data preprocessing needs to consider some random transformation operations on the original image, such as random cropping and random flipping. The purpose of these operations is to enhance the data and prevent over-fitting in subsequent training.

4.2 Implementation Details

Firstly, we use ClelebA to train a pre-train model for face detection. Because it's a little bit hard to directly train on WIDER FACE, even WIDERFACE-refine. It should be a big problem that there are too few publicly available face detection data sets.

After use the face bbox labels of CelebA to train a pre-train model, we continuously train on WIDERFACE-refine. We set the learning rate to 10^{-4} for the first 40k iterations, and decay it to $5 * 10^{-5}$ and $2.5 * 10^{-6}$ for training another 10k and 10k iterations, respectively. We use the default batch size 32 and inputsize $320 * 320$ in training, and only use ShffleNetV2 as the backbone network. Besides, we choose anchor generated by k-means clustering as 5 and use multi-scale training skills during training. What's more, we try compress the channels of network 0.5 times as original.

When testing, we not only test on GPU (GTX 1080), but also convert the caffemodel to ncnn in order to get a similar speed as arm. The results of caffemodel is same as ncnn but have little difference with ncnn-int8. We can see the results at 4.3.

4.3 Performance

We can see our method (1.0x-320) compare with some published face detection method on FDDB dataset in Figs. 2 and 3. Our method have well performance on both ContROC and DiscROC. It can be noticed that our discrete ROC curve and continuous ROC curve is almost superior to other method. Maybe some method a little bit superior to ours on one of ROC curve but behind us on another ROC curve. In general, our method has a good result on FDDB dataset. What's more, we through control some variables to compare some of our models. The results is in Table 2, we can see if compress our model by quantification or decreasing our feature channels, it will speed up but pay the price of losing accuracy. Our 0.5x model is double faster than 1.0x model, but loss three points of accuracy. Int8 quantification loss less accuracy than decreasing our feature channels, it's a good skill to improve the ability of models.

Table 2. We convert the model to ncnn and test on CPU, because we want to make it possible to close to test on ARM. We also try the int8 quantitative tool provided by ncnn to further compress our module, and evaluate all the modules with metric of f-score (IOU = 0.5) which combine precision and recall. Besides, our 1.0x module run at 18 ms on GTX 1080.

Network	CPU with ncnn	f-score ($\alpha = 1$)
Our module 1.0x-320	90 ms	0.882
Our module 0.5x-320	45 ms	0.857
Our module 1.0x-int8-320	50 ms	0.874
Our module 0.5x-int8-320	25 ms	0.848

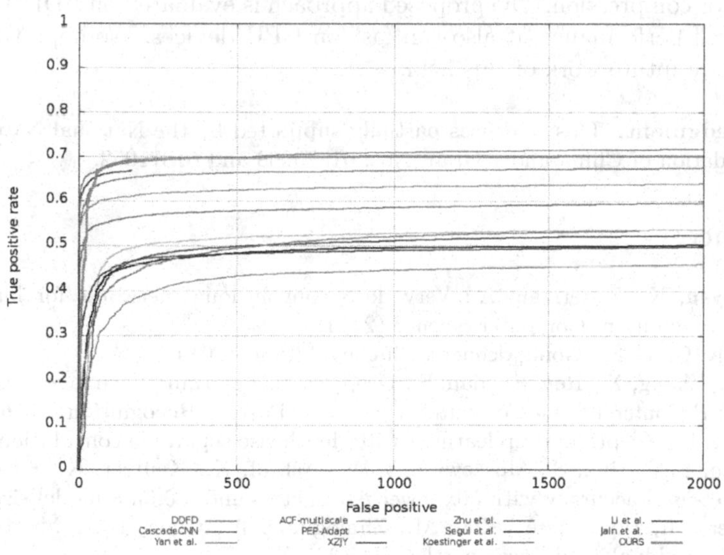

Fig. 2. Continuous ROC curve

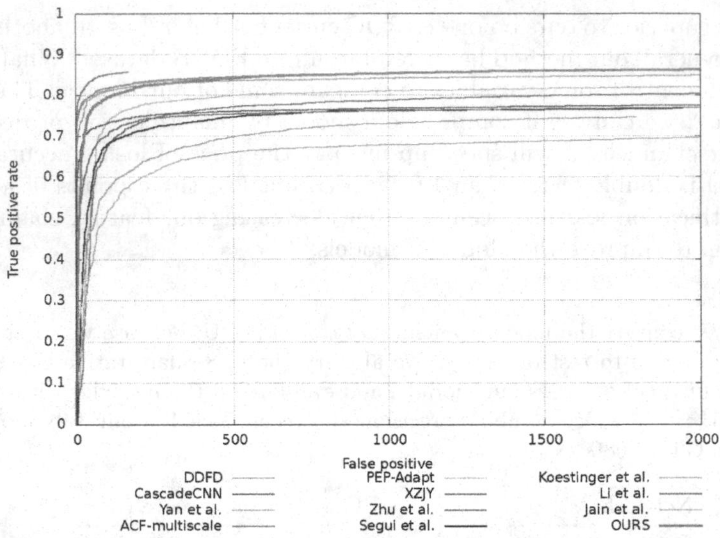

Fig. 3. Discrete ROC curve

5 Conclusion

We propose a simple light-weight network for face detection by integrating light-weight network, some detection method and several newly developed skill for detection or compression. The proposed approach is evaluated on FDDB dataset and get well performance, it also run fast on CPU devices. We hope this work could inspire future work of this field.

Acknowledgment. This work was partially supported by the National Natural Science Foundation of China under Grant Nos. 61573068 and 61871052.

References

1. Simonyan, K., Zisserman, A.: Very deep convolutional networks for large-scale image recognition. Computer Science (2014)
2. Szegedy, C., et al.: Going deeper with convolutions (2014)
3. He, K., Zhang, X., Ren, S., Jian, S.: Deep residual learning for image recognition. In: IEEE Conference on Computer Vision and Pattern Recognition (2016)
4. Chollet, F.: Xception: deep learning with depthwise separable convolutions (2016)
5. Iandola, F.N., Han, S., Moskewicz, M.W., Ashraf, K., Keutzer, K.: SqueezeNet: AlexNet-level accuracy with 50x fewer parameters and <0.5mb model size (2016)
6. Sandler, M., Howard, A., Zhu, M., Zhmoginov, A., Chen, L.C.: MobileNetV2: inverted residuals and linear bottlenecks (2018)
7. Howard, A.G., et al.: MobileNets: efficient convolutional neural networks for mobile vision applications (2017)
8. Zhang, X., Zhou, X., Lin, M., Sun, J.: ShuffleNet: an extremely efficient convolutional neural network for mobile devices (2017)

9. Ma, N., Zhang, X., Zheng, H.T., Sun, J.: ShuffleNet V2: practical guidelines for efficient CNN architecture design (2018)
10. Wang, M., Deng, W.: Deep face recognition: a survey. CoRR abs/1804.06655 (2018)
11. Li, S., Deng, W.: Deep facial expression recognition: a survey. CoRR abs/1804.08348 (2018)
12. Li, Z., Chao, P., Gang, Y., Zhang, X., Jian, S.: Light-head R-CNN: in defense of two-stage object detector (2017)
13. Ren, S., He, K., Girshick, R., Sun, J.: Faster R-CNN: towards real-time object detection with region proposal networks. IEEE Trans. Pattern Anal. Mach. Intell. **39**(6), 1137–1149 (2017)
14. Liu, W., et al.: SSD: single shot multibox detector. In: Leibe, B., Matas, J., Sebe, N., Welling, M. (eds.) ECCV 2016. LNCS, vol. 9905, pp. 21–37. Springer, Cham (2016). https://doi.org/10.1007/978-3-319-46448-0_2
15. Redmon, J., Farhadi, A.: YOLOv3: an incremental improvement (2018)
16. Redmon, J., Farhadi, A.: Yolo9000: better, faster, stronger. In: IEEE Conference on Computer Vision and Pattern Recognition (2017)
17. Deng, J., Dong, W., Socher, R., Li, L.J., Li, K., Li, F.F.: ImageNet: a large-scale hierarchical image database. In: IEEE Conference on Computer Vision and Pattern Recognition (2009)
18. Li, H., Zhe, L., Shen, X., Brandt, J., Gang, H.: A convolutional neural network cascade for face detection. In: Computer Vision and Pattern Recognition (2015)
19. Zhang, K., Zhang, Z., Li, Z., Yu, Q.: Joint face detection and alignment using multitask cascaded convolutional networks. IEEE Sig. Process. Lett. **23**(10), 1499–1503 (2016)
20. Yu, J., Jiang, Y., Wang, Z., Cao, Z., Huang, T.: UnitBox: an advanced object detection network (2016)
21. He, K., Gkioxari, G., Dollár, P., Girshick, R.: Mask R-CNN. In: 2017 IEEE International Conference on Computer Vision (ICCV) (2017)

Dairy Cow Tiny Face Recognition Based on Convolutional Neural Networks

Zehao Yang, Hao Xiong, Xiaolang Chen, Hanxing Liu, Yingjie Kuang, and Yuefang Gao(✉)

College of Mathematics and Informatics,
South China Agricultural University, Guangzhou, China
scau_xionghao@outlook.com, cxlcxlcxlang@163.com,
{lhx666, kuangyj, gaoyuefang}@scau.edu.cn

Abstract. In practical applications of cow face recognition, the accuracy is often lower than expected because of the influence of camera's low resolution and position. In this paper, we aim to develop and pilot a method for improving recognition accuracy and recovering identity information for generating cow faces closed to the real identity. Specifically, our network architecture consists of two parts: a super-resolution network for recovering a high-resolution cow face from a low-resolution one, and a face recognition network. The super-resolution network is cascaded with the recognition network. An alternately training strategy was introduced to ensure the stability of the training process. The cow face dataset was collected by us, which contains 85200 dairy cow face images from 1000 subjects. Experimental evaluations demonstrate the superiority of the proposed method. Our method has achieved 94.92% recognition accuracy on the small size (12×14) cow face.

Keywords: Cow recognition · Convolutional neural network · Super-resolution

1 Introduction

Recently, animal recognition has played a significant role in production management, controlling the outbreak of critical diseases, vaccination and traceability [1, 2]. The traditional animal recognition methods, such as ear-tagging, embedded microchips, ear tattoos and RFID-based identification systems, have been applied to recognize individual livestock animal [1]. But the performance of the conventional methods is not good due to their vulnerability to losses, sensor malfunction and fraud of tag number. These challenges hinder the application of the technologies.

In contrast, computer-vision-based methods do not have the disadvantages. As an emerging research field of computer vision, visual-based animal recognition is applied at various aspects to recognize and classify different species based on discriminatory set of features. For example, Li et al. [3] introduced an individual dairy cow identification approach by extracting shape features of the Region of Interest of the cow tail and head with Zernike moments, and classifying alternatively by four classifiers. Zin et al. [4] proposed a cow body recognition method based on a deep convolutional neural

Z. Sun et al. (Eds.): CCBR 2019, LNCS 11818, pp. 216–222, 2019.
https://doi.org/10.1007/978-3-030-31456-9_24

network, which was introduced for learning the black and white pattern of the dairy cow body. Hansen et al. [5] adapted convolutional neural network face recognition approaches from human literature to on farm pig-face recognition. However, due to the low resolution and high angle of the camera in the farm environment, it is usually impossible to obtain a high-quality cow face image, which causes severe damage to recognition performance.

There has been many researches into recovering and recognizing low quality faces [6]. For example, Chen et al. [7] proposed a deep end-to-end Face Super-Resolution Network (FSRNet) to make full use of the geometry prior such as facial landmark heatmaps and parsing maps. SICNN [8] introduced a super-identity loss function and a domain-integrated training approach to stable the joint training.

In order to recover identity information from low-quality cow face images, generate faces closed to the real ones and improve the performance of tiny face recognition, we propose a tiny cow face recognition framework, which consists of a super-resolution network and a face recognition network. We also use a training strategy adopted from the human face recognition literature for ensuring the stability of the training process. A farm cow face dataset collected by us is introduced for training the deep learning model.

The remainder of this paper is organized as follows. Section 2 outlines the data collection and introduces the background to the chosen approaches. The experimental comparisons over the state-of-the-art SR methods are presented in Sect. 3. Section 4 concludes our work.

2 Methodology

2.1 Dairy Cow Face Dataset

The dairy cow face dataset was collected by us over a period of two months in a dairy cow farm in China. The dataset contains 85200 cow face images from 1000 Holstein dairy cows. The images in the dataset are manually collected by mobile phone and digital camera or extracted from video sequences. The cow images with the same ear tag number are placed in the same folder. To avoid very similar data, the structural-similarity index measure (SSIM) [9] is employed to measure similarity between images. The images deemed too similar to one another will be discarded. Moreover, we used the object detection CNN model to crop the cow face region of each image. Some examples from dataset are shown in Fig. 1.

2.2 Tiny Cow Face Recognition Framework

Deep learning and convolutional networks have been applied in a wide range of both research areas and industrial settings. In this paper, we propose a tiny cow face recognition framework with coupling the super-resolution model and recognition model.

Super-resolution (SR) aims to convert a given low-resolution (LR) image with coarse details to a corresponding high-resolution (HR) image with better visual quality

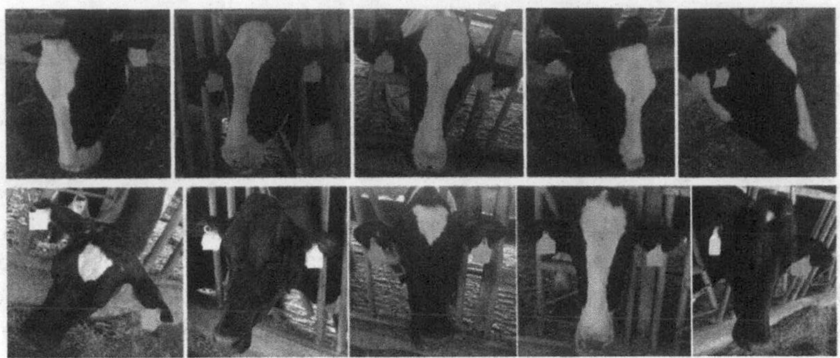

Fig. 1. Some dairy cow faces images from the proposed dataset.

and refined details. Thanks to the advances in deep learning techniques and the increasing size of training data in recent years, deep learning based SR models have been actively explored and frequently achieve the state-of-the-art performance on various benchmarks of SR [10]. However, most of existing works do not consider the recovery of identity information, so that they cannot generate faces closed to the real ones and do great damage to recognition performance. To verify the performance of different super-resolution models on recovering the identity information, we tested three state-of-the-art SR networks: Super-Resolution Convolutional Neural Network abbreviated as SRCNN [11], is the first successful attempt towards using only convolutional layers for super-resolution and only consists of three convolutional and two ReLU layers, stacked together linearly; Enhanced Deep Super-Resolution (EDSR) [12], was inspired by ResNet [13] architecture and demonstrated substantial improvements by removing Batch Normalization layers, achieve better performance compared to older architectures such as SRCNN; Residual Channel Attention Network (RCAN) [14], introduced a channel attention mechanism within each local residual block and a recursive residual design where residual connections exist within each block of a global residual network, and reached the top performance compared to contemporary approaches such as VDSR [15] and RDN [16].

Due to the superior classification performance of ResNet50 [13], we propose to use it as the recognition model.

The whole network structure is shown in Fig. 2.

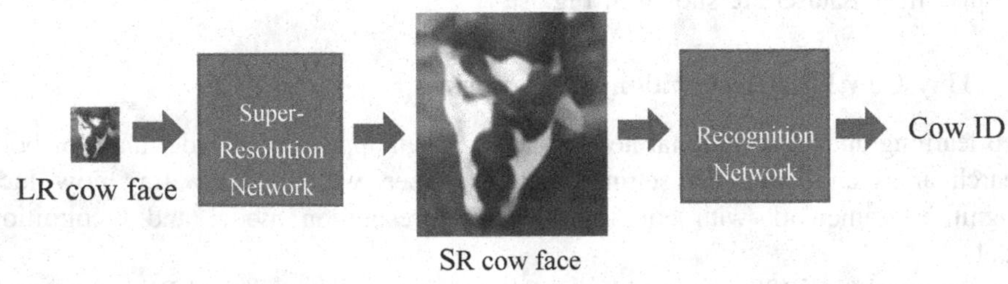

Fig. 2. Tiny cow face recognition framework

2.3 Training Strategy

Due to the different task between the SR and recognition, the model is difficult to converge if we simply train both SR network and recognition network from scratch. To facilitate the training difficulty, we adapt an alternately training method from human face hallucination literature [8].

Specifically, we divide the training process into two stages. First, we separately train a super-resolution model with the L1 loss and a ResNet50 classification model with cross-entropy loss from scratch. Then, we finetune recognition network and SR network alternately in each iteration. In each iteration, we first update the recognition network using the fused recognition loss,

$$L_R = C_{HR} + C_{SR} \tag{1}$$

where C_{HR} denotes the cross-entropy loss of original HR image and C_{SR} denotes the cross-entropy loss of SR image.

Next, we update the SR network by jointly using the super-resolution loss and super-identity loss,

$$L_S = L_{SR} + \alpha L_{SI} \tag{2}$$

where L_{SR} is L1 loss as super-resolution loss, and L_{SI} is super-identity loss. We use α to balance the weight of two loss functions, and in our experiment the α is set to 8. The L_{SI} is defined as:

$$L_{SI} = \left\| \frac{f_{SR}}{\|f_{SR}\|_2} - \frac{f_{HR}}{\|f_{HR2}\|_2} \right\| \tag{3}$$

where f_{SR} and f_{HR} denote the SR and original HR image identity features extracted from recognition model. For ResNet50, the feature is a 2048-dimensional feature vector. The alternative optimization process is conducted until the whole network converge.

3 Experiments and Analysis

3.1 Experimental Setup

We implement our models with the PyTorch 1.1.0 framework and train them using NVIDIA GeForce GTX Titan X on Ubuntu 18.04 LTS OS. Stochastic Gradient Descent (SGD) method is employed as the optimizer.

We use 82010 of 85200 cow face images as training set and 3190 images as test set for training the super-resolution network and recognition network separately and fine-tuning the whole network.

For SR network training, we preprocess the LR face images by bicubic interpolation downsampling to the input size, and then separately train SR model for 12 × 14 inputs with 8 × upscaling factor, 24 × 28 inputs with 4 × upscaling factor and 56 × 48 inputs with 2 × upscaling factor separately. The training and model parameters are set the same as the papers.

For face recognition network training, the input face images are resized to 112 × 96 pixels by bicubic interpolation and applied random horizontal flip and random crop. We use batch size of 128, set learning rate as 0.01 and set momentum as 0.5, train ResNet50 from scratch for 200 epochs to ensure model convergence.

For whole network fine-tuning, we use the same parameters as about except adjusting the batch size to 16, dividing the learning rate by 10, setting momentum as 0.9 and fine-tuning for 30 epochs.

3.2 Results

First, we test our tiny cow face recognition framework before fine-tuning, the results are listed in Table 1.

Table 1. Accuracy of frameworks before fine-tuning (%)

Scale	Bicubic	SRCNN	EDSR	RCAN	Ground-truth HR
8×	11.69	20.56	44.00	56.66	96.67
4×	61.61	81.67	89.53	90.10	96.67
2×	93.73	95.68	96.33	96.33	96.67

The comparison results of fine-tuned tiny cow face recognition framework with different super-resolution methods are presented in Table 2.

Table 2. Accuracy of framework with different super-resolution methods

Scale		LR	Bicubic	SRCNN	EDSR	RCAN	GT
8×	Output					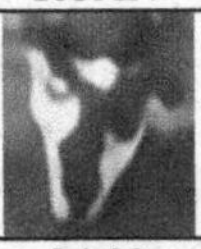	
	Acc. (%)	-	11.69	90.41	93.61	**94.92**	96.67
4×	Output						
	Acc. (%)	-	61.61	96.87	**97.37**	97.27	96.67
2×	Output		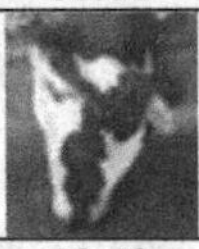				
	Acc. (%)	-	93.73	97.71	97.65	**98.43**	96.67

As shown in Table 2, our tiny cow face recognition framework achieves cow face recognition accuracy of 94.92% with 12 × 14 pixels input, 97.37% with 24 × 28 pixels input and 98.43% with 48 × 56 pixels input. The comparison results of Tables 1 and 2 demonstrate the effectiveness of the fine-tuning strategy. Interestingly, our framework even achieves better face recognition accuracy with 4 × and 2 × upscaling factor than ground-truth high-resolution images, indicate that SR network may be able to extract more useful features. RCAN shows the best visual quality and identity recovery quality, but its computation is also large. SRCNN, in contrast, has only three CNN layers, still achieves a decent result.

4 Conclusion

In this paper, we introduce a cow face dataset collected by us, and presents the 2 × , 4 × and 8 × upscaling results of tiny cow face recognition framework fine-tuning with three state-of-the-art super-resolution methods: SRCNN, EDSR and RCAN. The results show a superior visual quality and demonstrate that our tiny cow face recognition framework can significantly improve the recognizability of low-resolution dairy cow face.

Acknowledgement. This work is supported in part by the National Science Foundation of China (NSFC) under Grant No. 61702196.

References

1. Awad, A.I.: From classical methods to animal biometrics: a review on cattle identification and tracking. Comput. Electron. Agric. **123**, 423–435 (2016)
2. Gaber, T., Tharwat, A., Hassanien, A.E., Snasel, V.: Biometric cattle identification approach based on Weber's Local Descriptor and AdaBoost classifier. Comput. Electron. Agric. **122**, 55–66 (2016)
3. Li, W., Ji, Z., Wang, L., Sun, C., Yang, X.: Automatic individual identification of Holstein dairy cows using tailhead images. Comput. Electron. Agric. **142**, 622–631 (2017)
4. Zin, T.T., Phyo, C.N., Tin, P., Hama, H., Kobayashi, I.: Image technology based cow identification system using deep learning. In: Proceedings of the International MultiConference of Engineers and Computer Scientists, vol. 1 (2018)
5. Hansen, M.F., et al.: Towards on-farm pig face recognition using convolutional neural networks. Comput. Ind. **98**, 145–152 (2018)
6. Li, P., Prieto, L., Mery, D., Flynn, P.: Face recognition in low quality images: a survey. arXiv preprint arXiv:1805.11519 (2018)
7. Chen, Y., Tai, Y., Liu, X., Shen, C., Yang, J.: FSRNet: end-to-end learning face super-resolution with facial priors. In: Proceedings of the IEEE Conference on Computer Vision and Pattern Recognition, pp. 2492–2501 (2018)
8. Zhang, K., et al.: Super-identity convolutional neural network for face hallucination. In: The European Conference on Computer Vision (ECCV), pp. 183–198 (2018)
9. Wang, Z., Bovik, A.C., Sheikh, H.R., Simoncelli, E.P., et al.: Image quality assessment: from error visibility to structural similarity. IEEE Trans. Image Process. **13**, 600–612 (2004)
10. Wang, Z., Chen, J., Hoi, S.C.: Deep learning for image super-resolution: a survey. arXiv preprint arXiv:1902.06068 (2019)
11. Dong, C., Loy, C.C., He, K., Tang, X.: Learning a deep convolutional network for image super-resolution. In: Fleet, D., Pajdla, T., Schiele, B., Tuytelaars, T. (eds.) ECCV 2014. LNCS, vol. 8692, pp. 184–199. Springer, Cham (2014). https://doi.org/10.1007/978-3-319-10593-2_13

12. Lim, B., Son, S., Kim, H., Nah, S., Lee, K.M.: Enhanced deep residual networks for single image super-resolution. In: Proceedings of the IEEE Conference on Computer Vision and Pattern Recognition Workshops, pp. 136–144 (2017)
13. He, K., Zhang, X., Ren, S., Sun, J.: Deep residual learning for image recognition. In: Proceedings of the IEEE Conference on Computer Vision and Pattern Recognition, pp. 770–778 (2016)
14. Zhang, Y., Li, K., Li, K., Wang, L., Zhong, B., Fu, Y.: Image super-resolution using very deep residual channel attention networks. In: Proceedings of the European Conference on Computer Vision (ECCV), pp. 286–301 (2018)
15. Kim, J., Kwon Lee, J., Mu Lee, K.: Accurate image super-resolution using very deep convolutional networks. In: The IEEE Conference on Computer Vision and Pattern Recognition (CVPR), pp. 1646–1654 (2016)
16. Zhang, Y., Tian, Y., Kong, Y., Zhong, B., Fu, Y.: Residual dense network for image super-resolution. In: The IEEE Conference on Computer Vision and Pattern Recognition (CVPR), pp. 2472–2481 (2018)

Reconstructed Face Recognition

Xiaoning Liu(✉), Shanghao Zhao, Shixiong Wang, Yunpeng Jing, and Jun Feng

College of Information Science and Technology, Northwest University, Xi'an 710127, China
xnliu@nwu.edu.cn

Abstract. Computer-aided craniofacial reconstruction technology has very important application in the field of criminal investigation. But reconstruction a face from skull is not the end of work. The reconstructed face needs to be automatically identified in the missing population photo database. This paper proposed a reconstructed face recognition method based on deep learning. We trained a weighted fusion deep network for feature extraction, built two different neural network models for reconstructed face verification and use KNN for reconstructed face recognition. This paper uses 166 sets of data for experiments. In reconstructed face verification, the accuracy of using the Pseudo Siamese neural network is 98.33%. In reconstructed face recognition, the Top1 accuracy of the method using Pseudo Siamese neural network is 99.57%. Experiments show that the proposed method can effectively improve the accuracy of reconstructed face recognition.

Keywords: Craniofacial reconstruction · Reconstructed face recognition · Deep neural network

1 Introduction

Computer-aided craniofacial reconstruction technology has very important application in criminal investigation. When identifying an unknown skull, it is necessary to find a face image of the missing person that is most similar to the reconstructed face in the missing population photo database. Reconstructed face recognition combines the practical application needs of the criminal investigation field. Therefore, this research has very important significance.

Reconstructed face has the following characteristics: lack of texture information, no hair, closed eyes and large differences in illumination. Reconstructed face recognition is a process from 3D face to 2D face recognition. Huang et al. [1] proposed geometric feature based method to recognize face reconstructed from skull. Zhao et al. [2] improved the method based on feature point. Pu et al. [3] proposed method based on local feature. Li et al. [4] proposed method based on global feature. Zhao et al. [5] improved the method based on global feature. But the accuracy and robustness of traditional methods need to be improved.

The reconstructed face recognition mainly uses methods from the field of face recognition. With the successful application of deep learning in the field of face

Z. Sun et al. (Eds.): CCBR 2019, LNCS 11818, pp. 223–230, 2019.
https://doi.org/10.1007/978-3-030-31456-9_25

recognition [6–9], more and more excellent face recognition models have been proposed. The accuracy of face recognition based on deep learning has exceeded the human eyes. The face recognition method based on deep learning can be divided into two categories according to the loss function, one is metric learning [8] and the other is classification [7].

The face recognition method based on deep learning requires a large amount of data to train. In recent years, transfer learning [10], zero-sample learning [11] and single-sample learning [12] have been successfully applied in small datasets.

Inspired by the face recognition network model [7–9], single sample learning [12, 13], Siamese network model [14] and Pseudo Siamese network model [14–17]. We trained a weighted fusion deep network for feature extraction, built two different neural network models for reconstructed face verification and use KNN (K-Nearest Neighbors) for reconstructed face recognition.

2 Method

We use deep convolutional neural network for face feature extraction and the network called CNN (Convolutional Neural Network) deep architecture. This paper designs two different neural network models to measure the similarity between the two kinds of face. We called the neural network decision model. The overall architecture is shown in Fig. 1.

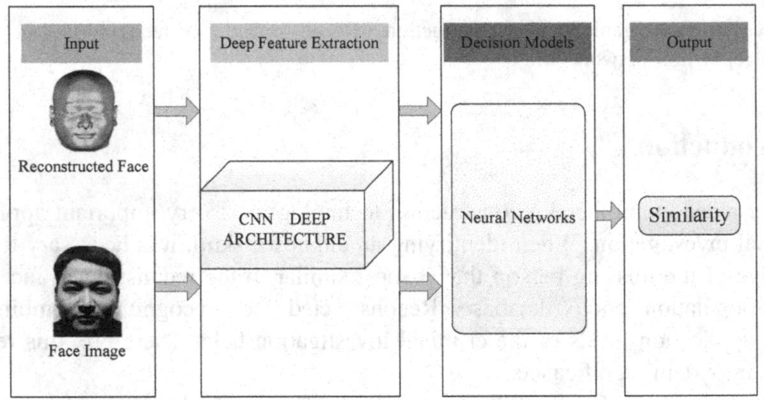

Fig. 1. The overall framework of reconstructed face verification

2.1 CNN Deep Architecture

CNN Deep architecture plays the role of feature extraction. We trained a weighted fusion deep network for feature extraction. InceptionV3 is a pre-trained model (Fig. 2).

Mini-CNN is mainly used to obtain the shallow features of LBP images. We borrowed the method from face recognition feature extraction. The shallow features can be used to enhance the feature representation of the reconstructed face. Mini-CNN architecture is shown in Fig. 3.

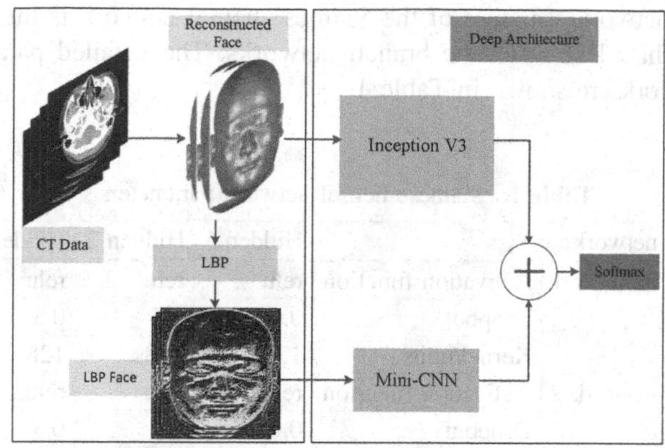

Fig. 2. The weighted fusion network

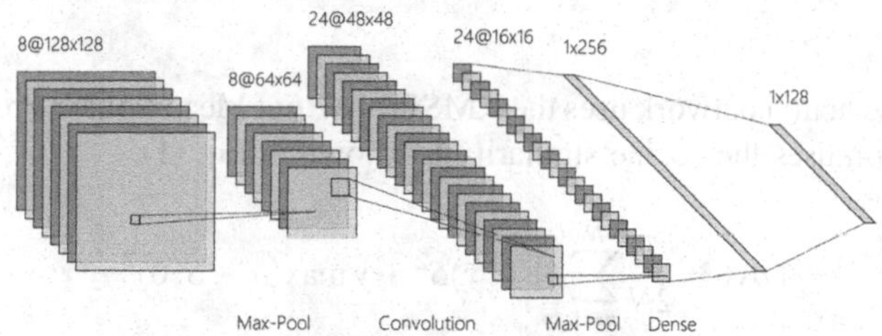

Fig. 3. Mini-CNN architecture

2.2 Decision Models

In order to obtain more suitable reconstructed face features, we designed two different neural network models to further train the face features obtained in Sect. 2.1.

Siamese neural network can process the face features obtained in Sect. 2.1 to obtain new face features. The architecture of the Siamese network is shown in Fig. 4.

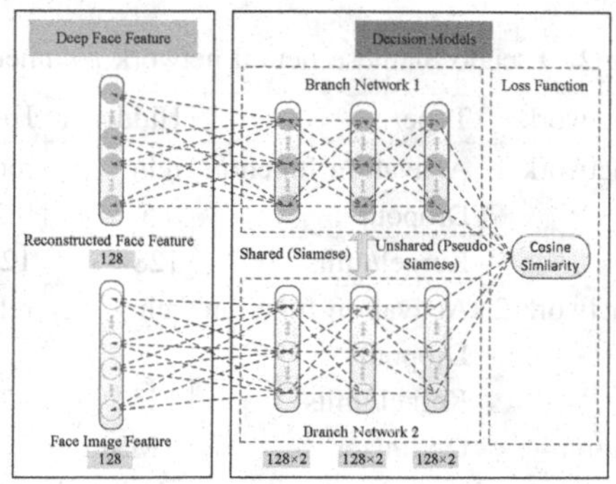

Fig. 4. Siamese neural network architecture

The branch network structure of the Siamese neural network is the same and the parameters are shared between the branch networks. The detailed parameters of the twin neural network are shown in Table 1.

Table 1. Siamese neural network parameters

Branch network	Type	Hidden 1	Hidden 2	Hidden 3
Branch network 1	Activation function	relu	relu	relu
	Dropout	0.6	0.5	0.3
	Kernel/units	128	128	128
Branch network 2	Activation function	relu	relu	relu
	Dropout	0.6	0.5	0.3
	Kernel/units	128	128	128
Optimization	Optimizer	RMSProp		
	Loss function	Cosine similarity		

The Siamese neural network uses the RMSProp (Root Mean Square Prop) optimizer. The loss function uses the cosine similarity as shown in Eq. (1).

$$Loss = \frac{1}{2N}\sum_{n=1}^{N}(1-y)S^2 + y\max(a-S,0)^2 \quad (1)$$

y indicates the prediction result, a is the boundary threshold the value is 0.78. S represents the cosine distance between two face feature vectors, as shown in Eq. (2).

$$S(X_1, X_2) = \frac{<F(X_1), F(X_2)>}{\|F(X_1)\|\ \|F(X_2)\|} \quad (2)$$

X1 represents the reconstructed of the face, *X2* represents the face image and *F(X)* represents the face features.

The detailed parameters of Pseudo Siamese neural network are shown in Table 2.

Table 2. Pseudo Siamese neural network parameters

Branch network	Type	Hidden 1	Hidden 2
Branch network 1	Activation function	relu	relu
	Dropout	0.5	0.3
	Kernel/units	128	128
Branch network 2	Activation function	relu	relu
	Dropout	0.5	0.3
	Kernel/units	128	128
Optimization	Optimizer	RMSProp	
	Loss function	Cosine similarity	

3 Experiments

Experiment used i3-2130 CPU 3.40 GHz, 8G memory and 64-bit operating system. 166 sets of data were used for experiments. The training set and test set were divided according to the ratio of 7:3.

3.1 Dataset

The reconstructed face data preprocessing is shown in Fig. 5. Face photos obtained by camera.

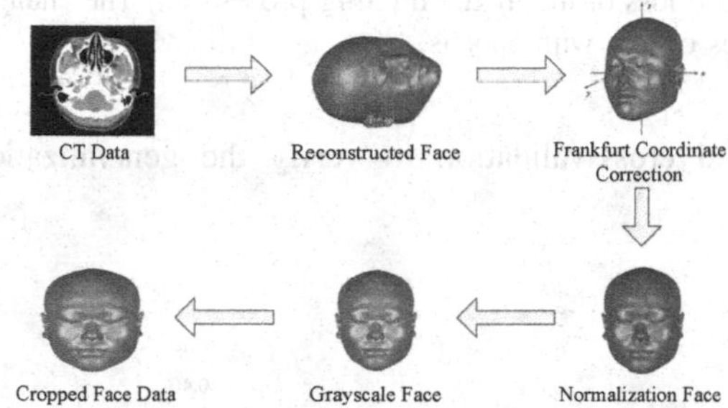

Fig. 5. Reconstructed face data preprocessing process.

3.2 Evaluation

The reconstructed face verification uses the accuracy, loss value for evaluation. The reconstructed face identifies uses accuracy for evaluation.

4 Result

4.1 Reconstructed Face Verification

The Siamese neural network trained 100 epochs. Test accuracy is 95% (Figs. 6, 7 and 8).

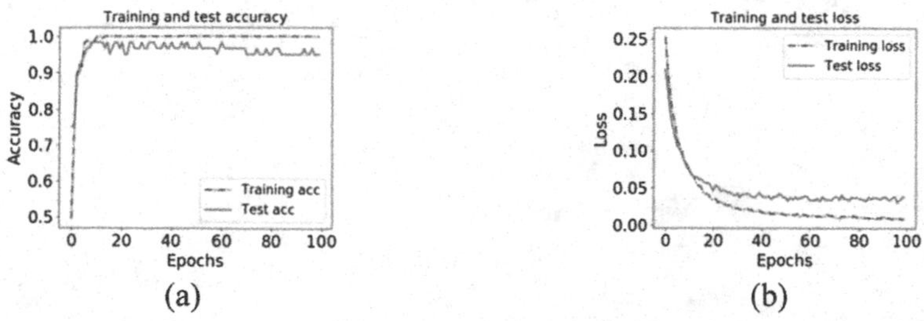

Fig. 6. The accuracy and loss of the model training process. (a) The changes of accuracy with epochs; (b) The changes of loss with epochs.

The Pseudo Siamese neural network trained 100 epochs. Test accuracy is 98.33%.

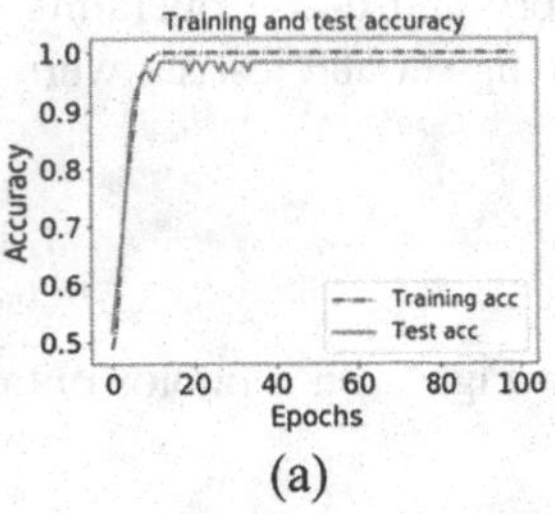

(a)

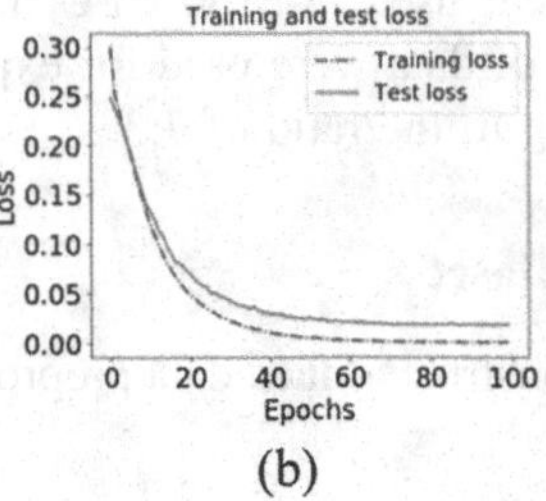

(b)

Fig. 7. The accuracy and loss of the model training process. (a) The changes of accuracy with epochs; (b) The changes of loss with epochs.

We used five-fold cross-validation to verify the generalization capabilities of model.

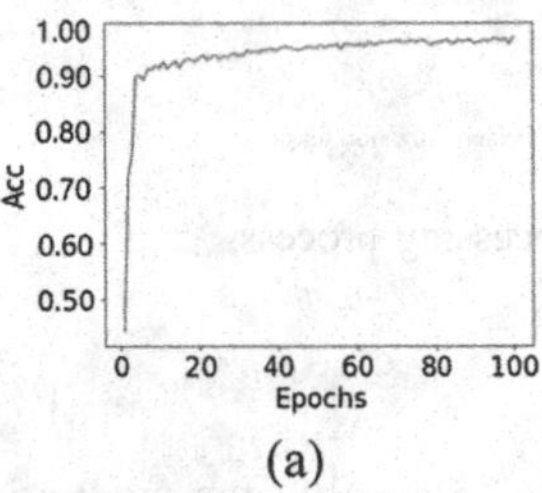

(a)

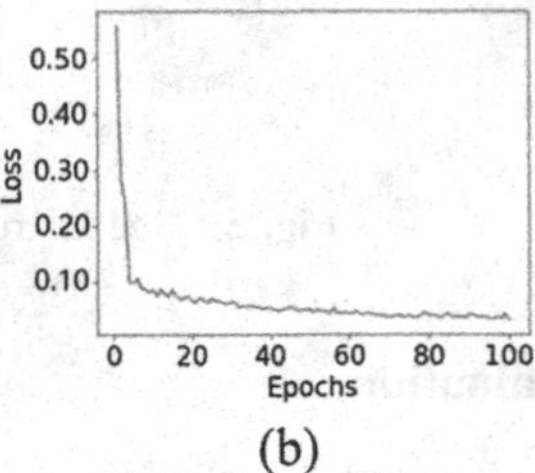

(b)

Fig. 8. The accuracy and loss of the model training process. (a) The changes of accuracy with epochs; (b) The changes of loss with epochs.

The model trained 100 epochs, it takes 158.32 s. The final test accuracy was 97.5%.

4.2 Reconstructed Face Recognition

In the reconstructed face recognition, we used Pseudo Siamese neural network for comparative experiments. The TOP1 accuracy are shown in Table 3.

Table 3. Comparison of different methods

Method	Accuracy(%)
Huang et al. [1]	95.00
Zhao et al. [2]	93.43
Zhao et al. [19]	94.87
Zhao et al. [9]	95.16
DeepFace [20]	98.35
DeepID [7]	98.72
DeepID3 [14]	99.23
FaceNet [8]	97.39
VGGFace [21]	99.15
Hu et al. [18]	99.31
Our	**99.57**

5 Conclusion

The research of reconstructed face recognition combines the practical application requirements in the field of criminal investigation. This paper inspired by transfer learning and small sample learning. We trained a weighted fusion deep network for feature extraction, built two different neural network models for reconstructed face verification and use KNN (K-Nearest Neighbors) for reconstructed face recognition.

Acknowledgment. This work is supported by Shaanxi Natural Science Foundation No. 2018JM 6061, Special Scientific Research Program of Shaanxi Education Department No. 2013JK1180 and Qingdao Municipality's Independent Innovation Major Project of China (2017-4-3-2-xcl).

References

1. Huang, J., Zhou, M., Duan, F., Deng, Q., Wu, Z., Tian, Y.: The weighted landmark-based algorithm for skull identification. In: Real, P., Diaz-Pernil, D., Molina-Abril, H., Berciano, A., Kropatsch, W. (eds.) CAIP 2011. LNCS, vol. 6855, pp. 42–48. Springer, Heidelberg (2011). https://doi.org/10.1007/978-3-642-23678-5_3
2. Zhao, J., et al.: 3D facial similarity measure based on geodesic network and curvatures. Math. Prob. Eng. **2017**, 17 (2014)
3. Pu, Y.-C., Du, W.-C., Huang, C.-H., Lai, C.-K.: Invariant feature extraction for 3D model retrieval: an adaptive approach using Euclidean and topological metrics. Comput. Math Appl. **64**, 1217–1225 (2012)
4. Li, P., Ma, H., Ming, A.: Combining topological and view-based features for 3D model retrieval. Multimedia Tools Appl. **65**, 335–361 (2013)
5. Zhao, J.-L., et al.: 3D face similarity measure by fr, chet distances of geodesics. J. Comput. Sci. Technol. **33**, 207–222 (2018)
6. Simonyan, K., Zisserman, A.: Very deep convolutional networks for large-scale image recognition (2014)

7. Sun, Y., Wang, X., Tang, X.: Deep learning face representation from predicting 10,000 classes. In: Proceedings of the 2014 IEEE Conference on Computer Vision and Pattern Recognition, pp. 1891–1898. IEEE Computer Society (2014)
8. Schroff, F., Kalenichenko, D., Philbin, J.: FaceNet: a unified embedding for face recognition and clustering (2015)
9. Sun, Y., Liang, D., Wang, X., Tang, X.: DeepID3: face recognition with very deep neural networks (2015)
10. Zhang, L.: Transfer adaptation learning: a decade survey (2019)
11. Li, Y., Zhang, J., Zhang, J., Huang, K.: Discriminative learning of latent features for zero-shot recognition (2018)
12. Vinyals, O., Blundell, C., Lillicrap, T., Kavukcuoglu, K., Wierstra, D.: Matching networks for one shot learning (2016)
13. Zhu, Y., Zhuang, F., Yang, J., Yang, X., He, Q.: Adaptively transfer category-classifier for handwritten chinese character recognition. In: Yang, Q., Zhou, Z.-H., Gong, Z., Zhang, M.-L., Huang, S.-J. (eds.) PAKDD 2019. LNCS (LNAI), vol. 11439, pp. 110–122. Springer, Cham (2019). https://doi.org/10.1007/978-3-030-16148-4_9
14. Zagoruyko, S., Komodakis, N.: Learning to compare image patches via convolutional neural networks (2015)
15. He, K., Zhang, X., Ren, S., Sun, J.: Spatial pyramid pooling in deep convolutional networks for visual recognition. In: Fleet, D., Pajdla, T., Schiele, B., Tuytelaars, T. (eds.) ECCV 2014. LNCS, vol. 8691, pp. 346–361. Springer, Cham (2014). https://doi.org/10.1007/978-3-319-10578-9_23
16. DZeiler, M., Fergus, R.: Visualizing and understanding convolutional neural networks (2013)
17. Zhang, K., Zhang, Z., Li, Z., Qiao, Y.: Joint face detection and alignment using multitask cascaded convolutional networks. IEEE Signal Process. Lett. **23**, 1499–1503 (2016)
18. Hu, G., et al.: Attribute-enhanced face recognition with neural tensor fusion networks. In: 2017 IEEE International Conference on Computer Vision (ICCV), pp. 3764–3773 (2017)
19. Zhao, J., Wu, Z., Liu, C., Duan, F., Zhou, M., Cao, J.: 3D facial similarity comparison in shape space (2015)
20. Taigman, Y., Yang, M., Ranzato, M., Wolf, L. DeepFace: closing the gap to human-level performance in face verification. In: 2014 IEEE Conference on Computer Vision and Pattern Recognition, pp. 1701–1708 (2014)
21. Mei, W., Deng, W.: Deep face recognition: a survey (2018)

A Two-Stage Method for Assessing Facial Paralysis Severity by Fusing Multiple Classifiers

Pengfei Li[1], Shune Tan[2], Xiurong Zhou[1], Sicen Yan[2], Qijun Zhao[1(✉)], Jicheng Zhang[2], and Zejun Lv[1]

[1] National Key Laboratory of Fundamental Science on Synthetic Vision, College of Computer Science, Sichuan University, Chengdu, China
qjzhao@scu.edu.cn

[2] Sichuan Integrative Medicine Hospital, Chengdu, China

Abstract. Facial paralysis is a disease that face can not do normal movement on the malfunctioned side. This paper proposes a novel two-stage method for automatically assessing the severity of facial paralysis in a coarse to fine manner. In the first stage, the method coarsely determines whether the query face has severe or mild facial paralysis by analyzing the symmetry of the face under neutral expression and the appearance of the closed eye on the malfunctioned side of the face. In the second stage, the face of severe facial paralysis is further classified into two levels by analyzing the motion feature in showing teeth, while the face of mild facial paralysis is classified into four levels by analyzing the motion feature in showing teeth and raising eyebrows. In both stages, support vector machines (SVMs) are employed to classify the face into different facial paralysis severity levels based on different features. The final assessment is obtained by fusing the results of the multiple SVMs. Evaluation experiments on a database collected by ourselves obtain promising results and prove the effectiveness of fusing the results of multiple classifiers that are based on different features.

Keywords: Facial paralysis · House-Brackmann grading system · Facial biometrics · Multiple classifiers

1 Introduction

Facial biometrics has been widely studied for forensics and security applications under the assumption that faces reveal people's identity. But lots of information besides identity can be also observed from faces, e.g., health status. Facial paralysis, also known as Bell's facial paralysis, is a disease caused by facial nerve abnormalities. Patients of facial paralysis can not complete daily facial expressions normally such as raising eyebrows, screwing-up nose and showing teeth. Patients with severe facial paralysis usually show obvious facial asymmetry even when they perform neutral expression. Consequently, the patient may not be able

Z. Sun et al. (Eds.): CCBR 2019, LNCS 11818, pp. 231–239, 2019.
https://doi.org/10.1007/978-3-030-31456-9_26

to do normal activities such as drinking water and eating food, and the saliva is often flowed out from the mouth on the malfunctioned side. This seriously affects the patient's appearance as well as the patient's daily life.

In clinic, the doctor's objective assessment of the severity of facial paralysis patients is usually based on manual measurements according to House-Brackmann(H-B) grading system [4] or electromyography (EMG) obtained by electrical stimulation. For manual measurements, the doctor will ask the patient to perform facial actions such as raising eyebrows and showing teeth (see Fig. 1), and estimate the facial paralysis severity by comparing the range of the motion with H-B grading system. The EMG diagnosis method is to let the patient perform facial EMG examination, and decide whether the face is normal or abnormal according to the reaction of the facial nerve. These methods both are complicated to apply and have low efficiency. Therefore, automatic assessment of facial paralysis severity using facial images or videos is highly demanded.

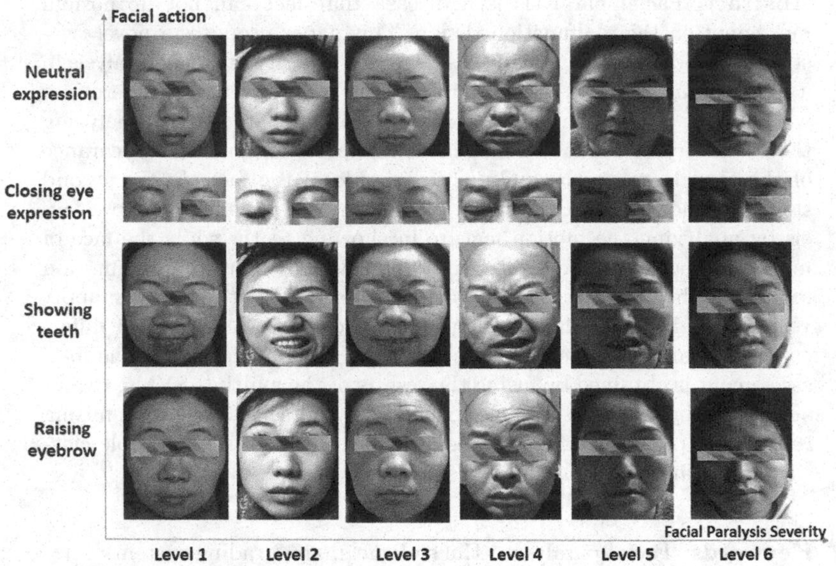

Fig. 1. Sample facial images displaying various actions that are of different facial paralysis severity levels according to House-Brackmann grading system

Thanks to the rapid development of image acquisition and analysis techniques, many automatic facial paralysis severity assessment methods have been proposed in the past years. As we will review in Sect. 2, although promising results have been obtained by these automatic methods, they mostly use single facial features (either static or motion features) or single classifiers. In this paper, we propose a novel two-stage method, which first coarsely classifies the query face into severe or mild facial paralysis based on static features, and then assigns fine severity levels for the query face based on motion features. Multiple classifiers are used in both stages. We will introduce in detail our proposed method in Sect. 3. Evaluation experiments are conducted in Sect. 4 on clinical data collected by ourselves, and the results show the promise of our method. Finally, the paper is concluded in Sect. 5.

2 Related Work

In this section, we briefly review prior work on automatic facial paralysis severity assessment based on the used source data.

Static Image Based. Some researchers use static images that record the maximum facial movement to predict the severity of facial paralysis. [1] proposed a method to extract symmetry region of interest, lines and points based on facial landmarks to assess facial paralysis severity. [6] combined distance features of facial landmarks and action unit (AU) features to assess the severity of facial paralysis. [10] regarded facial paralysis as a special expression, and used LBP descriptors [9] as facial paralysis features.

Video Based. Some researchers predict the facial paralysis severity based on facial videos which record the whole facial action process that begin and end with patient at rest. [3] used LBP features in temporal-spatial domain to extract motion information for facial paralysis severity assessment. [7,8] used Gabor filters and wavelet decomposition to extract features on LBP images, and then extracted motion feature of each frame and the first frame based on correlation matrix.

Infrared Thermal Image Based. [11] provided a quantitative clinical objective assessment of facial paralysis based on the temperature difference between the left and right sides of face. [5] proposed a method which segments the infrared thermal facial image automatically to extract the temperature distribution feature and uses a RBF neural network to assess facial paralysis severity.

3 Method

Figure 2 shows the block diagram of our proposed method. Unlike existing methods, we assess the facial paralysis severity in a coarse to fine manner by utilizing both static and motion features and based on multiple classifiers. First, we coarsely divide facial paralysis into severe and mild levels. The severe level corresponds to level 6 and level 5 in H-B grading system, while the mild level corresponds to levels 1 to 4 in H-B grading system. At first stage, static face images are used, and the assessment is completed by analyzing symmetry of face and appearance of closed eyes. The face with severe facial paralysis is further classified into level 6 and level 5 as defined in H-B grading system based on the motion feature extracted from video of showing teeth. If the face is classified as mild facial paralysis at the first stage, it will be further assessed by two

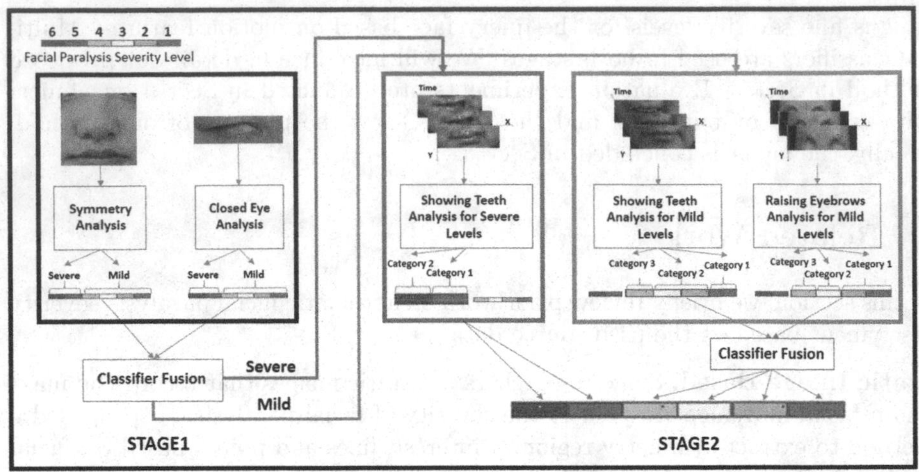

Fig. 2. An overview of the proposed two-stage method of automatic facial paralysis severity assessment using facial images and videos

classifiers. One classifier also analyzes the video of showing teeth, but classifies the face into three categories corresponding respectively to level 1, level 2 and level 3, and level 4 in H-B grading system. The other classifier is based on the video of raising eyebrows, and classifies the face into another three categories, i.e., level 1 and level 2, level 3, and level 4 in H-B grading system. The results of these classifiers are finally fused to give the specific facial paralysis severity level of the face.

3.1 First Stage: Coarse Assessment

Data Preprocessing and Static Feature Extraction. In this paper, we assume that it is known which side of the face suffers from facial paralysis. Hence, to simplify the subsequent analysis, we horizontally mirror the face image/video if the left-hand side of the face is malfunctioned. This way we have only to analyze the right hand-side of the face to assess facial paralysis severity. To extract features, we locate the facial landmarks on the query face image by using the method in [2]. Based on the landmarks, as shown in Fig. 3, the face is parsed into different local patches, including mouth and nose (MN), right eye (E), mouth (M), and eyebrows (EB). Local binary pattern features [9] are then extracted from these local patches and used as input for the classifiers to predict the facial paralysis severity levels. In this paper, nonlinear support vector machines with RBF kernels (SVMs)[1] are employed as the classifiers.

Symmetry Analysis. As can be seen from the sample images in Fig. 1, faces with severe facial paralysis appear obviously asymmetric while faces with mild

[1] https://www.csie.ntu.edu.tw/~cjlin/libsvm/.

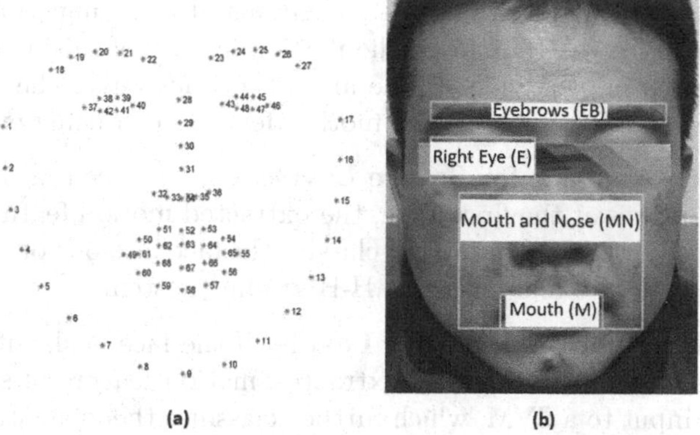

Fig. 3. (a) Facial landmarks and (b) local patches on the face used for facial paralysis severity assessment

facial paralysis do not. Based on this observation, we use the MN patches on face images of neutral expression for symmetry analysis. After segmenting the MN patch based on the landmarks on the input face image, we first normalize the patch to 224 × 224, then extract LBP feature from it, and finally use a SVM to classify the input face as either severe or mild facial paralysis.

Closed Eye Analysis. According to clinical symptom, faces with severe facial paralysis can not completely close eyes. Therefore, we analyze the appearance of the E patches when patient is in closed eyes state. Specifically, we normalize the E patch to 40 × 110, extract LBP feature from it, and use another SVM to classify the input face into severe or mild facial paralysis.

For the first stage, we will combine the results of the neutral expression classifier and closed eye classifier to give a judgment on the severity of the patient's facial paralysis. We treat the class label as a score. So if the sum of the classification results of the two classifiers is two, the patient is diagnosed as a severe facial paralysis, otherwise the patient is a non-severe facial paralysis.

Classifier Fusion. The final assessment result of stage one is obtained by combing the output of the two classifiers. Only if both classifiers say that the input face has severe facial paralysis, the input face is diagnosed as severe facial paralysis; otherwise, it is classified as mild facial paralysis.

3.2 Second Stage: Fine Assessment

Data Preprocessing and Motion Feature Extraction. Facial videos captured during the face performing specific actions of showing teeth and raising eyebrows are used in the second stage. We use the method in [2] to detect the faces in the video and locate their facial landmarks, and then crop and normalize the face regions to 300 × 300 pixels. To analyze the motion feature of showing teeth, we crop the M patch in each video frame, and extract LBP features for all the M patches in the video, which are concatenated as a single motion feature vector for showing teeth. To analyze the motion feature of raising eyebrows, we crop the EB patch in each video frame and also concatenate the LBP features extracted from the EB patches as the motion feature for raising eyebrows.

Showing Teeth Analysis for Severe Levels. For the face that is classified as severe facial paralysis at the first stage, the extracted motion feature of showing teeth is processed by a SVM to further classify the face into one of two categories corresponding to level 6 and level 5 in H-B grading system.

Showing Teeth Analysis for Mild Levels. If the face is classified into mild facial paralysis at the first stage, its extracted motion feature of showing teeth is taken as the input to a SVM, which further classifies the face into one of three categories of fine severity levels.

Raising Eyebrows Analysis for Mild Levels. For the face of mild severity levels, the motion feature of raising eyebrows is also used for fine assessment. Specifically, a SVM is employed to classify the face into one of three categories of fine severity levels based on the motion feature of raising eyebrows.

Classifier Fusion. For severe levels, i.e., level 6 and level 5 in H-B grading system, the output of the SVM classifier in showing teeth analysis is directly taken as the final assessment result. For mild levels, the outputs of the two SVM classifiers (one based on showing teeth analysis and the other based on raising eyebrows analysis) are fused in the following way. If both classifiers assign the face into category three, the face is diagnosed as level 4 facial paralysis; if one classifier assigns the face into category three and the other into category two, the face is diagnosed as level 3 facial paralysis; if both classifiers say that the face is in category two or if one classifier says that the face is in category two and the other says that it is in category one, the face is classified as level 2 facial paralysis; if both classifiers classify the face into category one, the face is diagnosed as level 1 facial paralysis.

4 Experiments

4.1 Database and Protocol

Because no image/video database of faces with facial paralysis is available in the public domain, we collected our own database at the Sichuan Integrative Medicine Hospital. The database consists of 39 samples of 23 facial paralysis patients. Each sample contains four videos captured when the patient displays neutral expression, and performs facial actions of closing eyes, showing teeth and raising eyebrows. The ground truth facial paralysis severity levels have been annotated for all the samples by doctors. Table 1 summarizes the number of samples of each of the six severity levels in H-B grading system.

Table 1. The number of facial paralysis samples of each of the six severity levels in House-Brackmann grading system

Severity level	1	2	3	4	5	6
Sample numbers	7	5	10	7	5	5

In the experiments, we do four-fold cross validation evaluation. In each fold, we randomly choose 80% of the samples for training and the rest for testing. To make the evaluation more reliable, when splitting the database, we ensure that the patients in the training subset are completely different from the patients in the testing subset.

Because of the small size of the database, we augment the training subset as follows. For stage one, we extract 95 images from the neutral expression video of each sample, and 15 images from the closing eye video of each sample. These images are then augmented by scaling, translation, and adding Gaussian noise. For stage two, we randomly perturb the detected facial landmarks in the videos. Finally, the training set for the classifier in symmetry analysis has 3,000 images for both severe and mild levels, while the training set for the classifier in closed eye analysis has 300 images for both severe and mild levels. The training set for the classifier in showing teeth analysis for severe levels consists of 15 videos for each of the two severe levels. The training sets for the classifiers in showing teeth analysis and raising eyebrows analysis for mild levels both have 15 videos for each of the three categories of mild levels.

Two performance metrics are used in the evaluation. One is recall rate. The recall rate for a specific severity level is defined as the percentage of testing images/samples whose severity levels are correctly predicted. The other is accuracy under specific disagreements. Taking a disagreement of d as an example, the accuracy is defined as the percentage of testing samples whose predicted severity levels differ from their ground truth levels by d.

4.2 Performance of Coarse Assessment

Table 2. Image-level recall rates (%) for severe and mild facial paralysis in coarse assessment

Facial paralysis severity level	Mild	Severe
Recall rates by symmetry analysis	66.0	89.9
Recall rates by closed eye analysis	68.6	91.7
Recall rates by fused classifiers	89.3	90.1

We first evaluate the performance of coarse assessment of stage one. Because the assessment at this stage is based on single static images, we can give a severity level assessment result for each image in a sample, and we can also make assessment for each sample by majority voting among the assessment results of all the images of the sample. Therefore, we compute recall rates for severe and mild facial paralysis at both image level and sample level, which are shown in Tables 2 and 3, respectively. According to the results, by fusing the results of symmetry analysis and closed eye analysis, the recall rates of mild facial paralysis are obviously improved. This demonstrates the effectiveness of combining multiple classifiers. Besides, sample-level assessment is generally better than image-level assessment. This is because multiple images are used for one query face in sample-level assessment.

Table 3. Sample-level recall rates (%) for severe and mild facial paralysis in coarse assessment

Facial paralysis severity level	Mild	Severe
Recall rates by symmetry analysis	65.0	100
Recall rates by closed eye analysis	70.0	100
Recall rates by fused classifiers	100	100

Table 4. Accuracy (%) of fine assessment of facial paralysis severity levels with respect to prediction disagreement

Disagreement (d)	0	1	2	3	4	5	≤ 1
Showing teeth analysis only	10.7	28.6	32.1	17.9	7.1	3.6	49.3
Raising eyebrows analysis only	10.7	17.9	35.7	21.4	3.6	7.1	28.6
Fusing multiple classifiers (Ours)	35.7	50.0	14.2	0.0	0.0	0.0	85.7

4.3 Performance of Fine Assessment

The final results of our proposed method are summarized in Table 4 in terms of fine assessment accuracy with respect to severity level prediction disagreement. As can be seen, our method achieves an accuracy of 85.7% under the requirement that the predicted severity levels differ from the true values by no more than one. With such accuracy, our method is promising to serve as a useful assistant for doctors in clinical diagnosis of facial paralysis. In Table 4, we also compare our method with assessment by showing teeth analysis or raising eyebrows analysis only. Not surprisingly, using single feature or single classifier, the assessment accuracy is substantially degraded compared with using multiple features or classifiers. This again proves the effectiveness of our proposed method.

5 Conclusions

In this paper, we propose a novel method for automatically assessing the facial paralysis severity levels based on facial images/videos. Unlike existing methods, our method completes the assessment in a coarse to fine manner with stage one coarsely classifies the input face into either severe or mild facial paralysis and stage two further classifies the face into fine severity levels. Multiple features and classifiers are used in both stages for more accurate assessment. Evaluation experiments on a benchmark database collected by ourselves show promising results. However, the database in this paper is still very small, and it is difficult (if not impossible) to fairly compare our method with others due to lack of public benchmarks. We are continuing collecting more clinical data to enlarge our database, and plan to release it in the future for academic usage to promote the literature of automatic facial paralysis diagnosis.

Acknowledgment. This work is supported by the National Natural Science Foundation of China (61773270, 61703077), the Miaozi Key Project in Science and Technology Innovation Program of Sichuan Province, China (No. 2017RZ0016), and Chinese Medicine Science and Technology Research Project of Sichuan Provincial Traditional Chinese Medicine Administration(2018LC031).

References

1. Anguraj, K., Padma, S.: Evaluation and severity classification of facial paralysis using salient point selection algorithm. Int. J. Comput. Appl. **123**(7), 23–29 (2015)
2. Feng, Y., Wu, F., Shao, X., Wang, Y., Zhou, X.: Joint 3D face reconstruction and dense alignment with position map regression network. In: Proceedings of the European Conference on Computer Vision (ECCV), pp. 534–551 (2018)
3. He, S., Soraghan, J.J., O'Reilly, B.F., Xing, D.: Quantitative analysis of facial paralysis using local binary patterns in biomedical videos. IEEE Trans. Biomed. Eng. **56**(7), 1864–1870 (2009)
4. House, J.W., Brackmann, D.E.: Facial nerve grading system. Laryngoscope **93**(8), 1056–1069 (2010)
5. Liu, X., Dong, S., An, M., Bai, L., Luan, J.: Quantitative assessment of facial paralysis using infrared thermal imaging. In 2015 8th International Conference on Biomedical Engineering and Informatics (BMEI), pp. 106–110. IEEE (2015)
6. Modersohn, L., Denzler, J.: Facial paresis index prediction by exploiting active appearance models for compact discriminative features. In: VISIGRAPP (4: VISAPP), pp. 271–278 (2016)
7. Hung Ngo, T., Chen, Y.-W., Seo, M., Matsushiro, N., Xiong, W.: Quantitative analysis of facial paralysis based on three-dimensional features. In: 2016 IEEE International Conference on Image Processing (ICIP), pp. 1319–1323. IEEE (2016)
8. Hung Ngo, T., Seo, M., Matsushiro, N., Chen, Y.-W.: Evaluation of facial paralysis based on spatial features of filtered images. Int. J. Biosci. Biochem. Bioinform. **6**(1), 1 (2016)
9. Ojala, T., Pietikäinen, M., Mäenpää, T.: Multiresolution gray-scale and rotation invariant texture classification with local binary patterns. IEEE Trans. Pattern Anal. Mach. Intell. **7**, 971–987 (2002)
10. Wang, T., Dong, J., Sun, X., Zhang, S., Wang, S.: Automatic recognition of facial movement for paralyzed face. Bio-Med. Mat. Eng. **24**(6), 2751–2760 (2014)
11. Zhang, D.: A method of selecting acupoints for acupuncture treatment of peripheral facial paralysis by thermography. Am. J. Chin. Med. **35**(06), 967–975 (2007)

Latent Spatial Features Based on Generative Adversarial Networks for Face Anti-spoofing

Jingtian Xia, Yan Tang, Xi Jia, Linlin Shen(✉), and Zhihui Lai

Computer Vision Institute, School of Computer Science and Software Engineering, Shenzhen University, Shenzhen 518060, China
{xiajingtian2018, tangyan2016, jiaxi}@email.szu.edu.cn, {llshen, laizhihui}@szu.edu.cn

Abstract. With the wide deployment of the face recognition system, many face attacks, such as print attack, video attack and 3D face mask, have emerged. Face anti-spoofing is very important to protect face recognition system from attack. This paper proposes a structure of generative adversarial networks with skip connection for face anti-spoofing. First, we obtain the latent spatial features of faces by training generative adversarial networks to reconstruct both real and spoof faces; second, we use the convolution neural networks to detect the spoofing faces. In this paper, the proposed method is evaluated by three public databases. The results suggest that our approach achieves as high as 98% accuracy on both CASIA-FASD and REPLAY-ATTACK databases.

Keywords: Face anti-spoofing · Generative adversarial networks · Latent spatial features

1 Introduction

Nowadays face recognition has been widely used in various real-world applications, such as access control, phone unlock, etc. However, attackers may easily spoof the face recognition systems by presenting a printed photo (i.e. print attack), a video (i.e. replay attack) or a 3D face mask of the client in front of the camera. Current anti-spoofing researches to detect these attacks can be classified into three categories, namely motion-based [1–3], texture/distortion [4, 5] analysis-based, and CNN-based methods [6]. Motion-based methods try to exploit explicit motions, such as eye blinking [1], head rotation [2] and lip movements [3], to distinguish genuine and spoofing faces. These approaches are effective for print attacks. The methods based on texture and distortion analysis assumes that texture artifacts and image quality distortion often appear in the spoof face images. The common flaw of the two approaches is that they cannot take into account all attacks. CNN-based methods utilize deep learning network to learn face features for face anti-spoofing. But now the spoofing face pictures are becoming more and more realistic, which makes the effect of the general deep learning model limited. Therefore, we hope to extract discriminative features of the image before presenting it into the deep learning model. It is a good way to use Generative Adversarial Networks (GAN) to implement feature extraction.

Z. Sun et al. (Eds.): CCBR 2019, LNCS 11818, pp. 240–249, 2019.
https://doi.org/10.1007/978-3-030-31456-9_27

In the development of computer vision, GAN's application is becoming more and more popular. GAN was first proposed by Goodfellow [7] in 2014 as an image generation network, which consists of two parts: generator and discriminator. Among them, the generation model's purpose is to generate realistic images to deceive the discriminator. The discriminant model aims to distinguish the real image and the generated pseudo-image. The training process of generator and discriminator is a kind of game process. GAN's applications include image generation, image translation and super resolution. Image generation is to generate an image from a gaussian noise, such as Attribute2image [8] and StackGAN [9]. Image translation generates images from one domain to another, such as CycleGAN [10], Pix2Pix [11] and StarGAN [12]. Super-resolution generates high-resolution images from low-resolution images, i.e. deblurring, as shown in [13]. Among them, Pix2Pix [11] is an extension of the condition GAN's [14], it is a typical method based on image to image conversion, and it designed a generator with skip connection which is to transfer low level in the whole network information, like U-Net [15], and a discriminant framework called PatchGAN (similar to the block constraint operation), and use the adversarial loss and the L1 loss.

As shown in Fig. 1, This paper proposed a GAN based on U-Net structure to learn the latent spatial features of human face, and then classifies the extracted features to realize face anti-spoofing. It uses the idea of image generation from image to find the differences between real and spoofing faces, which is significantly different with the traditional idea. The purpose of reconstructing the input image is to extract latent spatial features to better represent the original input image better. On the face anti-spoofing problem, Jourabloo et al. [16] made a similar GAN to model spoofing faces. But unlike the GAN of this paper, their network structure is original encoder-decoder (ENDEC), this paper used ENDEC with skip connection structure, so that we can convey information of deeper levels better, and retain more details.

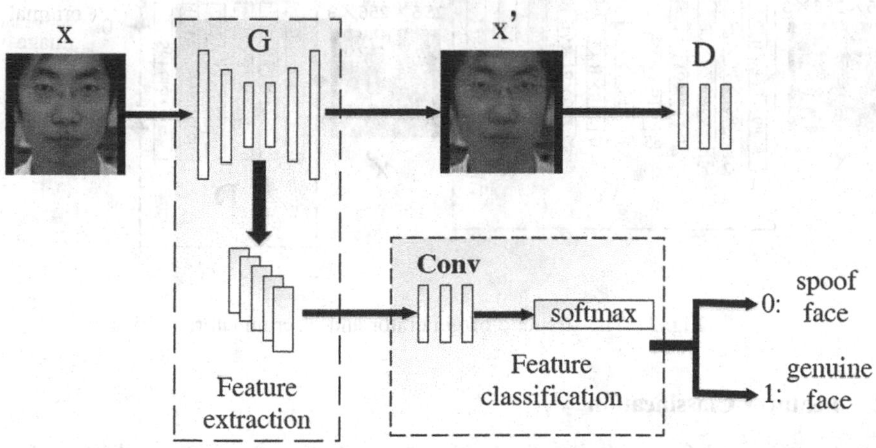

Fig. 1. The framework of GANs based latent spatial features for face anti-spoofing.

2 The Proposed Method

The method proposed in this paper is mainly divided into two parts: latent spatial features extraction and feature classification. The part of latent spatial features extraction mainly includes generator, discriminator and their losses. The part of feature classification mainly includes fusion and classification of multilayer latent spatial features.

2.1 Latent Spatial Feature Extraction

The latent spatial features are extracted from the structure of GAN. As shown in Fig. 2, the structure of GAN includes generator and discriminator. The generator structure in this paper is based on encoder-decoder network structure with skip connection, which consists of five convolution layers with strides equal to 2 for down-sampling, two residual blocks [17] and five convolution layers with strides equal to 2 for up-sampling. The blue arrows in Fig. 2 represent skip connection that can enhance the flow of information. For example, e2 and d2 are concatenated as the input of the next layer, that is, e2($64 \times 64 \times 128$) and d2($64 \times 64 \times 128$) are concatenated to be the input with size $64 \times 64 \times 256$ for features classification. The structure of discriminator is the same as that of PatchGAN [11], which discriminates each block of $N \times N$ to determine whether it is the feature of original image or generated image. Specifically, the discriminator obtains the final output by averaging the responses of all the blocks after the convolution operation of the image.

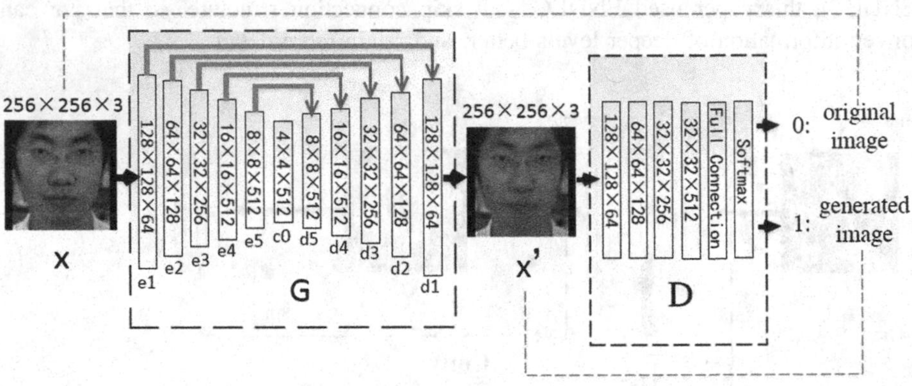

Fig. 2. The structure of generator and discriminator.

2.2 Features Classification

After latent spatial features extraction, we should classify the features through Convolution Neural Networks (CNN). Because the features of shallow layer are different from those of deep layer, five groups of features from generator, i.e. f1 (e1, d1), f2 (e2, d2), f3 (e3, d3), f4 (e4, d4) and f5 (c0), are extracted. While f5 directly extracts c0

(4 × 4 × 512), other groups of features combine two features together. For example, f2 is the concatenated feature of e2 and d2. Five groups of features (f1–f5) are input into convolution layers (Conv) for training, and the final classification result is obtained through cross entropy of the classifier. Each Conv here has 9 layers. The classification process of latent spatial features is shown in Fig. 3, among them Convs are convolution layers and FCs are fully connected layers. The output of the FC is the features with size 1 × 1 × 512. After concatenating the output from full connection layers, softmax classification can achieve good results.

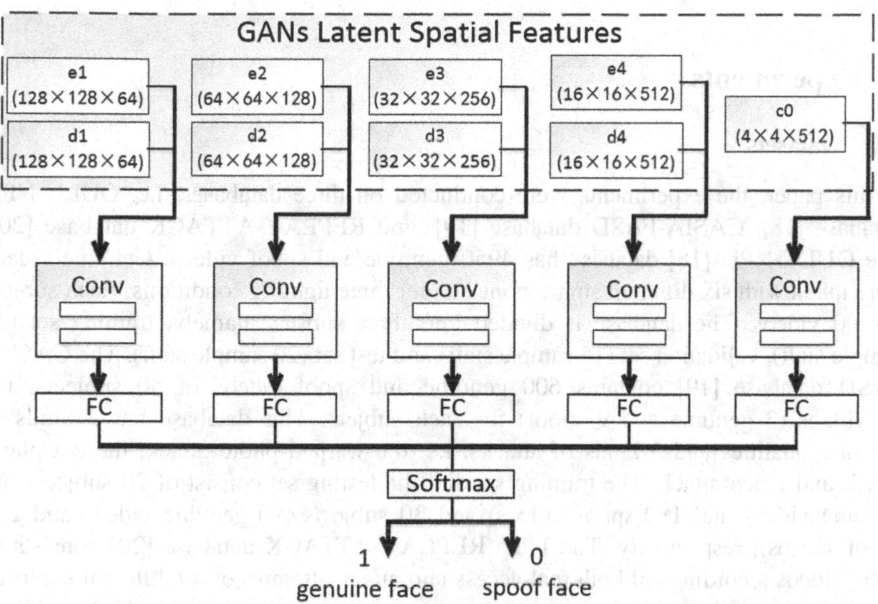

Fig. 3. The framework of classification.

2.3 Objective Function

In order to make the generated image more similar to the original image, L1 loss applied in this paper is similar to that of Pix2Pix [11]. The difference is that gaussian noise is not added in this method, but the target image is reconstructed from the original image. The formula is as follows:

$$L_{L1} = E_x\left[\|x - G(x)\|_1\right] \tag{1}$$

Where x is the input image, $G(x)$ is the generated image from x. Combining low frequency and high frequency information and can achieve better generation performance. The formula of the adversarial loss is as below:

$$L_{adv} = E_x[logD(x)] + E_x[\log(1 - D(G(x)))] \tag{2}$$

Where D is the discriminator. G tries to minimize this objective against an adversarial D that tries to maximize it. The final objective function is:

$$G^* = \arg\min_G \max_D L_{adv}(G,D) + \lambda L_{L1}(G) \tag{3}$$

The objective function is to make the generated image more similar to the original image. When the discriminator is unable to distinguish the generated image from the input image, the extracted latent spatial features are good representative of the original input image.

3 Experiments

3.1 Datasets

In this paper, the experiments were conducted on three databases, i.e. OULU-NPU database [18], CASIA-FASD database [19], and REPLAY-ATTACK database [20]. The OULU-NPU [18] database has 4950 genuine and spoof videos. Genuine videos were taken with six different smartphones under three lighting conditions. Each subject has 90 videos. The database is divided into three subsets, namely, training set (20 sample staff), validation set (15 sample staff) and test set (20 sample staff). The CASIA-FASD database [19] contains 600 genuine and spoof videos of 50 subjects, i.e. 12 videos (3 genuine and 9 spoof) for each subject. This database has 3 kinds of imaging qualities and 3 kinds of attacks, i.e. the warped photo attack, the cut photo attack and video attack. The training set and the testing set consist of 20 subjects (60 genuine videos and 180 spoof videos) and 30 subjects (90 genuine videos and 270 spoof videos), respectively. The Idiap REPLAY-ATTACK database [20] consists of 1200 videos recordings of both real-access and attack attempts of 50 different subjects. The training set, the validation set and the testing set consist of 15 subjects, 15 subjects and 20 subjects, respectively. Three types of attacks, i.e. printed photograph, mobile phone and tablet attacks, were designed.

3.2 Performance Metrics

In our experiment, the testing performance on the databases above are evaluated with the EER (Equal Error Rate) and HTER (Half Total Error Rate) [21]. The EER is the point in the ROC curve where the FAR (False Acceptance Rate) [21] equals the FRR (False Rejection Rate). The HTER is computed by

$$HTER(\tau) = \frac{FAR(\tau) + FRR(\tau)}{2} \tag{4}$$

where τ is the threshold.

3.3 Experimental Settings

The experiment in this paper first obtains each frame of image from video, detects face detection on each frame through MTCNN [22], and then aligns and scales the size of face images to 256 × 256. Finally, all the face images are input into the network structure of this paper and classified.

This experiment is implemented on pytorch. The difference between the encoder-decoder with skip connection (U-Net-like) and the original encoder-decoder, as well as the difference between convolution operation and direct flattening in the classification, were compared in Table 1. The approaches are named as GAN_encoder_decoder (GAN_E), GAN_UNet (GAN_U), GAN_UNet_Conv (GAN_U_Conv), GAN_encoder_decoder_Conv (GAN_E_Conv). "√" means with the component and "-" means without the component. For example, the network structure of GAN_U_Conv has the ENDEC structure with skip connection and the convolution layers in the classification operation. In addition, we obtain 5 groups of latent spatial features (f1–f5) from GAN. As we want to know which feature can best express the image, we test the accuracy of each feature on every database.

Table 1. The design of the comparative experiment.

Network Structure	U-Net_like	Encoder_decoder	Convolution layers
GAN_E	–	√	–
GAN_U	√	–	–
GAN_E_Conv	–	√	√
GAN_U_Conv	√	–	√

3.4 Results

In Fig. 4, we show the example images reconstructed using the different generators (the network without skip connection and the network with jump connection) with different iterations. According to Fig. 4, the generated image is closer to the input image when the iteration number increases. With the same iteration number, the image generated by GAN_U network structure is better than that by GAN_E.

The performance of different features on three different databases are shown in Table 2. Generally, the fused feature performs better than the single feature, which shows that the combination of shallow features and deep features contains useful information. For single features, the performance of f5 is the worst. The accuracies of other four sets of features varied for network structures and databases. Relatively speaking, the more information a feature contains, the more accurate it is. From the perspective of network structure, it can be seen that the encoder-decoder with skip connection and convolution operation in classification have the best effect of four structures. This indicates that the low-level information transmitted by skip connection is very important for face anti-spoofing. The reserved details are more conducive to the classification of genuine face and spoof face. Meanwhile the effect of adding convolution layers is better than that of not adding.

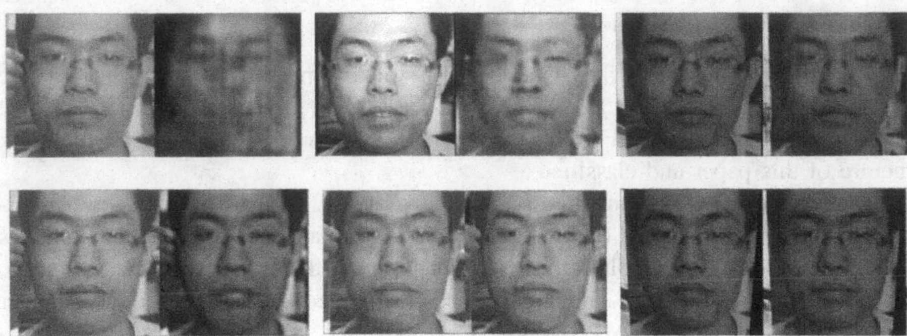

Fig. 4. The comparison of the images under two network structures with different iteration number. Each pair of images includes an original image and a reconstructed image. The first and second row shows the example images reconstructed by GAN_U and GAN_E, respectively. The second, fourth, sixth column show the example images generated at 1000, 5000 and 10000 iterations, respectively.

Table 2. The accuracy (%) of different features.

Databases	Networks structure	Features					
		f1	f2	f3	f4	f5	Fusion
CASIA-FASD	GAN_E	89.59	87.24	90.42	89.49	83.89	**93.00**
	GAN_U	96.20	94.56	95.73	83.85	81.39	**97.50**
	GAN_E_Conv5	95.90	95.10	93.40	92.40	85.40	**96.60**
	GAN_U_Conv5	96.00	96.70	96.10	94.90	89.60	**98.10**
REPLAY-ATTACK	GAN_E	90.16	97.96	87.80	93.77	85.21	**96.19**
	GAN_U	88.10	91.40	89.10	90.80	83.96	**93.00**
	GAN_E_Conv5	83.70	86.40	77.60	91.30	84.00	**92.00**
	GAN_U_Conv5	97.20	97.40	97.00	95.30	92.00	**98.10**
OULU-NPU	GAN_E	**88.31**	83.05	83.39	83.99	75.56	84.87
	GAN_U	90.20	91.50	90.00	93.40	80.40	**92.60**
	GAN_E_Conv5	**86.20**	72.80	80.10	75.40	79.90	83.10
	GAN_U_Conv5	92.70	88.60	90.80	91.70	81.70	**95.15**

The testing results of GAN_U_Conv on the three databases are shown in Table 3. While the result of “image-based” is calculated in terms of single image; “video-based” is the result calculated for the whole video. For example, if a segment of video contains 100 frames of images, “image-based” calculates the accuracy of all the images from all video, while “video-based” calculates the accuracy of each video by the average accuracy of the images from this video. In order to compare with other methods, three evaluation indexes – accuracy, EER and HTER – are adopted.

The comparison of this method with other methods on the CASIA-FASD and REPLAY-ATTACK databases is shown in Table 4. It can be seen that the method of this paper achieved better result than the existing method. This shows that GAN can

Table 3. Testing result of GAN_U_Conv.

Database	Image-based	Video-based		
	Accuracy (%)	Accuracy (%)	EER (%)	HTER (%)
CASIA-FASD	98.10	98.61	3.33	2.41
REPLAY-ATTACK	98.10	99.38	2.50	1.87
OULU-NPU	95.15	96.28	6.84	8.30

achieve better accuracy for face anti-spoofing. The REPLAY-ATTACK database itself is relatively simple, and its spoof type and photographic apparatus are not diverse enough. The video in the CASIA-FASD database contains more face movement, which lead to a decrease in the quality of the reconstructed face. Therefore, the performance of this method in REPLAY-ATTACK database is better than that in CASIA-FASD database.

Table 4. Results on CASIA-FASD and REPLAY-ATTACK databases.

Methods	CASIA-FASD	REPLAY-ATTACK	
	EER (%)	EER (%)	HTER (%)
IDA + SVM [22]	12.90	–	7.41
DPCNN [23]	4.50	2.90	6.10
LiveNet [24]	3.34	5.33	5.74
GAN_U_Conv	**3.33**	**2.50**	**1.87**

4 Conclusion

This paper proposed GAN based latent spatial feature for anti-spoofing, which was fully tested using CASIA-FASD and REPLAY-ATTACK databases. The results show that the proposed approach achieved reasonably good performance and is very competitive when compared with state of the art approaches in literature, in terms of EER and HTER.

References

1. Pan, G., Sun, L., Wu. Z., Lao, S.: Eyeblink-based antispoofing in face recognition from a generic webcamera. In: IEEE International Conference on Computer Vision, pp. 1–8 (2007)
2. De Marsico, M., Nappi, M., Riccio, D., Dugelay, J.L.: Moving face spoofing detection via 3D projective invariants. In: 5th IAPR International Conference on Biometrics, pp. 73–78 (2012)
3. Kollreider, K., Fronthaler, H., Faraj, M.I., Bigun, J.: Realtime face detection and motion analysis with application in liveness assessment. IEEE Trans. Inf. Forensics Secur. **2**(3), 548–558 (2007)

4. Boulkenafet, Z., Komulainen, J., Hadid, A.: Face spoofing detection using colour texture analysis. IEEE Trans. Inf. Forensics Secur. **11**(8), 1818–1830 (2016)
5. Wen, D., Han, H., Jain, A.K.: Face spoof detection with image distortion analysis. IEEE Trans. Inf. Forensics Secur. **10**(4), 746–761 (2015)
6. Liu, Y., Jourabloo, A., Liu, X.: Learning deep models for face anti-spoofing: binary or auxiliary supervision. In: IEEE Conference on Computer Vision and Pattern Recognition, pp. 389–398 (2018)
7. Goodfellow, I., Pouget-Abadie, J., Mirza, M., Xu, B.: Generative adversarial nets. In: 27th International Conference on Neural Information Processing Systems, pp. 2672–2680 (2014)
8. Yan, X., Yang, J., Sohn, K., Lee, H.: Attribute2Image: conditional image generation from visual attributes. In: Leibe, B., Matas, J., Sebe, N., Welling, M. (eds.) ECCV 2016. LNCS, vol. 9908, pp. 776–791. Springer, Cham (2016). https://doi.org/10.1007/978-3-319-46493-0_47
9. Huang, X., Li, Y., Poursaeed, O., Hopcroft, J.E.: Stacked generative adversarial networks. In: IEEE Conference on Computer Vision & Pattern Recognition (2017)
10. Zhu, J.Y., Park, T., Isola, P., Efros, A.: Unpaired image-to-image translation using cycle-consistent adversarial networks. In: IEEE International Conference on Computer Vision (2017)
11. Isola, P., Zhu, J.Y., Zhou, T., Efros, A.: Image-to-image translation with conditional adversarial networks. In: IEEE Conference on Computer Vision and Pattern Recognition, pp. 5967–5976. Honolulu, HI (2017)
12. Choi, Y., Choi, M., Kim, M.: StarGAN: unified generative adversarial networks for multi-domain image-to-image translation. In: IEEE Conference on Computer Vision and Pattern Recognition (2018)
13. Ledig, C., Theis, L.: Photo-realistic single image super-resolution using a generative adversarial network. In: IEEE Conference on Computer Vision and Pattern Recognition, pp. 105–114. Honolulu, HI (2017)
14. Mirza, M., Osindero, S.: Conditional generative adversarial nets. J. arXiv preprint (2014). arXiv:1411.1784
15. Ronneberger, O., Fischer, P., Brox, T.: U-Net: convolutional networks for biomedical image segmentation. In: Medical Image Computing and Computer-Assisted Intervention, pp. 234–241 (2015)
16. Jourabloo, A., Liu, Y., Liu, X.: Face de-spoofing: anti-spoofing via noise modeling. In: Ferrari, V., Hebert, M., Sminchisescu, C., Weiss, Y. (eds.) ECCV 2018. LNCS, vol. 11217, pp. 297–315. Springer, Cham (2018). https://doi.org/10.1007/978-3-030-01261-8_18
17. He, K., Zhang, X., Ren, S.: Deep residual learning for image recognition. In: IEEE Conference on Computer Vision and Pattern Recognition, pp. 770–778 (2016)
18. Zhang, Z., Yan, J., Liu, S., Lei, Z., Yi, D., Li, S.Z.: A face antispoofing database with diverse attacks. In: 5th IEEE IAPR International Conference on Biometrics, pp. 26–31 (2012)
19. Chingovska, I., Anjos, A., Marcel, S.: On the effectiveness of local binary patterns in face anti-spoofing. In: IEEE Biometrics Special Interest Group, pp. 1–7 (2012)
20. Boulkenafet, Z., Komulainen, J., Li, L.: OULU-NPU: a mobile face presentation attack database with real-world variations. In: 12th IEEE International Conference on Automatic Face & Gesture Recognition. pp. 612–618. IEEE Computer Society (2017)
21. Bengio, S., Mariéthoz, J.: A statistical significance test for person authentication. In The Speaker and Language Recognition Workshop (Odyssey), Toledo, pp. 237–244 (2004)
22. Wen, D., Han, H., Jain, A.K.: Face spoof detection with image distortion analysis. In: IEEE Transactions on Information Forensics and Security, pp. 746–761 (2015)

23. Li, L., Feng, X., Boulkenafet, Z.: An original face anti-spoofing approach using partial convolutional neural network. In: IEEE International Conference on Image Processing Theory, Tools and Applications, pp. 1–6. (2017)
24. Rehman, Y.A.U., Po, L.M., Liu, M.: LiveNet: improving features generalization for face anti-spoofing using convolution neural networks. J. Expert Systems with Applications, pp. 159–169 (2018)

Similarity Measurement Between Reconstructed 3D Face and 2D Face Based on Deep Learning

Shanghao Zhao, Xiaoning Liu(✉), Shixiong Wang, Yunpeng Jing, and Jun Feng

College of Information Science and Technology, Northwest University, Xi'an 710127, China
xnliu@nwu.edu.cn

Abstract. Craniofacial reconstruction technology is very important in the field of criminal investigation. But reconstruction a face from skull is not the end of work. The key technology is the similarity measurement between reconstructed 3D face and 2D face image. It can not only be used to retrieve the most similar face image from missing population database but also can be used to value the reconstruction methods. We built a 3D reconstructed face dataset, trained a deep face feature extraction model and built a neural network for similarity measurement. Firstly, the reconstructed 3D face and 2D face image need to be preprocessing. Secondly, deep network is designed for similarity measurement. Finally, we tested the proposed model. The accuracy of the similarity between two kinds of face images was 96.67%. Experiments show that the proposed neural network model can effectively measure the similarity between two kinds of face images.

Keywords: Craniofacial reconstruction · Similarity measurement · Deep neural network

1 Introduction

Craniofacial reconstruction techniques have been widely used in criminal investigation field. How to identify the reconstructed face is very important. The current method is to identify the reconstructed face by relatives. It is passive and time-waste. If we can retrieve the most possible photos from the database, it will be great helpful for identifying the unknown skull. So the similarity measurement between the reconstructed face and face image is valuable to be researched.

The early similarity measure method of reconstructed face was based on 3D model [1, 2]. They can be divided into two types, one is based on geometric features between 3D models [3] and the other is based on the topology [4], which is mainly used for 3D model retrieval.

Reconstructed face similarity measure method also use the method of face recognition, including methods based on physical features of surface features [5]. These methods use the features extracted by hand and data preprocessing takes a lot of time.

Z. Sun et al. (Eds.): CCBR 2019, LNCS 11818, pp. 250–257, 2019.
https://doi.org/10.1007/978-3-030-31456-9_28

With the development of deep learning in the field of computer vision, a large number of excellent network models have been proposed. Chopra [6] proposed the Siamese network architecture to measure the similarity of faces. Sergey [7] proposed the Siamese network architecture combined with spatial pyramid pooling [8] to measure the similarity between two images. At present, the accuracy of face recognition based on deep learning has exceeded the recognition level of the human eyes [9]. Florian [10] proposed using the triplet as a loss function to achieve the feature representation of the face. Zhu [11] used the method of transfer learning to recognize Chinese handwritten character.

Inspired by the ideas of face recognition network model [10], single-sample learning [12] and Siamese network model [7], this paper firstly proposes a method for measuring the similarity between reconstructed face and face image based on deep neural network. We built a 3D reconstructed face dataset, trained a deep face feature extraction model and built a neural network for similarity measurement. The experiment results shown the method can effectively measure the similarity between two kinds of face images.

2 Method

This section mainly explains the methods used in the paper. Figure 1 is the framework of face similarity measurement.

Firstly, data are preprocessed. Secondly, Improved Inception [13] model is used as deep architecture, which is used to extract the deep feature of the reconstructed face and face image. Thirdly, Considering there are too many features extracted by the deep learning, the method proposed by Chopra et al. [9] is used for feature reduction. Finally, taking the features as input, train the neural network model we built. The final similarity measurement model is obtained.

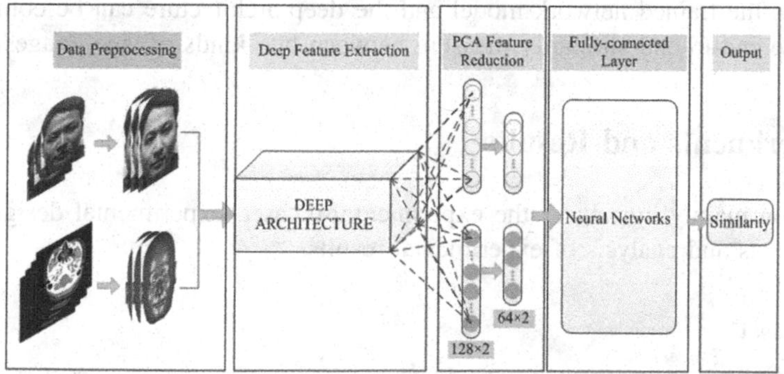

Fig. 1. The similarity measurement framework of reconstructed face and face image

2.1 Deep Architecture

The deep architecture is composed of CNN (Convolutional Neural Networks). The improved Inception model [13] is used as the deep architecture. We have improved the original network and added Batch Normalization. The inception module is shown in Fig. 2. We will introduce the details of the Inception model in Sect. 3.

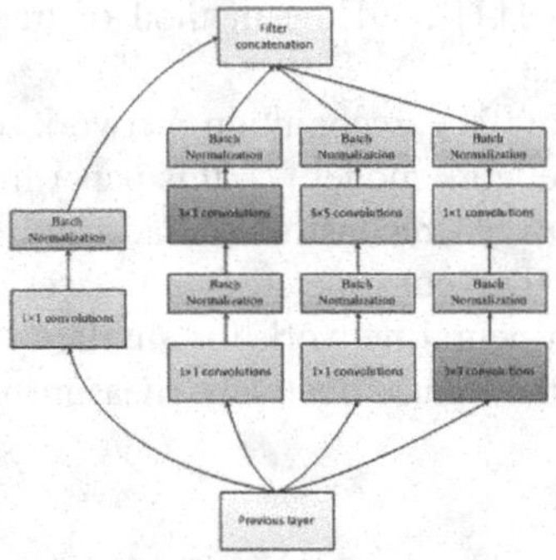

Fig. 2. The inception module

2.2 Neural Network

In order to obtain accurate similarity measurement results, we build a neural network model for further training. The details of the neural network we will introduce in Sect. 3. Binary cross entropy is used as the loss function:

$$Loss = -\sum_{i=1}^{N} y_i \log \hat{y}_i + (1 - y_i) \log(1 - \hat{y}_i) \tag{1}$$

Finally, the trained network model and the deep architecture can be combined to achieve the end-to-end similarity measure between two kinds of face images.

3 Experiments and Results

This section mainly introduces the experimental dataset, experimental design, evaluation methods and analysis of experimental results.

3.1 Dataset

3D faces constructed by CT are regarded as the reconstructed face. Face images are taken by camera. Positive samples indicate the same person's reconstructed face and face image, the negative sample indicates they are different person. We built 166 sets of data. The ratio of training set to test set is 7:3.

3.2 Experiment Design

In the experiment, the experimental equipment used i3-2130 CPU 3.40 GHz, 8G memory and 64-bit operating system. The details of the deep architecture are shown in Table 1.

Table 1. Details of the improved Inception model

Type	Output size	Depth	#1×1	#3 × 3 reduce	#3 × 3	#5 × 5 reduce	#5 × 5	Pool proj(p)	params	FLOPS
convl (7 × 7 × 3,2)	112 × 112 × 64	1							9 K	119 M
batch normalization										
max pool + norm	56 × 56 × 64	0						m 3 × 3, 2		
inception(2)	56 × 56 × 192	2		64	192				115 K	360 M
norm + max pool	28 × 28 × 192	0						m 3 × 3, 2		
inception(3a)	28 × 28 × 256	2	64	96	128	16	32	m, 32p	164 K	128 M
inception(3b)	28 × 28 × 320	2	64	96	128	32	64	L_2, 64p	228 K	179 M
inception(3c)	14 × 14 × 640	2	0	128	256,2	32	64,2	m 3 × 3, 2	398 K	108 M
inception(4a)	14 × 14 × 640	2	256	96	192	32	64	L_2, 128p	545 K	107 M
inception(4b)	14 × 14 × 640	2	224	112	224	32	64	L_2, 128p	595 K	117 M
inception(4c)	14 × 14 × 640	2	192	128	256	32	64	L_2, 128p	654 K	128 M
inception(4d)	14 × 14 × 640	2	160	144	288	32	64	L_2, 128p	722 K	142 M
inception(4e)	7 × 7 × 1024	2	0	160	256,2	64	128,2	m 3 × 3, 2	717 K	56 M
inception(5a)	7 × 7 × 1024	2	384	192	384	48	128	L_2, 128p	1.6 M	78 M
inception(5b)	7 × 7 × 1024	2	384	192	384	48	128	m, 128p	1.6 M	78 M
avg pool	1 × 1 × 1024	0								
fully conn	1 × 1 × 128	1							131 K	0.1 M
L2 normalization	1 × 1 × 128	0								
total									7.5 M	1. 6B

The details of the neural network are shown in Table 2.

Table 2. Neural network parameters

Heading level	Hidden 1	Hidden 2	Hidden 3	Output
Activation Function	relu	relu	relu	Sigmoid
Dropout	0.5	0.5	0.3	0
Kernel/units	100	30	10	1
Optimizer	Adam			
Loss function	binary_crossentropy			

3.3 Evaluation

We use the accuracy-loss values and ROC, AUC as the evaluation standard. We validate the generalization capabilities of the model using a five-fold cross-validation.

The vertical axis represents the TPR (True Positive Rate) and the horizontal axis is FPR (False Positive Rate), which is expressed as:

$$TPR = \frac{TP}{TP + FN} \quad (2)$$

$$FPR = \frac{FP}{TN + FP} \quad (3)$$

3.4 Results

The experimental results of 128-dimensional feature are shown in Fig. 3. The accuracy of the final test set reached 93.33%.

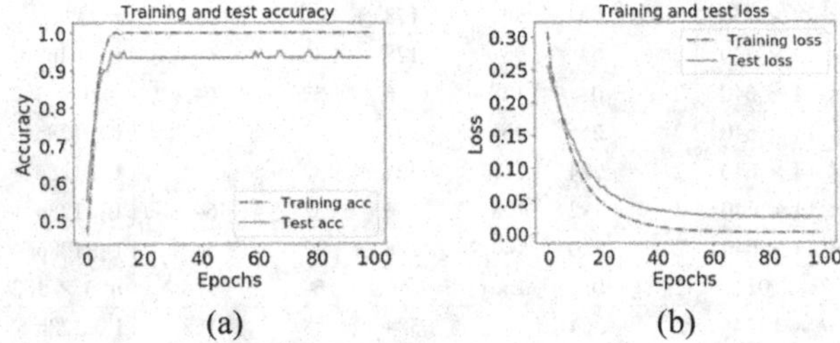

Fig. 3. The accuracy and loss of the model training using 128-dimensional features. (a) The changes of accuracy with epochs; (b) The changes of loss with epochs.

To test the influence of feature dimension reduction, we design another experiment. The experimental results are shown in Fig. 4. The accuracy of the final test set reached 96.67%.

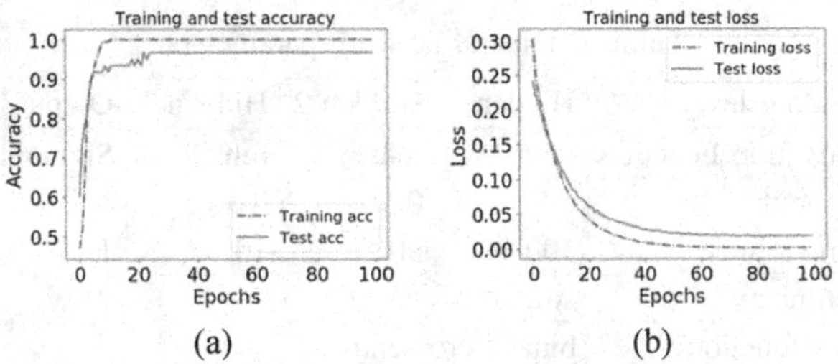

Fig. 4. The accuracy and loss values of the model training using 64-dimensional features. (a) The changes of accuracy with epochs; (b) The changes of loss with epochs.

From the 30 epochs, the performance of the model is gradually stabilized. The accuracy of the test set no longer increases and the model converges.

We use the ROC curve and the AUC value to further evaluate the model. The AUC value of the experimental results of the unreduced dimension facial features is 0.934. The AUC value of the experimental results of facial features after dimension reduction is 0.946. The experimental results are shown in Fig. 5.

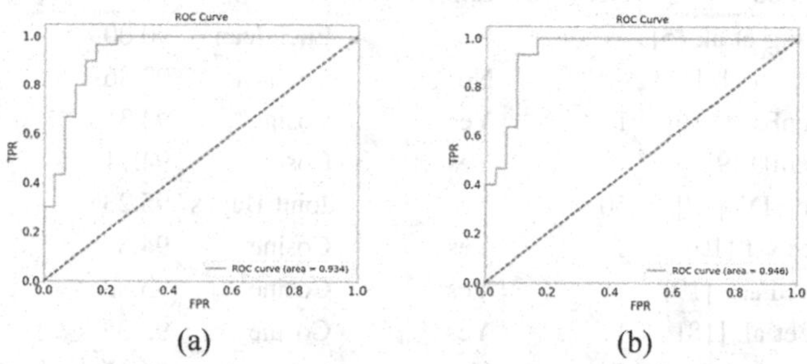

Fig. 5. ROC curve. (a) Using 128-dimensional face features; (b) Using 64-dimensional face features.

It can be seen from the experimental results that the face features after dimension reduction can achieve higher AUC values in the experimental results and the trained model performance is better than the model trained without the feature dimension reduction data.

In order to further verify the performance of the model and better evaluate the generalization ability of the model, we use the five-fold cross-validation method to cross-validate the model, the test accuracy rate is 95%. The experimental results are shown in Fig. 6.

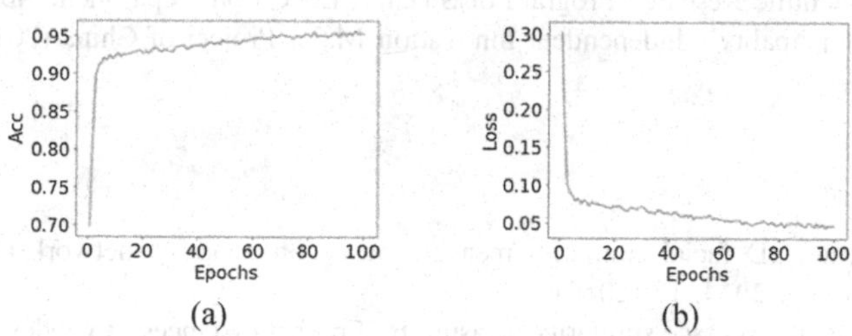

Fig. 6. Five-fold cross-validation experiment results. (a) Accuracy of Five-fold cross-validation; (b) Loss of Five-fold cross-validation.

The experiment was trained on the same machine configuration for 173.16 s. It can be seen from the experimental results that the performance of the model tends to be stable after 80 epochs of training. The experimental verification of the proposed model has good generalization ability.

We conducted comparison experiments without fine-tuned on the same dataset. The experimental results are shown in Table 3.

Table 3. Comparison of different methods

Method	Networks	Embedding	Metric	Accuracy (%)
Huang et al. [5]	–	No	Euclidean	90.00
Zhao et al. [15]	–	No	Geodesic	92.86
DeepFace [16]	1	Yes	Cosine	94.35
DeepID [9]	1	Yes	Cosine	94.71
DeepID3 [17]	50	No	Joint Bayes	95.23
FaceNet [10]	1	Yes	Cosine	94.87
VGGFace [19]	1	Yes	Cosine	95.68
Hu et al. [18]	1	Yes	Cosine	95.35
Our	**2**	**Yes**	–	**96.67**

Compared with other methods, the efficiency and accuracy of our method both have a good performance.

4 Conclusion

This paper firstly proposed a method of deep neural network to measure the similarity between reconstructed face and face image. Based on the ideas of transfer learning and small sample learning, the neural network model is built on the basis of pre-trained model. Experiments show that the proposed method can effectively measure the similarity between reconstructed 3D face and 2D face.

Acknowledgment. This work is supported by Shaanxi Natural Science Foundation No. 2018JM 6061, Special Scientific Research Program of Shaanxi Education Department No. 2013JK1180 and Qingdao Municipality's Independent Innovation Major Project of China (2017-4-3-2-xcl).

References

1. Zhao, J., et al.: 3D facial similarity measure based on geodesic network and curvatures. Math. Prob. Eng. **2014**, 17 (2014)
2. Zhao, J.-L., et al.: 3D face similarity measure by Fr, chet distances of geodesics. J. Comput. Sci. Technol. **33**, 207–222 (2018)
3. Pu, Y.-C., Du, W.-C., Huang, C.-H., Lai, C.-K.: Invariant feature extraction for 3D model retrieval: an adaptive approach using Euclidean and topological metrics. Comput. Math Appl. **64**, 1217–1225 (2012)
4. Liu, T., Gao, J., Zhao, Y.: An approach to 3D building model retrieval based on topology structure and view feature. IEEE Access **6**, 31685–31694 (2018)
5. Huang, J., Zhou, M., Duan, F., Deng, Q., Wu, Z., Tian, Y.: The weighted landmark-based algorithm for skull identification. In: Real, P., Diaz-Pernil, D., Molina-Abril, H., Berciano, A., Kropatsch, W. (eds.) CAIP 2011. LNCS, vol. 6855, pp. 42–48. Springer, Heidelberg (2011). https://doi.org/10.1007/978-3-642-23678-5_3

6. Chopra, S., Hadsell, R., LeCun, Y.: Learning a similarity metric discriminatively, with application to face verification. In: 2005 IEEE Computer Society Conference on Computer Vision and Pattern Recognition (CVPR'05), vol. 531, pp. 539–546 (2005)
7. Zagoruyko, S., Komodakis, N.: Learning to compare image patches via convolutional neural networks (2015)
8. He, K., Zhang, X., Ren, S., Sun, J.: Spatial pyramid pooling in deep convolutional networks for visual recognition. In: Fleet, D., Pajdla, T., Schiele, B., Tuytelaars, T. (eds.) ECCV 2014. LNCS, vol. 8691, pp. 346–361. Springer, Cham (2014). https://doi.org/10.1007/978-3-319-10578-9_23
9. Sun, Y., Wang, X., Tang, X.: Deep learning face representation from predicting 10,000 classes. In: Proceedings of the 2014 IEEE Conference on Computer Vision and Pattern Recognition, pp. 1891–1898. IEEE Computer Society (2014)
10. Schroff, F., Kalenichenko, D., Philbin, J.: FaceNet: a unified embedding for face recognition and clustering (2015)
11. Zhu, Y., Zhuang, F., Yang, J., Yang, X., He, Q.: Adaptively transfer category-classifier for handwritten Chinese character recognition. In: Yang, Q., Zhou, Z.-H., Gong, Z., Zhang, M.-L., Huang, S.-J. (eds.) PAKDD 2019. LNCS (LNAI), vol. 11439, pp. 110–122. Springer, Cham (2019). https://doi.org/10.1007/978-3-030-16148-4_9
12. Vinyals, O., Blundell, C., Lillicrap, T., Kavukcuoglu, K., Wierstra, D.: Matching Networks for One Shot Learning (2016)
13. Szegedy, C., et al.: Going deeper with convolutions. In: 2015 IEEE Conference on Computer Vision and Pattern Recognition (CVPR), pp. 1–9 (2015)
14. Zhang, K., Zhang, Z., Li, Z., Qiao, Y.: Joint face detection and alignment using multitask cascaded convolutional networks. IEEE Signal Process. Lett. **23**, 1499–1503 (2016)
15. Zhao, J., Wu, Z., Liu, C., Duan, F., Zhou, M., Cao, J.: 3D facial similarity comparison in shape space (2015)
16. Taigman, Y., Yang, M., Ranzato, M., Wolf, L. DeepFace: closing the gap to human-level performance in face verification. In: 2014 IEEE Conference on Computer Vision and Pattern Recognition, pp. 1701–1708 (2014)
17. Sun, Y., Liang, D., Wang, X., Tang, X.: DeepID3: face recognition with very deep neural networks (2015)
18. Hu, G., et al.: Attribute-enhanced face recognition with neural tensor fusion networks (2017)
19. Mei, W., Deng, W.: Deep face recognition: a survey (2018)

Real-Time Face Occlusion Recognition Algorithm Based on Feature Fusion

Xiangde Zhang, Bin Zheng, Yuanjie Li, and Lianping Yang(✉)

College of Sciences, Northeastern University, Shenyang, Liaoning, China
{zhangxiangde,yanglp}@mail.neu.edu.cn

Abstract. The real-time face occlusion recognition is an important computer vision problem, especially for the public safety field. In order to construct a real-time face occlusion recognition system, this paper first established a large occlusion face database. Then, this paper proposed a face occlusion recognition algorithm based on the fusion of histogram of oriented gradient(HOG) and local binary pattern(LBP), the experimental results show that the occlusion face recall rate and the unobstructed face recall rate are 92.03% and 93.58% respectively, the speed is about 12.26 ms. Finally, taking into account time factor, this paper established a lightweight deep neural network based on AlexNet with an occlusion face recall rate and an unobstructed face recall rate of 91.79% and 91.42% respectively, and the speed is approximately 22.92 ms. The experimental results show that the face occlusion recognition method based on HOG+LBP features not only improves the recognition rate of occlusion face, but also reduces the time complexity, and illustrates the effectiveness of the algorithm.

Keywords: Face occlusion recognition · Histogram of oriented gradient · Local binary pattern · Convolutional neural network

1 Introduction

Face occlusion recognition means to determining whether a given face is occluded. The definition of face occlusion is blurred, the lack of face occlusion data sets and the diversity of face occlusion types has brought great challenges to face occlusion recognition research. However, in applications such as ATM machines, it requires to quickly determine whether a given face belongs to an occlusion face to determine whether there is an abnormal behavior, and when abnormal behavior is detected. The system is very important because it can promptly alert and take appropriate measures to provide greater protection for public safety.

Generally, face occlusion recognition is mainly divided into a method based on statistical learning and a method based on face features. The methods based on statistical learning are mainly PCA [1] analytical detection methods [2, 3]; methods based on facial features such as detection of occlusion of hair styling [4] and detection of mask and sunglasses occlusion [5]. Whether it is based on facial features or statistical learning, it is often not possible to quickly and accurately detect different types of occlusion. In addition, the current occlusion recognition algorithm uses a small number of data sets

Z. Sun et al. (Eds.): CCBR 2019, LNCS 11818, pp. 258–265, 2019.
https://doi.org/10.1007/978-3-030-31456-9_29

and occlusion is obvious, which imposes great limitations on the generalization of the model. After analysis, the face occlusion recognition did not achieve rapid development, on the one hand because of the lack of data sets that can be used to recognize occluded face; on the other hand, the real-time requirements are very high when it is used to identify face occlusion in applications similar to security, which increases the challenge of face occlusion recognition. In order to solve these problems, this paper first constructs a face database containing multiple types of occlusions, and then combines HOG [6] and LBP [7] as feature vectors for face occlusion recognition, and finally uses SVM [8] to train and classify. At the same time, a lightweight convolutional neural network is constructed to identify the occluded face. The experimental results show the effectiveness and real-time of the HOG+LBP-based face occlusion recognition method.

2 Algorithm

2.1 Building an Occlusion Face Image Database

In order to identify the occluded face, this paper established a database containing 46,345 face images. There are 16,391 occluded faces in the database, and 29,954 faces are unobstructed. The obstructions that block the face mainly include hands, books, sunglasses and masks. The occlusion of the face image is mainly obtained in three ways: picking in the existing face database, collecting on the Internet and using the laptop to

Fig. 1. Some occluded face images

take pictures. Figure 1 shows the partially occluded face images in the database:

(1) Crop face area and normalize

MTCNN [9] is an open face detection and location model. The model has the following advantages: 1. The model meets the integration of detection and localization. 2. High precision and fast speed can meet the requirements of real-time. In this paper, the images in the database are processed by MTCNN to obtain the face area. According to the position of the two eyes of the face, the face is normalized to 100*100, and the positions of the two eyes are set to (25, 25) and (25, 75) respectively. Then using normalized occluded faces and unobstructed face images for model construction.

(2) Illumination preprocess

In order to reduce the influence of illumination on face occlusion recognition, the normalized image was preprocessed by local histogram equalization. The specific operation is as follows: the main idea of the histogram equalization process is to change the gray histogram of the original image from a certain gray interval in the comparative set to a uniform distribution in the entire gray range. Histogram equalization is to nonlinearly stretch the image and redistribute the image pixel values so that the number of pixels in a certain gray range is approximately the same. The principle of local histogram equalization is to divide the picture into several area blocks, and then separately perform equalization processing according to a certain output histogram distribution in each area, and finally the adjacent areas are spliced by linear interpolation, effectively reducing the boundary noise. In this way, the method effectively suppresses the noise and also effectively enhances the local contrast.

2.2 Face Occlusion Recognition Based on HOG+LBP

Training phase:

A. Input $T = \{(I_1, y_1), (I_2, y_2)\ldots(I_N, y_N)\}$, where N is the total number of training samples, I_i representing the ith training sample, and $i \in \{1, 2\ldots N\}$, $y_i \in \{0, 1\}$ representing that the sample is occluded or unobstructed;

B. Extracting the HOG feature of the face training sample;

C. Extracting the LBP feature of the face training sample;

D. Using the PCA method to reduce the dimension of the extracted HOG features and LBP features respectively to reduce the complexity of the model and further improve the recognition speed;

E. Combine the reduced-dimensional HOG features and LBP features then input them into the SVM to obtain an occlude face recognition classifier.

Testing phase:

Given the input image, the image preprocessing is first performed, then the HOG feature and the LBP feature are extracted separately, and the reduced dimension of the HOG feature and the LBP feature are merged into the trained SVM classifier, and test the new image finally. Figure 2 is a flow chart of face occlusion recognition test based on HOG and LBP features.

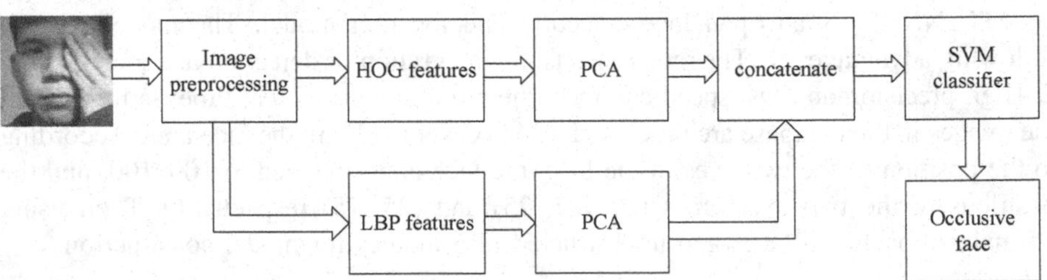

Fig. 2. Flow chart of face occlusion recognition

For step B in the training phase, the steps to extract the HOG feature are as follows:

(1) Data normalization: The input image is normalized by the Gamma correction method.

(2) Calculate the gradient at the pixel(x,y): extract the contour information and further weaken the illumination interference.

(3) Calculate the gradient size and direction according to the gradients obtained in (2):

$$M(x,y) = \sqrt{G_x^2(x,y) + G_y^2(x,y)} \tag{4}$$

$$\theta(x,y) = \arctan(\frac{G_y(x,y)}{G_x(x,y)}) \tag{5}$$

Normally, the gradient direction is defined by Eq. (5).

$$\theta(x,y) = \begin{cases} \theta(x,y) + \pi, \theta(x,y) < 0 \\ \theta(x,y), \theta(x,y) \geq 0 \end{cases} \tag{6}$$

(4) Divide the image into $c \times c$ small cells and count the gradient direction histogram in each cell, thus obtaining the histogram features of each $c \times c$ cell;

(5) The adjacent $b \times b$ cells are grouped into one block, and the features of all the cells in the block are connected in series to obtain the HOG feature vector of the block.

(6) The HOG feature of the image can be obtained by concatenating the HOG feature vectors of all blocks.

For step C in the training phase:

The basic idea of the classic LBP is: for the image I, the gray value of the central pixel is the threshold, and the gray value of the surrounding pixel is compared with it. If the gray value of the surrounding pixel is smaller than the gray value of the central pixel, the pixel position is marked as 0, otherwise it is marked as 1, and the binary code obtained by such comparison is read counterclockwise from the pixel point, and finally converted into a decimal value, which is the LBP value of the pixel. Given a 3×3 neighborhood, the gray value of the current pixel is $I(x,y)$, as the center point of the 3×3 neighborhood, the LBP value of the pixel is:

$$LBP(x,y) = \sum_{i=0}^{7} S[I_i(x,y) - I(x,y) \geq 0] \times 2^{7-i} \tag{7}$$

Where in, S[x] indicates the indication function, that is 1 when the condition is satisfied, and 0 if the condition is satisfied.

For the PCA method in step D of the training phase:

The core idea of PCA is to extract effective data information from a large number of occlusion face image data, reduce the amount of calculation, speed up the recognition, and ensure real-time requirements. The essence is to linearly transform the original features into low-dimensional spaces while representing the original features as well as possible. The process mainly solves the eigenvectors and eigenvalues of the covariance matrix. Under the generated new coordinate system, the spatial coordinates corresponding to the eigenvalues of a largest linearly independent group of samples can be obtained, and the main components are retained, and the secondary components are removed. By lowering the data dimension, you can fit the original data with less data.

For the SVM method in step E of the training phase:

SVM is a machine learning method based on statistical learning. It is based on the principle of structural risk minimization, which minimizes the risk of machine learning by selecting appropriate recognition functions, and ensures the classification of selected training samples and test samples with minimum error, looking for an approximate estimate of the relationship between the input variable and the output variable, predicting the outcome of the output variable with a higher accuracy.

2.3 Face Occlusion Recognition Based on Deep Neural Network

For deep neural networks, in order to obtain a better performance classifier, it is often necessary to use a deeper and larger convolutional neural network, but because of the high speed requirement on the face occlusion recognition, a high recognition accuracy is constructed. Identifying fast classifiers is a challenging task. In order to realize the real-time face occlusion recognition by means of the excellent recognition ability of convolutional neural network, this paper builds the neural network based on AlexNet [10].

3 Experiment and Result Analysis

3.1 Face Occlusion Recognition Experiment Based on HOG+LBP

The HOG feature focuses on extracting the edge information of the face image, and the LBP feature focuses on extracting the internal texture information of the face image. Therefore, the two features are combined to complement each other and improve the recognition performance. In order to verify the validity of the HOG+LBP feature and the SVM classifier, a research experiment was conducted on the database constructed in this paper.

After preprocessing the image of the database, the next step is extracting HOG feature on the face image. Different image sizes, different block sizes and different PCA principal components extract different HOG feature dimensions, which in turn affect the speed and recognition rate of face occlusion recognition. In the HOG feature of this experiment, each block consists of 2×2 cells. In this paper, the effects of different image sizes, different cell sizes and different PCA principal components on the recognition speed and accuracy of face occlusion are studied in turn. The experimental results are shown in Table 1:

As can be seen from lines 1, 2, and 3 of the table, when the image size is 128×96, the face occlusion recall rate is the highest.

It can be seen from the second, fourth, and fifth lines of the table that when the size of the block is too small, the HOG feature dimension increases sharply, and the occlusion face recall rate decreases. This shows that there is too much redundant information in the HOG feature, which interferes with the recognition performance of

Table 1. Influence of different factors on face occlusion recognition

Serial number	Feature operator	Image size	Block size	Feature dimension	Occlusion recall rate	Unblocked recall rate	Inference time(ms)
1	HOG	96 × 96	16 × 16	4356	83.82	87.50	140.26
2	HOG	128 × 96	16 × 16	5940	85.02	91.42	221.07
3	HOG	128 × 128	16 × 16	8100	84.54	90.50	269.18
4	HOG	128 × 96	32 × 16	2772	86.72	91.17	133.56
5	HOG	128 × 96	32 × 32	1260	90.34	88.92	47.68
6	LBP	128 × 96 128 × 96	16 × 16	2784	86.50	91.60	141.19
7	LBP	128 × 96	32 × 16	1392	88.41	90.17	44.72
8	LBP	128 × 96	32 × 32	696	78.26	89.67	33.88
9	PCA_HOG	128 × 96	32 × 32	200	89.86	92.92	10.57
10	PCA_HOG	128 × 96	32 × 32	300	91.55	93.33	24.23
11	PCA_HOG	128 × 96	32 × 32	400	90.82	92.42	15.21
12	PCA_HOG +PCA_LBP	128 × 96	32 × 32	200_200	90.58	93.08	9.56
13	**PCA_HOG +PCA_LBP**	**128 × 96**	**32 × 32**	**300_300**	**92.03**	**93.58**	**12.26**

the SVM. After weighing the recall rate and time, we select the block size to be 32 × 32. However, since the feature dimension is large and the required recognition time is long, it is considered to use the PCA method to first reduce the HOG feature vector and then use the SVM classifier to identify it.

It can be seen from lines 9, 10, and 11 of the table that the overall recognition rate of the PCA_HOG feature is higher than the recognition rate of the HOG feature, and the recognition time is greatly reduced. When the number of principal components of the PCA is 300 (up to 93.65% of the total), the PCA_HOG feature can better represent the original face image information, and reduce the interference of a large amount of redundant information in the HOG feature, and can ensure the recognition effectiveness.

In the 12th and 13th rows of the analysis table, the PCA method is used to reduce the dimensions of the HOG and LBP, and then the fusion features are input into the SVM classifier for identification. The results show that the feature dimensions of both HOG and LBP are taken as 300, the masked face recall rate and the unobstructed face recall rate reached the highest, respectively 92.03% and 93.58%. At the same time, the inference time was only 12.26 ms per image, which achieved real-time effects; thus verifying the effectiveness of the HOG+LBP method.

3.2 Face Occlusion Recognition Experiment Based on Convolutional Neural Network

In order to compare the classification performance of the face occlusion recognition method based on HOG+LBP, the data set of this paper is classified and tested by deep convolutional neural network. This paper slightly improves the original AlexNet model. In AlexNet, the number of neurons in the last three fully connected layers are 4096, 4096, 1000 respectively. In order to speed up the test speed of the model and ensure the accuracy of the model, the number of neurons in the last three fully connected layers are changed to 64, 64, 2 respectively; The final model size is 9.6 M, and the test results of 10,000 iterations show that the recall rate of the occlusive face is 91.79%, the recall rate of the unobstructed face is 91.42%, and the average time is 22.92 ms per image, compared to the traditional HOG+LBP's face occlusion recognition method, the recall rate of the face blocking and the recall rate of the unobstructed face are reduced by 0.24% and 2.16% respectively, and the test time of each image is increased by 10.66 ms, which indicates the traditional HOG+LBP's face occlusion identification method guarantees high recall rate and time control, which verifies the effectiveness and real-time of the method.

4 Conclusion

This paper proposes a face occlusion recognition algorithm based on feature fusion and SVM classifier. The algorithm firstly reduces the dimension of the extracted HOG features and LBP features by PCA, then cascades the reduced features to obtain the final feature vector, and finally combines the SVM classifier for occlusion identification. The experimental results show that the fusion of sparse HOG and LBP features can greatly reduce the time complexity and achieve feature complementation, improve the face occlusion recognition rate.

Acknowledgment. This work is supported by the Fundamental Research Funds for the Central Universities (Grant No. N160504007)

References

1. Jung, Y., Choi, J., Yu, B., et al.: A novel active frequency drift method of islanding prevention for the grid-connected photovoltaic inverter. In: 2005 IEEE Power Electronics Specialists Conference. Recife: IEEE, pp. 1915–1921 (2005)
2. Du, C., Su, G.: Eyeglasses removal from facial images for face recognition. J. Tsinghua Univ. (Nat. Sci. Ed.) **2005**(07), 928–930 (2005)
3. Wang, Z., Tao, J.: Face occlusion detection and reconstruction. Comput. Res. Dev. **47**(01), 16–22 (2010)
4. Wang, Z., Yang, D.: Research on detection method of hair-occlusion in face recognition. Microcomput. Appl. **35**(02), 32–34 (2016)
5. Yuan, B.: Location and recognition of abnormal faces. Nanjing University of Science and Technology, (2005)
6. Dalal, N., Triggs, B.: Histograms of oriented gradients for human detection. In: Proceedings of Computer Vision and Pattern Recognition, pp. 886–893 (2005)
7. Ojala, T., Harwood, I.: A comparative study of texture measures with classification based on feature distributions. Pattern Recogn. **29**(1), 51–59 (1996)
8. Cristianini, N., Shawe-Taylor, J.: An introduction to support vector machines and other kernel-based learning methods, pp. 1–28. Cambridge University Press, New York (2001)

9. Chen, D., Ren, S., Wei, Y., Cao, X., Sun, J.: Joint cascade face detection and alignment. In: Proceedings ECCV, p. 7 (2014)
10. Krizhevsky, A., Sutskever, I., Hinton, G.E.: ImageNet classification with deep convolutional neural networks. In: NIPS, pp. 1106–1114 (2012)
11. Jia, Y., et al.: Caffe: convolutional architecture for fast feature embedding. In: ACMMM, pp. 675–678 (2014)

Joint Face Detection and Alignment Using Focal Loss-Based Multi-task Convolutional Neural Networks

Rongsheng Wang, Jinzhao Tian, and Changlong Jin(✉)

Department of Computer Science, School of Mechanical Electrical & Information Engineering, Shandong University, Weihai, Shandong, China
wangrs1412@mails.jlu.edu.cn,
tianjinzhaothesixth@gmail.com, cljin@sdu.edu.cn

Abstract. In order to learn more hard negative example features of face, MTCNN increases the proportion of negative to positive examples. However, the training data of MTCNN suffer from the extreme foreground-background class imbalance, which results in a large number of well-classified negative examples overwhelming the detector during training. To solve this problem, we introduce Focal Loss to MTCNN to improve face classification performance. Besides, the Batch Normalization is adopted to speed up training and prevent network performance degradation caused by overfitting. The experimental results demonstrate that the proposed method has a better performance than MTCNN on face classification, and has a good comprehensive performance on facial landmark localization.

Keywords: Class imbalance · MTCNN · Face detection · Focal loss · Batch normalization

1 Introduction

MTCNN [1] is an effective combination of traditional cascade structure and Convolutional Neural Network(CNN), which is inspired by Cascade CNN [2]. MTCNN can detect faces quickly and locate facial landmarks accurately. To detect face precisely and exclude hard-negative examples of similar faces in complex backgrounds as far as possible, the MTCNN need to add a large number of negative examples in training set, which lead to an extreme foreground-background class imbalance, large amounts of easy negatives will overwhelm training and lead to degenerate models. Although algorithms like online hard example mining(OHEM) are used to maintain a manageable balance between foreground and background, they are inefficient, the training process is still dominated by large mounts of essay classified examples.

As a novel loss function, Focal loss [3] can be used as an effective way to deal with foreground-background class imbalance. Different from OHEM, Focal Loss didn't abandon the simple examples completely, it dynamically scales the cross entropy loss, and the scaling factor decreases as the increase of corresponding confidence that the sample is classified into its correct category. During training, this scaling factor can

Z. Sun et al. (Eds.): CCBR 2019, LNCS 11818, pp. 266–273, 2019.
https://doi.org/10.1007/978-3-030-31456-9_30

reduce the loss of well classified examples automatically, and focus on the training model that pays close attention to hard examples.

Based on MTCNN, this paper introduces Focal Loss to improve face classification performance and employs Batch Normalization(BN) [4] in front of each convolution layer to optimize the training process, as called **Focal MTCNN** in this work.

2 Network Architecture

The network structure of Focal MTCNN is similar to MTCNN. P-Net densely scans each level of the image pyramid with 12 × 12 sliding windows to reject more than 90% of the detection windows quickly. The rest of the detection windows are cropped out and resized into 24 × 24 as input to the R-Net. R-Net further removes more than 90% of non-face images. Finally, the remaining few windows are verified by inputting O-Net with an image size of 48 × 48. At each stage, face and partial face from CelebA [5] undergo facial landmark localization.

As the input image resolutions of the P-Net, R-Net, and O-Net increase, the depths of these networks gradually increase. The early low-resolution shallow network can quickly screen large-scale faces, and the late high-resolution deep network performs a small number of face screening and verification, therefore, it can be improved in both speed and accuracy.

3 Loss Function

Focal MTCNN requires Face Classification Loss, Bounding Box Regression Loss, and Facial Landmark Localization Loss to complete network training.

3.1 Face Classification Loss

Face classification is to judge whether an image is a human face or not, and the cross entropy loss(CE Loss) function is adopted in MTCNN:

$$L_{face,CE,1} = -\frac{1}{m}\sum_{i=1}^{m}\left(y_i^{face}\log(p_i) + \left(1 - y_i^{face}\right)\log(1 - p_i)\right) \tag{1}$$

where m is the number of examples, p_i is the probability that an image is a human face, and $y_i^{face} \in \{0, 1\}$ denotes the ground-truth label, respectively.

We modify the Eq. (1) and define the p_t as:

$$p_t = \begin{cases} p_i & y_i^{face} = 1 \\ 1 - p_i & y_i^{face} = 0 \end{cases} \tag{2}$$

Obviously, p_t indicates the probability that the sample is classified correctly. Then, $L_{face,CE}$ is:

$$L_{face,CE,2} = -\frac{1}{m}\sum_{i=1}^{m}\log(p_t) \tag{3}$$

In general, one way to address class imbalance is to add a CE balance factor $\alpha \in [0, 1]$, The weights of α and $1-\alpha$ are assigned to the positive and negative categories, respectively. For convenience, we define α_t in a way similar to the definition of p_t. then the α-balance $L_{face,CE}$ is:

$$L_{face,CE,\alpha_t} = -\frac{1}{m}\sum_{i=1}^{m}\alpha_t\log(p_t) \tag{4}$$

This Loss is a simple extension of CE Loss and is the original form of Focal MTCNN Face Classification Loss below.

As mentioned earlier, the class imbalance encountered during training overwhelms the cross entropy loss. Simple examples that are easy to classify, especially simple negative samples, accumulate most of the losses and dominate the gradient. Although α-balanced CE loss balances positive and negative samples in a certain degree, it does not distinguish between easy/hard examples. Therefore, we define Modified MTCNN's Face classification Loss as:

$$L_{face} = -\frac{1}{m}\sum_{i=1}^{m}\alpha_t(1-p_t)^{\gamma}\log(p_t) \tag{5}$$

where γ is focal loss factor.

Facial bounding box regression loss and facial landmark localization loss of Focal MTCNN are similar to MTCNN, as shown in Eqs. (6) and (7).

3.2 Bounding Box Regression Loss

The Bounding box regression Loss is defined as:

$$L_{bbox} = \frac{1}{m}\sum_{i=1}^{m}\left\|y_i^{bbox} - \hat{y}_i^{bbox}\right\|_2^2 \tag{6}$$

where $y_i^{bbox} \in R^4$ is coordinates of the predicted bounding box, $\hat{y}_i^{bbox}$ is ground-truth.

3.3 Facial Landmark Localization Loss

The Facial landmark localization Loss is defined as:

$$L_{landmark} = \frac{1}{m}\sum_{i=1}^{m}\left\|y_i^{landmark} - \widehat{y}_i^{landmark}\right\|_2^2 \tag{7}$$

where $y_i^{landmark} \in R^{10}$ denotes the coordinates of the predicted face landmark, $\widehat{y}_i^{landmark}$ is ground-truth.

3.4 Combination of Loss Functions

Since P-Net, R-Net, and O-Net have different tasks for each loss function, there are different training image types in the learning process. For example, the training set produced includes three types: face, non-face, and part-face. non-face only needs to calculate face classification loss L_{face}, the remaining two losses are set to 0. Therefore, the combination of the loss function is determined by the following equation:

$$\begin{aligned} L_{all} = \frac{1}{m}\sum_{i=1}^{m}\sum_{j\in\{face,bbox,landmark\}} & \omega_j\beta_i^j(-\alpha_t(1-p_t)^{\gamma}\log(p_t) \\ & + \left\|y_i^{bbox} - \widehat{y}_i^{bbox}\right\|_2^2 + \left\|y_i^{landmark} - \widehat{y}_i^{landmark}\right\|_2^2) \end{aligned} \tag{8}$$

where ω_j indicates the weight coefficient of different network loss functions, as shown in Table 1. $\beta_i^j \in \{0, 1\}$ is face type, when the image is face or part-face, $\beta_i^j = 1$, otherwise $\beta_i^j = 0$.

Table 1. ω_j in P-Net, R-Net, and O-Net.

	ω_{face}	ω_{bbox}	$\omega_{landmark}$
P-Net	0.60	0.20	0.20
R-Net	0.50	0.25	0.25
O-Net	0.30	0.30	0.40

Since the main task of P-Net and R-Net is face classification, face classification is given more weight in the Focal MTCNN stage. In the O-Net phase, the focus is on the facial landmark localization, thus giving $\omega_{landmark}$ a greater value.

4 Experimental Results and Analysis

4.1 Datasets and Training Data Making

We use WIDER FACE [6] as a training data set for face classification and facial bounding box regression, CelebA [5] is used as a training set for facial landmark localization, FDDB [7] as a face classification test set and AFLW [8] as a test set for facial landmark localization.

Table 2. Training data production rules.

Type of data	IoU
(a) Non-face	<0.3
(b) Face	>0.65
(c) Partial face	0.4–0.65

Because Focal MTCNN training tasks include face detection and facial landmark localization, it is necessary to make different data sets. Similar to MTCNN, we produce four kinds of image data. These data are determined by the IoU between the croped boxes and ground-truth: (a) non-face, (b) face, and (c) part-face, refer to Table 2. At the same time, we also made a dataset with only facial landmark location annotations denoted as (d). Where (a) and (b) are used for face classification tasks, (b) and (c) for facial bounding box regression(BBox reg), (d) is used for facial landmark localization.

P-Net:Randomly crop non-face, faces and partial faces from WIDER FACE, then take the face from CelebA for facial landmark localization.

R-Net:we use well-trained P-Net to generate training data for R-Net, and collect dataset for facial landmark localization from CelebA.

O-Net:we use well-trained R-Net to generate training data for O-Net.

Preprocessing: For the input images, some simple preprocessing is performed. Firstly, the images are flipped to expand the dataset, and the facial landmarks localization of the faces are also changed. Secondly, we deal with the random processing of image contrast, brightness, hue, and saturation. Finally, each pixel in RGB images is normalized by subtracting 127.5 then divided by 128.

Balance factor α: One of the strategies to improve the category imbalance is to add the balance factor α before the CE loss function, called α-balance CE Loss. As shown in Fig. 1, $\alpha = 0.5$ is equivalent to not adding a balance factor, and the model of α-balance CE Loss got the best performance with $\alpha = 0.7$.

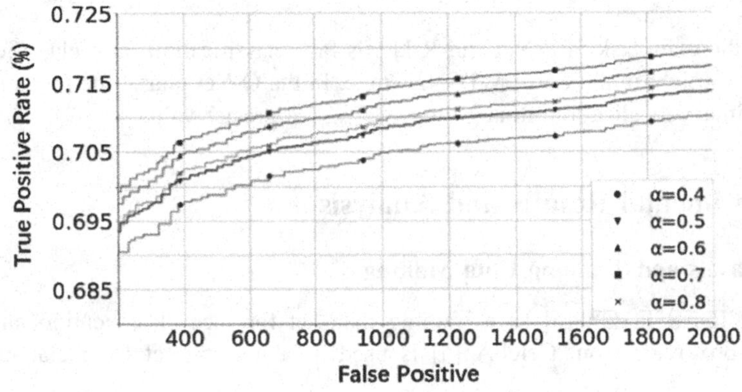

Fig. 1. ContROC under different α

Focal loss factor γ: We tested the performance of γ under $\alpha = 0.6$ and $\alpha = 0.7$. In order to simplify the experiment, we set the three networks in Focal MTCNN with the same α and γ. The specific data are shown in Table 3. Figure 2 shows that the facial classification performance based on Focal MTCNN is better than MTCNN.

Table 3. Verify the combined effect of α and γ.

α	γ	Cont accuracy
0.6	0	0.7172
0.6	1	0.7303
0.6	2	**0.7331**
0.6	5	0.7210
0.7	0	0.7193
0.7	0.5	0.7262
0.7	1	**0.7335**
0.7	2	0.7330
0.7	5	0.7227

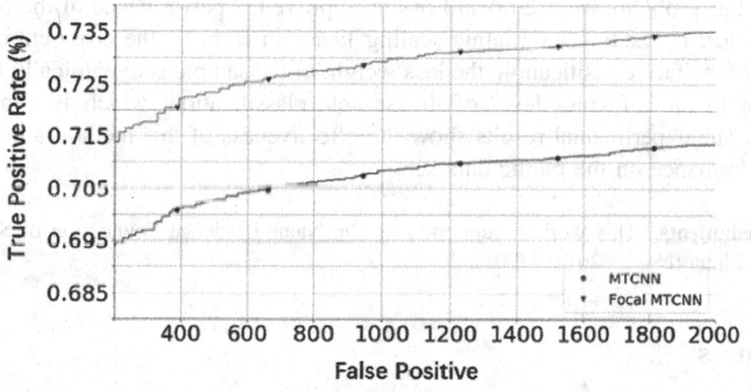

Fig. 2. ContROC of Focal MTCNN and MTCNN

Facial Landmark localization: The performance of fast facial landmark localization is compared among ESR [9], RCPR [10], SDM [11], TCDCN [12], MTCNN [1], and the proposed algorithm. Figure 3. shows that Focal MTCNN is superior to MTCNN in the accuracy of facial landmark localization.

Equation (8) shows that a large number of easy samples reduce the weight of the face classification loss function in the overall loss, and the weight of the face bounding box regression loss and the facial landmark localization loss is improved in the Easy Example. Therefore, in Focal MTCNN, the accuracy of facial landmark localization is higher than that of MTCNN. Figure 3 shows the comparisons between different algorithms.

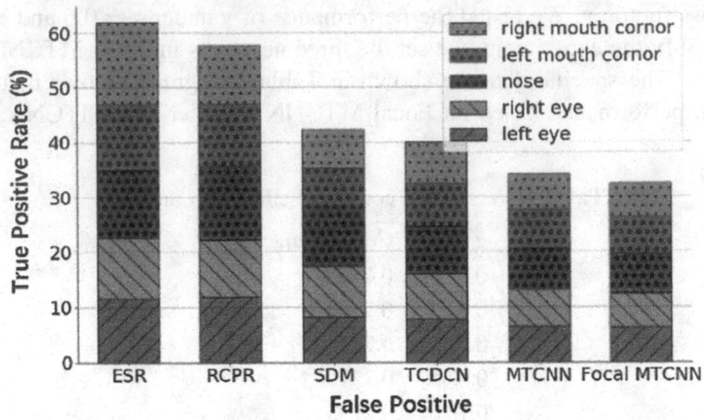

Fig. 3. Facial landmark localization evaluation on AFLW

5 Conclusion

We regard the training class imbalance as an obstacle to the performance of MTCNN. To solve this problem, we use Focal Loss to improve the performance of the MTCNN face detector. By adding a dynamic scaling factor in front of the cross-entropy loss function of the face classification, the loss weight of the sample is dynamically adjusted according to the difficulty level of the sample classification, which is simple and effective. The experimental results show the effectiveness of this method and achieve good performance on the public data set.

Acknowledgments. This work is supported by the Natural Science Foundation of Shandong Province, China (No. ZR2014FM004).

References

1. Zhang, K., Zhang, Z., Li, Z., Qiao, Y.: Joint face detection and alignment using multitask cascaded convolutional networks. IEEE Signal Process. Lett. **23**(10), 1499–1503 (2016)
2. Li, H., Lin, Z., Shen, X., Brandt, J., Hua, G.: A convolutional neural network cascade for face detection. In: CVPR, pp. 5325–5334 (2015)
3. Lin, T.-Y., Goyal, P., Girshick, R., He, K., Dollar, P.: Focal loss for dense object detection. In: ICCV (2017)
4. Ioffe, S., Szegedy, C.: Batch normalization: Accelerating deep network training by reducing internal covariate shift. arXiv preprint (2015). arXiv:1502.03167
5. Liu, Z., Luo, P., Wang, X., Tang, X.: Deep learning face attributes in the wild. In: CVPR, pp. 3730–3738 (2015)
6. Yang, S., Luo, P., Loy, C.C., Tang, X.: WIDER FACE: A Face Detection Benchmark. arXiv preprint (2016). arXiv:1511.06523
7. Jain, V., Learned-Miller, E.G.: FDDB: a benchmark for face detection in unconstrained settings. Technical Report UMCS-2010-009, University of Massachusetts, Amherst (2010)

8. Köstinger, M., Wohlhart, P., Roth, P.M., Bischof, H.: Annotated facial landmarks in the wild: a large-scale, real-world database for facial landmark localization. In: ICCV Workshops (2011)
9. Cao, X., Wei, Y., Wen, F., Sun, J.: Face alignment by explicit shape regression. IJCV **107** (2), 177–190 (2012)
10. Burgos-Artizzu, X.P., Perona, P., Dollar, P.: Robust face landmark estimation under occlusion. In: ICCV, pp. 1513–1520 (2013)
11. Xiong, X., Torre, F.: Supervised descent method and its applications to face alignment. In: CVPR, pp. 532–539 (2013)
12. Zhang, Z., Luo, P., Loy, C.C., Tang, X.: Facial landmark detection by deep multi-task learning. In: ECCV, pp. 94–108 (2014)

A Face Recognition Workflow Based Upon Similarity Measurement

Yigan Li(✉) and Zhaohui Wang

Hainan University, Haikou, Hainan Province, China
liyigan0324@vip.qq.com

Abstract. In order to combine with different feature extraction methods, in this paper, we propose a new method using similarity calculation between multiple features. We regard face recognition as a maximum-a-posteriori (MAP) problem and the de-pendency between different features is defined by a markov chain. We construct a matching similarity function T which helps us finding a better matching image. Experiments were tested using AR database and the results have shown that our recognition rate is higher, especially robust to small occlusion and noise.

Keywords: Face recognition · Multiple feature · Similarity calculation

1 Introduction

Face recognition mainly includes three steps: detection, feature extraction and recognition [1]. In particular, feature extraction is more difficult than the others in solving face recognition problems, which directly affects the recognition performance. To solve the different problems of recognition, many efficient and novel methods have been proposed, which can be divided into three types [2]: global approaches, local approaches and hybrid approaches.

In global approaches, such as Eigenface [3], kernel independent component analysis [4], support vector machine [5], etc., the entire face was considered as input data and modeled linearly or non-linearly. The local approaches, such as Brunelli et al. [6], Gabor filter [7], Local binary pattern [8] (LBP), etc., extract specific geometric features with accurate statistical models in the image. Therefore, their performance de-pends greatly on the effectiveness of feature extraction [9]. The hybrid approaches, such as Hidden Markov Model(HMM) [10], Directional LBP based wavelet [11], Local directional pattern [12], etc., fuse multiple features simultaneously, which shows more robust and accurate performance comparing to using a single feature.

In hybrid approaches, the image fusion can be carried out on three levels: pixel level, feature level and decision level [13]. In pixel level, Huang et al. [14] proposed a facial expression method based on multi-region evidence fusion. The face images were divided into different regions and a block histogram of gradient Gabor feature was extracted from every region. In final decision, different regions were combined to gain

Yigan Li, master student main research interests: image processing face recognition.

Z. Sun et al. (Eds.): CCBR 2019, LNCS 11818, pp. 274–283, 2019.
https://doi.org/10.1007/978-3-030-31456-9_31

the result with their own weights. Nefian et al. [15] grouped the face into 5 facial features i.e. mouth, eyes, nose, chin, forehead for frontal face images by using 5-state HMM. Miar-Naimi et al. [16] added eyebrows and chin as 7-state HMM. These methods could improve the accuracy, but less resistant to different interferences because of their limitation of a single feature. Therefore, in view of face complexity, face images could not be represented by a single feature completely. The fusion of feature level and decision level has gradually become the popular directions in face recognition [17].

Some researchers pay their attentions on feature level [18–20]. These methods [18–20] could significantly improve the performance of face recognition by combing different features. However, on decision level, they just simply obtained the final similarity score by a weighted summation of different features. In decision level, Kittler et al. [21] regarded different features as different classifiers and developed a common theoretical framework for combining classifiers, such as the product rule, sum rule, min rule, max rule, median rule, and majority voting. According to their experimental comparison, the sum rule gave the better accuracy and robustness. Based on the assumptions that classifier scores are distributed independently, Nandakumar et al. [22] proposed an optimal combination method of matching scores using likelihood ratio test by the product rule. But in practice, each classifier is not completely independent [23], and there are potential connections between the features used by each classifier. In the absence of a conditional dependent hypothesis, the posterior probability of the classifier can be calculated by joint distribution estimation [24–28]. The experimental and theoretical of these solutions are quite different while the environment is complicated.

In this paper, we develop a novel framework for dependency modeling in hybrid approach. We focus more on how to deal with the dependent between different features and believe feature extraction methods have less influence on decision level. We assume that different feature exactions are not independent of each other, the similarity calculations of the different results of the feature are performed. Finally, we propose a matching function T which helps us finding a better matching image. The proposal could reduce the mistakes according to experiments in the AR database [29].

2 MAP Problem

In this paper, we assume that different feature exactions are dependent of each other in a way and every process of the matching is independent in face recognition. So we define the problem of face recognition is a MAP problem and the dependency between different features is defined by a markov chain. In MAP problem, every face recognition X is defined as a Bernoulli distribution used to model the cases of being a true match. $X_i = (x_i, s_i)$, x_i means extracted features, s_i is the number of different feature, i is the sequence number. Compare to other multi-feature methods, we put all the match x_i together from different feature in the beginning of decision level, $T_K = \{X_{K_1}, X_{K_2}, \ldots, X_{K_I}\}, X_{K_I} \in X$. Without finding maximum similarity probability simply, we calculate a series of T to solve MAP under assuming X is conditionally independent.

$$
\begin{aligned}
T &= \arg\max_{T} P(T|\chi) \\
&= \arg\max_{T} P(\chi|\mathrm{T})P(T) \\
&= \arg\max_{T} \prod_{i} P(x_i|\mathrm{T})P(T)
\end{aligned} \tag{1}
$$

The number of T is huge, in order to reduce the time of calculation, we choose the first 10 X in every feature consist in T*, and we regulate that every X is chosen once in decision level. Formula (1) was decomposed as:

$$
\begin{aligned}
T^{*} &= \arg\max_{T} \prod_{\mathrm{i}} P(x_i|\chi) \prod_{T_k \in T} P(T_k) \\
&\mathrm{s.t.} T_k \cap T_o = \emptyset, T_k, T_o \in T
\end{aligned} \tag{2}
$$

$P(x_j|T)$ is a Bernoulli distribution which represents probability whether each matching process is true or not. $P(T_k)$ is a markov chain, including starting probability P_{entr}, ending probability P_{exit} and conversion probability $P_{link}(x_{k_{l_k}}|x_{k_{1_{k-1}}})$ of each match, as formula (3). Conversion probability models the connection of different feature, starting probability and ending probability are unified initialized.

$$
\begin{aligned}
P(T_k) &= P(\{x_{k_0}, x_{k_1}, \ldots, x_{k_{l_k}}\}) \\
&= P_{entr}(x_{k_0}) P_{link}(x_{k_1}|x_{k_0}) P_{link}(x_{k_2}|x_{k_1}) \ldots P_{link}(x_{k_{l_k}}|x_{k_{1_{k-1}}}) P_{exit}(x_{k_{l_k}})
\end{aligned} \tag{3}
$$

It is too difficult to find maximum of a function, so we change formula (2) as the logarithm of the matching function, the process of finding the maximum value is transformed to find the minimum value. The labels, δ_{i}, $\delta_{m,n}$, $\delta_{\mathrm{s,i}}$, $\delta_{\mathrm{e,i}}$ are put into the matching function so that we can use the labels finding the minimum value.

$$
\begin{aligned}
T &= \arg\min_{T} \sum_{T_k \in T} -\log P(T_k) + \sum_{\mathrm{i}} -\log P(x_i|T) \\
&= \arg\min_{T} \sum_{i}^{i=N} \delta_{\mathrm{i}}[-\log P(x_i|T)] + \sum_{i}^{i=N} \delta_{\mathrm{s,i}}[-\log P_{entr}(x_{k_i})] \\
&+ \sum_{i}^{i=N} \delta_{\mathrm{e,i}}[-\log P_{exit}(x_{k_i})] + \sum_{m,n}^{m,n=N} \delta_{\mathrm{m,n}}[-\log P_{link}(x_{k_1}|x_{k_2}) \ldots P_{link}(x_{k_n}|x_{k_m})]
\end{aligned} \tag{4}
$$

To simplify matching function and conveniently calculate, every term is transformed as the product between labels and different similarities C. It is detailed described in Sect. 3.2.

3 The Workflow

There are two face feature extraction methods, deep learning based face recognition algorithm [30–32] and hand-craft features [33–35]. Recently, the deep learning based face recognition algorithm is able to learn effective face features to obtain a very impressive performance. And hand-craft features have been researched for a long time, and the role of the hand-crafted face features is still effective. Both deep learning algorithms and hand-craft features play an important role in face recognition. In this section, we detailedly introduce a workflow which combines multi-features on decision level. In Sect. 3.1, we discuss how to calculate every probability in formula (4). In Sect. 3.2, we explain how to find better matching result by matching function T.

3.1 Similarity Calculation

The assumption of conditional independence between multiple feature classifiers is not applicable in most real environments. In order to satisfy the dependency among classifiers, we constructed a model to simulate the better face matching process by using feature extraction ① and feature extraction ②, as shown in Fig. 1.

Firstly, Manhattan distance were calculated in the same feature classifier and sorted from small to large which described similarity between the sample images with the test image. For Euclidean distance, the distance of same feature is too close between different face images, which is bad to discriminate. In this case, the selection of Manhattan distance can widen the distance, and has higher stability. Then, the chosen N feature vectors were extracted from feature vectors ① and feature vectors ②. N consisted of N_1 and N_2, and the number of N_1 and N_2 were set to 10 based on experiments. N_1 means the first N_1 feature vector number from Manhattan distance in feature vectors ①. N_2 means the first N_2 feature vector number from Manhattan distance in feature vectors ②. Next, the extracted feature vectors are calculated similarity with test feature vector and inter-similarity respectively. After the procedure of similarity calculation with test feature vector, normalized Manhattan distances were weighted and formed C_i from feature vectors ① and feature vectors ②. By the inter-similarity calculation, $C_{m,n}$ was processed as the same as C_i by using formula (5).

Under the assumption of dependence between different feature classifier results, the multi-classifier fusion algorithm based on multi-Agent weight adaptive adjustment [36] is used to find the weight of $C_{m,n}$ or C_i as:

$$C = q_1k_1 + q_2k_2 \tag{5}$$

Where C means $C_{m,n}$ or C_i.q_1, q_2 are different weights of each feature, k_1, k_2 obtained by normalized Manhattan distances from feature vectors ① and feature vectors ②. In $C_{m,n}$, k_1, k_2 were normalized to [I,0], I was determined by the number of classifiers, the value of I was set −0.5 based on experiments. In C_i, k_1, k_2 were normalized to [0,I], the value of I was set 1 based on experiments. The higher the similarity of the selected images, the smaller the value of $C_{m,n}$ or C_i are, which also means the closer the calculated distance between two different types of images, the greater the dependence is.

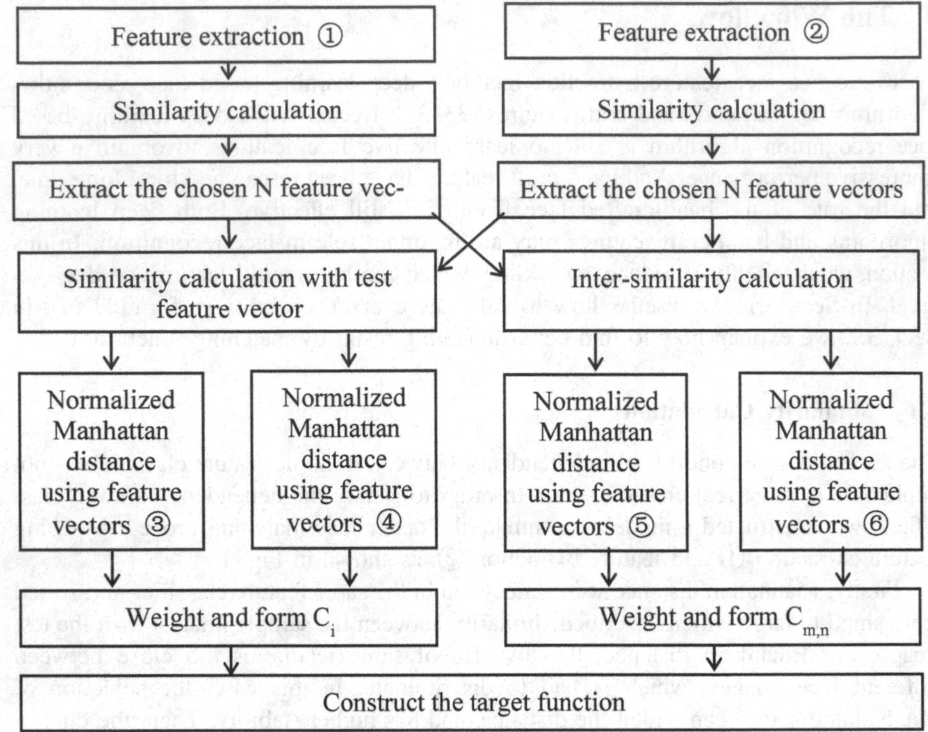

Fig. 1. Flow chart of similarity measurement

3.2 The Matching Results

In this section, we simplify a matching function T to find the best matching image type from multiple features. The formula is as follows:

$$T = \arg\min_{T} \sum_{i}^{i=N} \delta_{\mathrm{i}} C_i + \sum_{m,n}^{m,n=N} \delta_{\mathrm{m,n}} C_{m,n} + \sum_{i}^{i=N} \delta_{\mathrm{s,i}} C_{s,i} + \sum_{i}^{i=N} \delta_{\mathrm{e,i}} C_{e,i} \quad (6)$$

Where $C_{s,j}$ and $C_{e,j}$ are virtual similarities, were set to 1, which in order to helping to find the minimum of matching function T. δ_{i}, $\delta_{m,n}$, $\delta_{\mathrm{s,i}}$, $\delta_{\mathrm{e,i}}$ are labels, which mark whether similarities were chose, 1 means chose, 0 means no chose.

When $C_{m,n}$ is set to $[-0.5,0]$, matching function T will exist minimum value, which means there may be a set of images containing multiple image types. The process of calculating the minimum value is the process of finding the maximum similarity match. In the determination of the final match results, the sample image types are calculated by different values of δ_{i}, $\delta_{m,n}$, $\delta_{\mathrm{s,i}}$, $\delta_{\mathrm{e,i}}$. When the same type was found, the count is incremented by 1. If a sample type count is greater than the other sample types, this type is the desired match result. Otherwise, if several types of sample types are equal and higher than other sample types, the sample type with the highest ranking value and the highest count will be selected, this type is the matching result.

4 Experiments and Analysis

In order to verify the recognition rate in non-cooperating and uncontrolled environments. First, we evaluate the performance of the proposal with sum rule, minimum rule and mode rule according to Kittler et al [21] in AR database. Finally, we discuss our method with other single feature exaction methods.

In AR database, there are 126 people, divided into two sessions. Each session has 1638 images, divided into 13 conditions, and the image pixels are 165 × 120. We used the first 10 conditions in the first session in the experiments, as shown in Fig. 2.The recognition rate is shown in Table 1.

In order to test the influence of noise, the white noise and salt-pepper noise were chosen to carry out an experiment using AR database, and the formula (7) was used to identify the rate of decline.

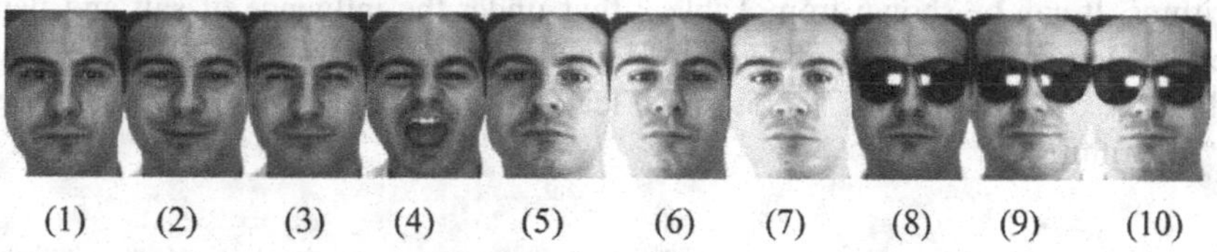

(1) (2) (3) (4) (5) (6) (7) (8) (9) (10)

Fig. 2. Example images from the AR database. From left to right: (1) Clean (2) Smile (3) Anger (4) Scream (5) Illum.Right (6) Illum.left (7) Illum.Both (8) Sunglasses (9) sg+Illum.Right (10) sg +Illum.left

$$\omega = \frac{\gamma - \alpha}{\gamma} \times 100\% \tag{7}$$

Where γ means the rate without noise, α means the rate after adding noise. ω means the decreasing ratio after adding noise. The smaller ω, the better robustness is. In the experiment, the white noise was selected with normalized variance δ of 0, 0.0008, 0.0015, 0.0031 and the salt-pepper noise with noise density d of 0.2, as shown in Fig. 3. The values were decided based on experiments. The result of experiments with salt and pepper noise is shown in Table 2.

Table 1. Comparison of each algorithm in white noise (%)

Algorithm	Noise(δ)				ω
	0	0.0008	0.0015	0.0031	
Sum rule	90.22	90.56	90.89	89.56	0.76
Minimum rule	90.22	90.11	90.44	88.56	1.84
mode rule	88.00	89.00	89.00	87.33	0.73
The proposal	91.56	90.56	90.22	90.33	1.34

Fig. 3. Noise-added face image. From left to right, the mean value is 0, the normalized difference is 0, 0.0008, 0.0015, 0.0031 white noise, and the noise density d is 0.2 salt and pepper noise.

Table 1 shows that compared with other algorithms, the proposal has higher recognition rates than second method approximately 1.34% without any noise, and when normalized variance δ of white noise is 0.0031, the recognition rate of the proposal is still 90.33%, ω is 1.34%. Under different white noise interference, the proposal maintains the highest rate and has acceptable performance than the other algorithms. It can be shown from Table 2 that under the influence of salt and pepper noise, the mode rule is greatly affected by noise, and the proposal is less affected. In the AR database 5–10 conditions, the proposal leads to an even larger improvement for the other algorithms.

Table 2. Face recognition rate of AR database with salt and pepper noise of 0.2 noise density (%)

Condition	Sum rule	Minimum rule	Mode rule	The proposal
2	**99**	**99**	**99**	**99**
3	98	98	**99**	98
4	68	**70**	66	66
5	98	98	96	**99**
6	96	96	96	**97**
7	84	84	79	**88**
8	91	88	88	**92**
9	78	81	74	**82**
10	69	69	62	**74**

In Table 3, the proposal leads to a higher face recognition rate than traditional feature exaction methods like LBP. But in more complex database LFW, the face images are not aligned which may lead the proposal to a worse recognition. And compare to [32, 33], our proposal doesn't use outside training data which also limits the performance.

Table 3. Face recognition rate of different feature exaction methods (%)

	LFW [37]	AR
LBP	88.33	87.22
SIFT	85.95	–
HOG	87.90	–
Gabor	84.93	80.22
The proposal	–	91.56
High-dim LBP [33]	95.17	–
Deep Representation [32]	96.13	–

5 Conclusion

We have presented a multiple features face recognition in non-cooperative and uncontrolled environment such as illumination changes, expression changes, occlusion, noise and etc. We propose a multiple features combined rule, in order to improve performance in a single feature classifier. Under the assumption that the results of multiple feature classifiers are dependent, the multiple feature classifiers were fused in an optimal solution which improves the accuracy of the recognition. When the environment is complicated, compared with other combined rules, the proposal can effectively reduce the rate of decline in recognition rate and enhance the robustness of the system. In the feature, we will test our method in more challenging database like LFW and combine with more advanced feature exaction methods next.

References

1. Mejda, C., Akram, E., Wajdi, B., et al.: A survey of 2D face recognition techniques. Computers **5**(4), 21 (2016)
2. Guofeng, Z., Guixia, F.U., Haitao, L.I., et al.: A survey of multi-pose face recognition. Pattern Recogn. Artif. Intell. **28**(07), 613–625 (2015)
3. Turk, M., Pentland, A.P.: Face recognition using Eigenfaces. In: Proceedings 1991 IEEE Computer Society Conference on Computer Vision and Pattern Recognition, pp. 586–591. Maui, HI, USA (1991)
4. Bach, F.R., Jordan, M.: Kernel independent component analysis. J. Mach. Learn. Res. **3**, 1–48 (2003)
5. Hoffmann, H.: Kernel PCA for novelty detection. Pattern Recogn. **40**(3), 863–874 (2007)
6. Brunelli, R., Poggio, T.: Face recognition: features versus templates. IEEE Trans. Pattern Anal. Mach. Intell. **15**(10), 1042–1052 (1993)
7. Lee, T.S.: Image representation using 2D gabor wavelets. IEEE Trans. Pattern Anal. Mach. Intell. **18**(10), 959–971 (1996)
8. Baochang, Z., Gao, Y., et al.: Local derivative pattern versus local binary pattern: face recognition with high-order local pattern descriptor. IEEE Trans. Image Process. A Publ. IEEE Signal Process. Soc. **19**(2), 533–544 (2010)
9. Yan, Y., Wang, H., Suter, D.: Multi-subregion based correlation filter bank for robust face recognition. Pattern Recogn. **47**(11), 3487–3501 (2014)

10. Samaria, F., Young, S.: HMM-based architecture for face identification. Image and Vis. Comput. **12**(8), 537–543 (1994)
11. Wu, F.: Face recognition based on wavelet transform and regional directional weighted local binary pattern. J. Multimedia **9**(8), 1017–1023 (2014)
12. Kim, D.J., Lee, S.H., Sohn, M.K.: Face recognition via local directional pattern[J]. Int. J. Secur. Appl. **7**(2), 191–200 (2013)
13. Liu, J., Zhang, L.-S., Xu, K.-X.: Multimodal face recognition based on images fusion on feature and decision levels. Nanotechnol. Precis. Eng. **7**(01), 65–70 (2009)
14. Huang, Z., Ren, F.: Facial expression recognition based on multi-regional D-S evidences theory fusion. IEEE J. Trans. Electric. Electron. Eng. **12**(2), 251–261 (2017)
15. Nefian, A., Hayes, M.: Face detection and recognition using hidden Markov models. In: Proceedings 1998 International Conference on Image Processing. ICIP98, pp. 141–145, vol. 1. Chicago, IL, USA (1998)
16. Miar-Naimi, H., Davari, P.: A new fast and efficient HMM-based face recognition system using a 7-State HMM along with SVD coefficients. Iran. J. Electric. Electron. Eng. **4**(1), 46–57 (2008)
17. Fuji, R., Yanqiu, L.I., Min, H.U., et al.: Face recognition method based on multi-features description and local fusion classification decision. Opto-Electron. Eng. **43**(09), 1–8 (2016)
18. Soodeh, N., Majid, A.: A modified technique for face recognition under degraded conditions. Vis. Commun. Image Representation **55**, 742–755 (2018)
19. Jing, L.I., Tao, Q., Chang, W., et al.: Robust face recognition using the deep C2D-CNN model based on decision-level fusion. Sensors **18**(7), 2080 (2018)
20. Hoda, M., Amirhossein, S., Benyamin, G.: Pixel-level alignment of facial images for high accuracy recognition using ensemble of patches. Journal of the Optical Society of America **35**(7), 1149 (2018)
21. Kittler, J., Hatef, M., Duin, R.P.W., et al.: On combining classifiers. IEEE Trans. Pattern Anal. Mach. Intell. **20**(3), 226–239 (2002)
22. Nandakumar, K., Chen, Y., Dass, S.C., et al.: Likelihood ratio-based biometric score fusion. IEEE Trans. Pattern Anal. Mach. Intell. **30**(2), 342–347 (2007)
23. Ma, A.J., Yuen, P.C., Lai, J.H.: Linear dependency modeling for classifier fusion and feature combination. IEEE Trans. Pattern Anal. Mach. Intell. **35**(5), 1135–1148 (2013)
24. Prabhakar, S., Jain, A.K.: Decision-level fusion in fingerprint verification. Pattern Recogn. **35**(4), 861–874 (2002)
25. Duda, R.O., Hart, P.E., Stork, D.G.: Pattern Classification, pp. 177–196. Wiley, New Jersey (2000)
26. Terrades, O.R., Valveny, E., Tabbone, S.: Optimal classifier fusion in a non-bayesian probabilistic framework. IEEE Trans. Pattern Anal. Mach. Intell. **31**(9), 1630–1644 (2009)
27. Gehler, P., Nowozin, S.: On feature combination for multiclass object classification. In: Proceedings IEEE International Conference Computer Vision, pp. 221–228 (2009)
28. Demiriz, A., Bennett, K.P., Shawe-Taylor, J.: Linear programming boosting via column generation. Mach. Learn. Res. **46**(1–3), 225–254 (2002)
29. Huang, G.B., Ramesh, M., Berg, T., et al.: Labeled faces in the wild: a database for studying face recognition in unconstrained environments, pp. 07–49. University of Massachusetts, Amherst, Technical Report (2007)
30. Sun, Y., Wang, X., Tang, X.: Deep learning face representation by joint identification-verification (2014)
31. Taigman, Y., Yang, M., Ranzato, M., et al.: DeepFace: closing the gap to human-level performance in face verification. In: Conference on Computer Vision and Pattern Recognition (CVPR). IEEE Computer Society (2014)

32. Zhu, X., Ramanan, D.: Face detection, pose estimation, and landmark localization in the wild. In: 2012 IEEE Conference on. IEEE Computer Vision and Pattern Recognition (CVPR) (2012)
33. Chen, D., Cao, X., Wen, F., et al.: Blessing of dimensionality: high-dimensional feature and its efficient compression for face verification. In: 2013 IEEE Conference on Computer Vision and Pattern Recognition (CVPR), IEEE (2013)
34. Déniz, O., Bueno, G., Salido, J., et al.: Face recognition using histograms of oriented gradients. Pattern Recogn. Lett. **32**(12), 1598–1603 (2011)
35. Liao, S., Jain, A.K., Li, S.Z.: Partial face recognition: alignment-free approach. IEEE Trans. Pattern Anal. Mach. Intell. **35**(5), 1193–1205 (2013)
36. Biao, T., Wei, J., Randi, F., et al.: Face recognition using decision fusion of multiple sparse representation-based classifiers[J]. Telecommun. Sci. **34**(4), 31–40 (2018)
37. Huang, G.B., Ramesh, M., Berg, T., et al.: Labeled faces in the wild: a database for studying face recognition in unconstrained environments (2008)

106-Point Facial Landmark Localization with Mobile Networks Based on Regression

Xiangyang Zhai, Yuqing He(✉), Qian Zhao, and Yutong Ding

Key Laboratory of Photoelectronic Imaging Technology and System, Ministry of Education of China, School of Optoelectronics, Beijing Institute of Technology, Beijing 10081, China
yuqinghe@bit.edu.cn

Abstract. Sparse facial landmark localization has lower precision for face reconstruction, while more point landmarks are competent to depict the structure of facial components. In this paper, the pipeline of detecting 106-point facial landmarks with regression is proposed. Based on the convergence and practical application of multi-points regression, we design MobileNetV2-FL and VGG16-FL. Besides, an effective data preprocessing strategy and some training tricks, such as the Online Hard Example Mining algorithm and Wing loss are applied to the issue. Experimental results show that the proposed method has lower failure rate, and is an effective and robust facial landmark localization method.

Keywords: Facial landmark localization · Regression · Mobile network

1 Introduction

Facial landmark localization aims to automatically identify the predefined locations of the facial key points on facial images or videos. It's an important and essential intermediary step for many face analysis applications, such as emotion estimation, facial pose estimation, and so on. Sparse facial landmark localization has been developed, such as 5 points [1, 2] and 68 points [3]. However, sparse facial landmark localization has lower precision for face reconstruction. It is incompetent to depict the structure of facial components e.g., there is no points defined on the lower boundary of eyebrow and the wing of nose. For example, face beautification need more accurate position of face shape. More facial key points bring difficulty to convergence and more semantic ambiguities emerge. This paper selects a relatively high number –106 points that are capable to describe the most application scenes. Figure 1 shows the position of the 106-point landmarks. These points are located at the semantic locations that describe discriminative texture information.

With the recent development of deep learning, the performance of facial landmark localization has been considerable improved. For dense facial landmark localization, the submitted methods of top three winners were described on the 106-point facial landmark localization competition and aimed at dense points [4], and relatively little research has been done on dense points. In recent years, different network structures are applied to sparse facial landmark localization. Sun firstly applied cascade convolutional neural network (CNN) to facial landmark localization problem [2]. Bulat proposed a novel

Z. Sun et al. (Eds.): CCBR 2019, LNCS 11818, pp. 284–292, 2019.
https://doi.org/10.1007/978-3-030-31456-9_32

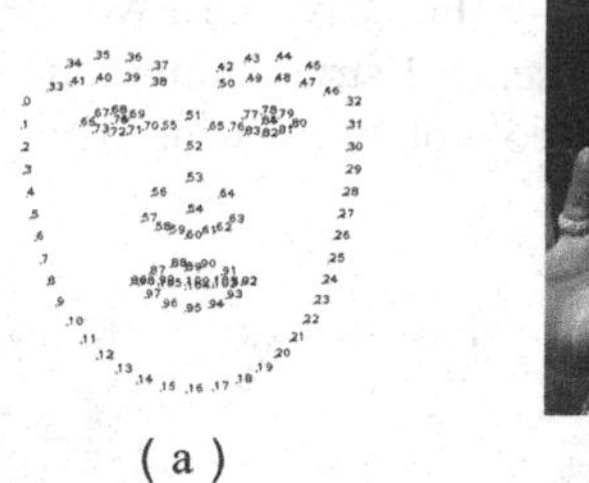

(a)

(b)

Fig. 1. 106-point facial landmarks (a) the order of 106-point facial landmarks (b) the position of facial landmarks on the image

hierarchical, parallel and multi-scale ResNet [5]. Instead of training multiple networks in a cascaded manner, Trigeorgis trained a deep convolutional Recurrent Neural Network (RNN) for facial landmark detection to mimic the cascaded behavior [6]. Bulat proposed Super-FAN, which incorporated structural information in a GAN-based super-resolution algorithm via integrating a subnetwork for face alignment through heatmap regression and optimizing a novel heatmap loss [7]. Since complex networks require high deployment and hardware and can't be applied to mobile devices, we make some corrections for mobile networks on the problem of multi-points regression.

Considering the practical application, we combine regression-based method and mobile network structure for the facial landmark localization to reduce algorithm complexity while retaining the accuracy of points detection. However, one issue for the regression-based method is that it may be sensitive to the face detector and the quality of the face bounding box since it learns the mapping from the facial appearance within the face bounding box region to the landmarks. Because the size and location of the initial face is determined by the face bounding box, algorithms trained with one face detector may not work well if a different biased face detector is used in testing. Here, we use a simple but effective data preprocessing method to solve this problem.

This rest of the paper is organized as follows. Section 2 describe the detail of 106-point facial landmark localization method, including network structure, data preprocessing and other training tricks. The advocated approach is validated experimentally in Sect. 3. The conclusion is given in Sect. 4.

2 106-Point Facial Landmark Localization

The method of implementing 106-point facial landmark localization mainly includes the strategy of modifying network structure, data preprocessing strategy, and some training tricks.

2.1 The Strategy of Modifying Network Structure

The basic self-designed CNN is described in Fig. 2. CNN-B stacks 5 layers of Module-A followed by FC-1024 and FC-212 (full connection 1024 and 212) as the regression output to generate 106-point landmarks. Based on CNN-B, we use Module-B to replace

Module-A and call the structure as CNN-F. For CNN-FL, we use avgpool to replace FC-1024 in CNN-F. The Conv3-2 represents 2-stride convolutions using 3 × 3 kernels, and the Conv-1 represents 1-stride convolutions using 3 × 3 kernels.

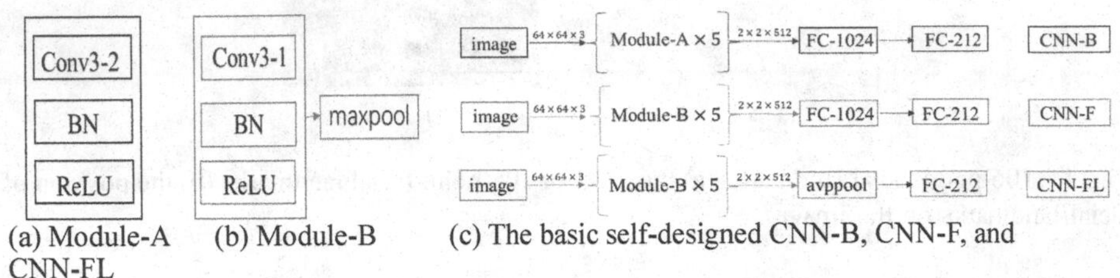

(a) Module-A (b) Module-B (c) The basic self-designed CNN-B, CNN-F, and CNN-FL

Fig. 2. The basic 106-point facial landmark localization structure

Theoretically, adding a layer of full connection layer will increase the convergence difficulty for the 106-point facial landmarks regression problem, specifically bringing difficulty of converging to the minimum. A lot of texture information that is important for landmarks localization will lose due to the operation of 2-stride convolution. We conduct facial landmark localization experiments with CNN-B, CNN-F and CNN-FL and get the results (Table 1). The mean-square error (MSE) and the number of parameters of CNN-FL are lower than that of CNN-B and CNN-F, and despite the increase of floating point operations (FLOPs), the FLOPs aren't still high, so the above analysis and the experiment results are consistent.

Table 1. The performance comparison of different network structures

ConvNet	Params (Million)	FLOPs (Billion)	MSE ($\times 10^{-3}$)
CNN-F	3.89M	0.08B	0.255
CNN-B	3.89M	0.02B	0.350
CNN-FL	**1.68M**	**0.08B**	**0.210**

Based on the strategy of improving CNN, the following modifications of the network components have been made to VGG16 and MobileNetV2 for multi-points regression:

(1) Replace 2-stride convolution with 1-stride convolution and maxpool;
(2) Use only one full connection layer.

Applying the above modification principle to VGG16 [11], VGG16-FL was born. Similarly, to obtain the modified MobileNetV2 [10], we adjust the MobileNetV2 according to the size of the input image and the above modifications. The modified MobileNetV2 (named MobileNetV2-FL) is illustrated in Table 2.

Table 2. MobileNetV2-FL: the notations are same as MobileNetV2

input	operator	t	c	n	s
64 × 64 × 3	conv2d	–	32	1	2
32 × 32 × 32	bottleneck	1	16	1	1
32 × 32 × 16	bottleneck	6	24	2	2
16 × 16 × 24	bottleneck	6	32	3	2
8 × 8 × 32	bottleneck	6	64	4	2
4 × 4 × 64	bottleneck	6	96	3	1
4 × 4 × 96	bottleneck	6	160	3	2
2 × 2 × 160	bottleneck	6	320	1	1
2 × 2 × 320	conv2d 1 × 1	-	512	1	1
2 × 2 × 512	AdaptiveAvgPool2d	-	–	1	–
1 × 1 × 512	FC212	–	–	1	–

2.2 Data Preprocessing Strategy

Whatever kind of face detector we utilize, the width, height and aspect ratio of the face is affected by face detector and face position in the image. So the data preprocessing strategies of center cropping, random cropping and random scaling are adopted to produce diversity samples and avoid overfitting.

As depicted in Fig. 3, a face box with the width of W and the height of H is padded 0.2-times corresponding to the width and height of the face box to get the initial image. For center cropping, the right, the left and the down are padded 0.1-times. For random cropping, based on the center of the face box, we randomly get the center of the patch of random cropping in the initial image.

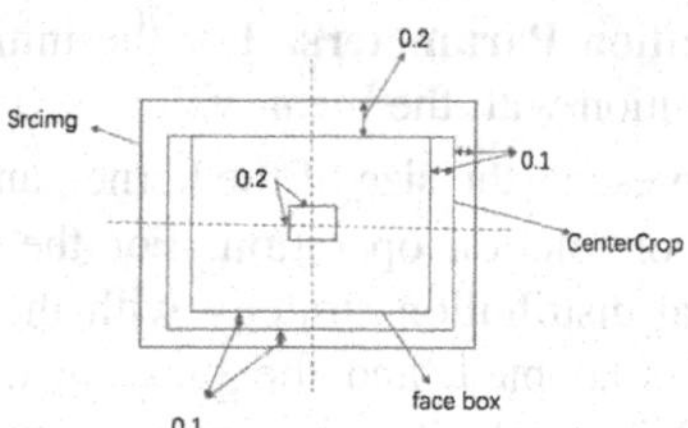

Fig. 3. Center cropping and random cropping

For random scaling, based on the aspect ratio of the face box, we can get the aspect ratio of the patch. The width and the height of the patch are defined as follows:

$$H_{new} = \text{randint}(0.9 \times H, 1.3 \times H) \quad (1)$$

$$ratio_{new} = \text{randint}(0.9 \times ratio, 1.1 \times ratio) \quad (2)$$

$$W_{new} = ratio_{new} \times H_{new} \tag{3}$$

Where randint(min, max) represents random integers from min to max.

Each training image is sequentially processed by the following procedure:

(1) Horizontal flipping: The image is horizontally flipped with probability of 0.5.
(2) Random cropping: The strategy is described as above. When testing an image, the center cropping replaces the random cropping.
(3) Random scaling: The strategy is described as above.
(4) Scale transformation: After the above processing, the image is resized to 64×64 using bilinear interpolation.

2.3 The Training Tricks

In order to make full use of samples and improve the accuracy of facial landmark localization, some tricks are used in training process.

Loss Function. Two kinds of loss function MSE and Wing Loss [12], are used in this experiment. Wing loss is a kind of loss function designed for facial landmark localization regression, so Wing loss is used as loss function in training, and MSE is used for comparison.

Online Hard Example Mining (OHEM). For most datasets, there is a question of sample imbalance, and simple samples are easy to fit in training. Therefore, in the later stage of training, we sort training samples by the loss values and pick the top ones in a certain proportion, and just use them as hard examples of forward and backward propagation. The trick aims to solve the problem of insufficient hard samples and improve the detection accuracy.

The Setting of Implementation Parameters. For the initial weights of convolution layer, we use normal distribution with the mean value of 0 and the standard deviation of $\sqrt{2/K^2C'}$, in which K represents the size of the kernel, and C' represents the number of output channels in the convolution operation. For the initial weights of the full connection layer, the normal distribution strategy with the mean value of 0 and the standard deviation of 0.01 is adopted, and the bias are directly assigned to 0. The weights and bias of the Batch Normalization layer are assigned to 1 and 0, respectively. The gradient descent algorithm (SGD) is used with 0.9 momentum and 0.0005 weight decay. ReLU is used as activation function. In our experiments, we choose 4 sets of parameters that is $\omega = 10\ or\ 15\ and\ \in = 4\ or\ 2$, and finally the parameters of Wing loss as $\omega = 10$ and $\in = 4$ has the optimal solution. The setting of implementation parameters improves the efficiency and accuracy of training model.

3 Experiments

We carried out 106-point landmark localization experiments with the proposed methods, and verified the effect of the proposed method and strategy.

3.1 Dataset

We used training dataset to train all models, and used MSE on the validation dataset to determine whether a model perform well or not. Finally we compared the results of different network structures on test dataset using strategies with positive effects.

Training Dataset. These images including single face annotated 106-point facial landmarks are from CelebFaces Attributes Dataset (CelebA) [8], which is a large-scale dataset of face attributes, including 202,599 face images of 10,177 individuals. The dataset covers large variations on pose and expression.

Validation and Test Dataset. The accessible JD-landmark dataset [4] is composed of LFPW, AFW and HELEN and re-annotate them with 106-point. In this paper, all images of LFPW dataset are used as validation dataset including 3082 single face images. The AFW and HELEN are used as the test dataset and include 1000 single face images and 6942 single face images respectively.

3.2 Evaluation Metric

For evaluation of facial landmark localization model, we adopted the widely used Normalized Mean Error (*NME*), and used diagonal distance of the face bounding box as the normalization term. For a dataset including N images with a single face, the Failure, the Error, and the area-under-the curve (AUC) can evaluate the model.

Failure rate is used to measure the robustness of a model. The proportion of failed detection is calculated to represent the capacity of handling the difficult images.

$$Failure = \frac{\sum_{j=1}^{N} Num(NME_j > T)}{N} \tag{4}$$

Here, the threshold T is set to 0.05 [9].

Error is the average of NME of every image, Error $= \frac{\sum_{j=1}^{N} NME_j}{N}$.

AUC provides a general qualitative result of how the model performs at progressive mean errors:

$$AUC_\alpha = \int_0^\alpha f(e)de \tag{5}$$

where e is the distance normalized error, $f(e)$ is the cumulative errors distribution curve (CED), function and α is the value of arithmetic sequence between 0 and 1 that is used to calculate the definite integration. The CED function is *NME* with respect to the proportion of *NME* of every image less than some bin value to all images, that is $\sum_{j=1}^{N} Num(NME \leq bin)/N$. A greater AUC value generally means that model has a better performance. In AUC, the abscissa represents e_{ji}, and the ordinate represents the proportion of detected landmarks less than some bin value to all detected landmarks, that is $\sum_{j=1}^{N} \sum_{i=0}^{105} Num(e_{ji} \leq bin)/N106$.

3.3 Experiment Results

For easy comparison on different platforms, we have given the FLOPs of these networks, and the FLOPs can represent the time cost to some extent. In addition, because the Multi-Stack Face Alignment method in literature [4] didn't give specific structural parameters and can't be realized to compare with our methods, we trained a big model as VGG16-FL based on regression. In our experiments, we compared the big model with the mobile model and report the results.

First, based on MobileNetV2-FL the experiments of trade-off between accuracy and efficiency. The parameter width_multiplier (*WM*) controls the number of output channels in the operator layer, and the parameter output_stride (*OS*) represents the reduction ratio 2^n in the feature map, and n is the number of 2-stride in the operator layer. The standard *OS* for the MobileNetV2-FL in Table 2 is 2^5. And we tested different parameters. And in practical application, we can choose the hyper-parameters according to the requirements of application platform and accuracy. Mainly based on the result of MSE, we choose the *WM* 1 and *OS* 8 to conduct the following experiments.

Second, we demonstrated the positive effect of multi-points regression using the modified network, Wing loss and OHEM. In Table 4, we can see that VGG16-FL and MobileNetV2-FL have lower MSE than that of VGG16 and MobileNetV2, respectively. So, the strategy of modifying network structures has positive effect on multi-points regression. As illustrated in Fig. 4(a), based on VGG16-FL, Wing loss effectively reduces the number of small error in facial landmark localization compared with MSE. OHEM slightly improves the accuracy of difficult samples (Table 3).

Table 3. The number of parameters, FLOPs and MSE in validation dataset

WM	1.25	1	0.5	1	1	**1**	1
OS	32	32	32	32	16	**8**	4
Params (M)	5.92	3.90	1.15	3.90	3.90	**3.90**	3.90
FLOPs (B)	0.05	0.03	0.01	0.03	0.11	**0.37**	1.05
MSE ($\times 10^{-3}$)	0.228	0.239	0.283	0.239	0.172	**0.148**	0.151

Table 4. The performance comparison of different network structures

ConvNet	Params (Million)	FLOPs (Billion)	MSE ($\times 10^{-3}$)
VGG16	17.04M	1.26B	0.218
VGG16-FL	**14.83M**	**1.26B**	**0.141**
MobileNetV2	4.31M	0.38B	0.161
MobileNetV2-FL	**3.90M**	**0.37B**	**0.148**

Finally, we trained CNN-FL, VGG16-FL and MobileNetV2-FL with the training tricks of Wing loss and OHEM and verified the results on test datasets. It can be concluded that VGG16-FL performs as well as MobileNetV2-FL, while both of them outperform CNN-FL from the AUC curve of Fig. 4(b) and (c) and the failure and error of Table 5. Although VGG16-FL has a larger of parameters and FLOPs than MobileNetV2-FL, MobileNetV2-FL obtains comparable results.

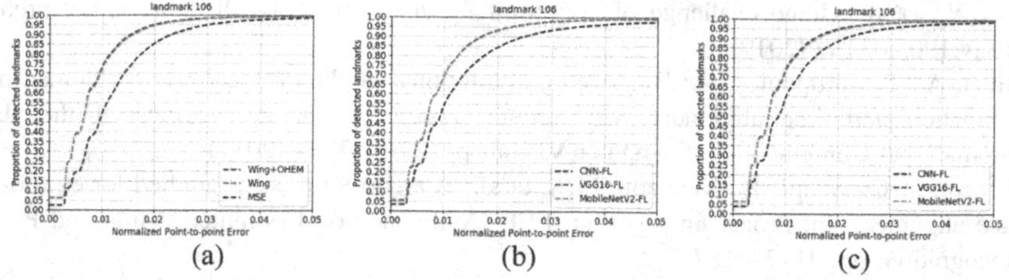

Fig. 4. The AUC curve (a) the AUC curve on AFW and HELEN dataset using Wing loss and OHEM or not (b) the AUC curve on AFW dataset (c) the AUC curve on HELEN dataset

Table 5. The failure and error of test dataset in different network

	AFW		HELEN	
	Failure	Error	Failure	Error
CNN-FL	1.81%	0.01656	0.91%	0.01356
VGG16-FL	0.70%	0.01277	0.46%	0.01065
MobileNetV2-FL	0.70%	0.01283	0.50%	0.01086

In conclusion, the strategies of modifying network structures, data preprocessing, Wing Loss and OHEM have positive impact on 106-point landmark localization. MobileNetV2-FL obtains comparable results with VGG16-FL, but the number of parameters and FLOPs are much lighter.

4 Conclusion

For 106-point landmark localization with regression-based method, we obtain a lightweight network structure with high accuracy by modifying the network adaptively and applying data preprocessing strategy, Wing Loss and OHEM.

Acknowledgments. This work is supported by National Science Foundation of China (No. 61573356) and National Key R&D Program of China (2018YFB0504900).

References

1. Zhang, K., Zhang, Z., et al.: Joint face detection and alignment using multitask cascaded convolutional networks. IEEE Signal Process. Lett. **23**(10), 1499–1503 (2016)
2. Sun, Y., Wang, X., Tang, X.: Deep convolutional network cascade for facial point detection. In: Proceedings of the IEEE Conference on Computer Vision and Pattern Recognition, pp. 3476–3483 (2013)
3. Zhou, E., Fan, H., Cao, Z., Jiang, Y., Yin, Q.: Extensive facial landmark localization with coarse-to-fine convolutional network cascade. In: Proceedings of the IEEE International Conference on Computer Vision Workshops, pp. 386–391 (2013)

4. Liu, Y., et al.: Grand challenge of 106-point facial landmark localization. arXiv preprint arXiv:1905.03469 (2019)
5. Bulat, A., Tzimiropoulos, G.: Binarized convolutional landmark localizers for human pose estimation and face alignment with limited resources. In: Proceedings of the IEEE International Conference on Computer Vision, pp. 3706–3714 (2017)
6. Trigeorgis, G., Snape, P., Nicolaou, M.A, et al.: A recurrent process applied for end-to-end face alignment. In: Proceedings of the IEEE Conference on Computer Vision and Pattern Recognition, pp. 4177–4187 (2016)
7. Bulat, A., Tzimiropoulos, G.: Super-FAN: integrated facial landmark localization and super-resolution of real-world low resolution faces in arbitrary poses with GANs. In: IEEE Conference on Computer Vision and Pattern Recognition, pp. 109–117 (2017)
8. Sagonas, C., Antonakos, E., et al.: 300 Faces In-The-Wild Challenge: database and results. Image Vis. Comput. **47**, 3–18 (2016)
9. Sandler, M., Howard, A., et al.: MobileNetV2: inverted residuals and linear bottlenecks. In: IEEE Conference on Computer Vision and Pattern Recognition, pp. 4510–4520 (2018)
10. Simonyan, K., Zisserman, A.: Very deep convolutional networks for large-scale image recognition. arXiv preprint arXiv:1409.1556 (2014)
11. Liu, Z., Luo, P., et al.: Deep learning face attributes in the wild. In: Proceedings of the IEEE international Conference on Computer Vision, pp. 3730–3738 (2014)
12. Feng, Z. H., Kittler, J., et al.: Wing loss for robust facial landmark localization with convolutional neural networks. In: IEEE Conference on Computer Vision and Pattern Recognition, pp. 2235–2245 (2017)

Eye-Based Biometrics

Long Range Pupil Location Algorithm Based on the Improved Circle Fitting Method

Yongliang Zhang[1(✉)], Xiaoxiao Qian[1], Zhongsu Luo[1], Keyi Zhu[2], and Minjun Yu[1]

[1] College of Computer Science and Technology, Zhejiang University of Technology, Hangzhou 310023, China
titanzhang@zjut.edu.cn

[2] Glasgow College, University of Electronic Science and Technology, Chengdu 611731, China

Abstract. Since the pupil will show abnormal contraction or expansion after taking drugs, the technology of long range pupil diameter detection can be used for rapid screening of drug users. In this paper, a long range pupil location algorithm is proposed based on the improved circle fitting method. Firstly, the improved histogram-based binarization method is used to obtain candidate pupil contours, and non-pupil contours are filtered according to the shape or size. Then, the ROI is extracted from the original image according to the pupil contours, and the facula contours are extracted and filled by the features, such as gray value, size and position. Finally, an improved circle fitting method is used to obtain an accurate pupil position. The experimental results on CASIA-IrisV4-Distance database show that the proposed algorithm can locate the pupil more accurately and the average deviation of center and radius is smaller compared with the existing pupil detection algorithms.

Keywords: Long range pupil detection · Ellipse fitting · ROI · Circle fitting · Contours screening

1 Introduction

The pupil, as a black hole located in the center of the iris, can adjust its size reflectively under the influence of different light intensities, mood or drugs. This passive change of pupil usually can be applied to criminal investigations, medical researches and many other aspects [1]. Since some drug users may have pupil dilations, pupil detection technology has become a potential direction in place of traditional blood, saliva and urine detection to detect of drug addicts.

In fact, many solutions have been proposed to cope with the pupil detection problem. The work presented in [2] proposes a novel method to detection the pupil of human eyes using Otsu threshold, which performs well on the pupil detection. However, the performance of this work degrades on the low-quality images. The reliable pupil detection and iris segmentation algorithm based on SPS proposed by Susitha [3] uses the parabolic and morphological operations to finish the eyelid detection, pupil detection and iris segmentation. It achieves a great performance in

Z. Sun et al. (Eds.): CCBR 2019, LNCS 11818, pp. 295–303, 2019.
https://doi.org/10.1007/978-3-030-31456-9_33

terms of segmentation and execution time. However, taking the above algorithms as a representative, many existing pupil detection algorithms perform well under laboratory conditions [4], but show great limitation facing with the non-ideal eye images collected at a distance. Inspired by learning from synthetic data in Parallel Vision framework, Gou et al. [5] propose a coarse-to-fine pupil detection framework based on shape augmented cascade regression models learning from the adversarial synthetic images.

Aiming at the scene of long range pupil location and detection, we propose an improved circle fitting based pupil location method. Firstly, the improved gray histogram-based method is applied to obtain candidate contours of the pupil, and then the unique pupil contour is determined by the screening method based on pupil features. Then the faculae in the pupil area is obtained and filled. Finally, the precise pupil position can be calculated with an improved fitting circle method. Compared with other pupil location algorithms, the experimental results show that the proposed method achieves better accuracy while dealing with eye images acquired from a long range where the problems of severe facula and eyelid occlusion occur.

2 Proposed Method

The flow chart of the proposed algorithm for long range pupil location is shown in Fig. 1. The first step is image preprocessing (including normalization and smoothing). The second is to detect the pupil contour. Next, the ROI of eyes is extracted in order to detect and fill the faculae. Lastly, the precise location of the long range pupil is obtained.

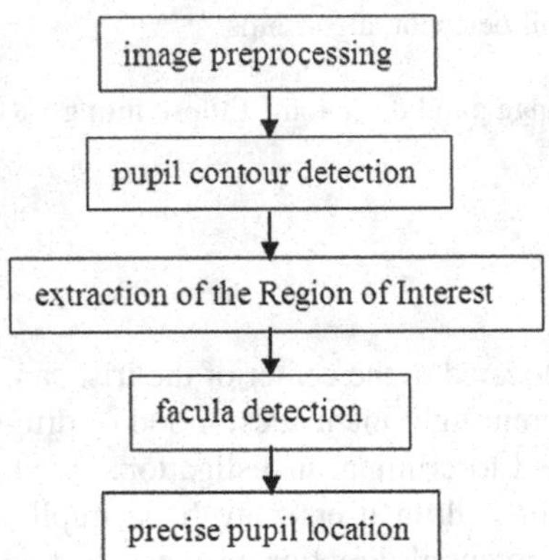

Fig. 1. The flow chart of the proposed algorithm.

2.1 Image Preprocessing

The estimation of the size of connected domains, such as pupil and facula, is necessary in the process of the proposed algorithm. We first normalize the size of the images according to the standard width, and then perform the Gaussian smoothing on the images after converting them into grey images to reduce noise.

2.2 Pupil Contour Detection

As the pupil is usually darker than the most surrounding parts of the image, the threshold segmentation method can be used to obtain the connectivity component of the pupil [6]. An improved histogram-based method is proposed to find an appropriate threshold value [7].

Obviously, the gray value distribution of the image collected under different illumination conditions is different for the same object, and the threshold is different as well. Therefore, we use the average gray value (*ave*) of the image to complete the preliminary estimation of the segmentation threshold as follows:

$$cutGray_{rough} = \begin{cases} 12 - \sin((50 - ave) * \pi/100) * 7, 0 \le ave < 50 \\ 35 - \sin((100 - ave) * \pi/100) * 4, 50 \le ave < 100 \\ 50, 100 \le ave < 150 \\ 50 + (ave - 150) * 19/25, 150 \le ave < 200 \\ 50 + (ave - 200) * 34/25, 200 \le ave < 255 \end{cases} \tag{1}$$

In the above formulas, the intermediate interval is taken as the standard interval, whose corresponding segmentation threshold is 50 [7], and the rest intervals' corresponding thresholds are various according to the value. In the intervals of $[0, 50)$ and $[50, 100)$ where the pupil and background gray value are close to each other, the formula is constructed by using the incremental section of the sinusoidal function. In contrast, in the intervals of $[150, 200)$ and $[200, 255)$ where the pupil is clearly distinguished from the background, the threshold value is calculate using a linear function easily.

Next, we obtain the gray histogram of the eye image, and smooth the histogram with a suitable step length such as 3. The result is shown in Fig. 2.

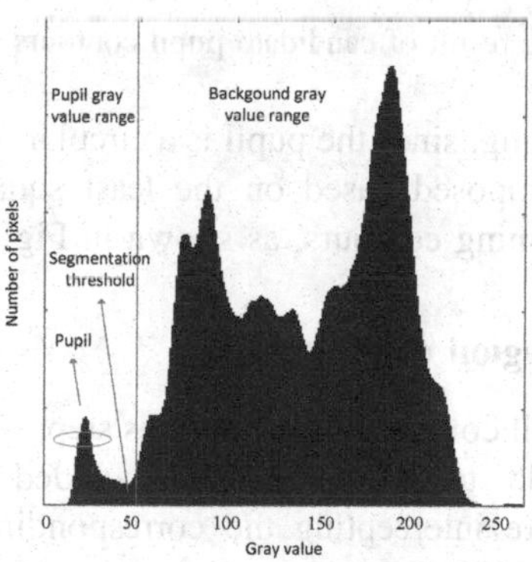

Fig. 2. The gray histogram of the eye image.

We can find that there is a peak value on the left side of $cutGray_{rough}$ in the histogram image, which is close to the pupil gray value, we record it as $gray_{pupil}$.Then the first valley value on the right side of $gray_{pupil}$ is exactly the segmentation threshold value $cutGray_{accurate}$. Next, we binary the image according to the value and extract all the contours in the image as the candidate pupil contours, as shown in Fig. 3.

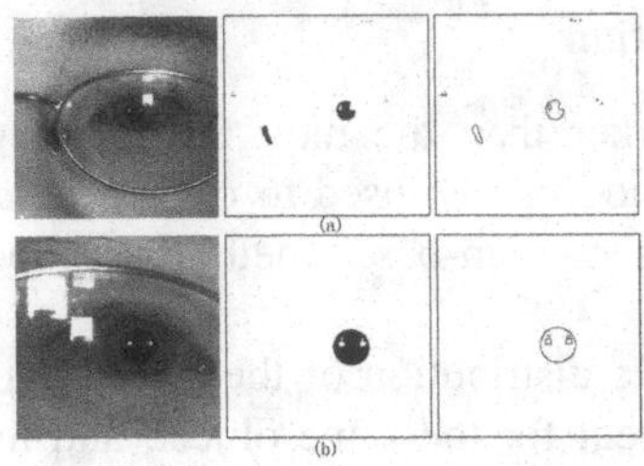

Fig. 3. The result of extraction of pupil contour.

It is inevitable that there are several interference contours in the candidate contours (as shown in Fig. 3), so we propose a pupil characteristic based contour screening method:

(1) Pixel number screening: for a fixed-size eye image, the pixel number of the pupil contours is always within a certain threshold range. Those contours with too few or too many pixels should be filtered, as shown in Fig. 4(a) and (b).

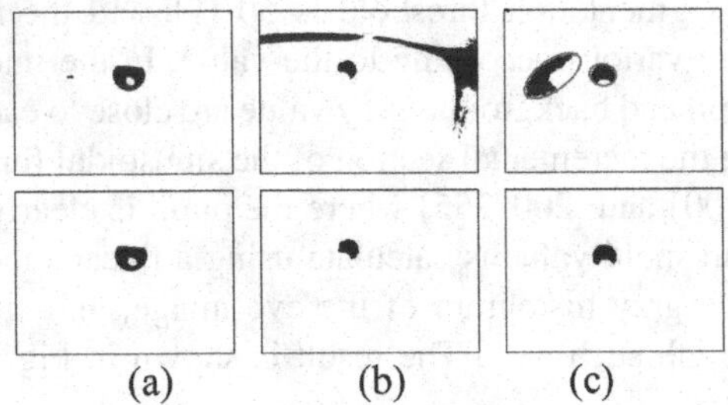

Fig. 4. The result of candidate pupil contours screening.

(2) Circular feature screening: since the pupil is a circular ellipse, an improved ellipse fitting algorithm is proposed based on the least squares method to check the circularity of all remaining contours, as shown in Fig. 4(c).

2.3 Extraction of the Region of Interest

Basing on the obtained pupil contour in the previous step, we can obtain the minimum enclosing rectangle. In order to ensure the ROI included the whole pupil area, we enlarge the rectangle before intercepting the corresponding rectangular area in the original image, as shown in Fig. 5.

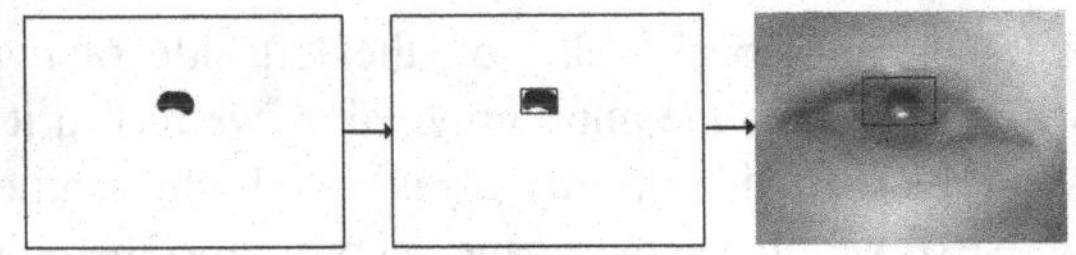

Fig. 5. The minimum external rectangle of pupil contour.

2.4 Facula Detection

Since the main components of the ROI are pupil and iris, and the faculae shows the characteristics of high gray value, we can simply estimate the gray value of the faculae using the histogram-based method. The histogram is shown in Fig. 6.

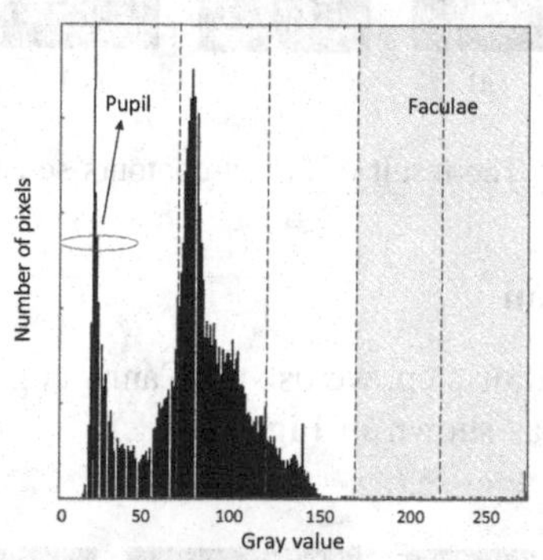

Fig. 6. The gray histogram of the ROI.

What we can observe is that the histogram has several distinct peak values, in which the smallest peak value $gray_{pupil}$ is an approximation value of the pupil gray value. Since the histogram shows a dense distribution on the left side, the segmentation threshold of facula $gray_{facula}$ is estimated based on $gray_{pupil}$ as follows:

$$gray_{facula} = 255 - (255 - gray_{pupil}) * 2/5 \quad (2)$$

According to the $gray_{pupil}$, the ROI is binarized to obtain candidate facula contours. There are several interference contours, so a facula characteristic is proposed based screening method to filter the interference contours as follows:

(1) Pixel number screening: since the size of faculae in pupil area is within a certain threshold range, the number of pixels of the contours are used as a screening condition, as shown in Fig. 7.
(2) Location screening: the faculae we want to process are located in the pupil area, so the position information can also be used for screening. We assume that the minimum y coordinate of the pupil edge point is $y_{pupil\text{-}leftUp}$, then any point $(x_{facula-contourn}, y_{facula-contourn})$ on the facula contour is required to satisfy the following formula:

$$y_{facula-contourn} \geq y_{pupil-leftUp} \quad (3)$$

If not, the contour needs to be filtered, as shown in Fig. 7(b) and (c).

After screening, we fill the facula contours on the basis of the binarized eye image.

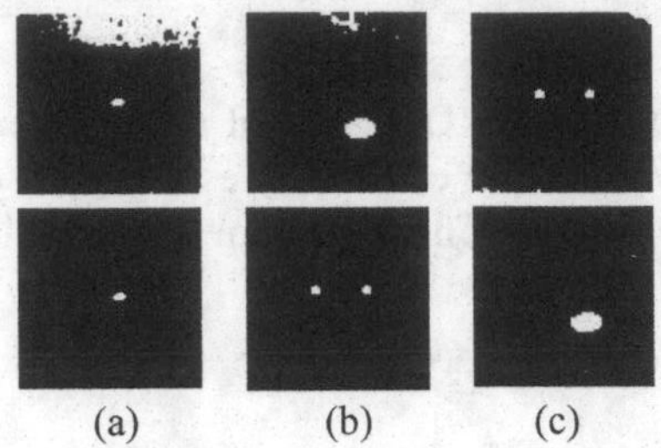

Fig. 7. The result of facula contours screening.

2.5 Precise Pupil Location

Before the precise pupil location step, we use the Canny edge detection algorithm to get the edge of the eye image, as shown in Fig. 8.

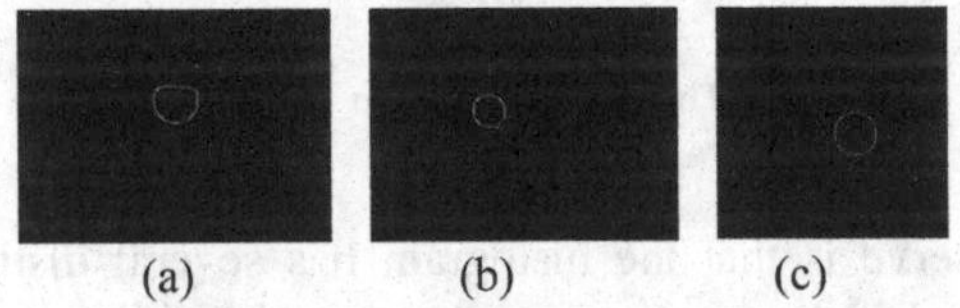

Fig. 8. Edge detection images.

We can find that the extracted pupil contours may have problems such as incomplete edges, as shown in Fig. 7(a) and (b). In response to this problem, we propose an improved circle fitting algorithm to fit the pupil contour:

(1) Randomly select 3 pixels on the contour for circle fitting and record the coordinates of the center of this circle as (x_c, y_c), the radius as r_c.

(2) Assume the fitting rate of the current circle as $fitRate_c$. For any point (x_p, y_p) on the contour, we calculate the distance between (x_p, y_p) to (x_c, y_c) as dis_p. And then calculate the $fitRate_c$ according to the relationship between dis_p and r_c as follows:

$$fitRate_c = \begin{cases} fitRate_c + 1, \left| dis_p - dis_c \right| \leq 1 \\ fitRate_c, others \end{cases} \quad (4)$$

(3) Repeat step (1) and (2) several times, and compare all fitting circles to obtain the best fitting circle as the accurate location result of the pupil.

After that, we mark the pupil in the original image, as shown in Fig. 9.

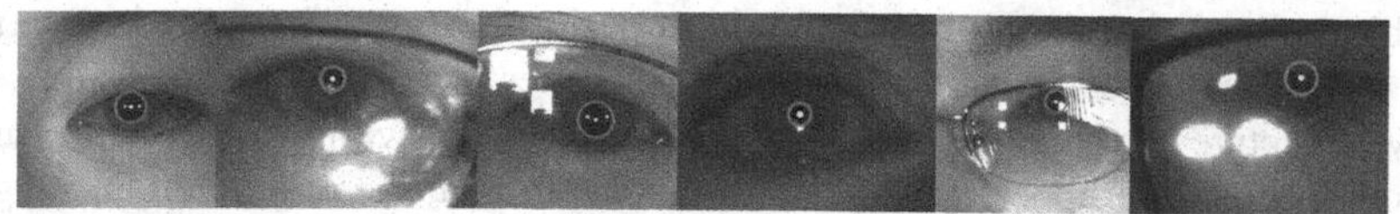

Fig. 9. Fitting result of several eye images.

3 Experimental Results

To verify the effectiveness of the proposed algorithm, we use the CASIA-IrisV4-Distance database for experiments. The CASIA-IrisV4-Distance database was published by the Institute of Automation, Chinese Academy of Sciences. It contains 2,567 half-face images of 142 volunteers. The images of the database were acquired by the Biometric Image Acquisition and Recognition System (LMBS) developed by the Chinese Academy of Science. The resolution of the images is 2352*1728 pixels.

In order to realize the accuracy of the quantitative analysis algorithm, the images were marked by a human expert. Define the center of the circle as (x_0, y_0), the radius of the circle as r_0. Assume the center and radius calculated the algorithm as (x, y) and r. Compared with the data obtained by the expert, we can get the deviation of center by formula $Q_c = |x_0 - x| + |y_0 - y|$ and the deviation of radius by formula $Q_r = |r - r_0|$. According to the comparison results of all the images, the average deviation of the center $\overline{Q_c}$ and the radius $\overline{Q_r}$ can be calculated. Taking some representative eye image as examples, the processed image results of the algorithm is shown in Fig. 10, and the location deviation result is shown in Table 1.

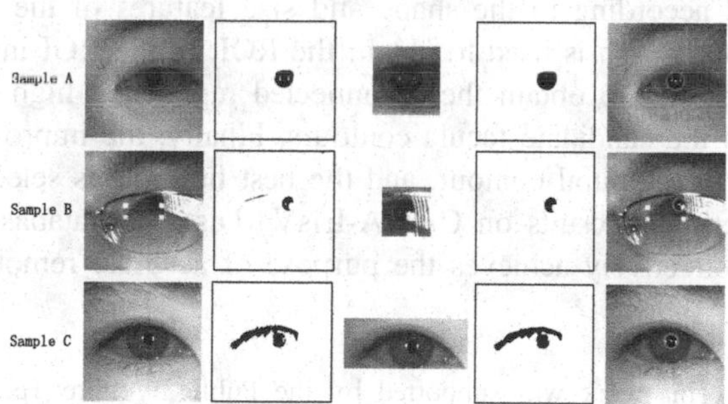

Fig. 10. The processed image results on the proposed algorithm.

Table 1. The deviation results of long range pupil location.

	Sample A	Sample B	Sample C
Q_c	0.00	2.00	5.00
Q_r	0.34	0.20	1.91

Table 1 shows that the proposed algorithm performs very well while dealing most of the images with good quality. It also shows better robustness when dealing with heavily reflective eye images. However, when dealing with images with severe adhesion between the upper eyelashes and the pupil area, there is a certain range of errors in the detection.

For a more comprehensive demonstration, the proposed algorithm has been tested on the whole database. Table 2 shows the comparison results between the proposed algorithm and some of the existing methods on CASIA-IrisV4-Distance.

Table 2. The comparison results between the proposed algorithm and the existing algorithms.

	Masek [8]	Ma [9]	Ivan Matveev [10]	Proposed
$\bar{Q}_c$	3.67	4.79	2.82	2.35
$\bar{Q}_r$	5.15	5.39	3.26	1.81

4 Conclusion

Different from the eye images collected at a close range, the eye images collected at a long range are more susceptible to environmental interference, which greatly increases the difficulty of pupil location and makes most of the pupil location algorithms not applicable. In this paper, a new pupil location algorithm is proposed. Firstly, we transform the image into gray image, normalize and denoise the image. Next, the improved histogram-based method is applied to binarize the images, and the connected domain edge is extracted as the candidate pupil contours. Then, we screen all the candidate contours according to the shape and size features of the pupil to get the unique pupil contour which is used to obtain the ROI. In the ROI image, we use the histogram-based method to obtain these connected regions of high gray value, and extract the edge as the candidate facula contours. Finally, the improved circle fitting method is used to fit the pupil contour, and the best fit circle is selected as the pupil location. The experiment results on CASIA-IrisV4-Distance database prove that the proposed method effectively achieves the purpose of accurate remote pupil location detection.

Acknowledgement. This work was supported by the Public Welfare Technology Research Program of Zhejiang Province under Grant LGF18F030008.

References

1. Wang, C.A., Munoz, D.P.: A circuit for pupil orienting responses: implications for cognitive modulation of pupil size. Curr. Opin. Neurobiol. **33**, 134–140 (2015)
2. Khan, T.Z., Podder, P., Hossain, M.F.: Fast and efficient iris segmentation approach based on morphology and geometry operation. In: International Conference on Software, Knowledge, Information Management and Applications, Bangladesh (2014)

3. Susitha, N., Subban, R.: Reliable pupil detection and iris segmentation algorithm based on SPS. Cogn. Syst. Res. **57**, 78–84 (2018)
4. Fuhl, W., Kübler, T., Sippel, K., Rosenstiel, W., Kasneci, E.: ExCuSe: Robust Pupil Detection in Real-World Scenarios. In: Azzopardi, G., Petkov, N. (eds.) CAIP 2015. LNCS, vol. 9256, pp. 39–51. Springer, Cham (2015). https://doi.org/10.1007/978-3-319-23192-1_4
5. Gou, C., et al.: Cascade learning from adversarial synthetic images for accurate pupil detection. Pattern Recogn. **88**, 584–594 (2019)
6. Chen, M.H., Wen, J., Zhu, Y., et al.: Multi-level thresholding for pupil location in eye-gaze tracking system. In: International Conference on Machine Learning & Cybernetics. IEEE (2017)
7. Keke, G.U., Weiwei, F.U., Yuefang, D.O.N.G., et al.: Rapid pupil detection based on improved contour tracking. Infrared Technol. **39**(6), 574–578 (2017)
8. Masek, L.: Recognition of human IRIS patterns for biometric identification (2007)
9. Ma, L., Tan, T., Wang, Y., et al.: Local intensity variation analysis for iris recognition. Pattern Recogn. **37**(6), 1287–1298 (2004)
10. Matveev, I., Novik, V., Novik, V.: Location of pupil contour by Hough transform of connectivity components. Pattern Recogn. Image Anal. **26**(2), 398–405 (2016)

Multi-source Heterogeneous Iris Recognition Using Locality Preserving Projection

Guang Huo[1], Qi Zhang[1(✉)], Huan Guo[1], Wenyu Li[1], and Yangrui Zhang[2]

[1] School of Computer Science, Northeast Electric Power University, Jilin 132012, China
yanhuo1860@126.com, zq2219321180@163.com, 1114619524@qq.com, 1260814407@qq.com

[2] School of Foreign Languages, Northeast Electric Power University, Jilin 132012, China
hata0420@sina.com
http://www.springer.com/lncs

Abstract. Multi-source heterogeneous iris recognition (MSH-IR) has become one of the most challenging hot issues. Iris recognition is too dependent on the acquisition device, causing have large intra-class variations, capture iris duplicate data more and more larger. The paper proposed the application of locality preserving projection (LPP) algorithm based on manifold learning as a framework for MSH-IR. Looking for similar internal structures of iris texture, MSH-IR is performed by measuring similarity. The new solution innovation aspects that LPP algorithm is used to establish the neighboring structure of the similar feature points of the iris texture, and the similarity between the MSH-IR structures is measured after mapping to the low-dimensional space, and using the SVM algorithm to find and establish the optimal classification hyperplane in low-dimensional space to implement the classification of multi-source heterogeneous iris images. The experiment based on the JLU-MultiDev iris database. The experimental results demonstrates the effectiveness of the LPP dimension reduction algorithm for MSH-IR.

Keywords: Iris recognition · Multi-source heterogeneous · Manifold learning · LPP

1 Introduction

Iris recognition has been widely used for personal identification due to the unique, complex, and stable texture patterns in iris [1]. MSH-IR means different acquisition devices result in different quality of the iris images of the same collector. As show in (Fig. 1). Hence, MSH-IR causes the low interoperability [2,3] between the captured devices. It is obvious that there are significant differences at iris texture details among these iris images acquired from

Z. Sun et al. (Eds.): CCBR 2019, LNCS 11818, pp. 304–311, 2019.
https://doi.org/10.1007/978-3-030-31456-9_34

different devices. MSH-IR has large intra-class variations, which challenge the conventional well-performed iris recognition systems [4]. Recently, in the some fields of researchers have addressed multi-source heterogeneous and proposed some solutions. In fingerprint recognition, Rose and Jain [1] first proposed cross-platform fingerprint feature extraction and matching algorithm is a problem to be solved in the future. Yang et al. [5] proposed a second-order feature evaluation method based on error rate, decision tree and analyzed the device independence problem in fingerprint image segmentation. In vein recognition, Wang et al. [6] proposed a recognition method based on Local Binary Pattern(LBP) and multi-level structure, better solved the problem caused by different parameters of the device for heterogeneous vein image recognition. In medical terms, Li et al. [7] first explained the importance of equipment independence in application problems such as classification and retrieval of medical images. In iris recognition, Ryan et al. [8] analyzed the inter-operability between different devices from a hardware perspective, in order to illustrate the impact of different types of acquisition equipment on iris recognition. Arora et al. [9] proposed the application of selective image enhancement algorithms to minimize the difference between two cross-device iris images. These methods only focus on how to adjust the sensors or directly process the images, and do not analyze the feature structure of the images, and can not extract more effective feature points. Currently, there are few researchers on MSH-IR at home and abroad. However, public paper on multi-source heterogeneous iris recognition based on manifold learning has not yet appeared.

Manifold learning is developed along with the development of nonlinear data dimensionality reduction [10]. The method is the discovery of potential low-dimensional manifold structures from high-dimensional observation data. Hence, the paper proposes the application of manifold learning to MSH-IR. Manifold learning since Tenenbaum et al. [11] and Belkin et al. [12] proposed Isometric mapping(ISOMAP) and Laplacian Eigenmaps(LE), such as nonlinear dimensionality reduction algorithms. More and more researchers study the dimensionality reduction of manifold learning [13–15], He et al. [16] proposed the Locality Preserving Projections (LPP) based on the LE algorithm. Dimension reduction of data based on local feature structure, The above manifold learning is successfully applied in face recognition. And the most important is these methods pays more attention to the local neighbor relationship between image features. Iris feature is composed of a local texture structure. Express these areas with neighbor graphs, and find similar neighbor structures of similar iris images under different devices, comparison of similarities between textures of multi-source heterogeneous iris images, improve MSH-IR accuracy. So, the paper will analyze the effect of LPP on MSH-IR.

2 Overview of the Proposed Approaches

In this section, a brief description of the proposed manifold learning approach is given, which incorporates two discriminative learning techniques: LPP and SVM classifier. The main aim here is to local iris texture structures and identify their strengths and weaknesses to enable the proposal of an iris recognition system that integrates the strengths of these two techniques. The overall architecture of this paper is shown in (Fig. 2).

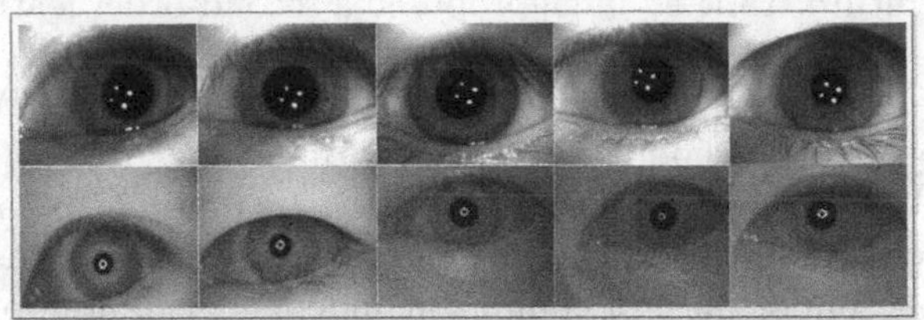

Fig. 1. Iris images captured by different parameters devices. Images in the first row are acquired by Lin Boshi S903, images in the second rows are captured by Sun Time 900A. In the two rows, images of the same columns belong to the same subject.

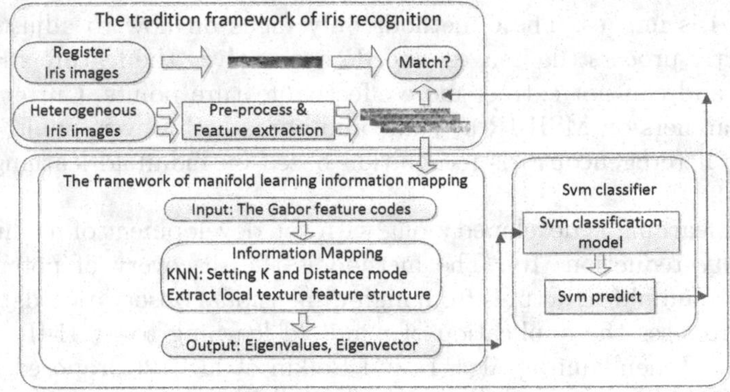

Fig. 2. Overall architecture

2.1 Pre-processing

Since the iris images contains redundant information, such as eyelids, eyelashes, sclera, etc, iris images need to be pre-processing, including quality evaluation, iris localization, enhancement, normalization, ROI interception.

Quality evaluation is a qualified iris images determined by a set of multiple indicators [16]. Iris location is binary image and Hough circle detection of iris images [17] to effectively determine the inner and outer boundaries of the iris. Iris normalization is through the mapping between polar and Cartesian coordinates [18] and iris enhancement is performed by histogram equalization. The approximate circular regions after positioning in the devices I and II are mapped into rectangular regions having a size of 512 * 64. Both devices I and II intercept an ROI (Region Of Interest) having a size of 256*32, since ROI has a lot of effective texture information. As shown in (Fig. 3).

2.2 Gabor Feature Extraction

2D Gabor filter analyzes information in different directions and scales, suitable for extracting local texture features [18–20]. The paper selected five scales and eight orientations to get forty filters by Gabor feature extraction as shown in (Fig. 4) direction-based feature coding of iris features, It can be seen that there are large differences in iris texture features under different devices.

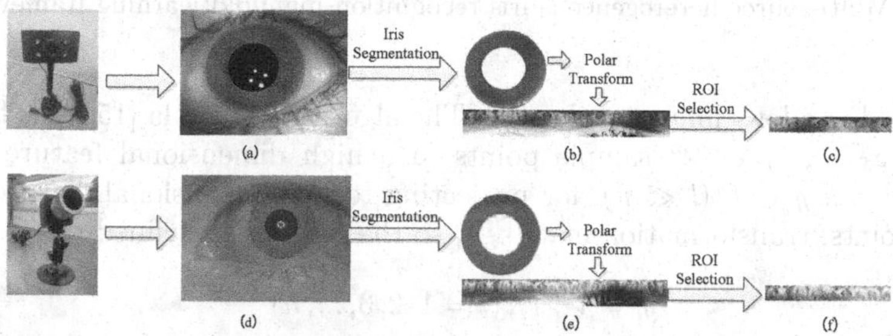

Fig. 3. Iris images pre-processing. (a)–(d) Pre-processing of iris images captured by device I. (e)–(h) Pre-processing of iris images captured by device II. (a)(e) different capture devices; (b)(f) iris location; (c)(g) normalization and enhancement; (d)(h) ROI

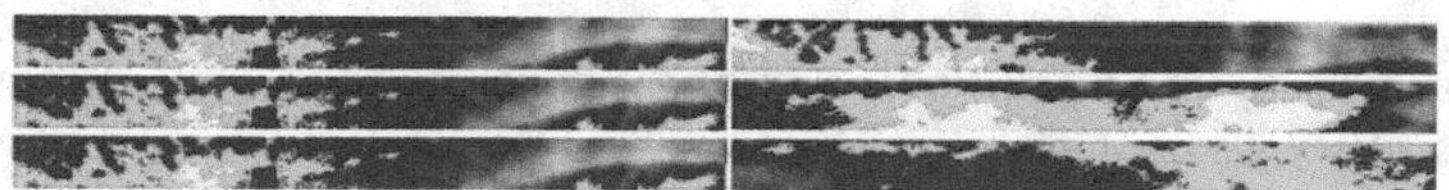

Fig. 4. Iris texture feature. The first row is the same class of iris images texture features captured by the same device; the second row is the different class of iris images texture features captured by the same device; the third row is the same class of iris images texture features captured by different device (multi-source heterogeneous iris images).

2.3 Manifold Learning

The Framework of Manifold Learning. The manifold structure of the paper is shown in (Fig. 5). Assumed that multiple types of iris samples are input, iris texture manifold is extracted by LPP algorithm, and the local geometry of the sample space is preserved. The optimal domain of each sample and the corresponding projection matrix are obtained by KNN (K-Nearest Neighbor) method, which improves the classification accuracy.

Locality Preserving Projection. The basic idea of the LPP algorithm: given a sample data arbitrarily, KNN method is used to construct a neighbor graph of sample points to form an internal structure. When this structure is projected into a low-dimensional space, the local neighbor structure of the original space

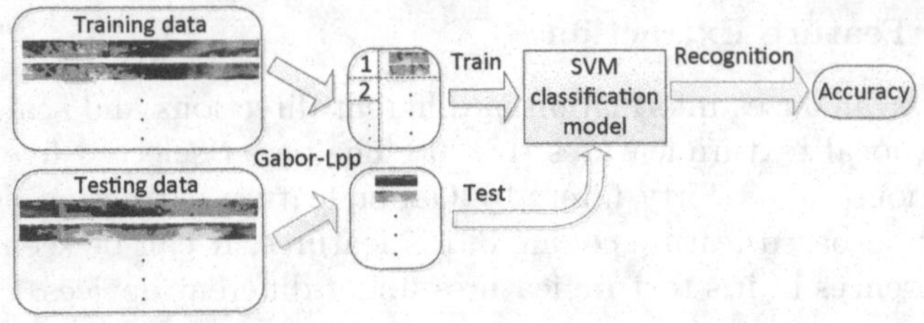

Fig. 5. Multi-source heterogeneous iris recognition manifold learning framework

is preserved in a low-dimensional space. The algorithm formula [15] is as follows: $X = x_1, x_2, ..., x_n \in R^n$ sample points in a high dimensional feature space, $Y = y_1, y_2, ..., y_l \in R^l (l \ll n)$, for projecting to low dimensional feature space sample points, transformation matrix V, so the formula is defined as:

$$y_i = V^T x_i, (i = 1, 2, 3, ..., n) \quad (1)$$

y_i and y_j is a pair of sample points of mutual neighborhood, W_{ij} is weight matrix, find the shortest point in the sample to create a local geometry as

$$\min \sum_{i,j} (y_i - y_j)^2 W_{i,j} \quad (2)$$

To prevent zero-direction solutions, add linear constraints $y^T D y = 1$, equivalent to $V^T x D x^T V = 1$. Laplacian matrix $L = D - W$, D is diagonal array, $D_{ii} = \sum_i W_{ii}$. Purpose function:

$$\min \sum_V V^T x L x^T V \quad (3)$$

$$s.t. V^T x D x^T V = 1 \quad (4)$$

Lagrangian constructor

$$L(V, \lambda) = V^T x L x^T V - \lambda (V^T x D x^T V - 1) \quad (5)$$

$$\frac{\partial L}{\partial V} = 0 \quad (6)$$

$$\frac{\partial V}{\partial \lambda} = 0 \quad (7)$$

$(XDX^T)^{-1}(XLX^T)$ obtained first d minimum eigenvalues $\lambda_1 < \lambda_2 < \lambda_3 < ... < \lambda_d$, then the feature vector corresponding to the eigenvalue is $W = (\omega_1, \omega_2, \omega_3, ..., \omega_d)$.

3 Cross Device Experiment

In order to analyze the influence of the combination of LPP and SVM on MSH-IR, the group of experiments used cross-device experiments. The model is shown in (Fig. 6). i = 7 is the optimal number of training samples. Hence, random selected 16 labels of iris images, random selected 7 images as training samples and 8 images as test samples.

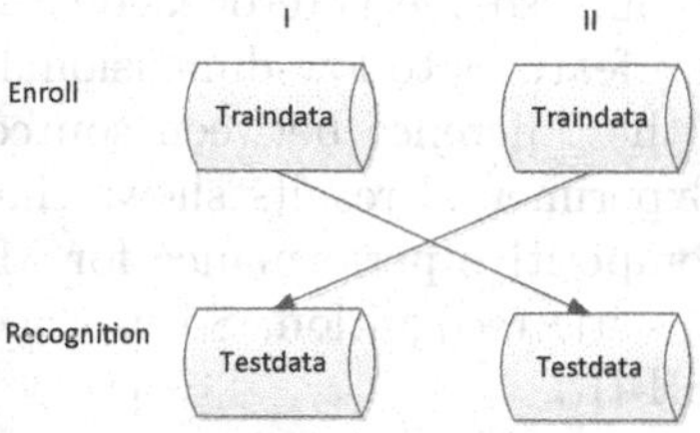

Fig. 6. Cross device model. The iris images captured by device I is used as the training set, the iris images captured by device II is used as the testing set, called I-II; the iris images captured by device II is used as the training set, and the iris image captured by device I is used as the testing set, called II-I.

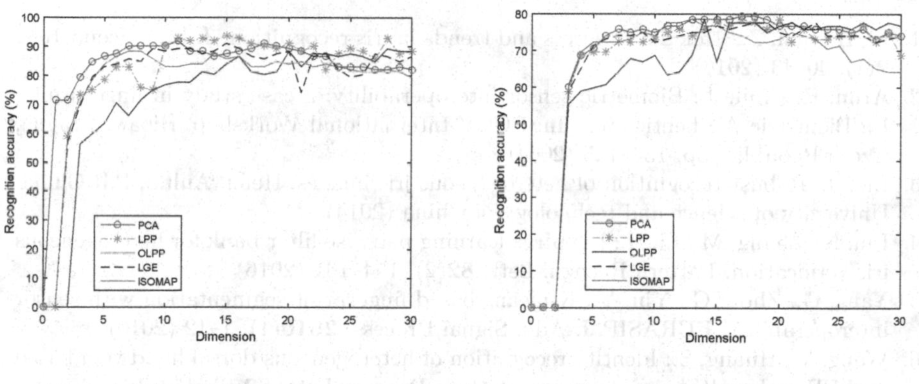

Fig. 7. I-II **Fig. 8.** II-I

As shown in Figs. 7 and 8 that the relationship between the number of projection vectors and the recognition accuracy of five different dimensionality reduction algorithms. Performed on I-II and II-I data sets. Recognition accuracy gradually increases as the data dimension decreases until it becomes gentle. It is shows to us that effective to use the dimensionality reduction algorithm to remove redundant information. However, the maximum recognition accuracy of the five kinds of dimensionality reduction algorithms are all in the projection vectors between 8–28. Therefore, when the number of projection vectors selected is 20, it can be seen that the recognition accuracy of the LPP algorithm is the highest.

4 Conclusions

In this paper, we have proposed a manifold learning to solve MSH-IR based on Locality Preserving Projective. Constructing the neighborhood structure of the iris local texture, and comparison of similar structures of multi-source heterogeneous iris in the low-dimensional space, realized the correct identification between multi-source heterogeneous iris images. The core contribution of the paper is based on the framework of manifold learning the relational features to express similarities for multi-source heterogeneous iris feature matrix. LPP reduce the local iris texture features to low-dimensional space and maintain its neighbor structure. Thus the difference between source are take into account for better performance. Experimental results shows that the proposed method achieves promising and competitive performance for MSH-IR. But MSH-IR is worse than the homologous iris recognition. So, we need to further study the new solution based on MSH-IR.

Acknowledgments. This work is supported by Science and technology project of the Jilin Provincial Education Department (Grant NO. JJKH20180448KJ and Grant NO. JJKH20170107KJ).

References

1. Li, H., Sun, Z., Tan, T.: Progress and trends in iris recognition. J. Info. Secur. Res. **2**(1), 40–43 (2016)
2. Arun, R., Anil, J.: Biometric sensor interoperability: a case study in fingerprints. In: Biometric Authentication. In: ECCV International Workshop, Bioaw, Prague, Czech Republic, pp. 134–145 (2004)
3. Liu, J.: Robust recognition of heterogeneous iris images. Hefei, Anhui, P.R.China. University of science and technology of China (2014)
4. Liu, N., Zhang, M., Li, H.: DeepIris: learning pairwise filter bank for heterogeneous iris verification. Pattern Recogn. Lett. **82**(2), 154–161 (2016)
5. Yang, G., Zhou, G., Yin, Y.: K-means based fingerprint segmentation with sensor interoperability. EURASIP J. Adv. Signal Process. **2010**(1), 1–12 (2010)
6. Wang, Y., Huang, S.: Identity recognition of heterogeneous dorsal hand vein based on LBP and multi-layer structure. Pattern Recogn. Lett. **82**(2), 154–161 (2016)
7. Li, H., Zhang, Q.: Identity recognition of heterogeneous dorsal hand vein based on LBP and multi-layer structure. Pattern Recogn. Lett. **82**(2), 154–161 (2016)
8. Connaughton, R.: A cross-sensor evaluation of three commercial iris cameras for iris biometrics. In: CVPR 2011 Workshops, pp. 90–97. IEEE (2011)
9. Arora, S.S., et al.: On iris camera interoperability. In: 2012 IEEE Fifth International Conference on Biometrics: Theory, Applications and Systems (BTAS). IEEE (2013)
10. Tenenbaum, J.B.: A global geometric framework for nonlinear dimensionality reduction. Science **290**(5500), 2319–2323 (2000)
11. Mikhail, B., Partha, N.: Laplacian eigenmaps and spectral techniques for embedding and clustering. Adv. Neural Inf. Process. Syst. **14**(6), 585–591 (2002)
12. Cai, D., He, X.: Orthogonal laplacianfaces for face recognition. IEEE Trans. Image Process. **15**(11), 3608–3614 (2006)

13. He, X.: Neighborhood preserving embedding. In: Proceedings of the ICCV, vol. 2, pp. 1208–1213 (2005)
14. Yan, S., Dong, X., Zhang, B.: Graph embedding and extensions: a general framework for dimensionality reduction. IEEE Trans. Pattern Anal. Mach. Intell. **29**(1), 40–51 (2007)
15. He, X., Niyogi, P.: Locality preserving projections. In: Advances in neural Information Processing Systems, pp. 153–160 (2004)
16. Shi, C., Zhou, F., Yulu, H.: Study for iris image quality assessment. Chin. J. Liq. Cryst. Displays **31**(12), 1131–1136 (2016)
17. Jun, M., Yan, J., Peng, Q.: Iris localization for visible-light images based on hough transform. Comput. Technol. Dev. **27**(5), 40–45 (2017)
18. Liu, X., Shen, L., Fan, H.: Face recognition algorithm based on Gabor wavelet and locality preserving projections. Mod. Phys. Lett. B **31**, 19–21 (2017)
19. Tai Sing Lee: Image representation using 2D Gabor wavelets. IEEE Trans. Pattern Anal. Mach. Intell. **18**(10), 959–971 (1996)
20. Li, H., Guo, L., Wang, X.: Iris recognition based on weighted Gabor filter. J. Jilin Univ. (Eng. Technol. Edn.) **44**(1), 196–202 (2014)

Iris Recognition Based on Adaptive Optimization Log-Gabor Filter and RBF Neural Network

Qixian Zhang[1,2], Xiaodong Zhu[2,3], Yuanning Liu[2,3](✉), Guang Huo[4], Guangyu Wang[5], Shuai Liu[2,3], Tong Ding[1,2], Kuo Zhang[2,3], Kiese Diangebeni Reagan[2,3], and Chaoqun Wang[1,2]

[1] College of Software, Jilin University, Changchun 130012, China
[2] Key Laboratory of Symbolic Computation and Knowledge Engineering of Ministry of Education, Jilin University, Changchun 130012, China
liuyn@jlu.edu.cn
[3] College of Computer Science and Technology, Jilin University, Changchun 130012, China
[4] College of Computer Science, Northeast Electric Power University, Jilin 132012, China
[5] College of Aviation Foundation, Aviation University of Air Force, Changchun 130022, China

Abstract. In order to improve the universality and accuracy of one-to-one iris recognition algorithm, there proposes an iris recognition algorithm based on adaptive optimization Log-Gabor filter and RBF neural network in this paper. Iris amplitude features are extracted with Log-Gabor filter. The selection mutation operator and particle swarm optimization algorithm are used to optimize the filter parameters. Then principal component analysis (PCA) are used to reduce dimensions, thereby reducing the noise and redundancy. Then the Euclidean distance between iris amplitude features are calculated, and the RBF neural network is built for iris recognition. Compared with other iris recognition algorithms on JLU-6.0 iris library and CASIA-Iris-Interval iris library, the recognition rate of this algorithm is higher, and the ROC curve is closer to the coordinate axis, so it has good stability and robustness.

Keywords: Log-Gabor filter · Selection mutation operator · RBF neural network · Euclidean distance · Iris recognition

1 Introduction

Iris recognition technology is a hot research direction of biometric recognition [1]. The key steps of iris recognition are feature extraction and recognition [2]. In feature extraction, the Gabor filter is usually used to extract features [3]. Especially, Daugman used Gabor filter method to extract the phase features of iris texture. However, Gabor filter has the obvious limitation that the maximum bandwidth is limited to double frequency. In this regard, Field proposed the Log-Gabor [4] filter which not only has the advantages of Gabor filter, but also overcomes the above shortcomings. In the traditional

Z. Sun et al. (Eds.): CCBR 2019, LNCS 11818, pp. 312–320, 2019.
https://doi.org/10.1007/978-3-030-31456-9_35

method, if the filter parameters are set improperly, it is easy to fall into the local optimal extreme value [5]. Hamming or other distance algorithms are greatly affected by the environment and may not accurately differentiate iris category. The recognition algorithm based on BP neural network [6] can improve the accuracy substantially. However, the BP neural network structure is complex, it has more parameters, and the convergence speed is slow.

For the small iris library (less than 200 categories, less than 30 iris images in a single category) shot in ideal state, this paper proposes an iris recognition algorithm based on adaptive optimization Log-Gabor filter and RBF neural network [7]. The selection mutation operator and particle swarm optimization (SM-PSO) are used to optimize the parameters of Log-Gabor filter. The iris amplitude features are extracted with Log-Gabor filter. RBF neural network is constructed to calculate the Euclidean distance between iris amplitude features for iris recognition.

2 Iris Image Processing

The iris image needs to be processed before feature extraction [8]. All pre-processed [9] iris images are taken in an ideal state. Through quality evaluation, iris localization, normalization processing and image enhancement, the iris area is mapped into a rectangle of 512 × 64 dimensions. Histogram equalization is used to enhance the rectangle. Then a 256 × 32 dimensions, which has the strongest and the least interfered texture region at the upper right corner of the enhanced image, is cut as the iris recognition area. Finally, horizontal shift is performed to eliminate iris rotation [10]. The images in iris image processing process are shown in Fig. 1.

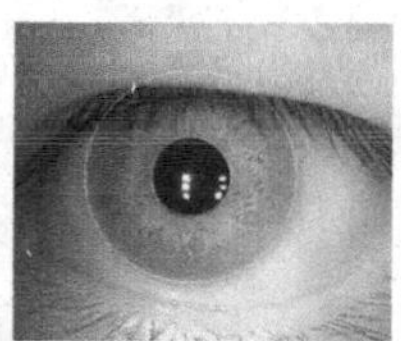

(a)Iris localization image

(b)Normalized and enhanced iris

(c)Iris recognition area

Fig. 1. Iris image processing process

3 Iris Feature Extraction and Recognition

3.1 Log-Gabor Filter and Iris Amplitude Features

The expression of 2D Log-Gabor filter in the frequency domain is shown as Eq. 1.

$$LG(r,\theta) = \exp\left(-\frac{[\log(r/f_0)]^2}{2[\log(\sigma_r/f_0)]^2}\right)\exp\left(-\frac{(\theta-\theta_0)^2}{2\cdot\sigma_\theta^2}\right) \quad (1)$$

f_0 is the central frequency of the filter, θ_0 is the orientation angle of the filter, σ_r determines the scale bandwidth and σ_θ determines the angular bandwidth. In this paper, different directions and scales of Log-Gabor filter are used to extract iris amplitude features. Since the θ_0 is fixed in six directions, as shown in Sect. 3.2, f_0, σ_r,σ_θ are selected as adaptive modification parameters.

There are two important characteristics to note. Firstly, Log-Gabor always has no DC component and the bandwidth is not limited. Secondly, the transfer function of the Log-Gabor function has an extended tail at the high frequency end, which enables us to preserve the real texture features in iris image. With the Log-Gabor filter to deal with the iris recognition area, in which the amplitude of each coordinate point is called iris amplitude feature, a 256 × 32 dimensions iris amplitude image is formed. As shown in Fig. 2.

Fig. 2. Iris amplitude image

3.2 RBF Neural Network and Iris Recognition

The RBF neural network usually has three layers: input layer, hidden layer and output layer. As in Fig. 3.

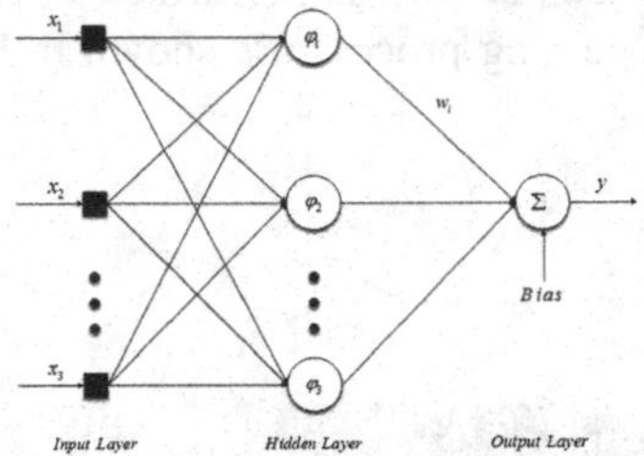

Fig. 3. RBF neural network structure

Through experimental results, this paper found that by dividing the iris recognition area into two parts horizontally, each of which is 256 × 16 dimensions, iris texture omission can be prevented and better recognition effect can be gotten. Each of these blocks corresponds to a RBF neural network, then the PCA is used to reduce the block to 256 × 1 dimensions, thereby reducing the noise and redundancy.

There are three parameters that need to be determined in the training phase of RBF neural network: the center value and variance of the hidden layer and the connection weights from the hidden layer to the output layer. By using the node deletion method [11], we find the optimal number of nodes in the input layer of the neural network is 24 and the number of nodes in the hidden layer is 40.

The Log-Gabor filters, with 6 directions and 4 scales, is used to construct the input layer. The directions are as follows:$\theta=[0, \pi/6, \pi/3, \pi/2, 2\pi/3, 5\pi/6]$, then we calculate the Euclidean distance for two blocks between the test and the template iris of 256×1 dimensions. Finally, the average value of the 256 Euclidean distances is taken as the input value of the input layer in this scale and direction. The values of these 24 inputs are calculated. The formula is shown in Eq. 2.

$$X = \frac{\sum_{i=1}^{256} \sqrt{(I_i - T_i)^2}}{256} \tag{2}$$

X is the input value, I_i and T_i represent the amplitude feature of the test iris and the template iris. Since the input layer only acts as a transmission of data, the connection weight between the input layer and the hidden layer is equivalent to 1. Use K-means algorithm [12] is used to determine the appropriate center vector X_j for 40 nodes in the hidden layer. The distance $r = \|X - X_j\|$ is the independent variable of the radial basis function. The hidden layer of RBF neural network selects 40 nodes, which are equivalent to 40 radial basis functions, and each basis function corresponds to a training data. The output of RBF neural network is 24 dimensions vector. The Gaussian function is chosen for the activation function of the hidden layer, as shown in Eq. 3.

$$\varphi(X_i) = \exp\left(-\frac{\|X_i - X_j\|}{2\sigma_j^2}\right) \tag{3}$$

The connection weight W_j between the hidden layer and the output layer is trained according to the gradient drop method. The output vector of the output layer is calculated as shown in Eq. 4.

$$y_i = \sum_{j=1}^{40} W_j \varphi_j(\|X^i - X^j\|) \tag{4}$$

The standard variance of the 24 dimensions output value is calculated in each neural network. The calculation is shown in Eq. 5.

$$\delta^2 = (\sum_{i=1}^{n} y_i^2 - (\sum_{i=1}^{n} y_i)^2/n)/(n-1) \tag{5}$$

Then the average value F of the variance of the two blocks neural networks is taken as the final value. Only when the value F is smaller than the threshold A can we determine that the test iris is in the same category as the template iris. Threshold A is set according to different iris libraries.

3.3 SM-PSO and Parameter Optimization

This paper uses SM-PSO to optimize f_0, σ_r, σ_θ of the Log-Gabor. The PSO algorithm in this paper uses 50 particles, each with an initial velocity range of [−1, 1]. Each particle contains a set of Log-Gabor filter parameters that need to be optimized, which is equivalent to 50 sets of initial Log-Gabor filters. The initial value of f_0, σ_r ranges from 0 to 1, and σ_θ ranges from 0 to π. The individual extreme value (P_{id}) and the global extreme value (P_{gd}) of the particles are set as the initial values.

One iris for testing and 20 iris for training of the same category and different categories are taken respectively. The iris amplitude features extraction algorithm mentioned above is used, and the standard variance after RBF neural network is obtained. The fitness G is calculated. The fitness function is shown in Eq. 6.

$$G = \sum_{i=1}^{20} (FD_i - 1)^2 / \sum_{i=1}^{20} (FS_i - 1)^2 \tag{6}$$

FD_i and FS_i respectively represent the final output values of different iris and same iris through RBF neural network. Under normal circumstances, the output value of different iris is far away from 1, while the same iris is close to 1. The higher value of G, the higher fitness. By 500 iterations, each time we calculate the new fitness G. If G is larger than the previous G, then the new P_{id} is set to the corresponding filter parameters for the new G, and filter parameters corresponding to the maximum G in the 50 group filters are set as the new P_{gd}. The constriction factor K is used. Then the update of velocity and position of the particle are carried out according to Eqs. 7, 8, and 9.

$$V^{d+1} = K[wV^d + c_1 r_1 (P_{id}^d - X^d) + c_2 r_2 \left(P_{gd}^d - X^d\right)] \tag{7}$$

$$X^{d+1} = X^d + V^{d+1} \tag{8}$$

$$K = \frac{2}{2 - c - \sqrt{c^2 - 4c}}, c = c_1 + c_2 \tag{9}$$

w is the inertia weight, set to 0.972. r_1 and r_2 are random numbers in the range of [0,1]. c_1 and c_2 are learning factors of self and group, set to 1.4945 [13]. P_{id}^d is the individual optimal particle position, P_{gd}^d is the global optimal particle position. V is the speed of the particle, and X is the position of the particle. After adding the contraction factor K, the velocity of particles can be effectively controlled [14].

Each particle evolution uses the selection mutation operator in the genetic algorithm. We calculate the fitness of 50 particles according to Eq. 6, and then two particles with the highest fitness were selected as the mutant particles. The mutation operation mainly determines whether the particle needs to mutate or not according to the mutation probability P_m. Five different variation intervals were used for the variable particles, and the fitness of each variation interval after 100 iterations was counted, and the maximum fitness was taken as the variation interval of the particle. After 500 iterations, the final P_{gd} is used as the parameter of Log-Gabor filter.

4 Experiment and Analysis

Since large iris libraries require higher acquisition devices and are rarely seen in practical applications, this paper mainly designs and recognizes the small iris libraries taken in ideal conditions. In the experiment, qualified iris images from CASIA-Iris-Interval iris library of Chinese Academy of Sciences [15] and JLU-6.0 [16] iris library of Jilin University were respectively selected to form two iris libraries, and each iris library was divided into training iris and testing iris, proportion of half. The experimental environment is as follows: CPU main frequency 3.2 GHZ, 16G memory, Windows10 operating system and programming tool MATLAB R2018a. In this experiment, the equivalent error rate (EER), ROC curve and correct recognition rate (CRR) are used to evaluate algorithms. EER is a value that false rejection rate (FRR) equal to false acceptance rate (FAR).

The algorithm in this paper is compared with the two iris libraries mentioned above in the following algorithm.

1. PSO algorithm is used to optimize the parameters of the filter, observe the effect of selection mutation operator in GA on recognition. (PSO + LG + RBF)
2. Don not optimize the filter parameters. Use the initial values, observe the effect of parameter optimization on recognition. (LG + RBF)
3. Gabor filter is used to extract iris texture features, SM-PSO algorithm is used to optimize the parameters of the filter, and observe the influence of Gabor and Log-Gabor on recognition. (SM-PSO + Gabor + RBF)
4. Random selection method (RSM) [17] is used for hidden layer center points in RBF neural network. And observe the effect of hidden layer center point selection mechanism on iris recognition. (SM-PSO + LG + (RSM)RBF)
5. BP neural network is used for iris recognition. BP neural network is set to three layers, according to the node deletion method, the number of nodes in each layer is set to 24. Choose the Sigmoid function [18] as activation function. (SM-PSO + LG + BP).

The matching times of Inter and Outer matching are calculated by matching algorithm. The number of irises, categories and match count in each iris library are shown in Table 1. Each algorithm CRR, EER are shown in Table 2.

Table 1. The number of matches within each iris library

Iris	Category	Sample	Total	Inter matching	Outer matching	Total match
JLU-6.0	160	30	4800	5152	10639	15791
CASIA-Iris-Interval	200	20	4000	3310	9140	12450

Table 2. CRR and EER of each algorithm

	JLU-6.0		CASIA-Iris-Interval	
	CRR	EER	CRR	EER
PSO + LG + RBF	98.25%	1.52%	96.01%	2.68%
LG + RBF	97.98%	1.77%	96.27%	2.64%
SM-PSO + Gabor + RBF	98.62%	1.39%	97.23%	2.01%
SM-PSO + LG + (RSM)RBF	98.98%	1.03%	97.83%	1.84%
SM-PSO + LG + BP	99.11%	0.89%	98.58%	1.46%
SM-PSO + LG + RBF	**99.68%**	**0.35%**	**98.87%**	**0.96%**

The ROC curves of JLU-6.0 and CASIA-Iris-Interval are shown in Fig. 4.

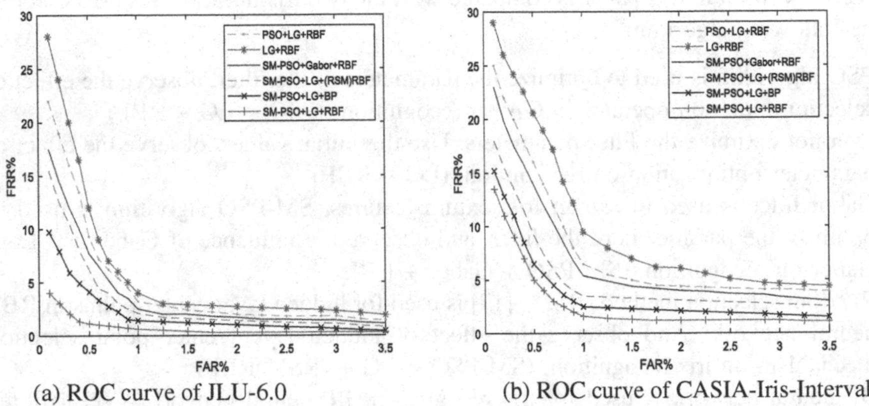

(a) ROC curve of JLU-6.0 (b) ROC curve of CASIA-Iris-Interval

Fig. 4. ROC curve of each iris libraries

The closer the ROC curve is to the coordinate axis, the smaller the EER, the higher the CRR, and the better the performance of the algorithm. As shown in Table 2 and Fig. 4, the result of parameter optimization for Log-Gabor is better than without optimization. The effect of using SM-PSO algorithm is better than only using particle swarm optimization, which also indicates that the selection mutation operation plays an improved role in avoiding the parameter falling into the local optimal solution. According to the experimental results, the recognition effect of using Log-Gabor to extract the texture feature of iris is better than using Gabor filter. This also indicates that the existence of DC component and bandwidth limitation will indeed interfere the iris recognition.

After using the RSM algorithm in the center point of the hidden layer in RBF neural network, CRR of the algorithm decreases and EER increases. In this paper, the hidden layer center of RBF can be located in an important area of input space through the redistribution of neural network resources. For RSM algorithm, the center point of hidden layer is randomly selected in the input sample, and the center is fixed. By contrast, the algorithm in this paper is more flexible.

Although BP neural network has a high recognition accuracy, it is still not as accurate as this algorithm. On the other hand, BP neural network has many parameters, the learning speed is slow and it is easy to fall into a local minimum.

5 Conclusions

Aiming at improving the universality and accuracy of one-to-one iris recognition algorithm, this paper proposes an iris recognition algorithm based on adaptive optimized Log-Gabor filter and RBF neural network. Log-Gabor filter is used to extract the amplitude features of iris, and SM-PSO algorithm is used to find the globally most suitable filter parameters. Finally, RBF neural network is used to classify and recognize iris dynamically. The CRR of JLU-6.0 iris library and CASIA-Iris-Interval iris library are 99.68% and 98.87%, EER respectively: 0.35% and 0.96%. The ROC curve is the closest to coordinate axis in many method comparisons and has good stability and universality.

However, this paper does not further study the weight from hidden layer to output layer of RBF neural network. Moreover, this algorithm is not tested in a larger iris library. These two points will be the focus of further research.

Acknowledgments. The authors would like to thank the referee's advice and acknowledge the support of the National Natural Science Foundation of China (NSFC) under Grant No. 61471181. Jilin Province Industrial Innovation Special Fund Project under Grant No. 2019C053-2. Science and technology project of the Jilin Provincial Education Department under Grant No. JJKH20180448KJ. Thanks also go to the Jilin Provincial Key Laboratory of Biometrics New Technology for supporting this project.

References

1. Wang, W., Zhu, Y., Tan, T.: Identification based on iris recognition. J. Autom. **28**(1), 1–10 (2002)
2. Li, X., Sun, Z., Tan, T.: Overview of iris image quality-assessment. Journal of Image and Graphics **19**(6), 813–824 (2014)
3. Liu, S., et al.: Gabor filtering and adaptive optimization neural network for iris double recognition. In: Zhou, J., et al. (eds.) CCBR 2018. LNCS, vol. 10996, pp. 441–449. Springer, Cham (2018). https://doi.org/10.1007/978-3-319-97909-0_47
4. Wang, R., Wu, X.: Riemannian manilold image set classification algorithm based on log-gabor wavelet features. Pattern Recogn. Artif. Intell. **30**(4), 377–384 (2017)
5. Gao, S., Zhu, X., Liu, Y., et al.: A quality assessment method of iris image based on support vector machine. J. Fib. Bioeng. Inf. **8**(2), 293–300 (2015)
6. Yuan, C., Sun, X., Wu, Q.J.: Difference co-occurrence matrix using BP neural network for fingerprint liveness detection. Soft. Comput. **13**(23), 5157–5169 (2019)
7. Dua, M., Gupta1, R., Khari, M., Crespo, R.G.: Biometric iris recognition using radial basis function neural network. Soft Comput. 1–23 (2019, in Press)
8. Si, G.: Research on Capture and Quality Evaluation of Iris Image. Jilin University, Changchun (2016)

9. Liu, S., Liu, Y., Zhu, X., Feng, J., Lu, S.: Iris location algorithm based on partitioning search. Comput. Eng. Appl. **54**(18), 212–217 (2018)
10. Liu, S., Liu, Y., Zhu, X., Lin, Z., Yang, J.: Ant colony mutation particle swarm optimization for secondary iris recognition. J. Comput. Aided Des. Comput. Graph. **30**(8), 1604–1614 (2018)
11. Zhu, J., Xun, Q., Yi, H., et al.: Virtual network mapping algorithm of node deletion. J. Anhui Univ. (Natural Sciences) **38**(5), 37–43 (2014)
12. Shi, K., et al.: Dynamic barycenter averaging kernel in RBF networks for time series classification. IEEE Access **47**(7), 564–576 (2019)
13. Liu, S., Liu, Y., Zhu, X., Huo, G., Liu, W., Feng, J.: Iris double recognition based on modified evolutionary neural network. J. Electr. Imaging **6**(6), 063023 (2017)
14. Ma, J., Wei, G.: Improved learning algorithm for RBF neural network. Comput. Syst. Appl. **24**(2), 84–87 (2013)
15. CASIA Iris Image Database. http://www.cbsr.ia.ac.cn/english/IrisDatabase.asp
16. JLU Iris Image Database. http://www.jlucomputer.com/index/irislibrary/irislibrary.html
17. Chun-yong, Y., Sun, Z.: Parallel implementing improved k-means applied for image retrieval and anomaly delection. J. Multimedia Tools Appl. **76**(16), 16911–16927 (2017)
18. Shao, X., Wang, H., Liu, J., et al.: Sigmoid function based integral-derivative observer and application to autopilot design. J. Mech. Syst. Sig. Process. **84**, 113–127 (2017)

Retinal Vessel Segmentation Method Based on Improved Deep U-Net

Yiheng Cai(✉), Yuanyuan Li, Xurong Gao, and Yajun Guo

Beijing University of Technology, Beijing, China
caiyiheng@bjut.edi.cn

Abstract. The automatic segmentation of retinal vessels plays an important role in the early screening of eye diseases. However, vessels are difficult to segment with pathological retinal images. Hence, we propose the use of deep U-net, a new retinal vessel segmentation method based on an improved U-shaped fully convolutional neural network. The method uses not only local features learned from the shallow convolution layers, but also abstract features learned from deep convolution layers. To improve the segmentation accuracy for thin vessels, we applied Gaussian matched filtering to the U-net. The batch normalization layer was added in the U-net network, which increased the speed of convergence. In the training phase, a new sample amplification method called translation-reflection was proposed to increase the proportion of blood vessels in the training images. Results of the experiments showed that the proposed method leads to better retinal vessel segmentation than other methods developed in recent years do for the SE, SP, Acc, Ppv, and AUC evaluation metrics.

Keywords: Deep learning · Segmentation · Gaussian matched filtering · U-net · Batch normalization

1 Introduction

Diseases such as glaucoma, cataracts, and diabetes cause retinal fundus blood vessel lesions and can cause pain and even blindness for long-term patients with these diseases [1]. Manual vessel segmentation is important for the detection of these eye diseases, but segmentation by experienced experts is cumbersome and time-consuming. Therefore, automatic extraction of retinal blood vessels from images is particularly important. Automatic segmentation is difficult because of inadequate contrast regions, pathological regions, and background noise.

Recently, deep learning has been used in retinal vessel segmentation, and it has achieved promising results [2, 3]. It classifies retinal vessel segmentation at the pixel level, and it uses deep learning to achieve semantic segmentation and end-to-end tuning. These convolutional neural network-based segmentation methods, in which the size of image blocks is usually much smaller than the size of the whole image, limits

The work was supported by the National Key Research and Development Program of China (No. 2017YFC170302) and the Science and Technology Project of Beijing Municipal Education Commission (No. KM201710005028).

Z. Sun et al. (Eds.): CCBR 2019, LNCS 11818, pp. 321–328, 2019.
https://doi.org/10.1007/978-3-030-31456-9_36

the size of the perceptual region; this approach can only extract some local features, thus limiting the performance of segmentation. Additionally, this type of method has a high storage cost and computation efficiency is relatively low. To solve these problems, Fu et al. [4] proposed a deep learning method that regarded retinal vessel segmentation as a border extraction problem. By combining the deep convolution neural network with a fully connected conditional random field (CRF), the fusion images of the four-sided output vessel probability maps were input into CRF to complete the segmentation of the whole retinal image. Luo et al. [10] and Orlando et al. [11] proposed retinal vessel segmentation methods that used deep neural network for training and CRF for fine tuning, and they achieved better segmentation results. However, using fully connected CRFs complicates the network with many parameters, which requires high-performance training equipment and long-term training.

Dasgupta et al. [5] proposed an end-to-end retinal vessel segmentation method in which the retinal vessel image was divided into small pieces and the full convolution network (FCN) was applied to segmented retinal vessels. A segmentation method based on FCN uses a de-convolution layer to sample the feature map of the last convolution layer to restore it to the same size as the input image; therefore, it can classify the image at the pixel level and address the issue of semantic segmentation. However, an FCN does not fully use the information obtained from the shallow convolution layers, which have smaller perception domains and can learn some local features. A new fully convolutional neural network [6], called U-net [7], has been successfully applied to cell image segmentation; in this study, we use deep U-net for retinal vessel image segmentation, and propose an improved U-net-based retinal vessel segmentation method to achieve end-to-end retinal vessel segmentation.

2 Materials and Methods

Our experimental method is outlined in Fig. 1. In the training phase, the preprocessing processes included green channel extraction, contrast limited adaptive histogram equalization (CLAHE), and gamma correction. Gaussian matched filtering was applied before the network training to enhance the contrast of small blood vessels. To increase the number of training samples, five sample amplification methods were used (i.e., rotation, translation, stretching, flipping, and, our newly developed method, reflection). Amplified samples were used as the input for the deep U-net.

The network consisted of convolution layers, lower sampling layers, and upper sampling layers, forming a left-right symmetrical, end-to-end, U-shaped network. It used a deeper network with four levels to expand the field of perception. At each level, the max-pooling operation was performed after the convolution layers and more abstract features were learned by down-sampling with maximum preservation. In the up-sampling stage, we used bilinear interpolation and the up-sampling network layer was connected with the corresponding shallow network layer at the same level; therefore, more information was maintained in the training process. Subsequently, we added the batch normalization (BN) layer in the U-net network to avoid over-fitting and to increase the speed of network convergence.

In the test phase, the test images were preprocessed using the same processes as the training phase. After Gaussian matched filtering, the image was input into the trained network model, and the output of the deep U-net was the segmentation result.

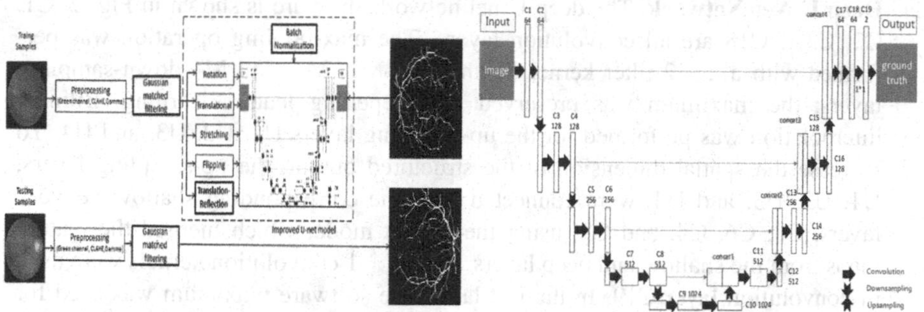

Fig. 1. Retinal vessel segmentation process based on an improved U-net

Fig. 2. Network construction graph for the deep U-net

2.1 Gaussian Matched Filtering Method

Gaussian matched filtering can simulate the gray distribution of retinal vessels [12]. Our previous work [13] proved that Gaussian matched filtering can enhance small blood vessels in the image, which can improve small blood vessel segmentation accuracy. In our framework, the Gaussian kernels in 12 different directions are used to filter the retinal image, and the corresponding maximum response is found as the response value of each pixel, which is used as an input to thc improved U-net. And the segmentation accuracy of the framework with and without filtering were compared to verify the validity of Gaussian matched filtering.

2.2 Image Amplification

Image amplification is usually required to enrich training samples because there are usually too few samples of retinal blood vessel segmentation images. In addition to the common image expansion methods, such as rotation, translation, stretching, and flipping, we used a new method, translation-reflection. When the translation amplification was performed, the images with 40 pixels translated in both horizontal and vertical directions always contained large background pixels. To overcome this problem, we use the reflection transformation along symmetrical axis of blood vessel distribution and its vertical direction at the circle boundary of the image. Therefore, the background parts were filled with vessel pixels of the symmetrical image, which increased the proportion of blood vessels in the image and moderately reduced the imbalance of positive and negative samples.

2.3 The Proposed Architecture: Improved Deep U-Net

The image samples after augmentation were input into the improved deep U-net, which extended the receptive field with a deeper network and extracted more abstract features.

(1). **Deep U-Net Network.** The deep U-net network structure is shown in Fig. 2. C1, C2, C3 …C18 are all convolution layers. The max-pooling operation was performed with a 2 * 2 filter kernel for the M1, M2, M3, and M4 down-sampling layers; the maximum was preserved for deepening feature learning. Bilinear interpolation was performed for the up-sampling layers U1, U2, U3, and U4. To increase the spatial dimension of the structured output, the up-sampling layers, U1, U2, U3, and U4, were connected with the corresponding shallow network layers, C8, C6, C4, and C2, using the concat mode, which merged the feature maps from the shallow and deep layers. Two 1 * 1 convolution kernels were used in convolution layer C19. In the last layer, the software maximum was used for classification.

(2). **Batch Normalization.** When the network becomes deeper, there are more parameters that need to be learned. In the U-net network training process, when the parameters of the previous layer changed, the data distribution received by the subsequent network layers also changed. With the deepening of the network, this change amplified, thus affecting the convergence rate of the network. To overcome this problem, a BN operation [14] was introduced before ReLU activation after convolution layers C1, C3, C5, C7, and C9, so the network layer data were normalized to a uniform distribution; this had minimal effect on the latter layers and it avoided slow network convergence caused by learning a different data distribution. Moreover, BN is very effective for gradient feedback transmission and has the effect of regularization, which prevents the network from over-fitting the data.

We chose a relatively large initial learning rate because the BN layer had an effect on the convergence speed of the network, so we did not need to adjust the learning rate incrementally. The convergence rates of the networks with and without BN were compared. We compared the convergence speeds of network training with BN and Dropout, a stochastic regularization strategy commonly used to prevent over-fitting of deep networks.

2.4 Databases and Evaluation Metrics

The retinal images used in the experiments were from the Digital Retinal Images for Vessel Extraction (DRIVE) and the Structured Analysis of the Retina (STARE) databases. The preprocessing processes included green channel extraction, CLAHE, and the gamma correction, which differentiate blood vessel from the background. In the evaluation of blood vessel segmentation methods, we used sensitivity (Se), specificity (Sp), accuracy (Acc), precision rate (Ppv), and the area under receiver operating characteristic curve (AUC) to evaluate the proposed method and compare it with other methods. Where, Sensitivity (Se) represents the proportion of correctly segmented vascular pixels in the total number of vascular pixels in the standard image, Specificity

(Sp) represents the proportion of non-vascular pixels correctly segmented in the segmented image in the total number of non-vascular pixels in the standard image, The precision rate (Ppv) represents the proportion of vascular pixels correctly segmented in the segmented image in the total number of vascular pixels segmented.

3 Result

3.1 The Effect of Translation-Reflection Transformation

Of the 4000 images selected from the training samples, the images after translation-reflection transformation accounted for 0, 1/4, 1/2, and 3/4 of the total samples. After network training, the segmentation accuracy of the test set was calculated. The results of the experiment are shown in Table 1.

The segmentation accuracy of the test set clearly increased with increasing translation-reflection samples, which shows that increasing the content of blood vessels (positive samples) in the image with translation-reflection transformation helps to distinguish blood vessels from the background in the whole training network. When the number of translation-reflection samples increased to 3000, the segmentation accuracy slightly decreased, indicating that the proportion of translation-reflection samples was not an improvement. It is necessary to work with other amplification methods to expand the network's ability to identify blood vessels in various situations. In subsequent experiments, we used Sample distribution.

Table 1. The effect of translation-reflection transformation

Amplification methods	Sample distribution1	Sample distribution2	Sample distributio3	Sample distribution4
Rotation, translation, stretching and flipping	4000	3000	2000	1000
Translation-reflection	0	1000	2000	3000
Acc	0.9653	0.9681	0.9713	0.9711

3.2 Merging the Gaussian Matched Filtering with the U-Net Network

The segmentation result using Gaussian matched filtering of retinal images as training samples is clearly closer to the blood vessel graph manually segmented by experts (Fig. 3). For example, in the red ellipse 2, Gaussian matched filtering successfully segmented the cross-vessel while the method without Gaussian matched filtering clearly did not segment the cross-vessel. Gaussian matched filtering can also improve the segmentation accuracy of small blood vessels. The micro-vessels in red ellipse 1 are not segmented without Gaussian matched filtering and during manual segmentation by an expert. However, Gaussian matched filtering provided a better result. In our specific region of interest, the segmentation results using Gaussian matched filtering distinguish the edge of this area (i.e., the position shown in the blue box); this also shows that using the images processed by Gaussian matched filtering on training samples has improved segmentation.

The evaluation of the Gaussian matched filtering is shown in Table 2. Each index of the non-Gaussian matched filtering is smaller than the index of the Gaussian matched filtering, which indicates that the Gaussian matched filtering method can effectively improve the accuracy of vessel segmentation.

Table 2. The evaluation index

	Se	Sp	Acc	Ppv	AUC
Non-Gaussian matched filtering	0.8018	0.9846	0.9685	0.8335	0.9814
With Gaussian matched filtering	0.8206	0.9891	0.9743	0.8788	0.9838

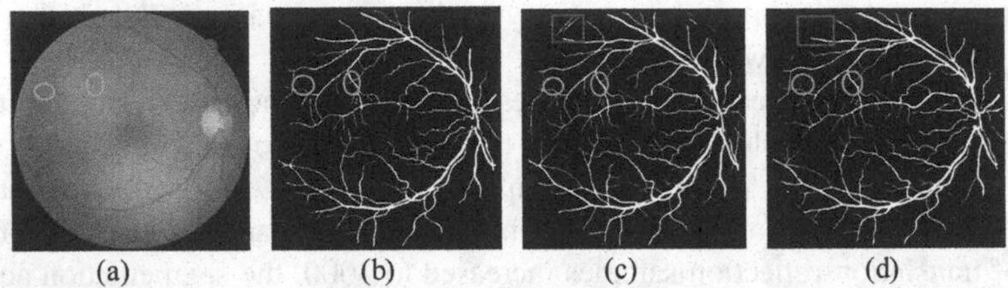

Fig. 3. Segmentation results of one example image (a) original image; (b) ground truth; (c) segmentation results of an image without Gaussian matched filtering; and (d) segmentation results of an image using Gaussian matched filtering (the red ellipses indicate specific areas where we compared the four images. The blue squares indicate specific areas where we compared the methods with or without Gaussian matched filtering (Color figure online)

3.3 Analysis for Batch Normalization

The results of the comparison between BN and Dropout are shown in Fig. 4. The green curve represents the training process of the network using Dropout. The red curve represents the training process of the improved U-net network with BN layers. The blue curve represents the accuracy of the training process after introducing the BN layers. The network using Dropout shows decreasing loss after 300 iterations. However, the convergence speed improved after adding BN layers and the loss stabilized to less than 0.1 after iterations less than 300; this can avoid over-fitting and save training time.

3.4 Comparison with Other Methods

Table 3 shows the comparison of our proposed vessel segmentation method with other deep learning methods [3, 5, 8, 9]. The results in Table 3 show that our proposed method is superior to the methods we studied for the SE, SP, Acc, Ppv, and AUC evaluation metrics. Our proposed algorithm applied a better training dataset and used an improved deep U-net network to obtain more abstract features, which combined shallow information to obtain better segmentation.

Our method may also be helpful for some difficult cases. It can achieve good results in the segmentation of small vessels, vessels in lesion images, and vessels with central reflection, as shown in Fig. 5. Figure 5(a) is an image with many small blood vessels in the vicinity of the macula; the reflex arcs near the optic disc were successfully identified as non-blood vessels using our method (e.g., the blue ellipse in Fig. 5(a)). Figure 5(b) shows successful separation of blood vessels from the background for an image containing a lesion using our proposed method, and our method did not incorrectly identify the lesion area as a dense vessel patch, which is a common error in traditional feature extraction methods. Figure 5(c) shows that our method identified the vessels with central reflex.

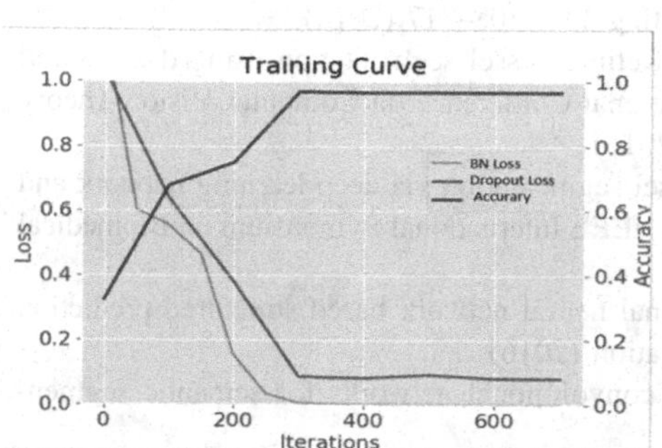

Fig. 4. The training curve before and after adding batch normalization

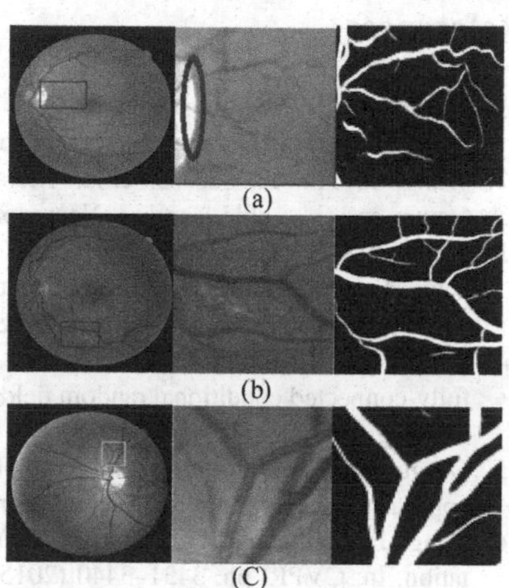

Fig. 5. Segmentation images with small blood vessels, lesions, and vessel central reflex (Color figure online)

Table 3. Comparative results of recent works on retinal vessel segmentation

Methods	Se	Sp	Acc	Ppv	AUC(ROC)
2nd human Observer	0.7760	0.9724	0.9472	–	–
Martina et al. [3]	0.7276	0.9785	0.9466	–	0.9749
Dasgupta et al. [5]	0.7691	0.9801	0.9533	0.8498	0.9744
Luo [8]	–	–	0.9600	–	–
Xie [9]	0.7761	0.9800	0.9536		
The proposed method	0.8206	0.9891	0.9743	0.8788	0.9838

4 Conclusions

We proposed and tested a retinal blood vessel segmentation method based on an improved U-net network. to segment blood vessels of retinal images quickly and accurately. We used a new sample amplification method, which increased the proportion of blood vessels in the image after translation using reflection transformation; this reduced the imbalance between positive and negative samples in the image. By introducing BN layers in the U-net network, we prevented over-fitting, and the convergence speed of the network was also accelerated. In addition, the combination of the deep U-net network and traditional Gaussian matched filtering improved the accuracy of the segmentation. This method achieved end-to-end vascular segmentation of the whole retinal image. Furthermore, it produced accurate results, and the efficiency of network training improved; it also achieved good results in the segmentation of small vessels, lesion images, and vessels with central reflex.

References

1. Fraz, M.M., Remagnino, P., Hoppe, A.: Blood vessel segmentation methodologies in retinal images–a survey. Comput. Methods Programs Biomed. **108**(1), 407–433 (2012)
2. Wang, S., Yin, Y., Cao, G., et al.: Hierarchical retinal blood vessel segmentation based on feature and ensemble learning. Neurocomputing **149**, 708–717 (2015)
3. Melinscak, M., Prentasic, P., Loncaric, S.: Retinal vessel segmentation using deep neural networks. In: Proceeding of the 10th International Conference on Computer Vision Theory and Applications (VISAPP), pp. 577–582 (2015)
4. Fu, H., Xu, Y., Wong, D.W.K.: Retinal vessel segmentation via deep learning network and fully-connected conditional random fields. In: IEEE International Symposium on Biomedical Imaging, pp. 698–701 (2016)
5. Dasgupta, A., Singh, S.: A fully convolutional neural network based structured prediction approach towards the retinal vessel segmentation (2016)
6. Long, J., Shelhamer, E., Darrell, T.: Fully convolutional networks for semantic segmentation. In: CVPR, pp. 3431–3440 (2015)
7. Ronneberger, O., Fischer, P., Brox, T.: U-Net: convolutional networks for biomedical image segmentation. In: Navab, N., Hornegger, J., Wells, W., Frangi, A. (eds.) MICCAI 2015. LNCS, vol. 9351, pp. 234–241. Springer, Cham (2015). https://doi.org/10.1007/978-3-319-24574-4_28
8. Luo, Y.S.: From retinal image to diabetic retinopathy diagnosis. University of Electronic Science and Technology of China, Sichuan, China (2017)
9. Xie, L.: Blood vessel segmentation method for fundus images based on deep learning. Shenzhen University, Shengzhen, China (2017)
10. Orlando, J., Prokofyeva, E., Blaschko, M.: A discriminatively trained fully connected conditional random field model for blood vessel segmentation in fundus images. IEEE Trans. Biomed. Eng. **64**(1), 16–27 (2016)
11. Luo, Y., Yang, L., Wang, L., Cheng, H.: CNN-CRF network for retinal image segmentation. In: The Third International Conference on Cognitive Systems and Information Processing (2016)
12. Chaudhuri, S., Chatterjee, S., Katz, N., et al.: Detection of blood vessels in retinal images using two-dimensional matched filters. IEEE Trans. Med. Imaging **8**(3), 63–269 (1989)
13. Cai, Y., Gao, X., Qiu, C., Cui, Y.: Retinal vessel segmentation method with efficient hybrid features fusion. J. Electron. Inf. Technol. **39**(8), 1956–1963 (2017)
14. Ioffe, S., Szegedy, C.: Batch normalization: accelerating deep network training by reducing internal covariate shift. In: ICML 2015 Proceedings of the 32nd International Conference on Machine Learning - Volume 37, Lille, France, 06–11 July 2015, pp. 448–456 (2015)

Multi-pyramid Optimized Mask R-CNN for Iris Detection and Segmentation

Huanwei Liang[1(✉)], Zilong Chen[2], Hui Zhang[1], Jing Liu[1], Xingguang Li[1], Lihu Xiao[1], and Zhaofeng He[1]

[1] Beijing IrisKing Tech Co., Ltd., Beijing, China
{lianghw,zhanghui,liujing,lixg,xiaolh,hezhf}@irisking.com

[2] Material Evidence Identification Center of the Ministry of Public Securit, Beijing, China
enoen@163.com

Abstract. Iris segmentation is an irreplaceable stage of iris recognition pipeline. The traditional segmentation methods are poorly robust, and the segmentation method using FCN runs very slowly. Therefore, in this paper, we propose an iris detection segmentation model based on multi-pysamid optimized Mask R-CNN. It is mainly realized by expanding the segmentation feature and performing the fusion operation on the segmentation feature obtained in the feature pyramid. This method enhances the expression of segmentation features and improves iris segmentation performance. Finally, experiments were conducted on two public datasets UBIRIS.v2 and CASIA.IrisV4-distance. Experimental results show that the proposed model achieves better results than state-of-the-art methods in the literature.

Keywords: Iris segmentation · Multi-pyramid · Convolutional neural network

1 Introduction

Iris recognition [2,9,11,20] has become an indispensable part of biometric identification due to uniqueness and reliability. Iris segmentation [2–4,7,9–11,20] is to locate and isolate the iris from other regions, it plays an important role in iris econgnition. Traditional iris segmentation algorithms usually adapt to linited centrain image condition, which show significant reducing in the actural complex situation.

There are many traditional iris segmentation methods [3,4,7,9,11,12,15,20, 21]. For example, based on edge detection [4], Hough transform [21], pixel [12], etc. These methods usually require sharp contours or some prior knowledge and are easily affected by noise. In recet year, due to the development of the deep convolutional neural networks (CNN), more and more segmentation methods based on CNN are proposed [1,10]. However, direct prediction using features extracted from convolutional neural networks does not completely separate the iris from the non-iris region. Due to these shortcomings, the ability of iris applications is limited.

Z. Sun et al. (Eds.): CCBR 2019, LNCS 11818, pp. 329–336, 2019.
https://doi.org/10.1007/978-3-030-31456-9_37

To solve the above problems, we introduce an multi-pysamid optimized network, which is an extension of Mask R-CNN [5]. The proposed network model achieves precise segmentation and accurate detection of the iris. The main contributions of this paper include:

(1) Appropriately expand the feature map of the mask, without adding too much calculation while retaining more segmentation information.
(2) The information of the multi-pyramid segmentatino is fused by taking the maximum value to improve the characterization ability of the feature map.

2 Related Work

2.1 Traditional Methods

Most of the traditional iris segmentation methods are adge based methods. Few studities are pixel level segmentation. Daugman's study [4] is one of the classic methods, Integral differential operator is used to approximate the iris boundary, but the calculation is large. Hough transform [21] is also often used to fit iris boundaries in traditional algorithms, mainly by using each point to vote to determine whether it is a boundary, and [9,11,20] use a similar method. Pulling and pushing method is proposed by he [7] is imspried by Hookes law, but it also can't fit the iris boundary of special cases. Shah and Ross [15] uses an active contour model to improve the accuracy of iris segmentation, but results are still sensitive to noise. There are also many uses of artificial design features to segment the iris, such as location and color features [12]. However artificial designed features are often limited, and the generalization performance of the model is poor.

2.2 Deep Neural Network Methods

With the development of deep learning, CNN makes great breakthroughs in instance segmentation. A large number of segmentation methods are proposed, such as Seg-Edge bilateral constraint network (SEN) [8], which is a network focused on iris segmentation. The full convolutional networks (FCN) [1,10] alse is used to achieve iris segmentation. For example, MFCN [10], using a full convolution network, fuses the different features of the upper and lower layers, and obtains accurate iris segmentation results. These methods illustrate the excellent performance of deep learning in iris segmentation, but due to the large amount of computation, the real-time iris recognition cannot be satisfied.

3 Proposed Method

This section describes the proposed iris segmentation method detaily. The base network structure is the Mask R-CNN framework. The proposed method achieves more accurate iris segmentation results on public datasets than other methods, and provides iris detection results with less computational load, it provides support for real-time iris recognition.

3.1 Overall Structure

The proposed method follows the Mask R-CNN framework on the overall architecture, and the backbone network is ResNet-50 [6], the feature pyramid network (FPN) structure is used to integrate the local texture details with the high-level abstract information. We found that the feature information of the input segmentation branch only uses the data of a single layer pyramid, and the input feature scale is small, which suppresses the segmentation performance. So we chose multi-pyramid fusion and expand size of feature map to improve accuracy without increasing the amount of computation. Detailed experiments are given in Sect. 4. The overall flowchart is shown in Fig. 1.

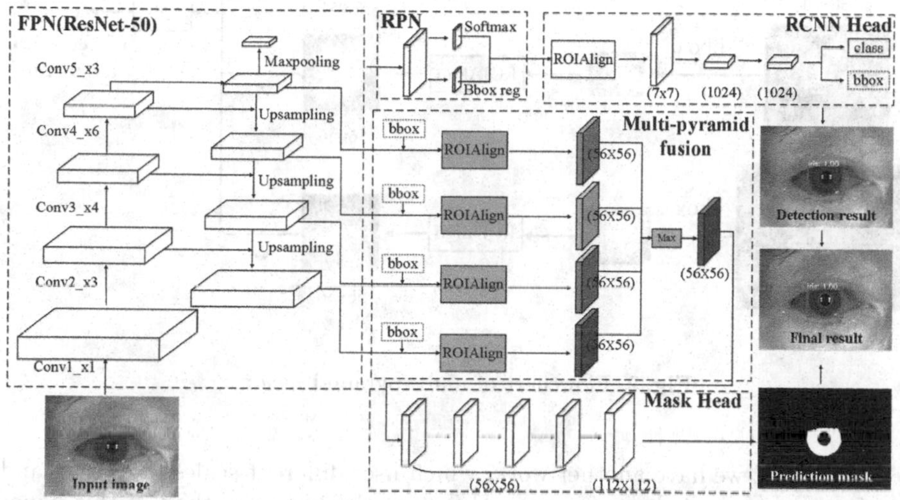

Fig. 1. Network architecture of the proposed method. The RPN, Mask Head and RCNN Head are standard components of Mask R-CNN. Multi-pyramid fusion module fuses feature maps with different pyramid.

3.2 Multi-pyramid Fusion Module

Multi-pyramid fusion implementation process is shown in Fig. 2. After detection branch output classification and location information, bbox is provided for the detection branch, and the size is predicted. Selecting the featrue of the iris region for ROIAlign operation from different pyramid, and obtaining feature maps of the same size. Max operation is performed on the corresponding points of the feature map acquired. Finally, segmentation feature maps of the fusion multi-layer pyramid feature are output. Since the max operation reflects the low-level texture information and the high-level semantic information into the same feature map to enrich the information.

In the ROIAlign operation, the required feature map is normalized to a larger scale of 56 × 56, it retains more useful information for segmentation in Fig. 2. Larger scale feature maps are not tested due to time. This work is supported by National Key R&D Program of China [2018YFC0807303].

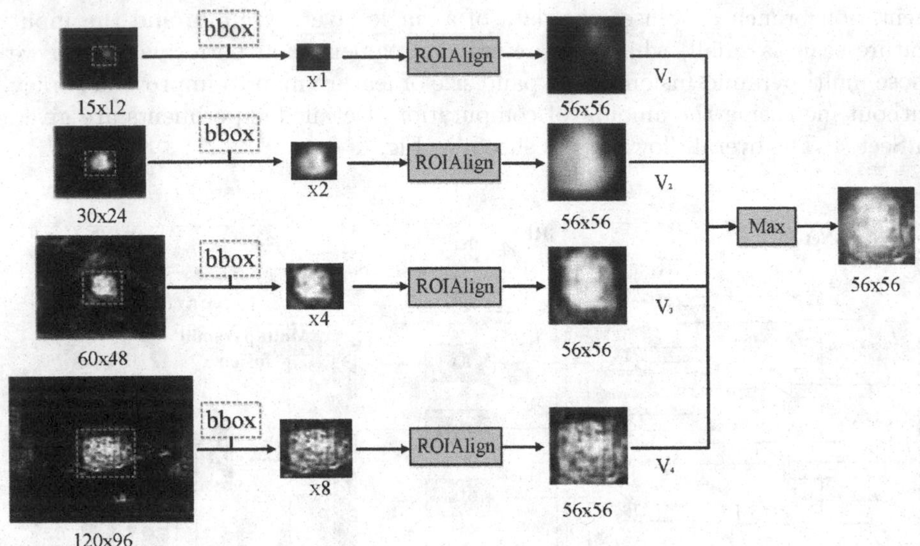

Fig. 2. Flowchart of multi-pyramid fusion.

Meanwhile, we have another work, which uses different scales to extract and fuse features of single-layer features. However, the fusion method of this paper is more direct to obtain features of different scales from multi-pyramids, it can obtain richer segmentation information.

There are two main branches in the overall framework for detection and segmentation. We use multitask loss $L = L_{class} + L_{reg} + L_{mask}$ to jointly train the model, L_{class} and L_{reg} use the loss function of Faster R-CNN [14], L_{mask} uses binary cross entropy loss, the formula is as follows:

$$L = \sum_{i=0}^{N} y_i log\hat{y}^i + (1 - y^i) log(1 - \hat{y}^i) \tag{1}$$

$$\hat{y}^i = g(\max(V_1(x, y), V_2(x, y), V_3(x, y), V_4(x, y)))$$

where $\hat{y}^i$ represents the probability of each pixel. $g(*)$ uses the sigmod function, V_* indicates that the pixel value of the defferent pyramid.

4 Experiment

4.1 Datasets

The proposed method is validated on two public datasets, UBIRIS.v2 [13] and CASIA.v4-Distance [19]. The UBIRIS.v2 dataset has 500 images for training, and 445 images for testing. The CASIA.v4-Distance dataset has 300 images are used for training and 100 images are used for testing, mask size is the same as the original picture size, and the bounding box of the iris is obtained according to the mask.

4.2 Data Augmentation

We augmente the data in the two datasets by adding illumination, filtering, and the image is randomly scaled by 1 to 2 times to simulate the iris image of the real scene. Finally, the images of the UBIRIS.v2 and CASIA.v4-Distance training datasets are 5000 and 15000, respectively. All iris images in both datasets are croped with the size of 480×360 pixels as experimental input.

4.3 Implementation Details

The model is implemented using the pytorch framework, and the hyperparameter settings are as follows: momentum is 0.9 and weight decay is 0.0001, the maximum number of iteration steps is 90k, learning rate is 0.0025, which is divided by a factor of 10 at the 60k and 80k iteration, respectively.

4.4 Experimental Results

The average segmentation error (ASE) is generated by comparing pixels to pixels between the real mask and the predicted mask, and is the main evaluation index of the segmentation quality. It is computed as follow:

$$ASE = \frac{1}{H \times W} \sum_{i,j \in (H,W)} M(i,j) \oplus GT(i,j) \tag{2}$$

H and W are the image length and width, $M(i,j)$ and $GT(i,j)$ are the prediction result and real mask, and $\oplus$ is the XOR operation.

Baseline. The proposed method is an extension of maskrcnn, so using it as the iris segmentation baseline. In the segmentation branch, the feature is adjusted to a 14×14 size feature map after ROIAlign, and then a 28×28 prediction mask is generated by a small FCN. The experimental results show that the segmentation errors are 1.01% and 0.739% in the UBIRIS.v2 and CASIA.v4-Distance databases, respectively.

In order to verify the influence of different size feature maps on segmentation, we designed two feature maps of size 28×28 pixels and 56×56 pixels for comparison experiments. The experimental results are shown in Table 1. Expanding the feature map helps improve segmentation accuracy.

Table 1. Segmentation results of different size feature maps.

Method	UBIRIS.v2		CASIA.v4-Distance	
	ASE (%)	time (s)	ASE (%)	time (s)
Mask R-CNN (14 × 14)	1.010	0.038	0.739	0.038
Mask R-CNN (28 × 28)	0.890	0.039	0.452	0.039
Mask R-CNN (56 × 56)	0.883	0.040	0.444	0.040

Multi-pyramid Fusion Module. In order to improve the richness of the features of the segmentation branch, we designed a multi-pyramid fusion module, features that need to be segmented are acquired on the pyramid feature layer of the backbone network, and the fusion mode is to take the max of the corresponding position as an output. simultaneously, we designed another additive fusion method, which is to accumulate different layer features as input. The experimental results are shown in Table 2. Using the maximum value as the output has better segmentation effect.

Table 2. Multi-pyramid fusion results. (add) and (max) indicates the way of fusion.

Method	UBIRIS.v2		CASIA.v4-Distance	
	ASE (%)	time (s)	ASE (%)	time (s)
Fusion (add)	0.861	0.0421	0.437	0.0421
Fusion (max)	**0.858**	0.0420	**0.421**	0.0420

Table 3. Comparisons of the proposed methods and other iris segmentation method. '-' indicates the result is not reported in their work.

Method	UBIRIS.v2		CASIA.v4-Distance	
	ASE (%)	time (s)	ASE (%)	time (s)
Our method	**0.86**	0.042	**0.42**	0.042
SEN [8]	0.88	0.200	0.46	0.200
MFCN [10]	0.90	0.200	0.59	–
RTV-L1 [22]	1.21	–	0.68	–
Tan et al. [18]	1.31	–	–	–
Tan and Kumar [17]	1.72	0.750	0.81	1.530
Proenca [12]	1.87	0.780	–	–
Tan and Kumar [16]	1.90	–	1.13	–

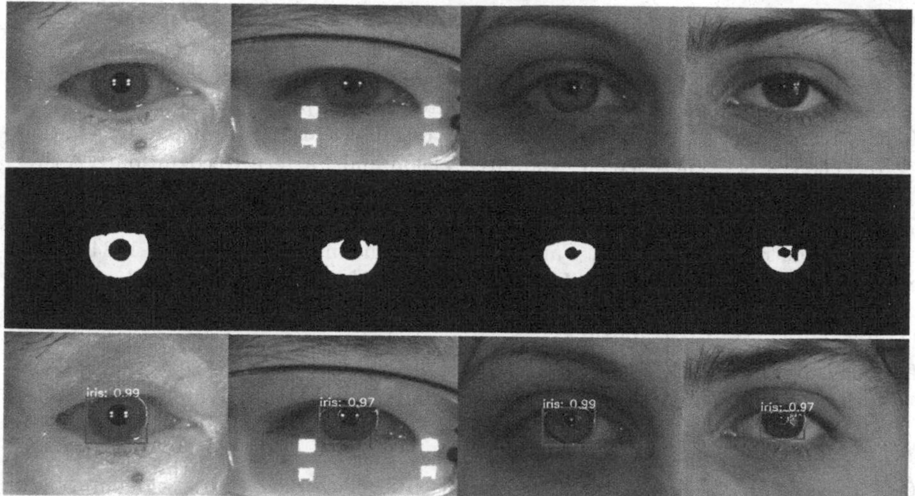

Fig. 3. The first row is the original image, the second row is the prediction mask, and the third row is the final result. The red pixels indicate non-iris pixels are predicted as iris pixels, and the green pixels are the opposite. (Color figure online)

Comparison with Other Iris Segment Algorithms. The proposed method is compared with other published state-of-the-art iris segmentation methods. The experimental results are shown in Table 3. In the two datasets UBIRIS.v2 and CASIA.v4-Distance, our method has a great improvement in speed and segmentation accuracy compared with other methods. Finally, the experimental results are shown in Fig. 3. The different results have different scales for the images, and the time results are only used as a reference.

5 Conclusions

In this paper, we propose an iris detection and segmentation model that combines accuracy and speed. By the appropriate expansion of the segmentation features and the fusion of segmentation features on different pyramids, the current best segmentation results are achieved on the two public iris datasets UBIRIS.v2 and CASIA.v4-Distance.

References

1. Bazrafkan, S., Thavalengal, S., Corcoran, P.: An end to end deep neural network for iris segmentation in unconstrained scenarios. Neural Netw. **106**, 79–95 (2018)
2. Daugman, J.: Statistical richness of visual phase information: update on recognizing persons by iris patterns. Int. J. Comput. Vis. **45**(1), 25–38 (2001)
3. Daugman, J.: New methods in iris recognition. IEEE Trans. Syst. Man Cybern. Part B (Cybern.) **37**(5), 1167–1175 (2007)

4. Daugman, J.: How iris recognition works. In: The Essential Guide to Image Processing, pp. 715–739. Elsevier (2009)
5. He, K., Gkioxari, G., Dollár, P., Girshick, R.: Mask R-CNN. In: Proceedings of the IEEE International Conference on Computer Vision, pp. 2961–2969 (2017)
6. He, K., Zhang, X., Ren, S., Sun, J.: Deep residual learning for image recognition. In: The IEEE Conference on Computer Vision and Pattern Recognition (CVPR), pp. 770–778 (2016)
7. He, Z., Tan, T., Sun, Z., Qiu, X.: Toward accurate and fast iris segmentation for iris biometrics. IEEE Trans. Pattern Anal. Mach. Intell. **31**(9), 1670–1684 (2009)
8. Hu, J., Zhang, H., Xiao, L., Liu, J., He, Z., Li, L.: Seg-edge bilateral constraint network for iris segmentation. In: 2019 International Conference on Biometrics (ICB), pp. 1–8. IEEE (2019)
9. Kong, W., Zhang, D.: Accurate iris segmentation based on novel reflection and eyelash detection model. In: Proceedings of 2001 International Symposium on Intelligent Multimedia, Video and Speech Processing. ISIMP 2001 (IEEE Cat. No. 01EX489), pp. 263–266. IEEE (2001)
10. Liu, N., Li, H., Zhang, M., Liu, J., Sun, Z., Tan, T.: Accurate iris segmentation in non-cooperative environments using fully convolutional networks. In: 2016 International Conference on Biometrics (ICB), pp. 1–8. IEEE (2016)
11. Ma, L., Wang, Y., Tan, T.: Iris recognition using circular symmetric filters. In: Object Recognition Supported by User Interaction for Service Robots, vol. 2, pp. 414–417. IEEE (2002)
12. Proenca, H.: Iris recognition: on the segmentation of degraded images acquired in the visible wavelength. IEEE Trans. Pattern Anal. Mach. Intell. **32**(8), 1502–1516 (2010)
13. Proenca, H., Filipe, S., Santos, R., Oliveira, J., Alexandre, L.: The UBIRISv.2: a database of visible wavelength images captured on-the-move and at-a-distance. IEEE Trans. PAMI **32**(8), 1529–1535 (2010)
14. Ren, S., He, K., Girshick, R., Sun, J.: Faster R-CNN: towards real-time object detection with region proposal networks. In: Advances in Neural Information Processing Systems, pp. 91–99 (2015)
15. Shah, S., Ross, A.: Iris segmentation using geodesic active contours. IEEE Trans. Inf. Forensics Secur. **4**(4), 824–836 (2009)
16. Tan, C., Kumar, A.: Unified framework for automated iris segmentation using distantly acquired face images. IEEE Trans. Image Process. **21**(9), 4068–4079 (2012)
17. Tan, C., Kumar, A.: Towards online iris and periocular recognition under relaxed imaging constraints. IEEE Trans. Image Process. **22**(10), 3751–3765 (2013)
18. Tan, T., He, Z., Sun, Z.: Efficient and robust segmentation of noisy iris images for non-cooperative iris recognition. Image Vis. Comput. **28**(2), 223–230 (2010)
19. Biometrics Ideal Test: CASIA.v4-database. http://www.idealtest.org
20. Tisse, C.l., Martin, L., Torres, L., Robert, M., et al.: Person identification technique using human iris recognition. In: Proceedings of Vision Interface, vol. 294, pp. 294–299. Citeseer (2002)
21. Wildes, R.P.: Iris recognition: an emerging biometric technology. Proc. IEEE **85**(9), 1348–1363 (1997)
22. Zhao, Z., Ajay, K.: An accurate iris segmentation framework under relaxed imaging constraints using total variation model. In: The IEEE International Conference on Computer Vision (ICCV) (2015)

Constrained Sequence Iris Quality Evaluation Based on Causal Relationship Decision Reasoning

Liu Shuai[1,2], Liu Yuanning[1,2], Zhu Xiaodong[1,2(✉)], Zhang Hao[1,2], Huo Guang[4], Wang Guangyu[5], Cui Jingwei[2,3], Li Xinlong[2,3], Wu Zukang[1,2], and Dong Zhiyi[1,2]

[1] College of Computer Science and Technology, Jilin University, Changchun 130012, China
zhuxd@jlu.edu.cn
[2] Key Laboratory of Symbolic Computation and Knowledge Engineering of Ministry of Education, Jilin University, Changchun 130012, Jilin, China
[3] College of Software, Jilin University, Changchun 130012, China
[4] College of Computer Science, Northeast Electric Power University, Jilin 132012, China
[5] College of Aviation Foundation, Air Force Aviation University, Changchun 130022, China

Abstract. In order to select as many available irises as possible for recognition through the same indicators, a quality evaluation algorithm for constrained sequence iris is proposed in this paper. In the case where other indicators are set idealization, a variety of iris quality indicators are set from the perspective of sharpness, iris region nature, and offset degree. According to the causal relationship among quality indicators, the order of indicators evaluation will be adjusted, and then a quality decision reasoning process can be formed. The results of experiments used the JLU iris library of Jilin University indicate that the algorithm can effectively improve the survival rate of available iris in the sequence iris and play an active role in improving iris recognition accuracy.

Keywords: Constrained sequence iris · Quality evaluation · Quality indicator · Causal relationship · Quality decision reasoning process

1 Introduction

In the process of iris recognition, poor quality iris may make iris information not be well extracted, then the effect of recognition will be affected. The sequence iris [1] is a collection of irises taken continuously by the same person over a period of time. Even the constrained state iris of shooting posture is standard, iris performance status is also uncertain. How to select as many available irises as possible from sequence irises through the same indicators is a difficult research point. Iris images under different states of the same person with poor quality are shown in Fig. 1.

The current researches about sequence iris quality evaluation mainly through fixed order by fixed indicators, including: Daugman proposed an algorithm based on high

Z. Sun et al. (Eds.): CCBR 2019, LNCS 11818, pp. 337–345, 2019.
https://doi.org/10.1007/978-3-030-31456-9_38

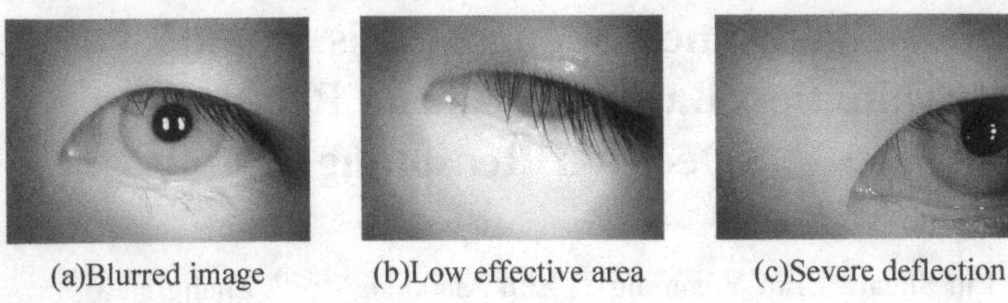

(a)Blurred image (b)Low effective area (c)Severe deflection

Fig. 1. Iris images under different states of the same person with poor quality

frequency energy in the 2-D Fourier spectrum to evaluate iris quality [2]. Gao proposed an iris evaluation algorithm based on secondary evaluation [3]. Pan proposed an iris quality evaluation algorithm based on BP neural network [4].

In the multi-state sequence iris, the fixed order evaluation ignores the causal relationship among each indicator, the available iris survival rate may be decreased. In this paper, a quality evaluation algorithm based on causal relationship decision reasoning is proposed for constrained sequence iris. Qualified iris quality indicators are set from the perspective of sharpness, iris region nature and offset degree on the basis of other indicators have been identified as ideal. According to the causal relationship of quality evaluation indicators, the order of quality evaluation indicators will be adjusted, which evaluate iris quality by means of decision reasoning.

2 Evaluation Indicators and Decision Reasoning

The algorithm preconditions are as follows: sequence iris is the living eye image; other factors are set in ideal states; the iris collection equipment does not change, the collection person posture is standard. The iris can be normalized to the 514 × 64 dimensional region [5]. The iris intercept region of 256 × 32 dimensional in the upper left corner is intercepted. The example of Iris processed images is shown in Fig. 2.

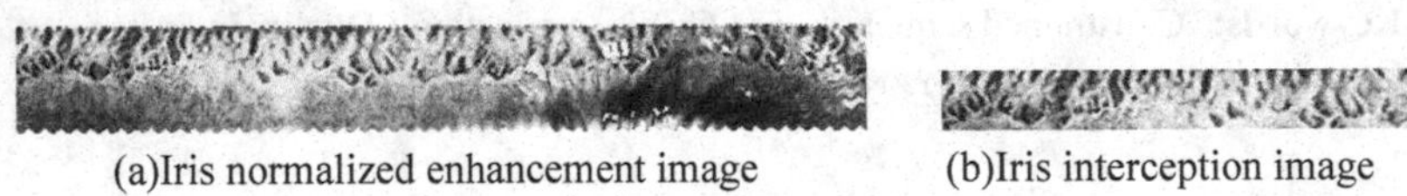

(a)Iris normalized enhancement image (b)Iris interception image

Fig. 2. Iris processed images

2.1 Sharpness

The definition of sharpness is divided into rough sharpness and accuracy sharpness. The rough sharpness is based on the gradient change. Because the clear iris texture is strong and the amount of information carried is large, the neural network is used to accurately discriminate sharpness according to the amount of iris information.

Rough Sharpness: Rough sharpness is used to exclude very blurred images by Tenengrad gradient method [6], classify by threshold.

Accuracy Sharpness: The neural network with four layers is used to calculate accuracy sharpness of iris intercepted image. The number of nodes at each layer is 128, 32, 8 and 1, respectively. The iris intercepted image is divided into 16 × 8 sub-blocks of 16 × 4 dimensions. The Tenengrad gradient value of 128 sub-blocks are used as the input values of neural network. The improved Sigmoid function [7] is used as the excitation function of neural network. The input layer (T_a) are set to four nodes for one group and divided into 32 groups. Connection weights between the first hidden layer input value and the input layer corresponding number group are set to 1, and other connection weights are 0. Input value (F_i) and output value (Y_i) of each node in the first hidden layer are shown in Eq. 1.

$$F_i = \sum_{b=1}^{4} 1 \times T_{4\times i-b} \quad Y_i = \frac{1}{1+e^{a_1-F_i}} \quad i = 1,2,\ldots,32 \tag{1}$$

a_1 represents the first hidden layer adjustment threshold.

First hidden layer (Y_i) is set to four nodes for one group and divided into eight groups. Connection weights between the second hidden layer input value and the first hidden layer corresponding number group are set to 1, and other connection weights are 0. Input value (S_i) and output value (Q_i) of each node in the second hidden layer are shown in Eq. 2.

$$S_i = \sum_{b=1}^{4} 1 \times F_{4\times i-b} \quad Q_i = \frac{1}{1+e^{a_2-S_i}} \quad i = 1,2,\ldots,8 \tag{2}$$

a_2 represents the second hidden layer adjustment threshold.

Second hidden layer (Q_i) is set to four nodes for one group. Connection weights between the output layer input value and the second hidden layer are set to 1, and other connection weights are 0. Input value (Z) and output value (W) of each node in the output layer is shown in Eq. 3.

$$Z = \sum_{b=1}^{8} 1 \times Q_i \quad W = \frac{1}{1+e^{a_3-Z}} \tag{3}$$

a_3 represents the output layer adjustment threshold.

The final output value W is the value of accuracy sharpness result and the value of W is close to 1, iris image is considered to be clear. The neural network structure is shown in Fig. 3. The solid line represents the connection weight is not 0, and the dotted line represents the connection weight is 0.

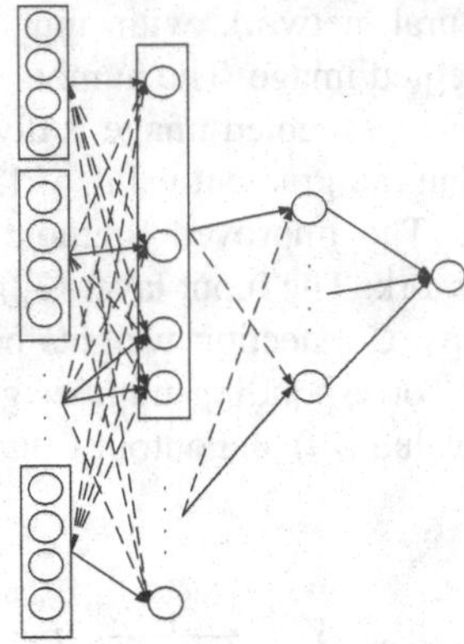

Fig. 3. Neural network structure

2.2 Iris Region Nature

The iris region nature is composed of three parts: iris distribution ratio, ratio of inner circle to outer circle, gray value sub-block variance. The three indicators mainly focus on the problem of eyelid interference, uneven distribution of iris gray scale caused by illumination, and excessively narrow iris area caused by excessive pupil, which can help to find iris with appropriate iris size and sufficient effective information.

Iris Distribution Ratio: The ratio of the points where grayscale value belongs to iris in the 512 × 64 dimensional normalized enhancement image is calculated. A high ratio value indicates that the most part of normalized enhancement image is iris area and eyelashes and eyelids have less interference with iris. The result is below the proportional threshold will considered as unqualified image.

Ratio of Inner Circle to Outer Circle: When shooting an eye image, the pupil may be too expanded or compressed because people have different sensitivity to light, the effect of iris recognition may be affected. Normally, iris width should be one to two times pupil radius [8]. The ratio of iris width to pupil radius is calculated.

Gray Value Sub-block Variance: In the actual iris acquisition process, uneven lighting of eye surface will cause the problem of uneven light distribution and uneven grayscale distribution. In addition, eyelashes also cause a large change of iris region gray value, which may interfere recognition process. For the 256 × 32 dimensional intercepted image, it is divided into 8 × 4 sub-blocks with 32 × 8 dimensional. The gray average of all sub-blocks is calculated to get variance R. The variance calculation is shown in Eq. 4.

$$R = \frac{\sum_{i=1}^{32} (X_i - \frac{1}{32} \times \sum_{i=1}^{32} X_i)^2}{32} \tag{4}$$

2.3 Offset Degree

The offset degree is composed of two parts: strabismus and over boundary. Two indicators are used to exclude situations where the image boundary is exceeded or the iris shape is changed too much because of squint. The partition region standard and schematic diagram of each point in the upper right area are shown in Fig. 4.

Upper left area	Top right area
Lower left area	Lower right area

(a) Partition region standard

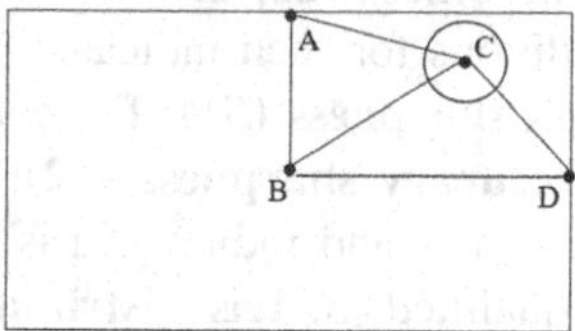

(b)Upper right area diagram

Fig. 4. The partition region standard & upper right area diagram

Strabismus: the strabismus problem refers to the phenomenon in which the eyes look to both sides when shooting. This kind of image is likely to cause system collapse in the subsequent processing process, so it need to be eliminated [9]. Strabismus eye is mostly elliptical in the constrained iris, the ratio A1 of the distance among pupil center and the iris left and right ends and the ratio B1 of the distance among iris center and pupils left and right ends are calculated. The values of A1 and B1 are closer to 1, the eye shape is more similar to circle, which represents there is no strabismus phenomenon.

Over Boundary: During the actual operation, it is find that once the pupil is close to the boundary, there may be cases where the outer circle is beyond image boundary or the outer circle is normalized collapse after being close to the boundary. It is necessary to determine whether the eye is over boundary or the outer circle is close to the boundary. First, eye image is divided into four regions according to the center point B$(M/2, N/2)$ of $M \times N$ dimensions image, which are upper left area, upper right area, lower left area and lower right area.

The upper right area is taken as an example. The center point B(x_b, y_b) is connected to iris inner circle center C(x_c, y_c), the rightmost midpoint D(x_d, y_d) of image center, and the uppermost midpoint A(x_a, y_a) of image center. The cosine of $\angle$BAC and $\angle$BDC are calculated to determine whether over boundary and set two cosine thresholds. When the cosines of two angles are greater than cosine thresholds, respectively, it is determined that the pupil image is close to the center point and no over boundary. The cosine of $\angle$BAC is shown in Eq. 5 and the cosine of $\angle$BDC is shown in Eq. 6.

$$\cos(\angle BAC) = \frac{(x_a - x_b)^2 + (y_a - y_b)^2 + (x_a - x_c)^2 + (y_a - y_c)^2 - (x_b - x_c)^2 - (y_b - y_c)^2}{2 \times \sqrt{(x_a - x_b)^2 + (y_a - y_b)^2} \times \sqrt{(x_a - x_c)^2 + (y_a - y_c)^2}} \quad (5)$$

$$\cos(\angle BDC) = \frac{(x_d - x_b)^2 + (y_d - y_b)^2 + (x_d - x_c)^2 + (y_d - y_c)^2 - (x_b - x_c)^2 - (y_b - y_c)^2}{2 \times \sqrt{(x_d - x_b)^2 + (y_d - y_b)^2} \times \sqrt{(x_d - x_c)^2 + (y_d - y_c)^2}} \quad (6)$$

2.4 Causal Relationship and Decision Reasoning

The reasoning order is adjusted in this paper based on the causality of each indicator. The preconditions for each indicator:

1. **Rough sharpness (*S*1):** Do not require preconditions, directly operate the eye image. 2. **Accuracy sharpness (*S*2):** The iris normalized enhanced and intercepted image; The center and radius of iris inner circle and outer circle; Rough sharpness evaluation qualified. 3. **Iris distribution ratio (*S*3):** The iris normalized enhanced image; Accuracy sharpness evaluation qualified. 4. **Ratio of inner circle to outer circle (*S*4):** The center and radius of iris inner circle and outer circle; Accuracy sharpness evaluation qualified. 5. **Gray value sub-block variance (*S*5):** The iris normalized enhanced and intercepted image; Accuracy sharpness evaluation qualified. 6. **Strabismus ratio (*S*6):** The center and radius of iris inner circle and outer circle; Rough sharpness evaluation qualified. 7. **Two cosine values (Over boundary) (*S*7):** The center of iris inner circle; Rough sharpness evaluation qualified.

According to preconditions of above indicators, the reasoning order of quality evaluation can be obtained.

***N*1:** The center of iris inner circle; ***N*2:** The radius of iris inner circle; ***W*1:** The center of iris outer circle; ***W*2:** The radius of iris outer circle; ***J*1:** The iris normalized enhanced image; ***J*2:** The iris normalized enhanced and intercepted image.

1. $J2 \cap N1 \cap N2 \cap W1 \cap W2 \cap S1 \rightarrow S2$; 2. $J1 \cap S1 \rightarrow S3$;
3. $N1 \cap N2 \cap W1 \cap W2 \cap S2 \rightarrow S4$; 4. $J2 \cap S2 \rightarrow S5$;
5. $N1 \cap N2 \cap W1 \cap W2 \cap S1 \rightarrow S6$; 6. $N1 \cap S1 \rightarrow S7$.

According to these reasoning formulas, the decision reasoning process is:

1. Calculate image rough sharpness; 2. Obtain the center and radius of iris inner circle by Canny edge detection and Hough circle detection; 3. Calculate two cosine values, judge whether to over boundary; 4. Obtain the center and radius of iris outer circle by Canny edge detection and Hough circle detection; 5. Calculate strabismus ratio; 6. Normalized and enhanced iris, get normalized enhanced images and intercepted images; Then calculate accuracy sharpness; 7. Calculate iris distribution ratio, ratio of inner circle to outer circle, and gray value sub-block variance.

The flow chart of reasoning process is shown in Fig. 5.

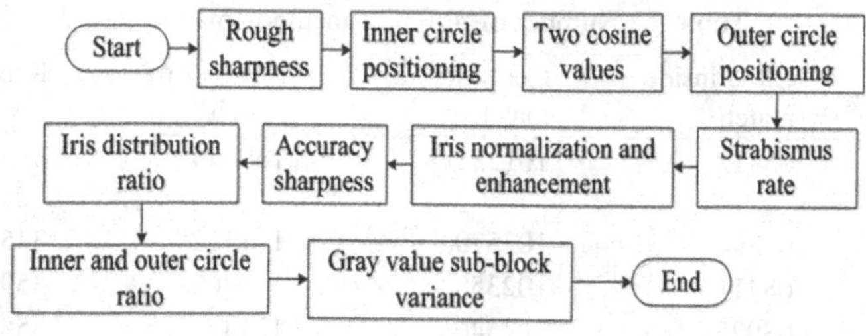

Fig. 5. Iris quality evaluation decision reasoning process

3 Experiment and Analysis

The CPU used in the experiment is dual-core 2.5 GHz, memory is 8 GB, and operating system is Windows. In order to ensure the consistency of iris collection and the quality evaluation is more in line with the prerequisites of this paper, 36,000 iris images sequential intercepted from JLU iris library [10] are taken as experimental sequence iris library. The comparison methods in this paper are the Fourier evaluation method of the literature [2]; the SVM evaluation method of the literature [3]; the neural network evaluation method of the literature [4]. The quality evaluation results are divided into four cases:

1, The method considers qualified, actual really qualified; 2, The method considers qualified, but actual unqualified; 3, The method considers unqualified, actual unqualified; 4, The method considers unqualified, but actual qualified.

Two-dimensional Gabor filtering in literature [11] is used to extract texture information of qualified images determined by four methods. Iris feature is converted to binary code. The iris category is determined by the Hamming distance [12]. The evaluation results of the four methods on the iris set are shown in Table 1.

Table 1. The evaluation results of four methods

Method	Method certified qualified	Unqualified in certified qualified	Method certified unqualified	Qualified in certified unqualified
This paper method	35998	0	9002	2
Daugman [2]	34718	135	10282	1417
Gao [3]	35934	34	9066	100
Pan [4]	35874	52	9126	178

The number of inside match, outside match, and total match for each method to recognizable iris are shown in Table 2. The CRR and EER of each method are shown in Table 3. The ROC curve is shown in Fig. 6.

Table 2. Number of different methods match

Method	Class inside match	Class outside match	Number of match	Recognizable iris
This paper method	68412	101232	169644	35998
Daugman [2]	67542	103570	171112	34583
Gao [3]	68411	102358	170769	35900
Pan [4]	68925	102546	171471	35822

Table 3. The CRR and EER of each method

Method	CRR	EER
This paper method	99.88%	0.28%
Daugman [2]	97.94%	2.26%
Gao [3]	99.47%	0.58%
Pan [4]	98.76%	1.51%

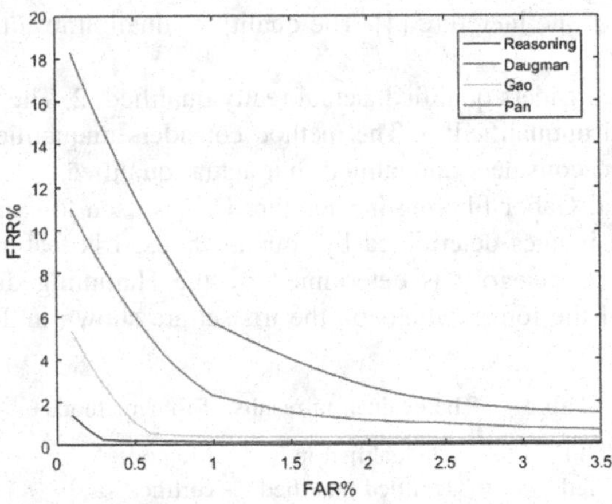

Fig. 6. ROC curve of each method

From Tables 1, 3 and Fig. 6, it can be seen that the qualified images screened by this paper method is the most and the situation of false accept and false reject are less, the effect of recognition is well, CRR is higher, EER is lower, ROC curve is also closer to horizontal and vertical axis. Because the order of indicators in this paper is adjusted according to the causal relationship of each indicator and compared with other multi-step quality assessment methods, the method in this paper has designed more comprehensive indicators based on the actual collection environment, which guarantee high flexibility and good inclusiveness for a large amount of sequence irises, which can improve available iris survival rate. In addition, multiple indicators designed in this paper also can ensure iris feature effective amount of information and recognition accuracy. However, the indicators of comparison methods are single and the processes are fixed. For the multi-state iris, the available iris may easily rejected because of the conflict of indicators.

4 Conclusions

In this paper, a method of constrained sequence iris quality evaluation is proposed. The evaluation indicators are set up in three aspects and the decision reasoning order is adjusted according to indicators causal relationship. Experiment results show that the proposed method can improve the survival rate of available iris while ensuring the accuracy of recognition. However, the type of iris in this paper is the constrained iris, the range of iris state change is still small, how to expand the scope of indicators is the next work step focus.

Acknowledgments. The authors would like to thank the referee's advice and acknowledge the support of the National Natural Science Foundation of China (NSFC) under Grant No. 61471181. Jilin Province Industrial Innovation Special Fund Project under Grant No. 2019C053-2, 2019C053-6. Science and technology project of the Jilin Provincial Education Department under Grant No. JJKH20180448KJ. Thanks to the Jilin Provincial Key Laboratory of Biometrics New Technology for supporting this project.

References

1. Liu, S., Liu, Y., Zhu, X., et al.: Sequence iris quality evaluation algorithm based on morphology and grayscale distribution. J. Jilin Univ. (Sci. Ed.) **56**(5), 1156–1162 (2018)
2. Daugman, J.: Statistical richness of visual phase information update on recognizing persons by iris patterns. Int. J. Comput. Vis. **45**(1), 25–38 (2001)
3. Gao, S., Zhu, X., Liu, Y.: A quality assessment method of iris image based on support vector machine. J. Fiber Bioeng. Inform. **8**(2), 293–300 (2015)
4. Pan, S.: Research on preprocessing algorithm of iris recognition. College of Computer Science and Technology, Jilin University, Changchun, China (2016)
5. Liu, S., Liu, Y.N., Zhu, X.D., et al.: Iris location algorithm based on partitioning search. Comput. Eng. Appl. **54**(18), 212–217 (2018)
6. Wang, Y., Tan, Y., Tian, J.: A new kind of sharpness evaluation function of image. J. Wuhan Univ. Technol. **29**(3), 124–126 (2007)
7. Liu, S., Liu, Y., Zhu, X., et al.: Iris double recognition based on modified evolutionary neural network. J. Electron. Imaging **26**(6), 063023 (2017)
8. Liu, Y., Liu, S., Zhu, X., et al.: Iris secondary recognition based on decision particle swarm optimization and stable texture. J. Jilin Univ. (Eng. Technol. Ed.) **49**(4), 1329–1338 (2019)
9. Liu, S., et al.: Gabor filtering and adaptive optimization neural network for iris double recognition. In: Zhou, J., et al. (eds.) CCBR 2018. LNCS, vol. 10996, pp. 441–449. Springer, Cham (2018). https://doi.org/10.1007/978-3-319-97909-0_47
10. JLU Iris Image Database. http://www.jlucomputer.com/index/irislibrary/irislibrary.html
11. Liu, Y., Liu, S., Zhu, X., et al.: LOG operator and adaptive optimization Gabor filtering for iris recognition. J. Jilin Univ. (Eng. Technol. Ed.) **48**(5), 1606–1613 (2018)
12. Liu, Y.N., Liu, S., Zhu, X.D.: et al. Iris recognition algorithm based on feature weighted fusion. J. Jilin Univ. (Eng. Technol. Ed.) **49**(1), 221–229 (2019)

Iris Image Super Resolution Based on GANs with Adversarial Triplets

Xiao Wang[1,2], Hui Zhang[2(✉)], Jing Liu[2], Lihu Xiao[2], Zhaofeng He[2], Liang Liu[1], and Pengrui Duan[1]

[1] School of Computer Science, Beijing University of Posts and Telecommunications, Beijing, China
{byr_wx,liangliu,dpr}@bupt.edu.cn

[2] Beijing IrisKing Tech Co., Ltd., Beijing, China
{zhanghui,liujing,xiaolh,hezhf}@irisking.com

Abstract. Iris recognition is a safe and reliable biometric technology commonly used at present. However, due to the limitations of equipment and environment in a variety of application scenarios, the obtained iris image may be of low quality and not clear enough. In recent years, there are many attempts to apply neural networks to iris image enhancement. This paper is inspired by SRGAN, and introduces the adversarial idea into the triplet network, finally proposing a novel iris image super-resolution architecture. With triplet loss, the Network can keep reducing intra-class distance and expanding inter-class distance during iris image reconstruction. The experiments on CASIA's several benchmark iris image datasets yield considerable results. This architecture makes a contribution to enhancing iris images for recognition.

Keywords: Biometric technology · Iris image super-resolution · GANs · Triplet network

1 Introduction

At present, biometric technology is applied in a diverse application scenario, which is the core technology of individual identification and verification systems including access control systems, attendance systems, identity systems, and enterprise security systems [5]. Iris texture is stable, and almost unchanged for life. Therefore, iris recognition is one of the most reliable and safe biometrics.

However, due to the limitations of the acquisition device or the long capturing distance, it is still difficult to obtain high-quality iris images directly in the realistic iris recognition scenes such as smart phones and surveillance videos. In these cases, iris image enhancement contributes to iris detection and identification. While the super resolution of iris image has following challenges. The texture of iris is complex and lack of structured information, which makes the reconstruction difficult. The texture of iris is very random and variable.

This work is supported by National Key R&D Program of China[2018YFC0807303].

Z. Sun et al. (Eds.): CCBR 2019, LNCS 11818, pp. 346–353, 2019.
https://doi.org/10.1007/978-3-030-31456-9_39

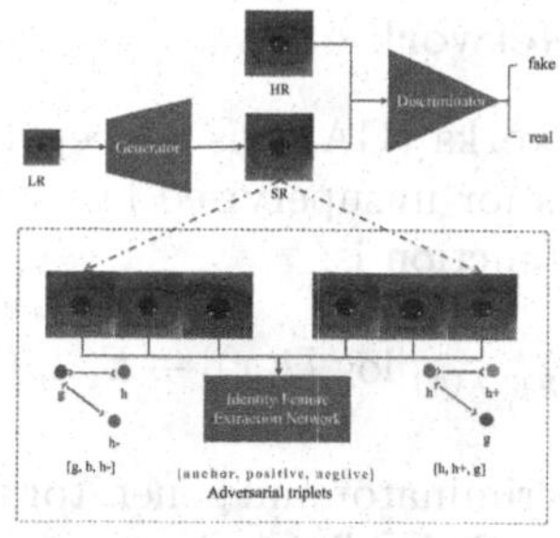

Fig. 1. The proposed architecture. The SR image is set as anchor or negative example of corresponding HR image when training the generator and classifier respectively. Different triplet combinations are developed resulting in adversarial relationship.

In recent years, with the development of machine learning, there are many studies devoted to iris super-resolution topics. These methods [1–3,15] require complex feature engineering, which are dependent on the trained data set and lacks strong generalization ability. Nowadays many end-to-end single image super resolution (SISR) methods based on deep learning have been produced. [6,10,14] all achieved satisfying results on super-resolution tasks. Iris image super-resolution is different from the general super-resolution task [11]. For the super-resolution of iris image, it is not only necessary to restore the image with good perception, but also to extract the feature information that is helpful for recognition [12].

In order to overcome the shortcomings of the previous iris super-resolution method and to generate iris images with better visual effect and more accurate recognition, a novel framework is proposed for iris image super-resolution in this article. The main contributions of this paper are as follows.

(1) A super-resolution (SR) network with GAN [7] is combined with an iris identity feature extraction network, which helps to preserve identity information.
(2) Triplet loss is added to the SR network, which is beneficial for the recognition of generated iris images.
(3) We provide a training method of the identity feature extraction network with adversarial relationship, bringing new ideas to the super-resolution task for images used for identifying.

2 Method

The network structure we proposed is shown in Fig. 1. The network consists of three models, a generator, a discriminator and an identity feature extraction network corresponding to the alignment network in super-FAN [4].

2.1 Super-Resolution Network

Generative Adversarial Networks (GAN) is a deep learning model and one of the most promising methods for unsupervised learning in complex distribution in recent years. The object function is:

$$\min_G \max_D V(D,G) = E_{x \sim p_{data}(x)}[\log D(x)] + E_{z \sim p_z(z)}[\log(1 - D(G(z))]. \quad (1)$$

where D and G represent discriminator and generator respectively. The generator is used to generate samples and the discriminator is used to determine whether the sample is real or generated by the generator.

The proposition in [10] is that super-resolution images generated by a deep network with MSE loss are often too smooth to conform to human visual perception. And more natural pictures can be produced if combining GAN with a super-resolution network. This paper follows the generation network structure of SRGAN and adopts the loss function it contributes. The perceptual loss consists of two parts:

$$L_G = -\mathrm{E}_{I^{LR} \sim p_{data}(I^{LR})} \log D(G(I^{LR})). \quad (2)$$

where $D(G(I^{LR}))$ is the probability that the reconstructed image $G(I^{LR})$ is a natural HR image.

$$L_{\text{content}} = \frac{1}{WH} \sum_{x=1}^{W} \sum_{y=1}^{H} \left(\phi(I^{HR})_{x,y} - \phi(G(I^{HR}))_{x,y} \right)^2. \quad (3)$$

where ϕ represents a feature map of some layer extracted by pre-trained VGG19, and W and H describe the dimensions of the respective feature maps within the VGG network.

2.2 Identity Feature Extraction Network with Adversarial Triplets

Iris Identity Feature Extraction Network. The enhanced iris images generated by deep neural networks have a certain decline in recognition effect, and they also fail to recover identity information on iris texture. To alleviate this, we integrate the iris identity feature extraction network into the super-resolution network to retain the identity features.

Triplet loss [13] is a loss function in deep learning. Its formula is as follows:

$$\sum_{\mathrm{i}}^{N} \left[\|f(x_i^a) - f(x_i^p)\|_2^2 - \|f(x_i^a) - f(x_i^n)\|_2^2 + \alpha \right]. \quad (4)$$

where $f(x_i)$ represents a feature vector, and the superscripts a, p and n represent anchor, positive and negative examples. α is the margin between intra-class distance and inter-class distance.

Triplet network is often used to train less sensitive samples such as faces, irises, etc. Our iris identity feature extraction network also adopt triplet loss to maintain iris identity uniqueness of different categories. The input is a triple consisting of an anchor example, a positive example, and a negative example. The anchor and the positive are from the same category, while the negative is from another. In order to distinguish each category, the model needs to get as long an inter-class distance as possible and as short an intra-class distance as possible.

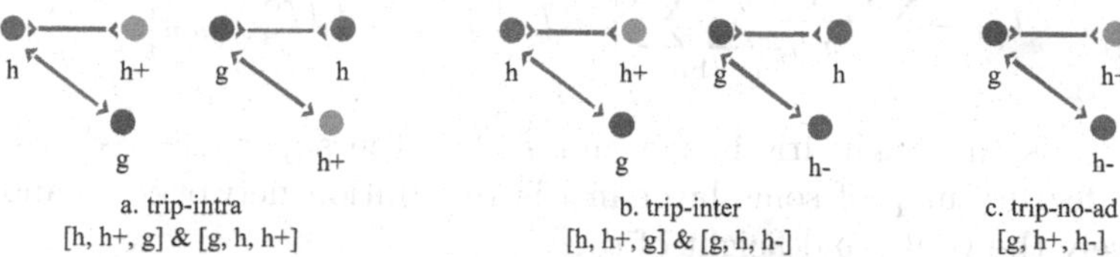

Fig. 2. Adversarial triplets. The structure of the triple is [anchor, positive, negative].

Identity Preserving with Adversarial Triplets. Further, our target is to enable features of the generated iris image extracted to be close to those of the corresponding original HR image, which helps reduce intra-class distance. On the Other hand, we should maintain separation of different categories to ensure that there is a long enough inter-class distance. So we absorbed the experience of adversarial network and maintain a adversarial relationship when extracting features.

Similarly, we alternately train the identity feature extraction network and the generator. The adversarial relationship is obtained by means of the selected triples when training the two models, so as to continuously enhance the capabilities of the identity feature extraction network and generator. Consider the following three ways of organizing, shown in Fig. 2 (g represents the generated image, h represents the high-resolution image corresponding to g, h+ represents the high-resolution image from the same category as g, and h− represents the high-resolution image from a different category.):

(1) Training the identity feature extraction network, the triples are composed of [h, h+, g]; Training the generator, the triples are composed of [g, h, h+]; It reduces the distance between the generated image and the original image, and promotes the identity information of the generated image to approximate that of the original image. We named this method *trip-intra* in this paper.
(2) Training the identity feature extraction network, the triples are composed of [h, h+, g]; Training the generator, the triples are composed of [g, h, h−]; The distance between classes is expanded. We named this method *trip-inter* in this paper.
(3) To validate the effectiveness of adversarial relationship, we will also use the [g, h+, h−] triples to train the identity feature extraction network and generator. We named this method *trip-no-ad* in this paper.

2.3 Overall Loss

An iris super-resolution network structure is proposed by [8] this year, which adds feature extraction network and calculates the feature distance between the original image and the generated image to optimize the recognition effect of the generated image. Its specific loss function called *identity preserving loss* is

$$L_{\text{id}} = \sum_{i} \frac{1}{w_i h_i} \sum_{m=1}^{w_i} \sum_{n=1}^{h_i} \left| \phi_i(I^{HR})_{m,n} - \phi_i(I^{SR})_{m,n} \right|^2. \quad (5)$$

where I^{HR} is the origin iris image and I^{SR} is the super-resolved iris image. ϕ_i is the feature map of some layer in iris recognition network. w_i and h_i are respectively the width and height of ϕ_i.

The loss function of the entire network includes the content loss and the adversarial loss in the SR Network, the triplet loss from the iris identity feature extraction network and the identity preserving loss. thus we get the overall loss function as

$$L = L_{content} + \alpha L_G + \beta L_{triplet} + \gamma L_{id}. \quad (6)$$

where overall loss L is the weighted sum of the above four loss functions. In the process of training, we set different trade-off parameters and balance the weight of each loss.

3 Experiment

3.1 Datasets

We use public iris datasets from CASIA iris database for training and testing. The training dataset consists of CASIA-Iris-Lamp dataset (16212 iris images of 819 classes from 411 subjects captured by a hand-held iris sensor with lamp on and off), CASIA-Iris-Interval dataset (2639 iris images of 395 classes from 249 subjects captured with the self-developed close-up iris camera of CASIA under near infrared light) and part of CASIA-Iris-Thousand dataset (first 18000 iris images of 1800 classes from 900 subjects collected by IKWMB-100 camera of IrisKing). The test dataset uses the last 2000 iris images of 200 classes from 100 subjects in CASIA-Iris-Thousand dataset.

3.2 Parameters

The original images are cropped into 224 × 224 centered around the center of pupil. We downsample the training set images as low resolution images with a downsampling factor of 4 and 8. A large number of experiments have shown that when the tradeoff parameters α, β and γ are set as 1e−3, the network can be stably trained and achieve better results. The network uses ADAM [9] optimizer and initial learning rate is 1e−4. All experiments are conducted with the TensorFlow framework on a GTX Titan Xp GPU.

3.3 Results

As mentioned in Sect. 2.2, we combine training the adversarial SR network and the iris identity feature extraction network, and there are several different ways of organizing triples and training models when introducing adversarial triplets relationship. These methods are named as:

Net-t: Introduced triplet loss for the SR network by adding the identity feature extraction network based on a triplet network. The triple is [g, h+, h−], non-adversarial.

Net-intra: Training the generator, the triple is [h, h+, g]; training the identity feature extraction network, the triple is [g, h, h+]; adversarial.

Net-inter: Training the generator, the triple is [h, h+, g]; training the identity feature extraction network, the triple is [g, h, h−]; adversarial.

Net-id: SR network in Sect. 2.1 with identity preserving loss.

Net-t, Net-intra, and Net-inter are without identity preserving loss. While Net-id is without triplet loss. In addition, we must also reduce the intra-class distance and expand the inter-class distance besides maintaining feature consistency, so we add identity preserving loss to Net-inter as follow.

INet: Integrated network of Net-id and Net-inter.

The above methods aim to explore which method can better generate deep identity information on the iris. Moreover, we also add some methods as comparative experiments.

bicubic: a traditional interpolation method.

SRCNN: a classic deep learning super-resolution network.

SRGAN: a state-of-the-art super-resolution network.

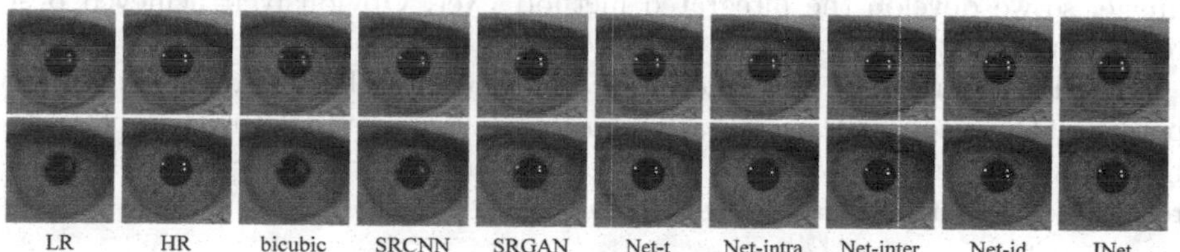

Fig. 3. SR results with 4× and 8×.

The first and second row in Fig. 3 are the LR input and SR results of the above model with upscaling factors of 4 and 8, which are denoted by 4× and 8×, respectively. It can be seen that the methods proposed in this paper have achieved better results than the ordinary super-resolution method. We train a lot of times using different loss weights and adjusting various parameters, and find that images generated by network without adversarial triplets are easy to produce grid-like textures, while images generated by Net-intra and Net-inter are more natural.

Figure 4 reports the ROC curves in a pre-trained triplet classifier comparison scheme. Origin represents original HR iris images' performance on the classifier.

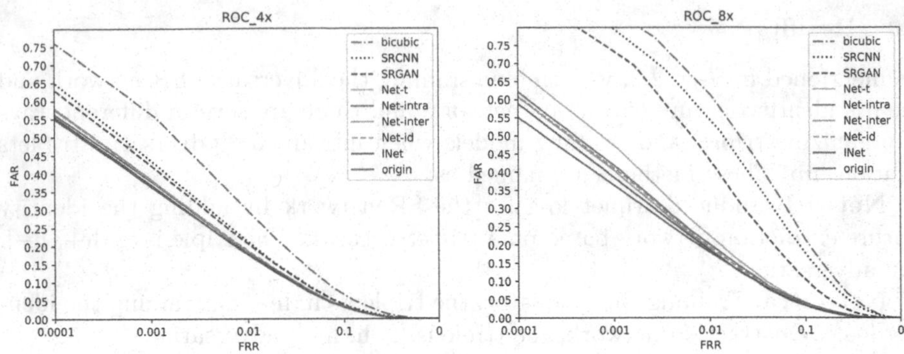

Fig. 4. ROC curves in 4× and 8× situations.

In the 4× super-resolution, Net-id, Net-inter and Net-t have achieved similar results, while Net-intra are slightly better, indicating that the iris features used to distinguish the different categories are not lost much when 4× upscaling. It shows that Net-intra has a powerful ability to approximate original features. A good recognition effect can be obtained by approximating the features of the generated image and the original image. In the case of 8× super-resolution, Net-intra does not perform as well as 4× upscaling. It can be inferred that Net-intra may alienate the inter-class distance, although this method narrows the intra-class distance. Net-inter keeps the distance between the classes while approaching the intra-class features and it performs very well. And through experiments we find that Net-id can stably restore the identity information close to the original image, so we develop the integrated method INet. Obviously it achieved best results in both cases.

The PSNR are listed in Table 1. Our SR network is based on SRGAN using perceptual loss, so PSNR is not particularly high. Compared with other methods, INet has a little improvement. And we can see that the effect of vision and recognition is not necessarily positively correlated with PSNR.

Table 1. PSNR

	scale	bicubic	SRCNN	SRGAN	Net-t	Net-intra	Net-inter	Net-id	INet
PSNR	4×	32.29	32.77	30.97	30.77	33.30	32.75	31.61	33.51
	8×	28.63	28.80	24.42	26.67	29.65	29.41	28.60	29.79

4 Conclusions

In this paper, we propose a novel method with adversarial triplets to enhance iris images for recognition. Through extensive experiments, the images generated methods with adversarial triplets have better visual effect and INet (Net-inter with identity preserving loss) achieves a better recovery effect. We can conclude that there are two points to note when performing iris image super-resolution. One is feature level similarity with origin images, and the other is to reduce the intra-class distance and expand the inter-class distance. In this way, iris images enhanced by INet restore good visual details and achieve remarkable improvement on iris recognition performance.

References

1. Aljadaany, R., Luu, K., Venugopalan, S., Savvides, M.: IRIS super-resolution via nonparametric over-complete dictionary learning. In: 2015 IEEE International Conference on Image Processing (ICIP), pp. 3856–3860. IEEE (2015)
2. Alonso-Fernandez, F., Farrugia, R.A., Bigun, J.: Eigen-patch iris super-resolution for iris recognition improvement. In: 2015 23rd European Signal Processing Conference (EUSIPCO), pp. 76–80. IEEE (2015)
3. Alonso-Fernandez, F., Farrugia, R.A., Bigun, J.: Iris super-resolution using iterative neighbor embedding. In: Proceedings of the IEEE Conference on Computer Vision and Pattern Recognition Workshops, pp. 153–161 (2017)
4. Bulat, A., Tzimiropoulos, G.: Super-FAN: integrated facial landmark localization and super-resolution of real-world low resolution faces in arbitrary poses with GANs. In: Proceedings of the IEEE Conference on Computer Vision and Pattern Recognition, pp. 109–117 (2018)
5. Chowhan, S., Shinde, G.: Iris biometrics recognition application in security management. In: 2008 Congress on Image and Signal Processing, vol. 1, pp. 661–665. IEEE (2008)
6. Dong, C., Loy, C.C., He, K., Tang, X.: Image super-resolution using deep convolutional networks. IEEE Trans. Pattern Anal. Mach. Intell. **38**(2), 295–307 (2015)
7. Goodfellow, I., et al.: Generative adversarial nets. In: Advances in Neural Information Processing Systems, pp. 2672–2680 (2014)
8. Guo, Y., Wang, Q., Huang, H., Zheng, X., He, Z.: Adversarial iris super resolution. In: the 12th IAPR International Conference on Biometrics (2019)
9. Kingma, D.P., Ba, J.: Adam: a method for stochastic optimization. arXiv preprint arXiv:1412.6980 (2014)
10. Ledig, C., et al.: Photo-realistic single image super-resolution using a generative adversarial network. In: Proceedings of the IEEE Conference on Computer Vision and Pattern Recognition, pp. 4681–4690 (2017)
11. Nguyen, K., Fookes, C., Sridharan, S., Tistarelli, M., Nixon, M.: Super-resolution for biometrics: a comprehensive survey. Pattern Recogn. **78**, 23–42 (2018)
12. Ribeiro, E., Uhl, A., Alonso-Fernandez, F.: Iris super-resolution using CNNs: is photo-realism important to iris recognition? IET Biom. **8**(1), 69–78 (2019)
13. Schroff, F., Kalenichenko, D., Philbin, J.: FaceNet: a unified embedding for face recognition and clustering. In: Proceedings of the IEEE Conference on Computer Vision and Pattern Recognition, pp. 815–823 (2015)
14. Tong, T., Li, G., Liu, X., Gao, Q.: Image super-resolution using dense skip connections. In: Proceedings of the IEEE International Conference on Computer Vision, pp. 4799–4807 (2017)
15. Zhang, Q., Li, H., He, Z., Sun, Z.: Image super-resolution for mobile iris recognition. In: You, Z., et al. (eds.) CCBR 2016. LNCS, vol. 9967, pp. 399–406. Springer, Cham (2016). https://doi.org/10.1007/978-3-319-46654-5_44

SDItg-Diff: Noisy Iris Localization Based on Statistical Denoising

Xiangde Zhang[1], Runan Zhou[1], Xiangyue Meng[1], and Qi Wang[1,2(✉)]

[1] Department of Mathematics, College of Sciences, Northeastern University, Heping District, Shenyang, Liaoning, People's Republic of China
{zhangxiangde,wangqimath}@mail.neu.edu.cn, 997554138@qq.com, 1550719374@qq.com

[2] Key Laboratory of Data Analytics and Optimization for Smart Industry (Northeastern University), Ministry of Education, Heping District, Shenyang, Liaoning, People's Republic of China

Abstract. It is quite challenging to localize noisy iris. In order to improve the stability and accuracy of noisy iris localization, this paper presents a statistical denoising integral difference operator (SDItg-Diff). Firstly, we use the Itg-Diff operator to produce several candidate boundaries with large Itg-Diff values. Then, the Pauta criterion is used to exclude the severe outlier pixels on each candidate boundary and the SDItg-Diff indicator is calculated after noise removal. The boundary with the max SDItg-Diff indicator is taken as the final localization boundary. The experimental result shows that, compared with the Itg-Diff operator, the proposed method can achieve more stable localization on noisy iris images.

Keywords: Iris localization · Itg-Diff · Pauta criterion · Statistical denoising · SDItg-Diff

1 Introduction

A typical iris recognition system [1,2] contains several stages: iris localization [3], iris normalization [4], feature extraction [5] and template matching [6]. The iris localization is to determine the inner and outer boundaries of iris. The traditional iris localization algorithm is easily affected by noise. Wojciech et al. [7] point out that existing localization methods easily produce wrong results on noisy iris images with spots. Figure 1 shows a noisy iris image and its localization results by classical Itg-Diff and proposed SDItg-Diff.

The iris localization methods can be classified according to the boundary models are determined and flexible. The circular [8] and elliptical [9] boundary are determined models, while active contour [10,11] and spline curve [12] are more flexible. In localizing noisy iris images, the flexible models are easily affected by different kinds of noise leading to mis-localization. In real applications, the

Z. Sun et al. (Eds.): CCBR 2019, LNCS 11818, pp. 354–363, 2019.
https://doi.org/10.1007/978-3-030-31456-9_40

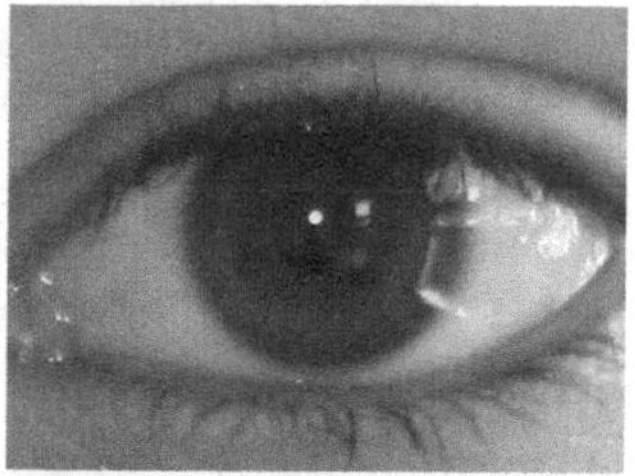

(a) An illustration of noisy iris images (In this image, iris is covered by a facula, which easily leads to mis-localization)

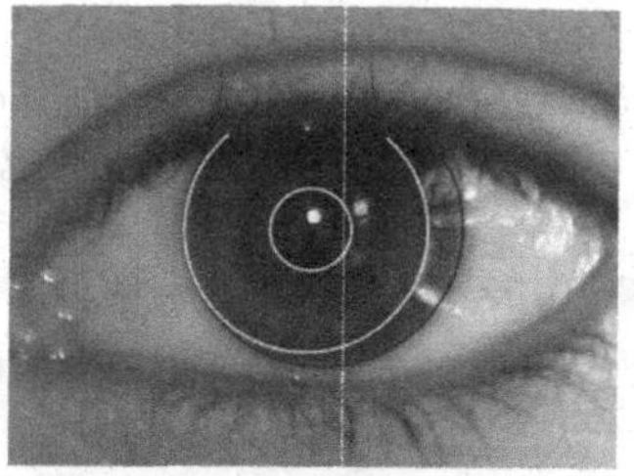

(b) The segmentations results by Itg-Diff and proposed SDItg-Diff (The yellow circle is the localization result by classical Itg-Diff and the blue circle is generated by the proposed SDItg-Diff)

Fig. 1. Example of noisy iris image and its localizations by Itg-Diff and proposed SDItg-Diff

determined boundary model is more robust, but it still easily produces wrong segmentations because of noises.

In order to segment the noisy iris image stably, the circular model is adopted for inner and outer boundaries of iris. Further more, Statistical Denoising Integral Differential (SDItg-Diff) is proposed for a robust iris localization. Firstly, the Integral Differential operator (Itg-Diff) is adopted to produce several candidate boundaries with top K Itg-Diff indicators. Then, the Pauta criterion is used to exclude the severe outlier pixels on each candidate boundary and the SDItg-Diff indicator is calculated after denoising. The boundary with the largest SDItg-Diff indicator is taken as the final localization result. The experiment shows that, compared with the Itg-Diff operator, the proposed method can achieve more stable localization for noisy iris images.

2 Statistical Denoising via Pauta Criteria

Based on the analysis of ideal iris image, the distribution of outer boundary [13] is modeled by normal distribution. In this paper, Pauta criterion is adopted [14] to exclude outlier pixels of boundary.

2.1 Intensity Distribution of Iris's Outer Boundary

The texture of iris is mainly located near the inner boundary of an iris. The variation of intensity is smaller near the outer boundary. In this paper, the intensity distribution of the outer boundary is modeled by normal distribution for an ideal iris, which is $N(\mu, \sigma^2)$, where μ and σ are the mean and variance of intensities of a given boundary.

2.2 Noise Pixel Detection Based on Pauta Criterion

When the iris boundary is affected by noise, it is equivalent to adding outliers to the normal distribution samples. To separate outliers, Pauta criterion is adopted in this paper.

Suppose that $\{(x_i, y_i) \mid i = 1, 2, \cdots, T\}$ is a set of vectors, where T is the total count of vectors. $x_i \sim N(\mu, \sigma^2)$. Some x_i are affected by noise. y_i is the outlier indicator for x_i. For any given i, $y_i = 0$ if x_i is an outlier, otherwise, $y_i = 1$.

According to Pauta criterion,

$$y_i = \begin{cases} 0 \mid X_i - \mu \mid \geq \lambda\sigma \\ 1 \ otherwise \end{cases} \tag{1}$$

where μ and σ are the mean and variance of samples. Generally, $\lambda = 3$. While in this paper, $\lambda = 2$.

Figure 2 illustrates the outlier detection process of outer boundary. Figure 2(a) shows the estimation of normal distribution of boundary intensities and the normal distribution when outlier are excluded by Pauta criterion. Figure 2(c) presents the histogram obtained when $\lambda = 2$. In this figure, the blue curve is normal distribution $N(\mu_1, \sigma_1^2)$ of the original boundary. The red and black dashed line are $y = \mu_1 \pm 2\sigma_1$. Figure 2(e) illustrates the location of outlier pixels in the iris image. Figure 2(c) shows that the detected outlier pixels are near the eyelashes and upper eyelids.

Figure 2(b), 2(d) and 2(f) illustrate the second iteration and outliers excluded by Pauta criterion.

3 SDItg-Diff

SDItg-Diff is proposed by combining Pauta criterion with Itg-Diff operator.

3.1 Itg-Diff

The Itg-Diff operator [8] is widely used in iris localization. It calculates the intensity difference of different circular boundaries and takes the maximum from all the Itg-Diff indicators as the final localization. The formula is given as follows:

$$max_{(a,b,r)} \left| G_\sigma(r) * \frac{\partial}{\partial r} \oint_{a,b,r} \frac{I(x,y)}{2\pi r} ds \right| \tag{2}$$

where, $G_\sigma(r)$ is a smooth function. $*$ is a convolution operation. I is an image. (a, b) is the circular center. r is the radius.

Let $f_{a,b}$ be the polar transformation of iris image with center (a, b) [8]. $N_{a,b}$ is the polar transformation of noise template with center (a, b). $N_{a,b}(r, \theta) = 0$ if pixel $f_{a,b}(r, \theta)$ is noise. $N_{a,b}(r, \theta) = 1$ if pixel $f_{a,b}(r, \theta)$ is not noise. Let $g_{a,b}$ be the Sobel gradient of $f_{a,b}$ along r.

Vector $p = (a, b, r)$ is the parameter of a circle, where (a, b) is the central coordinate and r is the radius. Let $f_p(\theta) = f_{a,b}(r, \theta)$, $g_p(\theta) = g_{a,b}(r, \theta)$ and $N_p(\theta) = N_{a,b}(r, \theta)$. The set of effective boundary pixels is $\Gamma_p = \{\theta | N_p(\theta) = 1, \theta \in \{2\pi j/M, j = 0, 1, \cdots, M-1\}\}$, where M is the total count of divisions.

$$Gr_p = Gr(a, b, r) = \frac{\sum_{\theta \in \Gamma_p} [|g_p(\theta)| \times (sign(g_p(\theta)) + 1)]}{\sum_{\theta \in \Gamma_p} (sign(g_p(\theta)) + 1)} \tag{3}$$

where $sign(\cdot)$ is a sign function.

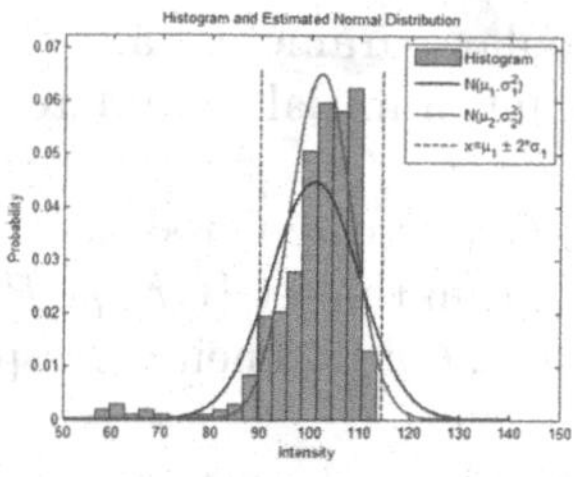

(a) Histogram of outer boundary and its normal distribution estimation before and after iteration

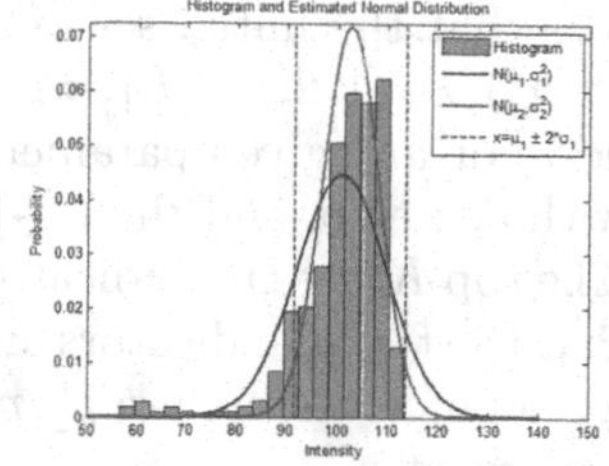

(b) Histogram of outer boundary and its normal distribution estimation before and after the second iteration

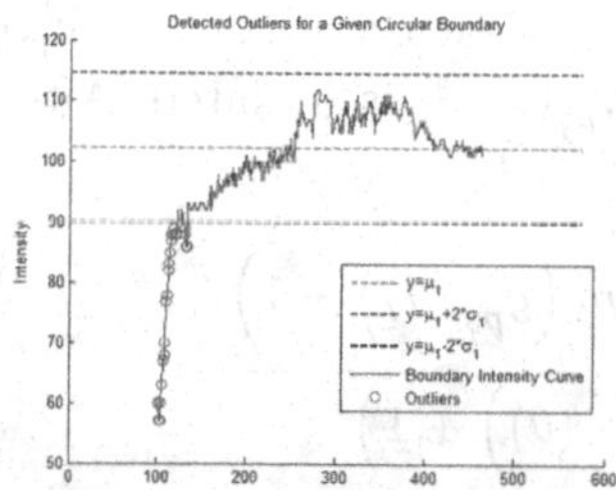

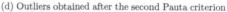

(c) Outliers obtained after Pauta criterion

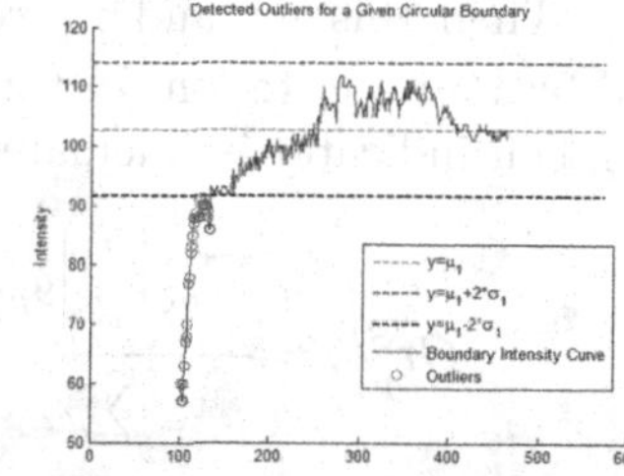

(d) Outliers obtained after the second Pauta criterion

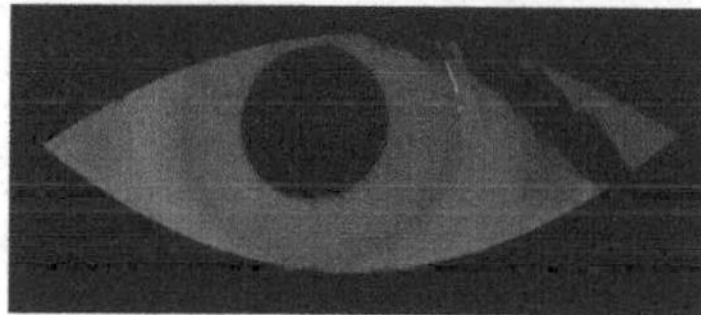

(e) Excluded outliers of iris outer boundary after iteration

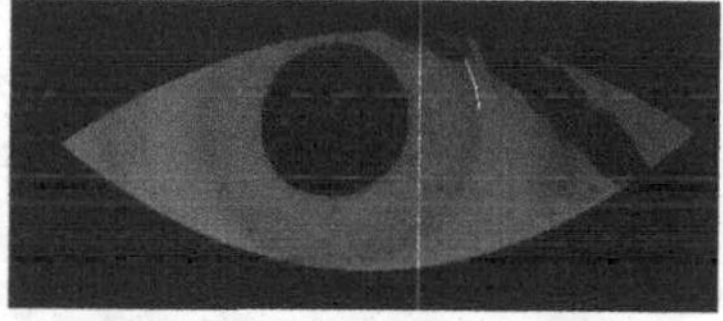

(f) Excluded outliers of iris outer boundary after the second iteration

Fig. 2. Illustration of outlier detection process of outer boundary based on Pauta criterion (Color figure online)

According to Eq. (3), the Itg-Diff indicator of any given vector $p = (a, b, r)$ can be calculated. The final circular parameter can be obtained by maximizing Itg-Diff indicators:

$$p_{Itg-Diff} = \arg\max_{p} \{Gr_p | p = (a, b, r)\} \tag{4}$$

3.2 SDItg-Diff

Itg-Diff is still easily affected by outlier pixels, leading to mis-localization. The proposed SDItg-Diff chooses iris boundaries with the top K Itg-Diff indicators. Then the outliers of these selected boundaries are excluded by Pauta criterion. Finally, the SDItg-Diff indicators of these selected boundaries are calculated and the circle with max SDItg-Diff indicator is selected as the final iris localization.

Suppose that the initial set of candidate circular parameters are $P = \{p_i \mid p_i = (a_i, b_i, r_i), i = 1, 2, \ldots, L\}$, where L is the count of initial candidate circular boundaries. For any given parameter $p = (a, b, r) \in P$, f_p is the polar transformation with center p, and the Itg-Diff indicator Gr_p is calculated according to Eq. (3). The top K Itg-Diff indicators are selected from the set $\{Gr_p|p{\in}P\}$. Let's assume that the top K indicators are $Gr_{p'_1}, Gr_{p'_2}, \cdots, Gr_{p'_K}$. Their corresponding circular parameter vectors are $p'_1, p'_2, \cdots, p'_K$.

For any given $p'_j \in \{p'_1, p'_2, \cdots, p'_K\}$, $f_{p'_j}$ is the polar transformation of iris image corresponding to parameter p'_j. $\Gamma_{p'_j} = \{\theta|\theta{\in}\{2\pi j/M, j = 0, 1, \cdots, M-1\}$ and $N_{p'_j}(r'_j, \theta) = 1\}$. So the pixel set corresponding to parameter p'_j is $\{f_{p'_j}(\theta) \mid \theta \in \Gamma_{p'_j}\}$. Then this set and its corresponding noise template $N_{p'_j}(r'_j, \theta)$ are processed by Pauta criterion. In this process, $N_{p'_j}(r'_j, \theta)$ is updated. After that, the SDItg-Diff indicator is calculated as follows:

$$Gr^{SD}_{p'_j} = \frac{\sum_{\theta\in\Gamma_{p'_j}} \left|g_{p'_j}(\theta)\right| \times \left(sign\left(g_{p'_j}(\theta)\right) + 1\right)}{\sum_{\theta\in\Gamma_{p'_j}} \left(sign\left(g_{p'_j}(\theta)\right) + 1\right)} \tag{5}$$

Finally, the parameter vector with the largest SDItg-Diff indicator is taken as the final localization:

$$p_{SDItg-Diff} = \arg\max_{p'} \left\{Gr^{SD}_{p'_1}, Gr^{SD}_{p'_2}, \cdots, Gr^{SD}_{p'_K}\right\} \tag{6}$$

4 Experiment

4.1 Experimental Database

NICE: II is a visible-light noise iris database [15] established by University of Beira Interior, which is suitable for testing the robustness of localization algorithm. The proposed method is tested on this database.

4.2 Experimental Process

In the experiment, the R-layer of a given image of NICE: II is selected for localization. The preprocess of iris image [16] is as follows: Firstly, the iris image is smoothed by 3 × 3 median filter. Secondly, two-dimensional circular Gabor filter is used to detect the spot area. Linear interpolation method is used to fill the spot area. Then Adaboost algorithm is used to detect the iris region. After that, the parabolic boundaries of the upper and lower eyelids are determined.

Figure 3 shows a typical result of image preprocessing. The black region is the noise of the image. The pupil and outer boundary of iris are localized by Itg-Diff and the proposed SDItg-Diff, separately.

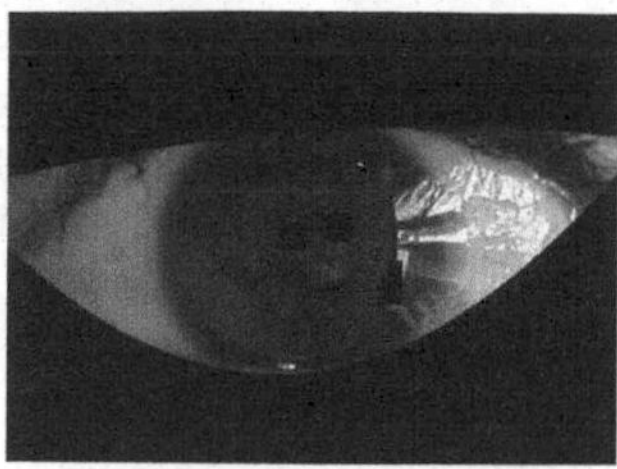

Fig. 3. Noisy iris image after excluding preliminary noise

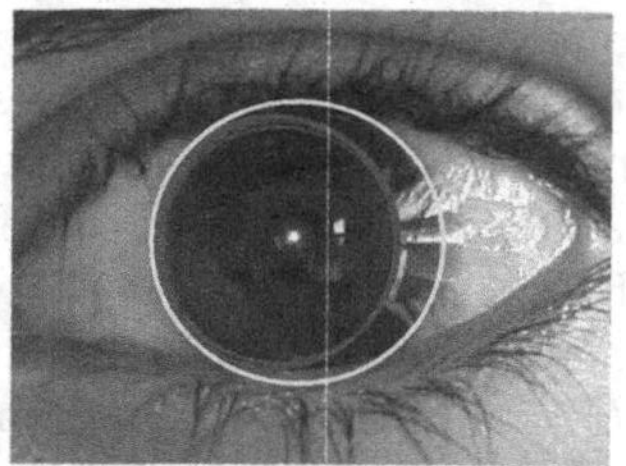

Fig. 4. The results of Itg-Diff and proposed SDItg-Diff (The red thick circle is obtained by Itg-Diff, which is labeled as $Idx = 1$ in Table 1. The yellow circular boundary is got by proposed SDItg-Diff, which is labeled as $Idx = 9$ in Table 1.) (Color figure online)

4.3 Experimental Result and Analysis

Table 1 presents the circles with top K Itg-Diff indicators in localizing iris image of Fig. 3, ($K = 15$) (The result is presented in Fig. 4). The first column is the order of boundaries. The columns 2–4 are the parameters of circles (a, b, r). The columns 5–6 present Itg-Diff and SDItg-Diff indicators.

Table 1. Circular boundaries with top K Itg-Diff indicators ($K = 15$)

Idx	a	b	r	Itg-Diff	SDItg-Diff
1	**156**	**178**	**79**	**60.77193**	**35.00635**
2	153	178	81	58.64343	35.07882
3	154	179	80	58.14349	31.82352
4	153	176	81	57.0877	30.60941
5	154	178	80	56.93172	35.76294
6	152	177	81	56.45655	34.4124
7	153	177	81	55.52018	32.08134
8	152	178	81	55.51509	35.3985
9	**155**	**193**	**95**	**54.82636**	**47.17127**
10	156	179	78	54.6633	30.0527
11	154	193	95	54.29974	42.04334
12	152	176	81	54.19631	32.00599
13	155	178	79	54.15938	33.6774
14	161	193	96	54.13157	41.56077
15	155	194	95	54.11543	45.33087

Figure 4 presents the circles obtained in Table 1. The red thick circle is obtained by Itg-Diff, which corresponds to $Idx = 1$ in Table 1. The yellow circular boundary is got by proposed SDItg-Diff, which is labeled as $Idx = 9$ in Table 1. Obviously, the localization result of SDItg-Diff is more reasonable than Itg-Diff.

Figure 5 shows the calculation processes of the two boundaries of $Idx = 1$ and $Idx = 9$. Figure 5(a) shows the localized boundary $Idx = 1$ by Itg-Diff. The gradient of the spot's boundary is large. When the large gradient is accumulated to Itg-Diff indicator, it is easily leads to mis-localization. Figure 5(c) presents the

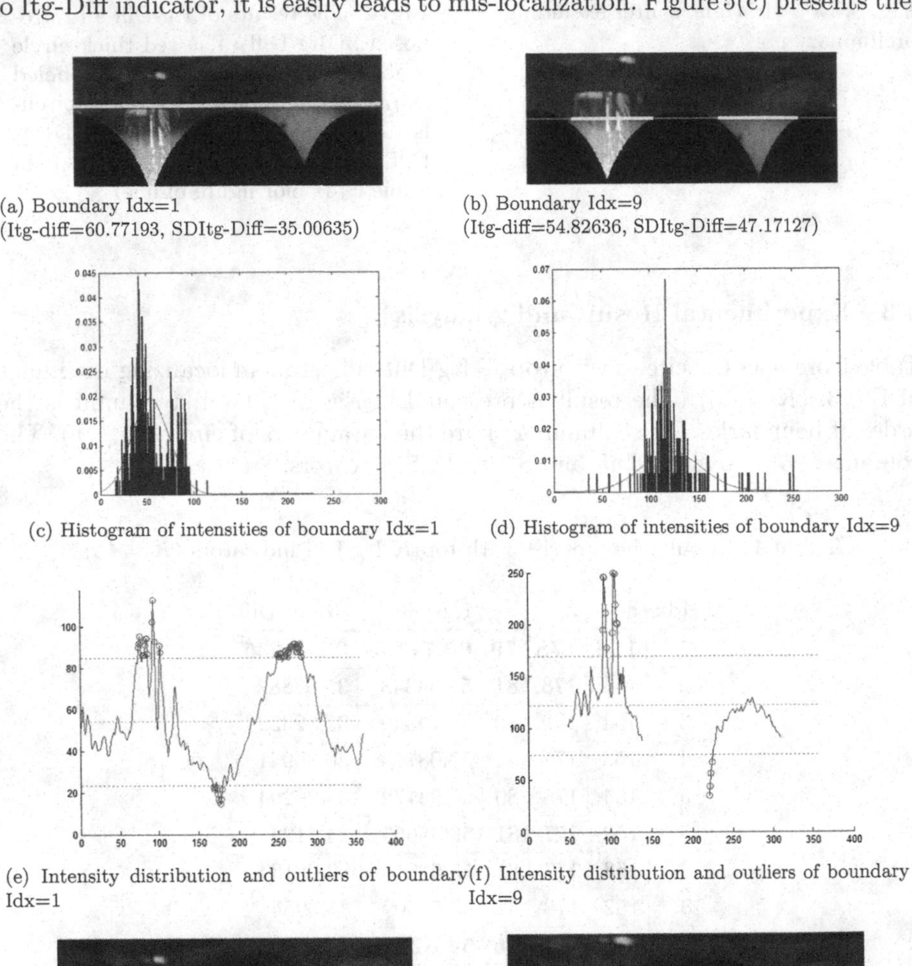

(a) Boundary Idx=1 (Itg-diff=60.77193, SDItg-Diff=35.00635)

(b) Boundary Idx=9 (Itg-diff=54.82636, SDItg-Diff=47.17127)

(c) Histogram of intensities of boundary Idx=1

(d) Histogram of intensities of boundary Idx=9

(e) Intensity distribution and outliers of boundary Idx=1

(f) Intensity distribution and outliers of boundary Idx=9

(g) Outliers of boundary Idx=1 (Red pixels)

(h) Outliers of boundary Idx=9 (Red pixels)

Fig. 5. Illustration of noise detection for two boundaries Idx = 1 and Idx = 9 (Color figure online)

intensity distribution of boundary pixels and its normal estimation. Figure 5(e) displays the intensity curve of the entire boundary with $\lambda = 2$ and the detected outliers. The green dotted line is $y = \mu$, where μ is the mean intensity of boundary. The red dotted line is $y = \mu \pm 2\sigma$. The hollow red dots on the blue curve show the outliers of boundary. Figure 5(g) shows the detected outliers (red pixels) on the normalized iris image. As can be seen, the pixels on the spot are detected and excluded.

Figure 5(b), (d), (f) and (h) illustrate the processing process on boundary $Idx = 9$.

According to Table 1 and Fig. 5, it can be found that the pixels with larger or smaller intensities are excluded. For the non-iris boundaries, the noise pixels usually have larger gradients. So excluding outliers can lower down the Itg-Diff indicator (as shown in Fig. 5(a), (c), (e) and (g)). While for the real iris boundary, the gradient of outlier pixels is not very large generally. So the outlier detection process has a greater impact on the non-iris boundary and a smaller impact on the iris boundary (as shown in Fig. 5(b), (d), (f) and (h)). The proposed SDItg-Diff can eliminate the serious outliers and improve the accuracy of localization.

Table 2 shows the performance of different methods on NICE: II database. Compared with Itg-Diff and RTV [17], SDItg-Diff achieves a more robust and accurate iris localization. Figure 6 shows some localization results of noisy iris images of NICE: II.

Table 2. Performance of different methods

Algorithms	mIoU (%)
Itg-Diff [8]	54.6
RTV [17]	53.0
Proposed SDItg-Diff	88.2

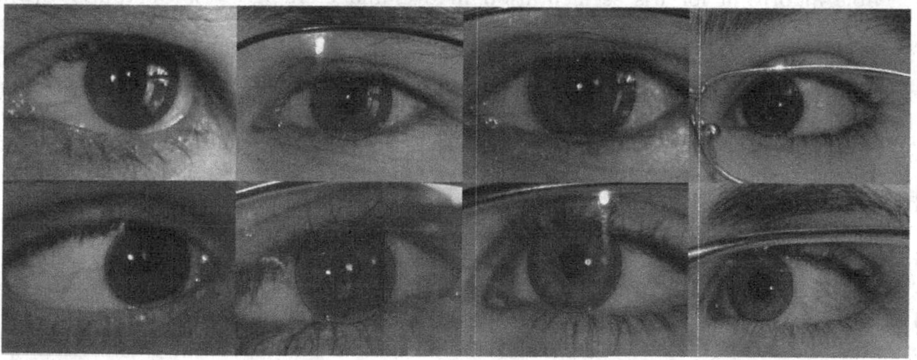

Fig. 6. Localization results of NICE: II Database

5 Conclusion

The main contributions of this paper are as follows: (1) The intensity distribution of boundary pixels of ideal iris image is modeled by normal distribution; (2) The Pauta criterion is used to eliminate serious noisy pixels on the boundary. The experiment on NICE: II indicates that the proposed method is more robust for iris localization.

Acknowledgement. This work is supported by National Natural Science Funds of China, No. 11371081 and No. 61703088, the Doctoral Scientific Research Foundation of Liaoning Province, No.20170520326 and "the Fundamental Research Funds for the Central Universities", N160503003.

References

1. Daugman, J.G.: High confidence visual recognition of persons by a test of statistical independence. IEEE Trans. Pattern Anal. Mach. Intell. **15**(11), 1148–1161 (2002)
2. Bowyer, K.W.: The results of the nice. II iris biometrics competition. Pattern Recogn. Lett. **33**(8), 965–969 (2012)
3. Cui, J., Wang, Y., Li, M., Sun, Z.: A fast and robust iris localization method based on texture segmentation. In: Proceedings of SPIE - The International Society for Optical Engineering, vol. 5404, pp. 401–408 (2004)
4. Proenca, H., Alexandre, L.A.: Iris recognition: an analysis of the aliasing problem in the iris normalization stage. In: International Conference on Computational Intelligence and Security (2009)
5. Bae, K., Noh, S., Kim, J.: Iris feature extraction using independent component analysis. In: Kittler, J., Nixon, M.S. (eds.) AVBPA 2003. LNCS, vol. 2688, pp. 838–844. Springer, Heidelberg (2003). https://doi.org/10.1007/3-540-44887-X_97
6. Rathgeb, C., Uhl, A.: Bit reliability-driven template matching in iris recognition. In: Fourth Pacific-rim Symposium on Image and Video Technology (2010)
7. Sankowski, W., Grabowski, K., Napieralska, M., Zubert, M., Napieralski, A.: Reliable algorithm for iris segmentation in eye image. Image Vis. Comput. **28**(2), 231–237 (2010)
8. Daugman, J.: High confidence visual recognition of persons by a test of statistical independence. IEEE Trans. Pattern Anal. Mach. Intell. **15**, 1148–1161 (1993)
9. Ryan, W.J., Woodard, D.L., Duchowski, A.T., Birchfield, S.T.: Adapting starburst for elliptical iris segmentation. In: 2008 IEEE Second International Conference on Biometrics: Theory, Applications and Systems, pp. 1–7, September 2008
10. McInerney, T.: Sketchsnakes: Sketch-line initialized snakes for efficient interactive medical image segmentation. Comput. Med. Imaging Graph. **32**(5), 331–352 (2008)
11. Daugman, J.: New methods in iris recognition. IEEE Trans. Syst. Man Cybern. Part B (Cybern.) **37**(5), 1167–1175 (2007)
12. He, Z., Tan, T., Sun, Z., Qiu, X.: Toward accurate and fast iris segmentation for iris biometrics. IEEE Trans. Pattern Anal. Mach. Intell. **31**(9), 1670–1684 (2009)
13. Chhikara, R.S.: The inverse gaussian distribution: theory, methodology, and applications. Appl. Stat. **39**(2), 259 (1988)
14. Shen, C., Bao, X., Tan, J., Liu, S., Liu, Z.: Two noise-robust axial scanning multi-image phase retrieval algorithms based on pauta criterion and smoothness constraint. Opt. Express **25**(14), 16235 (2017)

15. Proenca, H., Alexandre, L.A.: The nice. I: Noisy iris challenge evaluation - Part I. In: IEEE International Conference on Biometrics: Theory (2007)
16. Dong, W., Sun, Z., Tan, T.: Iris matching based on personalized weight map. IEEE Trans. Pattern Anal. Mach. Intell. **33**(9), 1744–1757 (2011)
17. Zhao, Z., Kumar, A.: An accurate iris segmentation framework under relaxed imaging constraints using total variation model. In: 2015 IEEE International Conference on Computer Vision (ICCV), pp. 3828–3836, December 2015

End to End Robust Recognition Method for Iris Using a Dense Deep Convolutional Neural Network

Ying Chen, Zhuang Zeng(✉), and Fei Hu

Nanchang Hangkong University, Nanchang 330063, JiangXi, China
c_y2008@163.com, z_z2019@163.com, 13093628315@163.com

Abstract. Many algorithms of iris recognition have been proposed in academic field. Due to the iris image is obscured by illumination, blur and occlusion, iris recognition has not been widely adapted in life, the robustness of iris recognition algorithm is required to be higher. Hence, this paper proposes an end to end dense deep convolutional neural network (DDNet) for the iris recognition. DDNet used a deeper network structure and used the segmented images as input images without prior preprocessing or other conventional image processing techniques. The performance of the DDNet is tested on CASIA-Iris-V3 and IITD, from 138 and 224 different subjects respectively. Experiment results showed that DDNet is adapted and robust in different parameters, and its performance over most existing algorithms.

Keywords: Deep convolutional neural network · End to end · Iris recognition

1 Introduction

Biometric technology has become increasingly integrated into our daily life, from unlocking the smartphone to access control system. Iris recognition has proven to be an innovative and reliable biometric technology which is widely used in safety, identification and authentication systems. There are generally two factors that lower the recognition performance in iris recognition systems: non-ideal iris image, accuracy and robustness of the algorithm. In ideal iris image, iris area is unaffected by the eyelids and eyelashes, and the image is under ideal lighting conditions. In fact, iris image contains blurs, off-angles and obstructions, which will greatly affect the accuracy of iris recognition system. A good recognition algorithm has an important influence on the accuracy of the entire iris recognition system, and owns robust and accurate.

2 Related Work

2.1 Conventional Iris Segmentation Algorithms

These methods are usually developed for iris texture or gradient. Sun et al. [1] used ordinal measures for iris feature representation and developed multilobe differential filters to compute ordinal measures. Abhyankar et al. [2] proposed and compared a

Z. Sun et al. (Eds.): CCBR 2019, LNCS 11818, pp. 364–375, 2019.
https://doi.org/10.1007/978-3-030-31456-9_41

method to perform iris encoding using bi-orthogonal wavelets and directional bi-orthogonal filters. Minaee et al. [3] used scattering transform and textural features for iris recognition, which applied PCA for the extracted features to reduce the dimensionality of the feature vector. This kind of algorithm has fast recognition speed and high performance in high quality iris image. However, some useful information is lost in feature extraction which leads to the appearance of algorithm accuracy bottleneck.

2.2 Method Based on CNN

Image recognition methods based on Deep learning, which show high recognition performance through extensive data learning and are being applied to various fields. Al-Waisy et al. [4] proposed an efficient real-time multimodal biometric system for iris detection. Gangwar et al. [5] proposed DeepIrisNet which is bases on very deep architecture and various tricks from recent successful CNNs, and used in cross-sensor iris recognition. Dat et al. [6] proposed an iris recognition rendering attack detection method, which used a convolutional neural network based on a near-infrared optical camera sensor and a support vector machine. These schemes have better accuracies compared to traditional methods while the robustness is not strong enough. Table 1. shows the comparisons between proposed and previous researches.

Table 1. Comparisons between proposed and previous studies on iris recognition.

Methods	Strength	Weakness
Conventional iris segmentation algorithms [1–3]	Fast processing speed and accurate in ideal iris image	(1) Some useful information is lost (2) Iris recognition accuracy is greatly affected by image noise
Method based on CNN [4–6]	The higher accuracy than traditional methods	(1) Large training parameters (2) Not robust enough
Proposed method	(1) Without prior preprocessing (2) Robust	High performance requirements for computers

The aim of the study is solving the problem of precise recognition without prior preprocessing and developing robust solutions for near-infrared illumination environment. The main contributions of our work can be summarized as follows:

(1) This study proposes an end to end dense deep convolutional neural network (DDNet) and the result of it show that DDNet is adapted and robust.
(2) DDNet uses the segmented images as input images without prior preprocessing or other conventional image processing techniques.
(3) DDNet is tested with CASIA-Iris-V3 [7] and IITD [8] datasets, this study used LabelMe [9] to manually mark the eyelashes as non-iris areas by using marks which would help us to analyze the effect of eyelashes on iris recognition.

3 Proposed Method

3.1 Description of the Proposed System

The iris collection will be affected by illumination, attitude and occlusion, which will limit the performance of the iris recognition algorithm. It usually undergoes more preprocessing methods before the iris image is sent to the iris recognition algorithm, such as morphological corrosion expansion, blurring, denoising and multi-scale image transformation which would greatly increases the time of iris recognition. In reference [20], we have done research on iris segmentation. In this study, the iris recognition process is shown in Fig. 1, we use segmented iris images as an input images without prior preprocessing for the aim of making our theme more focused.

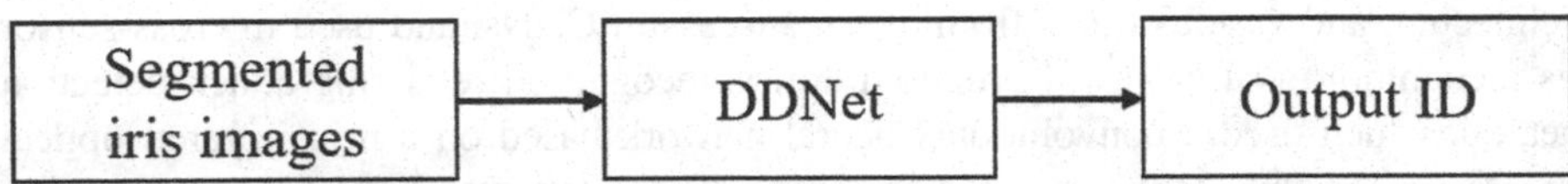

Fig. 1. Flowchart of the proposed method

3.2 Iris Recognition Based on CNN

In this study, we propose an end to end dense deep convolutional neural network (DDNet) which is consists of two parts: transition layers and dense block. Transition layers is consists of two dense blocks, and the main part of dense block is multiple bottleneck layers which is consists of Batch Normalization (BN), rectified linear unit (Relu), Convolution (Conv), and connected in the form of BN-Relu-Conv1x1-BN-Relu-Conv3x3. Bottleneck layers would directly transmit the output feature map to the subsequent bottleneck layer, and the subsequent bottleneck layer combines multiple feature maps as their own outputs owing to that Conv1x1 and Conv3x3 in the bottleneck layer do not change the height and width of the feature map. This dense connection shortens the connection between the front and back layers.

As shown in Fig. 2, the network model is mainly composed of convolution layer, Dense block, transition layer and fully connected layer. The Transition layer consists of BN, Relu, Conv1x1, and average pooling layer, which effectively reduces network redundancy. In order to ensure the flow of information between the network layers, the dense blocks are connected by the translation layer.

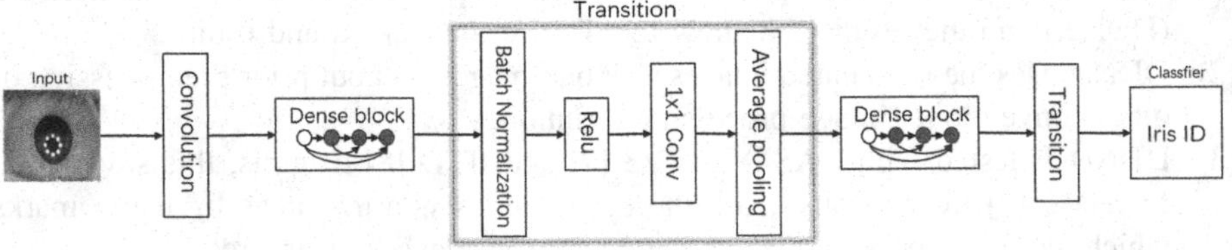

Fig. 2. Structure of the proposed model

As shown in Table 2 and Fig. 3, proposed method is composed of 1 convolutional layer, 7 dense blocks, 7 transition layers, 2 full connected layers (FCL) and 1 softmax layer. In the 1st convolutional layer, 64 filters of size 5 × 5 are used so that the size of the feature map is 128 × 128 × 64 in the 1st convolutional layer. As with the dense block 1, the filter size of 3 × 3, the padding of 1, and the stride of 1 are applied to the BN-Relu-Conv. The height and width of the feature map are unchanged, and the channel increases the number of filters. In addition, the number of filters of conv1x1 in the dense block is the same as the channel of the input feature map.

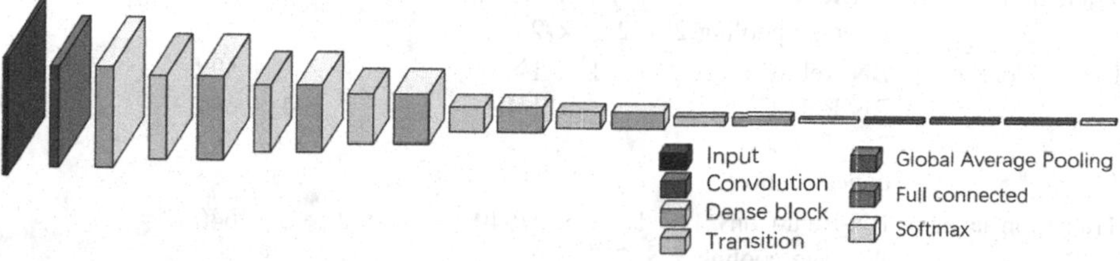

Fig. 3. Structure of DDNet.

Table 2. Detailed layer-wise structure of DDNet.

Name	Layer type	Number of stride/filter	Size of feature map Height × Width × Channels
Input Conv1	Convolution 5 × 5	2 × 2/64	128 × 128 × 3 128 × 128 × 64
Dense block 1	BN-Relu-Conv 1 × 1 BN-Relu-Conv 3 × 3 X2 concatenation	1 × 1 1 × 1/48	128 × 128 × 112 128 × 128 × 160
Transition layer 1	BN-Relu-Conv 1 × 1 Average pooling 2 × 2	1 × 1/160 2 × 2	64 × 64 × 160
Dense block 2	BN-Relu-Conv 1 × 1 BN-Relu-Conv 3 × 3 × 2 concatenation	1 × 1 1 × 1/48	64 × 64 × 208 64 × 64 × 256
Transition layer 2	BN-Relu-Conv 1 × 1 Average pooling 2 × 2	1 × 1/256 2 × 2	32 × 32 × 256
Dense block 3	BN-Relu-Conv 1 × 1 BN-Relu-Conv 3 × 3 × 2 concatenation	1 × 1 1 × 1/48	32 × 32 × 304 32 × 32 × 352
Transition layer 3	BN-Relu-Conv 1 × 1 Average pooling 2 × 2	1 × 1/352 2 × 2	16 × 16 × 352
Dense block 4	BN-Relu-Conv 1 × 1 BN-Relu-Conv 3 × 3 × 2 concatenation	1 × 1 1 × 1/48	16 × 16 × 400 16 × 16 × 448

(*continued*)

Table 2. (*continued*)

Name	Layer type	Number of stride/filter	Size of feature map Height × Width × Channels
Transition layer 4	BN-Relu-Conv 1 × 1 Average pooling 2 × 2	1 × 1/448 2 × 2	8 × 8 × 448
Dense block 5	BN-Relu-Conv 1 × 1 BN-Relu-Conv 3 × 3 × 2 concatenation	1 × 1 1 × 1/48	8 × 8 × 496 8 × 8 × 544
Transition layer 5	BN-Relu-Conv 1 × 1 Average pooling 2 × 2	1 × 1/544 2 × 2	4 × 4 × 544
Dense block 6	BN-Relu-Conv 1 × 1 BN-Relu-Conv 3 × 3 × 2 concatenation	1 × 1 1 × 1/48	4 × 4 × 592 4 × 4 × 640
Transition layer 6	BN-Relu-Conv 1 × 1 Average pooling 2 × 2	1 × 1/640 2 × 2	2 × 2 × 640
Dense block 7	BN-Relu-Conv 1 × 1 BN-Relu-Conv 3 × 3 × 2 concatenation	1 × 1 1 × 1/48	2 × 2 × 688 2 × 2 × 736
Transition layer 7	BN-Relu-Conv 1 × 1 Max pooling 2 × 2	1 × 1/736 2 × 2	1 × 1 × 736
FC1	Fully Connected		4096
Dropout1	Dropout-(50%)		
FC2	Fully Connected		4096
Dropout2	Dropout-(50%)		
FC3	Fully Connected		Class numbers
Cost	Softmax		

Compared to DenseNet, the DDNet have three key differences as follows:

(1) DenseNet is using 3 dense blocks for CIFAR and SVHN datasets and 4 dense blocks for ImageNet classification, whereas DDNet uses 7 dense blocks for each dataset.
(2) In DenseNet, all dense blocks have four convolutional layers while DDNet has two convolutional layers in all dense blocks.
(3) In DenseNet, all transition layers use max pooling, whereas DDNet use average pooling in transition layers. In addition, we add the BN layer and the Relu layer in front of the convolution layer in all transition layers.

4 Experiments and Results

4.1 Data Augmentation

In this study, the CASIA-Iris-V3 Interval and IITTD dataset are used as iris images in near-infrared illumination environment. CASIA-Iris-Interval collected 2,639 iris images from 249 subjects, but 123 subjects had fewer than 10 iris images. Therefore, we selected 1900 images from 138 subjects. IITD iris dataset collected 2,240 iris images from 224 subjects. Each subject selected 5 images of the left and right eye irises. In this study, we used LabelMe [9] to manually mark the datasets, as shown in Fig. 4. In (a), the red area is the iris area and we used green lines to mark the eyelashes and set them to non-iris areas. (b) is the mark obtained by parsing.

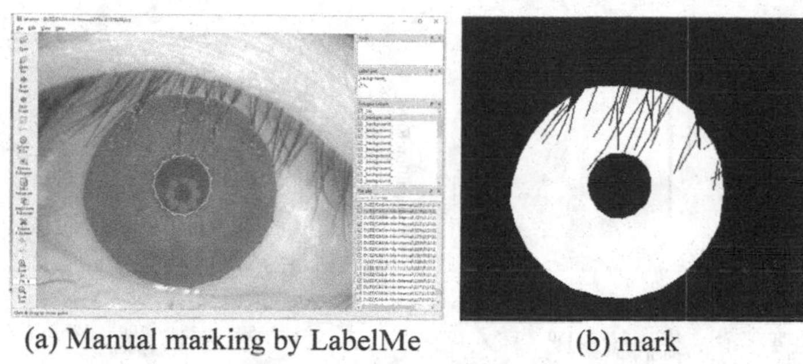

(a) Manual marking by LabelMe (b) mark

Fig. 4. Manual mark the dataset by LabelMe (Color figure online)

Each image of training data is augmented 5 times by Cropping and resizing with interpolation. We use interpolation to resize the image to 135 × 135, then crop five 128 × 128 areas from the four corners and the middle of these images. Finally, the datasets divide into training set and testing set by 8:2, as shown in Table 3, and the testing images do not participate in model training.

Table 3. Details of augmentation datasets.

Property	CASIA-Iris-V3	IITD
Number of training image	7600	8960
Number of testing images	1900	2240
classes	138	224
Image size	128 × 128 pixels	128 × 128 pixels

4.2 Experimental Data and Environment

In this study, Tensorflow is used as the deep learning framework. The specific parameters of the experimental equipment as follows:

CPU: Intel (R) Core (TM) i9-7900X CPU @ 3.30 GHz 3.31 GHz
GPU: NVIDIA GeForce GTX 1080 Ti
Memory: 32.0 GB

Considering that the memory is not large enough, the batch size is set to 32. Because the dataset is relatively small which is not only avoids the overfitting of dropout layer but also improves the generalization performance of the training model during the training process, and the dropout rate is set to 0.5. One epoch refers to train all the training set images at once.

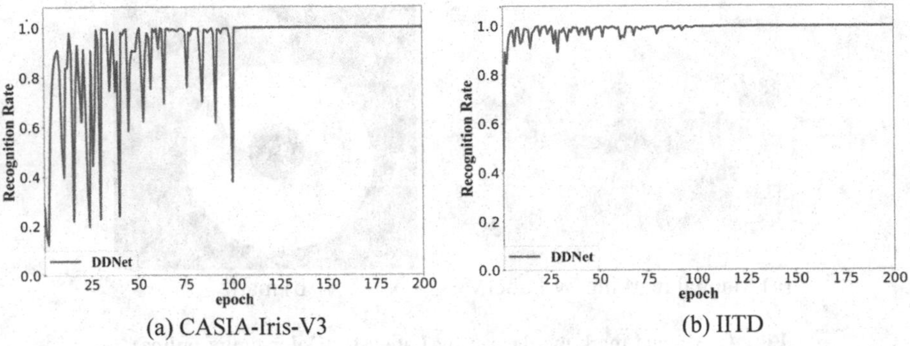

Fig. 5. The validation rank-1 identification curves of two adopted iris datasets

In this study, the initial learning rate is set to 0.0001 which would be reduced by a tenth every 50 epochs after it trains 100 epochs. Meanwhile, the experiment set the epoch to 200 making sure the training convergence enough. The validation rank-1 identification curves of two adopted iris datasets is shown as Fig. 5. The oscillation range of the curve gradually decreases, which means the training loss is converging. In addition, when the value of epoch increases to 125, the curves have almost no oscillation until the training end. Hence, 150 epochs are taken as the initial value of epoch in all remaining experiments, since it can save computer resource.

4.3 Analysis of Parameters

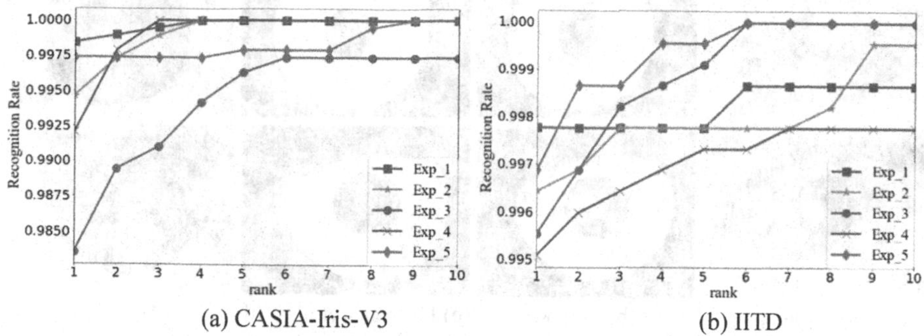

(a) CASIA-Iris-V3 (b) IITD

Fig. 6. Performance analysis using CMC

Table 4. Effects of different parameters on Rank1 identification rate (%)

Dataset	Exp_1	Exp_2	Exp_3	Exp_4	Exp_5
CASIA-Iris-V3	99.84	99.46	98.35	99.21	99.74
IITD	99.78	99.64	99.55	99.51	99.69
Attribute	Original	64 × 64	Eyelashes	Max Pooling	Without cropped

As shown in Table 4 and Fig. 6, Exp_1 uses average pooling in transition layers and meanwhile, its input image owns following characteristics: size is 128 × 128 and the eyelashes in the iris have been marked and cut in this image.

Effect of Input Image Size
Using our network, we evaluated the effect of input image size on 2 different settings: 64 × 64 and 128 × 128. It can be seen from the results that there is a significant drop in accuracy in the case of 64 × 64 image size compared to the 128 × 128 input image.

Effect of Eyelashes
The eyelashes in the iris will interfere iris recognition and it is a pity that ground-truth provided by Hofbauer et al. [10] not marked the eyelashes in the iris. As shown in Fig. 7, the green area in the result is marked as an iris area in (c), but is marked as a non-iris area in (b). And the red area in the result is marked as an iris area in (b), but is marked as a non-iris area in (c). As shown in Table 4 and Fig. 6, the results show that removing eyelashes within the iris can steadily improve the recognition accuracy.

Effect of Average Pooling
To investigate the effect of average pooling on accuracy, the effects are shown in Table 4 and Fig. 6. Exp_1 used the network structure of Table 2. In the Exp_4, we use Max pooling in all transition layers. In CASIA-Iris-V3. It can be seen from the results that average pooling can effectively improve the performance of DDNet.

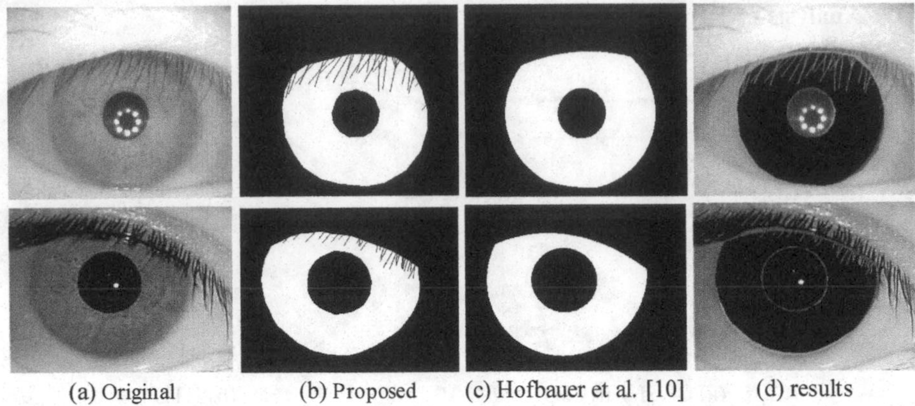

(a) Original (b) Proposed (c) Hofbauer et al. [10] (d) results

Fig. 7. Some compare results of two different ground-truth (Color figure online)

Effect of Input Cropped Image

In this study, we have cropped the original image of the iris dataset according to ground-truth. Only the eyeball image containing the iris portion is retained and other portions such as the eyelids and sclera are eliminated, which reduces computational resource consumption and training time. As shown in Fig. 8 (a)(b) from CASIA-Iris-V3, and (c)(d) from IITD. Image as (a)(c) are the cropped image. Exp_1 uses a dataset as (a)(c), and Exp_5 uses a dataset as (b)(d). It can be seen from the results that the accuracy would be improved by cropping images.

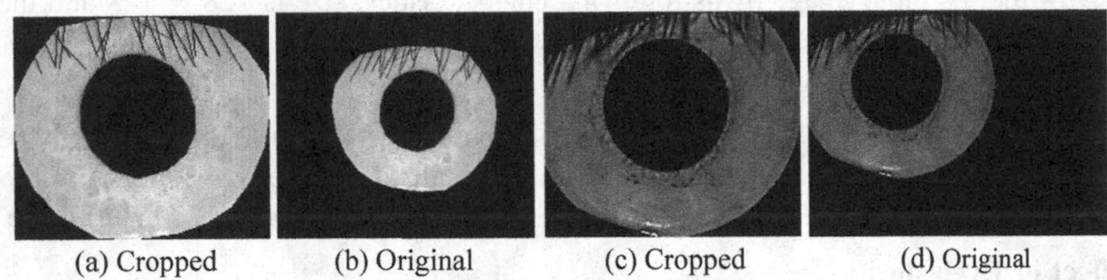

(a) Cropped (b) Original (c) Cropped (d) Original

Fig. 8. Cropped image and original image

4.4 Comparison with Other Methods

The comparison of the iris recognition method using the CASIA-Iris-V3 and IITD datasets with the existing methods is shown in Table 5. In order to verify the superiority of the proposed structure, we use the correct recognition rate (CRR) to compare the results of the proposed algorithm with the excellent results obtained by other algorithms and meanwhile, the CRR of the Rank-1 recognition rate is used as a criterion for judging the performance of the algorithm. In addition, for comparison, we cite the results of the existing methods in the literature from various datasets in Table 5. To show the performance of the proposed method, we compare its performance to various methods which are based on respective datasets. It can be seen from Table 5 that on the CASIA-Iris-V3 iris dataset, the test set CRR obtained by the proposed method is 99.84%, which is lower than the results in the literature [11] and [16]: 99.85% and 100%. Umer et al. [16] used the feature fusion algorithm of the left and right eyes to obtain 100% CRR. In the literature [11] and [16], there are only 109 and 99 individuals were used for testing respectively, which were less than the 138 individuals used in this chapter. Therefore, the dataset we selected is more challenging. On the IITD iris dataset, the proposed method has a test set CRR of 99.78% which is already higher than any other existing algorithms. Moreover, DDNet is an end-to-end method without conventional image processing techniques. The experiment verifies the superiority of the proposed method and the excellent learning ability of the deep convolutional neural network structure.

Table 5. The Rank1 identification rate (%) for Iris datasets

Dataset	Methods	CRR (%)
CASIA-Iris-V3	Ma et al. [11]	99.85
	Costa et al. [12]	99.10
	Vatsa et al. [13]	97.21
	Kerim et al. [14]	99.40
	Nabti et al. [15]	99.00
	Umer et al. [16]	100.00
	Proposed	99.84
IITD	Minaee et al. [3]	99.20
	Bharath ct al. [17]	95.93
	Elgamal et al. [18]	95.00
	Dhage et al. [19]	97.81
	Umer et al. [16]	99.52
	Proposed	99.78

4.5 Robustness Analysis

DDNet is tested with CASIA-Iris-V3 and IITD datasets, The Rank1 identification rate are 99.84% and 99.78% respectively. It is obviously that the precision gap of DDNet between two data set is small, only 0.06%. Meanwhile, Umer et al. [16] obtained the identification rate in CASIA-Iris-V3 and IITD datasets is 100% and 99.52% respectively which exists 0.48% difference and owns larger difference than DDNet.

IITD is a more challenging dataset, in shown as Fig. 9(a) and (b) are the same individual, we can see that (a) is obviously affected by ambiguity while (b) is not. Meanwhile, (c) and (d) are also the same individual, (d) is severely affected by upper eyelid cover. Hence, image of the same individual exists big difference in IITD and the demand for algorithm robustness is higher.

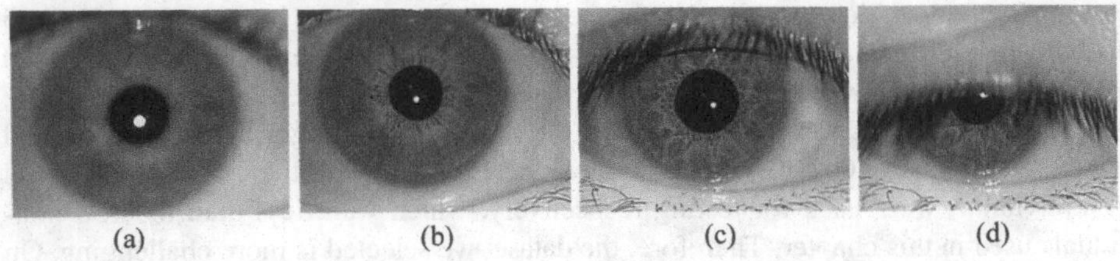

(a) (b) (c) (d)

Fig. 9. Original image of IITD

Umer et al. [16] used 99 individuals for testing in CASIA-Iris-V3. However, CASIA-Iris-V3 have 249 individuals, they may use relatively better image and exists small difference among these images. In IITD, they used all images which lead to the algorithm accuracy is significantly reduced. Owing to this, it is insufficient robustness.

DDNet used 138 individuals for testing in CASIA-Iris-V3 and used total images in IITD. However, although the accuracy of DDNet is lower than Umer et al. [16] owing to it used more individuals in CASIA-Iris-V3 while the accuracy of DDNet in IITD only down 0.06% so as to the method's accuracy is already higher than any other existing algorithms. Hence, DDNet owns high adaptability and robustness.

5 Conclusion

In this paper, our contribution is threefold. First, we introduced an end to end dense deep convolutional neural network (DDNet) for iris recognition and meanwhile, we can see from the results that our proposed method is satisfactory and robust. Second, DDNet uses the segmented images as input images without prior preprocessing or other conventional image processing techniques. Third, we not only provide two manually mark ground-truth for CASIA-Iris-V3 and IITD but also mark eyelashes in iris areas which is aims to analyze the effect of eyelashes on iris recognition. The results show that removing eyelashes within the iris can steadily improve the recognition accuracy. However, the image of CASIA-Iris-V3 and IITD is near-infrared illumination image so that designing a visible illumination iris recognition system is still an open and challenging problem, meanwhile, it is also an extremely important matters.

References

1. Sun, Z., Tan, T.: Ordinal measures for iris recognition. IEEE Trans. Pattern Anal. Mach. Intell. **31**(12), 2211–2226 (2008)
2. Abhyankar, A., Schuckers, S.: Iris quality assessment and bi-orthogonal wavelet based encoding for recognition. Pattern Recogn. **42**(9), 1878–1894 (2009)
3. Minaee, S., Abdolrashidi, A.A, Wang, Y.: Iris recognition using scattering transform and textural features. In: IEEE Signal Process. and Signal Process. Educ. Workshop, pp. 37–42. IEEE (2015)
4. Al-Waisy, A.S., Qahwaji, R., et al.: A multi-biometric iris recognition system based on a deep learning approach. Pattern Anal. Appl. **21**(3), 783–802 (2018)

5. Gangwar, A., Joshi, A.: DeepIrisNet: deep iris representation with applications in iris recognition and cross-sensor iris recognition. In: Proceedings of the IEEE International Conference on Image Processing, pp. 2301–2305. IEEE (2016)
6. Dat, N., Tuyen, P., Young, L., et al.: Deep learning-based enhanced presentation attack detection for iris recognition by combining features from local and global regions based on NIR camera sensor. Sensors **18**(8), 2601 (2018)
7. Chinese Academy of Science—Institute of Automation, CASIAIRISV3 Iris Image Database Version 3.0. http://biometrics.idealtest.org/dbDetailForUser.do?id=3
8. Kumar, A., Passi, A.: Comparison and combination of iris matchers for reliable personal authentication. Pattern Recogn. **43**(3), 1016–1026 (2010)
9. LabelMe [EB/OL], 16 January 2016. https://github.com/wkentaro/LabelMe
10. Hofbauer, H., Alonso-Fernandez, F., Wild, P., et al.: A ground truth for iris segmentation. In: International Conference on Pattern Recognition, pp. 527-532. IEEE (2014)
11. Ma, L., Wang, Y., Tan, T.: Iris recognition using circular symmetric filters. In: International Conference on Pattern Recognition. IEEE (2002)
12. Costa, R.M.D., Gonzaga, A.: Dynamic features for iris recognition. IEEE Trans. Syst. Man Cybern. B Cybern. **42**(4), 1072–1082 (2012)
13. Vatsa, M., Singh, R., Noore, A.: Improving iris recognition performance using segmentation, quality enhancement, match score fusion, and indexing. IEEE Trans. **38**(4), 1021–1035 (2008)
14. Kerim, A.A., Mohammed, S.J.: New iris feature extraction and pattern matching based on statistical measurement. Int J Emerg Trends Technol Comput Sci. **3**(5), 226–231 (2014)
15. Nabti, M., Bouridane, A.: New active contours approach and phase wavelet maxima to improve iris recognition system. In: European Workshop on Visual Information Processing, pp. 238–244. IEEE (2013)
16. Umer, S., Dhara, B.C., Chanda, B.: Texture code matrix-based multi-instance iris recognition. Pattern Anal. Appl. **19**(1), 283–295 (2016)
17. Bharath, B.V., Vilas, A.S., Manikantan, K., et al.: Iris recognition using radon transform thresholding-based feature extraction with Gradient-based Isolation as a pre-processing technique. In: International Conference on Industrial and Information Systems, pp. 1–8. IEEE (2015)
18. Elgamal, M., Al-Biqami, N.: An efficient feature extraction method for iris recognition based on wavelet transformation. Int. J. Comput. Inf. Technol. **2**(03), 521–526 (2013)
19. Dhage, S.S., Hegde, S.S., Manikantan, K., et al.: DWT-based feature extraction and radon transform based contrast enhancement for improved iris recognition. Procedia Comput. Sci. **45**, 256–265 (2015)
20. Chen, Y., Wang, W., Zeng, Z., et al.: An adaptive CNNs technology for robust iris segmentation. IEEE Access **7**, 64517–64532 (2019)

Emerging Biometrics

X-Ray Image with Prohibited Items Synthesis Based on Generative Adversarial Network

Tengfei Zhao[1,2], Haigang Zhang[1,2], Yutao Zhang[1,2], and Jinfeng Yang[1,2](✉)

[1] Tianjin Key Lab for Advanced Signal Processing, Civil Aviation University of China, Tianjin, China

[2] Shenzhen Polytechnic, Shenzhen 518055, China

jfyang@szpt.edu.cn

Abstract. Using deep learning to assist people in recognizing prohibited items in X-Ray images is crucial to improve the quality of security inspections. However, these methods require lots of data and the data collection usually takes much time and efforts. In this paper, we propose a method to synthesize X-ray image to support the training of prohibited items detectors. The proposed framework is built on the Generative Adversarial Networks (GAN) with multiple discriminators, trying to synthesize realistic X-Ray prohibited items and learn the background context simultaneously. In the other hand, a guided filter is introduced for detail preserving. The experimental results show that our model can smoothly synthesize prohibited items on background images. To quantitatively evaluate our approach, we add the generated samples into training data of the Single Shot MultiBox Detector (SSD) and show the synthetic images are able to improve the detectors' performance.

Keywords: Image synthesis · Generative Adversarial Network · X-ray baggage security

1 Introduction

Baggage inspection with X-ray machines is a priority task, which can reduces the risk of crime and terrorist attacks [1]. Security and safety screening with X-ray scanners has become an important process in the transportation industry and at border checkpoints [2]. However, inspection is a complex task and the detection for prohibited items relies mainly on the human. Missed inspection is an unavoidable mistake, when the security inspector has worked for a long time. This will cause security risks. Therefore, this type of task is more suitable for computer processing, freeing human from this heavy work.

With the advances of Convolutional Neural Networks(CNN), the realization of intelligent security check is no longer out of reach [3]. However, most prohibited items detection models require lots of images and manually collecting images usually takes much time and efforts. There are currently almost no public data sets containing prohibited items on the web. Therefore, it is very important

Z. Sun et al. (Eds.): CCBR 2019, LNCS 11818, pp. 379–387, 2019.
https://doi.org/10.1007/978-3-030-31456-9_42

to design approaches that automatically synthesize images for extending new datasets. Motivated by recent promising success of GANs [4] in several applications [5–7], we propose to build a GAN-based model to synthesize realistic prohibited items images in real scene and utilize them as the augmented data to train the CNN-based prohibited items detector. We denominate it as X-ray image-Synthesis-GAN(XS-GAN). Compared with adopting the regular GAN, the XS-GAN synthetic images are more realistic and retain more details.

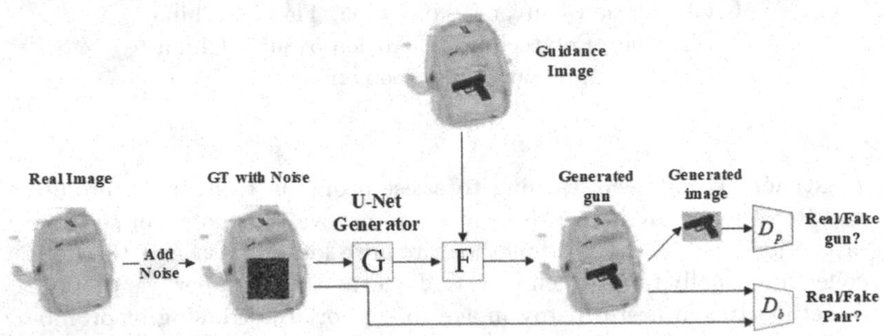

Fig. 1. The XS-GAN model.

XS-GAN adopts the adversarial learning recipe and contains multiple discriminators: D_b for background context learning and D_p for prohibited items discriminating (the gun as an example), as shown in Fig. 1. We replace the prohibited items with the bounding boxes with random noise and train the generator G to synthesize new prohibited items within the noise region. The discriminator D_b, learns to discriminate between real and synthesized pair. Meanwhile, the discriminator D_p learns to judge whether the synthetic prohibited item cropped from the bounding boxes is real or fake. D_b aims to force G to learn the background information. It leads to smooth connection between the background and the synthetic prohibited items. In order to makes G to generate real prohibited items with more realistic shape and details, we introduce guided filters into the proposed XS-GAN. After training, the generator G can learn to generate photo-realistic prohibited items in the noise box regions.

2 Related Work

2.1 Generative Adversarial Network

GANs [4] have achieved great success in generating realistic new images from either existing images or random noises. The main idea is to have continuing adversarial learning between a generator and a discriminator, where the generator tries to generate more realistic images while the discriminator aims to distinguish the newly generated images from real images. It is like a game, and will reach a state of balance. The generate image is consistent with the original image.

2.2 Image Synthesis with GAN

The work of image synthesis using GAN is generally based on the image-to-image translation work. The Pix2pix-GAN [5] is the earliest image-to-image translation model based on the condition GAN [8]. CycleGAN [6], DiscoGAN [9], and DualGAN [10] are similarly in principles. CycleGAN replaces the traditional one-way generated GAN with a loop-generated ring network and changes the traditional input method of paired images. Therefore, the input to the model becomes available for any two images. GAWWN [11] introduced a new synthesis method, which can synthesizes higher resolution images given instructions describing what content to draw in which location. PS-GAN [7] proposed an algorithm that can smoothly synthesize pedestrians on background images of varying and different levels of detail.

2.3 Guided Filter

Guided Filters [12,13] use one image as a guide for filtering another image, which exhibits superior performance in detail preserving filtering. The filtered output is a linear transformation of the guided image, where the guided image can be the input image itself or another different image. Guided filtering has been used for a variety of computer vision tasks. [14] uses guided filter for weighted averaging and image fusion. [15] uses a rolling guidance to fully control the detail smoothing in an iterative manner. [16] uses guided filtering to suppress heavy noise and structural inconsistency. [17] uses guided filtering as a non-convex optimization problem and proposes solutions via majorize-minimization.

Most GANs for image-to-image translation can synthesize high-resolution images, but the appearance transfer usually suppresses image details such as edges and textures. The proposed XS-GAN introduces guided filter into the generator network, which enables both appearance transfer and detail retention.

3 The Proposed Method

Unlike the regular GAN, our method leverages an adversarial process between the generator G and two discriminators: D_b for background context learning and D_p for discriminating prohibited items. In this section, we will give a detailed formulation of the overall objective.

3.1 Model Architecture

U-Net for Generator G**.** The Generator G learns a mapping function $G{:}x \rightarrow y$, where x is the input noise image and y is the ground truth image. In this work, we adopt the enhanced encoder-decoder network (U-Net) [5] for G. It follows the main structure of the encoder-decoder architecture, where the input image x is passed through a series of convolutional layers as down-sampling layers until the bottleneck layer. Then the bottleneck layer feeds the encoded information of original inputs to the deconvolutional layers to be up-sampled. U-Net uses the skip connections to connect the down-sampling and up-sampling layers to symmetric locations relative to the bottleneck layer, which can preserve richer local information (Fig. 2).

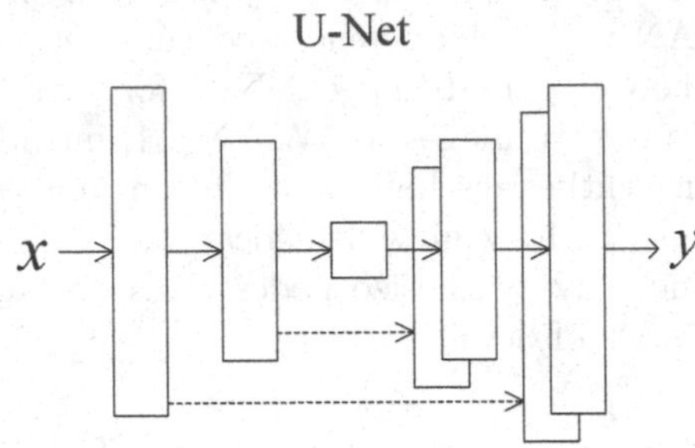

Fig. 2. The U-Net structure of the Generator G.

D_p to Discriminate Fake/Real Prohibited Items. For this discriminator D_p, we crop the synthetic prohibited items from the generated image as a negative sample, while the real prohibited items y_p from the original image y as a positive sample. Therefore, D_p is used to classify whether the generated prohibited item is real or false in the noise area. It forces G to learn the mapping from z to the real prohibited items y_p, where z is the noise region in the noise image x.

D_b to Learn Background Context. The goal of our model is to not only synthesize real prohibited items but also smoothly fill the synthetic prohibited items into the background. Thus our model needs to learn context information. Following the pair-training recipe from Pix2Pix-GAN [5], D_b is used to classify between real and synthetic pairs. The real pair is the noise image x and the ground truth image y, while the synthesized pair is the noise image x and the generated image. The overall framework is shown in Fig. 3.

Guided Filter. Guided filter is designed to perform edge-preserving image smoothing by using the structure in the guidance image. We introduce the guided filter into the proposed XS-GAN and formulate the detail-preserving as a joint up-sampling problem. In particular, the synthetic images (image detail loss) output of G is the input image I to be filtered and the initially input image act as the guidance image R to provide edge and texture details. Therefore, the detail-preserving image T can be derived by minimizing the reconstruction error between I and T, subjects to the linear model:

$$T_i = a_k I_i + b_k, \forall i \in \omega_k \tag{1}$$

where i is the index of the pixel and ω_k is a local square window centered at pixel k .

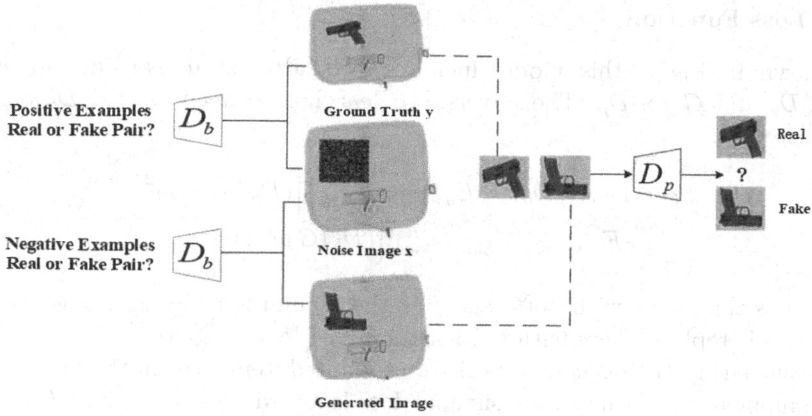

Fig. 3. The overall structure of discriminator.

In order to determine the coefficients of the linear models a_k and b_k, we seek a solution that minimizes the difference between T and filter input R, which can be derived by minimizing the following cost function in the local window:

$$E\left(a_k, b_k\right) = \sum_{i \in \omega_k} \left(\left(a_k I_i + b_k - R_i\right)^2 + \in a_k^2\right) \tag{2}$$

here $a_k I_i + b_k$ represents the output of the filter. Since the output of the filter combines the characteristics of the guidance image and the input image, $\left(a_k I_i + b_k - R_i\right)^2$ is used here to measure the similarity between the output image and the input image. And $\in$ is a regularization parameter that prevents a_k from being too large. It can be solved by linear regression:

$$a_k = \frac{\frac{1}{|\omega|}\sum_{i \in \omega_k} I_i - \mu_k \bar{R}_k}{\bar{\sigma}_k + \in} \tag{3}$$

$$b_k = \bar{R}_k - a_k \mu_k \tag{4}$$

where μ_k and σ_k^2 are the mean and variance of I at ω_k, $|\omega|$ is the number of pixels in ω_k, and $\bar{R}_k = \frac{1}{|\omega|}\sum_{i \in \omega_k}$ is the average of R in ω_k.

By applying a linear model to all ω_k windows on the image and calculating (a_k, b_k), the filter output can be derived by averaging all possible values of T_i:

$$T_i = \frac{1}{|\omega|} \sum_{k: i \in \mu_k} \left(a_k I_i + bk\right) = \bar{a} I_i + \bar{b}_i \tag{5}$$

where $\bar{a}_i = \frac{1}{|\omega|}\sum_{k \in \omega_k} a_k$ and $\bar{b}_i = \frac{1}{|\omega|}\sum_{k \in \omega_i} b_k$. We integrate the guided filter into the generator network structure to implement an end-to-end trainable system.

3.2 Loss Function

As shown in Fig. 1, this model includes two adversarial learning processes $G \Leftrightarrow D_b$ and $G \Leftrightarrow D_p$. The adversarial learning between G and D_b can be formulated as:

$$\begin{aligned}\mathcal{L}_{LSGAN}(G, D_b) = E_{y \sim p_{gt \cdot image}(y)}\left[(D_b(y) - 1)^2\right] \\ + E_{x,z \sim p_{noise \cdot image}(x,z)}\left[(D_b(G(x,z)))^2\right]\end{aligned} \tag{6}$$

where x is the image with noise and y is the ground truth image. The original GAN loss is replaced here with the least squared loss of LSGAN.

To encourage G to generate realistic prohibited items within the noise box z in the input image x, another resistance loss is added between G and D_p:

$$\begin{aligned}\mathcal{L}_{GAN}(G, D_p) = E_{y_p \sim p_{prohibiteditems}(y_p)}[\log D_p(y_p)] \\ + E_{z \sim p_{noise}(z)}[\log(1 - D_p(G(z)))]\end{aligned} \tag{7}$$

where z is the noise box in x and y_p is the crop prohibited items in the ground truth image y. The negative log-likelihood targets are used to update the parameters of G and D.

GAN training can benefit from traditional losses [5]. In this paper, the L loss is used to control the difference between the generated image and the real image y:

$$\mathcal{L}_{\ell_1}(G) = E_{x,z \sim p_{noise \cdot image}(x,z), y \sim p_{gt \cdot image}(y)}\left[\|y - G(x,z)\|_1\right] \tag{8}$$

Finally, combining the previously defined losses results in a final loss function:

$$\mathcal{L}(G, D_b, D_p) = \mathcal{L}_{LSGAN}(G, D_b) + \mathcal{L}_{GAN}(G, D_p) + \lambda \mathcal{L}_{\ell_1}(G) \tag{9}$$

4 Experimental Results

4.1 Datasets

The datasets used in our experiments are collected from the laboratory. We experiment with several types of prohibited items, such as guns, fruit knives, forks, hammers and scissors.

4.2 Contrast Experiment

In this section, We conducted several synthetic experiments on prohibited items and evaluated the synthesized images. The experimental results are shown in Fig. 4.

As can be seen from Fig. 4, our XS-GAN model with guided filtering has a better effect on the synthesis of security image prohibited items. The pix2pix-GAN model hardly the generated prohibited items. The PS-GAN can generate

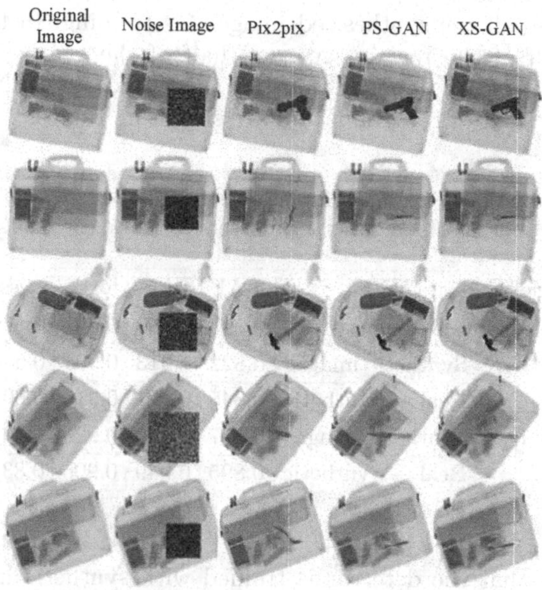

Fig. 4. Columns 1–2 are the input images, columns 3–5 show the images synthesized by pix2pix-GAN, PS-GAN and XS-GAN.

prohibited items, but the synthesis image is not clear enough. The images generated using our improved XS-GAN network model are not only clearer but also can retain more details.

In order to evaluate the quality of synthetic images, we test Fréchet Inception Distance (FID) score. The smaller the value of FID, the closer the synthetic image is to the real image. The test results are shown in Table 1.

Table 1. FID Score Test.

Model	Score
Pix2pix	69.73
PS-GAN	57.44
XS-GAN	47.21

As shown in Table 1, the XS-GAN synthesized images has the lowest FID score, which proves that the images synthesized by our method are closer to the real images.

To analyze the effect of the data augmentation, we combine the real and synthesized data to train the SSD [18] detectors and evaluate the performance. We experimented with images of three prohibited items, pistols, forks, and scissors. In the first experiment we use all the real images for training. In the second experiment we use all the synthesized images for training. In the third experiment we use half of the real images and half of the synthesized images for training. We use synthetic images from PS-GAN and XS-GAN to train SSD, separately. The results of the evaluation are shown in Table 2.

Table 2. Results of the SSD algorithm evaluation. Experimental evaluations were performed using real data sets, synthetic data sets, and mixed data sets, respectively.

Model	Data	mAP	gun	fork	scissor
	Real images	0.793	0.909	0.891	0.579
PS-GAN	Synthetic images	0.822	0.913	0.901	0.654
	Real + Synthetic	0.845	0.921	0.916	0.697
XS-GAN	Synthetic images	0.877	0.936	0.929	0.767
	Real + Synthetic	0.895	0.949	0.906	0.831

Table 2 shows that the detector is trained with synthetic images from XS-GAN can improve 8% mAP, and the detector is trained with mixed images can improve 10% mAP. However, the detector is trained with synthetic images from PS-GAN can improve 3% mAP, and the detector is trained with mixed images can improve 5% mAP. Thus by adding the synthetic images, the AP rate can be improve, and the image synthesized by our method has better data enhancement effect.

5 Conclusion

This paper introduces the XS-GAN model to synthesizes realistic X-Ray images in certain bounding boxes. The experimental results show that the network model with guided filtering can retain more details when synthesizing images. Our model can generate high quality prohibited items images, and the synthetic images can effectively improve the abilities of CNN based detectors. We use this model to synthesize different prohibited items images, which demonstrates the ability of generalization and transferring knowledge. We will continue to study XS-GAN for prohibited items image synthesis for training better detection models.

References

1. Mery, D., Svec, E., Arias, M., Riffo, V., Saavedra, J.M., Banerjee, S.: Modern computer vision techniques for x-ray testing in baggage inspection. IEEE Trans. Syst. Man Cybern. Syst. **47**(4), 682–692 (2016)
2. Mendes, M., Schwaninger, A., Michel, S.: Does the application of virtually merged images influence the effectiveness of computer-based training in x-ray screening? In: 2011 Carnahan Conference on Security Technology, pp. 1–8. IEEE (2011)

3. Rogers, T.W., Jaccard, N., Griffin, L.D.: A deep learning framework for the automated inspection of complex dual-energy x-ray cargo imagery. In: Anomaly Detection and Imaging with X-Rays (ADIX) II, vol. 10187. International Society for Optics and Photonics, 101870L (2017)
4. Goodfellow, I., et al.: Generative adversarial nets. In: Advances in Neural Information Processing Systems, pp. 2672–2680 (2014)
5. Isola, P., Zhu, J.Y., Zhou, T., Efros, A.A.: Image-to-image translation with conditional adversarial networks. In: Proceedings of the IEEE Conference on Computer Vision and Pattern Recognition, pp. 1125–1134 (2017)
6. Zhu, J.Y., Park, T., Isola, P., Efros, A.A.: Unpaired image-to-image translation using cycle-consistent adversarial networks. In: Proceedings of the IEEE International Conference on Computer Vision, pp. 2223–2232 (2017)
7. Ouyang, X., Cheng, Y., Jiang, Y., Li, C.L., Zhou, P.: Pedestrian-synthesis-gan: Generating pedestrian data in real scene and beyond. arXiv preprint arXiv:1804.02047 (2018)
8. Mirza, M., Osindero, S.: Conditional generative adversarial nets. arXiv preprint arXiv:1411.1784 (2014)
9. Kim, T., Cha, M., Kim, H., Lee, J.K., Kim, J.: Learning to discover cross-domain relations with generative adversarial networks. In: Proceedings of the 34th International Conference on Machine Learning, vol. 70, pp. 1857–1865. JMLR. org (2017)
10. Yi, Z., Zhang, H., Tan, P., Gong, M.: Dualgan: Unsupervised dual learning for image-to-image translation. In: Proceedings of the IEEE International Conference on Computer Vision, pp. 2849–2857 (2017)
11. Reed, S.E., Akata, Z., Mohan, S., Tenka, S., Schiele, B., Lee, H.: Learning what and where to draw. In: Advances in Neural Information Processing Systems, pp. 217–225 (2016)
12. He, K., Sun, J., Tang, X.: Guided image filtering. In: Daniilidis, K., Maragos, P., Paragios, N. (eds.) ECCV 2010. LNCS, vol. 6311, pp. 1–14. Springer, Heidelberg (2010). https://doi.org/10.1007/978-3-642-15549-9_1
13. He, K., Sun, J.: Fast guided filter. arXiv preprint arXiv:1505.00996 (2015)
14. Li, S., Kang, X., Hu, J.: Image fusion with guided filtering. IEEE Trans. Image Process. **22**(7), 2864–2875 (2013)
15. Zhang, Q., Shen, X., Xu, L., Jia, J.: Rolling guidance filter. In: Fleet, D., Pajdla, T., Schiele, B., Tuytelaars, T. (eds.) ECCV 2014. LNCS, vol. 8691, pp. 815–830. Springer, Cham (2014). https://doi.org/10.1007/978-3-319-10578-9_53
16. Liu, W., Chen, X., Shen, C., Yu, J., Wu, Q., Yang, J.: Robust guided image filtering. arXiv preprint arXiv:1703.09379 (2017)
17. Ham, B., Cho, M., Ponce, J.: Robust guided image filtering using nonconvex potentials. IEEE Trans. Pattern Anal. Mach. Intell. **40**(1), 192–207 (2018)
18. Liu, W., et al.: SSD: single shot multibox detector. In: Leibe, B., Matas, J., Sebe, N., Welling, M. (eds.) ECCV 2016. LNCS, vol. 9905, pp. 21–37. Springer, Cham (2016). https://doi.org/10.1007/978-3-319-46448-0_2

A Deep Learning Approach to Web Bot Detection Using Mouse Behavioral Biometrics

Ang Wei, Yuxuan Zhao, and Zhongmin Cai(✉)

MOE KLINNS Lab, Xi'an Jiaotong University, Xi'an 710049, China
zmcai@sei.xjtu.edu.cn

Abstract. Web bots are automated scripts that perform online tasks like human. Abuse of bot technology poses various threats to the security of websites. Recently, mouse dynamics has been applied to bot detection by analyzing whether recorded mouse operations are consistent with human operational patterns. In this paper, we introduce a deep neural network approach to bot detection. We propose a new representation method for mouse movement data, which converts every mouse movement into an image containing its spatial and kinematic information. This representation method makes it possible to utilize CNN models to automate feature learning from mouse movement data. Experimental results demonstrate that our method is able to detect 96.2% of bots with statistical attack ability while traditional detection methods using hand-crafted features or RNN can only detect less than 30% of them.

Keywords: Bot detection · Mouse movement · CNN

1 Introduction

Web bots are automated scripts that run tasks without human intervention on the Internet. Malicious bots pose a serious threat to Internet users. They influence the results of online polls, spread spams, and commit various types of online crimes and frauds. According to Bot Traffic Report 2016 [1], malicious bots comprise 28.9% of online traffic and have caused considerable loss for the users and owners of websites.

Recently, mouse dynamics, a behavioral biometric, has been investigated for bot detection [2,3]. The basic idea is to analyze whether the mouse operation data is consistent with human operational patterns. Although web bots can generate mouse events, it's difficult for bots to perform mouse operations in a human manner. This makes it possible to differentiate bots from human users according to mouse dynamics.

Previous works relied on hand-crafted features and feed the features into a shallow machine learning model. In this paper, we introduce deep learning method to detect web bots using mouse dynamics. To do this, We tackle the

Z. Sun et al. (Eds.): CCBR 2019, LNCS 11818, pp. 388–395, 2019.
https://doi.org/10.1007/978-3-030-31456-9_43

difficulty of converting mouse movement sequences into suitable inputs for deep learning models by proposing a new representation method of mouse movements data. We transform every mouse movement sequence into an image containing its spatial and kinematic information. The representation makes it possible to apply CNN models to web bot detection using mouse dynamics. We build an experimental website and collect mouse movement data from both human subjects and web bots. The experimental results demonstrate that our method outperforms both traditional classifiers using hand-crafted features and RNN based approach in the detection of web bots with statistical attack [4,5] ability. The major contributions of this paper are listed as follows:

(1) We propose to employ deep neural networks to solve the problem of web bot detection using mouse dynamics.
(2) We introduce a new representation method for mouse movement data. It makes it possible to automate feature learning from mouse movement data using deep learning models.
(3) We establish a dataset of web accessing behaviors for both human and web bots by collecting their mouse operational data from an experimental website.
(4) Experimental results demonstrate that our method achieves an accuracy of 96.2% in detecting web bots with statistical attack ability while the accuracies of conventional methods are less than 30%.

2 Related Work

Mouse dynamics is a useful biometric for authentication. In recent years, it has also been applied in web bot detection. Gianvecchio et al. [6] proposed a non-interactive approach based on human observational proofs (HOPs) for continuous game bot detection. They monitored mouse and keystroke actions when users were playing an online game. Seven action metric features were used to train a cascade-correlation neural network for distinguishing bots from humans. In [3], the author used mouse dynamics to strengthen image CAPTCHA based bot detection. He extracted 20 features to create feature vectors for each session's data. In [2], the author employed mouse and keystroke dynamics to distinguish between human and bot in blog service Scenario. Eight features were defined to characterize mouse and keystroke actions. A classifier based on C4.5 algorithm was trained using the features of raw data collected from blog site.

Previous works made important progresses in behavioral based web bot detection. However, the widely-used features are usually coarse-grained features such as statistics of mouse movement sequences (e.g., mean and variance of velocity, acceleration, step size, angle). There is no feature proposed to accurately characterize the shape information of mouse trajectory. As a consequence, when facing more advanced human mimicry web bots with statistical attack abilities [7], existing detectors have a large chance to be deceived.

Motivated by the above analysis, in this work, we introduce a deep learning approach to web bot detection and propose an image representation of mouse movement data for deep CNN models. A deep learning approach can address the discussed issues and automate the complex feature engineering process.

3 Overview of Our Approach

The framework of our approach is shown in Fig. 1, which depicts the training as well as the online testing process of web bot detection. In online testing, the decision that whether a user is a bot or human depends on classification results of most mouse movement sequences extracted from his operation data. If a majority of mouse movement sequences are classified as bot-generated, the user will be classified as a bot. Thus in the rest of paper, we will focus on the analysis of individual mouse movement sequence and discuss the situation of single mouse movement sequence based classification.

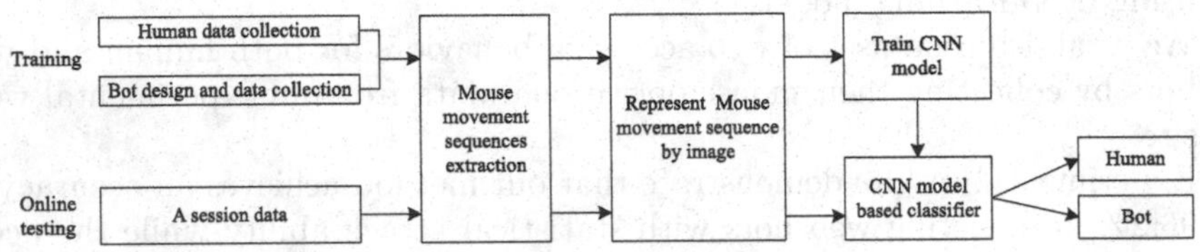

Fig. 1. Framework of our approach

To avoid confusion in the subsequent discussion, we at first introduce some notations that will be used throughout the paper.

1. *A mouse movement sequence* is the records of a series of consecutive mouse move events. It has the form $\{(x_1, y_1, t_1), \ldots, (x_i, y_i, t_i), \ldots, (x_n, y_n, t_n)\}$, where (x_i, y_i, t_i) denotes the coordinates and timestamp of a mouse move event.
2. *A Mouse trajectory* is a time-space curve corresponding to a mouse movement sequence.
3. *Step size* denotes the distance between two consecutive points.
4. *Event interval* denotes the time difference between two consecutive points.

3.1 Representation of Mouse Movements

The first step in processing mouse behavioral data is to separate the continuous sequence of mouse events into sequence segments corresponding to individual mouse movements. This is performed based on the observation that the event intervals between consecutive points in a mouse movement do not exceed 100 ms. In our study, we discard mouse movements having less than 15 events, which contain not enough information for bot detection. Then, we propose a two-step method to transform a mouse movement sequence into an image that can be an input for a CNN model.

Map Spatial Information into Image. One step is to map the spatial information such as shape and distances between consecutive events into an image. Firstly, we determine the size of the input image. We denote the max_range of a mouse movement as the maximal difference between x coordinates or y coordinates of two arbitrary points on its trajectory. Figure 2(a) shows most max_ranges of human mouse movements are smaller than 600 pixels. So we set the size of image to be 600 * 600. Secondly, we translate mouse movement sequence to the center of image. Thirdly, we zoom in or out mouse movement sequences according to the ratio of its max range and the image size (600 pixels). This transforms all different mouse movement sequences into similar sizes. At last, we represent every point in mouse movement sequence by a dot in the image according to its x and y coordinates. In order not to make an input image too sparse, the radius of dots in an image is set to 4 pixels. Although there are translation and zooming operation in the conversion process, we don't change the overall shape of mouse movement sequence.

Map Kinematic Information into Image. The distinguishing characteristics of a mouse movement for web bot detection also contain kinematic information. This information is reflected in its event interval series and step size series, which are denoted as $(\Delta t_1, \ldots, \Delta t_{n-1})$ and $(\Delta d_1, \ldots, \Delta d_{n-1})$ respectively. We employ the color information, BGR (Blue, Green and Red), of a dot for a mouse trajectory point in the input image to embed the kinematic information. We use Δd_i and Δt_i to set the G and R color values of the corresponding dot. The mapping function from step size to G color value is denoted as g(x) and the mapping function from event interval to R color value is denoted as f(x). g(x) and f(x) map Δd_i and Δt_i into an integer ranging from 0 to 255. Figure 2(b) is the converted input image of a human mouse movement sequence.

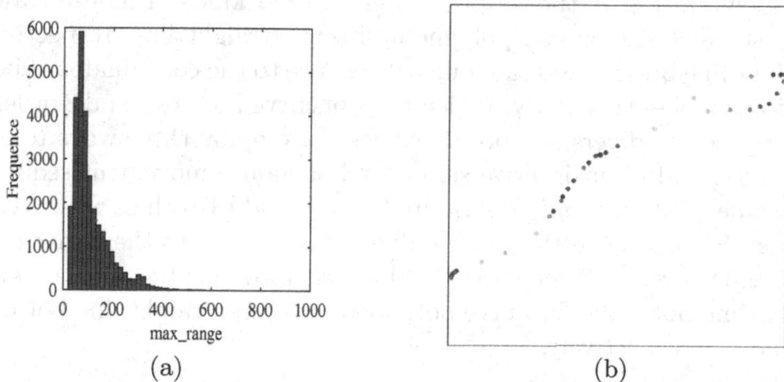

Fig. 2. (a) Max_range distribution of human mouse movement sequences. (b) A conversion results of human mouse movement sequences

3.2 Deep Classification Model

We choose ResNet [8], a classical CNN model, as our bot detection classifier. Specificly, we use the ResNet50 architecture from PyTorch. Data augmentation technique is employed by randomly rotating the image by 0, 90, 180, 270°, which can increase the variety of training samples and prevent overfitting. Besides, we load a pre-trained model from ImageNet to initialize the weights instead of training our model from random initializations.

4 Mouse Movement Data Collection

4.1 Data Collection Scenario

We use user registration process as our web bot detection scenario and build a registration website to collect mouse movement data. The website is a Java web application that consists of a front-end webpage and a back-end service program. There are three input fields, including username, password and password confirmation, and a submission button, on the front-end webpage. An event logger implemented by JavaScript is embedded in the front-end webpage, which silently collects a user's mouse operations when she accesses the website.

4.2 Human and Web Data Collection

There are 6 rounds of data collection during 2 months. Every subject is asked to finish the registration task ten times in each round. All subjects are told to operate mouse in a natural way according to their habits. Totally, 50 subjects participated in our data collection and we obtained over 3000 sessions of human data.

We use 4 kinds of bot scripts to generate the experimental data from web bots. As shown in Fig. 3, the scripts will generate 4 kinds of mouse trajectories including: straight-line, curve, polyline and semi-straight line, respectively. For semi-straight line bot, we add random disturbance to the coordinates of points on a straight-line mouse trajectory. Trajectories of curve bot are 2 and 3 order Bezier curves. To generate diversified bot activities, we employ three ways to generate step size series and event interval series for bot mouse movement sequence: (1) constant values, (2) uniformly distributed values and (3) values with a Gaussian distribution. Parameter settings are configured according to the norms of human activities. In this way, we generate 10000 mouse movement sequences with 2000 for straight-line bot, 3000 for curve bot, 3000 for semi-straight line bot and 2000 for polyline bot respectively.

4.3 Statistical Attack Dataset

The basic idea of statistical attack is to estimate the probability density functions of features from a group of people and then use the most probable feature values to generate the forgery [9]. According to the method shown in [4,5,9], we generate bot samples with statistical attack ability. Kernel density estimation is used to calculate the probability density estimate of step size series and event interval series of human mouse movement sequences respectively. In the process of synthesizing bot mouse movement sequences, the step size series and event interval series are generated according to the corresponding probability density estimate. This can guarantee that the step size series and event interval series of bots have similar distribution of human's. In this way, we generate 4000 mouse movement sequences for statistical attack dataset, with 1000 for each kind of bot.

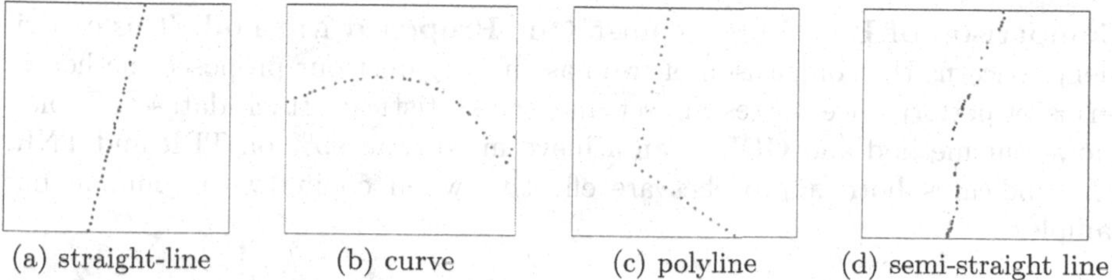

(a) straight-line (b) curve (c) polyline (d) semi-straight line

Fig. 3. Examples of 4 kinds of bot mouse trajectories

5 Experiment

5.1 Baselines for Comparison

The first baseline is the Gradient Boosting Decision Tree (GBDT) classifier using nine hand-crafted features. The nine features are defined in related work [2] and [3]. These features are movement efficiency, the average and the standard deviation of speed, acceleration, step size, and movement angle. Movement angle means supplementary angle of the angle that between three consecutive points and movement efficiency is displacement over distance.

The second baseline is an RNN model based method. Mouse movement sequence element for one time step is 3-dimensional vector (x, y, t). We convert element for one time step to $(\frac{dx}{dt}, \frac{dy}{dt})$ according to [10] and pad the sequence to length 60 as the input for RNN model.

5.2 Dataset Preparation

We extract over 10000 mouse movement sequences from human mouse movement data. The number of mouse movement sequences of bots is 10000. They are randomly partitioned into 5 complementary subsets. In every run of experiment, we use four of the five subsets for training. The validation set consists of half of the remaining subset and the testing set consists of the other half. We also use the statistical attack dataset discribed in Sect. 4.3 for further test. To remove the interference of the authentication effect, mouse movements from the same human subject are either used for training or testing, but not for both.

5.3 Experimental Results

In the testing phase, we choose true positive rate (TPR) and true negative rate (TNR) as evaluate metrics, which are used in related bot detection work [2]. TPR is the ratio of the number of human samples which are correctly classified to the number of all the human samples. TNR is the ratio of the number of bot samples which are correctly classified to the number of all the bot samples.

Comparison of Baselines Against Our Proposed Method. This experiment concerns the comparison of two baselines against our proposed method in terms of performance on testing set and the statistical attack dataset. Table 1 shows our method and GDBT can achieve more than 99% on TPR and TNR. This indicates both approaches are effective when coping with common bot samples.

Table 1. Comparison on test set

Model	Avg TPR	Avg TNR
GDBT	0.9934	0.9925
RNN	0.934	0.974
Our method	0.9981	0.9984

Table 2. Comparison on statistical attack dataset

	Avg TNR				
	Straight-line	Curve	Polyline	Semi-straight line	Overall
GDBT	0.186	0.503	0.210	0.063	0.240
RNN	0.205	0.427	0.368	0.172	0.293
Our method	0.936	0.999	0.989	0.924	0.962

Further more, we compare three methods on statistical attack dataset. Table 2 shows that our method can still detect 96.2% bot samples while two baselines only detect 24.0% and 29.3% bot samples respectively. As discussed in Sect. 4.3, for statistical attack dataset, some features of bot samples accord with distribution of human samples. Thus, methods using hand-craft features fail to detect these bot samples. In addition, it's hard for RNN model to learn the spatial information contained in mouse movement data, so the performance of RNN model decreases a lot. Our representation method directly visualize the difference of the distinguishing information containing in a mouse movement sequence. This makes it easier for a CNN model to learn the difference between human and bot samples, and thus has a better performance against statistical attack dataset.

6 Conclusion

In this paper, we propose a new method to represent mouse movement data by images and apply CNN model to web bot detection using mouse dynamics. This method makes it possible to automate feature learning from mouse movement data and improve the detection performance of more advanced bots. The experimental results demonstrate our method is effective in detecting bots with statistical attack ability.

Acknowledgments. This work is supported by NSFC (Grant No. 61772415).

References

1. Zelfman, I.: Bot traffic report 2016. Imperva Incapsula Blog (2017)
2. Chu, Z., Gianvecchio, S., Koehl, A., Wang, H., Jajodia, S.: Blog or block: Detecting blog bots through behavioral biometrics. Comput. Netw. **57**(3), 634–646 (2013)
3. D'Souza, D.F.: Avatar captcha: telling computers and humans apart via face classification and mouse dynamics. Electronic theses and dissertations. paper 1715 (2014)
4. Serwadda, A., Phoha, V.V.: Examining a large keystroke biometrics dataset for statistical-attack openings. ACM Trans. Inf. Syst. Secur. (TISSEC) **16**(2), 8 (2013)
5. Stanciu, V.D., Spolaor, R., Conti, M., Giuffrida, C.: On the effectiveness of sensor-enhanced keystroke dynamics against statistical attacks. In: Proceedings of the Sixth ACM Conference on Data and Application Security and Privacy, pp. 105–112. ACM (2016)
6. Gianvecchio, S., Wu, Z., Xie, M., Wang, H.: Battle of botcraft: Fighting bots in online games with human observational proofs. In: Proceedings of the 16th ACM Conference on Computer and Communications Security, pp. 256–268. ACM (2009)
7. Jin, J., Offutt, J., Zheng, N., Mao, F., Koehl, A., Wang, H.: Evasive bots masquerading as human beings on the web. In: 2013 43rd Annual IEEE/IFIP International Conference on Dependable Systems and Networks (DSN), pp. 1–12. IEEE (2013)
8. He, K., Zhang, X., Ren, S., Sun, J.: Deep residual learning for image recognition. In: Proceedings of the IEEE Conference on Computer Vision and Pattern Recognition, pp. 770–778 (2016)
9. Song, Y., Cai, Z., Zhang, Z.L.: Multi-touch authentication using hand geometry and behavioral information. In: 2017 IEEE Symposium on Security and Privacy (SP), pp. 357–372. IEEE (2017)
10. Chong, P., Tan, Y.X.M., Guarnizo, J., Elovici, Y., Binder, A.: Mouse authentication without the temporal aspect–what does a 2d-cnn learn? In: 2018 IEEE Security and Privacy Workshops (SPW), pp. 15–21. IEEE (2018)

Multi-task Deep Learning for Child Gender and Age Determination on Hand Radiographs

Mumtaz A. Kaloi[1,2], Xiaosen Wang[1], and Kun He[1](✉)

[1] Huazhong University of Science and Technology, Wuhan, China
brooklet60@hust.edu.cn
[2] Sukkur IBA University, Sukkur, Sindh, Pakistan

Abstract. In anthropology, especially in medico-legal or forensic investigation, the determination of gender and age of the subjects is typically a preliminary and compulsory obligation. State-of-the-art methods for gender determination use dimensions of the bones around the skull and pelvis area. Whereas age is determined on the basis of the degree in which bones have grown, for instance, dental eruption, epiphyseal fusion, tooth mineralization, and diaphyseal length. In this paper, we propose a convolutional neural network model with multi-task learning to determine the gender and age using left-hand radiographs. The model performs well by determining gender and age simultaneously. The results produced by the model specify that there is a relationship between gender and age which is with an increase in age, gender-related features become prominent. Phalanges and Metacarpals are the most significant parts of hand for gender detection based on a certain age group and age detection based on gender respectively. To our knowledge, our method is the first one to determine the gender and age of children simultaneously.

Keywords: Child gender · Child age · Multi-task learning

1 Introduction

In a forensic investigation, the identity of the deceased becomes a huge challenge when the subject is not only a juvenile but also a victim of a disastrous situation [1]. The incidents which occur due to criminal and deliberate actions are difficult to investigate, because in such situations usually the remains of the victims are destroyed by the culprits to mislead the forensic investigators in the identification of the deceased. To cope with such situations, a largely automated mechanism is needed.

In ideal circumstances, the state-of-the-art techniques may be suitable to be used for gender and age determination. But customary techniques may fail in scenarios when there is only a small portion of the body available for investigation. Usually, the extremities of the human body persist intact even in a disastrous condition. Therefore bones in the hand of a subject, as shown in Fig. 1, may play a crucial role in forensic investigation to determine gender and age. This research focuses on gender and age determination based on hand radiographs of children. From Fig. 1, it can be seen that a human hand has different kinds of bones at different levels. This anatomy of the human hand may be different in a boy as compared with a girl and these features of hands

Z. Sun et al. (Eds.): CCBR 2019, LNCS 11818, pp. 396–404, 2019.
https://doi.org/10.1007/978-3-030-31456-9_44

might be easily detected by convolutional neural networks. To utilize the features of the hands, deep learning techniques with convolutional neural networks are very suitable to be used.

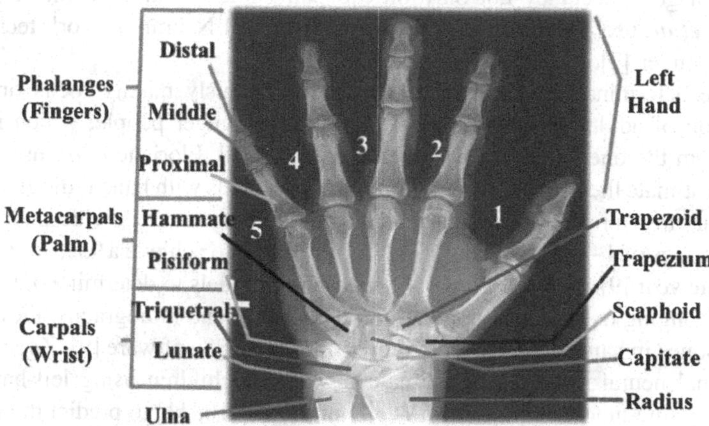

Fig. 1. Bones in the left hand of a child, there are 19 bones in the hand, and five major areas are Phalanges, Metacarpals, Carpals, Ulna and Radius [2].

We use multi-task learning to determine the gender and age of children on left-hand radiographs. Empirical results and visualization of gradient-based activations are analyzed to identify the most significant regions of hand to determine the age of a child by considering his/her gender and vice versa. Our work is based on three main facets. The first facet is to use multi-task learning for child gender and age detection simultaneously on hand radiographs. The second facet is to show the portions of hand which play a significant role in gender and age detection. The third one is to show a relationship between gender and age that gender has an impact on age detection and vice versa. We successfully train and test the model to detect the gender and age of children. Visualization of attention maps reveals the significance of Phalanges and Metacarpals portions of hand in gender and age detection.

2 Related Work

Before this research, many works try different techniques to determine the gender or age (mostly the gender of adults and age of children separately). In order to determine the gender, some works try to devise manual techniques to extract features of the hands [3]. For instance, Mahrous *et al.* investigate the hand dimensions of 600 individuals [4]. They use length, breadth and hand dimensions, and investigate the ratio between index and ring fingers. Their results show that the ratio of index and ring finger is higher in females as compared with males. Abdullah *et al.* [5] determine the gender by calculating hand dimensions, index finger and ring finger ratio in upper Egyptians. They claim in their results that the average male hands are 1.3 cm larger than females.

Manual techniques sometimes lead to costly mistakes. Therefore most recent works incorporate automated techniques to determine gender. Afifi *et al.* use convolutional neural networks to determine the gender of the individuals by biometric tracts found in hands [2, 6]. They use the images of hands, on both sides (Palm and Dorsal) and claim to achieve a good accuracy not only on the palm side but also on the dorsal side. Darmawan *et al.* use a Hybrid Particle Swarm Artificial Neural Network technique to determine gender [7].

For age determination, the techniques used previously mainly focus on the age identification of adults. However, age detection on younger people, which is greatly different from the one on adults, has been rarely studied. Floriane *et al.* use a manual method to estimate the age of 451 living French individuals with hand radiographs. They use a manual measurement technique to determine the age. They divide their data into three age groups of 1–13, 14–18 and 19–21. They claim to achieve a 95% accuracy with a bias of one year [9]. Yusuf *et al.* use 12 regression models to determine the age of the children belonging to the Asian population. Using left-hand radiographs, they measure all the 19 bones in hand and then apply regression on SPSS software [9]. Zhou *et al.* use convolutional neural networks to estimate the age of children using left-hand radiographs. They fine-tune the pre-trained VGGNet model [10, 11] to predict the bone age.

3 Gender and Age Determination with Multi-task Learning

In this paper, we propose to use convolutional neural networks [12] with multi-task learning [12] to determine the gender and age of children simultaneously. The purpose is to classify the left-hand radiographs of children in the age between one month and 18 years. Gender and age can be determined with two different models but it can be a time consuming and less effective task. Multi-task learning is a method that learns features simultaneously for multiple outputs [12, 13]. The task of gender and age detection on hand radiographs is well suited for multi-task learning.

Multi-task learning significantly improves the learning process for the convolutional neural networks when there is a very little inter-class deviation [13]. The multi-task learning network learns by sharing the weights for different tasks simultaneously.

3.1 Network Architecture

The architecture of the proposed model is based on deep convolutional neural networks, and the block diagram of the model is depicted in Fig. 2. The proposed model is based on 6 convolutional layers which learn the features for gender detection and age detection simultaneously using multi-task learning. The size of input images is 100×100 and we use kernels of 5×5 for each convolutional layer. The kernel size for max-pooling layers is 2×2. Activation function for each convolutional layer is Relu [11]. After the dense layer, there is a softmax layer for each task [10]. In order to cope with over-fitting, we use dropout [14] layers as depicted in Fig. 2. The proposed model shares all the layers (except for the dense layers) for gender and age detection. We use Adamax [14] method as an optimizer with 0.02 learning rate.

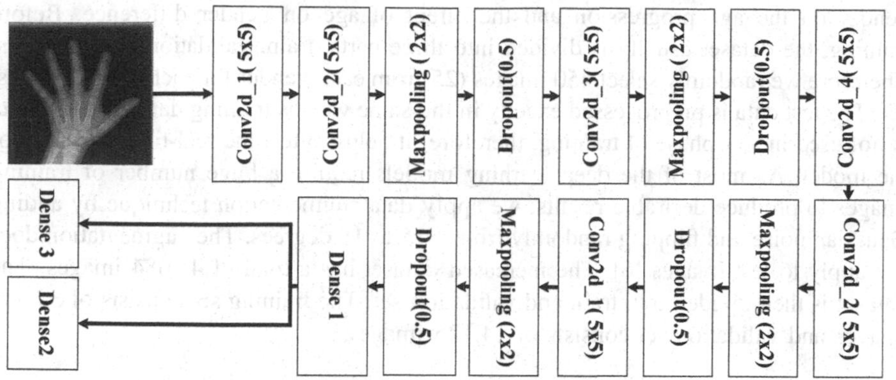

Fig. 2. The proposed network architecture. conv2d: 2-dimensional convolutional neural networks, the input image size is 100 × 100.

3.2 Loss Function

We construct the loss function with two components. Firstly, $\boldsymbol{L_g}$ aims to predict gender correctly.

$$L_g = H\big(f(X), y_g\big) \tag{1}$$

where f is the classifier, y_g is the gender label of data **X.** $H(a, b)$ is the entropy between a and b.

Secondly, $\boldsymbol{L_a}$ aims to give the correct prediction of age,

$$L_a(X, y_a) = H(f(x), y_a) \tag{2}$$

where y_a is the age label of data X. Thus, the total loss can be written as,

$$L(X, y_g, y_a) = \alpha L_g(X, y_g) + \beta L_a(X, y_a) \tag{3}$$

here, α and β are the hyperparameters to control the training process.

4 Experimental Results

We train the network using Keras 2.2.4 [12] with TensorFlow 1.12.0 backend on a Personal Computer operating on Windows 10 and powered with a GPU (Geforce GTX TitanX 1060), RAM of 16 GB and Intel Ci7 64 bit 8th generation CPU. All the data pre-processing tasks are performed using Python 3.6.

We use the dataset of the Radiological Society of North America (RSNA) Pediatric Bone Age Machine Learning Challenge [8, 16], which consists of 12,611 samples. We divide the data initially into 18 classes named as a_1 to a_{18}. Due to the fewer number of images for lower age groups, we reduce the number of classes to only 9 classes as shown in Fig. 3. The main reason for reducing the classes is to observe the effect of gender on the age progression and the effect of age on gender difference. Before training, the dataset usually is divided into three parts, train, validation, and test sets. Therefore we randomly select 450 images (25 from each gender for each class) as a test set. The test data is preprocessed exactly in the same way as training data. The test data is not used in any phase of training, therefore, it helps to test the real-time accuracy of the model. As most of the deep learning models require a huge number of training images to produce desirable results, we apply data augmentation technique by adding Gaussian noise and flipping randomly from −15 to 18 degrees. The augmentation does not apply to test images [6]. The increased dataset has a total of 47,084 images. The dataset is then divided into train and validation set. The training set consists of 32,959 images and validation set consists of 14,125 images.

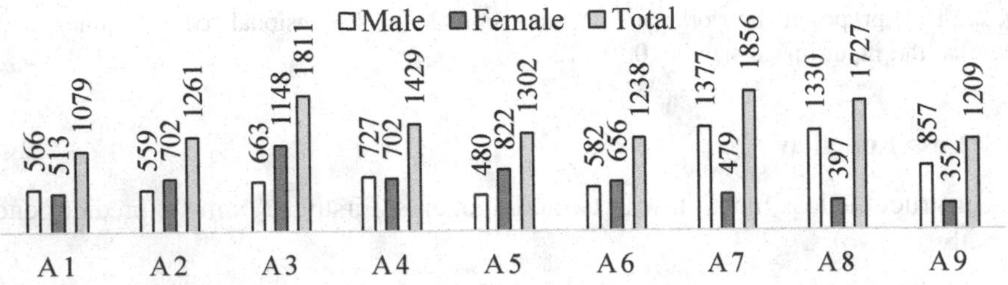

Fig. 3. The number of male and female samples in each reduced class. Initially, there are 18 classes of for age detection that is a_1 to a_{18}, a_1: One-year-old, a_2: Two-year-old, and so on. After reducing number of classes to only 9, A1 = (a_1-a_5), A2 = (a_6-a_7), A3 = (a_8-a_9), A4 = (a_{10}), A5 = (a_{11}), A6 = (a_{12}), A7 = (a_{13}), A8 = (a_{14}), and A9 = (a_{15}- a_{18}).

4.1 Training the Network

We train the network up to 180 epochs. The model achieves training accuracy of 98% for gender detection part and 93% for age detection part. Validation accuracy for gender detection part is 95% and age detection part is 88%. The hyperparameters α is 0.01 and β is 1.0.

The main reason for adding weight loss is to limit the gender detection part from dominating the learning process. As gender detection part has only two classes, therefore, it may influence the learning process, in such a situation static weight loss reduces the imbalance in the training process in the multi-task learning model. Along with multi-task learning, the model is trained independently for gender and age detection to observe the effectiveness of multi-task learning. We name both parts as MTL (Multi-task Learning) and WMTL (Without Multi-task Learning).

4.2 Results and Analysis

Table 1 illustrates the experimental results for the model with MTL and the models without MTL (WMTL). Table 1 is generated with the help of a confusion matrix for all the classes. There are 25 images for each gender in each class. We find that the model with multi-task learning performs better on male images to detect age as compared with female samples. It can be observed from Table 1 that as age progresses, the gender-based features become prominent therefore model performs well on older samples than younger samples. The models trained independently without multi-task learning have good accuracy but their accuracy is lower than the model trained with multi-task learning. For instance, A1 class in MTL part has 39 true positive samples and 36 true positive samples in WMTL part.

Table 1. Accuracy, precision, recall and F1 score for gender detection and age detection. MTL: Multi-Task Learning, WMTL: Without Multi-Task Learning, TN: True Negative, TP: True Positive, FN: False Negative, FP: False Positive, P: Precision, R: Recall, A: Accuracy, F1: F1 Score.

		TP	TN	FP	FN	P	R	A	F1
MTL	M	191	186	34	39	0.85	0.84	0.84	0.85
	F	186	191	39	34	0.83	0.85	0.84	0.84
	A1	39	390	10	11	0.80	0.78	0.96	0.79
	A2	35	380	20	15	0.64	0.70	0.93	0.67
	A3	36	386	14	14	0.72	0.72	0.94	0.72
	A4	33	384	16	17	0.68	0.66	0.93	0.67
	A5	32	389	11	18	0.75	0.64	0.94	0.70
	A6	36	389	11	14	0.77	0.72	0.95	0.75
	A7	39	388	12	11	0.77	0.78	0.95	0.78
	A8	43	390	10	7	0.82	0.86	0.97	0.84
	A9	47	394	6	3	0.89	0.94	0.98	0.92
WMTL	M	187	178	38	47	0.84	0.80	0.82	0.82
	F	178	187	47	38	0.80	0.83	0.82	0.82
	A1	36	390	10	14	0.79	0.72	0.95	0.76
	A2	33	387	13	17	0.72	0.66	0.94	0.69
	A3	36	382	18	14	0.67	0.72	0.93	0.70
	A4	30	380	20	20	0.60	0.60	0.92	0.60
	A5	31	381	19	19	0.62	0.62	0.92	0.62
	A6	28	381	19	22	0.60	0.56	0.91	0.58
	A7	35	382	18	15	0.67	0.70	0.93	0.69
	A8	39	386	14	11	0.74	0.78	0.95	0.76
	A9	45	394	6	5	0.89	0.90	0.98	0.90

Similarly, if we observe the Table 1 for gender detection, MTL part has 191 true positive male samples and WMTL has 187 true positive male samples. It proves the MTL model has higher accuracy as compared with WMTL models. Note that the comparison of the MTL model with state-of-the-art models is not suitable due to the fact that none of the previous models applies multi-task learning for gender and age detection simultaneously.

4.3 Area of Attention Detection

To determine the portions of the hand to which the model pays more attention, we use Grad-Cam [15], a gradient-based feature map visualization technique. Table 2 and Fig. 4 illustrate that the model learns most of its features for gender and age detection from Phalanges portion of the hands as age progresses. The gender-wise difference is mostly at the Phalanges portion and the difference for age detection is around different parts of the hand as depicted in Fig. 4.

Table 2. Visualization of the activation maps for gender detection part and age detection part.

	Input Image	Grad-CAM		Input Image	Grad-CAM
Male			Female		
A1			A9		

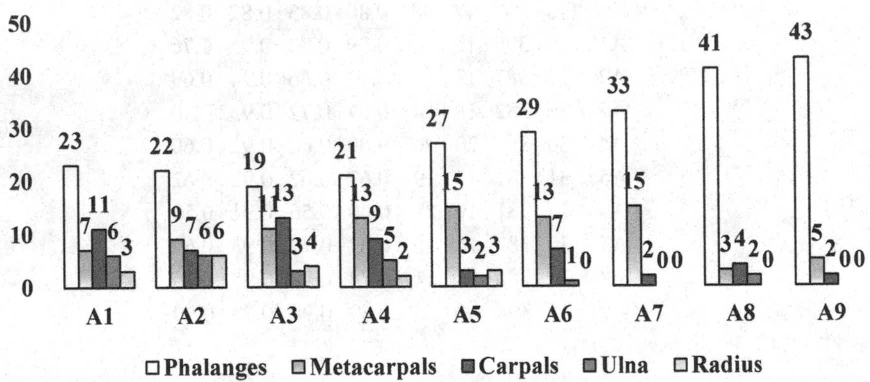

Fig. 4. Grad-Cam based area of attention for age detection from class A1 to A9. Most of the classes pay more attention to the Phalanges and Metacarpals areas.

5 Conclusion

The proposed multi-task learning-based model predicts gender and age with acceptable accuracy simultaneously. Our method contributes in three ways by proposing a novel technique for child gender and age detection. The first contribution is to propose a multi-task learning-based model to determine the gender and age of children simultaneously using left-hand radiographs only. The second contribution is the identification of important parts of the hand (Phalanges and Metacarpals) with Gras-CAM for gender-based age and age-based gender identification. The third contribution is to show a relationship between gender and age detection. In future, the model may be trained with not only left-hand radiographs of the children but it can also be trained with radiographs of right hands, which may help the forensic investigators in gender and age determination. Further, the hand radiographs of adults can also be used to train the network to test its efficacy in gender and age determination.

References

1. Pinto, S.C.D., Urbanová, P., Cesar-Jr, R.M.: Two-dimensional wavelet analysis of supraorbital margins of the human skull for characterizing sexual dimorphism. IEEE Trans. Inf. Forensics Secur. **11**(7), 1542–1548 (2016)
2. Afifi, M.: 11 k hands: Gender recognition and biometric identification using a large dataset of hand images (2018). arXiv:1711.04322
3. Garvin, H.M., Ruff, C.: Sexual dimorphism in skeletal brow ridge and chin morphologies determined using a new quantitative method. Am. J. Phys. Anthropol. **147**(4), 661–670 (2012)
4. Ibrahima, M.A.B., Khalifa, A.M., Hagras, A.M., Alwakid, N.I.: Sex determination from hand dimensions and index/ring finger length ratio in north Saudi population: medico-legal view. Egypt. J. Forensic Sci. **6**(4), 435–444 (2016)
5. Abdullah, H., Jamil, M.M.A., Nor, F.M.: Automated haversian canal detection for histological sex determination. In: 2017 IEEE Symposium on Computer Applications and Industrial Electronics (ISCAIE), Langkawi, pp. 69–74 (2017)
6. Zur, R.M., Jiang, Y., Pesce, L., Drukker, K.: Noise injection for training artificial neural networks: a comparison with weight decay and early stopping. Med. Phys. **36**(10), 4810–4818 (2009)
7. Darmawan, M. F., et al.: Hybrid PSO-ANN for sex estimation based on the length of the left-hand bone. In: 2015 IEEE Student Conference on Research and Development (SCOReD), pp. 478–483. Kuala Lumpur (2015)
8. Remy, Floriane, Hossu, Gabriel, et al.: Development of a biometric method to estimate age on hand radiographs. Forensic Sci. Int. **271**, 113–119 (2017)
9. Yusuf, S., Haron, H., et al.: Age estimation based on bone length using 12 regression models of left-hand x-ray images for Asian children below 19 years old. Legal Med. **17**, 71–78 (2015)
10. Zhou, J., et al.: Using convolutional neural networks and transfer learning for bone age classification. In: 2017 International Conference on Digital Image Computing: Techniques and Applications (DICTA), pp. 1–6. Sydney, NSW (2011)

11. Akcay, S., Kundegorski, M.E., Willcocks, C.G., Breckon, T.P.: Using deep convolutional neural network architectures for object classification and detection within x-ray baggage security imagery. IEEE Trans. Inf. Forensics Secur. **13**(9), 2203–2215 (2018)
12. Han, H., et al.: Heterogeneous face attribute estimation: a deep multi-task learning approach. IEEE Trans. Pattern Anal. Mach. Intell. **40**, 2597–2609 (2018)
13. Su, C., Yang, F., Zhang, S., Tian, Q., Davis, L.S., Gao, W.: Multi-task learning with low-rank attribute embedding for multi-camera person re-identification. IEEE Trans. Pattern Anal. Mach. Intell. **40**(5), 1167–1181 (2018)
14. Kotikalapudi, R.: Contributors, keras-vis (2017). https://github.com/raghakot/keras-vis
15. Zhou, B., et al.: Learning deep features for discriminative localization. In: 2016 IEEE Conference on Computer Vision and Pattern Recognition (CVPR), pp. 2921–2929. Las Vegas, NV (2016)
16. Safwan, S., et al.: The RSNA Pediatric Bone Age Machine Learning Challenge. https://doi.org/10.1148/radiol.2018180736

Shoe Pattern Recognition: A Benchmark

Mengjing Yang, Heng Jiang, and Yunqi Tang[✉]

School of Forensic Science, People's Public Security University of China, Beijing 100038, China
tangyunqi@ppsuc.edu.cn

Abstract. In this paper, we propose a benchmark of shoe recognition based on convolutional neural network. To meet the training and testing needs, we also set up a shoe database which contains 50 pairs of shoes and 160231 images. The Caffe framework is applied in combination with different network models to train and test the image data of shoes, which could obtain the best network model, and the similarity measurement between different shoe pictures is estimated for shoe verification. At the same time, the error recognition image analysis and robustness test are performed. The experimental results show that the proposed method achieves good performance with an accuracy of 95.31%. The proposed method provides a new way for shoe recognition.

Keywords: Criminal investigation · Shoe recognition · Convolutional neural networks

1 Introduction

With the wide application of video monitoring technology, it creates a new opportunity for the development of footprint examination to trace the source of criminal suspects by combining the video data of static footprint monitoring and surrounding dynamic monitoring. The existing "National Public Security Organs Shoe Sample Query System" can obtain the shoe type image according to the scene footprint, and the investigators can find the criminal suspect in the monitoring video according to the shoe type images obtained according to the analysis in the case investigation work. The continuous construction and improvement of video monitoring field have also enabled the development and maturity of video detection technology, which plays an increasingly significant role in case detection. However, at present, the process of finding and locking the shoe type in video and even obtaining the information of criminal suspects still mainly relies on the manual operation of public security technicians, which leads to low investigation efficiency and makes it easy to miss the best opportunity for investigation and arrest. Therefore, it is urgent to develop a method for automatic matching and identifying of shoe pattern images in video monitoring scenes around the crime scene based on the shoe pattern images obtained based on the footprints of the crime scene, thereby improving the degree automation of shoe pattern analysis and providing fast and effective information for tracking and locking criminal suspects.

In this paper, we propose a fast and automatic recognition benchmark based on convolutional neural network to monitor the shoe shape image in a video. In this

Z. Sun et al. (Eds.): CCBR 2019, LNCS 11818, pp. 405–414, 2019.
https://doi.org/10.1007/978-3-030-31456-9_45

method, the feature is extracted by a convolutional neural network, and then the similarity measurement between different samples is calculated to verify the shoe shape. Since there have been many mature algorithms for automatic retrieval and segmentation of human body in the video in the early stage [1, 2], and the cutting of shoe type can also be realized, this paper will focus on the research of classification and recognition algorithm after the establishment of a temporary database. In this paper, video monitoring around the crime scene is simulated and set up. After monitoring video, experimental data are collected for format conversion, frame classification, shoe type area cutting and normalization processing to build the experimental database, which contains a total of 50 shoe types with 160231 data images. Based on Caffe framework, the network structure is designed to build an adaptive network model, and the network identification rate and robustness are improved by debugging the network structure and other methods. An accurate and efficient classification and identification network is obtained and the network model and method applicable for shoe type recognition are improved.

2 Related Work

The integration of footprint and the monitoring around the crime scene video to trace the source of criminal suspects was proposed with the popularity of monitoring, so there are few relevant studies. Yuan [3] firstly proposed to enter the shoe sample query system of the national public security organs based on the footprints extracted from the crime scene to query the shoe type image, and then search for the suspected shoe type in the surrounding video to find the criminal suspect. However, in this paper, the traditional technology method of artificial shoe pattern recognition of video around the crime scene is very labor-intensive, and the investigation efficiency is low. Xu et al. [4] compared and analyzed the suspicious shoe images in video monitoring with the simulated shoe images in video simulation experiment, and found that the suspicious shoe images basically matched the characteristics of the simulated shoe images, thus narrowing the detection scope. In this paper, the artificial search for features and comparisons is carried out which is difficult to avoid errors and easy to be affected by subjective factors. Shoes appearance shape feature extraction and matching, is the key of the recognition of the shoe image automatic feature extraction and intelligent decision can realize automatic recognition of the problem, which requires image recognition technology, through the image processing analysis to identify the different patterns of the target or object (e.g., face, iris, flowers plant, remote sensing images, etc.). In recent years, with the continuous development of image recognition technology, it has been applied in various fields, among which face recognition [5–7], gait recognition [8, 9] and other technologies have been relatively mature.

Image recognition technology originated in the 1950 s, and was first applied to character recognition in office automation tasks, mainly for the analysis and recognition of two-dimensional images. In the 1960s, Roberts [10] proposed to extract 3d features from digital images, which initiated the research on image recognition to understand 3d scenes. In the next few decades, the Gaussian mixture model, k-means clustering, support vector machine and other shallow structures used in the early image recognition technology can solve some simple problems in various fields such as medicine, industry, transportation, security and so on, but it is difficult to solve complex real-world problems. Later, with the advent of deep neural network, especially since 2011, a large number of image recognition methods based on convolution neural network have emerged as the computing power of computers has been significantly enhanced and various algorithms have been well applied [11–17].

Along with the development of the classic network, network deep in the deepening, and the application effect of ImageNet data set is also getting better and better. From the 4-layer network structure of Lenet to the 8-layer network structure of AlexNet, the top-5 error rate is 16.4%. As for the 19-layer network structure of VGG, the top-5 error rate drops to 7.3%, and the 21-layer network structure of GoogLeNet [18], the top-5 error rate drops to 6.7%. Even later ResNet reached 152 layers, with a top-5 error rate of only 3.57%. Although the introduction of dropout layer, small convolution kernel, residual network and other factors makes the application effect continue to improve the application effect, with the deepening of the network structures, the network has more non-linear functions, making the decision function more decisive and achieving better classification effect.

Given the good applied results of convolution neural network, this paper will introduce convolution neural network into the shoe type analysis, which could not only avoid the artificial selection to determine the type of shoe features of subjective factors, but also increase the speed of automatic identification and matching to effectively improved the investigation efficiency. To avoid the error of the artificial search, the matching results can be rapidly applied to the next phase of the investigation work.

3 Proposed Method

Network Structure and Parameters

In this experiment, we set up four different network structures according to the comparison of the unique characteristics of shoe pattern recognition. The practical difference between these four network structures is the difference in network depth. The ConvNet configurations are outlined in Table 1. DeepID program [12] of the Chinese University of Hong Kong achieved a face recognition accuracy rate of 97.45% on the LFW database. The problem of shoe recognition is similar to face recognition, so DeepID network structure is one of the four network structures set in this paper. DeepID network framework includes four layers of convolution layer, three layers of pooling layer, and two layers of full connection layer. The penultimate full-connected layer is connected to the fourth layer of convolution and the third layer of pooling, which increases the number of output neurons and gives consideration to both local and global characteristics. However, DeepID solves a wide variety of data sets, and this experiment only simulates a small number of database types. Considering the computational complexity, it does not refer to this full connection strategy. We also refer to lenet-5 network structure with fewer network layers to enhance network depth contrast. The most effective application is DeepID network structure deepening, and the network structure is defined as DeepIDadd-network. The network structure of DeepIDadd-network structure is shown in the Fig. 1.

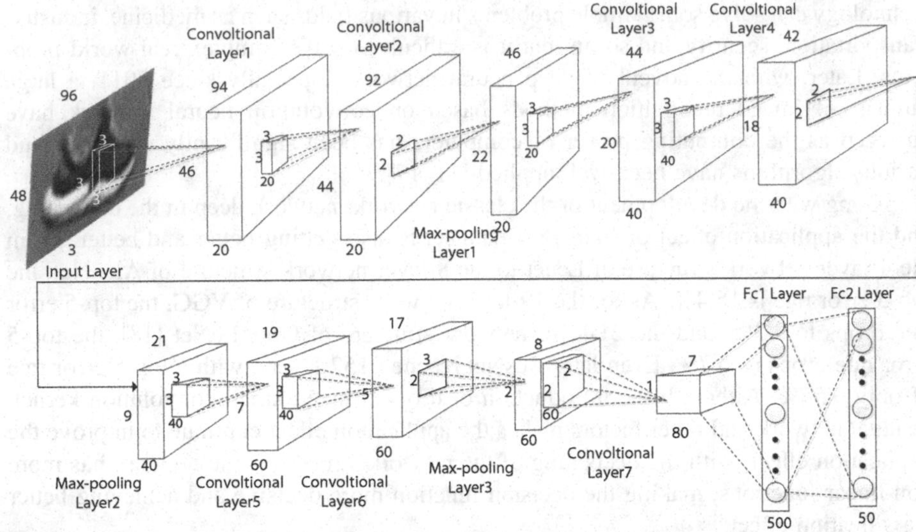

Fig. 1. DeepIDadd-network structure. The length, width, and height of each cuboid denotes the map number and the dimension of each map for all input, convolutional, max-pooling layers. The inside small cuboids and quadrangles denote the 3D convolution kernel size and the 2D pooling region sizes of convolutional and max-pooling layer, respectively.

Table 1. ConvNet configurations (shown in columns). Our network configuration is from 4 weight layers in the network LeNet (2 conv. And 2 FC layers) to 9 weight layers in the network DeepIDadd (7 conv. And 2 FC layers). The step size of convolution is 1, and the step size of pooling is 2.

ConvNet configuration			
LeNet	LeNetadd	DeepID	DeepIDadd
4 weight layers	6 weight layers	6 weight layers	9 weight layers
Input (96 * 48 RGB image)			
Conv1 5 * 5	Conv1 3 * 3 Conv2 3 * 3	Conv1 5 * 5	Conv1 3 * 3 Conv2 3 * 3
Maxpool1 2 * 2			
Conv2 5 * 5	Conv3 3 * 3 Conv4 3 * 3	Conv2 5 * 5	Conv3 3 * 3 Conv4 3 * 3
Maxpool2 2 * 2			
–	–	Conv3 5 * 5	Conv5 3 * 3 Conv6 3 * 3
–		Maxpool3 3 * 2	
–	–	Conv4 2 * 2	Conv7 2 * 2
Fc1-500			
Fc2-50			

Since the two layers 3 * 3 convolution kernel has the same receptive field as 5 * 5 convolution kernel, but with the same receptive field, the smaller convolution kernel can be used to increase the number of network layers and the extracted features are more elaborate. Therefore, the convolution kernel with the size of 5 * 5 in two classical networks is converted into the convolution kernel with the size of 2 layers of 3 * 3, and other parameters remain unchanged.

4 Experiments

4.1 Datasets

In this experiment, video data were collected in the footprint laboratory. A total of 8 volunteers (6 males and 2 females) wore 50 pairs of shoes for video data collection. A light blue carpet was laid on the experimental site to reduce background interference. For analog video monitoring in shoe angle and ensure the reliability of the experiment, from different angles for data acquisition (0°, 5°, 10°, 15°, 180°, etc.), at the same time by adjusting the indoor lamplight makes video data is not affected by light intensity. The volunteers walked successively in the 1.2-m-wide walking area. The collection device is the HIKVISION monitoring camera, and the frame rate is set at 50FPS, with the frame size of 1920 pixels * 1080 pixels, and the collection time of each type of sample is about 80 s (Fig. 2).

After the completion of video data collection, HMSTranscoder software was used to convert video format and cut video material of each pair of shoes into a sample video. At the same time, video brightness was set to 12 and the contrast was set to 15. Matlab (R2016a) software was used to batch frame each video sample. In order to ensure the data volume of the video frame by frame, 50 video frame folders were established and named 1–50. As the size of video frame was large, the proportion of the shoe type was very small. In order to eliminate invalid interference and reduce the amount of calculation, the proportion of the shoe in video frame was cut at a ratio of 2:1, which was normalized to 96 pixels * 48 pixels and saved. Video frame interception of shoe shape process is simulated automatic detection and cutting, using Matlab (R2016a) to write the program, we can achieve the manual click on the upper left corner of the shoe shape position to obtain coordinates, automatic interception ratio of 2:1 shoe shape picture, and save it to the specified folder. The interception process is shown in Fig. 4.

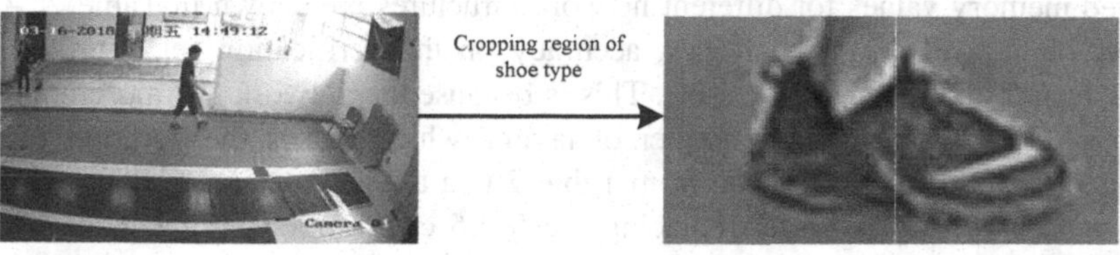

Fig. 2. Schematic diagram of interception process.

Video frame will be separate right and left foot interception process. Overlap with foot, there are other distractions and 45° angle is greater than the video frames to be deleted, to 50 class shoe image data obtained by intercepting filter, choose different illumination, angle sample images, a total of 160231 copies. Various sample data are shown in Fig. 3.

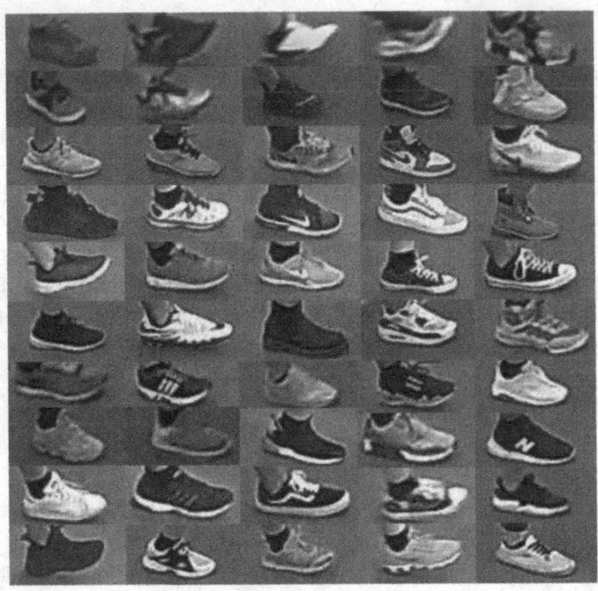

Fig. 3. Examples of various experimental data. The datasets included common shoe shapes in similar colors and different style categories.

4.2 Experimental Results and Analysis

4.2.1 Different Network Structures

By comparing the two classical neural network structures and deepening the layers of the two classical networks, four network structures were obtained. The variation trend of the accuracy and loss of different trainings with the number of traversal times of the training set are shown in Fig. 4. It can be seen from the figure that, although DeepI-Dadd network structure improves the accuracy slowly in the training process, it finally gets the highest accuracy. Except for the slight oscillation of each network when traversing the training set for 190 times, it tends to converge. Test accuracy and required memory values for different network structures are shown in Table 2. As the number of network layers increases, accuracy on the verification set improves continuously and finally reaches 95.31%. This is because the network has more non-linear functions after increasing the number of layers, which makes the decision function more decisive. It can also be seen from Table 2 that the memory value required by the new network constructed after replacing the 5 * 5 convolution kernel with two convolution kernels of 3 * 3 size each time will greatly increase during the training, and at the same time, the training time will also increase.

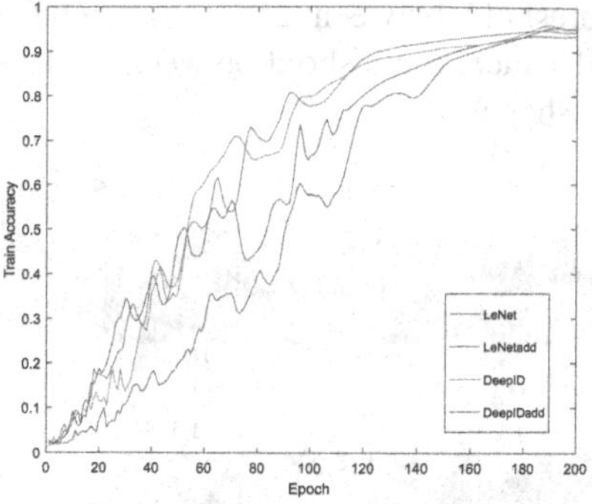

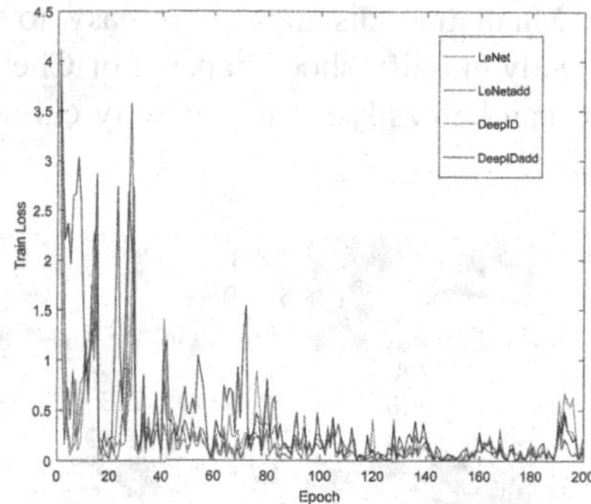

Fig. 4. Train Accuracy and Loss Vs epoch. These two figures show that the training accuracy and loss of different network structures increase with the number of traversal times of the training set.

Table 2. Network impact on performance. This table compares the performance of the execution test set between different network structures, or the effect of increasing the number of network layers on the recognition performance of shoe type is compared.

Network	The number of layers	Memory	Train time (min)	Val-Acc (%)	Loss
LeNet	6	83622404	50	91.91	0.2807
LeNetadd	8	150428164	67	93.63	0.2348
DeepID	9	82173444	44	94.36	0.1866
DeepIDadd	12	148559364	65	95.31	0.1539

4.2.2 Robustness of Different Pixel Images

In the actual practice of public security work, the shoe type pictures appearing in the video monitoring are different due to the different pixel quality of the monitor camera and the size of the shoe type displayed in the video. Therefore, the pixel robustness of DeepIDadd on the best network we set is shown in Table 3. DeepIDadd has strong pixel robustness because the accuracy of different pixel images has little change.

Table 3. Shows the robustness of DeepIDadd model

Pixels	2304	4608	9216
Val-rate (%)	94.63	95.31	95.19

4.2.3 Verification of Shoe Shape

Figure 5 shows the similarity distance between the 50-dimensional features outputted by DeepIDadd network structure. 0.0 indicates that the two pairs of shoes have exactly the same figure. The larger the distance, the lower the similarity. For Euclidian distances, a threshold between 38.6 and 97.6 makes it easy to classify shoe types correctly.

For Manhattan distance, it is easy to set a threshold between 218.8 and 566.6 to correctly classify shoe shapes. For Chebyshev distance, a threshold between 13.4 and 29.6 can be easily set to correctly classify shoe shapes.

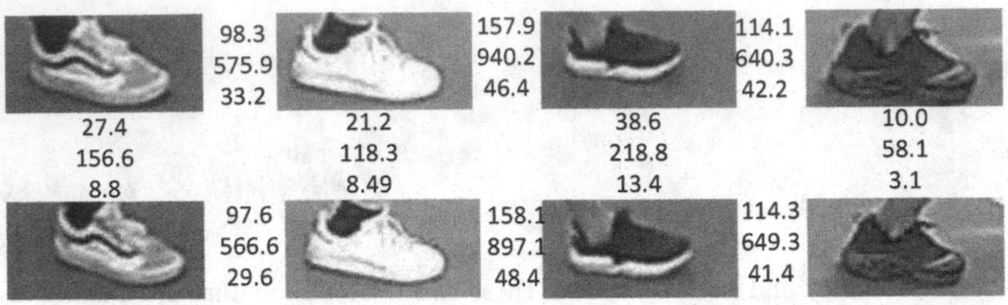

Fig. 5. Verification of shoe shape. The numbers between every two pictures successively represent Euclidean distance, Manhattan distance and Chebyshev distance where DeepIDadd model extracts 50-dimensional features.

4.2.4 Performance on VAL

When DeepIDadd was selected to train and classify the self-built shoe type database, the recognition error rate was 4.69%. The misidentification errors are mainly caused by the similar contour and color of the shoe type, image blurring and lighting factors, etc. Part of the wrongly identified shoe type picture is shown in Fig. 6.

Fig. 6. Partial misidentify of shoe type picture. This image shows some of the misidentified images

5 Conclusion

In this paper, after the large-scale data collection and the establishment of a database, four network structures were set up for comparative analysis, and the best network model DeepIDadd was obtained to be the benchmark of shoe recognition. The recognition accuracy could reach 95.31%. The pixel robustness of the network model was tested and good results were obtained. However, the experimental data used in this paper are all shoe shapes on a pure blue background. There are often interferences such as complex background, deformation and partial occlusion in actual investigation cases. At present, the structure of the experimental network is relatively simple, and the recognition effect of samples with similar shoe shape colors and contours is not good. In the next step, the network will be improved, which could improve the recognition accuracy of similar samples, and a robust shoe type recognition network model which is suitable for complex scenes will be built.

Acknowledgements. This work is supported by National Key Research and Development Program of China (Grant No. 2017YFC0822003), the Fundamental Research Funds for the Central Universities of China (Grant No. 2018JKF217).

References

1. Wang, X., Liu, Y., Li, G.: Moving object detection algorithm based on improved visual background extractor algorithm. Acta Opt. Sin. **56**(01), 011007 (2019)
2. Chen, C., Xuan, S., Xu, J.: Pedestrian detection and segmentation under background clutter. Comput. Eng. Appl. **48**(30), 177–181 (2012)
3. Yang, C., Yu, S.: Preliminary study on the application of footprint analysis in video investigation. Guangdong Pol. Technol. **25**(2), 61–63 (2017)
4. Xu, L., Li, Z., Li, Z., et al.: Application of video investigation simulation experiment in case detection. Forensic Sci. **43**(04), 330–333 (2018)
5. Wu, C., Ding, J.: Occluded face recognition using low-rank regression with generalized gradient direction. Pattern Recogn. **80**, 256–268 (2018)
6. Weng, R., Lu, J., Hu, J., Yang, G., Tan, Y.: Robust feature set matching for partial face recognition. In: IEEE International Conference on Computer Vision (ICCV), pp. 601–608. IEEE Computer Society, Sydney (2013)
7. Dewan, M., Granger, E., Marcialis, G.L., Sabourin, R., Roli, F.: Adaptive appearance model tracking for still-to-video face recognition. Pattern Recogn. **49**, 129–151 (2016)
8. Alotaibi, M., Mahmood, A.: Improved Gait recognition based on specialized deep convolutional neural networks. In: IEEE Applied Imagery Pattern Recognition Workshop (AIPR), pp. 1–7. IEEE, Lodz (2016)
9. Wu, Z., Huang, Y., Wang, L., et al.: A comprehensive study on cross-view gait based human identification with deep CNNs. IEEE Trans. Pattern Anal. Mach. Intell. **39**(2), 209–226 (2016)
10. Roberts, L.G.: Machine perception of three-dimensional solids (1965)
11. Krizhevsky, A., Sutskever, I., Hinton, G.: ImageNet classification with deep convolutional neural networks. In: Proceeding of the 26th Annual Conference on Neural Information Processing Systems, pp. 1097–1105 (2012)
12. Du, J., Hu, B., Zhang, Z.: Gastric carcinoma classification based on convolutional neural network and micro-hyperspectral imaging. Acta Opt. Sin. **38**(06), 0617001 (2018)
13. Simonyan, K., Zisserman, A.: Very deep convolutional networks for large-scale image recognition. Comput. Sci. (2014)
14. Sun, Y., Wang, X., Tang, X.: Deeply learned face representations are sparse, selective, and robust. In: IEEE Conference on Computer Vision and Pattern Recognition (CVPR), pp. 2892–2900 (2015)

15. Taigman, Y., Yang, M., Ranzato, M., Wolf, L.: DeepFace: closing the gap to human-level performance in face verification. In: IEEE Conference on Computer Vision and Pattern Recognition (CVPR), pp. 1701–1708 (2014)
16. Kumar, N., Berg, A., Belhumeur, P., Nayar, S.: Attribute and simile classifiers for face verification. In: IEEE International Conference on Computer Vision, pp. 365–372. IEEE (2010)
17. He, K., Zhang, X., Ren, S., et al.: Deep residual learning for image recognition. In: IEEE Conference on Computer Vision and Pattern Recognition (CVPR), pp. 770–778 (2016)
18. Szegedy, C., Liu, W., Jia, Y., et al.: Going deeper with convolutions. In: IEEE Conference on Computer Vision and Pattern Recognition (CVPR), pp. 1–9 (2015)

Learning Discriminative Representation for ECG Biometrics Based on Multi-Scale 1D-PDV

Yanwen Sun[1], Gongping Yang[1,2(✉)], Yuwen Huang[2], Kuikui Wang[1], and Yilong Yin[1]

[1] School of Software, Shandong University, Jinan 250101, China
gpyang@sdu.edu.cn

[2] School of Computer, Heze University, Heze 274015, China

Abstract. ECG has drawn increasing attention in the biometrics and achieves great success compared with other biological characteristics. However, ECG cannot satisfy the requirements of mobile application owing to the poor quality. In this paper, we learn discriminative representation for ECG biometrics based on multi-scale 1D-PDV feature. First, we choose PDV as the base feature and attempt to convert PDV to the one-dimensional and multi-scale in the ECG biometrics. Second, our method learns a mapping to project the multi-scale 1D-PDV to a low dimensional feature vector and capture discriminative information of ECG. Then each feature vector is pooled in the codebook and represented as a histogram feature. Last, we apply principal component analysis (PCA) to reduce the histogram feature dimension and compute the matching score with cosine similarity. We evaluate our method on two public databases and the results prove our method achieves superior performance than other existing methods.

Keywords: ECG biometrics · Multi-scale 1D-PDV · Discriminative representation · Cosine similarity

1 Introduction

As an important biomedical electrical signal, ECG reflect the essence of heart and life activities, and have important research significance. ECG can not only apply in clinical diagnosis, but also an emerging modality for biometrics [1, 2]. An ECG records the electrical activity of the heart. The electrical signals are acquired by electrodes placed on the body surface of the person [3]. This method of acquisition makes ECG superior to several other biometric systems were acquiring the biometric signal may distract the user. For example, the user may need to look at the camera in face recognition; the user may need to swipe his/her finger in fingerprint recognition. Another advantage of ECG is quasi-periodic; hence, observations are continuously available.

Z. Sun et al. (Eds.): CCBR 2019, LNCS 11818, pp. 415–423, 2019.
https://doi.org/10.1007/978-3-030-31456-9_46

Features are critical to the performance of biometrics. The Local Binary Pattern (LBP) features are regarded as an effective and discriminative texture descriptor. Also, these LBP features can be used in ECG biometrics. Louis et al. [4] proposed a 1DMRLBP feature is an adaptation of the two dimensional image based on LBP to suit one dimensional (1D) ECG. In this paper, we calculate the difference between the current point value and its neighbors to obtain a point difference vector (PDV). Because the PDV save the difference between the current point and its neighbors, so we can obtain actual differences of ECG and those information is useful in the ECG biometrics. However, PDV has a disadvantage: the scope of extraction is limited. If this extraction range is wide, the PDV will be long. Although a long code can exploit the rich information, the computational cost and storage requirement are increased [5].

In order to solve the disadvantages of PDV, many authors use learning methods to extract the discriminative information and achieve promising results in the field of biometrics. In the face biometrics, Lu et al. [6,7] proposed a compact binary feature descriptor by learning a hashing map to project PDV extracted from training images into binary codes. Liu et al. [8] proposed anchor-based manifold binary pattern for finger vein recognition, which learns the manifold information in the binary code. Inspired by the above work, we introduce a discriminative method aims to learn K hash functions that map high dimensional multi-scale 1D-PDV into a low dimensional feature vector and achieves a better performance [9].

In this work, we learn discriminative representation for ECG biometrics based on multi-scale 1D-PDV feature. First, considering that PDV is widely used in the biometrics domain, we extract the PDV from each heartbeat. Second, in order to capture PDV feature in different scale, we introduce a window size, w, and window shift steps, s, to design a new feature vector multi-scale 1D-PDV. Third, we design an objective function to learn a map that projects each multi-scale 1D-PDV into a code. In the learning process, the variance of the learned feature matrix is maximized and the quantization error between the multi-scale 1D-PDV and the learned feature matrixes is minimized. Due to the bag-of-words framework has successfully been used in the field of biometrics [10,13], we represent each ECG heartbeat as a histogram by the bag-of-words framework. We apply principal component analysis (PCA) to reduce the histogram feature dimension and compute the matching score with cosine similarity. Finally, experimental results on two public ECG databases are used to compare the performance of the proposed method to other existing ECG biometrics methods [15].

The rest of this paper is organized as following. Our proposed method is described in detail in Sect. 2. The experimental results that validate the proposed methods in comparison with the conventional methods are given in Sect. 3. Section 4 concludes this work.

2 Proposed Method

2.1 Multi-Scale 1D Point Difference Vector Feature Extraction

PDV feature has been widely used in the face and finger vein biometrics domain because it achieves better computational cost and considers the differences among neighbor subject. We take the center point of the window and calculate the difference between this point with its neighbors to construct a PDV vector. However, the above PDV is limited to the application of 2-D image. In this paper, PDV is applied to 1-D ECG signals and we propose multi-scale 1D-PDV to extract the feature.

(1) One Dimensional Point Difference Vector (1D-PDV)
In [6,7], the authors apply LBP to 1 dimension and use it as a feature for ECG biometrics. Inspired by this idea, we use the following method to apply PDV to the ECG. The neighbors are before and after a given point in a $2 \times p$ sizes. Figure 1 illustrates the extraction of 1D-PDV from the ECG, where p is set to 4 in this example.

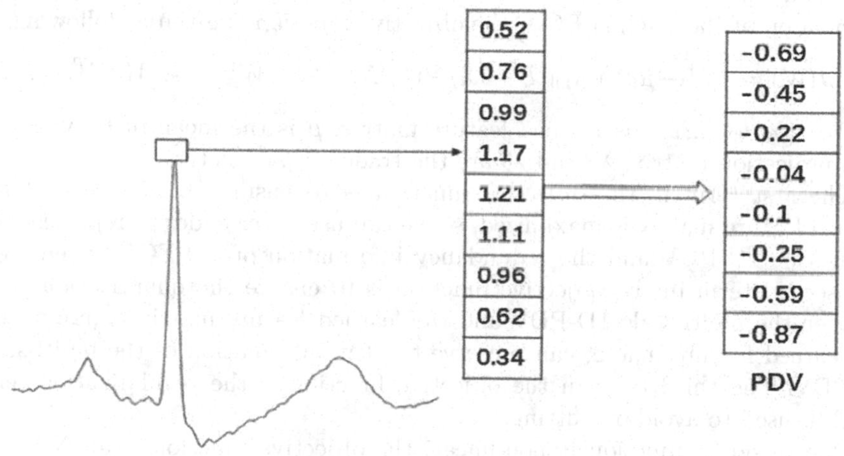

Fig. 1. Illustration of PDV operator in our method (with p=4)

(2) Multi-Scale 1D-PDV
Although the 1-D PDV features achieve better computational cost and consider the differences among neighbor subject, each feature vector only considers a fixed temporal change and the correlation between each PDV feature vector is not considered [11]. So, we design a window sizes w and window shift steps s to capture different scale PDV feature. For example, each person has 24 PDV feature vectors. When w is set to 3, s is set to 2, those

feature vectors are grouped as $1, 2, 3; 3, 4, 5; 5, 6, 7; \cdots; 20, 21, 22; 22, 23, 24$, the new feature vector has three different PDV feature vector. So, the window shift steps decide each window is overlapped or not. With different p, w and s, multiple scale can be captured for the same time-sample and this new structure can get more information than the single scale.

2.2 Discriminative Representation Learning

After getting the multi-scale 1D-PDV $X = \{x_1, x_2, ..., x_N\}$, where N is the person number, $x_i \in \Re^{t\times d}$, t is windows number of each person, $t = [1+(m-w)/s]\times num$, m is the sample number of heartbeat, num is the heartbeat number of a person. d is the dimensionality of a PDV feature vector, $d=2\times p\times w$, w, s and p are introduced above. The proposed method aims to learn K hash functions that map high dimensional multi-scale 1D-PDV x_i into a low dimensional feature codes vector [12] $b_i = \{b_{i1}, b_{i2}, ..., b_{ik}\}$. We can use $W = \{w_1, w_2, ..., w_n\}$ to represent this hash function and the feature vector b_{ik} of x_{ik} can be computed by the w_i.

$$b_{ik} = 0.5 \times (sgn(w_k^T x_i) + 1); \tag{1}$$

sgn(h) is a signum function, and if $h \geq 0$, $sgn(h) = 1$ and -1 otherwise.

In order to make learned feature vector b_n discriminative and retain the information of the original ECG, the objective function is given as following:

$$minJ(W) = -\|B-\mu\|^2 + \lambda_1\|(B-0.5) - W^T X\|^2 + \lambda_2\|W^2\| \quad s.t. WW^T = I \tag{2}$$

$B = \{b_1, b_2, ..., b_n\}$ is learned feature matrix, μ is the mean of B, W is the hash projection matrix, λ_1 and λ_2 are the trade-off parameters.

The first term in the objective function is to ensure the variance of the learned feature matrix is maximized, so we can use fewer codes to represent the multi-scale 1D-PDV and the redundancy information of the ECG is removed. The second term in the objective function is to ensure the quantization error between the multi-scale 1D-PDV and the learned feature matrix is minimized, the learned feature matrix can preserve the key information of the multi-scale 1D-PDV. The third term in the objective function is the regularization term which is used to avoid overfitting.

Due to sgn(.) function is non-linear, the objective function is an NP-hard problem. In order to solve this problem, we use signed magnitude to relax it [16]. We can write the formula (2) in the following matrix form:

$$minJ(W) = tr(W^T CW) + \lambda_1\|(B - 0.5) - W^T X\|^2 + \lambda_2\|W^2\| \quad s.t. WW^T = I \tag{3}$$

$$C = \frac{1}{N} \times (XX^T - 2X\mu^T + \mu\mu^T)$$

While formula (3) is not convex, we can adopt an alternate method to optimize W and B by following method [13]:

Fix W and update B: When W is a given matrix, (3) can be written as:

$$B = 0.5 \times (sgn(W^T x) + 1); \tag{4}$$

Algorithm 1. Discriminative representation learning

Require:

X= Multi-Scale 1D-PDV ;
λ_1 and λ_2 = parameters;
K = length of the Multi-Scale 1D-PDV codes;
T = iteration number;
ε = convergence parameter;

Result :

W = projection matrix W;

Initialize W :the top K eigenvectors of $XX^T = I$; t = 1 ;
repeat
    t = t+1;
    Fix W and update B with (1);
    Fix B and update W with (2);
until $|W\text{-} W^T| \leq \varepsilon$ *and* $t \geq 2$;
Return W;

Fix B and update W: When B is a given matrix, (3) can be written as

$$minJ(W) = tr(W^T CW) + \lambda_1(tr(W^T XX^T W) - 2 \times tr((B - 0.5) \times X^T W)) + \lambda_2\|W^2\| \quad (5)$$

We use the gradient descent method with curvilinear search algorithm in [14] to solve this problem to update W. The detailed procedure of the proposed method in Algorithm 1.

2.3 Representation Based on Bag-of-Words Model

The bag-of-words (BOW) model is a simplified representation used in natural language processing and information retrieval [13]. Since the BOW model can utilize statistical information while its simple and effective performance, so we select BOW model to represent the ECG.

Having the hash mapping matrix W, we map each multi-scale 1D-PDV from the training set and testing set into a low dimensional feature vector. Then we use k-means to cluster those feature vectors from the training set into a codebook. Then each feature vector is pooled in the codebook and all multi-scale 1D-PDV from a same ECG heartbeat are represented as a histogram feature for the ECG representation. Finally, we apply principal component analysis (PCA) to reduce the histogram feature dimension and compute the matching score with cosine similarity. Figure 2 shows our method how to represent ECG.

3 Experiments and Results

3.1 Databases

In our experiments, we select one channel of all of recordings in the MIT-BIH and MIT-ST database. Before the multi-scale 1D-PDV extraction, we use

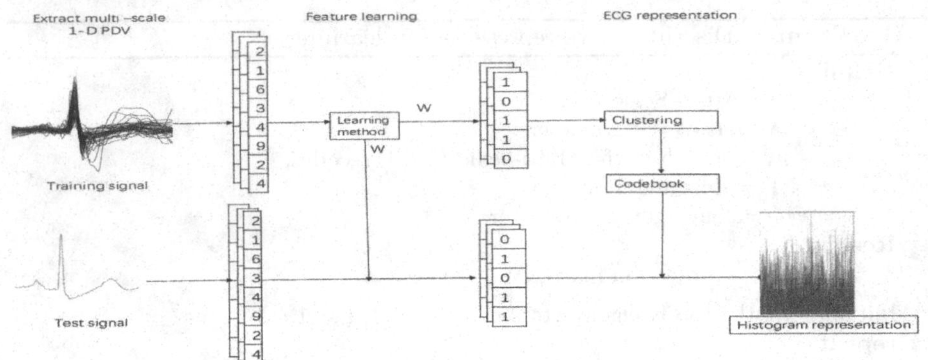

Fig. 2. Schematic of our proposed method based ECG representation

preprocessing to select the valid record. For each valid subject, we segment it into heartbeats. Each heartbeat in our experimental data consists of 130 points on the left of R peak and 130 points on the right. For each subject, we randomly select 24 heartbeats and the first 12 heartbeats are used as the training set while the other 12 heartbeats are used as the testing set.

3.2 Evaluation of the Method

In this section, we evaluate the ECG recognition performance of our proposed method. The performance is evaluated by the recognition rate and the computational time. We define the computational time are consisted of training time and matching time.

Table 1 shows that the multi-scale 1D-PDV achieves better performance than LBP and 1-D PDV on two public databases. The main reason for this result is that multi-scale 1D-PDV consider a fixed temporal change and the correlation between each PDV feature vector, the multi-scale 1D-PDV can capture more discriminative information than the other methods. Table 2 shows the training time and matching time per ECG. PDV-based methods are better than LBP-based method. This is because the PDV-based methods only need to calculate the difference between this point with its neighbors, but the LBP-based method need convert the binary sequence to a decimal number, and this process cost lots of computational time. Compared multi-scale 1D-PDV with 1-D PDV, we can see that the training time and matching time per ECG are little more. The reason is that multi-scale 1D-PDV combine 1-D PDV to a new feature and multi-scale 1D-PDV length is longer than 1-D PDV. So, the multi-scale 1D-PDV feature can largely enhance the accuracy of recognition rate and slightly reduce the computational time.

Table 1. Recognition rate of LBP, 1-D PDV, Multi-Scale 1D-PDV on MIT-BIH and MIT-ST database

Methods	Recognition rate on MIT-BIH	Recognition rate on MIT-ST
LBP	97.4	96.40
1-D PDV	98.65	98.47
Multi-Scale 1D-PDV	99.78	99.87

Table 2. Training time and Matching time of LBP, 1-D PDV, Multi-Scale 1D-PDV

Methods	Training time	Matching time per ECG
LBP	125.62 s	20.61 ms
1-D PDV	67.68 s	14.47 ms
Multi-Scale 1D-PDV	75.62 s	15.56 ms

3.3 Comparison with State-of-the-Art ECG Biometrics

In this part, we make a comparison between our method with the state-of-art methods on the MIT-BIH and MIT-ST database. We can see from Table 3 that our method achieves better performance than the previous methods. Especially in the MIT-ST database, the convincing performance proves our method can be applied in real world scenarios.

Table 3. EER and Recognition rate of different methods on MIT-BIH and MIT-ST database

Database	Method	EER	Recognition
MIT-BIH	[4]	20.4%	97.2%
	[17]	–	99.2%
	Ours	0.85%	99.78%
MIT-ST	[18]	–	99%
	[17]	–	98%
	Ours	0.92%	99.87%

4 Conclusion and Future Work

In this paper, we learn discriminative representation for ECG biometrics based on multi-scale 1D-PDV feature. Experiments on two public ECG databases to verify that our methods by introducing multi-scale 1D-PDV and our objective function achieve better performance than the state of-the-art method. The main contributions of our work are summarized as follows: (1) This is the first attempt to convert PDV to the one-dimensional and multi-scale in the ECG biometrics. With the extracted feature, the accuracy of recognition rate is enhanced and the computational time is reduced. (2) By the proposed objective function, we can learn a map that projects the multi-scale 1D-PDV to a low dimension and capture discriminative information of ECG. (3) We consider bag-of-words framework to present each heartbeat. (4) By testing on MIT-ST database, our method attains convincing performance in a real world scenarios and can be used in the actual ECG biometrics. In the future work, we plan to test the proposed method on a larger number database and apply the method on other biometrics.

Acknowledgements. This work was supported in part by the National Natural Science Foundation of China under Grant 61703235,61876098 and in part by the Key Research and Development Project of Shandong Province under Grant 2018GGX101032 and 2019GGX101056.

References

1. Biel, L., Pettersson, O., Philipson, L., Wide, P.: ECG analysis: a new approach in human identification. IEEE Trans. Instrum. Meas. **50**, 808–812 (2001)
2. Jain, A.K., Nandakumar, K., Ross, A.: 50 years of biometric research: accomplishments, challenges, and opportunities. Pattern Recogn. Lett. **79**, 80–105 (2016)
3. Kun, S., et al.: Human identification using finger vein and ECG signals. Neurocomputing **332**, 111–118 (2019)
4. Louis, W., Komeili, M., Hatzinakos, D.: Continuous authentication using one-dimensional multi-resolution local binary patterns (1DMRLBP) in ECG biometrics. IEEE Trans. Inf. Forensics Secur. **11**(12), 2818–2832 (2016)
5. Liu, H.Y., Yang, L., Yang, G.P., et al.: Discriminative binary: descriptor for finger vein recognition. IEEE Access **6**, 5795–5804 (2018)
6. Lu, J.W., Liong, V.E., Zhou, X.Z., et al.: Learning compact binary face descriptor for face recognition. IEEE Trans. Pattern Anal. Mach. Intell. **37**, 2041–2056 (2015)
7. Lu, J.W., Liong, V.E., Zhou, J.: Simultaneous local binary feature learning and encoding for homogeneous and heterogeneous face recognition. IEEE Trans. Pattern Anal. Mach. Intell. **40**, 1979–1993 (2018)
8. Liu, H., Yang, G., Yang, L., Su, K., Yin, Y.: Anchor-based manifold binary pattern for finger vein recognition. SCIENCE CHINA Inf. Sci. **62**(5), 52104:1–52104:16 (2019)
9. Liu, F., Yin, Y.L., Yang, G.P., et al.: Finger vein recognition with super-pixel based features. In: Proceedings of IEEE International Joint Conference on Biometrics (2014)
10. Agrafioti, F., Hatzinakos, D.: ECG based recognition using second order statistics. In: 6th Annual IEEE Communication Networks and Services Research Conference, CNSR 2008 (2008)
11. Pan, J., Tompkins, W.J.: A real-time QRS detection algorithm. IEEE Trans. Biomed. Eng. **3**, 230–236 (1985)
12. Wang, J., Kumar, S., Chang, S.-F.: Semi-supervised hashing for scalable image retrieval. In: Proceedings of the IEEE Computer Society Conference on omputer Vision and Pattern Recognition, pp. 3424–3431 (2010)

13. Gong, Y., Lazebnik, S., Gordo, A., Perronnin, F.: Iterative quantization: a procrustean approach to learning binary codes for large-scale image retrieval. IEEE Trans. Pattern Anal. Mach. Intell. **35**(12), 2916–2929 (2013)
14. Wen, Z., Yin, W.: A feasible method for optimization with orthogonality constraints. Math. Program. **142**(1), 397–434 (2013)
15. Dong, L., Yang, G., Yin, Y., Liu, F., Xi, X.: Finger vein verification based on a personalized best patches map. In: Proceedings IEEE International Joint Conference on Biometrics (IJCB), pp. 1–8, October 2014
16. Berkaya, S.K., Uysal, A.K., Gunal, E.S., Ergin, S., Günal, S., Bilginer Gülmezoglu, M.: A survey on ECG analysis. Biomed. Signal Process. Control **43**, 216–235 (2018)
17. Zhao, Z.D., Chen, D.D., Luo, Y.: A human ECG identification system based on ensemble empirical mode decomposition. Sensors **13**(5) (2013). https://doi.org/10.3390/s130506832
18. Lu, W., Hou, H.H., Chu, J.H.: Feature fusion for imbalanced ECG data analysis. Biomed. Signal Process. Control. **41**, 52–160 (2018)

Off-Line Handwritten Signature Recognition Based on Discrete Curvelet Transform

Long-Fei Mo[1], Mahpirat[2], Ya-Li Zhu[1], Hornisa Mamat[1], and Kurban Ubul[1](✉)

[1] School of Information Science and Engineering, Xinjiang University, Urumqi 830046, China
kurbanu@xju.edu.cn

[2] Academic Affairs Division, Xinjiang University, Urumqi 830046, China

Abstract. In order to improve the offline handwritten signature recognition effect, an offline handwritten signature recognition method based on discrete curvelet transform is proposed. First, the necessary pre-processing of offline handwritten signatures is carried out, including grayscale, binarization, smooth denoising, etc. The pre-processed signature image is subjected to curvelet transform to obtain real-numbered curve coefficients in the cell matrix, and a total of 82-dimensional energy features are extracted, and multi-scale block local binary mode (MBLBP) is combined on the cell matrix of discrete curvelet transform to form a new signature feature, use the SVM classifier for training and classification. Experiments on two databases, Uyghur and Kirgiz, the highest accuracy was 97.95% and 97.42% respectively. The experimental results show that the proposed method has better accuracy in offline handwritten signature recognition.

Keywords: Offline signature recognition · Discrete curvelet transform · Multi-scale block local binary mode · Support Vector Machines

1 Introduction

As a stable and easy to acquire biological behavioral feature, handwritten signature is now widely used in finance, public security, judicial and administrative fields, and is one of the important means of personal identity authentication. Handwritten signature recognition is divided into two types by different acquisition methods: online handwritten signature [1] recognition and offline handwritten signature [2] recognition. Online signature recognition often uses handwriting board, touch screen and other devices to collect signatures, and extract dynamic information such as pressure and speed, because the point sequence of signature writing can be clearly obtained in online signature samples, its technology has become mature. Off-line handwritten signature is a kind of document which is written in paper and formed by scanner. It often extracts its shape and location, because it only has static characteristics, it is more difficult to recognize off-line signature than on-line handwritten signature recognition, and it is still in the developing stage.

Z. Sun et al. (Eds.): CCBR 2019, LNCS 11818, pp. 424–434, 2019.
https://doi.org/10.1007/978-3-030-31456-9_47

For many years, domestic scholars have studied the problem of handwritten signature recognition and identification, and proposed many algorithms and theories to make the technology more and more mature. Kumar et al. [3] proposed the chord moment feature of the upper and lower envelopes of the offline signature, and obtained the correct recognition rate of 93.98%. Narkhede et al. [4] extracted wavelet features and used feedforward neural network to obtain 97.61% accuracy. Joshi et al. [5] extracted the wavelet transform features and used Hamming distance to identify and classify, and obtained 95% recognition rate. Chen [6] identified the Lagrangian Support Vector Machine (LSVM) algorithm and obtained an average recognition rate of 84.83%. Pham et al. [7] extracted histogram features and geometric features and classified them by similarity measure. The accuracy rates of 97.67% and 80.04% were obtained on Dutch and Chinese signature datasets, respectively.

The recognition of the signatures of the minority nationalities in Xinjiang has been slow, and there have been related studies in recent years. Abri et al. [8] took multiple features such as directional features, three-dimensional baseline features and baseline displacement features, using different classifiers such as K-NN classifier, Euclidean distance and chi-square distance. Get a recognition rate of up to 96%. Ubul et al. [9] extracted the density characteristics of signatures and classified them with K-NN classifier, which obtained a recognition rate of 96%. Yimin et al. [10] extracted and combined the 128-dimensional local center feature and the 112-dimensional ETDT feature of the signature, and used the distance metric and similarity to identify and obtain 97.1% recognition rate.

2 Offline Handwritten Signature Recognition

The research of off-line handwritten signature recognition is a research field in biometric research and a research direction in the field of pattern recognition. As a research direction in pattern recognition, like most pattern recognition problems, offline handwriting is divided into four steps, data acquisition, preprocessing, feature extraction, training and testing, respectively. The flow chart is shown in Fig. 1.

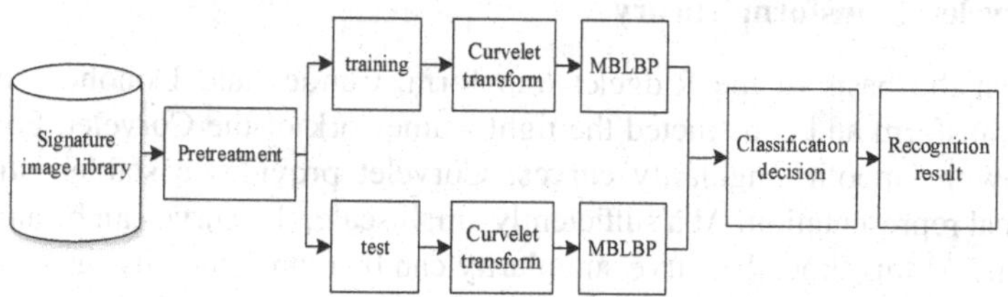

Fig. 1. Offline handwritten signature recognition process

In the data collection part, this paper uses two kinds of offline signature databases, Uyghur and Kirgiz, each database collects the signatures of 100 Uyghurs, each writing 20 true signatures and a total of 4000 signature samples. In order to better preserve the differentiated information of the signature image, it needs to be processed before the feature extraction of the image. In this paper, the image is first normalized in size, and then the weighted average method is used for grayscale processing. The signature image is binarized by the OTSU algorithm [11], and the image is denoised using bilateral filtering. In this way, the internal information and edge information of the image can be better preserved. The preprocessed image is shown in Fig. 2 below:

(a) Original signature image

(b) Grayscale

(c) Binarization

(d) Double sideband filtering

Fig. 2. Preprocessed signature image

In the feature extraction part, feature extraction is an important part of the signature recognition process. Only the feature extracted from the signature that can represent the identity of the signer can continue to be identified. In this paper, the non-subsampled curvelet transform is used to extract the energy of the curvelet coefficients, and the multi-scale block local binary mode features are combined to form the feature vector used in the experiment. In the training and testing part, the eigenvectors are trained from the training signature samples to form the training model, and then the training model is used for classification test. In this paper, the support vector machine algorithm is used to classify and identify the signature.

3 Curvelet Transform

The curvelet transform [12] is a further development based on the theory of ridgelet transform, multi-scale ridgelet transform theory and bandpass filter theory.

3.1 Curvelet Transform Theory

In 1999, on the basis of the Ridgelet transform, Candes and Donoho proposed the Curvelet transform and constructed the tight framework of the Curvelet. For objective functions with smooth singularity curves, Curvelet provides a stable, efficient, and near-optimal representation. At a sufficiently small scale, the curve can be analyzed as a straight line. At this time, the curve singularity can be represented by linear singularity. The schematic diagram is shown in Fig. 3.

Comparing Fig. 3(a) with Fig. 3(b), it can be seen that when the scale is getting thinner, several long strips of support can cover the entire singularity curve, which has directionality and wavelet Compared to the transformation, it can make a more sparse representation of the curve singularity.

The frequency window U_j in the continuous domain smoothly divides the frequency domain into rings of different angles. Such segmentation is not suitable for the

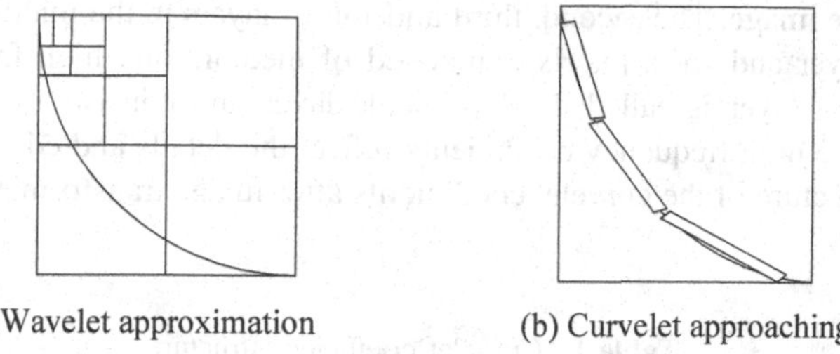

(a)Wavelet approximation (b) Curvelet approaching

Fig. 3. Schematic diagram of wavelet approximation and Curvelet approximation

two-dimensional Cartesian coordinate system of the image, so the discrete curvelet transform uses the concentric square region $\widetilde{U}_j$ instead of the annular region U_j. Taking the Cartesian coordinate system $f[t_1, t_2](0 \leq t_1, t_2 \leq n)$ as input, the discrete form of the curvelet transform is:

$$C^D(j, l, k) = \sum_{0 \leq t_1, t_2 < n} f[t_1, t_2] \overline{\varphi^D_{j,l,k}[t_1, t_2]} \quad (1)$$

$\varphi^D_{j,l,k}$ is a discrete Curvelet function. Angle segmentation is not equally spaced, but the slopes are equally spaced. In the implementation of two discrete curvelet transforms proposed by Candes et al., this paper chooses the fast algorithm based on Wrap. The scale angle division diagram of the discrete curvelet transform scale is shown in Fig. 4.

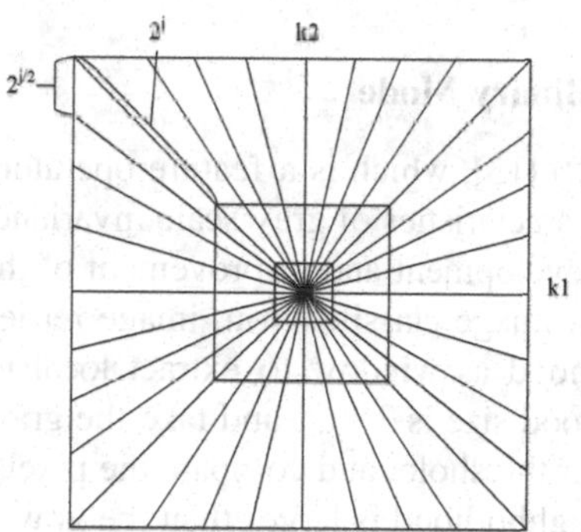

Fig. 4. Scale angle segmentation diagram of discrete curvelet transform

3.2 Curvelet Coefficient Analysis

After transformation, the curvelet coefficient structure is C{j}{l}(k_1, k2), l representing the scale, l representing the direction, and (k_1, k_2) representing the matrix coordinates of the l direction on the scale layer. After the discrete curvelet transform, the image is divided into five scale layers. The first layer is called the Coarse layer, the matrix is composed of low frequency coefficients, and the low frequency coefficients contain an overview of the image. The second, third and fourth layers in the middle are called the Detail scale layer and are a matrix composed of medium and high frequency coefficients; The fifth layer is called the Fine scale layer and consists of high frequency coefficients. The high frequency coefficients reflect the details and edge features of the image. The structure of the curvelet coefficients after image transformation is shown in Table 1.

Table 1. Curvelet coefficient structure

Level	Scale factor	Number	Form			
Coarse	C{1}	1	21 * 21			
Detail	C{2}	16	18 * 22	16 * 22	22 * 18	22 * 16
	C{3}	32	34 * 22	22 * 34	32 * 22	22 * 32
	C{4}	32	67 * 44	44 * 67	64 * 43	43 * 64
Fine	C{5}	1	256 * 256			

Using the real curve coefficients in the cell matrix obtained by the curvelet transform, a total of 82 matrices can extract 82-dimensional energy features at most, and the calculation formula is as shown in Eq. (2).

$$E = \sum_{x=1}^{m}\sum_{y=1}^{n} C^2\{i\}\{j\} \tag{2}$$

Where m and n are the size of the cell.

3.3 Multi-scale Local Binary Mode

Local Binary Pattern (LBP) [13], which is a feature operator mainly describing image texture features, has the characteristics of gray scale invariance and rotation invariance. Through the continuous development and improvement of the operator over the years, it has been widely used in image classification, image retrieval and other fields. LBP algorithm takes neighborhood as window to extract local texture of image. Select a window whose neighborhood size is 3 * 3, and take the gray value of the center point in the window as the center threshold, and compare the pixels of eight points around it. If the gray value of the neighborhood is larger than the gray value, the point is marked as 1, and vice versa, as 0. Taking the upper left corner of the neighborhood as the starting point, an octal binary number can be obtained clockwise. The decimal representation of the binary number is obtained, that is, the LBP value of the point. The calculation method is shown in Fig. 5

Figure 6 below shows a 9 × 9 MB-LBP operator [13] generation process. The 9 × 9 image block is divided into 9 small blocks of size 3 × 3, and the gray average value of each 3 × 3 small block is obtained to obtain a 3 × 3 gray matrix, and the remaining MB-LBP operator is extracted. Same as the original LBP operator process. When a 3 × 3 MB-LBP operator is used, it is equivalent to a basic 3 × 3 LBP operator.

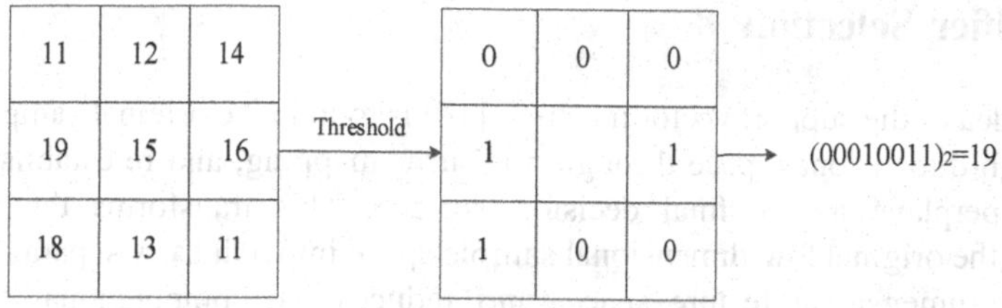

Fig. 5. Basic LBP operator generation process

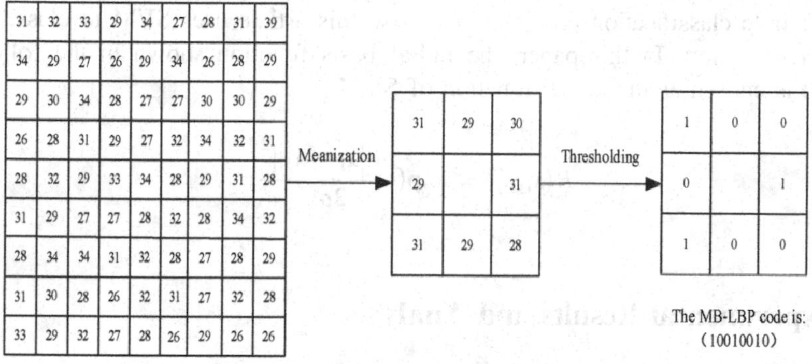

Fig. 6. MBLBP operator generation process

MB-LBP filtered images with different block sizes are shown in Fig. 7.

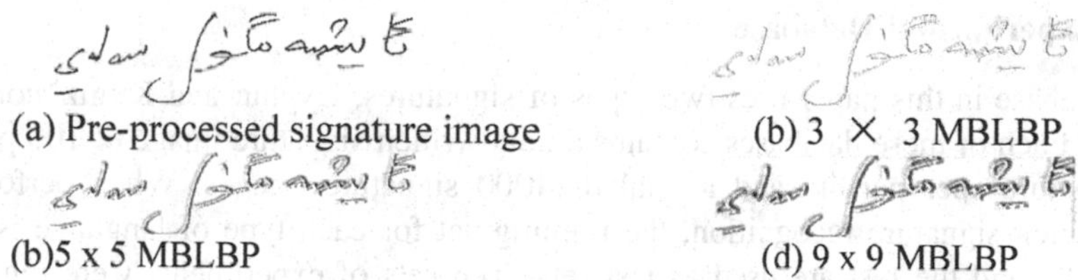

Fig. 7. MBLBP filtered signature image of different sizes

It can be seen from Fig. 7 that the images of MB-LBP filtering of different sizes are quite different. When conducting an experiment, you should choose the right scale. In this paper, a 5 × 5 MB-LBP operator was selected for the experiment. When the MB-LBP operator is extracted for training recognition, its histogram is extracted to form an MB-LBP histogram feature.

4 Classifier Selection

The main idea of the support vector machine [14] is to map the original sample space to another high-dimensional space through nonlinear mapping, and re-establish a classification hyperplane as the final decision surface. This transforms the indivisible problem of the original low-dimensional sample space into a linearly separable problem in the high-dimensional feature space, and reduces the computational complexity through the introduction of the kernel function. Compared with traditional artificial neural networks based on empirical risk minimization, SVM has strong generalization ability and can avoid over-fitting. It shows many advantages in solving nonlinear and small sample classification problems. Because this article uses SVM to classify signature recognition. In this paper, the radial basis function shown in the following formula is chosen as the kernel function of SVM.

$$K(x_i, x_j) = \exp(\frac{-\left\|x_i - x_j\right\|^2}{2\sigma^2}) \tag{3}$$

5 Experimental Results and Analysis

5.1 Experimental Equipment Environment

The CPU of the experimental platform of this paper is Intel(R) Core(TM) i5-6500 @3.20 GHz 3.20 GHz processor, 8 GB memory, the system is Windows 10 64 bit, and the programming environment is MATLAB 2016b.

5.2 Experimental Database

The database in this paper uses two types of signatures, Uyghur and Kirgiz, collected locally. Each of these databases contains a handwritten signature image of 100 people, 20 signatures per person, and a total of 4000 signature images. When performing handwritten signature recognition, the training set for each type of language is 1000 and 1600, and the rest are used as test sets. Ten sets of experiments were randomly selected from two different databases, and the average of the experimental results was obtained as the result of the experiment.

5.3 Signature Recognition Experiment Based on Discrete Curvelet Transform

In this paper, when extracting the features of discrete wavelet transform, the preprocessed image is firstly subjected to discrete curvelet transform. The transformed image is obtained by three levels of curvelet coefficients, among which the low frequency sum The high frequencies each contain one cell matrix, and the middle and high frequencies contain 80 cell matrices. By finding the energy of each cell matrix coefficient, a total of 82-dimensional energy characteristics can be obtained.

Table 2. Experimental results of Uyghur signature recognition based on discrete curve transform

Training Curve wave level	Dimension	Training 1000	Training 1600
Coarse	18	56.7%	58.75%
Coarse+Detail	50	75.6%	79.25%
Coarse+Detail+Fine	82	80.4%	**85.75%**

Table 3. Experimental results of Kirgiz signature recognition based on discrete curve transform

Training Curve wave level	Dimension	Training 1000	Training 1600
Coarse	18	60.4%	66.5%
Coarse+Detail	50	78.9%	83.5%
Coarse+Detail+Fine	82	81.6%	**87%**

It can be seen from Tables 2 and 3 that for the Uyghur database and the Kirgiz database, when extracting the same curve layer energy characteristics, the number of training sets of the signature is increased, and the recognition rate is improved, and the signature can be obtained. The performance of the recognition system depends on the size of its training set. When the curvelet level is increased, the extractable energy feature dimensions are 18-dimensional, 50-dimensional, and 82-dimensional, respectively. It can be seen that for the two languages, when only the curve coefficient of the Coarse layer is extracted, the training is 1600. The highest recognition is 58.75% and 66.5%, the effect is relatively poor, because the first layer only contains the profile features of the image, the texture features are not obvious. When the experiment extended the Detail layer and the Fine layer, the recognition rate increased, and the highest recognition rate reached 85.75% and 87% at 1600, indicating that the mid-high frequency and high frequency contain detailed edge features of the image, which can be well represented. The texture features of the signature image enhance the recognition.

5.4 Signature Experiment Based on MBLBP

In this paper, when MBLBP features are extracted, because of the large difference between the MBLBP filter signature images of different scales, in order to find the MBLBP filtering suitable for the signature image size, this paper selects six different scales for experiments and obtains MBLBP in the image. After that, the statistical histogram is extracted to form the MBLBP statistical histogram feature, and the experimental results are shown in Tables 4 and 5.

Table 4. Experimental results of Uyghur signature recognition based on MBLBP

Training Scale	Training 1000	Training 1600
1	75.3%	80.5%
3	93.1%	96.25%
5	96.5%	**97.75%**
7	95.7%	97.75%
9	96.2%	97.75%
11	95.7%	97.75%

Table 5. Experimental results of Kirgiz signature recognition based on MBLBP

Training Scale	Training 1000	Training 1600
1	74.4%	78.75%
3	91%	93.75%
5	96.9%	**97.25%**
7	96.1%	96.5%
9	95.7%	96.5%
11	95.5%	96.28%

It can be seen from Tables 4 and 5 that, similar to 2 and Table 3, when the number of training sets is increased or decreased, the recognition rate is improved. When the filtering scale of MBLBP is increased, the recognition rate becomes higher. When the scale is 5, the highest recognition rate is 97.75% and 97.25% in training, respectively. When the scale is increased, the recognition accuracy will not increase but will increase. Decline, so this paper selects the MBLBP filter with a size of 5 for the subsequent feature fusion experiment.

5.5 Signature Recognition Experiment Based on Discrete Curvelet Transform and MBLBP Fusion

In order to extract better texture features in the discrete curvelet transform coefficients, this paper extracts the discrete curvelet coefficients from the signature image by curvelet transform, and then fuses the MBLBP features. The experimental results are shown in Tables 6 and 7.

Table 6. Experimental results of Uyghur handwritten signature based on discrete curve transform and MBLBP fusion

Training	Training 1000	Training 1600
Recognition rate	96.74%	97.95%

Table 7. Experimental results of Kirgiz handwritten signature based on discrete curve transform and MBLBP fusion

Training	Training 1000	Training 1600
Recognition rate	97.2%	97.42%

It can be seen from Tables 6 and 7 that when the curvelet transform and the MBLBP feature are combined, the recognition effect is improved. The best result is that when the training is 1600, the recognition rate is up to 97.95% and 97.42%, respectively. When the recognition rate of 0.2% and 0.17% is improved by using Discrete Curvelet Transform and MBLBP features, the experimental results show that this method has a good effect on Uyghur signature recognition.

6 Summary

In this paper, an off-line handwritten signature recognition method based on discrete curvelet transform is proposed. The real-time curvelet coefficients obtained in the cell matrix after curvelet transform are used to extract energy features, form feature vectors, and extract MBLBP features. The feature, using a database of 2,000 Uyghur and Kirgiz handwritten signatures, respectively, achieved a recognition rate of 97.95% and 97.42%. In the future research work, the sample type and data volume will be expanded, and the curvelet transform and MBLBP algorithm of this paper can be improved to expand the data volume to improve the accuracy of offline handwritten signature recognition.

Acknowledgment. This work was supported by the National Natural Science Foundation of China under Grant (No. 61862061, 61563052, 61163028), and 2018 years Scientific Research Initiate Program of Doctors of Xinjiang University under Grant No. 24470.

References

1. Tanwar, S., Obaidat, M.S., Tyagi, S., Kumar, N.: Online signature-based biometric recognition. In: Obaidat, M.S., Traore, I., Woungang, I. (eds.) Biometric-Based Physical and Cybersecurity Systems, pp. 255–285. Springer, Cham (2019). https://doi.org/10.1007/978-3-319-98734-7_10. Chapter 10
2. Das, S.D., Ladia, H., Kumar, V., et al.: Writer independent offline signature recognition using ensemble learning (2019)
3. Puhan, N.B., Manoj Kumar, M.: Off-line signature verification: upper and lower envelope shape analysis using chord moments. IET Biometrics **3**(4), 347–354 (2014)
4. Narkhede, P., Ingle, V.R.: Offline handwritten signature recognition using artificial neural network techniques. In: International Conference on Quality Up-gradation in Engineering, Science and Technology, pp. 21–24 (2015)
5. Joshi, S., Kumar, A.: Feature extraction using DWT with application to offline signature identification. In: Mohan, S., Suresh Kumar, S. (eds.) ICSIP 2012. LNEE, vol. 222, pp. 285–294. Springer, India (2013). https://doi.org/10.1007/978-81-322-1000-9_27

6. Chen, J.: Research on offline recognition of handwritten signature based on Lagrangian support vector machine. Guangxi University (2012). (in Chinese)
7. Pham, T.-A., Le, H.-H. Toan, D.: Offline handwritten signature verification using local and global features. Ann. Math. Artif. Intell. **75** (2014). https://doi.org/10.1007/s10472-014-9427-5
8. Abri, G.L.: Uyghur offline signature recognition technology research. Xinjiang University (2012). (in Chinese)
9. Ubul, K., Yadkar, N., Aysa, A., Ibrahim, T.: Uyghur based on density characteristics offline Signature recognitio. Comput. Eng. Des. **37**(08), 2200–2205 (2016). (in Chinese)
10. Yimin, A.H., Muti, M.L.M., Aisha, A., Ibira, T., Kurban, W.: High-dimensional statistical feature fusion of Uyghur offline Handwritten Signature Recognition. Comput. Sci. Explor. **12**(02), 308–317 (2018). (in Chinese)
11. Sun, J., Song, J., Wu, X., et al.: Image segmentation method of lettuce leaf based on improved Otsu algorithm. J. Jiangsu Univ. **2**, 179–184 (2018)
12. Sahare, P., Chaudhari, R.E., Dhok, S.B.: Word level multi-script identification using curvelet transform in log-polar domain. IETE J. Res. **2**, 1–23 (2018)
13. Nath, V.K., Hatibaruah, R., Hazarika, D.: An efficient multiscale wavelet local binary pattern for biomedical image retrieval (2018)
14. Li, J., Weng, Z., Xu, H., et al.: Support Vector Machines (SVM) classification of prostate cancer Gleason score in central gland using multiparametric magnetic resonance images: a cross-validated study. Eur. J. Radiol. **98**, 61–67 (2018)

Research on Automatic Classification Method of Footwear Under Low Resolution Condition

Heng Jiang[1], Mengjing Yang[1], Zhongliang Mi[2], and Yunqi Tang[1](✉)

[1] School of Forensic Science, People's Public Security University of China, Beijing 100038, China
tangyunqi@ppsuc.edu.cn
[2] Shanghai Key Laboratory of Scene Evidence, Shanghai 200083, China

Abstract. On the basis of the shoe prints left by the suspects at the crime scene, it can be inferred that the specific type of shoes worn by the suspects, and then the type of suspected shoes can be searched in the monitoring around the crime scene, which is a common investigative technique used by public security organs. However, this technique is less automated and intelligent, and in most cases, the shoes under video monitoring are small and mostly fuzzy. An automatic classification method of footwear for pedestrians under low resolution video monitoring is proposed. A footwear database has been constructed with 149,199 footwear images; Then, based on the convolutional neural network, a network model suitable for automatic footwear classification is designed. The experimental results show that the accuracy of the automatic footwear classification network model in the test stage is up to 98.47%.

Keywords: Low resolution · Convolutional neural network · Automatic footwear classification

1 Introduction

At present, although the crime situation is constantly changing, criminals will still leave footprints at the crime scene. In the course of investigation and litigation, the footprint is getting more and more attention from the public security organs and judicial departments, because the types of shoes worn by suspects can be inferred from the footprints. If the footprints can be combined with other evidence, it will play a huge role in solving the case [1]. For example, it has become an important means for public security organs to solve various cases that integrating the scene footprint and the surrounding video to realize the tracing of criminal suspects. Firstly, the shoeprints at the crime scene are used to infer the kind of shoes. Then, check whether the same kind of shoes appeared in video monitoring during the time of the crime. Finally, the kind of shoes at the crime scene are compared with the kind of shoes in video to narrow the scope of investigation. However, judging the kind of shoes under video monitoring generally by criminal technicians based on subjective experience. Artificial judgment error is easy to occur when the monitor screen is blurred. Especially when the color of two kinds of shoes are same or similar, it is easier to make subjective judgment errors, which is time-consuming and laborious.

Z. Sun et al. (Eds.): CCBR 2019, LNCS 11818, pp. 435–443, 2019.
https://doi.org/10.1007/978-3-030-31456-9_48

The essence of automatic footwear classification is computer image classification [2]. Image classification is a technology that uses computer to process, analyze and understand images and automatically classify objects in different modes. It is a main research direction in the field of computer vision. If the image classification can be introduced into the classification of shoes under video monitoring, then it can reduce the error rate of manual judgment, the workload of technicians will be greatly reduced, and the scope of detection can be narrowed and determined as soon as possible, so that the case can be solved in a short time.

In recent years, convolutional neural network (CNN) has gradually become a hot topic in the field of image classification. Different from the traditional recognition method based on feature matching technology, it can automatically extract more abstract and essential features. The performance of CNN is far better than that of traditional manual or semiautomatic extraction. It has been widely used in face recognition [3], commodity classification, commodity recommendation, user behavior analysis and other aspects. In this paper, an automatic footwear classification model based on CNN is designed to realize the automatic footwear classification under low resolution monitoring. Specifically, the main contributions of this paper are as follows:

- In combination with the characteristics of the crime scene, the footwear classification standards formulated by the national technical committee of footwear and the limitations of recognition accuracy, this paper temporarily divides shoes into leather shoes and athletic shoes.
- A low-resolution footwear database was established, including 149,199 footwear images.
- A suitable network model was designed for footwear classification, the ability of the designed network model was tested and compared with other network models.

2 Related Work

Image classification was seem as a way to classify the image into one of several categories by the image analysis. It mainly emphasizes the semantic judgment of the whole image. There are many ways to classify images. Before 2012, traditional image classification algorithms, such as SIFT and LBP [4], were mainly adopted. Then, the extracted features were used for training. Finally, classifiers such as support vector machine (SVM) [5] were used to classify the extracted features. The error rate was 28.2% [6].

In 2012, it was an important turning point in the field of large-scale image classification. AlexNet [7] proposed by Alex Krizhevsky et al. applied deep learning to large-scale image classification for the first time and achieved an error rate of 16.4%, which was about 10% lower than the traditional algorithm. Since then, deep learning has become a hot topic in image classification. The GoogleNet [8] proposed by the Google team in 2014 also applies the idea of deep learning, with an error rate of 6.7%. They reduced the error rate of the image classification contest to half of the previous best record. In 2014, Karen Simonyan discussed the influence of the depth of convolutional networks on the accuracy of large-scale image recognition. The author compared five convolutional neural networks of different depths with vgg-16 which has become a classical network architecture. Many networks remove and add layers on top of vgg-16 [2]. In 2015, the team of Microsoft research in Asia proposed a deep residual network with 152 layers, which achieved an error rate of 3.57% in the dataset of ILSVRC2015 [9]. With the deepening of CNN layers, the training process of the network becomes more difficult, which leads to the saturation or even decline of accuracy.

In early 2015, the prelu-nets proposed by researchers from Microsoft research in Asia became the first network model that exceeded the human eye recognition effect (error rate about 5.1%) in the ILSVRC data set. Compared with the previous convolutional neural network model, this model is improved in two aspects. On the one hand, the traditional rectified linear units (ReLU) [4] is extended, and the parameterized rectified linear units (PReLU) [10] is proposed. The activation function adaptively studies the parameters of rectified linear units and improves the recognition accuracy when the extra calculation cost is ignored. On the other hand, by modeling the rectified linear units (ReLU/PReLU), this model deduces a set of initialization methods with robustness, which can make models with more layers (such as models with 30 weighted layers) converge.

3 The Standards for Shoes Classification

A clear criteria of footwear should be determined before automatic classification of footwear. Today, with advanced shoemaking techniques and abundant types of shoes, there are various ways of classification, which is not conducive to the study in this paper. Therefore, the shoemaking standards formulated by the national technical committee in 2017 was referenced [11]. Footwear were divided into four categories: "daily wear footwear", "functional footwear", "children and infants footwear" and "other footwear". Among them, "daily wear footwear" can be divided into "formal footwear", "casual footwear" and "other footwear" according to functions, "functional footwear" were divided into "rehabilitation footwear", "occupational footwear", "professional sports footwear" and "other footwear". It can be seen that footwear classification by function has been widely accepted and adopted, and will be improved in the process of use according to the actual situation. At present, the mainstream classification of shoes in China [12] also verifies this point.

4 Design of CNN Model

Details of Footwear Classification Networks (FCNet) will be presented in this section. It includes three key components: Inception architecture, Parametric Rectified Linear Unit (PReLU) and Local Response Normalization (LRN).

4.1 Inception Architecture

Inception is mainly to reduce parameters while increasing network depth and width. The channel dimension of feature map can be reduced by the convolution kernel of 1 * 1. The basic structure of Inception is made up of four components. 1 * 1 convolution, 3 * 3 convolution, 5 * 5 convolution and 3 * 3 max pooling. The results of four component operation are combined on the channel. This is the core idea of Inception. Multiple convolution nuclei are used to extract information of different scales of images, and finally image features can be better represented. Although the network of Inception is deep, the number of parameters is not large. Inception V1 has 22 floors but just has 5 M parameters. VGGNet performance is similar to Inception V1 over the same period, but the number of parameters is much larger than Inception V1. Inception is introduced into Footwear Classification Network (FCNet) proposed. Architecture of FCNet and Inception are shown in Fig. 1.

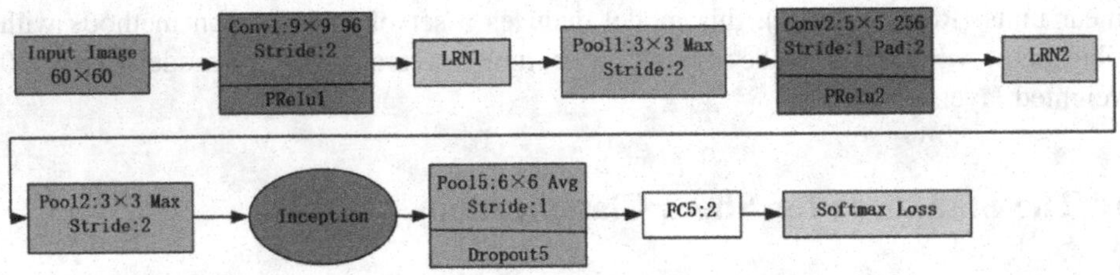

Fig. 1. Architecture of FCNet

4.2 Parametric Rectified Linear Unit (PReLU)

PRelu function is a function used to activate neurons in deep learning. It develops from Relu activation function and further restricts Relu. The Relu activation function is a unary piecewise linear function that returns the input when the input value is greater than zero, and returns zero when the input value is not greater than zero. This activation operation is known as unilateral inhibition, which makes neurons sparsely activated and enables them to better explore their relevant features. Meanwhile, the gradient of Relu function is constant in both segments, so there is no defect of gradient disappearance. Compared with nonlinear activation function, the convergence speed of training model parameters is more stable. The expression of Relu function is as follows:

$$\mathrm{Re}lu(x) = \max(0, x) = \begin{cases} x, x > 0 \\ 0, x \leq 0 \end{cases} \tag{1}$$

A linear term is add to PRelu activation function on the basis of Relu, so that the gradient of the function in the negative interval is not zero. This linear parameter is obtained by training. Since the number of parameters in PRelu layer learning is very small, it will not cause over-fitting during training. The expression of PRelu activation function is as follows:

$$PRelu(x) = \begin{cases} x, x > 0 \\ ax, x \leq 0 \end{cases} \tag{2}$$

4.3 Local Response Normalization (LRN)

Local response normalization layer is also called LRN layer and the lateral inhibition thought of biological nervous system has been referred. The activity of neurons is inhibited by LRN with small response, the response of neurons with high response value is relatively higher, so the robustness of the model has been improved. The calculation formula of LRN is:

$$b^i_{x,y} = a^i_{x,y} / \left(k + \alpha \sum_{j=\max(0,i-n/2)}^{\min(N-1,i+n/2)} (a^j_{x,y})^2 \right)^\beta \tag{3}$$

The total number of the layer characteristics is represented by N, the number of nuclear neighbors is represented by n, the cores in the coordinates of $(x\ y)$ value after PRelu is represented by $a^i_{x,y}$, convolution, pooling and activation function of the output, the output of the structure is a four dimensional array[batch, height, width, channel], batch is seen as batch number (each batch as a picture), height is seen as the picture height, width is seen as image width, the channel is seen as channel number, Remaining $k\ \alpha$, β for super parameters, these parameters are custom, in our designed network, $k = 5$, $\alpha = 0.0001$, $\beta = 0.75$.

5 Experimental Results and Analysis

Next, the experimental results of this paper will be presented from the following aspects: construction of shoe database, data preprocessing, details of the experimental configuration, result analysis and the analysis of misclassification.

5.1 Database Construction

63 pairs of shoes with high occurrence rate in crime scene had been collected, 30 pairs of leather shoes and 33 pairs of sneakers were included. The color of sneakers under video monitoring is same or similar with leather shoes, criminal technicians are easily confused. Leather shoes include formal leather shoes, casual leather shoes, high heels and boots. Sneakers includes general athletic shoes and professional athletic shoes. general athletic shoes include cloth shoes, board shoes and slippers. professional athletic shoes include run shoes, mountaineering shoes, basketball shoes and badminton shoes. The sample shoes are shown in Fig. 2.

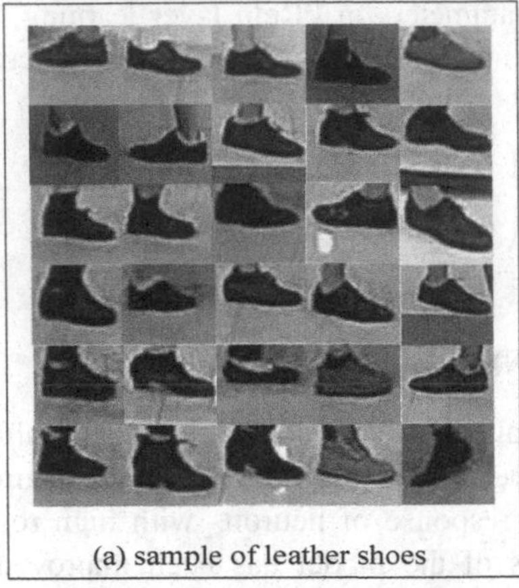
(a) sample of leather shoes

(b) sample of sneakers

Fig. 2. Sample of leather shoes and sneakers. we can find that Sneakers are shoes with the same or similar color as leather shoes, which are easily confused with leather shoes under video monitoring.

5.2 Data Preprocessing

Five volunteers were called for, 47 pairs of different shoes were collected, then volunteers wore these shoes walking in far away from the camera by the mean of simulating the criminal suspects or pedestrians. Selected Angle was 0°, 15° and 30°, the fuzzy conditions had been created. Then Matlab (R2016a) software was used to frame the acquired video. Since the obtained image contains all the characteristics of pedestrians, interference of other irrelevant areas should be eliminated to extract the effective areas. In order to speed up the training and testing, the size of all images was normalized to 60 * 60.

5.3 Results Analysis

A quantitative evaluation is also given to compare designed networks with others. Six performance indices are used in this study: Accuracy (ACC), True Positive Rate (TPR), False Positive Rate (FPR), Precision (Pr), Recall (Re) and F-measure (Fm). In this experiment, athletic shoes are represented positive example.

Images of 63 pairs of shoes are contained in data D, which are divided into two parts: D_1 and D_2. There are 47 pairs of shoes in D_1, with a total of 122,302 images. D_1 is divided into five equal parts on average (D_{11}, D_{12}, D_{13}, D_{14}, D_{15}), and all shoe samples are covered in each equal part. Then, one part is used as the test set and the rest is used as the training set. Images of 16 pairs of shoes are contained in D_2. Different from D_1, D_2 is the shoes that did not appear during the training, with a total of 26,897 images. The data set in detail is shown in Table 1.

Table 1. The data set in detail

The data set	D_1	D_2
Train set	97842 images	97842 images
Test set	24460 images	26897 images

Experimental results on D_1

D_{11} is used as the test set to test the four network models introduced above. The quantitative evaluation that used to compare with different network models is shown in Table 2. The ACC of the designed FCNet is up to 98.36%, higher than the other three network models. It is worth noting that although AlexNet's TPR is up to 99.04%, exceeding that of FCNet, its FPR is also high. It shows that AlexNet has superior performance in the identification of sneakers, but poor performance in the identification of leather shoes.

Table 2. Comparison of quantitative evaluation using different network models on D_1

Network model	TPR (%)	FPR (%)	ACC (%)
AlexNet	99.04	41.73	87.67
VGG-16	95.37	11.29	95.64
GoogleNet	97.21	8.70	97.33
FCNet	**98.44**	**2.68**	**98.36**

The test set D_{11}, D_{12}, D_{13}, D_{14}, D_{15} was used as the test set to test FCNet by the mean of five-fold cross validation respectively. The results are shown in Table 3, with an average accuracy of 98.47%.

Table 3. The first line represents the accuracy in the case of D_{11} as the test set, The last column represents average accuracy of five different test sets.

The data set	The test set	ACC (%)	Average ACC (%)
D_1	D_{11}	98.36	98.47
	D_{12}	98.74	
	D_{13}	98.47	
	D_{14}	98.96	
	D_{15}	97.83	

Experimental results on D_2

In order to further evaluate the model of FCNet, D_2 is used to test each network model collected in the simulated real environment. Pr and Re are contradictory. Generally speaking, when the Pr is high, the Re is often low; When the Re is high, the Pr is often low. When Pr and Re are both high, the model performs well. In addition, the performance of the model can be judged by the score of Fm. The quantitative evaluation is shown in Table 4. The Fm of FCNet is up to 95.73, higher than the other three network models. It is worth noting that although AlexNet's Re is up to 99.11%, exceeding that of FCNet, its Pr is too low. The performance of FCNet is better than the other three network models.

Table 4. Comparison of quantitative evaluation using different network models on D_2

Network model	Pr (%)	Re (%)	Fm (%)
AlexNet	64.80	99.11	83.98
VGG-16	77.37	93.97	84.87
GoogleNet	92.41	95.85	89.21
FCNet	**93.37**	**98.22**	**95.73**

Misclassification analysis

Finally, the misclassified images for analysis are exported. Part of representative images are shown in Fig. 3. The main reasons for misclassification are as follows: (a) Motion blur due to moving too fast; (b) The brightness is too low to produce a blur, so that the machine can't extract the features of the shoe; (c) The interference of background factors. In this experiment, there are three backgrounds of white, black and blue, and some images even have multi-color backgrounds.

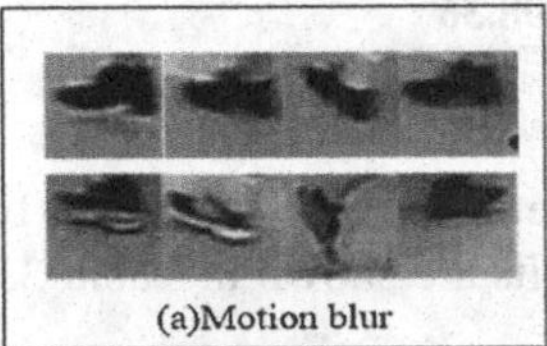
(a)Motion blur

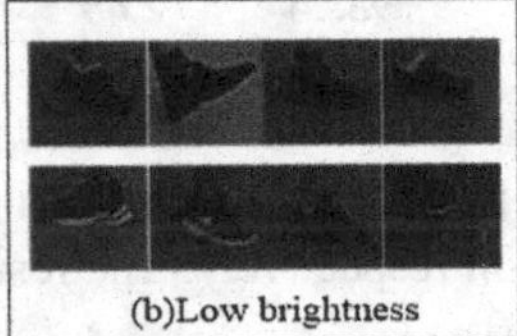
(b)Low brightness

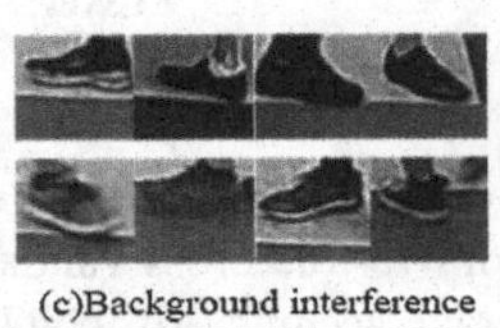
(c)Background interference

Fig. 3. Part of representative images of misclassification

6 Conclusion

In real cases, there are a large number of low-resolution video monitoring, resulting in poor image quality of video, and it is easy to make subjective judgment errors. In this case, the method of deep learning is used in this paper. Automatic classification of footwear is a basic dichotomy. Based on Caffe deep learning framework, convolutional neural network has been applied to automatic classification of footwear for the first time, the test accuracy reaches over 98% on D_1 and the test Fm reaches over 95% and the effectiveness of this network model has been verified. However, there are little shortcomings. The focus of this paper is on the automatic classification of footwear, and the automatic detection of footwear has not been involved. Extracting the shoe image in video can only be done by hand, a lot of time and energy has been taken. The database used in this paper is not complete, only leather shoes and sports shoes contained. The automatic detection of pedestrian shoes in video will be the next research work, experiments will be added to complete the database as much as possible.

Acknowledgements. This work is supported by National Key Research and Development Program of China (Grant No. 2017YFC0822003), the National Natural Science Foundation of China (Grant No. 61503387), the Opening Project of Shanghai Key Laboratory of Crime Scene Evidence.

References

1. Xiao, J.H., Liu, M.L.: A brief discussion on the relevant role of footprint inspection technology in investigation and solving cases. Technol. Innov. Appl. **36**, 15–16 (2014)
2. Simonyan, K., Zisserman, A.: Very deep convolutional networks for large-scale image recognition. Computer Science (2014)
3. Shui, W.J., Xu, W., Yang, M., Kai, Y.: 3D convolutional neural networks for human action recognition. IEEE Trans. Pattern Anal. Mach. Intell. **35**(1), 221–231 (2013)
4. Ahonen, T., Hadid, A., Pietikainen, M.: Face description with local binary patterns: application to face recognition. IEEE Trans. Pattern Anal. Mach. Intell. **28**(12), 2037–2041 (2006)
5. Niu, X.X., Suen, C.Y.: A novel hybrid CNN–SVM classifier for recognizing handwritten digits. Pattern Recogn. **45**(4), 1318–1325 (2012)
6. Russakovsky, O., Deng, J., Su, H., et al.: Imagenet large scale visual recognition challenge. Int. J. Comput. Vision **115**(3), 211–252 (2014)
7. Krizhevsky, A., Sutskever, I., Hinton, G.E.: Imagenet classification with deep convolutional neural networks. In: International Conference on Neural Information Processing Systems, pp. 1097–1105 (2012)
8. Szegedy, C., Liu, W., Jia, Y., et al.: Going deeper with convolutions. In: 2015 IEEE Conference on Computer Vision and Pattern Recognition (CVPR). IEEE (2015)
9. He, K., Zhang, X., Ren, S. et al.: Deep residual learning for image recognition. In: Computer Vision and Pattern Recognition (2016)
10. He, K., Zhang, X., Ren, S. et al.: Delving deep into rectifiers: surpassing human-level performance on imagenet classification. In: Computer Vision and Pattern Recognition (2015)
11. Shao, L.J.: Fourth meeting in the second session of the national technical committee on shoemaking of standardization administration of China was successfully held. Chinese-foreign Footwear (2017)
12. Chen, S.: Brief talk of classification and nomenclature of footwear products. Chinese-foreign Footwear (2016)

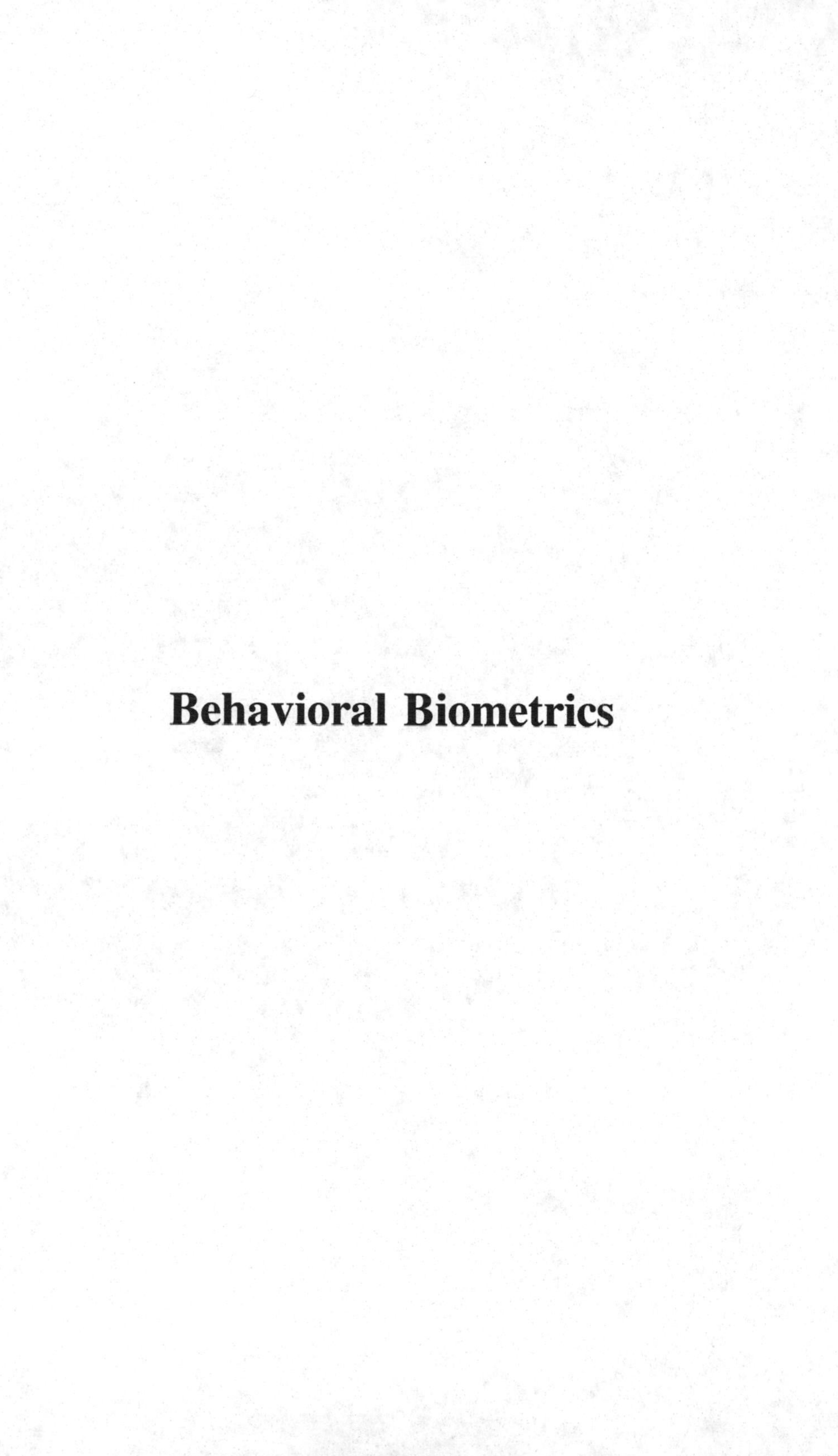

Behavioral Biometrics

Low-Resolution Person Re-identification by a Discriminative Resolution-Invariant Network

Tongtong Guo[2,3,4], Jianhuang Lai[1,3,4](✉), Zhanxiang Feng[1,3,4], Zeyu Chen[1,3,4], Xiaohua Xie[1,3,4], and Weishi Zheng[1,4]

[1] School of Data and Computer Science, Sun Yat-sen University, Guangzhou, China
{stsljh,fengzhx7,xiexiaoh6}@mail.sysu.edu.cn,
chenzy5@mail2.sysu.edu.cn, sunnyweishizheng@gmail.com

[2] School of Electronics and Information Technology, Sun Yat-sen University, Guangzhou, China
guott3@mail2.sysu.edu.cn

[3] Guangdong Key Laboratory of Information Security Technology, Guangzhou, China

[4] Key Laboratory of Machine Intelligence and Advanced Computing, Ministry of Education, Guangzhou, China

Abstract. Person Re-identification (re-id) needs to tackle with the problem of changing resolutions because the pedestrians from surveillance systems or public datasets have low-resolution problem (LR-REID) including low quality, blurry textures and so on, which results in a difficult challenge to extract the identity information under various resolutions. However, most existing re-id models are trained by high-resolution (HR) images, which will achieve poor performance when conducted directly on low-resolution images. In this paper, we propose a novel Discriminative Resolution-invariant Network (DRINet) to explore the subspace where LR and HR features are highly correlated and we can extract discriminant features in the commonly shared feature space. Firstly, we adopt ResNet as the backbone and impose the softmax loss together with the triplet loss to learn distinguishing features. Secondly, we impose the KL divergence loss on the backbone features to minimize the discrepancies between LR and HR features. Finally, we integrate the sparse auto-encoder (SAE) structure to find a subspace which is robust to the resolution variations. Experimental results verify the effectiveness of the DRINet in improving the LR-REID performance and the superiority of the DRINet against the state-of-the-art methods.

Keywords: Person Re-identification · Low resolution · Sparse auto-encoder · KL divergence

1 Introduction

Person Re-identification (re-id) is a task of image retrieval which matches pedestrians captured by non-overlapping cameras. At present, the re-id techniques

Z. Sun et al. (Eds.): CCBR 2019, LNCS 11818, pp. 447–454, 2019.
https://doi.org/10.1007/978-3-030-31456-9_49

have widespread applications in security domain. The existing researches pay more attention to solving the cross-view variants which assume that the pedestrians are with sufficiently high resolution. Therefore, the problem of resolution variations is largely ignored by the current literature. LR images have lost essential identity information including the sharp edges and clear details, which makes the LR-REID very challenging.

Naturally, there are three categories to address the LR-REID problem. (1) The first approach is to down-sample the HR gallery images and conduct matching between with LR images. (2) The second approach is to recover the high-frequency details of the LR images. However, wrong details may be generated during reconstruction, leading to unsatisfactory recognition performance. (3) The third approach is to find an optimal common space where LR and HR images are highly correlated, from which we can extract discriminative features that are beneficial for enhancing the LR-REID task.

In this paper, we propose a discriminative resolution-invariant network (DRINet) to learn the discriminative information. Firstly, we adopt the ResNet as the backbone with shared parameters for LR and HR domains to extract features. Then some discriminative losses, including the softmax loss and the triplet loss, are implemented over the backbone features to learn the distinguishing identity information. Secondly, we impose the KL divergence loss, an unsupervised constraint, between the LR and HR backbone features to ensure that the distributions of LR and HR features are consistent from the backbone network. Thirdly, we attach a SAE structure behind the backbone feature and implement a resolution-invariant loss on the hidden layer, which contains semantic structure information, to project the features into a common resolution-free subspace. Experimental results verify the effectiveness of our approach.

2 Related Work

2.1 General Re-id Methods

Re-id has drawn increasing research attention in the past 10 years. The existing works such as [3] focus on addressing the re-id challenges resulting from many uncontrolled variances. Many studies [16,18] focus on designing discriminative features, while others [17] pay attention to constructing more robust metric learning algorithms. With the development of deep convolution neural network, researchers are willing to design deep networks to learn more powerful representations. Zheng et al. [19] proposes an IDE model with simple ResNet-50 backbone as baseline for modern deep re-id systems. A number of methods [15,20] are proposed to improve the performance for deep re-id.

2.2 Low-Resolution Images Recognition

To tackle with the resolution mismatch, Chakrabarti et al. [1] suggest using person priors for image reconstruction. Jiao et al. [6] propose SING model which jointly conducts super-resolution and identity learning. Another choice is coupled mapping. A basic idea is to learn coupled transformations such that a LR image can directly match a HR image. Shi et al. [9] propose an optimization objective function associated with the LR/HR consistency, intra-class compactness and inter-class separability. Wang et al. [14] introduce a scale-distance function learning model. Coupled mapping methods generally achieve better recognition performance than super-resolution methods.

3 Methodology

3.1 Overall Architecture

Figure 1 demonstrates the overall structure of the proposed DRINet. Here we use ResNet50 [4] pretrained on ImageNet as the backbone to extract powerful features. We implement the softmax loss and the triplet loss to learn discriminant features. Furthermore, we impose the KL divergence loss on the backbone features to shrink the margin of LR and HR features. Finally, inspired by the existing LR-REID methods which search a common space using coupled linear mapping, we integrate a SAE structure into the proposed approach, which targets on exploring the resolution-invariant common space in an end-to-end manner. Particularly, we implement a resolution-invariant loss between the hidden-layer features (en_h and en_l) of LR and HR images to ensure that the features of the same identity under different resolutions are as similar as possible. Then the reconstruction loss is adopted for both LR and HR images to avoid mode collapse.

3.2 Loss Function

We employ multiple losses to obtain features that are both discriminative and resolution-free.

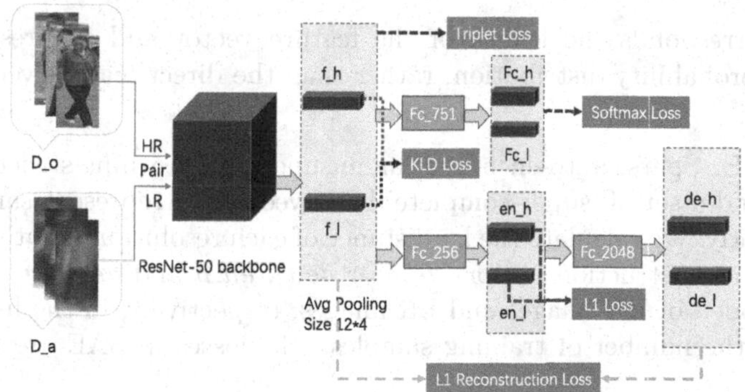

Fig. 1. The framework of the Discriminative Resolution-Invariant Network (DRINet).

Softmax Loss. For the backbone feature f. Softmax loss is formulated as:

$$L_{softmax} = -\sum_{i=1}^{N} log \frac{e^{W_{y_i}^T f}}{\sum_{k=1}^{C} e^{W_k^T f}} \tag{1}$$

where W_k means a weight vector for class k, with the size of mini-batch and C is the class number. Different from the softmax loss according to [12], we abandon bias terms in linear multi-class classifier.

Triplet Loss. We use the batch-hard tripletloss [5] to increase the inter-class spacing, and reduce the intra-class spacing. This loss function is formulated as follows:

$$\begin{aligned} L_{triplet}(f_a, f_p, f_n) = -\sum_{i=1}^{P}\sum_{a=1}^{K}\Big[\alpha + \max_{p=1...K}\left\|f_a^{(i)} - f_p^{(i)}\right\|_2 \\ - \min_{\substack{n=1...K \\ j=1...P \\ j\neq i}}\left\|f_a^{(i)} - f_n^{(j)}\right\|_2\Big]_+ \end{aligned} \tag{2}$$

where $f_a^{(i)}$, $f_p^{(i)}$, $f_n^{(i)}$ are anchor, positive and negative samples features, respectively. α is a margin between intra-class and inter-class distance. P is the number of identities selected in a batch and K is the number of images from each identity.

KLD Loss. We add KL divergence loss to increase the similarity between the distributions of LR and HR features. q and p means the distributions of LR and HR features, seperately. We expect distribution q to be as similar to distribution p as possible. The KLD loss is formulated as:

$$L_{KLD}(p||q) = \sum_{i=1}^{N} p(x_i) \cdot (logp(x_i) - logq(x_i)) \tag{3}$$

where N corresponds the length of the feature vector and x_i presents every element of probability distribution, rather than the direct feature vector.

Loss in SAE. Sparse auto-encoder is an unsupervised learning structure, which is used to find a set of 'super-complete' basis vectors to represent sample datas more efficiently. We calculate the L1 distance of each resolution input vector (f_h or f_l) and reconstruction vector (de_h or de_l). en_h and en_l are the feature vectors encoded of HR images and LR images, respectively, in the hidden-layer space. N is the number of training samples. The losses in SAE are formulated as follows:

$$L_{re}(f, de) = \frac{1}{N}\sum_{i=1}^{N} \left\|f^i - de^i\right\| \tag{4}$$

$$L_{inv}(en\_h, en\_l) = \frac{1}{N}\sum_{i=1}^{N} \left\| en\_h^i - en\_l^i \right\| \tag{5}$$

$$L_{SAE} = \frac{1}{3}\sum_{i=1}^{N} L_{reh} + L_{rel} + L_{inv} \tag{6}$$

Total Loss. The total loss of the constrains is formulated as follows:

$$L_{total} = a \cdot L_{Softmax} + b \cdot L_{Triplet} + c \cdot L_{KL} + d \cdot L_{SAE} \tag{7}$$

where a, b, c, d are the different weights of the losses. The value will be discussed in Sect. 4 by comparing these experiments.

4 Experiments

4.1 Training Set

LR-Market1501. The LR-Market1501 dataset includes images of 1501 identities collected by 6 different surveillance cameras. The pedestrians are extracted from the original image by DPM detector [2]. The LR images are synthetic by down-sampling the HR images using a gaussian pyramid by a magnification factor of 4 and then up-scaling back to the original image size, which refers to the study [11]. We organize the input data as follows: (1) HR person images are captured by cameras with views (1/2/3) while LR images are from views (4/5/6). (2) We put both resolutions images of the same identity together. Then we match pairs before training (see Fig. 2).

Fig. 2. The antithetical training set.

MLR-CUHK03. This dataset was built from the CUHK03 [7]. It consists of five different pairs of camera views, and has more than 14,000 images of 1,467 pedestrians. Following the settings in [15], both the manually cropped automatically detected images were used. LR images are down-sampled by different rates, which are $\frac{1}{2}$, $\frac{1}{3}$, $\frac{1}{4}$.

4.2 Implementation Details

We take P as 16 and K as 4 so that the mini-batch is 64. We set margin parameter for Triplet loss to 1.2. Adam optimizer is adopted to train the proposed network. The weight decay factor is set to be 0.0005. We set the initial learning rate to 0.01, and decay the learning rate twice in the rest epoches. We take the single-query mode. For Market1501, we refer to the multi-shot re-id setting. For MLR-CUHK03, we adopt standard single-shot re-id setting. Our approach is implemented on PyTorch framework.

4.3 Effectiveness of the DRINet

We conduct ablation experiments to validate the effectivenss of the DRINet. Table 1 demonstrates the results of each combination of losses in our method given a typical mAP and CMC values. Our method gets the best mAP/rank-1 0.7416/0.8076 on 4x dataset. We also verify the generative ability of DRINet on other down-scaling factors of 2 using the corresponding models trained on 4x LR and HR images.

Table 1. The results of various combination of losses on 4x and 2x LR query images.

The combination of Loss functions	map-4x	rank-1-4x	map-2x	rank-1-2x
Softmax	0.3234	0.4341	0.3362	0.4611
Softmax + KLD	0.4820	0.5716	0.4978	0.5989
Softmax + Triplet	0.4536	0.5576	0.4659	0.5597
Softmax + Loss in SAE	0.6148	0.7117	0.5868	0.6692
Softmax + KLD + Triplet	0.5072	0.6018	0.5276	0.6318
Softmax + KLD + Loss in SAE	0.6799	0.7426	0.6854	0.7527
Softmax + Loss in SAE + Triplet	0.7275	0.7925	0.7109	0.7797
DRINet	0.7416	0.8076	0.7335	0.7963

4.4 Comparisons with the Existing Methods

We compare the DRINet with three popular models on person reid [10,11,13] which are trained with HR images to evaluate the performance of the DRINet. Table 2 illustrates the comparison results. Apparently, the DRINet is powerful and competitive in dealing with LR images whereas the traditional re-id models perform poorly under low resolution settings. It also illustrates the comparison results with Resnet50 and SING [6] on LR-Market1501. The DRINet shows superior performance which validates the benifits of SAE and KLD. Furthermore, refering to the experiments in SING [6], we compare the DRINet method with three state-of-the-art LR-REID methods on one of datasets in this article (MLR-CUHK03 dataset): including JUDEA [8], SDF [14] and SING. Table 3 illustrates the comparison results. Apparently, the DRINet is powerful and superior in dealing with LR images.

Table 2. The results of various models on 4x LR images.

models	map	rank-1	rank-5	rank-10
HR_PCB	0.137	0.181	0.317	0.382
HR_MGN	0.3853	0.3031	0.5166	0.6134
HR_Part-aligned	0.358	0.429	0.607	0.682
Resnet50	0.3234	0.4341	0.6182	0.6945
SING	0.6255	0.7452	0.8432	0.8780
DRINet (ours)	0.7416	0.8076	0.8815	0.9086

Table 3. The results of various models on MLR-CUHK03.

models	rank-1	rank-5	rank-10
JUDEA	0.262	0.58	0.734
SDF	0.222	0.48	0.64
SING	0.677	0.907	0.947
DRINet (ours)	0.75	0.941	0.976

5 Conclusion

In this paper, we propose the Discriminative Resolution-invariant Network (DRINet) to explore the subspace where LR and HR features are highly correlated and extract discriminant features in the commonly shared feature space. The DRINet is effective in learning discriminative features from LR images by the constrains of KLD and SAE structure. The experimental results demonstrate the robustness of the DRINet for resolution-invariance. Extensive experiments indicate that our approach makes contribution to the LR-REID problem.

References

1. Chakrabarti, A., Rajagopalan, A., Chellappa, R.: Super-resolution of face images using kernel PCA-based prior. IEEE Trans. Multimedia **9**(4), 888–892 (2007)
2. Felzenszwalb, P.F., McAllester, D.A., Ramanan, D., et al.: A discriminatively trained, multiscale, deformable part model. In: CVPR, vol. 2, p. 7 (2008)
3. Feng, Z., Lai, J., Xie, X.: Learning view-specific deep networks for person re-identification. IEEE Trans. Image Process. **27**(7), 3472–3483 (2018)
4. He, K., Zhang, X., Ren, S., Sun, J.: Deep residual learning for image recognition. In: Proceedings of the IEEE Conference on Computer Vision and Pattern Recognition, pp. 770–778 (2016)
5. Hermans, A., Beyer, L., Leibe, B.: In defense of the triplet loss for person re-identification. arXiv preprint arXiv:1703.07737 (2017)
6. Jiao, J., Zheng, W.S., Wu, A., Zhu, X., Gong, S.: Deep low-resolution person re-identification. In: Thirty-Second AAAI Conference on Artificial Intelligence (2018)
7. Li, W., Zhao, R., Xiao, T., Wang, X.: DeepReID: deep filter pairing neural network for person re-identification. In: Proceedings of the IEEE Conference on Computer Vision and Pattern Recognition, pp. 152–159 (2014)

8. Li, X., Zheng, W.S., Wang, X., Xiang, T., Gong, S.: Multi-scale learning for low-resolution person re-identification. In: Proceedings of the IEEE International Conference on Computer Vision, pp. 3765–3773 (2015)
9. Shi, J., Qi, C.: From local geometry to global structure: learning latent subspace for low-resolution face image recognition. IEEE Signal Process. Lett. **22**(5), 554–558 (2015)
10. Suh, Y., Wang, J., Tang, S., Mei, T., Lee, K.M.: Part-aligned bilinear representations for person re-identification. In: Ferrari, V., Hebert, M., Sminchisescu, C., Weiss, Y. (eds.) Computer Vision – ECCV 2018. LNCS, vol. 11218, pp. 418–437. Springer, Cham (2018). https://doi.org/10.1007/978-3-030-01264-9_25
11. Sun, Y., Zheng, L., Yang, Y., Tian, Q., Wang, S.: Beyond part models: person retrieval with refined part pooling (and a strong convolutional baseline). In: Ferrari, V., Hebert, M., Sminchisescu, C., Weiss, Y. (eds.) ECCV 2018. LNCS, vol. 11208, pp. 501–518. Springer, Cham (2018). https://doi.org/10.1007/978-3-030-01225-0_30
12. Wang, F., Xiang, X., Cheng, J., Yuille, A.L.: NormFace: L2 hypersphere embedding for face verification. In: Proceedings of the 25th ACM International Conference on Multimedia, pp. 1041–1049. ACM (2017)
13. Wang, G., Yuan, Y., Chen, X., Li, J., Zhou, X.: Learning discriminative features with multiple granularities for person re-identification. In: 2018 ACM Multimedia Conference on Multimedia Conference, pp. 274–282. ACM (2018)
14. Wang, Z., Hu, R., Yu, Y., Jiang, J., Liang, C., Wang, J.: Scale-adaptive low-resolution person re-identification via learning a discriminating surface. In: IJCAI, pp. 2669–2675 (2016)
15. Xiao, T., Li, H., Ouyang, W., Wang, X.: Learning deep feature representations with domain guided dropout for person re-identification. In: Proceedings of the IEEE Conference on Computer Vision and Pattern Recognition, pp. 1249–1258 (2016)
16. Yang, Y., Yang, J., Yan, J., Liao, S., Yi, D., Li, S.Z.: Salient color names for person re-identification. In: Fleet, D., Pajdla, T., Schiele, B., Tuytelaars, T. (eds.) ECCV 2014. LNCS, vol. 8689, pp. 536–551. Springer, Cham (2014). https://doi.org/10.1007/978-3-319-10590-1_35
17. Yi, D., Lei, Z., Liao, S., Li, S.Z.: Deep metric learning for person re-identification. In: 2014 22nd International Conference on Pattern Recognition, pp. 34–39. IEEE (2014)
18. Zhao, R., Ouyang, W., Wang, X.: Unsupervised salience learning for person re-identification. In: Proceedings of the IEEE Conference on Computer Vision and Pattern Recognition, pp. 3586–3593 (2013)
19. Zheng, L., Yang, Y., Hauptmann, A.G.: Person re-identification: past, present and future. arXiv preprint arXiv:1610.02984 (2016)
20. Zhong, Z., Zheng, L., Cao, D., Li, S.: Re-ranking person re-identification with k-reciprocal encoding. In: Proceedings of the IEEE Conference on Computer Vision and Pattern Recognition, pp. 1318–1327 (2017)

DHML: Deep Heterogeneous Metric Learning for VIS-NIR Person Re-identification

Quan Zhang[1,3,4], Haijie Cheng[2,3,4], Jianhuang Lai[1,3,4(✉)], and Xiaohua Xie[1,3,4]

[1] School of Data and Computer Science, Sun Yat-sen University, Guangzhou, China
zhangq48@mail2.sysu.edu.cn, {stsljh,xiexiaoh6}@mail.sysu.edu.cn

[2] School of Electronics and Information Technology, Sun Yat-sen University, Guangzhou, China
chenghj3@mail2.sysu.edu.cn

[3] Guangdong Key Laboratory of Information Security Technology, Guangzhou, China

[4] Key Laboratory of Machine Intelligence and Advanced Computing, Ministry of Education, Guangzhou, China

Abstract. Narrowing the modal gap in person re-identification between visible domain and near infrared domain (VIS-NIR Re-ID) is a challenging problem. In this paper, we propose the deep heterogeneous metric learning (DHML) for VIS-NIR Re-ID. Our method explicitly learns a specific projection transformation for each modality. Furthermore, we design a heterogeneous metric module (HeMM), and embed it in the deep neural network to complete an end-to-end training. HeMM provides supervisory information to the network, essentially eliminating the cross-modal gap in the feature extraction stage, rather than performing a post-transformation on the extracted features. We conduct a number of experiments on the SYSU-MM01 dataset, the largest existing VIS-NIR Re-ID dataset. Our method achieves state-of-the-art performance and outperforms existing approaches by a large margin.

Keywords: Person re-identification · Cross-modal retrieval · Metric learning

1 Introduction

Person re-identification (Re-ID) is a very important issue in video surveillance. It searches for a target pedestrian in all of the visible cameras in a camera network with non-overlapping views. Traditional Re-ID can be considered as a single-modal matching task. However, when illumination becomes unavailable, the performance declines sharply. Among the types of data, near infrared (NIR) images are complementary to visible (VIS) images because of their low cost, robustness to light and abundant information. Thus, VIS-NIR Re-ID has received attention in recent years. Due to the data in the different modalities are

Z. Sun et al. (Eds.): CCBR 2019, LNCS 11818, pp. 455–465, 2019.
https://doi.org/10.1007/978-3-030-31456-9_50

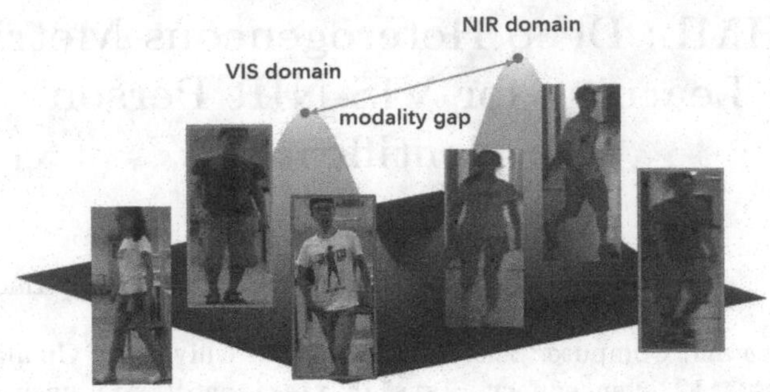

Fig. 1. Illustration of modality gap between VIS domain and NIR domain. Without any constrains, images from different modalities are always aggregated by modal-specific biases. Due to the large modal gap drowns out identity information, the distance of the same person in different modalities (the two images with green bounding boxes) is larger than that of different person (the image with red bounding box) in same modality. (Color figure online)

heterogeneous, there are significant intra-class differences and inter-class similarities in VIS-NIR Re-ID. As shown in Fig. 1, narrowing the gap between different modalities remains a critical challenge.

In this paper, we propose **d**eep **h**eterogeneous **m**etric **l**earning (DHML) for the VIS-NIR Re-ID. DHML is based on two simple motivations. First, in the Re-ID task, a common processing pattern is to map images from the original image space to the feature space though a feature extraction framework, and then to perform retrieval in this feature space. For example, the similarity metric in feature space between two images, I_x and I_y, can be described as

$$d(I_x, I_y) = ||\Phi(I_x) - \Phi(I_y)||_2, \tag{1}$$

where $\Phi(\cdot)$ is the feature extraction framework. However, it is impossible to measure the "perfect" similarity between heterogeneous images by Eq. 1. As we do not guide the model to consider the modal bias during the feature extraction, the feature appears to be aggregated by the modal information rather than by the identity information. This prompts us to adopt modal-specific projections for different modal features. In this way, we can transform the original feature space into a modal-independent feature space. Therefore, the similarity metric for the two heterogeneous images is further revised as follows:

$$d(I_x^m, I_y^n) = ||U^m(\Phi(I_x^m)) - U^n(\Phi(I_y^n))||_2, \tag{2}$$

where m and n represent the modal information of the image and U^i represents the transformation matrix under the corresponding modality i. As we explicitly teach the model to perform a domain-specific transformation, the model can focus on the modal deficiencies and narrow it. This heterogeneous metric can be robust enough to measure the identity similarity between images from different modalities.

Second, by Eq. 2, we can see that heterogeneous metric learning and feature extraction is a two-stage relationship, which means that feature extraction and metric learning are two independent operations. Transformation matrix U in Eq. 2 is essentially similar to a post-processing method for improving the results of map and ranking, but it does not optimize the features in the original feature space. Therefore, we further design the heterogeneous metric learning as a network structure, called **he**terogeneous **m**etric **m**odule (HeMM), into the feature extraction network, making it a complete end-to-end framework, which can be described as

$$d(I_x^m, I_y^n) = ||\Phi(I_x^m; U^m) - \Phi(I_y^n; U^n)||_2. \tag{3}$$

Such a strategy has two advantages. First, training the transformation matrices as parameters in the network is more accurate than the traditional optimization algorithm, because DHML captures more potential relationships within the data. Second, because of the end-to-end model framework, feature extraction can also be guided by DHML. The two modules can complement each other in the process of training, so the results are further improved.

To verify the performance of DHML, we have carried out abundant experiments on the largest available cross-modality Re-ID dataset [8], SYSU-MM01. Our best performance reach 63.7%, which is about 20% higher than the current best results.

In summary, the contributions of this paper are as follows.

1. We introduce deep heterogeneous metric learning (DHML) into VIS-NIR Re-ID. We explicitly perform a domain-specific transformation, and the model narrows the modal gap between two different modalities. Thus, DHML is more robust for measuring the identity similarity between heterogeneous images.
2. We further design the heterogeneous metric module (HeMM) and integrate it with the feature extraction module into an end-to-end network framework. A unified framework enables feature extraction to be supervised by both the classification module and the metric module, which makes the feature itself discriminating for modal interference. Compared with the independent operations, DHML has further improved the robustness of features.
3. We conduct multiple experiments on the largest available VIS-NIR Re-ID dataset, SYSU-MM01. The results fully verify the effectiveness of DHML and achieve state-of-art performance.

2 Related Works

Cross-Modality Re-ID: Currently, many Re-ID models [9,12,13] focus on VIS-VIS single-modality matching. For example, Jang et al. [3] have been shown to effectively extract color or appearance features in single-modality matching. However, VIS-VIS Re-ID methods are limited in surveillance applications when lighting is poor or unavailable. To avoid thenegative effects, some cross-modality retrieval methods were introduced into the process of person re-identification.

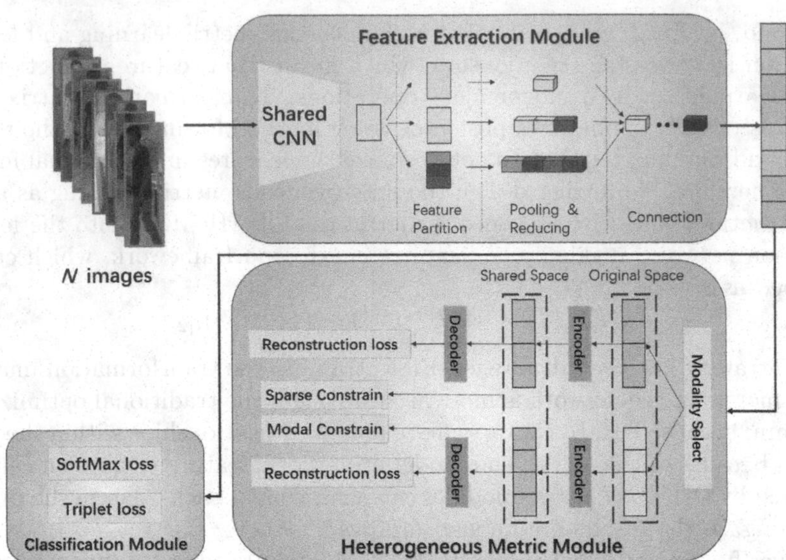

Fig. 2. Our end-to-end framework. Our approach consists of three modules: a feature extraction module, a heterogeneous metric module (**HeMM**) and a classification module. In the training stage, for a batch of images, the fixed-size feature vectors are obtained by the feature extraction module, and then the loss value is calculated by the HeMM module and the classification module, respectively. In the testing stage, we extract features in original feature space for input images.

Wu et al. [8] proposed deep zero-padding network for cross-modality matching and proposed the largest VIS-NIR Re-ID dataset, SYSU-MM01, but the performance of this method is unsatisfactory.

Metric Learning: Metric learning is usually used to measure similarity between samples. Recently, some metric learning methods have been proposed in Re-ID field. Chen et al. [1] formulated a distance model, named CVDCA, for teaching camera-specific projections to transform the unmatched features of each view into a common space. Compared with CVDCA, the proposed DHML have two advantages: (1) The CVDCA is a two-stage method, which leads to the fact that feature metric does not improve the quality of the original feature, but is just a kind of post-processing method. (2) The CVDCA is not a method of deep learning, and it only uses hand-craft features. DHML is a method of deep learning, and we extract features from the network, which produces more powerful features.

3 The Proposed Method

3.1 Network Structure

Our network consists of three modules: a feature extraction module, an heterogeneous metric module (HeMM) and a classification module, as shown in Fig. 2. For an input image I_d^m, the high-level feature is obtained by feature extraction module Φ. Then this feature is sent to the classification module, and simultaneously is constrained by the HeMM. We extract F as the whole evidence for Re-ID in the test stage.

Feature Extraction Module: Our feature extraction module draws lessons from a simple and efficient CNN framework [7]. The network is split into three branches. From top to bottom, we divide the feature map into one part, two parts and three parts separately. Then we conduct pooling and dimensionality reduction for each sub-feature in each branch. We compress each feature into a 256 dimensional vector. After that, we connect them in sequence. Finally, we get a feature representation ($256 \times 8 = 2048 dims$) of an input image, which combines a global feature with several local features.

Heterogeneous Metric Module: For a batch of features, $F = [f_1^m, \cdots, f_n^m], m \in \{V, N\}$[1], we first divide the features into two groups, F^V and F^N, according to modal labels through a modal selection layer. After that, each group is entered into its corresponding sparse autoencoder (SAE), and the features are projected from the original space to the shared space. Each SAE has two full connection layers with an activation function (ReLU), denoted as the encoder and decoder, respectively.

It is worth mentioning that, unlike the shared CNN in the feature extraction module, these two SAEs do not share parameters. This is the core idea of the DHML: for each modality, we make a modal-specific feature transformation. We explicitly teach the network to pay attention to the different modal information contained in the features, so that this module can guide the feature extraction module to ignore the modal information and focus on identity information, reducing the difference between the two modal features, and improving the representation of the features.

Classification Module: The classification module is a common and necessary structure in Re-ID tasks. Our classification module is composed of a series of softmax losses and triplet losses. Its function is to calculate the loss value of the input features and to use these data as supervisory information that is transmitted back to the network. In traditional models, the classification module is the only source of network supervised signals. As the classification module cannot remove the influence of modal information very well in our model, we add the HeMM to transmit effective supervised information for the network.

[1] V, N stand for VIS or NIR domains.

3.2 Optimization

As shown in Sect. 3.1, the supervisory information in our network mainly comes from the classification and HeMM. In the classification module, for the feature f of each input image, we use cross entropy loss and batch-hard triplet loss as follows:

$$l_{cross} = -\log \frac{\exp(W_y f)}{\sum_{k=1}^{C} \exp(W_k f)}, \tag{4}$$

where C represents the number of IDs in the training set, and W_k represents the classification weight for class k.

$$l_{triplet} = \left(\max_{p \in A(f)} d(f,p) - \min_{n \in B(f)} d(f,n) + \alpha \right)_+, \tag{5}$$

where $A(f)/B(f)$ represents a feature set that has the same/different ID label as f, $d(\cdot,\cdot)$ represents the Euclidean distance between two features, $(\cdot)_+$ means the function $max(0,\cdot)$, and α is a hyperparameter to control the distance between positive and negative sample pairs. To sum up, the loss function of the classification module can be rewritten uniformly as

$$L_{cls} = \frac{1}{N} \sum_{i=1}^{N} l_{cross} + l_{triplet}. \tag{6}$$

In the HeMM, we first use the reconstruction loss to constrain the output of each SAE to recover as much as possible for the input, which can be described as

$$l_r = ||f^V, D^V(E^V(f^V))||_2 + ||f^N, D^N(E^N(f^N))||_2, \tag{7}$$

where f^V, f^N, E^V, E^N, D^V and D^N represent the features, encoders, decoders of the two modalities, respectively. Then we propose modal constraints on the features of the shared space to enable them to focus on identity information. The modal constraints, l_{modal}, is similar to Eq. 5 in that it reduces the intra-class distance in a shared space and increases the extra-class distance. In addition, to make the heterogeneous metric more efficient, we impose a sparse constraint on the output of the hidden layer, that is, we expect the hidden layer to capture the most salient structure with a few neurons.

$$l_{sparse} = ||E^V(f^V)||_1 + ||E^N(f^N)||_1. \tag{8}$$

The total loss in this module can be represented as:

$$L_{metric} = l_r + l_{sparse} + l_{modal}. \tag{9}$$

Then, the loss function of the entire network can be represented as

$$L = \lambda_1 L_{cls} + \lambda_2 L_{metric}. \tag{10}$$

4 Experiments

4.1 Dataset

Due to VIS-NIR Re-ID is a novel problem, and many traditional datasets do not contain two modalities of image. Therefore, we choose the SYSU Multiple Modality Re-ID (SYSU-MM01) dataset proposed by Wu et al. [8]. To the best of our knowledge, this is the largest dataset in this field.

SYSU-MM01 contains 287,628 RGB images and 15,792 NIR images of 491 persons captured in six cameras. Cameras 1, 2, 4 and 5 operated under full illumination conditions, whereas cameras 3 and 6 operated under either low-light or non-illuminated conditions. In addition, cameras 1, 2 and 3 operated indoors, whereas cameras 4, 5 and 6 operated outdoors. Wu et al. also gave a fixed partition for SYSU-MM01: 296 identities for training, 99 identities for validation and 96 for testing. In the testing stage, there are two modes, the *all-search* mode and the *indoor-search* mode. In the all-search mode, cameras 1, 2, 4 and 5 are used for a gallery set and cameras 3 and 6 are used for a probe set. In the indoor mode, only cameras 1 and 2 are used for a gallery set, and the probe set is the same as in the all-search mode.

4.2 Implementation Details

During the training phase, we resize the input images to 384 × 128 and we use random horizontal flipping and random erasing [11] for data augmentation. Each mini-batch is sampled with randomly selected P identities, and each identity randomly selects K^V images in VIS domain and K^N images in NIR domain from the training set. Thus, for a mini-batch with N images, $N = P \times (K^V + K^N)$, where $P = 16, K^V = K^N = 2$. We set the α in the triplet loss of the classification module to 1.2 and the α in the modal constraint of the HeMM to 1.5. We set the weights of the loss function as $\lambda_1 = 2$ and $\lambda_2 = 0.1$. We choose Adam [4] as an optimizer. The weight decay factor is set to 5e-4. Our model is implemented on a PyTorch framework. To make the model converge, we train it for 8 h on the two NVIDIA TITAN X GPUs.

4.3 Results

We demonstrate the efficiency of DHML on the SYSU-MM01 and compare performance with other methods including hand-craft methods and deep learning methods. Table 1 shows the results of the MAP and the ranked accuracy of the various methods applied to this dataset. It is worth mentioning that several existing methods are trained on gray-scale images instead of RGB images, such as one-steam, zero-padding. To make a fair comparison, we conduct experiments on gray-scale and rgb images. In addition, to further demonstrate the effectiveness of DHML, we combine the feature extraction module and the classification module in the original network framework as a baseline. Baseline-50/101 denotes the Resnet-50/101 used in the feature extraction module as a shared CNN. *RGB* or

Table 1. Results on SUSY-MM01 dataset under all-search and indoor-search mode. Rank1, 10, 20 and mAP (%) are reported.

Method	All-search								Indoor-search							
	Single-shot				Multi-shot				Single-shot				Multi-shot			
	Rank1	Rank10	Rank20	mAP	Rank1	Rank10	Rank20	mAP	Rank1	Rank10	Rank20	mAP	Rank1	Rank10	Rank20	mAP
HOG+Euclidean	2.76	18.25	31.91	4.24	3.82	22.77	37.63	2.16	3.22	24.68	44.52	7.25	4.75	29.06	49.38	3.51
HOG+KISSME	2.12	16.21	29.13	3.53	2.79	18.23	31.25	1.96	3.11	25.47	46.47	7.43	4.10	29.32	50.59	3.61
HOG+LFDA	2.33	18.58	33.38	4.35	3.82	20.48	35.84	2.20	2.44	24.13	45.5	6.87	3.42	25.27	45.11	3.19
HOG+CCA	2.74	18.91	32.51	4.28	3.25	21.82	36.51	2.04	4.38	29.96	50.43	8.70	4.62	34.22	56.28	3.87
HOG+CDFE	2.09	16.68	30.51	3.75	2.47	19.11	34.11	1.86	2.80	23.39	44.46	6.91	3.28	27.31	48.61	3.24
HOG+GMA	1.07	10.42	20.91	2.52	1.03	10.29	20.73	1.39	1.84	17.97	36.14	5.64	1.80	18.10	35.79	2.63
HOG+SCM	1.86	15.16	28.27	3.57	2.40	17.45	31.22	1.66	3.30	25.82	46.23	7.52	3.90	28.84	51.64	3.22
HOG+CRAFT	2.59	17.93	31.50	4.24	3.58	22.90	38.59	2.06	3.03	24.07	42.89	7.07	4.16	27.75	47.16	3.17
LOMO+Euclidean	1.75	14.14	26.63	3.48	1.96	15.06	27.30	1.85	2.24	22.53	41.53	6.64	2.24	22.79	41.80	3.31
LOMO+KISSME	2.23	18.95	32.67	4.05	2.65	20.36	34.78	2.45	3.83	31.09	52.86	8.94	4.46	34.35	58.43	4.93
LOMO+LFDA	2.98	21.11	35.36	4.81	3.86	24.01	40.54	2.61	4.81	32.16	52.50	9.56	6.27	36.29	58.11	5.15
LOMO+CCA	2.42	18.22	32.45	4.19	2.63	19.68	34.82	2.15	4.11	30.60	52.54	8.83	4.86	34.40	57.30	4.47
LOMO+CDFE	3.64	23.18	37.28	4.53	4.70	28.23	43.05	2.28	5.75	34.35	54.90	10.19	7.36	40.38	60.33	5.64
LOMO+GMA	1.04	10.45	20.81	2.54	0.99	10.50	21.06	1.47	1.79	17.90	36.01	5.63	1.71	18.11	36.17	2.88
LOMO+SCM	1.54	14.12	26.27	3.34	1.66	15.17	28.41	1.57	2.86	24.34	44.53	7.06	2.89	25.81	48.33	3.02
LOMO+CRAFT	2.34	18.70	32.93	4.22	3.03	21.70	37.05	2.13	3.89	27.55	48.16	8.37	2.45	20.20	38.15	2.69
HIPHOP+CRAFT	1.80	14.56	26.29	3.40	1.92	16.00	28.31	1.77	2.86	23.40	41.94	7.16	3.01	25.53	44.97	3.43
Lin's [6]	5.29	33.71	52.95	8.00	6.19	37.15	55.66	4.38	9.46	48.98	72.06	15.57	11.36	51.34	73.41	9.03
One-steam [11]	12.04	49.68	66.74	8.00	6.19	37.15	55.66	4.38	9.46	48.98	72.06	15.57	11.36	51.34	73.41	9.03
Two-steam [11]	11.65	47.99	65.50	12.85	16.33	58.35	74.46	8.03	15.60	61.18	81.02	21.49	22.49	72.22	88.61	13.92
Asymmetric network [11]	9.30	43.26	60.38	10.82	13.06	52.11	69.52	6.68	14.59	57.94	78.68	20.33	20.09	69.37	85.80	13.04
Zero-padding [11]	14.80	54.12	71.33	15.95	19.13	61.40	78.41	10.89	20.58	68.38	85.79	26.92	24.43	75.86	91.32	18.64
HCML [5]	14.32	53.16	69.17	16.16	–	–	–	–	–	–	–	–	–	–	–	–
BDTR [10]	17.01	55.43	71.69	19.66	–	–	–	–	–	–	–	–	–	–	–	–
DGD [12]	22.77	65.90	80.66	23.76	27.81	72.46	85.95	17.30	23.70	69.48	86.10	33.36	29.34	77.17	90.23	23.35
cmGAN [2]	26.97	67.51	80.56	27.80	31.49	72.74	85.01	22.27	31.63	77.23	89.18	42.19	37.00	80.94	92.11	32.76
baseline-50(gray)	37.51	81.38	90.51	37.29	43.08	83.61	92.42	30.11	42.35	87.86	94.02	51.82	51.82	91.68	98.06	41.14
baseline-50(rgb)	29.94	75.70	87.20	30.70	34.44	79.28	89.35	24.13	30.70	84.98	95.66	42.05	36.94	87.98	96.65	32.02
baseline-101(gray)	39.11	82.87	93.18	38.43	45.88	87.50	95.44	31.10	43.41	87.69	94.79	50.73	53.43	93.51	97.53	40.84
baseline-101(rgb)	35.28	79.89	89.83	31.71	41.21	86.76	95.00	25.38	40.36	87.13	95.95	49.14	46.47	92.50	98.64	39.49
DHML-50(gray)	**49.74**	**89.63**	**96.26**	**48.44**	**57.21**	**92.33**	**97.38**	**41.87**	**55.73**	**95.29**	**99.02**	**63.86**	**67.94**	**98.13**	**99.76**	**54.59**
DHML-50(rgb)	**55.33**	**89.62**	**94.14**	**53.91**	**60.08**	**90.89**	**94.37**	**47.65**	**56.30**	**91.46**	**96.38**	**63.70**	**63.26**	**94.44**	**97.79**	**55.51**

Gray in our experiments indicate we use whether *RGB-NIR* or *Gray-NIR* data to train and test the models. If not emphasised in the following, the *RGB-NIR* data is adopted.

We can summarize the results given in the Table 1 as follows. (1) Our method achieves the state-of-art performance on this dataset. We use a very powerful feature extraction module as a very strong baseline and the model also extract a lot of supervisory information from our HeMM. (2) Without HeMM, the model training with Gray-NIR data achieves a better performance than the model training with RGB-NIR data, because the distribution of gray-scale data and NIR data is more similar than the distribution of RGB data and NIR data. As there is no HeMM to measure different modal differences, one of the ways to *explicitly* narrow the gap between the two modes is to use gray-scale data instead of RGB pictures for training. However, due to the lack of rich information in the gray-scale images, the accuracy of model is inaccurate. (3) The performance of our method with RGB data is better than that with NIR data. DHML has good structure and properties to solve the cross-modality metric problem. It also benefits from the fact that RGB images contain more information than gray-scale images, which makes our feature much more discriminative. (4) The effectiveness of the HeMM is not the result of the introduction of more parameters. To determine the influence of the number of parameters, we further calculate the total parameters for each structure in Table 2. DHML has less than 31.7% of the parameters as baseline-101, but its performance is almost 19% better than baseline-101 in mAP. This directly confirms that its effectiveness is due to HeMM's structure rather than the number of parameters.

Table 2. Number of parameters for three frameworks.

Network	Baseline-50	Baseline-101	DHML-50
Para Num	69.6M	126.6M	86.4M

4.4 Parameter Analysis

We analyse the influence of the size of the feature space generated by the encoder in HeMM on the performance of the model. Due to the input feature of the HeMM is a fixed 2048-dimensional vector, we test the performance of the model with 1024, 2048, 4096 and 8192 shared space dimensions in turn. It should be emphasized that the two SAEs in our HeMM are identical and do not share parameters. Table 3 shows that with the increase of the shared space dimension, the performance of the model first increases and then decreases. When the encoding space (1024 dims) is smaller than the input space (2048 dims), the autoencoder itself is an under-complete structure; when there are sparse constraints, it is difficult to get a complete representation of the input in the shared space. When the encoding space (8192 dims) is far beyond the input space, the capacity of the encoding space is far beyond the feature space, which results in over-fitting of the model on the training data. Finally, we choose 2048 as the best hyperparameters for HeMM.

Table 3. Analysis for different shared feature space dimension (%).

Shared space dims	Rank-1	Rank-5	Rank-10	mAP
1024	42.88	75.29	85.30	44.81
2048	**55.33**	**83.20**	**90.62**	**53.91**
4096	49.45	79.46	87.78	49.37
8192	47.31	77.97	85.51	47.86

5 Conclusion

This paper focus on the large modal gap between heterogeneous images. We propose the idea of deep heterogeneous metric learning into VIS-NIR Re-ID. An heterogeneous metric module, HeMM, is designed and integrated with feature extraction into an end-to-end framework, rather than as part of the post-processing operations. Our method effectively focuses on the inherent modal information inside the data and suppresses it, thus achieving the state-of-art performance when applied to the cross-modality Re-ID dataset SYSU-MM01.

References

1. Chen, Y.-C., Zheng, W.-S., Lai, J.-H., Yuen, P.C.: An asymmetric distance model for cross-view feature mapping in person reidentification. IEEE Trans. Circuits Syst. Video Technol. **27**(8), 1661–1675 (2016)
2. Dai, P., Ji, R., Wang, H., Wu, Q., Huang, Y.: Cross-modality person re-identification with generative adversarial training. In: Proceedings of the Twenty-Seventh International Joint Conference on Artificial Intelligence, IJCAI 2018, Stockholm, Sweden, 13–19 July 2018, pp. 677–683 (2018)
3. Jang, K., Han, S., Kim, I.: Person re-identification based on color histogram and spatial configuration of dominant color regions. Comput. Sci. **44**(3), 890–899 (2014)
4. Kingma, D.P., Ba, J.: Adam: a method for stochastic optimization. In: 3rd International Conference on Learning Representations, ICLR 2015, Conference Track Proceedings, San Diego, CA, USA, 7–9 May 2015
5. Liao, S., Hu, Y., Zhu, X., Li, S.Z.: Person re-identification by local maximal occurrence representation and metric learning. In: IEEE Conference on Computer Vision and Pattern Recognition, CVPR 2015, Boston, MA, USA, 7–12 June 2015, pp. 2197–2206 (2015)
6. Lin, L., Wang, G., Zuo, W., Feng, X., Zhang, L.: Cross-domain visual matching via generalized similarity measure and feature learning. IEEE Trans. Pattern Anal. Mach. Intell. **39**(6), 1089–1102 (2017)
7. Wang, G., Yuan, Y., Chen, X., Li, J., Zhou, X.: Learning discriminative features with multiple granularities for person re-identification. In: 2018 ACM Multimedia Conference on Multimedia Conference, MM 2018, Seoul, Republic of Korea, 22–26 October 2018, pp. 274–282 (2018)
8. Wu, A., Zheng, W.-S., Yu, H.-X., Gong, S., Lai, J.: RGB-infrared cross-modality person re-identification. In: IEEE International Conference on Computer Vision, ICCV 2017, Venice, Italy, 22–29 October 2017, pp. 5390–5399 (2017)

9. Xiao, T., Li, S., Wang, B., Lin, L., Wang, X.: End-to-end deep learning for person search. CoRR, abs/1604.01850 (2016)
10. Ye, M., Wang, Z., Lan, X., Yuen, P.C.: Visible thermal person re-identification via dual-constrained top-ranking. In: IJCAI, pp. 1092–1099 (2018)
11. Yi, D., Lei, Z., Liao, S., Li, S.Z.: Deep metric learning for person re-identification. In: 22nd International Conference on Pattern Recognition, ICPR 2014, Stockholm, Sweden, 24–28 August 2014, pp. 34–39 (2014)
12. Zheng, L., et al.: MARS: a video benchmark for large-scale person re-identification. In: Leibe, B., Matas, J., Sebe, N., Welling, M. (eds.) ECCV 2016. LNCS, vol. 9910, pp. 868–884. Springer, Cham (2016). https://doi.org/10.1007/978-3-319-46466-4_52
13. Zheng, L., Shen, L., Tian, L., Wang, S., Wang, J., Tian, Q.: Scalable person re-identification: a benchmark. In: 2015 IEEE International Conference on Computer Vision, ICCV 2015, Santiago, Chile, 7–13 December 2015, pp. 1116–1124 (2015)

Teager Energy Operator Based Features with x-vector for Replay Attack Detection

Zhenchuan Zhang, Liming Zhou, Yingchun Yang(✉), and Zhaohui Wu

College of Computer Science and Technology, Zhejiang University, Hangzhou, China
{11221052,21421210,yyc,wzh}@zju.edu.cn

Abstract. Audio replay attack poses great threat to Automatic Speaker Verification (ASV) systems. In this paper, we propose a set of features based on Teager Energy Operator and a slightly modified version of x-vector system to detect replay attacks. The proposed methods are tested on ASVspoof 2017 corpus. When using GMM with the proposed features, our best system has an EER of 6.13% on dev set and 15.53% on eval set, while the EER for the baseline system (GMM with CQCC) is 30.60% on eval set. When combined with the modified x-vector, the best EER further drops to 5.57% for dev subset and 14.21% for eval subset.

Keywords: Automatic Speaker Verification · ASV · Replay detection · Teager Energy Operator · x-vector

1 Introduction

Significant progresses have been made in the field of Automatic Speaker Verification (ASV) techniques in last two decades. This biometrics technology has become widely used in access systems, call-centers and mobile applications, but still not as popular as other biometrics authentication techniques such as face recognition or fingerprint recognition. One key factor impeding further application of ASV technique is that ASV systems are particularly vulnerable to *spoofing* attacks when compared to other biometrics techniques. Spoofing attacks can be categorized into 4 types: impersonation, replay audio (RA), speech synthesis (SA) and voice conversion (VC). Among these 4 types of spoofing attacks, RA poses the greatest threat in the sense of the ease of use and detection difficulty. Replay attackers are not required to have any expertise in audio signal processing or machine learning or ASV techniques. They don't even to have to get professional equipments or tools. And while the requirements to issue a replay attack are low, the false acceptance rate of state-of-the-art ASV systems would rise greatly when they are under replay attacks as evaluated in [1] and [2]. Thus a pre-step to detect whether the speech is genuine or replayed is crucial to the robustness of ASV systems.

This work is supported by NSFC 61602404 and the National Basic Research Program of China (973 Program) (No. 2013CB329504).

Z. Sun et al. (Eds.): CCBR 2019, LNCS 11818, pp. 466–473, 2019.
https://doi.org/10.1007/978-3-030-31456-9_51

Unlike the field of SV, what features best fit the task of RA detection is not settled yet. Being the most widely used feature in the field of ASV, MFCCs are tested for RA tasks in [3]. The baseline system of ASVspoof 2017 challenge uses CQCCs [4]. Some deep learning approaches directly operate on Fourier coefficients such as LCNN [5]. As suggested in [6], most of the cues that enable to detect the replay attacks can be found in the high-frequency band of the replayed recordings. Due to these reasons we consider using Teager Energy Operator since TEO is capable of expressing the energy information regarding speech generation [7] and the alterations introduced during replay are supposed to be reflected in terms of energy information. Hemant proposed a set of TEO based features which are called VESA-IFCC in [8], which used Variable length Teager Energy Operator based Energy Separation Algorithm and discarded amplitude information. Inspired by their work, we propose 3 simplified sets of TEO based features which require less computation and attempt to give comparable performance on ASVspoof 2017.

A few deep learning based methods [5,9] for replay attack detection have been proposed since the release of ASVspoof 2017. x-vector [10] is a DNN based state-of-the-art ASV technique. Like i-vector, x-vector embed speaker characteristics in fixed-length vectors for variable length utterances. As shown in [10], x-vector fits well in scenarios where the durations of utterances are short. These factors suggest that x-vector may be a powerful approach for replay attack detection, but as far as we know, there is no published paper investigating the possibility. Seeing this gap and inspired by the success of C3D [11] in the field of action recognition, we propose a temporal convolutional x-vector where the TDNN layers are replaced by temporal convolutional layers.

The remainder of this paper is organized as follows: Sect. 2 presents TEO based features and the temporal convolutional x-vector. Section 3 details the experimental setup and results. Section 4 gives some conclusions.

2 Proposed Method

In this section, we first introduce the basic idea of Teager Energy Operator, then give algorithms to extract 3 set of features based on TEO which we call as TEO Cepstral Coefficients (TEOCCs), TEO Amplitude Cepstral Coefficients (TEOACCs) and TEO Frequency Cepstral Coefficients (TEOFCCs). The x-vector architecture is given in the last subsection. These works are based on our previous studies [12].

Kaiser [7] gives a simple algorithm to calculate the 'energy' of a signal, which is

$$\psi[x(t)] = (\frac{dx}{dt})^2 - x(t)\frac{d^2x}{dt^2} \tag{1}$$

for continuous signals and

$$\psi[x(n)] = x^2(n) - x(n-1)x(n+1) \tag{2}$$

for discrete signals. And TEO could be extended to complex signals where the Teager Energy of a complex signal is the sum of the energy of the real and imaginary parts of the signal,

$$\psi[x(n)] = \psi[Re(x(n))] + \psi[Im(x(n))] \tag{3}$$

Using Eq. 2, one could get the energy for a *cosine* signal $x(n) = Acos(wn + \Phi)$ as:

$$\begin{aligned} \psi[x(n)] &= x^2(n) - x(n-1)x(n+1) \\ &= (Acos(wn + \Phi))^2 - Acos(w(n-1) + \Phi)Acos(w(n+1) + \Phi) \\ &= A^2 sin^2 w \\ &\approx A^2 w^2 \end{aligned} \tag{4}$$

This formula Eq. 4 shows that this energy estimate contains both amplitude and instantaneous frequency information. To separate these two information, Maragos proposed Energy Separation Algorithm (ESA) in [13].

In specific, ESA utilized two auxiliary functions $s(n) = x(n) - x(n-1)$ and $t(n) = x(n+1) - x(n-1)$. The final $a[n]$ for amplitude estimation and $w[n]$ for frequency estimation is

$$a[n] = \frac{2\psi[x(n)]}{\sqrt{\psi[x(n+1) - x(n-1)]}} \tag{5}$$

$$w[n] = arcsin\sqrt{\frac{\psi[x(n+1) - x(n-1)]}{4\psi[t(n)]}} \tag{6}$$

Note that all the above deductions are based on the assumption that the signal is a simple *cosine* signal while the speech signal is multi-component resonance. In [8], Hemant proposed a set of features which they called as Variable length Teager Energy OperatorEnergy Separation Algorithm-Instantaneous Frequency Cosine Coefficients (VESA-IFCC). The main idea is the use of Butterworth filters to extract narrowband components, and extracting VESA-IFCCs on these components respectively. And the VESA-IFCC discarded the amplitude information, because they thought that spectral envelope was the crucial part to distinguish between genuine and replayed speech, which however was not validated by experiments in their work and the improvements compared to ESA are not clear on replay attack detection. Seeing these gaps, we proposed 3 sets of features based on Teager Energy Operator.

2.1 TEOCC

The proposed TEO Cepstral Coefficients (TEOCCs) follow a similar process to the extraction of the commonly used MFCCs, which is shown in Fig. 1.

The speech signal is first transformed into frequency domain using short time discrete Fourier transform, where Hamming window is used and window size is

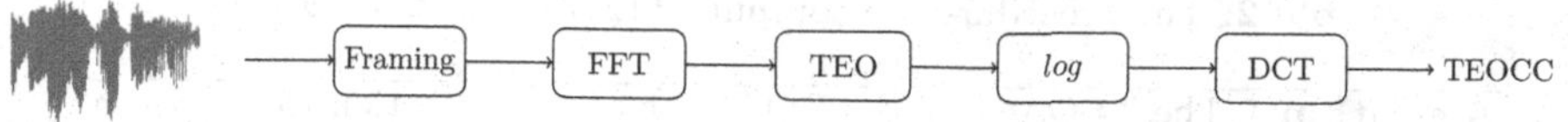

Fig. 1. The diagram of TEOCC estimation.

20 ms and the smoothing stride is 10 ms. Then TEO is used upon the resulting complex signal to get the energy spectrum. Then *log* function is applied on energy spectrum and DCT transform on *log* results to get the cepstral coefficients. This procedure is detailed in Table 1.

Table 1. The procedure to compute TEOCC.

Algorithm 1 The TEOCC feature extraction from speech

1: Speech signal: $s(n)$.
2: Bin and apply Hamming window function to get $x(n) = w(n) \times s(n)$.
3: Transform $x(n)$ into $X^{DFT}(n)$ using fast Fourier Transform.
4: Calculate the TEO energy $\psi[X^{DFT}(n)]$ according to Eq.3.
5: Apply *log* function: $log(\psi[X^{DFT}(n)])$.
6: Apply DCT on *log* to get TEOCCs:
$X^{TEOCC}(q) = \sum_{i=1}^{N}(X^{DFT}(i) \times cos(q\frac{\pi}{M}(i - \frac{1}{2})))$

2.2 TEOACC and TEOFCC

Figure 2 shows the diagram of TEOACC and TEOFCC estimation procedure.

The short time signal is decomposed using Butterworth filterbanks as in [8]. There are 40 linearly spaced 3rd-order Butterworth filters, each with a bandwidth of 195 Hz. The TEO is estimated for each of the decomposed signals. Then ESA is used to separate the TEO into amplitude signal AM and frequency signal FM. Then Hamming window is used to average these two signals where the window size is 20 ms and stride is 10 ms. DCT is applied directly on FM signals to get the TEOFCCs. For AM signals, *log* function is first applied on AM signals and then DCT is applied to get TEOACCs. This procedure is shown in Table 2.

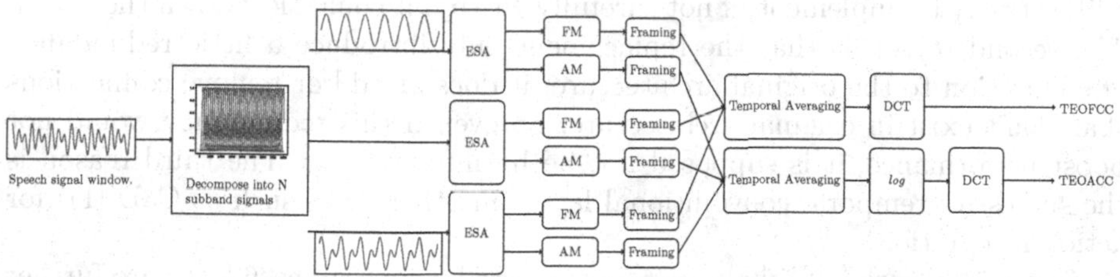

Fig. 2. The diagram of TEOACC and TEOFCC estimation.

Table 2. The procedure the compute TEOACC and TEOFCC.

Algorithm 1 The TEOACC and TEOFCC feature extraction from speech

1: Speech signal: $s(n)$.
2: Feed $s(n)$ into Butterworth filterbanks to get $x(n)$s for N sub-bands.
3: For each of the sub-band signal $x(n)$:
3.a: Construct auxiliary signal $t(n) = x(n+1) - x(n-1)$.
3.b: Compute the TEO energy $\psi[x(n)]$ and $\psi[t(n)]$ according to Eq.4.
3.c: Compute $a(n)$ and $w(n)$ according to Eq.5 and Eq.6.
3.d: Framing $a(n)$ and $w(n)$ to extract frame average:
$X^A = \frac{1}{N}\sum_{j=1}^{N} a(n)$ and $X^W = \frac{1}{N}\sum_{j=1}^{N} w(n)$
3.e: Applay log on X^A to get $log(X^A)$.
3.f: Apply DCT on $log(X^A)$ to get TEOACCs:
$X^{TEOACC}(q) = \sum_{i=1}^{N}(log(X^A(i) \times cos(q\frac{\pi}{M}(i-\frac{1}{2})))$
3.g: Apply DCT on X^W to get TEOFCCs:
$X^{TEOFCC}(q) = \sum_{i=1}^{N}(X^W(i) \times cos(q\frac{\pi}{M}(i-\frac{1}{2})))$
4: Concatenate the CCs for all the sub-bands.

2.3 x-vector Architecture

Like i-vector, x-vector extracts embeddings termed as x-vectors for an utterance, the difference is that x-vector uses a temporal pooling layer upon several time delay neural network (TDNN) layers to extract embeddings. This temporal pooling layer is how x-vector extract fix-sized embeddings for utterances of different durations. The main advantage of x-vector is that it could handle short utterances better than i-vector which is shown in [10] for utterances less than 10 s. This ability implies x-vector's fitness in replay attack detection where the utterances are often quite short.

We make two major modifications compared to the original architecture [10]. The new architecture is shown in Table 3. The first modification is obvious, the last fully connected layer in [10] whose output number is the number of enrolled speaker number which is often quite big, is replaced with a fully connected layer with only two outputs which imply the possibilities of the utterance is genuine and replayed respectively. The second modification is that we replaced the TDNN layers with 1-d temporal convolutional layers. The reasons for this modification are three-fold. First is the implementation reason. TDNN layers are a little tricky to implement, if not carefully written it could slow down the speed. The second reason is that the replacement only introduce a little redundancy of connection to the original architecture, it doesn't add or remove connections that don't exist in original architecture. So even if this redundancy would not boost performance, it is supposed not be harmful anyway. The third reason is the success of temporal convolutional layers in other fields such as C3D [11] for action recognition.

In original work [10], the x-vectors extracted from segment6 layer are further fed into LDA and PLDA algorithms to accomplish speaker recognition. Due to

Table 3. The x-vector DNN architecture. The TDNN layers in [10] are replaced with temporal convolutional layers, and they focus on frame level features. The stats pooling layer gives segment level statistics, thus the following layers focus on segment level features. f is number of features for each of the feature sets.

Layer	Layer context	Total context	Output size
input	–	–	$T \times f$
conv1	$[t-2, t+2]$	5	$512 \times T$
conv2	$[t-2, t+2]$	9	$512 \times T$
conv3	$[t-3, t+3]$	15	$512 \times T$
conv4	$\{t\}$	15	$512 \times T$
conv5	$\{t\}$	15	$1500 \times T$
stats pooling	$[0, T)$	T	3000
fc6	$\{0\}$	T	512
fc7 + softmax	$\{0\}$	T	2

task differences, these steps are omitted. Instead, the whole network is used to distinguish between replay and genuine, where the last layer, softmax, gives these two likelihoods.

3 Experiments

3.1 Dataset and Model Training

ASVspoof 2017 corpus is used. It is derived from text-dependent RedDots corpus [14] and its replayed version [4]. The former serve as the source of genuine recordings and the latter are derived using various configurations of environments, replay devices and recording devices. The whole corpus is divided into 3 subsets: *train*, *dev* and *eval*. The replay configurations for these subsets are mostly not overlapped, which is done on purpose to simulate the actual replay attacks where replay configurations are unknown to system developers. Please refer to [4] for more detailed information regarding ASVspoof 2017 corpus.

The GMM and x-vector are all trained using the *train* subset and evaluated on *dev* and *eval* subset. There are 512 components for GMM models.

3.2 Results

The resulting EER estimates (%) for all the TEO features are shown in Table 4a. The upper half is two reference systems: The CQCC system is the baseline system provided by ASVspoof 2017 in [4], and the VESA-IFCC system is the best subsystem proposed in [8]. The lower half shows features proposed in this paper. As stated in previous section, GMM system is used for all these features.

Table 4. EER(%) on dev and eval subset of ASVspoof 2017 for different features. The systems are GMMs and x-vectors respectively.

Features	dev	eval
CQCC[4]	10.35	30.60
VESA-IFCC[8]	4.61	15.50
TEOACC	**6.13**	**15.53**
TEOFCC	9.64	18.6
TEOAFCC	9.45	19.71
TEOCC	9.26	18.17

(a) GMM results.

Systems	dev	eval
$LCNN_{FFT}$[5](Original)	4.53	7.37
$LCNN_{FFT}$(Our implementation)	7.3	20.5
TEOACC	**5.57**	**14.21**
TEOFCC	9.11	17.97
TEOAFCC	8.82	18.69
TEOCC	8.76	18.1

(b) x-vector results.

It could be observed that all TEO features surpass the CQCC baseline system, and the best TEOACC feature give almost identical EER with VESA-IFCC system on eval subset although the EER on dev subset is quite worse.

The results for TEO feature based x-vector systems are shown in Table 4b. The upper part is some reference methods based on deep learning. Please note that although hard as we tried, we could not reproduce the results reported in [5], this phenomenon is also encountered in [15] where the EER is even worse than our implementation, hence we also included the results of our implementation of $LCNN_{FFT}$. As can be observed, our systems give comparable results with some of the deep models. We didn't elaborately adjust the architecture or tune the parameters for x-vector, there should still be some room for improvements since the gaps between x-vector and GMM both using TEO features are much less than the gaps between deep models and GMM both using CQCCs.

4 Summary and Conclusions

In this study, we investigate the ability of the proposed TEO based features to capture characteristics to distinguish between replayed and genuine speech. The TEO based features surpass CQCC in a great scale when using GMMs as backend classifiers, EER drops from 30.60% on eval subset to 15.53% which is comparable with VESA-IFCC. And our modified version of x-vector further improve the EER on eval subset to 14.21%. Our future work will focus on more appropriate deep networks and other novel mechanisms such as attention as in [16].

References

1. Ergünay, S.K., Khoury, E., Lazaridis, A., Marcel, S.: On the vulnerability of speaker verification to realistic voice spoofing. In: 2015 IEEE 7th International Conference on Biometrics Theory, Applications and Systems (BTAS), pp. 1–6. IEEE (2015)
2. Alegre, F., Janicki, A., Evans, N.: Re-assessing the threat of replay spoofing attacks against automatic speaker verification. In: 2014 International Conference of the Biometrics Special Interest Group (BIOSIG), pp. 1–6. IEEE (2014)

3. Villalba, J., Lleida, E.: Detecting replay attacks from far-field recordings on speaker verification systems. In: Vielhauer, C., Dittmann, J., Drygajlo, A., Juul, N.C., Fairhurst, M.C. (eds.) BioID 2011. LNCS, vol. 6583, pp. 274–285. Springer, Heidelberg (2011). https://doi.org/10.1007/978-3-642-19530-3_25
4. Kinnunen, T., et al.: ASVspoof 2017: automatic speaker verification spoofing and countermeasures challenge evaluation plan. Training **10**(1508), 1508 (2017)
5. Lavrentyeva, G., Novoselov, S., Malykh, E., Kozlov, A., Kudashev, O., Shchemelinin, V.: Audio replay attack detection with deep learning frameworks. In: INTERSPEECH, pp. 82–86 (2017)
6. Witkowski, M., Kacprzak, S., Zelasko, P., Kowalczyk, K., Galka, J.: Audio replay attack detection using high-frequency features. In: INTERSPEECH, pp. 27–31 (2017)
7. Kaiser, J.F.: On a simple algorithm to calculate the 'energy' of a signal. In: International Conference on Acoustics, Speech, and Signal Processing, pp. 381–384. IEEE (1990)
8. Patil, H.A., Kamble, M.R., Patel, T.B., Soni, M.H.: Novel variable length Teager energy separation based instantaneous frequency features for replay detection. In: INTERSPEECH, pp. 12–16 (2017)
9. Nagarsheth, P., Khoury, E., Patil, K., Garland, M.: Replay attack detection using DNN for channel discrimination. In: INTERSPEECH, pp. 97–101 (2017)
10. Snyder, D., Garcia-Romero, D., Povey, D., Khudanpur, S.: Deep neural network embeddings for text-independent speaker verification. In: INTERSPEECH, pp. 999–1003 (2017)
11. Tran, D., Bourdev, L., Fergus, R., Torresani, L., Paluri, M.: Learning spatiotemporal features with 3D convolutional networks. In: Proceedings of the IEEE International Conference on Computer Vision, pp. 4489–4497 (2015)
12. Zhou, L.: Research on audio replay detection method for speaker recognition. Master's thesis, Zhejiang University (2019)
13. Maragos, P., Kaiser, J.F., Quatieri, T.F.: Energy separation in signal modulations with application to speech analysis. IEEE Trans. Signal Process. **41**(10), 3024–3051 (1993)
14. Lee, K.A., et al.: The RedDots data collection for speaker recognition. In: Sixteenth Annual Conference of the International Speech Communication Association (2015)
15. Chettri, B., Mishra, S., Sturm, B.L., Benetos, E.: A study on convolutional neural network based end-to-end replay anti-spoofing. arXiv preprint arXiv:1805.09164 (2018)
16. Zhu, Y., Ko, T., Snyder, D., Mak, B., Povey, D.: Self-attentive speaker embeddings for text-independent speaker verification. In: Proceedings of the INTERSPEECH, vol. 2018, pp. 3573–3577 (2018)

Video Human Behaviour Recognition Based on Improved SVM_KNN for Traceability of Planting Industry

Wei Ni(✉), Quhua Rao, and Dingti Luo

College of Computer Science, Hunan University of Technology, Zhuzhou, China
4449015@qq.com

Abstract. Multivariate data acquisition is a difficult problem in traceability of planting industry. Video-based human behaviour recognition technology can automatically identify various human behaviors in the process of crops planting, and realize automatic data collection. A feature extraction method based on three-dimensional skeleton of human body and an improved SVM_KNN method has been proposed in this paper to classify human behavior and realize multi-target human behavior recognition based on video. The experiment results show that the human behavior recognition method proposed in this paper can effectively identify different human behaviors in crop planting.

Keywords: Human behaviour · SVM · KNN · Traceability · Planting industry

1 Introduction

Traceability system and technology of crop products is a key link of the food safety mechanism. Multivariate data acquisition is a difficult problem in traceability of crop products. Video-based human behaviour recognition technology can automatically identify various human behaviors in the process of agricultural products planting, and realize automatic data collection.

At present, video-based human behavior recognition has been widely used in video surveillance, virtual reality and patient monitoring [1]. However, multi-target behavior recognition in complex background needs further study.

Feature extraction is the first step of human behavior recognition process. Its accuracy directly affects the final recognition effect. Chaudhry and Bobick propose an optical flow-based method, which takes human body as the core area for analysis, and is suitable for ordinary scenes but not for complex scenes [2]. Rapantzikos proposes to apply discrete wavelet transform to three dimensions, and add color and motion information to calculate significant spatiotemporal points [3]. Klaser expands the HOG feature of local gradient direction histogram to 3D, and then forms HOG3D, which can be used for fast density sampling of space-time blocks at multi-scale [4].

Human behavior recognition is the second step of human behavior recognition process. It first trains the human behavior features extracted in the first step and gets the action template. Then it classifies the action process by analyzing the data. Support Vector Machine (SVM) proposed by Vapnik is the most widely used classification

Z. Sun et al. (Eds.): CCBR 2019, LNCS 11818, pp. 474–482, 2019.
https://doi.org/10.1007/978-3-030-31456-9_52

model in visual recognition [5]. The classification accuracy depends largely on the parameters of the model itself, such as penalty parameters and the bandwidth of the kernel function. It is easy to fall into local optimum in the process of seeking optimum. Huang proposed a parameter optimization method for SVM based on genetic algorithm, which effectively improved the classification accuracy of test sets [6]. Wang used artificial fish swarm algorithm to optimize the parameters of SVM to solve the regression problem [7]. The execution steps of the above methods are relatively numerous and the computational complexity is high, which makes the computational cost of global optimization process too high, and is not conducive to the application of large-scale video action data sets. *K* nearest neighbor algorithm (KNN) selects the nearest *K* samples from the samples near the tested samples [8]. Therefore, adding KNN algorithm to traditional SVM algorithm can effectively overcome the shortcomings of SVM.

In this paper, a three-dimensional skeleton model of human body has been extracted by Kinect, and a feature extraction method based on the three-dimensional skeleton of human body has been proposed. And an improved SVM_KNN method has been proposed to classify human behavior and realize multi-target human behavior recognition based on video.

2 Three-Dimensional Skeleton Model of Human Body

This paper use Kinect to establish three-dimensional skeleton model of human body. Kinect SDK is a Kinect for Windows software development toolkit, which can track up to 6 people, 25 joint points per person [9].

Not every joint is a key node, many of which are redundant in human body recognition. Therefore, some key joint points can be selected and the rest can be ignored. Seventeen joint points were selected as key nodes, including left/right ankle, left/right knee, left/right wrist, left/right shoulder, head, spine and spinal shoulder (neck), left/right palm, left/right hip joint, left/right elbow. The base of spine (hip) joint as origin was excluded. These joints are now numbered A-R (O as origin) (Fig. 1).

Taking 17 joint points in each depth image as feature points, the spatial distance of these 17 feature points relative to the joint points at the base of the spine (hip) as origin points constitutes 17 feature vectors of human behavior. Name the coordinates of each joint point $J_i = (x_i, y_i, z_i)$, the representation of these eigenvectors is as follows

$$\overrightarrow{JoJi} = \sqrt{(xi - xo)^2 + (yi - yo)^2 + (zi - zo)^2} \quad (1)$$

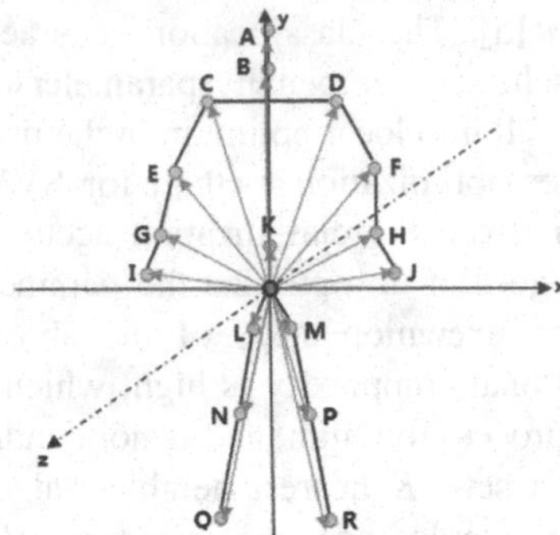

Fig. 1. Characteristic representation of human behavior.

3 Segmentation of Continuous Motion of Moving Human Body

Action segmentation is an indispensable step in human behavior recognition. This step divides continuous long video into different segments according to different actions [10].

Based on the temporal correlation between the three-dimensional human skeleton and the three-dimensional coordinates of the nodes, a continuous motion segmentation algorithm based on the dissimilarity of the three-dimensional human skeleton has been proposed.

The steps are as follows:

(1) Finding the Dissimilarity of two joint skeleton images

$$\text{Dissimilarity(i)} = \sum_{k=1}^{25} \sqrt{\text{DIFF(k)Z(i)} + \text{DIFF(k)Y(i)} + \text{DIFF(k)X(i)}} \quad (2)$$

In the formula, *K* denotes the *k*-th joint point, and Joint (*k*) *X* (*i*) denotes the *X* coordinates of the *k*-th joint point in the skeleton image of the *i*-th frame. Similarly, Joint (*k*) *Y* (*i*) and Joint (*k*) *Z* (*i*) can be inferred.

(2) For each moving window whose size is *m*, the local median *M* (*i*) calculated by the center is taken as the threshold value.

(3) Using normalization to convert dissimilarity and local median to (0, 1)

$$Dissimilarity'(i) = \frac{\text{Dissimilarity}(i) - \text{Dissimilarity}_{min}(i)}{\text{Dissimilarity}_{max}(i) - \text{Dissimilarity}_{min}(i)} \quad (3)$$

$$M'(i) = \frac{M(i) - M_{min}(i)}{M_{max}(i) - M_{min}(i)} \quad (4)$$

(4) If Dissimilarity′(*i*) >=*M*′(*i*), then frames I and I-1 are boundary transition frames for action segmentation.

This paper use MATLAB to calculate the inter-frame dissimilarity and local median of video clips and draw a graph. Then we can judge the segmentation points of continuous action according to the dissimilarity and the size of local median. Figure 2 shows the curve of the degree of dissimilarity between frames and the local median.

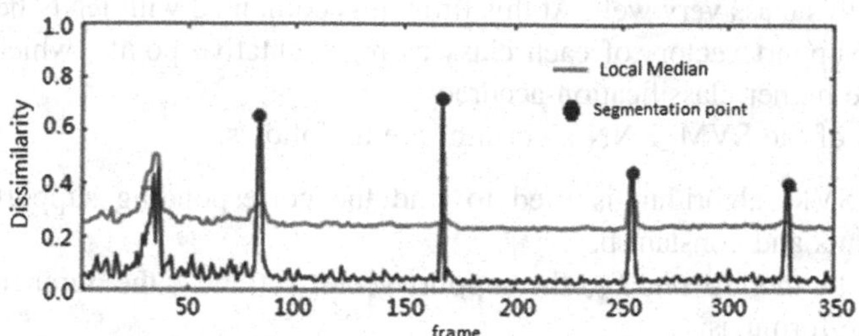

Fig. 2. Inter-frame dissimilarity and local median curve.

Figure 3 Shows the result of continuous motion segmentation algorithm based on dissimilarity degree. In order to observe the experimental results more intuitively, the segmented frames and the video frames before and after the segmented frames are output together in the form of pictures.

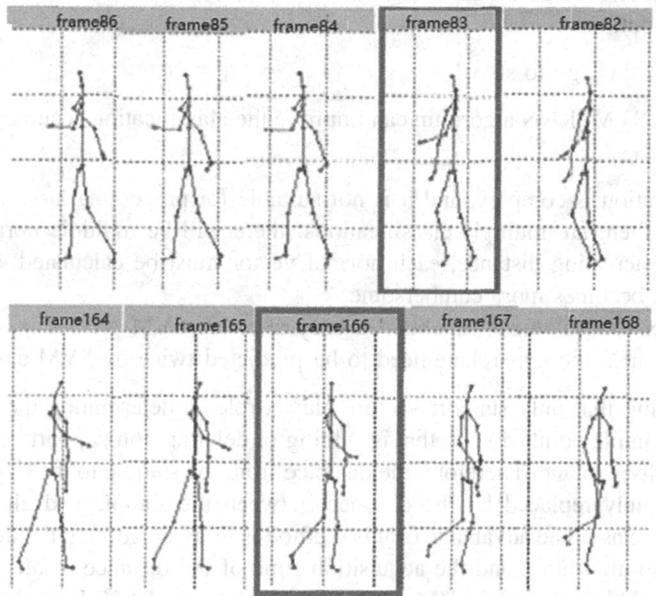

Fig. 3. Segmentation result graph of CMSBOD algorithms.

4 An Improved SVM_KNN Method

The combination of SVM and KNN classifier considers SVM as an INN classifier with only one representative point for each class. Because SVM only takes one representative point for each class of support vectors, sometimes this representative point can not represent this class very well. At this time, it is combined with KNN because KNN takes all the support vectors of each class as representative points, which makes the classifier have higher classification accuracy.

The steps of the SVM_KNN algorithm are as follows:

(1) Firstly, SVM algorithm is used to find the corresponding support vector, its coefficients and constant b.
(2) Set T to be the test set, T_{SV} the support vector set and k the number of KNN.
(3) Calculate formulas

$$\mathrm{g(x)} = \sum_{i} \propto_i K(x_i, x) - b \tag{5}$$

(4) If $|\mathrm{g}(x)| > \varepsilon$, Calculate formulas

$$\mathrm{f(x)} = \mathrm{sgn(g(x))} \tag{6}$$

As output, else Substitute KNN algorithm to classify, transfer parameters and return results to output.

(5) $\mathrm{T} \leftarrow \mathrm{T} - \{x\}$, go to step 1.

Although SVM_KNN algorithm can improve the classification accuracy, it also has some drawbacks.

(1) Computation is complex, and it is not suitable for processing large quantities of data. If there are multiple classifications, there will be multiple normal vectors. When calculating distance, each normal vector must be calculated, and the calculation becomes more cumbersome.
(2) The decision_value can be obtained only after the SVM prediction stage, so the samples near the hyperplane need to be predicted twice by SVM and KNN.

Considering that only support vectors play a role in determining the hyperplane, while other sample points do not, that is, adding or deleting non-support vectors has no effect on the hyperplane. Therefore, the distance from the sample to the hyperplane can be approximately replaced by the distance between the sample and all the support vectors of the class. The advantage of this method is to avoid solving the normal vector in the original algorithm, and the acquisition time of the distance results is advanced from the prediction stage of SVM to the training stage of SVM, thus avoiding the problem of secondary prediction.

The steps of the improved SVM_KNN algorithm are as follows:

(1) The existing sample set S is divided into training sample set S_T and testing sample set S_E. The training sample set S_T eigenvalue is input into the SVM

model for training, and the support vector set of each class sample is recorded as $V_1, V_2, \ldots, V_n$.

(2) Sample category labels are used to store the samples separately according to the action category and are recorded as $T_1, T_2, \ldots, T_n$.

(3) Extract an action sample from T_i (i = 1, 2, …, n), calculate the distance from the sample to all support vectors in V_i, and record the average value as D_i. Repeat step (3) until all samples are empty.

(4) Setting threshold ε. If $D_i < \varepsilon$, the action samples are close to the classification surface, using KNN algorithm and turning to step (5), else SVM algorithm is used and turn to step (6).

(5) Using all the support vectors obtained in step (1) to replace all the original training samples, and the distance between the action samples and the replaced training samples is calculated. Choose K classes with the smallest distance and count the corresponding support vector classes to complete the action sample classification.

(6) Classification results are obtained by using SVM algorithm.

Because the eigenvectors of human behavior have 17 dimensions and the distribution of each dimension component is different, the standard Euclidean distance is used to replace the traditional Euclidean distance when calculating the distance between the sample to be measured and the support vector. The normalized Euclidean distance formula is

$$D = \sqrt{\sum_{k=1}^{17} \left(\frac{x_{ik} - x_{jk}}{s_k}\right)^2} \tag{7}$$

5 Experiment and Results

The sample data set in this paper is obtained by Kinect 2.0 camera. Each human behavior has 100 samples, such as opening, ditching, sowing, watering, weeding and fertilization. The samples are divided into two parts, 60 samples used for training and others are used for testing.

Using the continuous motion segmentation algorithm based on the dissimilarity of the three-dimensional human skeleton proposed in Sect. 2 to realize action segmentation. And take 17 joint points in each depth image as feature points.

5.1 Parameter Setting

Set $K = 6$ in the KNN algorithm. Experiments show that when K value is between 1 and 6, the accuracy increases with the increase of K, but when $K > 6$, the accuracy decreases continuously. This is because too large K value will lead to interference points, too small will lack of classification basis, which will affect the accuracy of classification.

There are two parameters in SVM, one is the parameter σ in the RBF kernel function and the other is the penalty factor c. Over-fitting or under-fitting will occur if the value of σ is too large or too small. Too large c value will lead to low accuracy, and too small will not achieve results. So set the penalty factor $\sigma = 1$ and $c = 9$ by 10-fold cross-validation method.

The distance threshold e is generally between 0.4 and 0.8 or near 1. In this application, it is found that the accuracy is the highest when $e = 0.7$ through many tests. So the final determination is epsilon = 0.7.

5.2 Experimental Result

The experiment is programmed and simulated by MATLAB R2012b. The training set is input into SVM and SVM_KNN respectively, and the improved SVM_KNN is used to train the model and detect the sample set to be tested. The accuracy and running time are obtained. The comparison results of the three methods are shown in Table 1.

Table 1. The comparison results of the three methods.

Methods	Precision	Cost time
SVM	78%	0.350
SVM_KNN	87.1%	0.625
Improved SVM_KNN	88.2%	0.414

The results show that the accuracy of SVM_KNN algorithm is higher than that of SVM algorithm, but the time consumption is higher. The accuracy of the improved SVM_KNN algorithm is similar to that of the original SVM_KNN algorithm, but the time consumption decreases a lot.

The comparison results of different human behavior between SVM_KNN and improved SVM_KNN are shown in Table 2.

Table 2. Detail results of different behavior

Behavior	SVM_KNN	Improved SVM_KNN
Opening	89.1%	89.4%
Ditching	86.1%	88.4%
Sowing	88.2%	89.7%
Watering	80.2%	83.1%
Weeding	92.1%	93.2%
Fertilization	80.3%	82.9%

In Table 2, the recognition accuracy of each type of human behavior varies from one type to another because of whether there is a significant change in the behavior, whether there is a distinction between the behavior and other behavior, and the complexity of the environment in which the behavior is located. For example, the movement of watering itself does not change significantly, the posture is relatively fixed, and it has a certain degree with the fertilization behavior. Because of the overlap, the accuracy of behavior recognition is not high; the action of weeding changes greatly, and is different from other actions, so the accuracy is also high.

6 Conclusion

In order to automatically identify various human behaviors in the process of agricultural products planting, the Kinect has been used to extract the three-dimensional skeleton model of human body. And a feature extraction method based on three-dimensional skeleton of human body has been proposed. Based on the temporal correlation between the three-dimensional human skeleton and the three-dimensional coordinates of the nodes, a continuous motion segmentation algorithm based on the dissimilarity of the three-dimensional human skeleton is proposed to divides continuous long video into different segments according to different actions. Finally, an improved SVM_KNN method has been proposed to classify human behavior and realize multi-target human behavior recognition based on video. The experiment results show that accuracy of the improved SVM_KNN algorithm is similar to that of the original SVM_KNN algorithm, but the time consumption decreases a lot. The human behavior recognition method proposed in this paper can effectively identify different human behaviors in crop production.

Acknowledgements. This work was financially supported by Hunan science and technology project (No. 2016NK2211) and scientific research projects of Hunan education department (No. 17C0480).

References

1. Wang, S.G., Lu, F.J.: Action recognition based on line random forest voting. Opt. Precis. Eng. **24**(08), 2010–2017 (2016)
2. Bobick, A., Davis, A.: The recognition of human movement using temporal templates. IEEE trans. Pattern anal. Mach. Intell. **23**(3), 257–267 (2001)
3. Weinland, D., Ronfard, D., Boyer, D.: A survey of vision-based methods for action representation, segmentation and recognition. Comput. Vis. Image Underst. **115**(2), 224–241 (2011)
4. Wang, H., HKlaser, A.: Action recognition by dense trajectories. In: IEEE Computer Society Conference on Computer Vision and Pattern Recognition, vol. 7 (2011)
5. Song, R., Lin, Z.X., Yao, M.: Luminance uniformity evaluation for backlight based on ε–support vector regression. Chin. J. Liquid Cryst. Displays. **30**(05), 857–863 (2015)
6. Shen, L., Chen, H., Yu, Z.: Evolving support vector machines using fruit fly optimization for medical data classification. Knowl.-Based Syst. **96**, 61–75 (2016)
7. Huang, C.L., Wang, C.J.: A GA-based feature selection and parameters optimization for support vector machines. Expert Syst. Appl. **31**(2), 231–240 (2006)
8. Rogez, G., Rihan, J., Ramalingam, S., et al.: Randomized trees for human pose detection. In: 2008 International Conference on Computer Vision and Pattern Recognition (CVPR), pp. 1032–1039 (2008)

9. Ghojogh, B., Mohammadzade, H., Mokari, M.: Fisherposes for human action recognition using kinect sensor data. IEEE Sens. J. **18**(4), 1612–1627 (2018)
10. Knoop, S., Vacek, S., Dillmann, R.: Sensor fusion for 3D human body tracking with an articulated 3D body model. In: 2006 International Conference on Robotics and Automation (ICRA), pp. 1686–1691 (2006)

Application of Unscented Kalman Filter in Tracking of Video Moving Target

Qin Guo, Cuixia Zeng, Zhizhao Jiang, Xiaotong Hu, and Xiaofei Deng(✉)

School of Information Science and Engineering,
Jishou University, Jishou 416000, People's Republic of China
xiaofei0228@163.com

Abstract. The tracking of video moving target is actually an estimation problem of state variable. Kalman filter method is one of the classical estimators widely used in the field of state estimation. But in tracking system of video moving target, the classical Kalman filtering method has the problem of low tracking accuracy and divergence of filtering. In order to improve the tracking effect, a unscented Kalman filter algorithm is used to track moving target in video sequence. The application of unscented Kalman filter in tracking of video moving target is compared with that of Kalman filter by Matlab simulation software. The results show that unscented Kalman filter is more accurate and better than Kalman filter in tracking of video moving target.

Keywords: Untracked kalman filtering · Trackless transformation · Moving target tracking · Video sequence

1 Introduction

Moving target tracking technology in video sequence is the focus and hotspot [1–3]. Moving target tracking actually means to determine the moving target's position in each video image, and match the same target in different frames that is to estimate and predict the state of the target. In essence, when the system state model and observation equation are both linear and gaussian, and the noise is gaussian, the linear kalman filter (KF) is the best filter and the best filter for noise. For the nonlinear system filtering problem, the optimal solution of the classical kalman filter cannot be expressed, especially when the moving target in video sequence mutates, the target loss may occur, resulting in a large tracking error. S. Julier et al. proposed a nonlinear filtering method–

Fund Project: National College Student Innovation Training Project Funding (No. 201810531017, 201108531019); Jishou University School-level University Student Innovation Project Funding (No. JDCX2018040); Jishou University 13th Five-Year Communication Engineering Specialty Comprehensive Reform Pilot Construction Project; Hunan Province first-class undergraduate communication engineering professional construction project.

Z. Sun et al. (Eds.): CCBR 2019, LNCS 11818, pp. 483–492, 2019.
https://doi.org/10.1007/978-3-030-31456-9_53

Unscented Kalman Filter (UKF), by using unscented transform directly on the probability density approximation and accurately estimate the state of the mean and covariance, largely avoided the linearization error. Therefore, based on the defects of the classical kalman filtering algorithm in moving target tracking, this paper adopts untracked kalman filtering based on the unscented transform to track and estimate the moving target. Its core idea is use twice unscented transform to obtain the approximate sampling points (Sigma points) and reduce the linearization error. At the same time, kalman filter is used to calculate the gain matrix and update the state estimation and covariance estimation.

2 Analysis and Comparison of KF and UKF Algorithms

2.1 Discrete Kalman Filtering

Let the state equation and observation equation of the discrete time system be:

$$x(k+1) = \Phi(k+1,k)\,x(k) + \Gamma(k+1,k)\,w(k) \tag{1}$$

$$\mathrm{z}(k) = H(k)\,x(k) + v(k) \tag{2}$$

State noise and measurement noise are unrelated white gaussian noise sequences, and their statistical characteristics are:

$$E[w(k)] = 0, E\left[w(k)\,w^T(j)\right] = Q(k)\,\delta_{kj} \tag{3}$$

$$E[v(k)] = 0, E\left[v(k)\,v^T(j)\right] = R(k)\,\delta_{kj} \tag{4}$$

The statistical characteristics of the initial state are as follows

$$E[x(0)] = m_0, E\left\{[x(0)-m_0]\,[x(0)-m_0]^T\right\} = P_0 \tag{5}$$

When state noise w (k) and measurement noise v (k) are gaussian white noise, the filtering value of the system [4] is the unbiased minimum mean square error estimation of system state x (k/k), and $P(k/k)$ is the minimum mean square error matrix. When state noise $w(k)$ or measurement noise v (k) do not satisfy gaussian white noise distribution, filter value (k/k) is not an unbiased estimate of system state, nor is p (k/k) the minimum mean square error matrix.

The following equation can be obtained from the filter gain equation and one-step predictive mean square error equation:

$$K(k)\,R(k) = P(k/k)\,H^T(k) \tag{6}$$

Multiply $\mathrm{R}^{(-1)}(k)$ by both sides of this equation to get another expression for $K(k)$

$$K(k) = P(k/k)\,H^T(k)\,R^{-1}(k) \tag{7}$$

When $R(k)$ increases, this indicates that the observed value is unreliable, so the gain $K(k)$ should be smaller to weaken the correction effect of the new measurement on the estimation. On the contrary, when $Q(k-1)$ increases, means the random error of the step transition increases, and the state prediction correction should be strengthened, so $K(k)$ should increase. When $P(k/k)$ or $Q(k-1)$ and $R(k)$ increase or decrease the same multiplication, the gain matrix $K(k)$ remains unchanged. Therefore, we can say that the gain matrix K (k) depends on the signal-to-noise ratio $Q(k-1)/R(k)$ [5].

The state estimation equation says, the discrete kalman filtering algorithm has the filter value at time k equal to the prediction estimate at time k plus the correction term. This indicates that prediction is the basis of filtering in discrete kalman filtering algorithm, the accuracy of filtering estimation is better than prediction estimation.

2.2 Untracked Kalman Filtering

The Unscented Transform (UT) [6] implementation method is: in the original state, according to a certain rule select some sampling points, and make the mean and covariance of sampling points equal to the original state distribution. The obtained points are substituted into the nonlinear function, then obtain the point set of nonlinear function values and the mean and covariance of the transformation from these point sets finally.

There is a nonlinear transformation $y = f(x)$. The state vector is a dimensional random variable whose mean $\bar{x}$ and variance P are known. 2n+1 sigma points X and corresponding weight ω to calculate the statistical characteristics of y:

Step one: Calculate the sample points, $2n+1$ sigma points. N: dimension of a state.

$$\begin{cases} X^{(0)} = \bar{X}, \mathrm{i} = 0 \\ X^{(i)} = \bar{X} + \left(\sqrt{(\mathrm{n}+\lambda)P}\right)_i, i = 1 \sim n \\ X^{(i)} = \bar{X} - \left(\sqrt{(n+\lambda)P}\right)_i, i = n+1 \sim 2n \end{cases} \tag{8}$$

where, $\left(\sqrt{P}\right)^T\left(\sqrt{P}\right) = P$, $\left(\sqrt{P}\right)_{\mathrm{i}}$ represents the ith column of the square root of the matrix.

Step two: Calculate the corresponding weights of these sampling points

$$\begin{cases} \omega_m^{(0)} = \frac{\lambda}{\mathrm{n}+\lambda} \\ \omega_c^{(0)} = \frac{\lambda}{n+\lambda} + \left(1 - a^2 + \beta\right) \\ \omega_m^{(i)} = \omega_c^{(i)} = \frac{\lambda}{2(n+\lambda)}, i = 1 \sim 2n \end{cases} \tag{9}$$

From the above formula, superscript is the first sampling point. Parameter $\lambda = \mathrm{a}^2(n+k) - n$ is the scaling parameter, which is used to reduce the total prediction error. a is selected to control the distribution state of its sampling points, and k is the parameter to be selected. Although there is no boundary for its specific value, it is usually ensured that the matrix $(\mathrm{n}+\lambda)P$ is a semi-positive definite matrix. The selected parameter $\beta \geq 0$ is a non-negative weight coefficient, the moment difference of the higher order terms in the combination equation enables the effects of higher order terms to be included.

2.3 The Implementation of Unscented Kalman Filter Algorithm

For different moments k, Eq. (10)can describe the nonlinear system combining the random variable of gaussian white noise $W(k)$ and the observation variable Z of gaussian white noise $V(k)$.

$$\begin{cases} X(k+1) = \mathrm{f}(\mathrm{x}(k), W(k)) \\ Z(k) = h(x(k), V(k)) \end{cases} \tag{10}$$

Let $W(k)$ contain the covariance matrix Q and $V(k)$ contain the covariance matrix R. The basic program of unscented kalman filtering algorithm for random variable X at different moments k is as follows:
Step one: a set of sampling points (called Sigma point set) and their corresponding weights are obtained by using Eqs. (8) and (9).

$$X^{(\mathrm{i})}(k|k) = \begin{bmatrix} \hat{X}(k|k) \\ \hat{X}(k|k) + \sqrt{(n+\lambda)p(k|k)} \\ \hat{X}(k|k) - \sqrt{(n+\lambda)p(k|k)} \end{bmatrix}^T \tag{11}$$

Step two: one-step prediction of measuring 2n+1 sigma point set, i $= 1, 2 \cdots$ 2n + 1.

$$X^{(\mathrm{i})}(k+1|k) = f\left[k, X^{(i)}(k|k)\right] \tag{12}$$

Step three: the traditional kalman algorithm only needs to put the previous state into the equation of state to obtain the state prediction once. Here, a set of Sigma points are used for prediction and weighted average to obtain one-step prediction of system state quantity.

$$\hat{X}(k+1|k) = \sum_{i=0}^{2n} \omega^{(i)} X^{(i)}(k+1|k) \tag{13}$$

$$P(k+1|k) = \sum_{i=0}^{2n} \omega^{(i)} \left[\hat{X}(k+1|k) - X^{(i)}(k+1|k)\right]\left[\hat{X}(k+1|k) - X^{(i)}(k+1|k)\right]^{\mathrm{T}} + \mathrm{Q} \tag{14}$$

Step four: based on one-step prediction, UT transformation is used again to generate a new set of Sigma points.

$$X^{(\mathrm{i})}(k+1|k) = \begin{bmatrix} \hat{X}(\mathrm{k}+1|k) \\ \hat{X}(\mathrm{k}+1|k) + \sqrt{(n+\lambda)P(k+1|k)} \\ \hat{X}(\mathrm{k}+1|k) - \sqrt{(n+\lambda)P(k+1|k)} \end{bmatrix}^T \tag{15}$$

Step five: substitute the predicted Sigma point set in step four into the observation equation to obtain the predicted observation value $i = 1, 2 \cdots 2n + 1$.

$$Z^{(i)}(k+1|k) = h\left[X^{(i)}(k+1|k)\right] \tag{16}$$

Step six: the predicted value of Sigma point set was obtained from step five, and the mean value and covariance predicted by the system were obtained by weighted sum.

$$\bar{Z}(k+1|k) = \sum_{i=0}^{2n} \omega^{(i)} Z^{(i)}(k+1|k) \tag{17}$$

$$P_{z_k z_k} = \sum_{i=0}^{2n} \left[Z^{(i)}(k+1|k) - \bar{Z}(k+1|k)\right]\left[Z^{(i)}(k+1|k) - \bar{Z}(k+1|k)\right]^T + R \tag{18}$$

$$P_{z_k z_k} = \sum_{i=0}^{2n} \omega^{(i)} \left[X^{(i)}(k+1|k) - \bar{Z}(k+1|k)\right]\left[Z^{(i)}(k+1|k) - \bar{Z}(k+1|k)\right]^T \tag{19}$$

Step seven: calculate the kalman gain matrix.

$$K(k+1) = P_{x_k z_k} P_{z_k z_k}^{-1} \tag{20}$$

Step eight: calculate the covariance update and state update of the system.

$$\hat{X}(k+1|k+1) = \hat{X}(k+1|k) + K(k+1)\left[Z(k+1) - \hat{Z}(k+1|k)\right] \tag{21}$$

$$P(k+1|k+1) = P(k+1|k) - K(k+1) P_{z_k z_k} K^T(k+1) \tag{22}$$

It can be seen that UKF does not need to perform Taylor series expansion at the estimation point when dealing with nonlinear filtering, then perform the first n order approximation, but UT transformation is performed near the estimation point to obtain the mean and covariance. The Sigma point set matches the original statistical features, and the Sigma point set directly nonlinear mapping approximates the state probability density function. The essence of this approximation is a statistical approximation rather than a solution.

3 Simulation Results and Analysis of UKF in Tracking of Video Moving Target

3.1 The Establishment of Moving Target Tracking Model of Video Sequence

The establishment of mathematical model [7] in moving target tracking includes state model and measurement model. The state model of moving object tracking describes the state variable of moving object and the state noise as a function of time. The measurement model describes the functional relationship between measurement data, measurement noise and state variables. The measurement model of state model and target can be expressed as:

$$\dot{X}(t) = \varphi[X(t), t] + G(t)W(t) \tag{23}$$

$$Z(t) = H[X(t), t] + V(t) \tag{24}$$

where $X(t)$ is the target state vector; $Z(t)$ is the direction finding quantity. $\Phi[X(t), t]$ is a state variable; $H[X(t), t]$ is a measuring function, both of which have time-varying and non-time-varying states. $G(t)$ is state noise transfer matrix; $w(t)$ is state noise; $v(t)$ is measuring noise; The traditional assumption is that the white gaussian noise vector is irrelevant, its mean is zero, and the covariance matrix is $Q(t)$ and $R(t)$.

To detect the target in video, the target center, namely the center of gravity of the ball, can be abstracted into a particle with the coordinate of (x, y) when the model is established. The state of the falling ball is defined as $X(k) = \left[x\ y\ \dot{x}\ \dot{y}\right]^{\mathrm{T}}$, and the equation of state is as follows.

$$X(k+1) = \begin{bmatrix} 1 & dt & 0 & 0 \\ 0 & 1 & dt & 0 \\ 0 & 0 & 1 & 0 \\ 0 & 0 & 0 & 1 \end{bmatrix} X(k) + \begin{bmatrix} 0 \\ 0 \\ 0 \\ g \end{bmatrix} W(k) \tag{25}$$

$$Z(k) = \begin{bmatrix} 1 & 0 & 0 & 0 \\ 0 & 1 & 0 & 0 \end{bmatrix} X(k) + V(k) \tag{26}$$

Through this process could find the centroid vector (x, y). In this experiment, UKF is used to track video moving targets and adopt a relatively single background. For complex background or dynamic background, establish a relative motion model is necessary. Meanwhile, for a more complex background or dynamic background need a more complex target motion detection algorithm.

3.2 Experimental Results and Analysis

Matlab was used to track and process the video image of the ball repeatedly bouncing off the table in the free fall movement, and UKF and KF were used to track the moving target of video. Its resolution is 320 × 240, frame rate is 30 frames/s, and the total frame number in video is 60 frames. This experiment use a relatively single background. For complex background or dynamic background, a relative motion model needs to be established. At the same time, for video pictures with interference and lots of background clutter, a more complex target motion detection algorithm is needed.

Figures 1 and 2 are respectively the video track diagram of x axis and y axis. It can be seen from Fig. 1 that the trajectories of KF and UKF are basically the same along the x axis, and the tracking effect is good, and according Fig. 2 that UKF algorithm is more suitable to the actual track graph than KF tracking

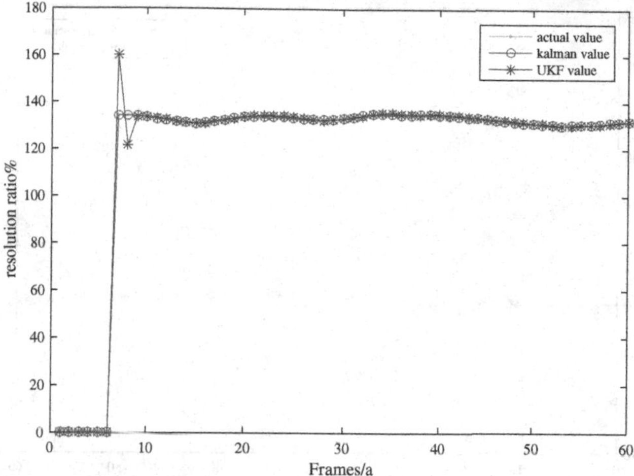

Fig. 1. The trajectory of X axis

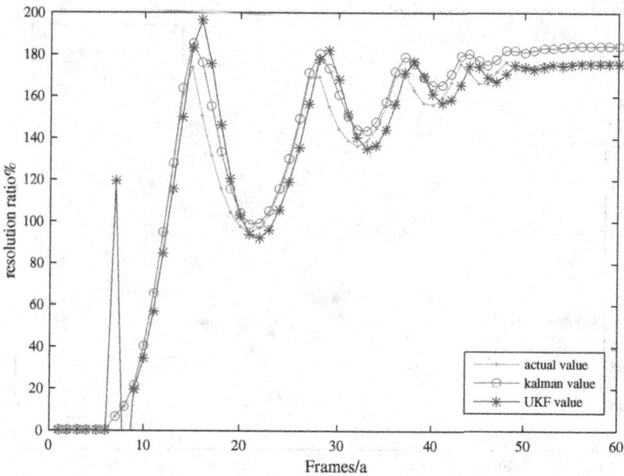

Fig. 2. The trajectory of Y axis

track, and the tracking effect is better. The tracking error along the X-axis is the difference between the actual position of the ball and the predicted value of the filter on the ball, as shown in Fig. 3. The tracking error along the Y-axis is the difference between the actual position of the ball and the predicted height value of the ball by the filter, as shown in Fig. 4. As can be seen from Fig. 3, the overall error values of KF and UKF algorithm in the X direction tend to zero. According to Fig. 4, in the Y direction, the error value of UKF and KF algorithm is zero before the 10th frame, which can accurately track moving targets in video sequence. Between frame 10 and frame 60, the overall KF tracking error value is

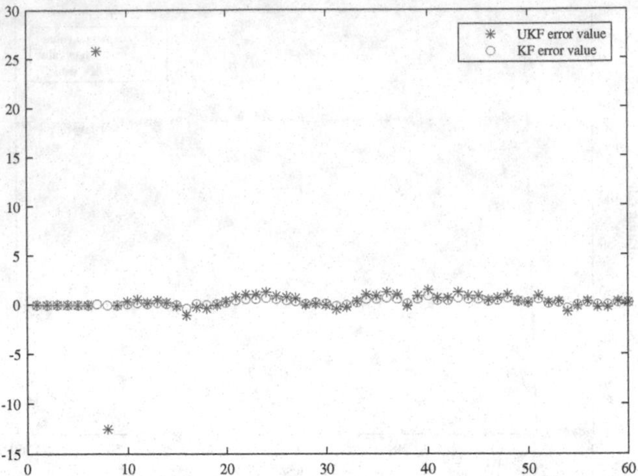

Fig. 3. The error graph of X axis

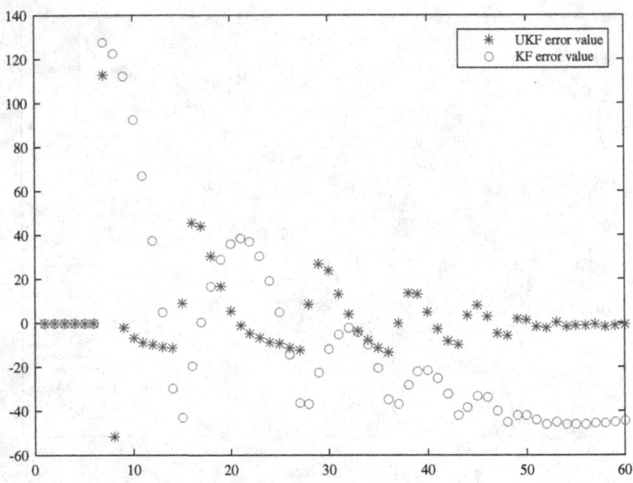

Fig. 4. The error graph of Y axis

larger than UKF, and ultimately cannot track the target ball. Between frames 50 and 60, the tracking error of UKF algorithm tends to zero, and finally tracks the target ball. The effect of the two methods is obviously compared. Therefore, by comparing the tracking error graph, it can be concluded that the UKF algorithm is more accurate in tracking moving targets in video with a smaller overall error.

3.3 Video Moving Target Tracking Results

Fig. 5. Tracking renderings of frames 10, 20, 30, 40, 50, and 60

The ball falls from a high place, is in free fall, hits the ground, bounces back up again, and repeats until the ball stops moving. The six images below are shown in Fig. 5. From left to right, from top to bottom, they are frame 10, 20, 30, 40, 50 and 60, and the red box is the tracking of the ball by KF algorithm, the blue box is the tracking of the ball by UKF filtering algorithm, and the green box is the outer box of the target ball. In the simulation results, it can be clearly seen that in video moving target tracking, for the previous frame number KF algorithm and UKF algorithm, accurate tracking can be carried out, while for the later frame number, KF algorithm and UKF algorithm tracking error, but UKF algorithm tracking effect is better, does not affect the overall moving target tracking. Therefore, in the process of the ball's free fall, UKF filter has a good tracking performance, with a small error in the estimated state and high accuracy. During the collision between the ball and the ground, it has better tracking performance and higher estimation accuracy.

Table 1. Statistical comparisons of the two methods

The algorithm	$E[\|\varepsilon\|]$	σ_ε	CC
The KF method	0.1042108447	0.1722379631	0.945766466
The UKF method	0.0641567021	0.0575184728	0.996833144

In order to evaluate performance of the algorithm in detail, their statistical properties are used to compare. The statistical properties include the mean absolute deviation $E[|\varepsilon|]$, the standard deviation of the estimation error σ_ε, and the CC (Correlation Coefficients). It can be seen from Table 1. that the average absolute deviation and the standard deviation of the estimation error of UKF algorithm are much smaller than those of KF algorithm, indicating that the estimation error of UKF algorithm is smaller than that of KF algorithm and the estimation accuracy is higher. The correlation coefficient of UKF algorithm is closer to 1 than that of KF, which indicates that UKF's tracking performance is better.

However, the magnitudes of the results are a bit small in Table 1, to clearly present the performance improvement, the performance improvement percentage I is used for evaluation. $I = \frac{0.1042108447-0.0641567021}{0.1042108447} = 0.624317$, the result of I shows that the proposed method improves the estimation results by 62.4317% points in the tracking of video moving target.

4 Conclusions

The exploration and application of tracking of video mobile target has a great impact. UKF algorithm is proposed to solve the problem of low accuracy and filtering divergence of the classical Kalman filter method used in tracking of video moving target. UKF is a standard kalman filtering algorithm, it takes a lossless transformation and applies the nonlinear system equations to the linear hypothesis, make the nonlinear system in kalman filter have higher accuracy and divergence. Papers from the moving target detection and tracking of moving targets with untracked kalman filter technology and combining the latest research results both at home and abroad, realize the UKF algorithm of video moving object detection and tracking. By qualitative analysis, especially statistical error analysis, the results show that UKF algorithm is more accurate than kalman filter algorithm. UKF algorithm is based on UT transformation and linear kalman filter framework with small linear error, which still plays a great influence in other applications. There may be some problems in the details of this paper and hopes to continue to study and improve in the future.

References

1. Zhao, X.M., Chen, K., Li, D.: Application of strong tracking Kalman filter in video target tracking. J. Environ. Sci. **47**(11), 128–131 (2016). 166
2. Jiang, D.: Research on target detection and tracking algorithm based on video monitoring. Master Dissertation (2018)
3. Xu, X.Y., Yao, H.M.: Detection and tracking of moving targets based on video image sequence. Electronic Technol. Softw. Eng. 1459–1460 (2018)
4. Dang, J.W.: Research on key technology of underwater guidance multi-target tracking. Master Dissertation (2004)
5. Zhao, L.P.: Research on the pursuit of fugitives based on wireless sensor network. Master Dissertation (2008)
6. Zhang, H.L.: SOC evaluation of power battery based on improved Thevenin model. Master Dissertation (2017)
7. Hou, L.: Research on maneuvering target tracking algorithm. Master Dissertation (2015)

Similarity Scores Based Re-classification for Open-Set Person Re-identification

Hongsheng Wang[1,2], Yang Yang[1,2], Shengcai Liao[3], Dong Cao[1,2], and Zhen Lei[1,2](✉)

[1] CBSR&NLPR, Institute of Automation Chinese Academy of Sciences, Beijing 100190, China
wanghongsheng2016@ia.ac.cn, {yang.yang,dong.cao,zlei}@nlpr.ia.ac.cn
[2] University of Chinese Academy of Sciences, Beijing 100049, China
[3] Inception Institute of Artificial Intelligence, Abu Dhabi, UAE
scliao@ieee.org

Abstract. In this paper, we propose a new similarity scores based re-classification method for open-set person re-identification, which exploits information among the top-n most similar matching candidates in the gallery set. Moreover, to make the cross-view quadratic discriminant analysis metric learning method effectively learn both the projection matrix and the metric kernel with open-set data, we introduce an additional regularization factor to adjust the covariance matrix of the obtained subspace. Our Experiments on challenging OPeRID v1.0 database show that our approach improves the Rank-1 recognition rates at 1% FAR by 8.86% and 10.51% with re-ranking, respectively.

Keywords: Open-set · Person re-identification · Re-classification · Metric learning

1 Introduction

Person re-identification aims to re-identify a query person across multiple non-overlapping cameras. It has been extensively studied [2,3,5,6,15]. Many earlier works focus on two fundamental problems: feature representation and metric learning. A large number of feature designing methods mainly focus on developing discriminative person representation to enhance the robustness of pedestrian images against pose, viewpoint and illumination. The classical representative descriptors include the Local Binary Pattern (LBP) [11], Ensemble of Local Feature [4], color names [13], Local Maximal Occurrence (LOMO) [6], Visibility-aware Part-level Features [10] etc. After the feature is extracted, metric learning is applied to learn a metric so that the same persons are close while different persons are far away from each other in the metric space. The popular metric learning methods include the relative distance comparison [14], Cross-view Quadratic Discriminant Analysis (XQDA) [6], Embedding Deep Metric [9], Joint Discriminative Learning [16] and large scale similarity learning [12], etc. In addition, the

Z. Sun et al. (Eds.): CCBR 2019, LNCS 11818, pp. 493–501, 2019.
https://doi.org/10.1007/978-3-030-31456-9_54

re-ranking technique (e.g., Sparse Contextual Activation [1], k-reciprocal Encoding [17], Expanded Cross Neighborhood [8], Deep Feature Ranking [7]) is often used as a post-processing step.

Problems. In practical application scenarios, person re-identification is usually an open-set test problem, that is, the subject of the probe image may not appear in the gallery set. Firstly, most of the conventional closed-set re-identification methods compute the feature distances between the query image and all the gallery images, which ignores the similarity information between candidate samples. Secondly, many previous metric learning methods have only been validated on the closed-set dataset. Limited effort has been devoted to answer whether similar effectiveness could be derived on the open-set scenario.

Contribution. This paper is dedicated to improving the open-set person re-identification. Firstly, we propose a regularization approach to improve the original XQDA metric learning, which introduces a independent regularization factor to adjust the metric space. Secondly, we propose a similarity scores based re-classification method for open-set person re-identification, which uses the similarity feature vector concatenated by the similarity scores between the probe image and the gallery image and those between gallery images to train a classifier to determine whether the query image exists in the gallery set.

2 Baseline Model

2.1 Feature Representations

For feature representation, a deep ID-discriminative Embedding (IDE) model proposed in [5] is adopted to validate the effectiveness of our proposed methods. It is trained with the ResNet-50 [5] network, which generates a 2,048-dimentional feature vector for each image.

2.2 Metric Learning

In this subsection, we use an improvement version of the Cross-view Quadratic Discriminant Analysis (XQDA) algorithm [6]. The derived distance function between two samples x_i and x_j by cross-view quadratic discriminant analysis is

$$d\left(x_i - x_j\right) = \left(x_i - x_j\right)^T \left(\sum\nolimits_I^{-1} - \sum\nolimits_E^{-1}\right)\left(x_i - x_j\right) \tag{1}$$

where $\sum_I$ and $\sum_E$ are the covariance matrices of the intrapersonal variations and the extrapersonal variations.

$$M = \sum\nolimits_I^{-1} - \sum\nolimits_E^{-1} \tag{2}$$

where $M_{r \times r}$ is $r \times r$ sized metric kernel learned on the derived subspace.

With two inverse matrices, the original cross-view quadratic discriminant analysis learns a distance metric kernel in the learned subspace, and then adjusts the covariance matrix $\sum_I$ of the intrapersonal variations in the original feature space, namely

$$\sum_I = \sum_I + \lambda \times I_{d \times d} \tag{3}$$

where λ is the regularization factor of $\sum_I$, $I_{d \times d}$ is identity matrix.

Through open-set person re-identification experiments, we found that the learned kernel matrix M of XQDA easily leads to overfitting. This is probably because a single regularization factor used in the original XQDA is not sufficient to regularize the learning of both the projection matrix W and the metric kernel M. Therefore, we introduce an additional regularization parameter ξ to the $\sum_E$ after the subspace learning to derive a better kernel matrix M, namely

$$\sum_{E'} = \sum_{E'} + \xi \times I_{r \times r} \tag{4}$$

2.3 Re-ranking

Due to re-ranking algorithms have boosted performance of person re-identification by a large margin, a typical re-ranking algorithm k-reciprocal Encoding is applied, which is introduced in this section.

The k-reciprocal nearest neighbors [17] encodes each image into a single vector as the k-reciprocal feature for re-ranking. Specifically, the k-nearest neighbors of a probe p is defined as

$$N(p,k) = \{g_1^0, g_2^0, ..., g_k^0\}, \tag{5}$$

where $|N(p,k)| = k$, and $|.|$ denotes the number of elements in the set. The k-reciprocal nearest neighbors $R(p,k)$can be defined as

$$R(p,k) = \{g_i | (g_i \in N(p,k)) \wedge (p \in N(g_i,k))\} \tag{6}$$

The $\frac{k}{2}$-reciprocal nearest neighbors of each candidate in $R(p,k)$ are added into a more robust set $R^*(p,k)$. By this operation, more positive samples similar to the candidates in $R(p,k)$ are added into $R^*(p,k)$.

3 Similarity Scores Based Re-classification

Existing closed-set re-identification methods compute the feature distances between the query image and all the gallery images and return a similarity ranking table. They ignore the similarity information between candidate samples. Thus, in this paper, the classification task and the sorting task in the open-set re-identification task are proposed to operate separately. Specifically, the classification task aims to distinguish the query sample between the genuine probe and the impostor probe, and get the maximum score of the matching gallery corresponding to each genuine probe and the location of the matches by the sorting task. Then, the similarity feature vector concatenated by the similarity scores between the probe image and the gallery image and those between gallery images is used to train a classifier to determine whether the query image exists in the gallery set, and then operates the classification task by using the genuine probes classified by the learned classifier.

We name the proposed method as similarity scores based re-classification and it mainly includes the following three processes:

1. Sorting Task
   To boost the performance, the re-ranking score list based on the respective initially obtained rank list is employed to implement the sorting task. The specific implementation steps are as follows:
   (a) Computing the feature similarity score between the probe image and the gallery image, and then obtaining the re-ranking score list.
   (b) Sorting the scores of each genuine probe.
   (c) Determining whether the genuine probe matches the gallery. If not, assigning the corresponding score to negative infinity. If there is a match, getting the maximum genuine score of the matches and the location of the matches.
2. Classification Task
   The classification task is to identify the genuine probe and the impostor probe by fully mining the score distribution of the original score list. The specific implementation steps are as follows:
   (a) Using the $n \times (n+1)$ sized feature similarity score vector concatenated by the $n \times 1$ sized top-n scores in the original score list between the probe image and the gallery image, and the $n \times n$ sized scores between those top-n gallery images to train a classifier to determine whether the query image exists in the gallery set.
   (b) Predicting probability score of the query sample belong to the genuine probe by the learned classifier.
   (c) Sorting the scores of each impostor probe in the predicted probability score, and then using the sorted impostor scores to generate the decision thresholds.
3. Evaluation Task
   Detection and identification should be both satisfied simultaneously, including the following two steps:
   - Comparing the genuine scores with the decision thresholds, which has to meet the condition that the genuine scores are not less than the decision thresholds.
   - Comparing the matching ranks of the genuine probe to the interested rank points, and then satisfying the condition that the matching ranks locate in front of the interested rank points.

4 Experiments

We compare our proposed algorithm to a number of the existing methods. In order to have a systematic comparison, we also implement two baseline models.

We implement a version without classification operation as baseline, which is used to check the effectiveness of our proposed similarity scores based model. We simply refer to the baseline model and the proposed model as REID and REID+CLS respectively. Due to re-ranking algorithms have boosted performance of person re-identification to a large degree, a version with re-ranking is also conducted as the two models, namely REID+RE-RANKING and REID+CLS+RE-RANKING, respectively. In addition, we use the IDE features based on the ResNet-50 network [5]. The improved XQDA is applied as distance metrics.

4.1 Dataset Description

OPeRID v1.0 [6] contains 7,413 images for 200 identities, captured by 6 cameras. For each trial, we randomly select half of the persons under each camera. Specifically, the test data is divided into the gallery set G under a certain camera, the genuine probe set P_G, which contains the same persons as in G under the other five cameras, and the impostor probe set P_N, which contains different persons from G who appear in the other five cameras.

4.2 Experimental Setting

We evaluate our proposed model on the challenging open-set person re-identification dataset OPeRID v1.0. The experiment is repeated 10 trials containing training and testing procedures. In our paper, we randomly select half of the images of each person to train the improved XQDA metric learning, and the other half for the classifier. To train a classifier, we further divide the probe set into the genuine probe set and the impostor probe set. In addition, we design a $n \times (n+1)$ sized similarity score vector as our classifier feature, which is concatenated by the $n \times 1$ sized top-n scores between the probe image and the gallery image and the $n \times n$ sized scores between those top-n gallery images. For the parameter setting, we set the regularization factor λ of the projection matrix W to 0.001 and the penalty factor ξ of the learned kernel matrix M to 0.1 in the metric learning session. Besides, we set k1 to 20, k2 to 6 with the k-reciprocal Encoding. Besides, the top-n of the classifier feature is set to top-10, and the parameter nTree of the random forest classifier is set to 5.

4.3 Results and Analysis

In our paper, we evaluated the improved XQDA on the IDE feature as baseline, we added the k-reciprocal Encoding as the other baseline model with re-ranking. The ROC curves at Rank 1 are shown in Fig. 1. From the figures we can see that the two baseline models, REID and REID+RE-RANKING, both of them get worst accuracy among the method combinations. Comparing with the two baseline models without the classifier to distinguish the query sample between the genuine probe and the impostor probe, the proposed REID+CLS model gains

8.86% improvement in Rank 1 accuracy and significant 10.51% improvement with the model of REID+CLS+RE-RANKING under FAR = 1%, which verifies the effectiveness of our proposed classifier for open-set identification. Moreover, for both models of the REID+CLS and the REID+CLS+RE-RANKING, they perform better than the respective baseline with the increasing FARs, but the advances they achieve are not as impressive as at low FARs, which indicates that the proposed method perform better under practical scenarios like re-identification at low FARs and the open-set task in surveillance. Especially that FAR = 100% corresponding to the closed-set person re-identification, our identification results are almost equivalent to the results of the respective baseline. It is reasonable that our approach does not work. Since there is only the genuine probe set, our proposed classifier could not obtain sufficient similarity information. Hence, it also proves that the proposed classifier is mainly attributed to the improvement of the open-set identification accuracy from another aspect.

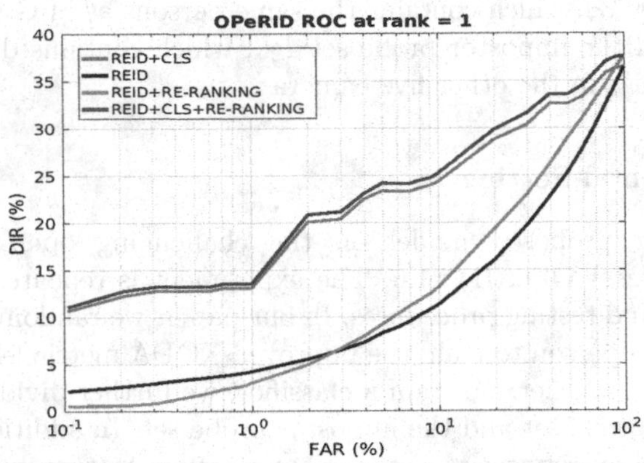

Fig. 1. ROC curves at Rank 1. Performances are measured in $\mu - \sigma$ of 10 trials.

We also evaluated the performances at fixed FARs, and the Cumulated Matching Characteristics (CMC) curves of several models under $FAR = 1\%$ and $FAR = 10\%$ are shown in Fig. 2. Comparing with two baseline models, REID and REID+RE-RANKING, our method impressively outperforms them and achieves large margin advances in a wide range of Rank accuracy at both FAR=1% and FAR=10%. It should be noted that, the improvement our proposed method achieve is more and more obvious with the increasing Rank, showing the identification capability of our approach under open-set conditions. Especially that the REID+CLS+RE-RANKING becomes the best one among the evaluated re-identification methods, indicating that our approach is more practical and effective to the open-set identification when combined with re-ranking algorithm.

Furthermore, we evaluated the recognition performance of the random forest classifier for distinguishing between the genuine probe and the impostor probe.

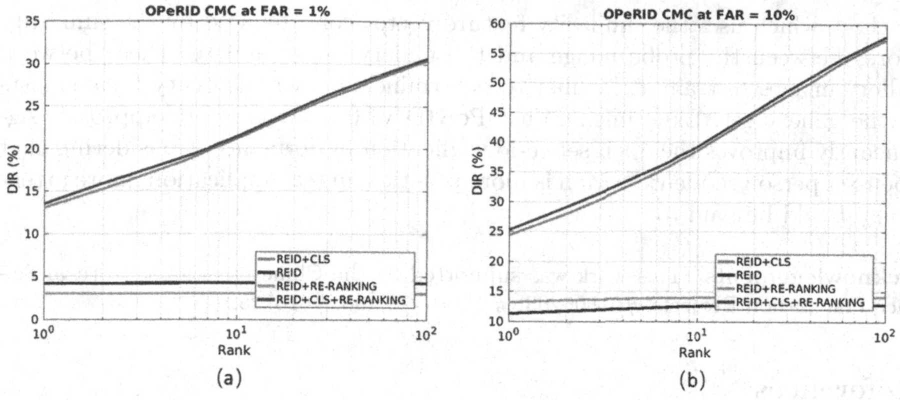

Fig. 2. CMC curves at FAR = 1 % (a) and FAR = 10 % (b). Performances are measured in $\mu - \sigma$ of 10 trials.

The experiment selects two groups of the test set, one group is constructed with the images under camera 2 as the gallery set, the other cameras as the probe set, the other group consists of the images under camera 6 as the gallery set, the rest of cameras as the probe set. The test partition is repeated for ten times, and the final performance is measured by the average value of the 10 trials. The results are shown in Table 1.

Table 1. Evaluating the accuracy (%) of random forest binary classifier for identifying between the genuine probe and the impostor probe.

numTrial	1	2	3	4	5	6	7	8	9	10	Avg
Camera 2	86.72	86.45	87.09	86.90	86.20	86.52	87.02	86.37	86.27	86.40	86.59
Camera 6	80.86	80.11	80.38	78.37	80.45	80.28	81.67	81.03	80.11	81.34	80.46

The results are in Table 1 show that, the average precision of our proposed classifier can reach over 80% under the open-set test protocol, which verifies the effectiveness of the classifier for determining whether the query image exists in the gallery set. Besides, each of the ten classification results shows that the result of each test experiment is close to the average value of 10 trials, which indicates that our approach is efficient and robust.

5 Conclusion

In this paper, we have presented an efficient and effective method for open-set person re-identification. We have proposed a novel regularization approach for the XQDA metric learning, which introduces an additional regularization factor to adjust the covariance matrix on the derived subspace. We have also proposed similarity scores based re-classification for open-set person re-identification method, which uses the similarity feature vector concatenated by the similarity scores between the probe image and the gallery image and the those between gallery images to train a classifier to determine whether the query image exists in the gallery set. Experiments on OPeRID v1.0 show that our approach significantly improves the open-set re-identification performance. Considering that open-set person re-identification is more practical in real application, more attentions should be paid to it.

Acknowlegements. This work was supported by the Chinese National Natural Science Foundation Projects #61806203, #61876178 and #61672521.

References

1. Bai, S., Bai, X.: Sparse contextual activation for efficient visual re-ranking. IEEE Trans. Image Process. **25**(3), 1056–1069 (2016)
2. Chen, Y.C., Zhu, X., Zheng, W.S., Lai, J.H.: Person re-identification by camera correlation aware feature augmentation. IEEE Trans. Pattern Anal. Mach. Intell. **40**(2), 392–408 (2018)
3. Chung, D., Tahboub, K., Delp, E.J.: A two stream siamese convolutional neural network for person re-identification. In: IEEE International Conference on Computer Vision, pp. 1992–2000 (2017)
4. Gray, D., Tao, H.: Viewpoint invariant pedestrian recognition with an ensemble of localized features. In: Forsyth, D., Torr, P., Zisserman, A. (eds.) ECCV 2008. LNCS, vol. 5302, pp. 262–275. Springer, Heidelberg (2008). https://doi.org/10.1007/978-3-540-88682-2_21
5. He, K., Zhang, X., Ren, S., Sun, J.: Deep residual learning for image recognition, pp. 770–778 (2015)
6. Liao, S., Hu, Y., Zhu, X., Li, S.Z.: Person re-identification by local maximal occurrence representation and metric learning. In: IEEE Conference on Computer Vision and Pattern Recognition, pp. 2197–2206 (2015
7. Nie, J., Huang, L., Zhang, W., Wei, G., Wei, Z.: Deep feature ranking for person re-identification. IEEE Access **7**, 15007–15017 (2019)
8. Saquib Sarfraz, M., Schumann, A., Eberle, A., Stiefelhagen, R.: A pose-sensitive embedding for person re-identification with expanded cross neighborhood re-ranking (2017)
9. Shi, H., Yang, Y., Zhu, X., Liao, S., Lei, Z., Zheng, W., Li, S.Z.: Embedding deep metric for person re-identification: a study against large variations. In: Leibe, B., Matas, J., Sebe, N., Welling, M. (eds.) ECCV 2016. LNCS, vol. 9905, pp. 732–748. Springer, Cham (2016). https://doi.org/10.1007/978-3-319-46448-0_44
10. Sun, Y., Xu, Q., Li, Y., Zhang, C., Li, Y., Wang, S., Sun,J.: Perceive where to focus: learning visibility-aware part-level features for partial person re-identification. In: IEEE Conference on Computer Vision and Pattern Recognition, IEEE Computer Society (2019)
11. Xiong, F., Gou, M., Camps, O., Sznaier, M.: Person re-identification using kernel-based metric learning methods. In: Fleet, D., Pajdla, T., Schiele, B., Tuytelaars, T. (eds.) ECCV 2014. LNCS, vol. 8695, pp. 1–16. Springer, Cham (2014). https://doi.org/10.1007/978-3-319-10584-0_1

12. Yang, Y., Liao, S., Lei, Z., Li, S.Z.: Large scale similarity learning using similar pairs for person verification. In: Proceedings of the Thirtieth AAAI Conference on Artificial Intelligence, 12–17 February 2016, Phoenix, Arizona, USA, pp. 3655–3661 (2016
13. Yang, Y., Yang, J., Yan, J., Liao, S., Yi, D., Li, S.Z.: Salient color names for person re-identification. 模式识别国家重点实验室 **8689**(9), 536–551 (2014)
14. Zheng, W.S., Gong, S., Xiang, T.: IEEE Trans. Pattern Anal. Mach. Intell. **35**(3), 653–668 (2013)
15. Zheng, W.-S., Gong, S., Xiang, T.: Group association: assisting re-identification by visual context. In: Gong, S., Cristani, M., Yan, S., Loy, C.C. (eds.) Person Re-Identification. ACVPR, pp. 183–201. Springer, London (2014). https://doi.org/10.1007/978-1-4471-6296-4_9
16. Zheng, Z., Yang, X., Yu, Z., Zheng, L., Kautz, J.: Joint discriminative and generative learning for person re-identification. In: IEEE Conference on Computer Vision and Pattern Recognition, IEEE Computer Society (2019)
17. Zhong, Z., Zheng, L., Cao, D., Li, S.: Re-ranking person re-identification with k-reciprocal encoding, pp. 3652–3661 (2017)

The GMM and I-Vector Systems Based on Spoofing Algorithms for Speaker Spoofing Detection

Hui Tang[1], Zhenchun Lei[1](✉), Zhongying Huang[1], Hailin Gan[1], Kun Yu[2], and Yingen Yang[1]

[1] School of Computer and Information Engineering, Jiangxi Normal University, Nanchang, China
Tanghui.th@foxmail.com, zhenchun.lei@hotmail.com, huangzhongying1996@163.com, hailingan@foxmail.com, ygyang@jxnu.edu.cn

[2] China Ship Development and Design Center, China Shipbuilding Industry Corporation, Wuhan, China
kunyu2013@163.com

Abstract. Automatic Speaker Verification (ASV) systems are more vulnerable to being attacked than other biometric systems, such as speech synthesis, voice conversion, and replay. In this paper, two frameworks (Gaussian mixture model based and i-vector based) are used to detect a variety of specific attack types. Three scoring methods (probabilistic normalization, linear regression and support vector machine) are used for the Gaussian Mixture Model (GMM) model. And three different classifiers (cosine distance, probabilistic linear discriminant analysis, support vector machine) are used for the i-vector system. Furthermore, the cosine classifier based on the i-vector system which uses three scoring methods is proposed in this paper. Experiments on the ASVspoof 2019 challenge logical access scenario show that the GMM classifier with the Support Vector Machines (SVM) scoring method based on different spoofing algorithms obtains the best performance on the evaluation set with EER of 7.03%. Moreover, SVM scoring is also useful for improving the i-vector system based on different spoofing algorithms.

Keywords: Spoofing detection · Spoofing algorithms · Speaker verification

1 Introduction

Automatic Speaker Verification (ASV) aims to automatically confirm the identity of the speaker by a given speech segment [1]. ASV technology has been widely used in many applications, such as online banking, intelligent home, and secure access control. For the security of these applications, ASV systems urgently need to improve the ability of detecting malicious attacks and thwarting unauthorized access attempt.

The four well-known attacks that present a serious threat to ASV systems are mimicry [2], text-to-speech (TTS) [3, 4], voice conversion (VC) [5, 6], replay [7].

Z. Sun et al. (Eds.): CCBR 2019, LNCS 11818, pp. 502–510, 2019.
https://doi.org/10.1007/978-3-030-31456-9_55

In this paper, we only focus on TTS and VC attacks detection on ASVspoof 2019[1] challenge and aim to develop generalized countermeasures for ASV anti-spoofing research. Today, well-trained synthetic speech and converted voice are as good as perceptually indistinguishable from bona fide speech [8]. A considerable volume of studies [9–13] has confirmed that TTS and VC attacks remain a serious concern to speaker verification systems. In real scenarios, fraudsters can easily manipulate an ASV system by utilizing more advanced voice conversion or speech synthesis algorithms to generate particularly effective spoofing attacks.

Meanwhile, a multitude of different spoofing technologies has been put forward to improve detection performance. Most existing countermeasures focus on designing discriminative features (front-end) with a simple GMM back-end [14–18]. As for antecedent anti-spoofing detection based on i-vectors systems, attention was paid to the feature selection process. For example, in [19], three different features (Mel-frequency cepstral coefficients, Mel-frequency principle components (MFCC), and cosine phase features) were used to extract i-vectors and concatenated as the features of SVM classifier. In [20], i-vectors were extracted from five feature extraction techniques (MFCC, phoneme posterior probability (PPP), MFCC-PPP, modified group delay (MGD) combined with tailored features PPP, and MGD-MFCC-PPP) and score fusion was applied to five subsystems. Motivated by the preliminary observations, we pay more attention to classifiers and score fusion in this paper.

In this paper, we established GMMs for spoofing detection based on different spoofing algorithms. Then three scoring methods (support vector machines, probabilistic normalization, multiple linear regression) were applied to make final decisions of the GMMs system. We focused on improving the performance of the i-vector system based on different spoofing algorithms. Moreover, three back-end classifiers (cosine distance, probabilistic linear discriminant analysis, support vector machines) were used for the i-vector system. And we also investigated the effect of scores fusion method. The cosine distance scoring in i-vector systems with three scoring methods was proposed for finding the optimal scoring methods.

2 Spoofing Detection

In this section, GMM and i-vector systems based on different spoofing algorithms have been considered for the spoofing detection task.

[1] https://datashare.is.ed.ac.uk/handle/10283/3336.

2.1 Classical GMM System

Gaussian mixture model (GMM) is a well-known generative model for speaker recognition [21, 22]. It represents a weighted sum of *k* multivariate Gaussians given by the equation:

$$p(x) = \sum_{k=1}^{k} \pi_k N(x|m_k, \Sigma_k), \tag{1}$$

where π_k is the weight of the *i*th mixture component and $N(\cdot)$ is a Gaussian probability density function with mean vector m_k and covariance matrix Σ_k. The parameters of GMM can be estimated using the expectation maximization (EM) algorithm.

In the typical spoofing detection task, we train two GMMs: one for bona fide speech and one for spoofed speech. For each speech signal *S*, where *S* is characterized by CQCC feature vectors, $\mathbf{X} = \{\mathrm{x}_1, \mathrm{x}_2, \ldots \mathrm{x}_\mathrm{T}\}$, the task is to determine whether *S* is a bona fide or spoofed speech, $\lambda_{\mathrm{bonafide}}$ and λ_{spoof} are the corresponding GMM models' parameters. Usually the log-likelihood ratio (LLR) is used as spoofing detection score, the decision between two hypotheses can be made:

$$S_{GMM}(\mathrm{X}) = \log p(\mathrm{X}|\lambda_{bonafide}) - \log p(\mathrm{X}|\lambda_{spoof}) \tag{2}$$

2.2 GMM System Based on Different Spoofing Algorithms

We propose to train different GMMs based on different spoofing algorithms. Six spoofing algorithms plus bona fide class in training set, are treated as different classes which yields a total of seven classes. For a new speech, we obtain seven different likelihood values. During testing, three scoring methods (PNorm, SVM, linear regression) are used for the final decision.

- **PNorm method:** The probabilistic normalization (PNorm) method is presented in [23]. Maximum spoofing scores among six GMM spoofing classifiers in the test set are selected, and then subtract from scores of the bona fide GMM, where is defined as follows:

$$S_{PNorm}(\mathrm{X}) = \log p(\mathrm{X}|\lambda_{bonafide}) - \max_{k \neq bonafide} (\log p(\mathrm{X}|\lambda_k)) \tag{3}$$

- **SVM method:** Seven GMM classifiers' likelihood scores on the train set are input to train the SVM model with radial basis function (RBF). And we make the final decision based on the output probability values.
- **Multiple linear regression method:** Multiple linear regression uses least squares. Under the equation for regression, the output provides least-squares estimates for each parameter. When trained on the training set, it returns the matrix of regression estimates. In the test phase, we multiply the GMM's likelihood score of the test set by the matrix of estimates.

2.3 Classical I-Vector System

Recently, the identity vector (i-vector) feature extraction method has become state-of-the-art in speaker recognition [24]. An i-vector is a mapping from a sequence of the feature vectors to a fixed-dimensional vector. A GMM supervector $\mathbf{M}$ is factorized as:

$$\mathbf{M} = \mathbf{m} + \mathbf{T}\mathbf{w}, \tag{4}$$

where $\mathbf{m}$ is the speaker- and channel-independent supervector, $\mathbf{T}$ is a low-rank matrix containing speaker and channel variability, and $\mathbf{w}$ is a latent variable which has a standard-normal distribution. The total variability matrix $\mathbf{T}$ defines the i-vector dimensionality.

2.4 I-Vector System Based on Different Spoofing Algorithms

In the i-vector system based on different spoofing algorithms, i-vectors are directly used as features of three different classifiers to compute scores: (i) Cosine distance scoring (CDS), (ii) Probabilistic linear discriminant analysis (PLDA), and (iii) Support vector machine (SVM). The following, w_{targt} and w_{test} are the i-vectors extracted from the target and the test utterances, respectively.

- **Cosine-based model:** The simple cosine similarity scoring has been applied successfully to compare two i-vectors for making a speaker spoofing detection decision. The cosine distance scoring between them is computed as follows:

$$score_{\mathbf{cosine}}(w_{target}, w_{test}) = \frac{w_{target}^{T} w_{test}}{\left\| w_{target} \right\| \left\| w_{test} \right\|} \tag{5}$$

- **PLDA-based model:** Given the amount of training data, the standard PLDA model is a probabilistic framework. For PLDA classification scoring, we compute the likelihood ratio (LLR) for the probability in Eq. (6). $p(w_{target}, w_{test}|H_1)$ is the probability that the test i-vectors w_{test} and the target i-vectors w_{target} share the same latent identity.

$$score_{\mathbf{PLDA}}(w_{target}, w_{test}) = \log \frac{p(w_{target}, w_{test}|\mathrm{H}_1)}{p(w_{target}|\mathrm{H}_0)p(w_{test}|\mathrm{H}_0)} \tag{6}$$

- **SVM-based model:** Different from the abovementioned classification scoring methods, the output score of the SVM classifier can be used for spoofing detection directly. Using i-vectors of bona fide and six spoofed classes from the training set to train an SVM model. The SVM with Radial Basis Function (RBF) is computed as Eq. (7). The following, the a_i, b is the SVM parameter, and $k(\cdot)$ is a kernel function. The RBF is expressed as Eq. (8), where the width σ^2 is specified a priori. In the experiments, we use the output of decision values to directly made final decisions from LIBSVM[2] package.

[2] https://www.csie.ntu.edu.tw/~cjlin/libsvm/.

$$f(x) = \sum_{i=1}^{m} a_i y_i k(x, x_i) + b, \quad (7)$$

$$k(x, x_i) = \exp\left\{\frac{-\|x - x_i\|^2}{2\sigma^2}\right\} \quad (8)$$

3 Experiments

3.1 Datasets

In the experiments, we used the ASVspoof 2019 database consisting of bona fide and spoofed speech signals generated by logical access (LA) use-case scenario with various text-to-speech (TTS) and voice conversion (VC) techniques. ASVspoof 2019 corpus is divided into three no speakers overlap subsets: training, development, and evaluation. And three data subsets are all split into two parts, namely the bona fide and the spoofed speech. There are 6 algorithms (3 speech synthesis algorithms, 1 TTS system implementation, and 2 voice conversion) included in training and development data. To obtain more generalized systems under mismatched conditions, the evaluation contains 14 kinds of spoofed speech generated by unseen spoofing algorithms. A more detailed description of the three subsets can be found in [8].

3.2 Results of GMM Systems

Classical GMM System

For ASVspoof 2019 challenge, the organizers offer the baseline system which is based on CQCC acoustic frontends and used a GMM binary classifier. In the baseline system, each utterance scores against two GMMs which trained separately on bona fide and spoofed speech to compute the likelihood ratio given in Eq. (2) during the test phase.

GMM System Based on Different Spoofing Algorithms

In the GMM system based on different spoofing algorithms, seven GMM models are trained and used three scoring methods (PNorm, SVM, linear regression) to compute the final score. To evaluate the proposed model performance, we use the following metrics: equal error rate (EER, %) and the tandem decision cost function (t-DCF) [25]. The following Table 1 shows the results of the baseline system and the final scoring methods in GMM systems based on different spoofing algorithms.

Table 1. Results for GMM-based systems on development and evaluation dataset.

Model	Dev		Eval	
	EER (%)	t-DCF^{min}	EER (%)	t-DCF^{min}
GMM (baseline)	0.24	0.007	8.97	0.214
GMM-PNorm	0.75	0.019	10.98	0.311
GMM-SVM	0.78	0.020	**7.03**	**0.187**
GMM-Linear regression	1.41	0.041	12.66	0.310

From Table 1, experiments conducted on the development and evaluation dataset, clearly demonstrate that the method of based on different spoofing algorithms improves the system performance. We compare a two-class (bona fide/spoofed) GMM of the baseline, and found that multi-class GMMs trained by the training set based on different spoofing algorithms can capture more details of unseen spoofing attack conditions. It is observed that SVM gave better spoofing detection performance than the baseline system. Based on different spoofing methods, the binary classification task is transformed into multiclass problems. For this, the performance of SVM method is better than PNorm and linear regression methods.

3.3 Results of I-Vector Systems

We use ASVspoof 2019 dataset for training UBM model with 512 Gaussian components, and the total variability matrix T. The normalization methods of principal component analysis (PCA), within-class covariance normalization (WCCN) [26] followed by length normalization (LN) [27] are applied together to the extracted 400-dimension i-vectors.

Three Classifiers Used for Classical I-Vector System
The results of the three models obtained on development and evaluation sets are summarized in Table 2. We use three different classifiers to compute scores. As can be seen that the SVM classifier always outperforms Cosine and PLDA classifiers. The PLDA classifier is inferior in comparison with the other two classifiers by EER estimates. And on the evaluation dataset, the SVM classifier yields approximately 10% and 4% better performance than PLDA and Cosine, respectively.

Table 2. Performance summary of the three classifiers in classic i-vector systems, on development and evaluation dataset.

Model	Dev		Eval	
	EER (%)	t-DCF^{min}	EER (%)	t-DCF^{min}
i-vector + cosine	1.57	0.045	16.44	0.406
i-vector + PLDA (2 classes)	1.84	0.046	17.63	0.441
i-vector + SVM (2 classes)	1.81	0.033	**15.79**	**0.393**

Two Classifiers Used for I-Vector System Based on Different Spoofing Algorithms
For systematically analyzing, we consider based on different spoofing algorithms to train the abovementioned models. Each algorithm plus bona fide speech is considered as a class. Then each class can be represented by its average i-vectors of the training set. From Table 3, It is observed that two classifiers when based on different spoofing algorithms perform better in comparison to the results of Table 2. Like findings on the GMM system (Table 1), the SVM classifier based on different spoofing algorithms achieves further improvement. The fact is that SVM trained on all training i-vectors helps to generalize better.

Table 3. Results for spoofing algorithms based on i-vector systems, and the performance comparison of two classifiers on the development and evaluation dataset.

Model	Dev		Eval	
	EER (%)	t-DCF^{min}	EER (%)	t-DCF^{min}
i-vector + PLDA (7 classes)	2.91	0.079	16.21	0.410
i-vector + SVM (7 classes)	0.55	0.012	**11.56**	**0.307**

Final Scoring Methods Used for Cosine Classifier in I-Vector System Based on Different Spoofing Algorithms

Spoofing detection performance of the final scoring methods present in the evaluation set is given in Table 4. For Cosine, an EER of 13.96% is obtained when using SVM methods on evaluation dataset, which demonstrates the high effectiveness of the method. However, the linear regression scoring method seems no benefit to improve the system performance.

Table 4. The results of three different scoring methods for cosine classifier sets based on different spoofing algorithms, on development and evaluation.

Model	Scoring methods	Dev		Eval	
		EER (%)	t-DCF^{min}	EER (%)	t-DCF^{min}
i-vector + cosine	PNorm	0.67	0.017	15.23	0.389
	SVM	0.66	0.019	**13.96**	**0.353**
	Linear regression	1.64	0.049	16.64	0.411

4 Discussion and Conclusion

In this paper, we establish GMM based and i-vector based systems for spoofing detection based on different spoofing algorithms. Three scoring methods (PNorm, linear regression and SVM) are used for the GMM model. And three different classifiers (cosine distance, PLDA, SVM) are used for the i-vector system. Furthermore, we propose to model cosine classifier based on i-vectors using three scoring method. In the ASVspoof 2019 experiments, it was found that a simple GMM system yields lower EER than the i-vector system. The best result (EER = 7.03%) was obtained using GMM classifiers with the SVM scoring method based on different spoofing algorithms. According to the results, it can be suggested that the SVM scoring method outperformed PNorm and linear regression in the GMM system. The i-vector system is state-of-the-art for speaker recognition, but to spoofing detecting, it is less effective in both development and evaluation datasets.

For future work, it is essential to explore new technologies to obtain more effective models and to find the optimal score methods to achieve robust performance on unknown attacks.

Acknowledgements. This work is supported by National Natural Science Foundation of P.R. China (61365004, 61662030), and by Educational Commission of Jiangxi Province of P.R. China (GJJ170205).

References

1. ZhiZheng, W., Evans, N., Kinnunen, T., Yamagishi, J., Alegre, F., Li, H.: Spoofing and countermeasures for speaker verification: a survey. Speech Commun. **66**, 130–153 (2015)
2. Hautamäki, R.S., et al.: Automatic versus human speaker verification: the case of voice mimicry. Speech Commun. **72**, 13–31 (2015)
3. Zhizheng, W., Leon, P.L., Demiroglu, D., Khodabakhsh, A., et al.: Anti-spoofing for text-independent speaker verification: an initial database comparison of countermeasures and human performance. IEEE/ACM Trans. Audio Speech Lang. Process. **20**(8), 768–783 (2016)
4. Zhizheng, W., Yamagishi, J., Kinnunen, T., Sahidullah, Md, et al.: ASVspoof: the automatic speaker verification spoofing and countermeasures challenge. IEEE J. Sel. Top. Sign. Process. **11**(4), 588–604 (2017)
5. Yamagishi, J., Kinnunen, T., Evans, N., De Leon, P.L.: Introduction to the issues on spoofing and countermeasures for automatic speaker verification. IEEE J. Sel. Top. Sign. Process. **11**(4), 585–587 (2017)
6. Xiaohai, T., SiuWa, L., Zhizheng, W., Eng Siong, C., Haizhou, L.: An example-based approach to frequency warping for voice conversation. IEEE/ACM Trans. Audio Speech Lang. Process. **25**(10), 1863–1876 (2017)
7. Rohan Kuman, D., Haizhou, L.: Instantaneous phase and excitation source features for detection of replay attacks. In: Asia-Pacific Signal and Information Processing Association (APSIPA) Annual Summit and Conference (ASC) 2018, November 2018
8. ASVspoof 2019: Automatic speaker verification spoofing and countermeasures challenge evaluation plan. http://www.asvspoof.org/asvspoof2019/asvspoof2019evaluation/plan.pdf
9. Kinnunen, T., Wu, Z.-Z., Lee, K.A., Sedlak, F., Chng, E.S., Li, H.: Vulnerability of speaker verification systems against voice conversion spoofing attacks: the case of telephone speech. In: ICASSP (2012)
10. Lorenzo Trueba, J., et al.: The voice conversion challenge 2018: promoting development of parallel and nonparallel methods. In: The Speaker and Language Recognition Workshop, Odyssey, pp. 195–202 (2018)
11. Leon, P.L.D., Apsingekar, V.R., Pucher, M., Yamagishi, J.: Revisiting the security of speaker verification systems against imposture using synthetic speech. In: Proceedings ICASSP, pp. 1798–1801 (2010)
12. Farrús, M.: Voice disguise in automatic speaker recognition. ACM Comput. Surv. **51**(4), 681–6822 (2018)
13. Alegre, F., Vipperla, R., Evans, N.W.D., Fauve, B.G.B.: On the vulnerability of automatic speaker recognition to spoofing attacks with artificial signals. In: Proceedings EUSIPCO, pp. 36–40 (2012)
14. Sahidullah, M., Kinnunen, T., Hanilci, C.: A comparison of features for synthetic speech detection. In: Proceedings INTERSPEECH, pp. 2087–2091 (2015)
15. Gomez-Alanis, A., et al.: Performance evaluation of front-and back-end techniques for ASV spoofing detection systems based on deep features. In: Proceedings IberSPEECH 2018, pp. 45–49 (2018)

16. Alam, M.J., Kenny, P., Bhattacharya, G., Stafylakis, T.: Development of crim system for the automatic speaker verification spoofing and countermeasures challenge 2015. In: Proceedings INTERSPEECH, pp. 2072–2076 (2015)
17. Kannangola, D., et al.: Factor analysis methods for joint speaker verification and spoof detection. In: Proceedings ICASSP, pp. 5385–5389 (2017)
18. Todisco, M., Delgado, H., Evans, N.: A new feature for automatic speaker verification anti-spoofing: constant Q cepstral coefficients. In: Proceedings Odyssey (2016)
19. Novoselov, S., Kozlov, A., Lavrentyeva, G., Simonchik, K., Shchemelinin, V.: STC anti-spoofing systems for the ASVspoof 2015 challenge. In: Proceedings IEEE International Conference Acoustics, Speech and Signal Processing (ICASSP), pp. 5475–5479 (2016)
20. Weng, S., et al.: The SYSU system for the interspeech 2015 automatic speaker verification spoofing and countermeasures challenge. In: Proceedings APSIPA, pp. 152–155 (2015)
21. Reynolds, D.A., Quatieri, T.F., Dunn, R.B.: Speaker verification using adapted Gaussian mixture models. Digit. Signal Process. **10**(1–3), 19–41 (2000)
22. Wang, L., Yoshida, Y., Kawakami, Y., Nakagawa, S.: Relative phase information for detecting human speech and spoofed speech. In: Proceedings INTERSPEECH, pp. 2092–2096 (2015)
23. Nanxin, C., et al.: Robust deep feature for spoofing detection—The SJTU system for ASVspoof 2015 challenge. In: Sixteenth Annual Conference of the International Speech Communication Association (2015)
24. Dehak, N., Kenny, P., Dehak, R., Dumouchel, P., Ouellet, P.: Front-end factor analysis for speaker verification. IEEE Trans. Audio Speech Lang. Process. **19**(4), 788–798 (2011)
25. Kinnunen, T., et al.: t-DCF: a detection cost function for the tandem assessment of spoofing countermeasures and automatic speaker verification. In: Proceedings Odyssey, Les Sables d'Olonne, France, June 2018
26. Hatch, A.O., Kajarekar, S.S., Stolcke, A.: Within-class covariance normalization for SVM-based speaker recognition. In: Proceedings ICSLP (2006)
27. Garcia-Romero, D., Espy-Wilson, C.Y.: Analysis of i-vector length normalization in speaker recognition systems. In: Proceedings INTERSPEECH, pp. 249–252 (2011)

Feature Enhancement for Joint Human and Head Detection

Yongming Zhang[1,2], Shifeng Zhang[1,2], Chubin Zhuang[1,2], and Zhen Lei[1,2](✉)

[1] CBSR & NLPR, Institute of Automation,
Chinese Academy of Sciences, Beijing, China
{yongming.zhang,shifeng.zhang,chubin.zhuang,zlei}@nlpr.ia.ac.cn
[2] University of Chinese Academy of Sciences, Beijing, China

Abstract. Human and head detection have been rapidly improved with the development of deep convolutional neural networks. However, these two detection tasks are often studied separately, without taking advantage of the relationship between human and head. In this paper, we present a new two-stage detection framework, namely Joint Enhancement Detection (JED), to simultaneously detect human and head based on enhanced features. Specifically, the proposed JED contains two newly added modules, *i.e.*, the Body Enhancement Module (BEM) and the Head Enhancement Module (HEM). The former is designed to enhance the features used for human detection, while the latter aims to enhance the features used for head detection. With these enhanced features in a joint framework, the proposed method is able to detect human and head simultaneously and efficiently. We verify the effectiveness of the proposed method on the CrowdHuman dataset and achieve better performance than baseline method for both human and head detection.

Keywords: Human detection · Head detection · Feature enhancement

1 Introduction

In object detection, there are many methods based on deep convolutional neural networks that have been proposed and made great progress. The current object detection methods are divided into two types, one is the one-stage detection [1–4], and the other is the two-stage detection [5–10]. As two subtasks of object detection, human detection and head detection are important research directions in computer vision. They have been used in some applications, such as person recognition, vehicle assisted driving, intelligent video surveillance and so on.

In human detection, Wang *et al.* [11] design a repulsion loss, which detects pedestrians in the crowd scenes. Zhou *et al.* [12] propose a network to simultaneously detect pedestrians by regressing two bounding boxes for full body and visible part estimation respectively. Zhang *et al.* [13] design an occlusion-aware R-CNN to improve the pedestrians detection accuracy, and propose an aggregation loss to enforce proposals to be close and locate compactly to the corresponding objects.

Z. Sun et al. (Eds.): CCBR 2019, LNCS 11818, pp. 511–518, 2019.
https://doi.org/10.1007/978-3-030-31456-9_56

In addition, head detection has experienced tremendous development in recent years. Vu *et al.* [14] propose a pairwise CNN to model pairwise relations among heads. Stewart *et al.* [15] propose a proposal-free head detector that is produced from CNN encoders using a regression module. Chen *et al.* [16] present a method utilizing spatial semantic relations between the pedestrian head and other body parts.

In this paper, we find that the human body and the head have certain similarities and commonalities, so we detect the human and the head in a unified framework. Most of the features of the human body and the head are shared, but there are still a small number of features that are exclusive, *i.e.*, the human body has its unique features and the head also has its own unique features different from the human body. In order to get better human features and head features, our core idea is introducing a method of feature enhancement. Specifically, we present a new two-stage detection framework, namely Joint Enhancement Detection (JED), to simultaneously and efficiently detect human and head based on enhanced features. The proposed JED contains two newly added modules, *i.e.*, the Body Enhancement Module (BEM) and the Head Enhancement Module (HEM). The former is designed to enhance the features used for human detection, while the latter aims to enhance the features used for head detection. Our motivation is to enhance the different features of human and head separately to better detect human body and head. For clarity, the main contributions of this work can be summarized as three-fold:

- We propose a two-stage detection way to jointly detect human and head in a unified framework.
- We design feature enhancement modules to purposefully learn better features of human and head for better detection performance.
- We achieve state-of-the-art performance on the CrowdHuman dataset.

2 Related Work

Human Detection. The CNN-based detectors have become a predominating trend in the field of pedestrian detection. Cai *et al.* [17] propose an architecture which uses different levels of features to detect persons at various scales. Mao *et al.* [18] propose a multi-task network to further improve detection pedestrians performance. Zhou *et al.* [19] propose to jointly learn part detectors so as to exploit part correlations and reduce the computational cost. Wang *et al.* [11] introduce a novel bounding box regression loss to detect pedestrians in the crowd scenes. Zhang *et al.* [20] propose to utilize channel-wise attention in convnets allowing the network to learn more representative features for different occlusion patterns in one coherent model. Zhou *et al.* [12] design a method to simultaneously detect pedestrians by regressing two bounding boxes for full body and visible part estimation respectively. Zhang *et al.* [13] design an occlusion-aware R-CNN to improve the pedestrians detection performance in the crowd, and propose an aggregation loss to enforce proposals to be close and locate compactly to the corresponding objects.

Head Detection. Early head detectors are used for crowd counting. Merad *et al.* [21] combine positive points of all previous techniques in the head detector. Venkatesh *et al.* [22] train a head detector using a state-of-the-art cascade of boosted integral features. Currently, with the arrival of deep learning, some CNN-based methods are proposed. Stewart *et al.* [15] present a proposal-free head detector that is produced from CNN encoders using a regression module, where the regression is generally composed of LSTM so that the variable-length output prediction is possible. Sun *et al.* [23] propose to investigate the influence of head scale and contextual information and design a scale-invariant method to dynamically detect heads depending on the complexity of the image. Le *et al.* [24] introduce a pairwise head detector based on key parts context of human head and shoulder, and assisted by priority of scene geometry structure.

3 Joint Enhancement Detection (JED)

This section presents the details of JED. It includes three key components: the overall framework, two-parallel feature enhancement modules and the implementation details.

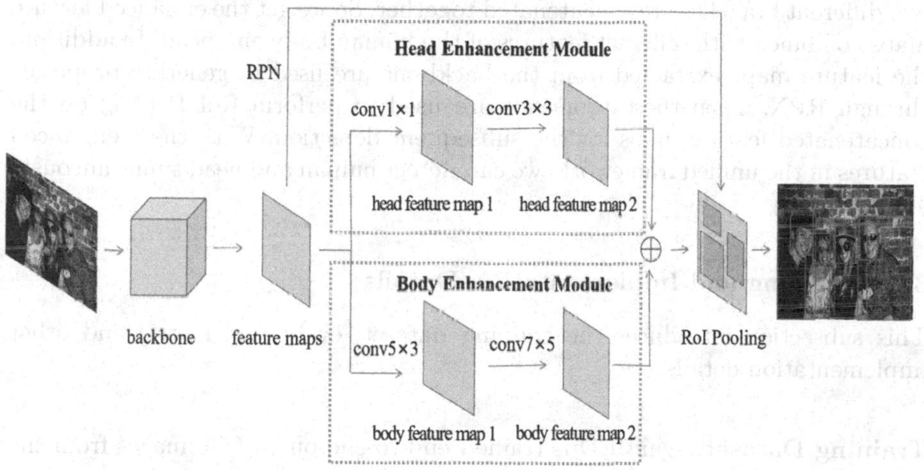

Fig. 1. The detection framework of JED.

3.1 Overall Framework

The whole architecture of Joint Enhancement Detection (JED) is illustrated in Fig. 1, it consists of RPN, two parallel branches that are Body Enhancement Module (BEM) and Head Enhancement Module (HEM), and RoI Pooling. The backbone is based on ResNet-50 with Faster R-CNN.

3.2 Two-Parallel Feature Enhancement Modules

Body Enhancement Module (BEM). The image is sent to the backbone network, and we get the feature maps. The BEM is used to enhance the features for human and get the enhanced feature maps for better human detection. We consider that the human body detection bounding box is rectangular, so the convolution kernel size of these two convolution layers is set as 5×3 and 7×5 respectively. The feature maps extracted from the backbone are fed into these two convolution layers. Then we obtain the enhanced feature map, which is more suitable to be used for human detection than head detection.

Head Enhancement Module (HEM). The HEM is used to enhance the features for head and get the enhanced feature maps for better head detection. The same as in BEM, we also get the feature maps from the backbone. We set the convolution kernel size of these two convolution layers is 1×1 and 3×3 respectively. Then the feature maps are fed into these two convolution layers. And we obtain the enhanced feature map, which is more suitable to be used for head detection than human detection.

Finally, the two kinds of enhanced feature maps obtained separately from the two different branches are concatenated together. So we get the enhanced feature maps combined with different features of the human body and head. In addition, the feature maps extracted from the backbone are used to generate proposals through RPN. Then these proposals are used to perform RoI Pooling on the concatenated feature maps for the subsequent detection. With these enhanced features in the unified framework, we can detect human and head simultaneously and efficiently.

3.3 Training and Implementation Details

This subsection introduces the training dataset, evaluation metric and other implementation details.

Training Dataset. Our JED is trained end-to-end on 15,000 images from the CrowdHuman [25] training set. There are ∼340 k persons and ∼99 k ignore region annotations in the CrowdHuman [25] training set. The number is more than 10× boosted compared with previous challenging pedestrian detection dataset like CityPersons [26]. The total number of persons is also noticeably larger than the others. We use human visible body bounding-box and head bounding-box to detect human and head respectively. Every image includes 22.6 persons with various kinds of occlusions in the dataset. To increase the robustness of training data, each training image is sequentially processed by random cropping, horizontal flipping and finally gets the short edge of input images to 800 pixels and caps the long side at 1, 400 pixels.

Evaluation Metric. We report the detection performance for instances in visible body (*i.e.*, human) and head categories. We follow the evaluation metric used in [27], the log-average miss rate (MR) over 9 points ranging from 10^{-2} to 10^{0} FPPI is used to evaluate the performance of our method. Besides, Average Precision (AP) and Recall of the algorithms are also provided for reference.

Other Implementation Details. We adopt ResNet-50 with a 5-level feature pyramid structure as the backbone network. We initialize the parameters of the base layers from the pre-trained ResNet-50. And the next additional convolution layers are initialized by the "xavier" method. We fine-tune the model using SGD for optimization with 0.9 momentum, 0.0001 weight decay and a mini-batch 2 per GPU. We train all models for 25 epochs with the initial learning rate of 0.01 and decrease it by a factor of 10 after 16 and 22 epochs. We implement Joint Enhancement Detection (JED) using PyTorch [28] framework.

4 Experiments

In this section, we firstly compare the performance between our proposed joint detection framework and the baseline of human detection and head detection on CrowdHuman [25] dataset. Then we verify the effectiveness of our proposed joint detection framework based on enhanced features.

4.1 Model Analysis

We firstly analyze the performance of our proposed joint human and head detection framework, which is denoted as JED w/o EM via removing BEM and HEM. We evaluate our proposed joint detection framework on 4,370 images from the CrowdHuman [25] validation set. It consists of 100,097 human visible bodies and 100,097 heads. We use the anchors scales to $8S$, where S represents the stride size of each pyramid level, and we set the height *vs.* width ratios of anchors as {1:2, 1:1, 2:1} in all our experiments.

As shown in Table 1, the baseline of human detection in CrowdHuman [25] denoted as Human-Original, obtains 91.51% Recall, 85.60% AP and 55.94% MR. The baseline of head detection in CrowdHuman [25] denoted as Head-Original, obtains 81.10% Recall, 77.95% AP and 52.06% MR. Our proposed joint human and head detection method (*i.e.*, JED w/o EM) obtains 91.52% Recall, 84.30% AP, 55.89% MR for human detection, and 81.60% Recall, 77.20% AP, 52.04% MR for head detection, which are 0.01% higher on Recall (91.52% *vs.* 91.51%), 0.05% lower on MR (55.89% *vs.* 55.94%) than the Human-Original, and 0.50% higher on Recall (81.60% *vs.* 81.10%), 0.02% lower on MR (52.04% *vs.* 52.06%) than the Head-Original. Compared with separate human detection and head detection baselines, the proposed detection framework achieves similar human and head detection performance, indicating that it can joint detect human and head effectively, with some shared feature extraction and thus more efficient inference operation.

Table 1. Human and head detection performance (%) of different methods on Crowd-Human dataset.

Method	Human			Head		
	Recall	AP	MR	Recall	AP	MR
Human-original	91.51	85.60	55.94	–	–	–
Head-original	–	–	–	81.10	77.95	52.06
JED w/o EM	91.52	84.30	55.89	81.60	77.20	52.04
JED only w BEM	91.81	85.00	55.18	81.40	76.72	52.01
JED only w HEM	91.40	83.70	55.93	83.70	78.40	51.88
JED	**91.90**	**85.90**	**53.59**	**84.20**	**79.20**	**50.85**

4.2 Feature Enhancement Verification

Before delving into our proposed framework of joint human and head detection based on enhanced features, we firstly analyze the performance of individual modules (*i.e.*, BEM and HEM) respectively. When JED only has BEM, the HEM is replaced by a 1×1 convolution layer. Similarly, when JED only has HEM, the BEM is replaced by a 1×1 convolution layer.

As illustrated in Table 1, our module BEM achieves 91.81% Recall, 85.00% AP, 55.18% MR for human detection, and 81.40% Recall, 76.72% AP, 52.01% MR for head detection, which are 0.29% higher on Recall (91.81% *vs.* 91.52%), 0.70% higher on AP (85.00% *vs.* 84.30%) and 0.71% lower on MR (55.18% *vs.* 55.89%) than the JED w/o EM for human detection. The module HEM achieves 83.70% Recall, 78.40% AP, 51.88% MR for head detection, and 91.40% Recall, 83.70% AP, 55.93% MR for human detection, which are 2.10% higher on Recall (83.70% *vs.* 81.60%), 1.20% higher on AP (78.40% *vs.* 77.20%) and 0.16% lower on MR (51.88% *vs.* 52.04%) than the JED w/o EM for head detection. The results demonstrate the performance of our proposed the Body Enhancement Module and the Head Enhancement Module has improved the detection performance respectively. In this paper, we combine BEM and HEM into the joint human and head detection framework, which is named Joint Enhancement Detection (JED). From Table 1, one can see that JED achieves 91.90% Recall, 85.90% AP, 53.59% MR for human detection, and 84.20% Recall, 79.20% AP, 50.85% MR for head detection. It is 0.38% higher on Recall (91.90% *vs.* 91.52%), 1.60% higher on AP (85.90% *vs.* 84.30%), 2.30% lower on MR (53.59% *vs.* 55.89%) than the JED w/o EM for human detection, and 2.60% higher on Recall (84.20% *vs.* 81.60%), 2.00% higher on AP (79.20% *vs.* 77.20%), 1.19% lower on MR (50.85% *vs.* 52.04%) than the JED w/o EM for head detection. The results validate the effectiveness of our proposed joint detection framework based on enhanced features.

5 Conclusion

In this paper, we present a new two-stage detection framework, namely Joint Enhancement Detection (JED), to simultaneously detect human and head based on enhanced features. JED contains two parallel modules, *i.e.*, the Body Enhancement Module (BEM) and the Head Enhancement Module (HEM). The BEM is designed to enhance the features used for human detection, and the HEM aims to enhance the features used for head detection. With these enhanced features in a joint framework, the proposed method is able to detect human and head simultaneously and efficiently. Preliminary experiments on the CrowdHuman dataset validate the effectiveness of the proposed method and we achieve better performance on both human detection and head detection than baseline method.

Acknowledgements. This work was supported by the Chinese National Natural Science Foundation Projects #61876178, #61806196, #61872367, #61572501.

References

1. Redmon, J., Divvala, S., Girshick, R.: You only look once: unified, real-time object detection. In: IEEE Conference on Computer Vision and Pattern Recognition, CVPR (2016)
2. Liu, W., et al.: SSD: single shot multibox detector. In: Leibe, B., Matas, J., Sebe, N., Welling, M. (eds.) ECCV 2016. LNCS, vol. 9905, pp. 21–37. Springer, Cham (2016). https://doi.org/10.1007/978-3-319-46448-0_2
3. Lin, T., Goyal, P., Girshick, R.: Focal loss for dense object detection. In: IEEE International Conference on Computer Vision, ICCV (2017)
4. Zhang, S., Wen, L., Bian, X., Lei, Z., Li, S.Z.: Single-shot refinement neural network for object detection. In: CVPR (2018)
5. Girshick, R., Donahue, J., Darrell, T.: Rich feature hierarchies for accurate object detection and semantic segmentation. In: IEEE Conference on Computer Vision and Pattern Recognition, CVPR (2014)
6. He, K., Zhang, X., Ren, S., Sun, J.: Spatial pyramid pooling in deep convolutional networks for visual recognition. In: Fleet, D., Pajdla, T., Schiele, B., Tuytelaars, T. (eds.) ECCV 2014. LNCS, vol. 8691, pp. 346–361. Springer, Cham (2014). https://doi.org/10.1007/978-3-319-10578-9_23
7. Girshick, R.: Fast R-CNN. In: IEEE International Conference on Computer Vision, ICCV (2015)
8. Ren, S., He, K., Girshick, R.: Faster R-CNN: towards real-time object detection with region proposal networks. In: TPAMI (2017)
9. Dai, J., Li, Y., He, K.: R-FCN: object detection via region-based fully convolutional networks. In: Advances in Neural Information Processing Systems, NIPS (2016)
10. Lin, T.Y., Dollár, P., Girshick, R., He, K., Hariharan, B., Belongie, S.: Feature pyramid networks for object detection. In: CVPR (2017)
11. Wang, X., Xiao, T., Jiang, Y., Shao, S., Sun, J., Shen, C.: Repulsion loss: detecting pedestrians in a crowd. In: CVPR (2018)
12. Zhou, C., Yuan, J.: Bi-box regression for pedestrian detection and occlusion estimation. In: ECCV (2018)

13. Zhang, S., Wen, L., Bian, X., Lei, Z., Li, S.Z.: Occlusion-aware R-CNN: detecting pedestrians in a crowd. In: Ferrari, V., Hebert, M., Sminchisescu, C., Weiss, Y. (eds.) ECCV 2018. LNCS, vol. 11207, pp. 657–674. Springer, Cham (2018). https://doi.org/10.1007/978-3-030-01219-9_39
14. Vu, T., Osokin, A., Laptev, I.: Context-aware CNNs for person head detection. In: ICCV (2015)
15. Stewart, R., Andriluka, M., Ng, A.Y.: End-to-end people detection in crowded scenes. In: CVPR (2016)
16. Chen, G., Cai, X., Han, H., Shan, S., Chen, X.: Headnet: pedestrian head detection utilizing body in context. In: FG (2018)
17. Cai, Z., Fan, Q., Feris, R.S., Vasconcelos, N.: A unified multi-scale deep convolutional neural network for fast object detection. arXiv preprint arXiv:1607.07155 (2016)
18. Mao, J., Xiao, T., Jiang, Y., Cao, Z.: What can help pedestrian detection?. In: CVPR (2017)
19. Zhou, C., Yuan, J.: Multi-label learning of part detectors for heavily occluded pedestrian detection. In: ICCV (2017)
20. Zhang, S., Yang, J., Schiele, B.: Occluded pedestrian detection through guided attention in CNNs. In: CVPR (2018)
21. Merad, D., Aziz, K., Thome, N.: Fast people counting using head detection from skeleton graph. In: AVSS (2010)
22. Venkatesh, B.S., Descamps, A., Carincotte, C.: Counting people in the crowd using a generic head detector. In: AVSS (2012)
23. Sun, Z., Peng, D., Cai, Z., Chen, Z., Jin, L.: Scale mapping and dynamic re-detecting in dense head detection. In: ICIP (2018)
24. Le, C., Ma, H., Wang, X., Li, X.: Key parts context and scene geometry in human head detection. In: ICIP (2018)
25. Shao, S., Zhao, Z., Li, B.: CrowdHuman: a benchmark for detecting human in a crowd. arXiv preprint arXiv:1805.00123 (2018)
26. Zhang, S., Benenson, R., Schiele, B.: Citypersons: a diverse dataset for pedestrian detection. In: CVPR (2017)
27. Dollár, P., Wojek, C., Schiele, B., Perona, P.: Pedestrian detection: a benchmark. In: CVPR (2009)
28. Paszke, A., Gross, S., Chintala, S., Chanan, G.: Pytorch (2017)

Author Index

Printed in the United States
By Bookmasters

Printed in the United States
By Bookmasters